P9-BYL-400

Romanticism

By the same author

Chinoiserie: The Vision of Cathay

Neo-classicism

The New Golden Land

The Penguin Dictionary of Architecture
(with Nicolaus Pevsner and John Fleming)

Dictionary of the Decorative Arts
(with John Fleming)

Romanticism

by Hugh Honour

Icon Editions

Harper & Row, Publishers

New York, Hagerstown, San Francisco, London

 For information address Harper & Row, Publishers, Inc., 10 East 53rd Street, New York, N.Y. 10022.

FIRST U.S. EDITION

ISBN: 0-06-433336-1 (cloth); 0-06-430089-7 (paper)

LIBRARY OF CONGRESS CATALOG CARD NUMBER: 78-2146

Designed by Gerald Cinamon

81 82 83 84 10 9 8 7 6 5 4 3

Acknowledgements

I am indebted to many friends for help and information, especially Dr Hans Aurenhammer, Professor L. D. Ettlinger, Dr John Gage, Professor Nigel Glendinning, Dr Carlo Pietrangeli, Dr Alex Potts, Mr Nicolas Powell, M. Pierre Rosenberg, Professor Robert Rosenblum and Professor Richard Wollheim. I am, of course, also deeply indebted to previous writers on Romanticism, from many of whom I have derived ideas as well as factual information: they are all, I hope, gratefully mentioned either in the Notes, Catalogue of Illustrations or Books for Further Reading. For permission to reproduce works of art I am indebted to the private collectors and the trustees and directors of galleries and museums mentioned in the Catalogue of Illustrations. To Dr Keith Andrews, M. Jean-Pierre Babelon, Dr H. G. Evers, M. Jean Feray, Fln Aasta Fischer, Dr Manfred F. Fischer, Mr John Harris, Mrs Francis Haskell, Mrs Dyveke Helsted, Miss Catherine Kruft, Mr Denys Sutton and Dr W. Wolters, I am grateful for help in obtaining photographs. I profited greatly from permission to consult the *documentation* of the department of paintings at the Louvre. Jon Whiteley allowed me to consult his subject index of French paintings in the Dept of the History of Art at Oxford and to read his unpublished thesis. Dr William Vaughan let me see the proofs of his book *Romantic Art* and kindly read my typescript, as did Professor Michael Podro to whose comments I am much indebted. I have greatly benefited from many conversations with Professor Francis Haskell and am additionally grateful to him for reading my typescript and suggesting improvements. At Penguins, Nikos Stangos was very helpful while I was working on the book and Peter Carson made valuable comments when I eventually delivered it. My greatest debt of all is to John Fleming: the book is as much his as mine.

H.H.
November 1977

Introduction

In *Neo-classicism* (1968) I discussed the artistic revolution which began in the 1750s and reached its climax in the early 1790s. The present volume is the sequel, concerned with the consequences during the next half-century of a still more momentous revolution in attitudes to the arts. It is about Romanticism as an historical phenomenon, not as a state of mind found in all periods and cultures. The urge to categorize artists as romantic or classic, introvert or extrovert, oral or anal, began with the Romantics themselves and their revaluation of the arts of the past. But such binary systems always remind me of the old epigram: 'I divide the world into two classes: those who divide the world into two classes and those who do not. I prefer the latter.'

Attempts to isolate concurrent Neo-classical and Romantic tendencies, even within the limited period from 1750 to 1850, have been unrewarding, especially when one is associated exclusively with the Antique Revival and the other with Medievalism or, at a more sophisticated level, with a preference for line rather than colour or for open rather than closed form. Regarded in this way, Neo-classicism and Romanticism are no more than figments of our logical modes of thought. More helpful and interesting are the studies which have tried to penetrate the cultural realities beneath the art-historical packaging and reveal the inner tensions. In their light the period has come to be seen – with much justification – as one of continuous development from the rejection of the Rococo in the mid-eighteenth century to the emergence of Realism in the mid-nineteenth. It is often called the 'age of Romanticism', sometimes sub-divided by the use of the terms 'pre-Romanticism' and 'Romantic classicism'. Yet such a view tends to obscure the disruptive effect of the fundamental changes in attitude, not only to the arts but to life in general, which inevitably flowed from the French Revolution and from the subsequent diffusion of Kant's philosophy, perhaps the most important intellectual event since the Protestant Reformation.

As we are the heirs to all the changes which took place in the 1790s, a considerable intellectual effort is needed to think our way back into previous centuries when it was assumed that literature and the visual arts had reached unsurpassable peaks of excellence in classical antiquity; when a mimetic theory of the arts prevailed, when music was still regarded as an inferior means of artistic expression and landscape an inferior type of painting; when such words as imagination, genius, originality or, indeed, revolution, reaction and romantic had yet to take on their modern connotations; and when the idea of a left and right in politics had still to be evolved. Significantly, the desire to achieve historical empathy emerged at the very same moment. But failure to distinguish between nineteenth-century and earlier attitudes and meanings of words has vitiated many historical studies, and none more than those of the origins of Romanticism and of the French Revolution.

The first use of the word 'romantic' (derived from *romance*, a composition in the French vernacular 'Romance' language as distinct from one in Latin) has been found in seventeenth-century England. Many of the ideas cherished by early nineteenth-century thinkers have been traced back to Vico, to Jakob Böhme, to the Hermetic philosophers and far beyond. Admiration for the wilder natural phenomena – mountains, waterfalls, storms at sea – has been detected in the eighteenth century and earlier: similarly the fascination of esoteric religions and superstitious beliefs in ghosts, vampires, werewolves, nightmares and so on. Interest in, and even the imitation of, medieval literature and architecture extends far back from the nineteenth century, back to the Middle Ages, in fact. Exoticism, especially the lure of the mysterious East, which appealed so strongly to several painters and writers of the early nineteenth century, is now seen to have been, like so many other 'Romantic' tendencies, a recurrent element in Western culture ever since Antiquity.

Another approach to Romanticism has been to work backwards from the art and aesthetics of the twentieth century and unravel threads of *avant-garde* continuity from the tangled web of nineteenth-century culture. As we inevitably seek in the arts of the past the qualities which seem most vital and meaningful in those of the present, it is hard to escape the pitfalls in this approach which was, of course, marked out by the Romantics themselves. It has inevitably falsified the picture of late eighteenth-century art by creating an unreal division between doctrinaire Neo-classics and forward-looking 'pre-Romantics' striving against the conventions of their time to become Romantics, if not Impressionists or Expressionists. In studies of the early nineteenth century, emphasis has similarly been placed on works which seem to look forward – to Monet, Picasso, Jackson Pollock or Mark Rothko. But it is one thing to say that Constable's large sketches appeal to us more than his highly finished pictures, another to suggest that Constable shared our views.

Yet there is much in Romanticism that does seem uncannily 'modern': the large, almost abstract, late paintings by Turner, for instance; Grandville's weird, almost surrealist, *Zoomorphoses* and *Métempsychoses*; some severe, almost 'Internationally Modern' buildings by Schinkel – almost, but not quite. The experimental nature of much modern literature seems to be prefigured in several Romantic productions. In Tieck's satiric comedy *Der gestiefelte Kater* (*Puss in Boots*) the 'audience' participates in the play, arguing about the performance, while the actors complain about their parts. E. T. A. Hoffmann's novel *Lebensansichten des Katers Murr* alternates without warning (often in the middle of a sentence) pages from the poignant autobiography of a crazed musician with sheets from the memoirs of his smug self-satisfied tom-cat. In Clemens Brentano's novel *Godwi*, the characters discuss how the author has misinterpreted them and finally describe his death. But similar devices had been adopted earlier by Sterne and (in a more limited way) by Cervantes. All that is specifically innovatory in these writings is the Romantic irony, underlying the play with levels of reality, which also distinguishes them from more recent experiments.

Definitions of Romanticism tend to be so general as to include a bewildering number of characteristics, most of which are to be found in other periods and cultures, or so specific that they exclude the majority of those commonly ascribed to the Romantics. In a celebrated essay, A. O. Lovejoy proposed that the word 'Romantic' should be used only in the sense of Friedrich Schlegel's definition of '*romantische Poesie*', published in 1798, and that all other 'romanticisms' should be distinguished from it and from one another.[1] As Friedrich Schlegel's own use of the term was far from consistent, this reduced a loosely connected group of ideas to an almost infinite number of statements made by individuals at different moments. Lovejoy has been much criticized for placing too much weight on this definition of 1798. But, as the first of many, it has outstanding importance, not only, nor primarily, for what it says but simply as a symptom of a strongly felt need to define qualities barely mentioned in the then accepted theories of the arts –

a need which perhaps indicates one valid approach towards a definition of Romanticism.

But, in general, definitions of Romanticism formulated during the early nineteenth century are so contradictory that they cannot be reduced to a single coherent system. And the same, of course, can be said of the major works of art and literature – paintings by Turner, Constable, Delacroix and Caspar David Friedrich, for example, or in England alone the poetry of Wordsworth, Shelley, Byron and Keats. Their diversity is their most obvious characteristic, yet they all present attitudes to art and life which differ fundamentally from those previously expressed. As Lévi-Strauss has remarked in another context: 'It is not the similarities but the differences which resemble one another.' To the Romantic artist – by nature essentially and intimately a passionate individualist, a spontaneous creator – any norm was deeply antipathetic.

Baudelaire said that 'Romanticism is precisely situated neither in choice of subject nor in exact truth, but in a way of feeling.' And, of course, this '*manière de sentir*' can be detected only subjectively. Hence the difficulty of defining Romanticism which led its first historian to declare, in 1829, that it is 'just that which cannot be defined'.[2] The underlying motives of the Romantics are too complex to be encapsulated in a simple formula. For if many were inspired by opposition to the aesthetic doctrines of classicism, to the rationalism of the Enlightenment, or to the political ideals of the French Revolution, many others were not, and they included both

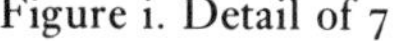
Figure i. Detail of 7

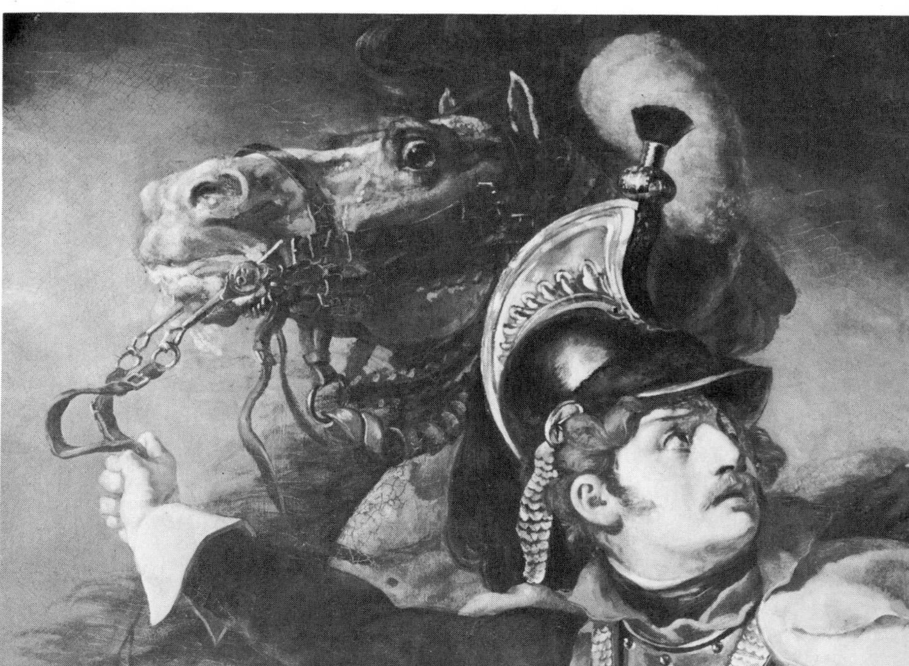

Delacroix and Turner. Neither in literature nor in the visual arts can Romanticism be regarded simply, or even primarily, as an expression of anti-rationalism in thought or reactionary illiberalism in politics.

Moreover, there is no Romantic 'style' in the visual arts, if by that is meant a common language of visual forms and means of expression, comparable with the Baroque or Rococo. There is no single work of art which exemplifies the aims and ideals of the Romantics as does, for example, David's *Oath of the Horatii* those of Neo-classical painters. There is no great paradigmatic Romantic masterpiece. Romantic ideals and visions of the world were conveyed – in fact had to be conveyed because of their Romantic nature – in such a variety of visual languages that the term Romantic can be applied to works which, in a formal sense, have nothing whatever in common: Géricault's *Wounded Cuirassier* of 1814 and Friedrich Overbeck's portrait of Franz Pforr of 1810, for instance [Figs. i and ii]. The one is as boldly and freely rendered, with sweeping brush-strokes and splashes of pigment dashed on with apparently exuberant spontaneity, as the other is meticulously, meditatively worked over with a miniaturist's precision of touch. Géricault's forms emerge out of the canvas, modelled with shifting contrasts of light and shade, light pigments dramatically superimposed over dark. Overbeck's forms are precisely, coolly articulated with firm outlines, drawn rather than painted, and deftly filled in with gently modulated colours of a subdued autumnal tonality, 'sweet though in sad-

Figure ii. Detail of 103

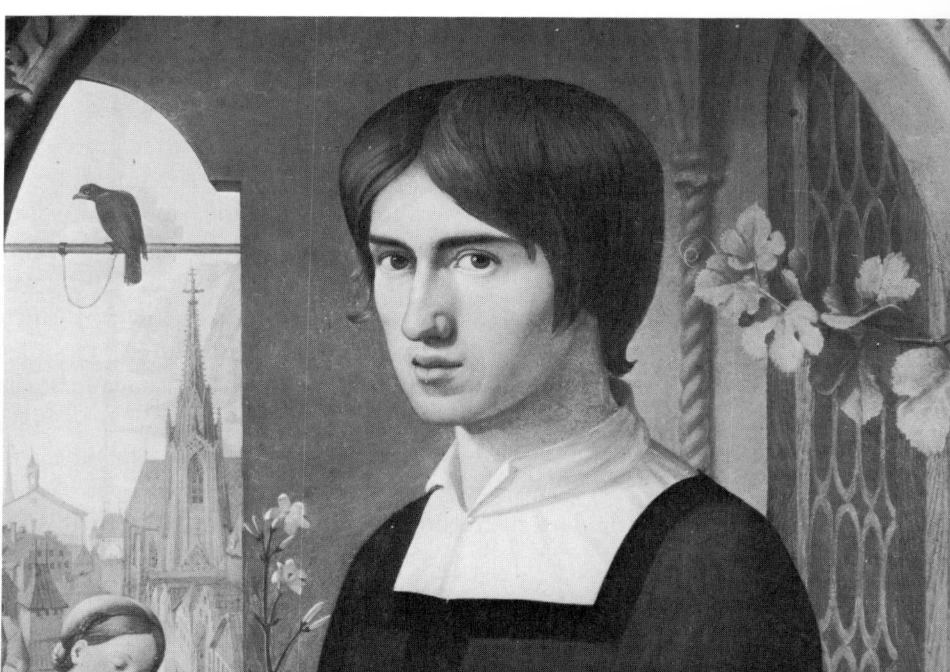

ness'. The systems of composition are equally diverse: Géricault's dynamic and open – it might have been cut out of some sprawling battle-piece, Overbeck's static and claustrally closed. It is therefore impossible to write about Romanticism as about Neo-classicism or any earlier international style, and the present book is necessarily very different from its predecessor.

The Neo-classical style was gradually transformed and fragmented in the early years of the nineteenth century, rather than rejected outright as the Rococo, for example, had been. An articulate and highly intelligent (though not a very gifted) artist of the time, Victor Schnetz, traced the origin of Romantic painting in France to the studio of the great Neo-classic Jacques-Louis David, who encouraged his pupils to develop their own individual talents. The Romantic movement was a revolution, he said, 'not an insurrection'.[3] Neo-classicism had been a regenerative movement, an attempt to purify the arts and create a style of universal relevance and eternal validity, deeply coloured by its anti-Rococo origin. Those who strove to realize its austere, logically conceived ideal of perfection were said to be on '*la bonne route*'. But from the mid-1790s this 'right road' came increasingly to be regarded as a cul-de-sac. Thus, while the Romantics inherited the high seriousness of Neo-classicism and its revulsion against frivolous or merely decorative art, they sought to express ideals which could be sensed only in the individual soul and lay beyond the bounds of logical discourse. The Romantic followed a 'mysterious way' which, in Novalis's phrase, 'leads inwards' – and sometimes led to solipsism.

For the Romantics, the individual sensibility was the only faculty of aesthetic judgement. The rules of art had to be submitted to it, just as the dogmas of the Church had been weighed, accepted or rejected according to the Protestant's inner light. Works of art previously accepted as models by universal consent were committed for re-trial. Caspar David Friedrich declared the artist's only law to be his feelings. 'Trust your own genius,' wrote the American painter Washington Allston, 'listen to the voice within you, and sooner or later she will make herself understood not only to you, but she will enable you to translate her language to the world, and this it is which forms the only real merit of any work of art.' Hence the new attitudes to artistic theory and to artistic education (the word academic began to acquire opprobrious overtones). Hence, too, the belief that the artist must express the beliefs, hopes, fears of his own time and country, for nationalism is a corporate form of individualism closely linked with the idea of freedom. And when this idea was taken to its illogical extreme in fiction, and perhaps also in real life, the feelings of the artist could count for more than the works he produced – or failed to produce. The hero of Charles Nodier's *Peintre de Salzbourg* claims to be, and is accepted as, a genius, although he never manages to paint anything. Another tragic hero, in Balzac's story *Le Chef-d'œuvre inconnu*, captures the essence of life in a 'masterpiece' which to his friends seems to be no more than a chaotic mess of pigment, and he commits suicide. One may wonder if Nodier and Balzac knew of Philipp Otto Runge, who devoted most of his brief career as a painter to the creation of what he called 'an abstract painterly fantastic-musical poem with choirs, a composition for all the arts collectively, for which architecture should raise a unique building', but lived to paint only one part which he instructed his brother to destroy. Nathaniel Hawthorne's story *The Artist of the Beautiful* was certainly inspired partly by the vast unfinished *Belshazzar's Feast* on which Washington Allston had worked during the last twenty-five years of his life. 'The poet leaves his song half sung, or finishes it beyond the scope of mortal ears, in a celestial choir,' Hawthorne wrote.

> The painter – as Allston did – leaves half his conception on the canvas to sadden us with its imperfect beauty, and goes to picture forth the whole, if it be no irreverence to say so, in the hues of heaven. But rather such incomplete designs of this life will be perfected nowhere. This so frequent abortion of man's dearest projects must be taken as a proof that the deeds of earth, however etherealised by piety or genius, are without value, except as exercises and manifestations of the spirit.

These ideas tended to set a new importance on the sketch – as the least premeditated form of art, in which the painter's or sculptor's feelings might seem to be recorded with spontaneous directness – and thus to the free handling of pigment or clay which revealed in the most direct manner possible the individuality of the artist's 'touch', his or her unique manner of expression. But meticulously detailed, delicately precise drawings and paintings could also present an unmistakably personal, sometimes almost myopically close-sighted, vision of the world – a hypersensitive response to the exquisite uniqueness of natural forms, rendered in nervously frail lines. What the Romantics sought at all costs to avoid were the blandly impersonal compositions, the glabrously smooth bodies and anonymous 'licked' surfaces of academic art. Similarly, they rejected the notion that symbolical images had codified meanings laid down in emblem books. They felt free to use symbols either in traditional or new ways, to give personal significance to those

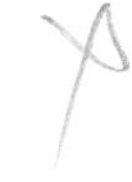

which had long been familiar, or to find others to express the constant preoccupations of the human spirit. Nothing could be further from their ideals than Renaissance or Baroque allegories with a one-to-one relationship between emblems and ideas, painted according to programmes often devised by patrons or men of letters. A Romantic work of art expresses the unique point of view of its creator. As Novalis claimed, 'The more personal, local, peculiar, of its own time, a poem is, the nearer it stands to the centre of poetry.'

A new significance was thus given to autobiography, which had attracted increasing interest during the eighteenth century. Rousseau's *Confessions* (written 1765–70 and published 1782) is a declaration of singularity – '*si je ne vaux pas mieux, au moins je suis autre*'. But the Romantics believed that they were worth more precisely *because* they were different from other men. The explicitly autobiographical character and intimate, almost confessional tone of so many of their greatest poems and paintings (Wordsworth's *The Prelude* and Constable's views of his childhood home; nearly all the poetry of Leopardi; Caspar David Friedrich's paintings, especially those of himself and his wife) is largely responsible for the persistent (and misguided) tendency to seek similarly intimate statements in the literature and art of other periods – the plays of Shakespeare, for example, or the paintings of Watteau.

The eighteenth century had been an age of classification. Insects, plants, animals and the races of man were divided into genera, species and sub-species. It was commonly supposed that this would lay bare the Divine Order or rational structure beneath the face of nature, but the result was entirely contrary. Intensive study of individual specimens only revealed their differences, encouraging speculation about the conflicts of opposed forces and the mysterious processes of growth and mutation. Intuition was called in to solve the problems which empiricism had brought to the surface. Gradually the mechanistic and static conception of Creation was replaced by one that was organic and dynamic. At the same time attitudes to human nature underwent a no less momentous change. The old idea that it had been at all times and in all places the same could not be maintained in the light of increasing knowledge, whether of the history of political institutions, religions or the arts. And as the differences became more strongly marked, each civilization came to be judged on its own merits and each historical character according to the standards of his or her own time. History began to play in Western thought the dominant part it was to have throughout the nineteenth century. 'The best theory of art is its history,' Friedrich Schlegel wrote in 1812. It was at about this time, too, that works of art were first seen – and, indeed, displayed in museums – as expressions of historical styles on a par with one another, rather than as deviations from a single norm, the one true style.

In this way, what began as an enlightened inquiry into the assumptions of the Enlightenment, conducted by such daring thinkers as Herder and Kant, suddenly acquired a greater urgency and a more general significance in the 1790s. The course of the French Revolution enormously sharpened historical consciousness. It revealed the complexity of what had previously seemed to be simple ideas – that ideals of personal and political liberty, for example, were not identical and could be mutually exclusive. It demonstrated the frailty of reason and the force of passion, the insufficiency of theories, and the power of circumstances to shape events. As Wordsworth wrote:

> a shock had then been given
> To old opinions; and the minds of all men
> Had felt it.

Romanticism was, very largely, the response to this situation, or, rather, the diversity of individual responses to it, united only at their point of departure and constantly subject to revision in a constantly changing world.

For there is no linear progression in Romanticism. Romantic styles in the visual arts radiate outwards in all directions from the still centre of Neo-classicism. In French painting, for instance, it is possible to trace currents leading from Jacques-Louis David to Gros, Prud'hon and Ingres, from Gros to Géricault and Delacroix, and so on; though a graph of them would seem feverishly inconsequent and, in any case, too simplistic by half, revealing little of interaction and nothing of the influence of contemporary foreign painters or of the old masters. The relationships between the Romantics were always complex. Conscious opposition by one artist to the work of another helped to mould individual styles (and not only in works of art: contemporaries noted that as the collars worn by Monsieur Ingres grew higher and stiffer those of Delacroix became looser and softer). And the similarities which have been seen between the works of artists who sometimes knew nothing of one another (Blake and Philipp Otto Runge), or between painters and poets (Turner and Shelley), or between painters and musicians (Delacroix and Berlioz), derive from common preoccupations. Similarly, the aesthetic theories which proliferated in the period did not so much influence works of art as attempt to provide philosophical answers to the problems which perplexed artists.

The shock of the intellectual and political upheavals of the late eighteenth century was felt throughout the Western world. No artists were wholly immune to it, least of all those who sought to re-establish the status quo. All the art of the first half of the nineteenth century was to some extent coloured by Romantic ideas, which were much more pervasive than those of the Enlightenment had been in the eighteenth century. But the distinction that had then been drawn between artists who pursued the right road and those who complaisantly satisfied the whims of frivolous patrons was now understood in an entirely different way. The substitution of an expressive for a mimetic theory of the arts put a new emphasis on the authenticity of the emotions expressed and, consequently, on the artist's sincerity and integrity. Spontaneity, individuality and 'inner truth' came in this way to be recognized as the criteria by which all works of art, literature and music, of all periods and countries, should be judged. It is here, perhaps, that one essential, distinguishing characteristic of Romantic art becomes evident – the supreme value placed by the Romantics on the artist's sensibility and emotional 'authenticity' as the qualities which alone confer 'validity' on his work. Instead of reflecting the timeless, universal values of classicism, every Romantic work of art is unique – the expression of the artist's own personal living experience. Thus many paintings of ostensibly 'romantic' subjects – of wild or exotic landscapes, of supernatural phenomena or scenes from medieval literature and history – and also those which imitate the styles of the great Romantic artists were, and still are, rejected for their lack of individual authenticity. As a character remarks in an early work by Victor Hugo: '*Distinguons, Monsieur; il y a des romantiques et romantiques.*'

1. For Lack of a Better Name

In the 1790s, under the double impact of the final stage of the Enlightenment and the French Revolution, misgivings and doubts which had gradually begun to be felt in the eighteenth century suddenly acquired deeper and more perplexing significance. Old orthodoxies were shaken, old certainties were undermined. Weapons forged by the *philosophes* to assault superstition were now turned against their own most cherished beliefs about the sufficiency of human reason, the perfectibility of man and the logical order of the universe. Problems which they had raised but left unsolved, because they were insoluble empirically, now seemed to be those which most urgently called for answers. From a tumult of anguished doubts, new convictions, which could not be reduced to simple formulae, began to emerge – belief in the primacy of imagination, the potentialities of intuition, the importance of the emotions and emotional integrity, and, above all, the uniqueness and unique value of every human being in a constantly changing cosmos.

The arts were both influenced by and played a part in this radical transformation of Western thought. For now the work of art – painting, poem, novel or musical composition – came to be regarded not simply as a reflection of reality or the embodiment of an immutable and rationally conceived ideal, but as an insight into the life of things and, perhaps, a means of lightening the 'burthen of the mystery ... the heavy and the weary weight of all this unintelligible world'. The age-old mimetic theory of the arts was replaced by an expressive one. For the first time in Western thought, aesthetics moved from the periphery to the centre of philosophical systems, and the meaning and purpose of the arts were more profoundly questioned than ever before. To explain the change in attitude that was taking place and to revalue the arts in its light a new critical vocabulary had to be created: hence the proliferation of artistic theories in the 1790s and the first decades of the nineteenth century – many of them couched in the form of definitions of Romanticism.[1]

These definitions can be misleading if they are read as straightforward statements or manifestos. As early as 1824 Émile Deschamps remarked that Romanticism had so often been defined, and the whole question reduced to such confusion as a result, that he hesitated to make darkness still darker by a fresh attempt.[2] His words have been echoed by innumerable writers ever since. But Deschamps had a particular reason for raising the issue. He was spokesman for a group of young poets, including Victor Hugo and Alfred de Vigny, who had been attacked and dubbed *romantiques* by the guardian of French artistic morals, the permanent secretary of the Académie française. Instead of embroiling himself in a discussion of Romanticism, Deschamps parried the attack by simply listing other writers who had been described as Romantics during the previous two decades – Chateaubriand, Byron, Mme de Staël, Goethe, Schiller, Joseph de Maistre, Vincenzo Monti, Thomas Moore, Walter Scott and Lamennais.

Victor Hugo, Alfred de Vigny and the other writers whom Deschamps defended did not call themselves Romantics. In the same year Hugo professed 'profound ignorance' of the terms 'romantic' and 'classic', saying that he could distinguish in literature as in everything else only the good and the bad, the beautiful and the deformed, the true and the false.[3] Two of the writers on Deschamps's list, Goethe and Byron, explicitly dissociated themselves from Romanticism.[4] There were, in fact, relatively few self-styled Romantic writers (Stendhal and Pushkin are the most notable[5]), and still fewer artists. When called 'the Victor Hugo of painting', Delacroix provocatively replied: '*Je suis un pur classique.*' But his objection to being called a Romantic was itself the expression of a characteristically Romantic belief in the uniqueness of his own individuality, and of a reluctance to allow it to be submerged in any school or coterie – any 'associations of mediocrities', as he termed them. He was prepared to accept the Romantic badge when he could wear it as a mark of difference, and told Théophile Silvestre in 1854: 'If one understands by my Romanticism the free manifestations of my personal impressions, my aversion for the stereotypes of the schools and my repugnance for academic formulae, I must admit not only that I am Romantic but that I was so at the age of fifteen: I already preferred Prud'hon and Gros to Guérin and Girodet.'[6]

The young writers and artists in Paris who were called Romantics had no programme, no common goal: they did not offer new dogmas for old. '*Tous les systèmes sont faux,*' wrote Hugo, '*le génie seul est vrai.*' In 1825 the *classique* Delécluze commented: 'They differ so much in opinions, have such different points of departure and reach such contrary conclusions that it is really impossible to extract an *idée-mère* from all this chaos.'[7] They were, and still are, identified because they differed – both from their predecessors and from the majority of their contemporaries. The only constant and common factor in their ever-shifting attitudes and scales of value was belief in the importance of individuality – of the individual self and its capacity for experience – and the rejection of all values not expressive of it. This emphasis on the supreme value of the personal sensibility of the artist is, of course, closely allied to those notions of genuineness and sincerity and 'living experience' (or *Erlebnis* in German philosophy) which led to the Romantic conception of personal authenticity or what, for want of a better word, one may call personal truth. In this way the work of art becomes self-validating. For it is by the degree to which the work expresses the artist's personal, living experience that it acquires inward coherence.

The word Romantic has come to be used in a bewildering variety of ways, as a term of abuse or praise, as a chronological, aesthetic or psychological category, to describe erotic emotions or purely cerebral processes. As none of these forms of usage is indefensible, and all may be traced back to the early nineteenth century, those who have attempted to establish a precise definition have often given up in despair. 'It is impossible to think seriously if one uses words like *Classicism*, *Romanticism*, *Humanism* or *Realism*,' wrote Paul Valéry. 'Nobody can get drunk or quench his thirst on labels.'[8]

Unfortunately, there is no word other than 'Romantic' which can be, or has been, used to describe that new attitude to art and life which began to emerge in the 1790s, what Isaiah Berlin has called a 'shift of consciousness' which 'cracked the backbone of European thought'. When, in 1819, the German historian of European poetry Friedrich Bouterwek came to describe the work of his younger contemporaries, he referred to 'the new school, which for lack of a better name might as well be called Romantic'.[9] Similarly, a few years later, a French art critic found himself obliged to call Géricault the leader of 'that new school which aims at the faithful representation of strong and affecting emotions which is rightly or wrongly called the Romantic school'.[10] For want of another, the word stuck and was soon applied not only to a group of poets in Germany and a new school of painters in France, but to musicians, artists, philosophers, novelists and even scientists of the same period in England, Italy, Spain, Russia, Scandinavia and America. In this mainly chronological sense, it has at least as clear a meaning as 'Renaissance'. Nor is it entirely meaningless even in its loosest and most colloquial usage – as in the advertising slogan 'tiny glints of gold make dull hair romantic'.[11]

In 1818 Giovanni Berchet claimed that the two words most frequently heard in Milan were *classico* and *romantico*. To clarify the meaning of the latter he wrote an entertaining imaginary interview with an Englishman, My lord P., who says:

> I have heard a woman lament that the form of her fan was classic rather than romantic, *all nonsense*... Another was examining a landscape painting by Gozzi and complained that it was too classical, *all nonsense*. The poor little thing believed perhaps that classic was the antithesis of our old English adjective romantic which has a significance entirely different from that of the new literary epithet of today...[12]

But the original meaning of the 'old English adjective' is not without importance.[13] In 1755 Dr Johnson defined 'Romantick' as: 'resembling the tales or romances; wild ... improbable; false ...; fanciful; full of wild scenery'. None of these meanings was lost during the next half century; but each acquired a more positive significance as romances were revalued, as the qualities of wild scenery came to be more sensitively appreciated and, especially, as the words *wild*, *improbable*, *false* and *fanciful* were opposed not to *civilized*, *historical*, *true* and *logical* so much as to *constrained*, *superficially apparent*, *dogmatic* and *unimaginative*.

The many definitions of Romanticism published between the 1790s and the 1830s are symptomatic of an obsessive urge to explore, to describe and account for, the qualities in works of art and literature which had suddenly come to be most highly valued. They reflect a desire to discover why some works of art made a strong emotional appeal and others did not, even though they seemed to observe all the rules which had been derived from the masterpieces then accepted as the greatest products of the human mind and hand. The word Romantic, so often used to describe the former, thus acquired a qualitative sense. For E. T. A. Hoffmann, writing in 1810, Beethoven was '*ein rein romantischer ... Komponist*', because his music 'sets in motion the lever of fear, of awe, of horror, of suffering, and awakens that infinite longing which is the essence of Romanticism'.[14]

That there is no disputing about matters of taste was a well-established cliché, though one which had seldom prevented disputes. Eighteenth-century theorists discussed the question rationally, also investigating that *je ne sais quoi* which was seen to lie beyond the rules of art. But for them the final appeal was always to the court of common consent; the canon of masterpieces was composed of works which had been approved by the best critics. The Romantics appealed only to their own sensibilities – to their own 'living experience' which alone could grant value and authenticity to the work. They were the first to appreciate that – to quote the sculptor Auguste Préault – '*jamais deux personnes n'ont lu le même livre, ni vu le même tableau*'. Individuality conditioned both the creation of the work of art and the response of the reader, spectator or listener. Washington Allston, the American painter who had sat at the feet of Coleridge, declared that 'the several characteristics, Originality, Poetic Truth, Invention, each imply a something not inherent in the objects imitated, but which must emanate alone from the mind of the Artist'.[15]

The Romantics were more deeply concerned with qualities than rules, with integrity of feeling than with rectitude of judgement – with poetry than with prosody. They gave a new significance to the distinction between poetry and verse (rather than poetry and prose) inherited from earlier criticism. They were also obsessed by such similarly imprecise distinctions as those between genius and talent, imagination and fancy, originality and novelty, truth and verisimilitude, sensibility and sentimentality. As a result, the words acquired, if not entirely new meanings, new implications which they retain to the present day.

'We were the last Romantics,' wrote W. B. Yeats in 1931. But it is no easier to escape from Romantic attitudes nowadays, or even to recognize them for what they are. The Romantics were, for example, largely responsible for relativism in appreciating the arts of other periods or places – for the belief that they should be judged strictly according to their own standards, though, ironically, they also erected barriers which hinder such relative judgements. Wordsworth's often misunderstood declaration that 'poetry is the spontaneous overflow of powerful feelings' still colours attitudes to literature in general, and often to the visual arts and music as well. It requires, strangely enough, less of a conscious effort to understand Schelling's emotionally subjective statement that 'architecture is frozen music' than to comprehend the Renaissance theory of harmonic proportions in architecture, although the latter is a product of rational modes of thought.

For many people the terms 'poetry' and 'Romantic poetry' are almost synonymous. Englishmen brought up on Keats, Shelley and Wordsworth often seem able to appreciate in earlier poetry only the qualities which were emphasized by the Romantics, so that they respond half-heartedly to the allegory of Spenser, the wit of Shakespeare, or the polish and elegance of Pope. Similarly, the music of Beethoven, Schubert and Schumann all too often conditions attitudes to – and sometimes the performance of – Monteverdi, Vivaldi or Bach, just as, in the visual arts, the paintings of Turner, Constable, Blake, Caspar David Friedrich, Géricault and Delacroix brought about a complete transformation in our ways of seeing both nature and art. They made it increasingly difficult for subsequent generations to respond to the art of the Renaissance or of Antiquity in a pre-nineteenth-century manner – to see, as it were, Raphael's *Stanze*, the Apollo Belvedere or the Medici Venus from Winckelmann's viewpoint, still less through a contemporary's eyes. Though it was, of course, the great Neo-classical theorist Winckelmann who, more than anyone else, taught Europe to look at Antiquity in a new 'subjective' manner, and thereby initiated a revolution which was soon to topple from their pedestals the very statues on which he had based his aesthetic.[16]

Whether or not certain late eighteenth-century works of art should be called 'Neo-classical', 'pre-Romantic', 'early Romantic', 'Romantic-Classic' or simply 'Romantic' may be endlessly debated. There is no scientific system of stylistic taxonomy. But many of the intellectual preoccupations and emotional fixations, the attitudes to life and art, which characterize the mainstream of early nineteenth-century painting, are already clearly evident in such pictures of the first decade as Caspar David Friedrich's *The Cross in the Mountains*, J. M. W. Turner's *The Fall of an Avalanche in the Grisons* and A.-J. Gros's *Napoleon on the Battlefield of Eylau*. These three great paintings are entirely dissimilar works by artists of diverse nationalities. And each one reveals a different kind of break – and continuity – with established traditions.

Caspar David Friedrich's *The Cross in the Mountains* [1] might at first sight be mistaken for an essay in the eighteenth-century tradition of 'sublime' prospects, a depiction of a crucifix of the type often erected in Catholic countries as a memorial or an object of pilgrimage. But although the smooth grass of the hill-top, the dark fir-trees and the clouds flushed with a sunset glow are rendered with meticulous truth to nature, the picture conveys a feeling of rapt stillness, an unearthly quiet which is almost hallucinatory. A devout Protestant, Friedrich painted it without a commission, apparently intending to send it to the Protestant King of Sweden, but was later persuaded to sell it to the Catholic Graf and Gräfin von Thun-Hohenstein, as an altarpiece for their private chapel in Schloss Tetschen.[17] This is not without significance, if only because it

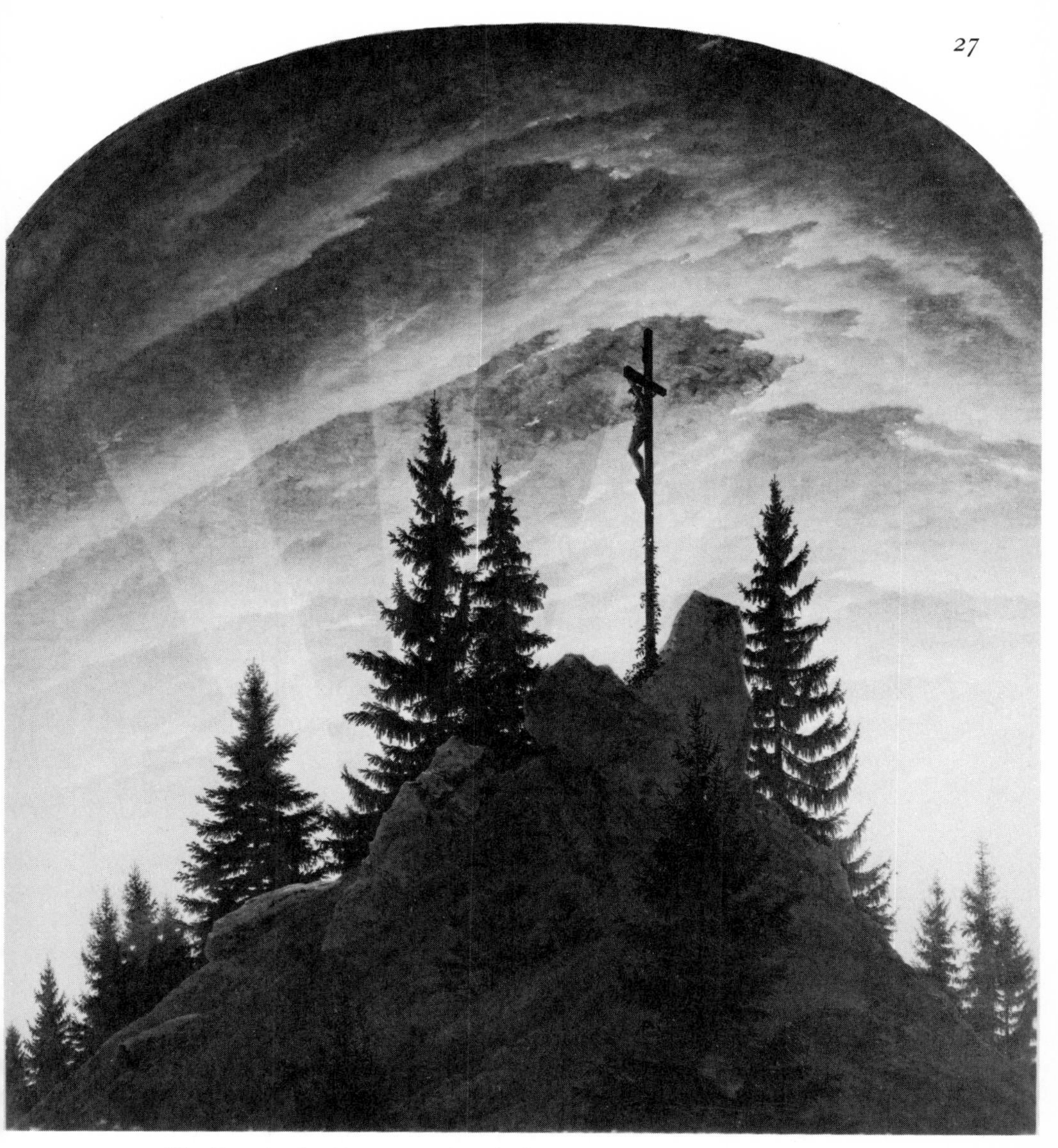

1. *The Cross in the Mountains*, 1807–8. Caspar David Friedrich

emphasizes the painting's underlying ambiguity. Expressing a new attitude to religion which transcends sectarianism and makes conventional eighteenth-century acceptance or rejection of the Christian creeds seem equally shallow, this deeply moving and, at the same time, perplexing work is unlike any earlier or later devotional image. It is so undogmatic that it holds its potency even in the present age of unbelief.

When the picture was first exhibited in Friedrich's studio in Dresden, at Christmas 1808, a visitor noted that everyone who came into the room was moved: 'Even loud-mouths ... spoke seriously and in quiet tones as if they were in a church.' Not so Friedrich Wilhelm Basilius von Ramdohr, Chancellor of the Saxon court, who was so incensed by the painting and its success that he published a denunciation in the *Zeitung für die elegante Welt*. Ramdohr, author of a treatise on aesthetics entitled *Charis* (Leipzig, 1793), which included a chapter summarizing the Neo-classical theory of landscape painting, was particularly well qualified to recognize the bold innovatory qualities of *The Cross in the Mountains*. To him it was the manifestation of a 'hitherto unknown notion of the art of landscape' which could endanger 'good taste' and rob painting of its 'specific excellence'. He associated it, moreover, with the 'calamitous spirit of the present times' and the horrible events of recent history. 'To keep silent would be pusillanimous,' he solemnly announced.

Citing the examples of Claude, Poussin and Ruisdael, and quoting from the French theorist Pierre-Henri de Valenciennes, Ramdohr indicated how Friedrich had set his face against all the accepted rules of landscape painting – in his manner of composition, his use of light and shade ('he has cast the earth into darkness') and his ignorance of, or reluctance to employ, aerial perspective. But he found the picture's implications still more disturbing. Was it a happy notion to make use of landscape to allegorize a religious idea? Should the pious be summoned to prayer by such a work? He contrasted Friedrich's symbolical picture with the long tradition of 'atmospheric' landscapes, instancing with approval Ruisdael's *Jewish Cemetery*.[18] He also drew a very firm distinction between the emotions which, in his view, could or should be aroused by art and by nature.

The innovations which shocked Ramdohr become clearly apparent when *The Cross in the Mountains* is set beside such an Alpine landscape as Caspar Wolf's *Lauteraargletscher* of 1776 [2]. Unlike Friedrich's picture, this is a topographically exact view, skilfully composed according to eighteenth-century conventions. Human figures set the scale, mark the perspective recession and provide a comforting contrast with the desolation of the scene. Apprehensive dogs indicate the terror of the bare mountain, but men are in command of the situation, apparently engaged in rational discussion of the beauties and wonders of nature: one of them has prudently provided himself with a parasol. It is an appealing picture, which might serve to illustrate many an eighteenth-century account

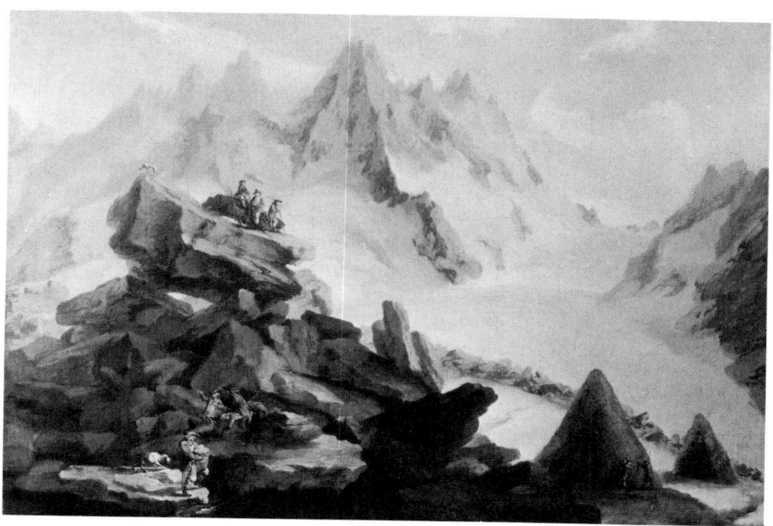

2. *The Lauteraargletscher*, 1776. Caspar Wolf

of Alpine travels, full of feeling for the sublime and reflecting enlightened intellectual curiosity in natural phenomena. But it contains no hint of what Coleridge was to call 'inner goings-on', no suspicion of a profounder meaning, of 'something far more deeply interfused'. Wolf's mountains are not seen as 'temples of Nature built by the Almighty', as 'natural cathedrals, or natural altars . . . with their clouds resting on them as the smoke of a continual sacrifice'.[19] The view is presented quite objectively – with logical visual clarity so that the spectator can respond to it as he would before the scene itself.

Friedrich broke the structure of the eighteenth-century landscape with its nicely measured planes which lead the eye gently into the far distance. His painting is without a foreground: the lower line of the frame cuts through hill and trees. The view is thus presented as if the spectator were suspended in mid-air or gazing out of a high window. But it departed still further and more obviously from traditional religious paintings. The very idea of installing such a picture in the place of a conventional devotional image above an altar must have seemed extraordinary if not shocking.

Ramdohr concluded his article by associating Friedrich with 'Jena mysticism which like a narcotic vapour is at present insinuating itself everywhere, in art as in science, in philosophy as in religion'. A decade earlier, Fichte had raised a storm by affirming his equation of God with the moral order of the universe in an article which cost him his professorial chair at Jena but profoundly influenced a group of young thinkers, including Novalis, Schleiermacher and the Schlegel brothers.[20] Some of his ideas were summarized in Novalis's strange mystical novel *Heinrich von Ofterdingen*, published in 1802:

> *Eins in allem und alles im Einen*
> *Gottes Bild auf Kräutern und Steinen*
> *Gottes Geist in Menschen und Tieren,*
> *Dies muss man sich zu Gemüte führen.**[21]

And *The Cross in the Mountains* might well be interpreted as an expression of this transcendental pantheism which had many adherents in Dresden but was bitterly opposed by Ramdohr (partly perhaps for personal reasons[22]).

In order to reply to Ramdohr, Friedrich was persuaded by his friends to write a description and interpretation of the picture[23]:

> *Description of the Picture.* On the peak of the rock the cross is raised high, surrounded with evergreen firs and with evergreen ivy entwining its base. The sun sinks radiating beams of light and in the crimson glow of evening the Saviour gleams on the Cross.
>
> *Interpretation of the Picture.* Jesus Christ, nailed to the wood, is turned towards the sinking sun, as to the image of the eternal life-giving Father. The old world – the time when God the Father moved directly on the earth – died with the teaching of Jesus. This sun sank and the earth was no longer able to comprehend the departing light. The purest, the most precious metal of the Saviour's figure on the Cross shines forth in the gold of the evening light and thus reflects it on the earth in softened brilliance. The Cross stands erected on a rock unshakably firm as our faith in Jesus Christ. Evergreen, enduring through all ages, the firs stand round the Cross, like the hope of mankind in Him, the Crucified.[24]

The vagueness and complexity of this passage only serve to emphasize that the painting cannot be adequately described in words. Like all Friedrich's mature works, *The Cross in the Mountains* demands and beggars description, calls for explanation yet defies analysis. For it is a symbolical rather than an allegorical picture – to use a distinction popular at the period – and Friedrich's prose does not provide an iconographical programme, but an aid to the interpretation of a spiritual idea which he was able to formulate only in paint. Later he was to commend a fellow artist for expressing 'through colour and form what words cannot render'.[25]

* 'One in everything and everything in one, God's image in leaves and stones, God's spirit in men and beasts, this must be impressed on the mind.'

The painting may, perhaps, be interpreted as an expression not so much of any positive belief but rather of that mood of doubt which was to characterize so much nineteenth-century thought – the gnawingly insistent, agonizing doubt and longing for faith which might be palliated, though seldom overcome, either by a resort to nihilism or by conversion to one of the more authoritarian creeds. The picture's ambiguities, the questions it poses but does not answer, suggest doubt of both rationalism and Christianity. The spectator is obliged to ponder whether it represents a wayside cross or Golgotha, whether Christ has turned his back on the world, whether the sun that is setting will rise again and – more subtly – whether the faith to which Friedrich refers in his explanation will be cut down by chance or change, like the fallen trees in so many of his later paintings. It is an image of that 'honest doubt' in which, paradoxically, nineteenth-century faith lived most fully and painfully. That Friedrich was sometimes able to wrench faith from doubt is suggested by a slightly later picture, *Morning in the Riesengebirge* [3], where the crucifix on a rock reappears in the clear light of sunrise, with the figure of a woman leading the painter himself to its foot. The spiritual turbulence of *The Cross in the Mountains* has been quelled in this serene windless landscape with white mists

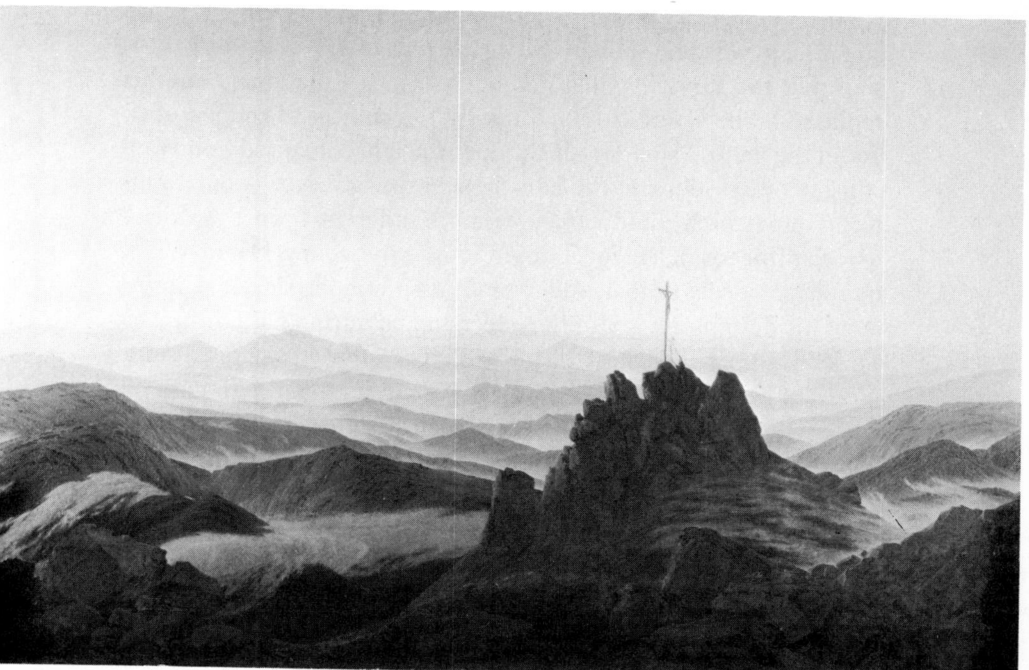

3. *Morning in the Riesengebirge*, 1810–11. Caspar David Friedrich

hanging over the sloughs, a majestic aerial view in which the purity of light and infinity of the horizon seem close to God. It also expresses a characteristically Romantic attitude to nature – one close, perhaps, to Fichte's *Naturphilosophie* and 'Jena mysticism' – but lacks the strange power of the earlier picture to move and trouble the soul.

Friedrich was one of the most withdrawn and isolated of all painters, living in a private world of his own creation. He was not of a theorizing turn of mind, and his epigrammatic remarks hardly constitute the basis of a coherent aesthetic or any consistent view of the world.[26] For art theorists as for connoisseurs he had little but contempt, which deepened with the years. Thinking in line and colour, rather than words and phrases, he evolved his extraordinary personal style as if by the guidance of his own 'inner light'. He may well have been unaware of the width of the gulf he had leaped in painting *The Cross in the Mountains*. Nor were his admirers as fully conscious of its revolutionary nature as his opponents. His detractor Ramdohr was the first to recognize that the whole fabric of art, as he understood it, had been shaken.

At about the same time in England, conservative critics were expressing their dismay at the innovations of a painter one year younger than Friedrich – J. M. W. Turner, born in 1775. 'That is madness,' said one of them of his *Falls of the Rhine at Schaffhausen*, shown at the Royal Academy in 1806. 'He is a madman,' another replied.[27] They were troubled not by the subject of the picture – one of the natural wonders of Europe which had inspired numerous effusive descriptions in the late eighteenth century[28] – but by its technique (which could hardly be more different from Friedrich's dry, flat linearity). 'As for Turner,' wrote the young David Wilkie in 1805, 'I really do not understand his methiod [sic] of painting at all his designs are grand the effect and colouring natural but his workmanship is the most obominable [sic] I ever saw and some pieces of his pictures you cannot make out at all and although his pictures are not large yet you must be at the other end of the room before they can satisfy the eye.'[29] His almost brutal handling of pigment with bold scumbling and much use of the palette knife was condemned as a 'vicious practice'. 'It is the scribbling of painting,' a critic complained in 1806, 'so much of the *trowel* – so *mortary* – surely a little more finishing might be borne?'[30]

Turner used his 'obominable' technique to still greater effect in a picture as violent in subject-matter as in handling: *The Fall of an Avalanche in the Grisons* [4], first exhibited in his own gallery

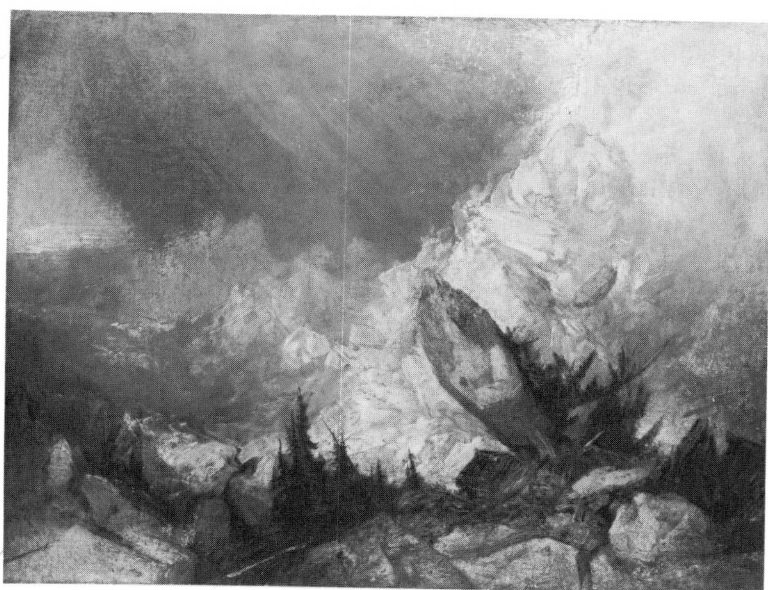

4. *The Fall of an Avalanche in the Grisons*, 1810. Turner

in 1810. Although he had been to Switzerland, he had not visited the Grisons, nor had he seen an avalanche. His immediate sources of inspiration seem to have been pictorial and literary. Philippe de Loutherbourg, to whom he was much indebted at this period, had shown an *Avalanche in the Alps in the Valley of Lauterbrunnen* at the Royal Academy in 1804. And James Thomson, one of his favourite poets, had described an avalanche in the Grisons in *The Seasons*.[31] There is, indeed, a strong echo of this passage in the verses Turner supplied as a catalogue entry for his picture. Yet the mood of *The Fall of an Avalanche in the Grisons* differs from the complacent Leibnitzian optimism of Thomson's poem, with its invocation to 'kindred glooms' and 'congenial horrors',[32] as much as its manner of handling does from Loutherbourg's sensuously painted work with its delicately balanced pattern of scrolls in massed cloud and rushing water.

Loutherbourg's picture is of a type which became increasingly popular in late eighteenth-century England. It seems to have been designed, almost too neatly, to satisfy the same taste for the sublime as the spectacles he staged in his Eidophusikon – a theatre without actors which showed, as he advertised it in the press in 1781, 'imitations of Natural Phenomena, represented by Moving Pictures'.[33] Here, audiences which included Reynolds and Gainsborough were thrilled by such spectacles as 'Storm at Sea and Loss of the Haleswell Indiaman', in which a painted scene was animated by coloured lights while the rumble of thunder, the rush of waves and the whistle of wind were simulated by shaking copper sheets, rattling peas in a box and waving silk streamers. Though sometimes cited as precocious manifestations of Romanticism, these curious entertainments reflect attitudes to nature and art totally at variance with those of the nineteenth-century Romantics. Descriptions of them recall Charles Lamb's comments on performances of *King Lear*: 'The contemptible machinery by which they mimic the storm which he goes out in, is not more adequate to represent the horrors of the real elements, than any actor can be to represent Lear: they might more easily propose to personate the Satan of Milton on the stage.'[34] Under the influence of the new expressive, rather than mimetic, theory of the arts, such spectacles as those of the Eidophusikon (which included 'Satan arraying his troops ... from Milton') and such pictures as those by Loutherbourg, which merely mimicked the visible world, came to be regarded as a very lowly form of art.[35] Turner's painting, on the other hand, powerfully conveys the sense of the artist's identification with nature – and with nature as a destructive as well as a creative force.

Neo-classical theorists had taught artists to look beneath the face of common nature and reveal in their pictures the underlying order of the universe. The Romantics were to find that superficial appearances concealed not so much order as impenetrable depths of inexplicable mystery. It was his overwhelming feeling for the senseless violence of nature and the helplessness of man in the face of the chaotic and cataclysmic that Turner expressed in *The Fall of an Avalanche in the Grisons*, by the use of such compositional devices as the jaggedly opposed diagonals of the foreground and the louring oppressive indistinctness of the background, no less than by his choice of subject. His first major masterpiece, *Snow Storm: Hannibal and his Army Crossing the Alps* [5], conveys, even more powerfully, the same experience – a disturbing insight into the futility of heroism in the face of history as well as nature, with diminutive figures perilously poised on the verge of a vortex which seems to suck them back into the primal chaos. In later works Turner was to express his tragic vision of the world by subtler means – in preternaturally bright and fleeting colours and in forms which merge and change, or are shrouded in the all engulfing blackness of despair – though never more forcefully than in this early masterpiece.

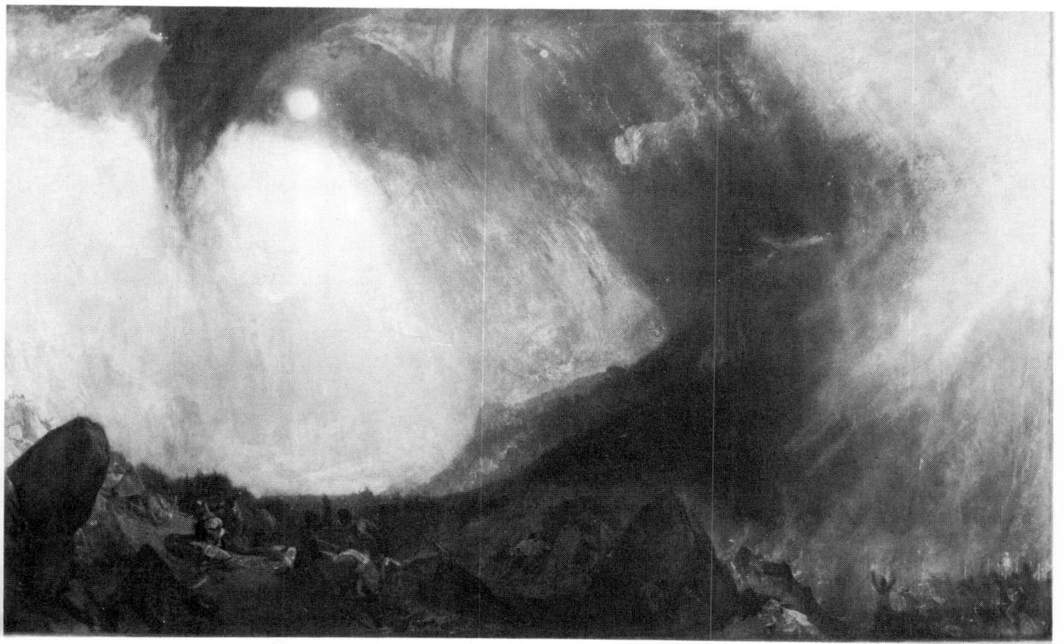

5. *Snow Storm: Hannibal and his Army Crossing the Alps*, 1812. Turner

Turner's extraordinary and constantly developing technique was an expression of his meaning. His starting-point seems to have been a Neo-classical abhorrence for the delicacy of *matière* and sweetness of colouring in Rococo painting and the deceitfulness of *trompe l'œil*. But he responded to these notions in his own way, rejecting not merely exquisite brush-work but smoothness of finish, not only illusionism but any device which would disguise his means. Other artists followed a similar process of development, to the consternation of conservative amateurs of art. In the 1820s a critic remarked: 'It is evident that Mr Constable's landscapes are like nature: it is still more evident that they are like paint.' Whether this was meant as praise or censure is not entirely clear, presumably the latter – though by this period, Lawrence Gowing suggests, painting was required to resemble itself before anything else, the operations portrayed being first and foremost the painter's.[36] Thus, it might be claimed that the autonomy of the work of art and the independence of its creator, for which Neo-classical artists had striven, were achieved, if in a different sense, by the Romantics.

To pass from the work of Caspar David Friedrich in Germany and Turner in England to that of Antoine-Jean Gros in France is to move from private lives to the public stage. Gros's *Battlefield of Eylau* [6], exhibited in 1808, the same year as Friedrich's *The Cross in the Mountains* and Turner's *Falls of the Rhine at Schaffhausen*, was an official commission for the series of *grandes machines* devised by Vivant Denon to celebrate Napoleon and the benefits of his régime. It thus presents a diametrically opposed political point of view to Turner's *Hannibal*, which seems to have an undertone of sardonic comment on the crossing of the Alps by the *Armée d'Italie* (for the French were often associated with the Carthaginians

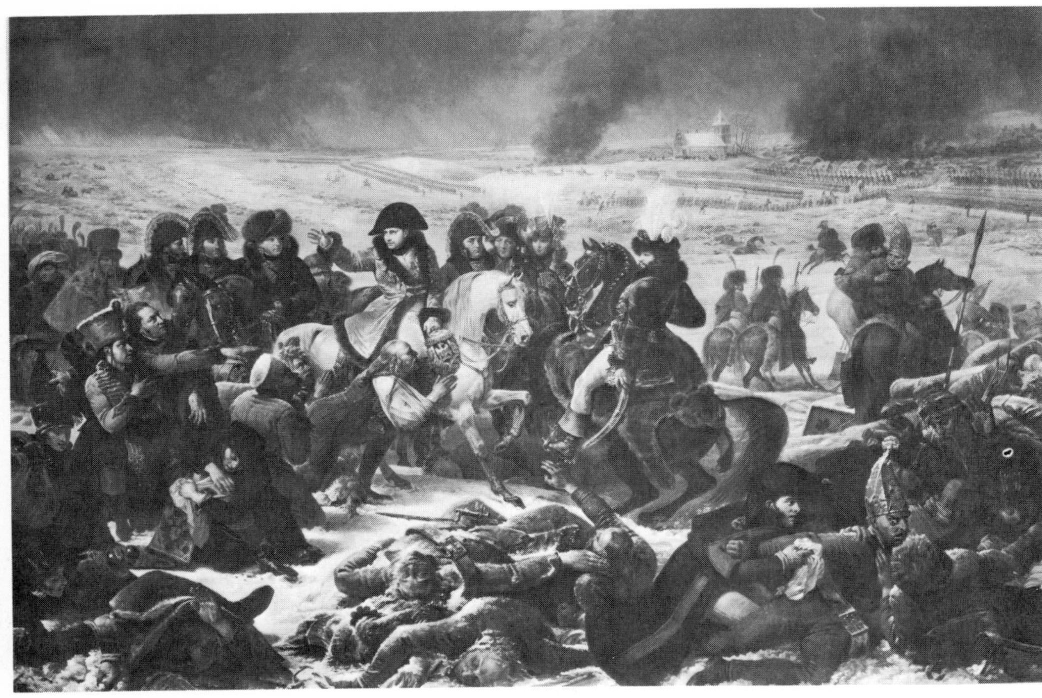

6. *Napoleon on the Battlefield of Eylau*, 1808. A.-J. Gros

at this period[37]). The battle fought between the French and the Russians at Eylau in Friedland, on 8 February 1807, was one of the bloodiest in the war and some 25,000 men are said to have been killed in it. Gros was required to commemorate an incident of the following morning: Napoleon revisiting the field and remarking that 'if all the kings of the world could contemplate such a spectacle, they would be less avid for wars and conquests.' This did not, needless to say, imply the least self-criticism. Napoleon regarded the Battle of Eylau, though fought far from French territory, as a defensive action. It was the Tsar, not he, who had been taught a lesson.

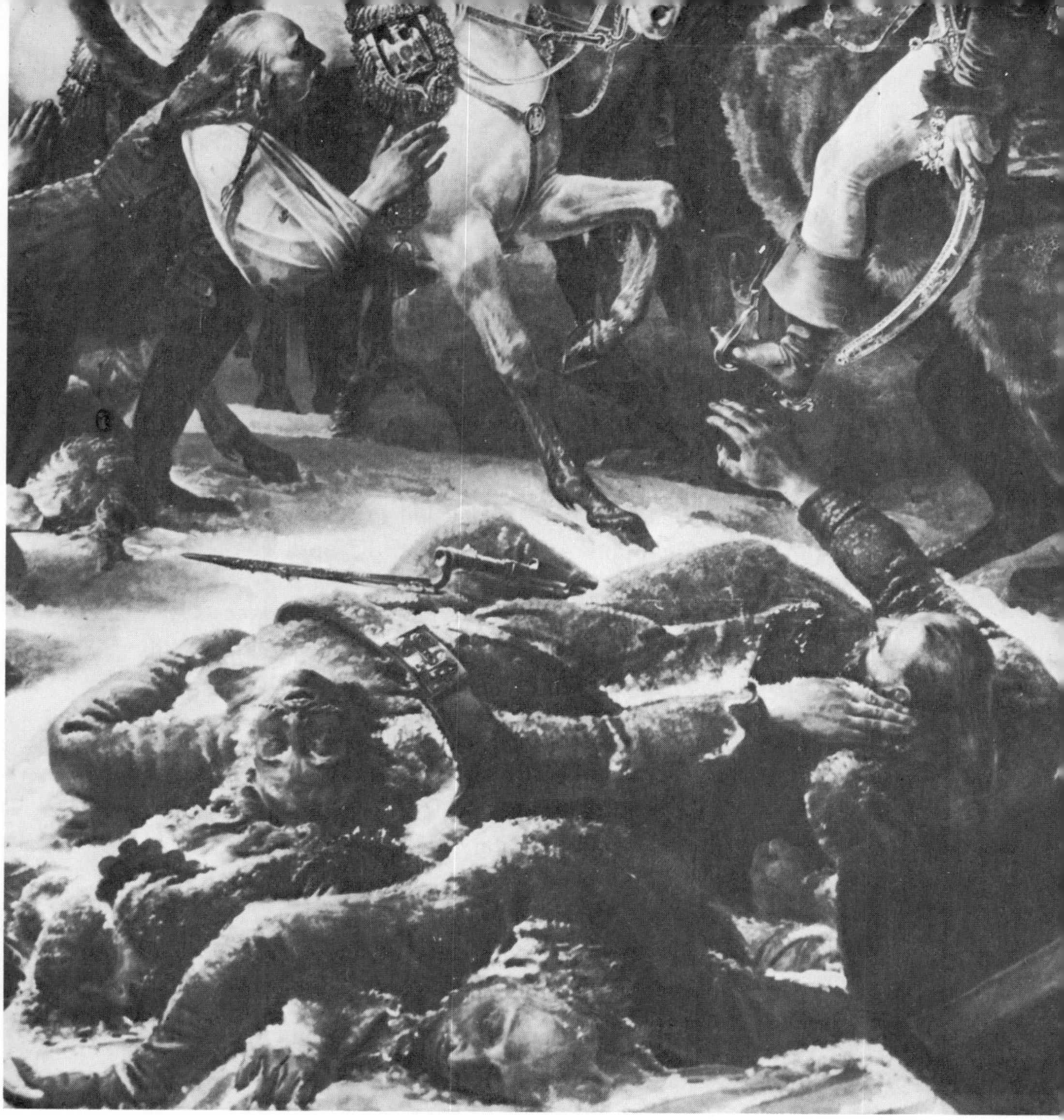

6a. Detail of 6

He could thus well afford to appear in the role of a pacific humanitarian – as Gros was to paint him.[38] And Gros was free to depict the horrors of war without any hint of disaffection.

Gros's previous Napoleonic picture *The Battle of Aboukir* had been criticized and compared unfavourably with the battle-pieces painted by Charles Le Brun for Louis XIV,[39] but the *Battlefield of Eylau* won general acclaim. Napoleon himself was more than satisfied and, after examining it in the Salon, took the cross of the Legion of Honour from his own coat and pinned it on to Gros's, creating him a baron of the Empire on the spot.[40] The gigantic canvas, eight metres wide, was carefully composed according to the established conventions for history painting in the grand style. Gros's debts to Rubens and, still more, to David are very evident. And although it gives an impression of realism, almost of reportage, it is as intricately constructed as any allegory, with every detail adroitly devised and placed to spell out the picture's meaning – from the burning houses on the sky-line and the distant lines of the army drawn up for Imperial review, to an abandoned bayonet with drops of blood congealed on its blade.

Gros was generally considered to be David's outstanding pupil, and one from whom David himself claimed to have learned, calling him a 'rival who reanimated his spirit and extended the compass of his ideas'.[41] The pupils of whom David disapproved were the group of radical painters known as *Barbus* or *Primitifs* who greatly influenced Ingres. Yet it was from Gros that the young *Romantiques* took their lead. This was accepted as an established fact by the 1830s. '*N'en doutons pas, c'est dans* Napoléon sur le champ de bataille d'Eylau *qu'est la naissance de l'école romantique*,' wrote Victor Schoelcher in 1831 in the pro-romantic periodical *L'Artiste*.[42] Similarly, Alfred de Musset drew his readers' attention to Gros's *Napoleon in the Plague House at Jaffa* [Fig. iv, p. 330]. 'Look at that vast and admirable composition; look at *Eylau*,' he exclaimed, 'and remember Géricault.'[43]

The foreground figures in the *Battlefield of Eylau* still command attention [6a]. Painted twice the size of life, as if they were fallen Titans, yet rendered with spine-chilling realism, this group of snow-sprinkled, blood-spattered corpses dominates the whole canvas. Partly because of their scale they are depicted in a broader manner and with greater boldness and virtuosity of handling than any other figures in the work of Gros. It is hardly surprising that they should have impressed young artists – as much as they initially shocked conservatives – whose eyes were accustomed to the smooth perfection of idealized marmoreal nudes by Neo-classical painters.[44] It was only to these figures that a few critics objected when the canvas was shown in the Salon of 1808, though none suggested that Gros had made a significant break with the teaching of David. And it may be questioned how far later attitudes to them were coloured by non-artistic sentiments.

When the *Battlefield of Eylau* was painted, Napoleon was at the height of his power, but within a few years the tide of fortune began to turn against him. As French attitudes to war were modified by a succession of Pyrrhic victories and then defeats – the retreat from

Moscow, the battles of Vittoria, Leipzig and finally Waterloo – attention shifted from the glory of the victors to the plight of the vanquished. It was, of course, in France that, almost for the first time in European history, the army was recognized as a representative part of the nation and not as a separate class.[45] Thus Frenchmen began, as it were, to identify themselves with the fallen figures in the foreground of Gros's picture rather than with the magnanimous Napoleon, the swaggering Murat and the plump self-satisfied fur-clad Marshals who constitute the central group. The process can be clearly traced in the work of Théodore Géricault.

In the Salon of 1812 Géricault exhibited a painting of an officer of the Imperial Guard (now in the Louvre), as jaunty and proud as Murat in the *Battlefield of Eylau*, thrilling to the music of battle, the boom of cannon and the whistle of grape-shot. His next Salon exhibit of 1814, no less strongly indebted to Gros, depicts a wounded cuirassier retreating from the field [7]. Whereas the earlier work had been a celebration of recklessly dashing bravado, the second is a picture of nobility, courage, endurance. This cuirassier is no mere symbol, Louis Aragon writes, 'but a man. Man. The tragic destiny of man. In the end there is only defeat.'[46] Géricault had

7. *Wounded Cuirassier*, 1814. Géricault

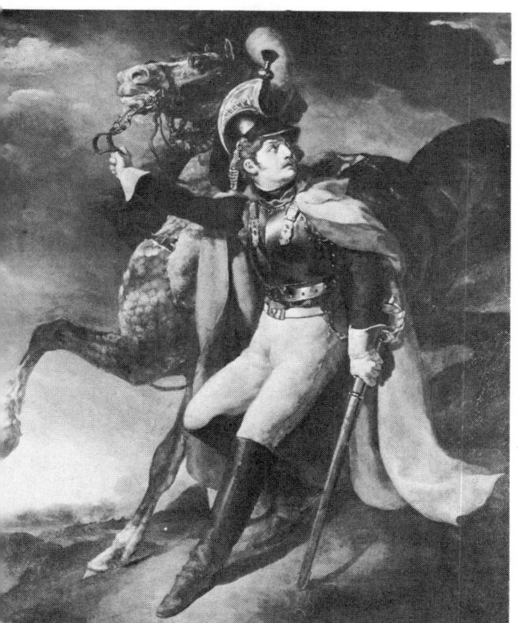

8. *The Return from Russia*, 1818. Géricault

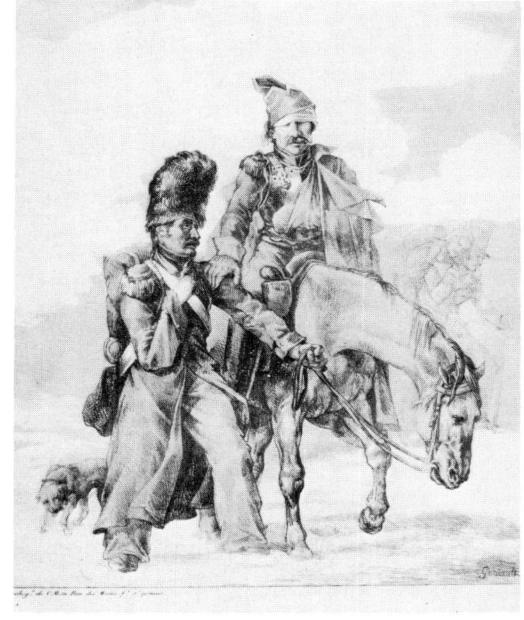

rendered what was conventionally regarded as a very un-heroic incident on a monumental scale, giving it an epic quality. But the poignancy of defeat is still more strongly emphasized in his lithographs of *A Cartload of Wounded Soldiers* and *The Return from Russia* [8] – emotionally charged images of the *servitude* rather than the *grandeur de la vie militaire*.

Only shortly after making these prints Géricault painted his masterpiece *The Raft of the 'Medusa'* [9], in which – as Lorenz Eitner succinctly put it – he 'took the foreground of human misery from one of Gros's pictures and omitted the apotheosis above'. Here

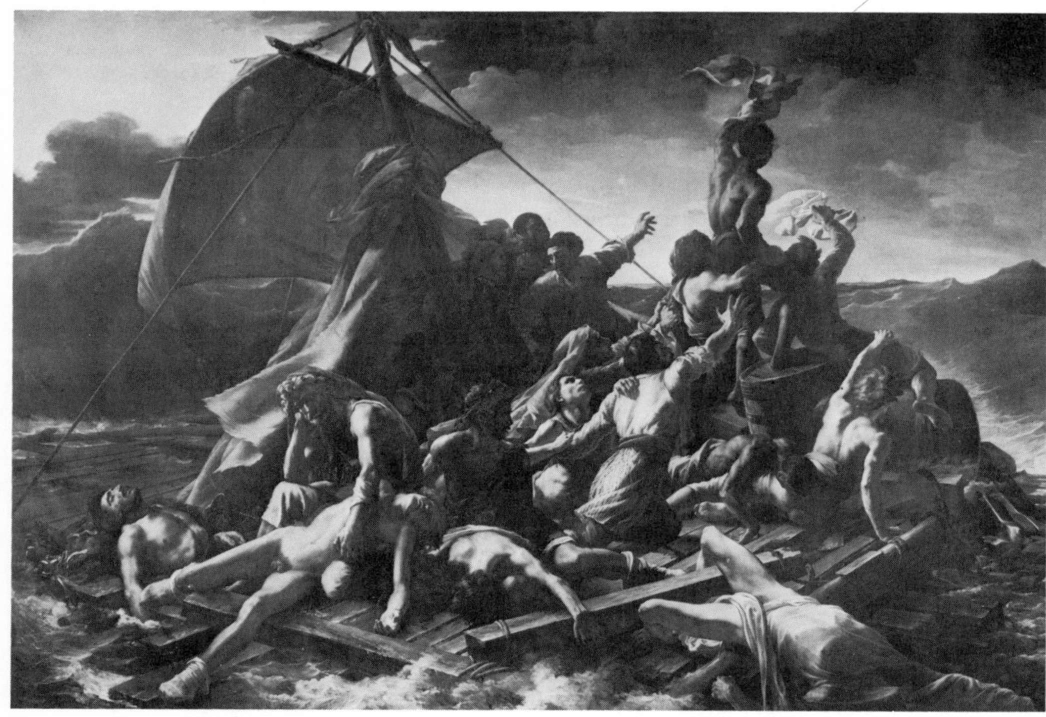

9. *The Raft of the 'Medusa'*, 1819. Géricault

the grand style and the heroic scale, hitherto reserved for grand and heroic themes – stories from the Bible, the exploits of Greek and Roman heroes, the deeds of rulers and their generals – were for the first time adopted to record the sufferings of ordinary people. The incident Géricault chose from the story of the shipwreck is highly significant. He began by considering several possible scenes: a mutiny on the raft, the survivors eating the bodies of their dead companions, as well as such obvious moments as those of the raft being cut adrift, and the final rescue. He rejected them all in favour of a subject of greater psychological tension and perplexing ambiguity: the false dawn of hope when the survivors sighted a distant ship, rallied their strength to signal to it, and then fell into profound despondency as it disappeared. Whether or not Géricault's choice carried any political significance as well, is difficult to determine. Simply by elevating a subject from 'low life', previously considered suitable only for a small-scale picture, he might seem to have been attacking both the long-established academic hierarchy of genres and the recently restored structure of society. But there can be no doubt that the picture came to be regarded as a political allegory. In a course of lectures suspended by the authorities of the tottering July Monarchy in 1847, Jules Michelet was to cite it as a symbol of France. '*C'est la France elle-même, c'est notre société toute entière qu'il embarqua sur ce radeau*,' he declared.

As published accounts of the wreck made abundantly plain, the men on the raft were not heroes in any normal sense of the word. Neither Spartan courage nor Stoic self-control was displayed by any of them: they had behaved as men all too frequently do in moments of crisis, and those who survived did so simply from a crude and animal urge to live. They suffered atrociously, but in no good or noble cause: they were victims of jobbery and incompetence, not of human or divine malevolence. But, by painting them as he did, Géricault raised the plight of the ship-wrecked to a level of universal significance, compelling the public to question their attitudes to the perennial problems of heroism, hope, despair and suffering, and providing only a disturbingly ambiguous answer.

In *La confession d'un enfant de siècle* (1836), Alfred de Musset describes the youth of France saying in the years of the Restoration: 'There is no more love. There is no more glory. A thick night covers the earth. And we shall be dead before the dawn.'[47] Géricault seems to have shared in this general depression, though without de Musset's sobbing self-pity. But lesser artists continued to indulge it throughout the years of the July Monarchy as well. Gros's dead and dying soldiers in the snow have an extensive progeny in pictures of incidents on the retreat from Russia – among which those by J.-F. Boissard de Boisdenier [10] and N.-T. Charlet are perhaps the most notable. Another painter, E.-A. Odier, produced a work [11] which conflated – and sentimentalized – Géricault's *Wounded Cuirassier* and lithograph *Return from Russia*. Such pictures owed their popularity and power to move partly to the haze of nostalgia which spread over the entire Empire period and partly to new attitudes to, or interpretations of, failure and success. For the Romantics had transformed the Christian doctrine of spiritual victory in physical defeat into a cult of failure – a cult not only of the defeated hero but of the unfulfilled genius, the poet who died young and neglected (Gilbert, Chatterton, André Chénier, Keats), of the incomplete masterpiece and the unconsummated passion. In this new pantheon Géricault himself was accorded an honoured place. (The otherwise reliable Charles Clément stated quite erroneously and very significantly that *The Raft of the 'Medusa'* was universally condemned when first exhibited, presumably in the belief that contemporary failure was almost a prerequisite for posthumous success.) Metaphorically, and often physically, a cast of Géricault's

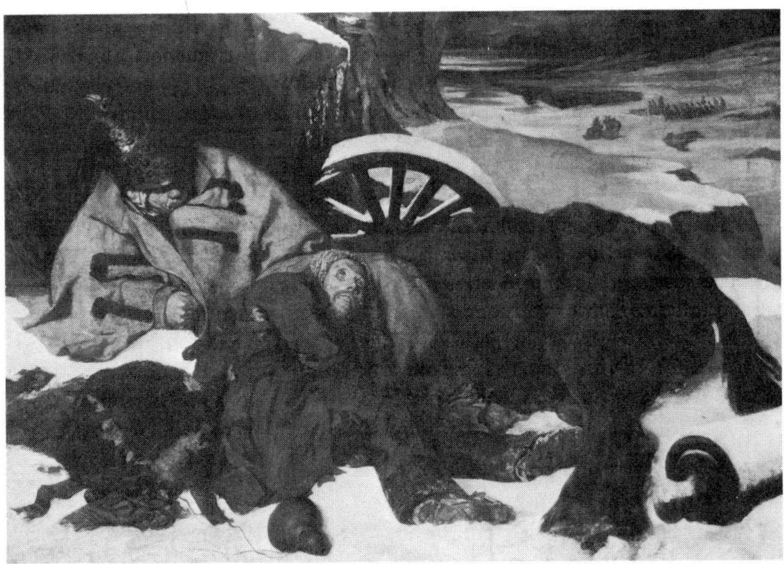

10. *The Retreat from Russia*, 1835. Boissard de Boisdenier

death-mask presided over the studios of young Parisian painters of the 1830s and 1840s.

The *mal de siècle* was a French disease (German *Weltschmerz* was spread by a different virus). And outside France Gros's Napoleonic paintings were seen in a different light, most notably by Goya whose *The Second of May 1808* and *The Third of May 1808* may almost be read as replies to them. The former, a scene of street fighting with the death of a Mameluke in the French service, is in many ways reminiscent of Gros's *The Battle of Aboukir*, the difference

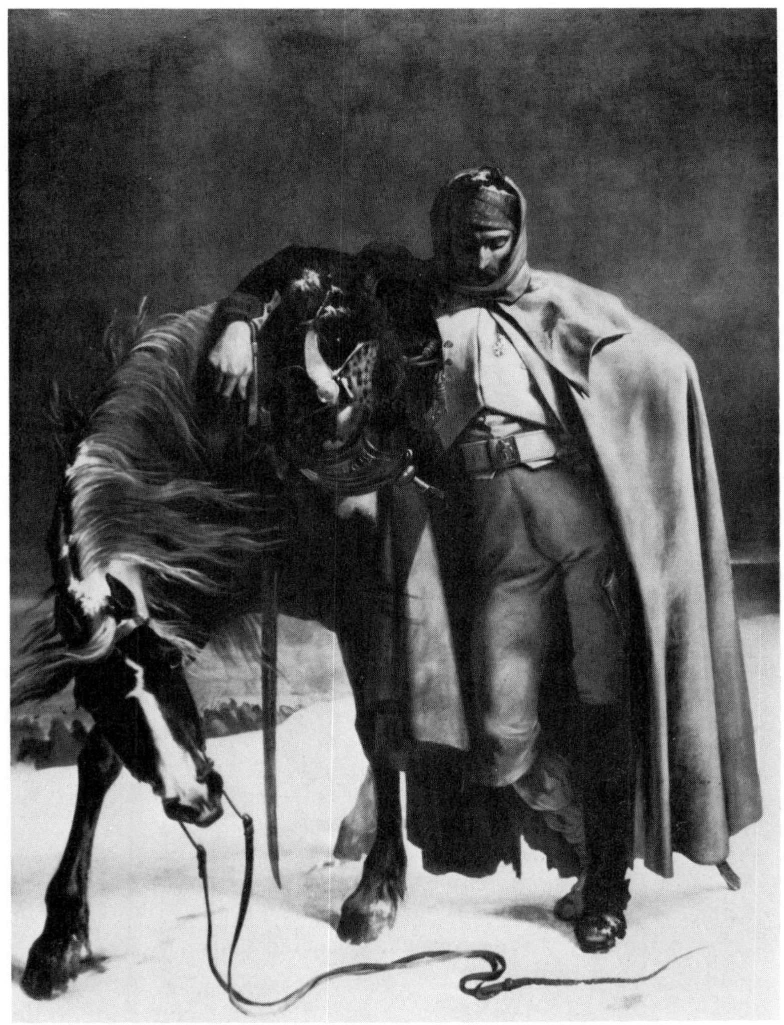

11. *Dragoon of the Imperial Guard*, 1832. E.-A. Odier

in subject being merely one of politics. Ironically, however, a fallen soldier in *The Battle of Aboukir* seems to reappear as a victim of the firing squad in the second of Goya's paintings [12] which is, both in composition and subject-matter, a direct riposte to the faintly absurd *Capitulation of Madrid* by Gros; and perhaps a disenchanted comment on the heroism of the great Neo-classical masterpiece, David's *Oath of the Horatii*, with which it has striking compositional similarities. There can be no doubt that in *The Third of May 1808* the emphasis is placed on, and the spectator's sympathy directed

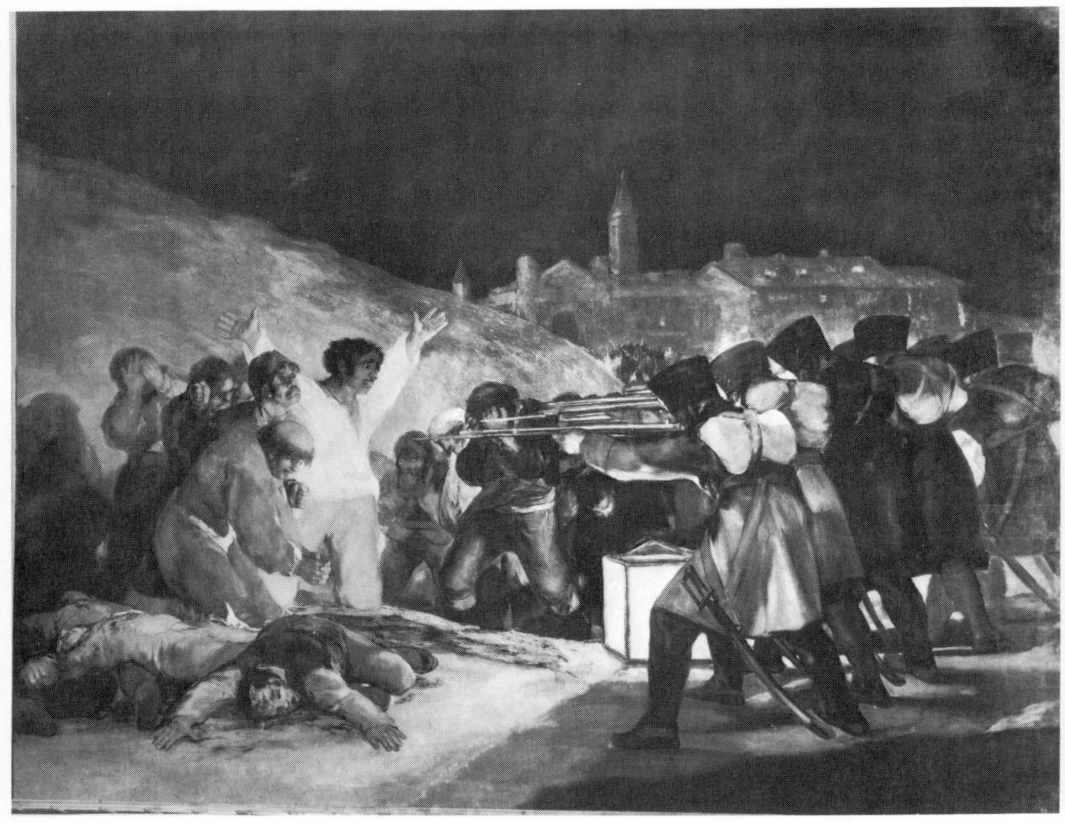

12. *The Third of May 1808*, 1814. Goya

exclusively to, the victims, especially the man in the white shirt who stands with outstretched arms before the ominously faceless firing-squad. Yet the picture is disturbingly ambiguous. Goya painted it just after the Bourbon Restoration of 1814, to commemorate the beginning of the Spanish War of Liberation, and he evidently intended to suggest that the men who were shot by the French in 1808 had not died in vain. To the modern spectator, however, it may appear as a secular martyrdom without any ray of hope that the manifest evils of this world will be righted in the next. There is no light, no hint of bright reversion in the dark sky which hangs over the scene. The only source of illumination in the picture is the soldier's gigantic lantern, perhaps a symbol of the remorseless logic of the Enlightenment in which so many Spanish intellectuals – and probably Goya too – had previously seen salvation.

This shift in emphasis from victors to victims is an instance of the way in which ideas developed by the Romantics could influence the creation of new works of art and also modify attitudes to old ones. Gros's *Battlefield of Eylau* [6] is, however, of importance not only because its subject-matter was open to a Romantic interpretation. By stressing the realistic, at the expense of the idealistic or classic, elements in David's work, Gros evolved a new style eminently suitable for pictures of modern subjects. And although Géricault made a more decisive break with tradition in his choice of themes, he was in other respects more faithful than Gros to Neo-classical principles. Working in the approved academic manner, he proceeded systematically from numerous swiftly drawn sketches, in which he gradually determined the general composition, to wonderful nude studies of individual figures drawn with a precision of outline and volumetric clarity equalled by few Neo-classical draughtsmen. In the pursuit of truth he frequented dissecting rooms and made the extraordinary paintings of heads and limbs of corpses which Delacroix was to call 'the best argument for beauty as it ought to be understood' [13]. Yet, in the final work, he followed the conventions of the grand style by endowing the survivors on the raft with the healthy physique of Greek athletes, rather than depicting them as they appeared when rescued – bearded, emaciated, covered with sores and wounds.

13. *Severed Legs and an Arm*, 1818. Géricault

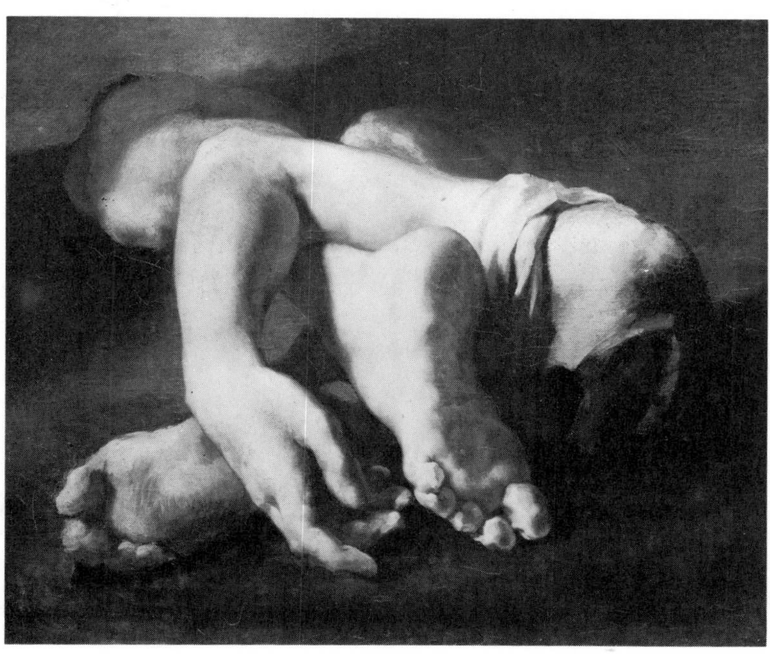

Despite its provocative subject, *The Raft of the 'Medusa'* was well received by the artistic establishment. Géricault was awarded a gold medal and given a commission for a large religious painting, which he passed on to the young Delacroix. In the Salon of 1819 it was Ingres, not Géricault, who aroused hostility, for his radical departure from the Davidian tradition in his *Grande Odalisque* and *Roger Freeing Angelica* [120].[48] *The Raft of the 'Medusa'* seems to have been criticized mainly for political rather than artistic reasons. And when the political scandal had died down, it was bought for the Louvre in 1824 and soon came to be seen as a kind of modern classic. By 1829, a writer in the ultra-reactionary *Journal des Artistes* could remark:

> The fate of all great things is to be eternally parodied and perverted by imitators and continuers. The religion of Christ, the writings of Chateaubriand, the paintings of Géricault, have engendered in our time, among other bizarre and monstrous products, the book of M. l'Abbé de la Mennais [sic], the writings of M. Victor Hugo, and the paintings of M. Eugène Delacroix.[49]

Many years later, Delacroix recalled his first reactions to *The Raft of the 'Medusa'*: 'The impression it gave me was so strong that as I left the studio I broke into a run, and kept running like a fool all the way back to the rue de la Planche where I lived.'[50] Its influence was very apparent in his first Salon exhibit, *The Barque of Dante* of 1822 [14]. And although David's disciple Delécluze called

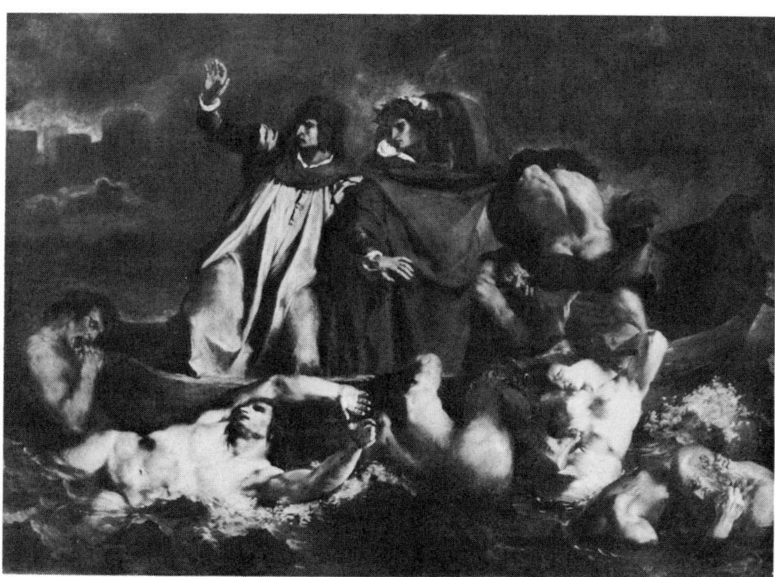

14. *The Barque of Dante*, 1822. Delacroix

this picture '*une vraie tartouillade*' ('a real daub'), it was well received and almost immediately acquired for the royal collection of contemporary paintings. The most enthusiastic of the critics was Adolphe Thiers (soon to emerge as a prominent politician), who descried in Delacroix 'the boldness of Michelangelo and the fecundity of Rubens'.

It is tempting to identify Delacroix with Balzac's Joseph Bridau (in *La Rabouilleuse*), the young painter, 'as gifted as Gros himself in the techniques of colour', who sets out with the intention of 'challenging the Classical school, of breaking down Greek conventions and doing away with the shackles with which art was bound – art to which Nature belongs, as it is, in the omnipotence of her creations and her fantasies'. But this is a view of the Romantic revolution developed after the event, on a par with Delécluze's account of *The Raft of the 'Medusa'* occasioning a 'raising of bucklers' against David, and encouraging young artists 'to rush into the fray with the impetuosity of youthful soldiers mounting a breach'.[51]

The Barque of Dante was conceived, like *The Raft of the 'Medusa'*, as a painting in the grand style, in the tradition of Michelangelo and Rubens. There are qualities in it which the severer Neo-classical theorists and artists (though not David himself) had abhorred – a love of rich dark colours, a dynamic energy, an emotional intensity and an almost erotic sensuality in the writhing nude figures. It made no decisive break away from the long line of European history paintings and was commended by Gros as 'a purified Rubens'. But Gros was appalled by *The Massacres of Chios* which Delacroix sent to the next Salon, in 1824 [15]. '*C'est la massacre de la peinture*,' he remarked.

As *The Massacres of Chios* owes a very obvious debt – which Delacroix himself acknowledged – to the *Plague House at Jaffa* [Fig. iv, p. 330] no one was better qualified than Gros to note the differences between the two works. Gros had exploited an oriental setting for a scene of horror, had adopted a broad painterly manner in handling and was equally bold in his treatment of human proportions. But his picture was integrated in such a way that every figure, every gesture and detail contributed to the central politico-didactic message. The pestilence is a foil to the all but immortal immunity of Napoleon. The emphasis is on his act, not on the sufferings of the plague-stricken, just as the *Battlefield of Eylau* celebrates his compassion for the dead and dying, not their misery. Neo-classical insistence on the moral purpose of art has simply been bent to a political end. Delacroix's picture was conceived in a very different

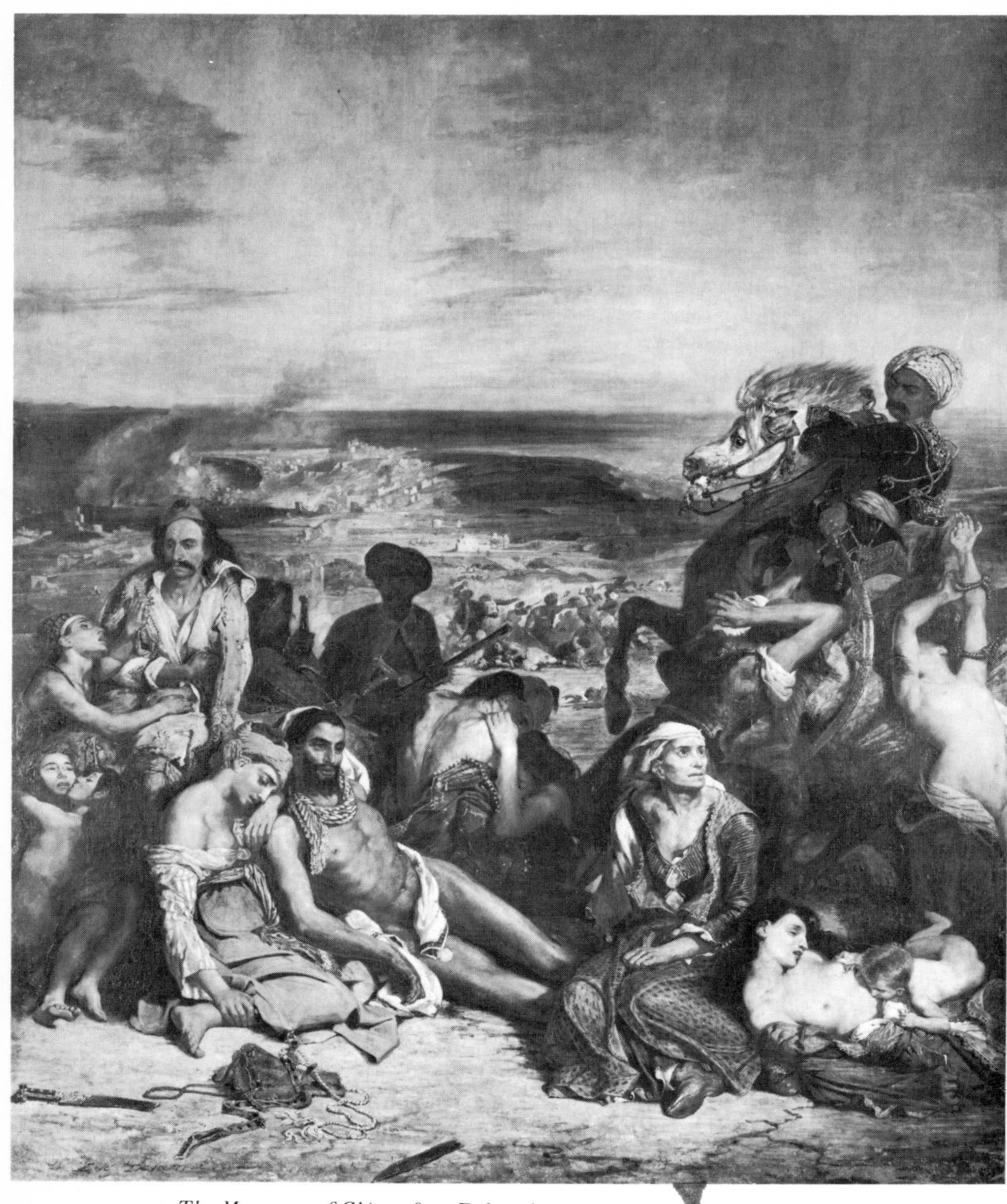

15. *The Massacres of Chios*, 1824. Delacroix

mood. It is a scene of horror unrelieved, inspired by sympathy with the Greeks in the War of Liberation from the Turks, but with no clear moral or social implications. As the original title, *Scènes des massacres de Scio*, reminds us, it depicts not one but several acts of violence: and the disorder of events is stressed by the apparently arbitrary vertical limits which cut through human figures. If the picture were to be extended to right or left, it would merely include more corpses, more rapacious Turks, more men and women hopelessly, helplessly awaiting their fate. In the complex pictorial composition there is no strongly defined pattern around a central axis, nothing to suggest a firm social or cosmic structure – rather the reverse.

Delacroix's debt to Gros and the school of David is still evident in the statuesque solidity of the figures. But where Gros had backed the protagonists of his Napoleonic dramas with 'drop-curtains' to close the scene, Delacroix painted a pellucid, sparkling, light-flooded landscape, which opens up the composition on to an almost limitless vista. Here, for the first time, he expressed his vision of the world as composed not of discrete elements, which could be combined with or detached from one another, but of an infinitely wide range of contrasting and merging colours, reflecting and absorbing light – a quintessentially pictorial vision which equates Creation with painting and reality with pigment. The technique in which he rendered it (and technique was to be for him often an end in itself and always more than a means) owes debts to Velasquez, and especially to Constable whose paintings he had recently seen and studied in Paris. After a visit to England in 1825, Delacroix painted a still more extraordinary landscape, as part of his *Still-Life with Lobsters*, which seems to have been both a tribute to, and comment on, the English school [16]. But it is only the distant view and the sky that are reminiscent of Constable. Nothing could be more remote from a Wordsworthian attitude to nature than the strange, almost surrealist assortment of dead birds, a hare, two lobsters and a tartan plaid which echo the sonorous colour schemes of early eighteenth-century still-lifes. And nothing could be further from Neo-classical didacticism than this essay in *l'art pour l'art*. Almost truculently he sent it to the Salon of 1827 in a refurbished Rococo frame.

Although far from advocating a return to '*les tons légers et charmants à l'œil*' associated with Boucher and Van Loo,[52] it was as a colourist that Delacroix made his most decisive break with the tradition in which he had been trained. Neo-classical theorists had ruled that to pay more attention to colour than to line was to rank the transient and variable above the eternal and sure, to appeal to the senses rather than to the mind. Immutable truths could be

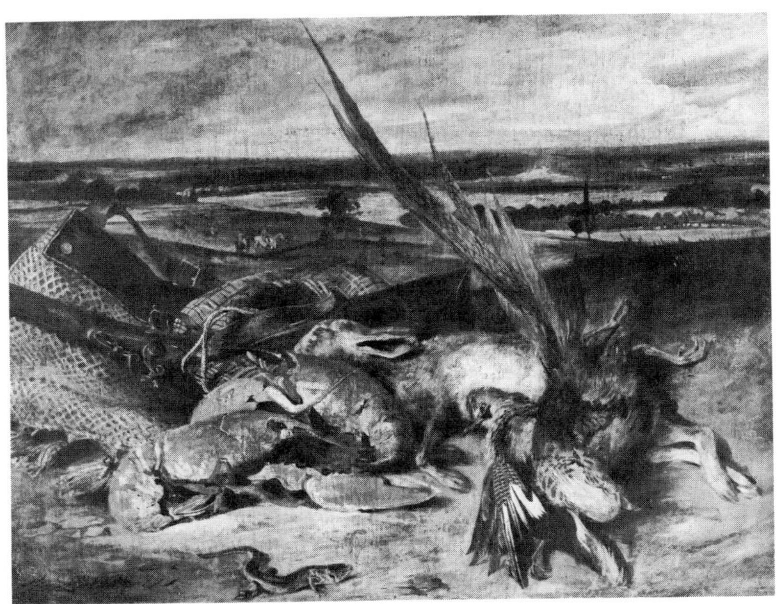

16. *Still-Life with Lobsters*, 1827. Delacroix

expressed only in pure forms with firmly defined contours. Delacroix seems to have grown increasingly sceptical of this view of art and also, perhaps, the notion of a static mechanistic cosmos on which it was based. 'Nature is sparing of decisive contours,' he told Chopin in 1841. 'Light which is its life, its manner of being, is always breaking silhouettes and instead of defining in the flat raises everything in the round.'[53] For him colour was life and light. In his view it appealed not merely to the senses but to the imagination – to what Baudelaire was to call '*la reine des facultés*', which assumed in Romantic aesthetics the place formerly assigned to the understanding.[54]

In January 1824, when he was working on *The Massacres of Chios*, Delacroix wrote in his journal: 'I find precisely in Mme de Staël the development of my idea about painting. This art, like music, is *higher than thought*; and both are superior to literature – in their vagueness.'[55] He was, of course, referring to Mme de Staël's *De l'Allemagne*, the main channel through which the ideas of the German Romantics (in a somewhat diluted form) reached both France and England. As his remark very clearly reveals, he found in this book the formulation of ideas which he had already developed as a painter, and it was to influence his artistic theory more than his practice. But by this date he was already being associated with the

French Romantic poets who owed a greater debt to Mme de Staël – '*notre grand' maman à tous*' as Rontiex called her in the first *Histoire du romantisme en France*, published in 1829.[56] Thus, Auguste Jal could praise Delacroix's *Christ in the Garden of Olives* as a 'poem which Chateaubriand or Nodier might analyse, which Lamartine might translate'.[57]

Delacroix and other painters were involved only involuntarily in the *bataille romantique* fought by writers. It began under the Empire with attacks on the new ideas imported into France from Germany. (*De l'Allemagne* was banned by the authorities in 1810 – '*Votre dernier ouvrage n'est pas français*,' the Duc de Rovigo told Mme de Staël.) In December 1814, immediately after the first Bourbon Restoration, the anti-royalist paper *Le Nain jaune* associated the victory of the Allies with the further spread of Romanticism, publishing a 'spoof' treaty of alliance between the literary powers of a *confédération romantique* (Germany, Austria, Switzerland, Holland, England, Sweden, Portugal, Spain and Italy), whose aim was to defile the purity of the French language and whose motto was '*mort aux classiques*'.[58] A decade later the work of young French Romantic poets was being denounced as un-French: at the Institut de France, Louis-Simon Auger protested that 'its main source is entirely Germanic'.[59] This chauvinism, ironically, was an outcome of a Romantic sense of nationalism. Auger identified the French genius with classicism and the Enlightenment; the *romantiques*, he declared,

> have presented mystical poetry to a people who have never seen in mysticism anything but a subject for pleasantries and epigrams; they have proffered vaporous odes to a nation with a particular genius for positive things; they have discussed superstitious beliefs seriously in front of a philosophical audience...

Those who favoured the *romantiques* saw the conflict from a different point of view – though one equally nationalistic, for they associated the genius of France with the vernacular poetry of the Middle Ages. In 1824 a writer in the *Globe* remarked that France was 'divided in literature as in politics and as in religion in two great parties, one taking Liberty as its device, that is to say hope for the future, and the other Authority, that is to say faith in the past'.[60] But the division was by no means clear cut, and this writer commented on the paradox that free thinkers in politics and religion were absolutists in literature, while most of those who protested against the Academy belonged to the political right wing. In the course of the next few years, however, nearly all the Romantic

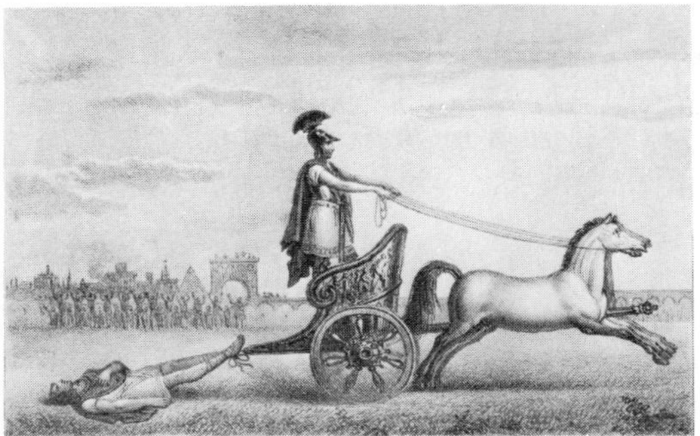

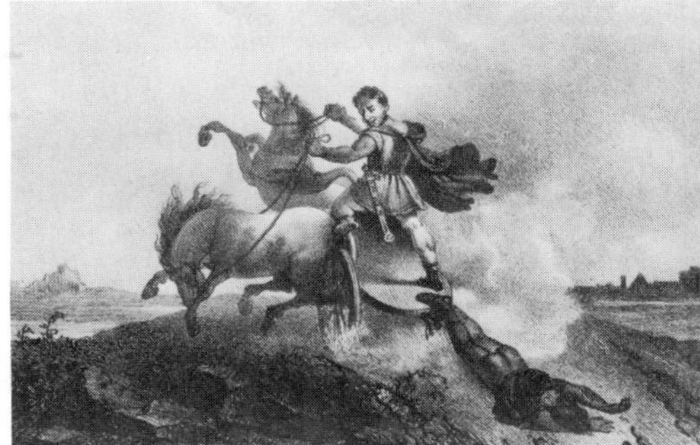

17a and b. *The Death of Hector*, *c.* 1824–30. Anonymous

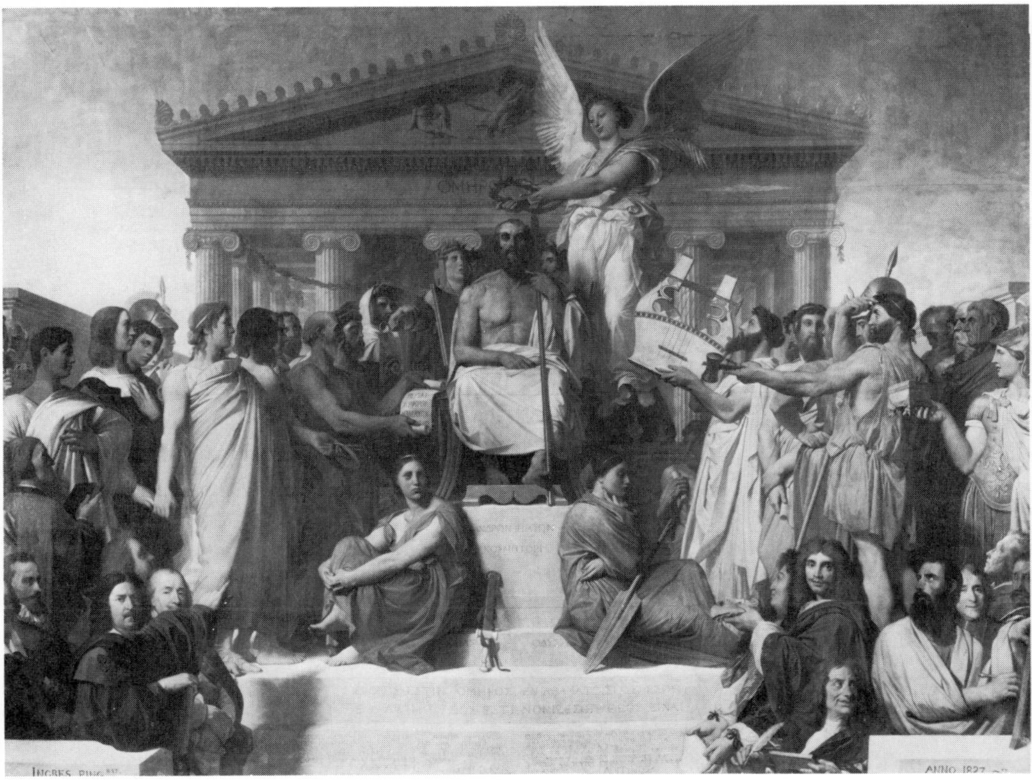

18. *The Apotheosis of Homer*, 1827. Ingres

writers joined the anti-Bourbon camp. The famous slogan '*le romantisme est le libéralisme en littérature*', which made its first appearance in a Belgian review in 1826, was soon taken up in France.[61]

That painters should also have been divided into two opposed parties by critics and the general public was almost inevitable. A pair of caricatures neatly illustrates their supposed polarity [17a and b]. Two paintings shown in the Salon of 1827–8 – *The Apotheosis of Homer* by Ingres [18] and *The Death of Sardanapalus* by Delacroix [19] – might seem to confirm this notion of mutually exclusive styles. The one is an extreme statement of faith in the classical values of repose, balance, clarity and nobility – Winckelmann's 'noble simplicity and calm greatness'. The other is an extreme expression of volatile dynamism, painterly bravura and dramatic tension of the disordered and unbridled. No more obviously Romantic picture than *The Death of Sardanapalus* was ever painted, even though it

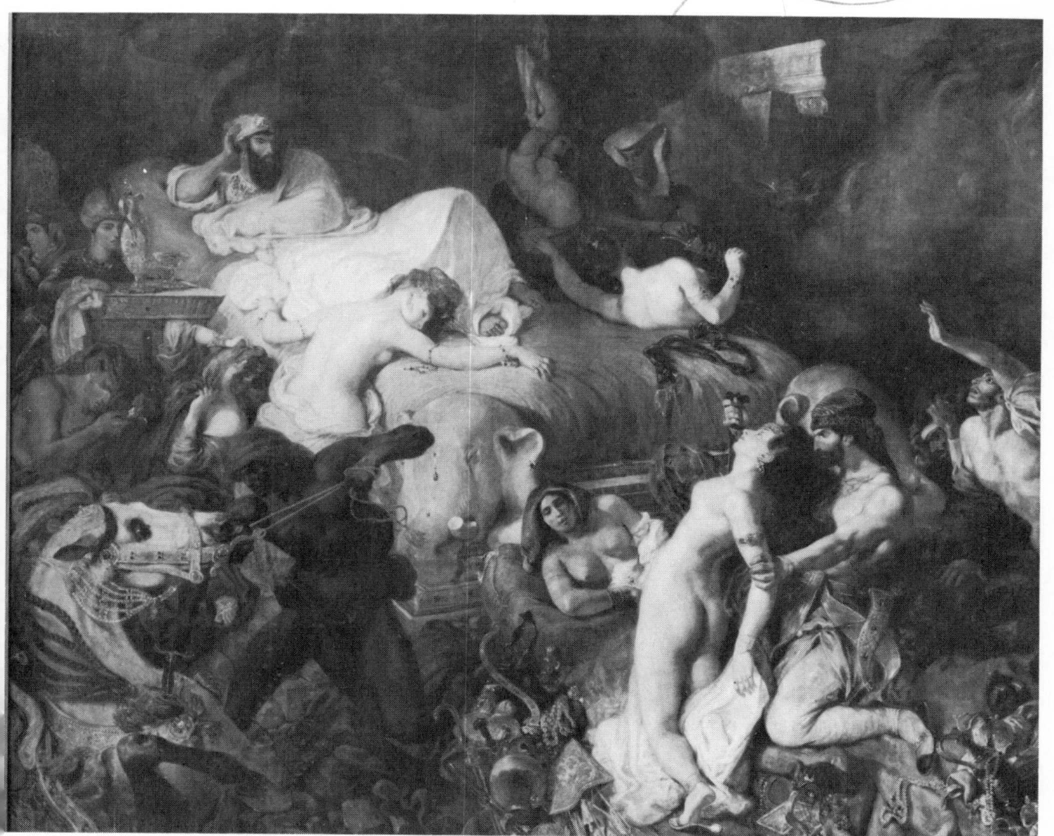

19. *The Death of Sardanapalus*, 1828. Delacroix

represents an Antique subject (Dionysian rather than Olympian) and owes obvious debts to the art of Antiquity. Stylistically it derives from the school of David by way of Gros and Géricault. *The Apotheosis of Homer*, on the other hand, illustrates the way in which Ingres – as his friend and pupil Amaury-Duval pointed out – overturned the teaching of David no less completely than David had that of his predecessors.[62] Its delicate and pallid colours, and intricate linear patterns, its contrasts between naturalistic and idealized representation, the sculptural modelling of some of the figures and the curious absence of spatial depth are all characteristic of Ingres's highly individual style. Nevertheless, such were the ambiguities and complexities of the artistic scene at this date that it was applauded by painters '*de l'école dite romantique*', according to a contemporary, Arnold Scheffer.[63] And the most enthusiastic

20. *Innovation romantique*, *c*. 1830. Anonymous

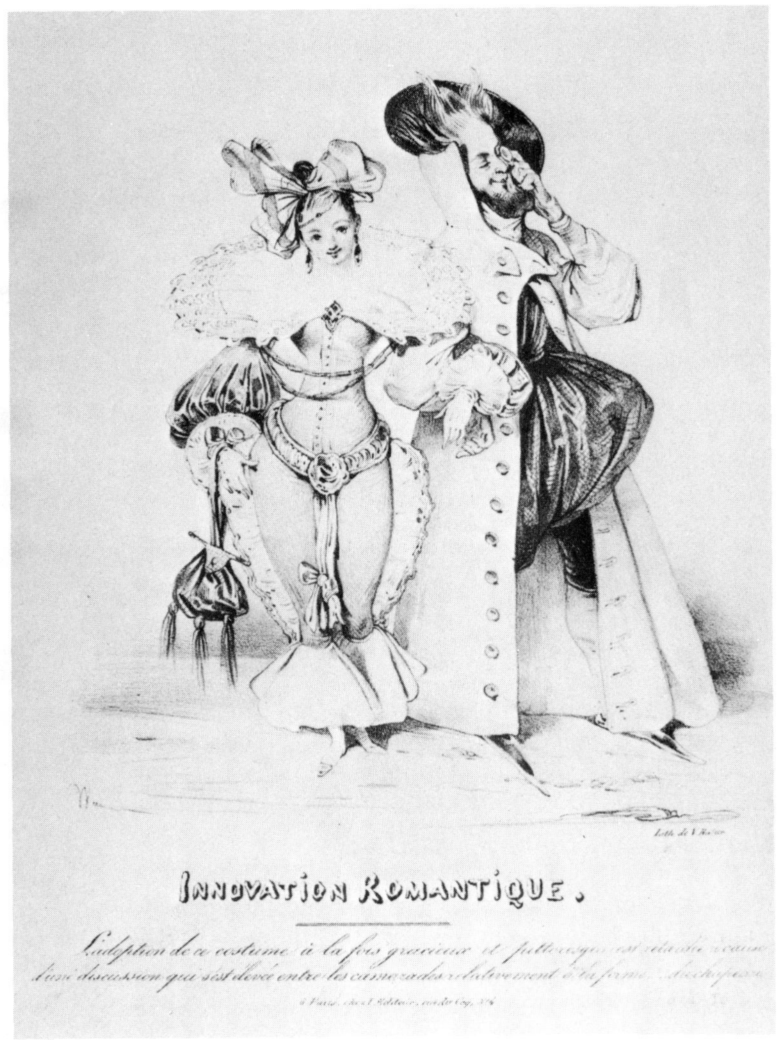

account of it appears in Alfred de Vigny's *Stello* (1832) – a key work of French Romantic literature, which gave to *The Apotheosis of Homer* a wholly Romantic interpretation as a kind of devotional image for the cult of genius. De Vigny described the poor, aged Homer enthroned and holding his blind beggar's staff like a sceptre, surrounded by great poets who constituted 'from his time to ours an almost unbroken chain of glorious exiles, of courageous victims of persecution, of thinkers crazed by misery'.[64]

In fact, by 1829 the term *romantique* had been reduced to a vogue word. Lady Morgan said that it was applied to Parisian tailors, milliners, pastry-cooks, and even doctors and apothecaries [20].[65] It was also used to describe trivial fashionable literature (especially novels), decorative pictures and *objets d'art* in the so-called Troubadour style [116]. Many artists and writers thus became increasingly anxious to dissociate themselves from the Romantic label. Significantly, the two most famous attacks on Romanticism were by authors who had begun in the Romantic camp: Heine's *Romantische Schüle* (first published in 1832–3 in a French translation) and de Musset's *Lettres de Dupuis et Cotonet* (1836). Neither attempted to advance a classicistic case. They objected not to the ideas which had given life to Romanticism, and which they tacitly accepted, but simply to their devaluation.

In 1864 Theophile Thoré turned a definition of this debased Romanticism against Ingres, whom he described as 'the most Romantic artist of the nineteenth century'.[66] Yet in the same year Baudelaire wrote, with reference to Delacroix: 'To say the word Romanticism is to say modern art – that is, intimacy, spirituality, colour, aspiration towards the infinite, expressed by every means available to the arts.'[67] Few other French writers of the day would have associated this shop-soiled word with such ideas. But Baudelaire clearly needed it – with all the range of serious and trivial significance it had by then acquired – to express his deeply felt view. And 'for lack of another' we are still obliged to use it too.

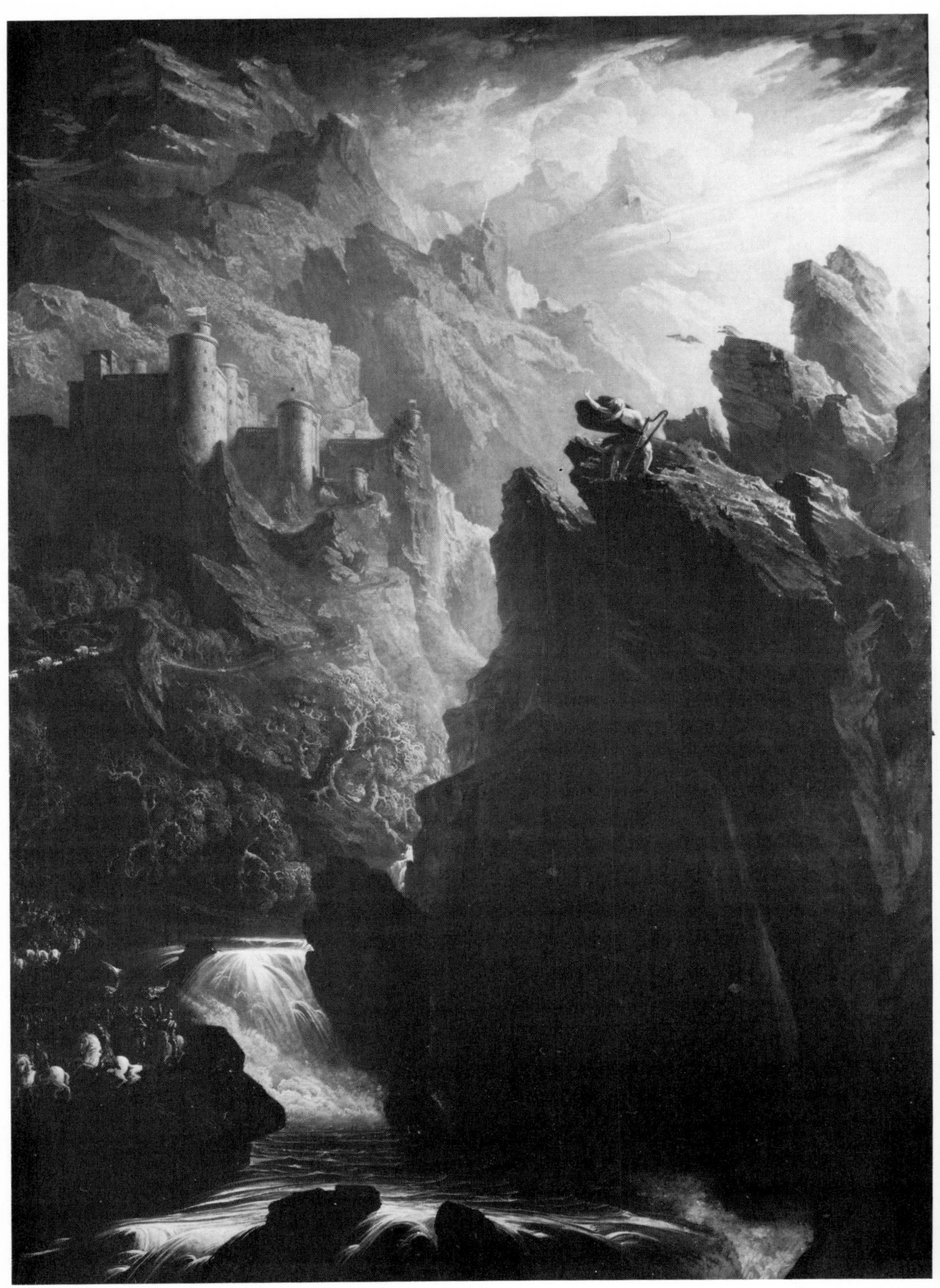

21. *The Bard*, 1817. John Martin

2. *The Morality of Landscape*

John Martin's *The Bard* of 1817 [21] and Thomas Cole's *A Scene from Byron's 'Manfred'* of 1833 [22] are both Romantic landscapes – by any definition of the term. They express that feeling for the sublimity of nature – the exhilarating terror inspired by rushing

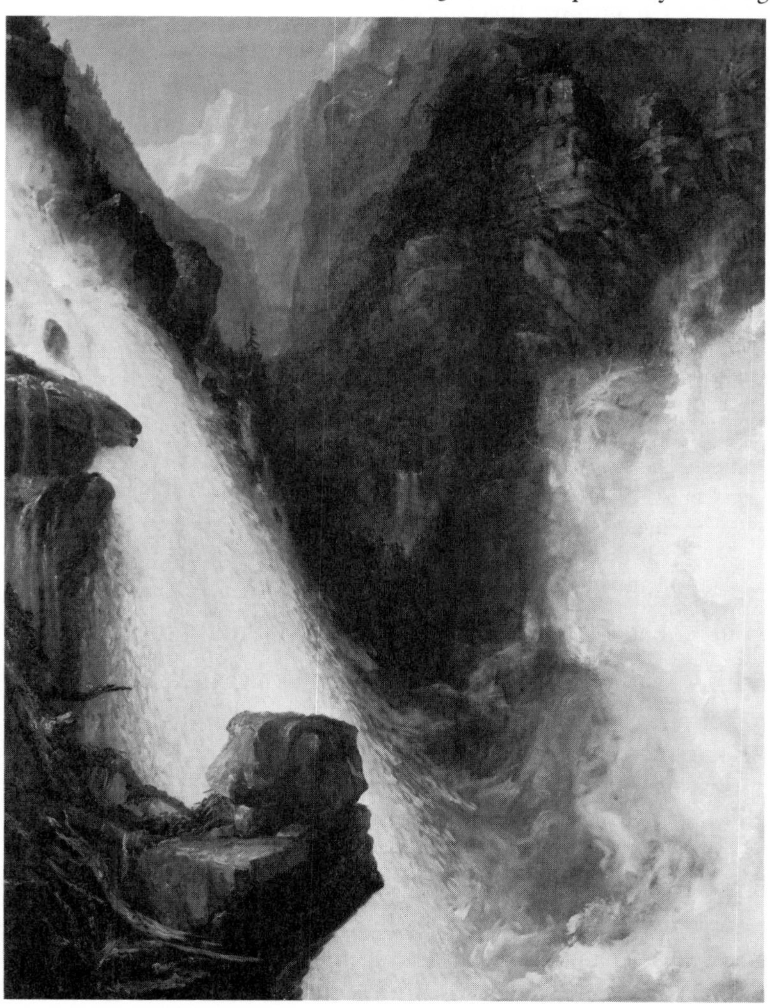

22. *A Scene from Byron's 'Manfred'*, 1833. Thomas Cole

torrents, roaring waterfalls, precipitous crags, unattainable mountain peaks – which had grown steadily stronger in the course of the eighteenth century.[1] Both call to mind a famous passage from Wordsworth's 'Lines composed a few miles above Tintern Abbey' of 1798:

> The sounding cataract
> Haunted me like a passion: the tall rock,
> The mountain, and the deep and gloomy wood,
> Their colours and their forms, were then to me
> An appetite: a feeling and a love,
> That had no need of a remoter charm,
> By thought supplied, or any interest
> Unborrowed from the eye...

But this describes only one of the two attitudes to nature which are the subject of the poem. For when he wrote these lines Wordsworth had outgrown the 'aching joys' and 'dizzy raptures', and learned:

> To look on nature, not as in the hour
> Of thoughtless youth, but hearing oftentimes
> The still, sad music of humanity,
> Nor harsh nor grating, but of ample power
> To chasten and subdue. And I have felt
> A presence that disturbs me with the joy
> Of elevated thoughts; a sense sublime
> Of something far more deeply interfused,
> Whose dwelling is the light of setting suns,
> And the round ocean and the living air,
> And the blue sky, and in the mind of man:
> A motion and a spirit, that impels
> All thinking things, all objects of all thought,
> And rolls through all things.

In nature he now recognizes:

> The anchor of my purest thoughts, the nurse,
> The guide, the guardian of my heart, and soul
> Of all my moral being.

It is no more than a coincidence that shortly after this was written Philippe de Loutherbourg painted a scene near Tintern, emphasizing those qualities which had made the Wye valley a Mecca for British and even Italian amateurs of landscape,[2] though it did not go beyond that feeling for the 'picturesque' he had so well expressed in an earlier painting incorporating the abbey ruins [188]. Closer affinity with Wordsworth's mature attitude to nature may be found in landscapes which John Constable was beginning to paint in a different part of England. His views of the Vale of Dedham [25, 45] might almost seem to have been prefigured by Wordsworth's description, at the beginning of the poem, of

> These plots of cottage-ground, these orchard tufts,
> Which, at this season, with their unripe fruits,
> Are clad in one green hue, and lose themselves
> Among the woods and copses...
> These hedgerows, hardly hedgerows, little lines
> Of sportive wood run wild; these pastoral farms
> Green to the very door: and wreaths of smoke
> Sent up, in silence, from among the trees!

Yet no one would have called these pictures 'Romantic landscapes' in the early nineteenth century. Nor was any one to describe Wordsworth as a Romantic poet for many years to come.[3]

The 'romantic landscape' had been fairly well defined as a category before the end of the eighteenth century. In 1793 Ramdohr, who, as we have seen, was to be shocked by Caspar David Friedrich's work, distinguished two main types of landscape: views of 'Arcadian places' and of 'romantic places, like those Poussin, Salvator Rosa, Everdingen and others have conceived. Rocks, waterfalls, woodland rivers etc.'[4] When Gainsborough exhibited an essay in the manner of Gaspar Poussin in 1783, it was described by a contemporary as a 'romantic view' [23]. Pictures in the style of Salvator

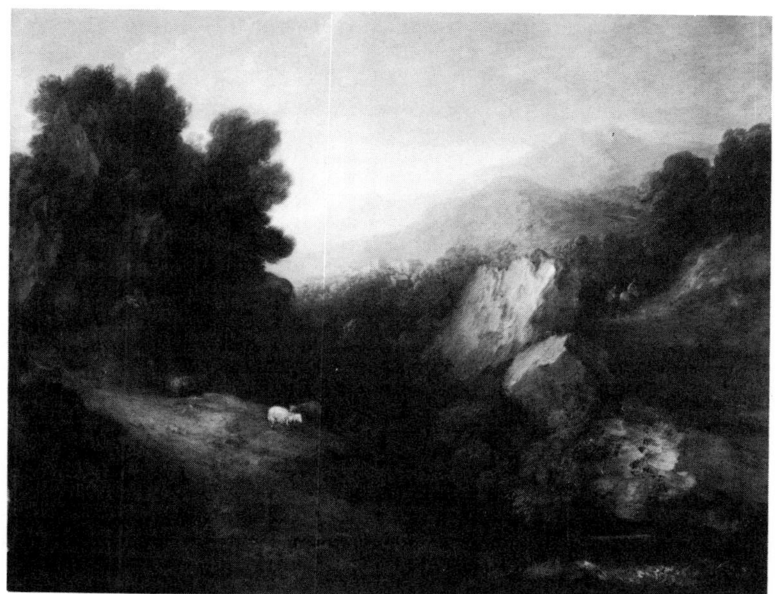

23. *Rocky Mountain with Landscape and Sheep*, 1783. Gainsborough

Rosa, and the Scandinavian landscapes of Allart van Everdingen (regarded as a kind of Salvator Rosa of the North), were still more obviously 'romantic' in the eighteenth-century meaning of the word.

The artists whom we nowadays think of as the great masters of the Romantic landscape certainly owed something to the work of these seventeenth-century painters, though less, paradoxically, than they did to pictures of 'Arcadian places', which included not only Claude's poetic evocations of the Roman Campagna but also Dutch pastoral scenes. Recalling the myth of the Golden Age which had haunted the European imagination since Antiquity, such pictures of quiet meadows with cows and flocks of sheep and shepherds had been given a new significance by Jean-Jacques Rousseau's pastoral primitivism. As images of man dwelling in the bosom of nature, they could recall the happy pastoral (pre-agricultural) stage of civilization which Rousseau believed to be 'the state least subject to revolutions, the best state for man'.[5] The craggy Apennine landscapes of Salvator Rosa, on the other hand, though regarded in the eighteenth century as 'romantic prospects' *par excellence*, had decreasing influence on artists. Constable slyly called Rosa 'a great favourite with the novel writers, particularly the ladies'.[6]

Ramdohr's classification of landscapes is an instance of the eighteenth-century desire to categorize, to treat both art and nature as orderly structures, divided and sub-divided in such a way that even disorderly elements could be isolated and kept firmly under control. There is no reason to believe that artists of the time objected to, or felt constrained by, such systems, any more than musicians or poets, who happily wrote within the framework of accepted genres. Richard Wilson, Gainsborough, Joseph Vernet and de Loutherbourg gave great freshness and beauty to pictures composed strictly according to long-established conventions. But the Romantics re-examined both the work of their predecessors and also the rules which had been derived from them, in the light of their own personal experience of art and nature.

Turner, the most personal and revolutionary of all Romantic landscape painters, seems to have been obsessed by the history of his art.[7] In one painting after another he challenged comparison with and, as it were, commented on, Claude and the Dutch masters. In *Dido Building Carthage* (which he bequeathed to the National Gallery on condition that it should be hung near works by Claude), he dissolved the Claudean structure of landscape in a blaze of what he called 'amber-coloured ether' – provoking a critic to complain that he 'did not understand his art'.[8] Aelbert Cuyp provided a point of departure for *Dordrecht: The Dort Packet-Boat from Rotterdam Becalmed* [24], an image of golden light and breathless calm evoking the reflective sadness of a summer day, which Constable called 'the most complete work of genius I ever saw'.[9] Constable is said to have

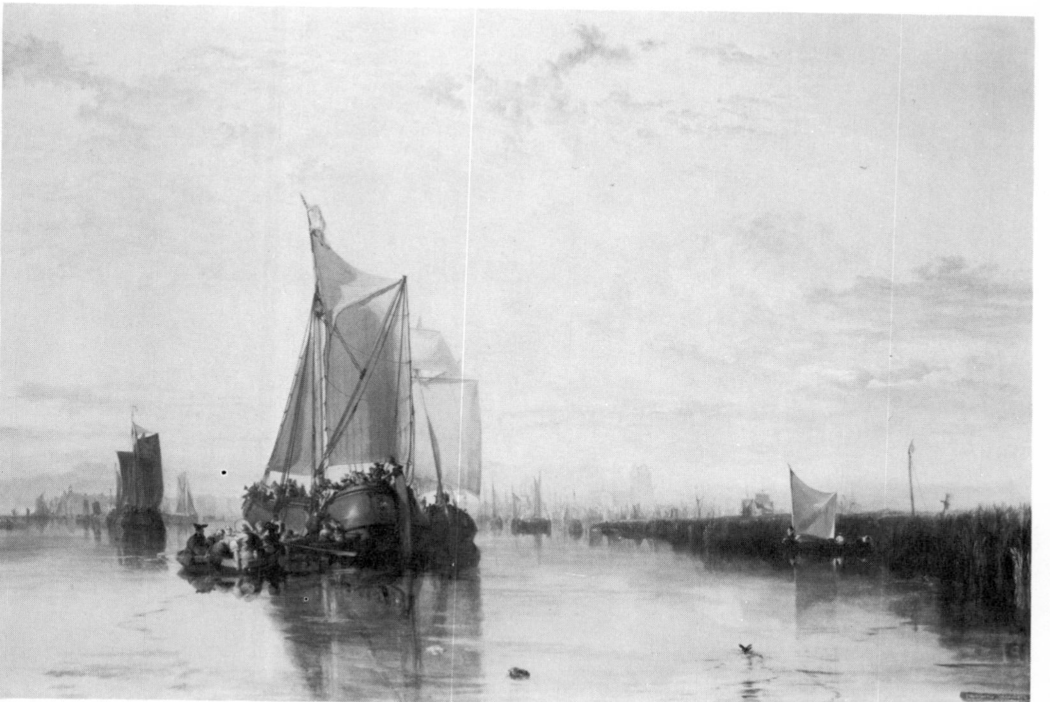

24. *Dordrecht: The Dort Packet-Boat from Rotterdam Becalmed*, 1818. Turner

remarked: 'When I sit down to make a sketch from nature, the first thing I try to do is to forget that I have ever seen a picture.'[10] Yet his debt to earlier landscape painters was no less great than Turner's. He made copies of pictures by Claude and Ruisdael in order to learn from them.[11] And his large view of *Dedham Vale* [25] betrays the influence of a painting by Claude which he particularly loved – but he succeeded in translating the Latin of the original into contemporary English, and endowing it with a new poetic intensity.

The hostility to imitation, for which Constable is notorious, was directed exclusively against pastiches of old masters which lacked 'the moral feeling of landscape' and deserved 'only to be classed with the showy and expensive articles of drawing room furniture'.[12]

Initially, Constable even opposed the foundation of the National Gallery because he feared that it would encourage 'manufacturers of pictures'.[13] He drew a firm distinction between painters who were 'intent only on the study of departed excellence, or what others

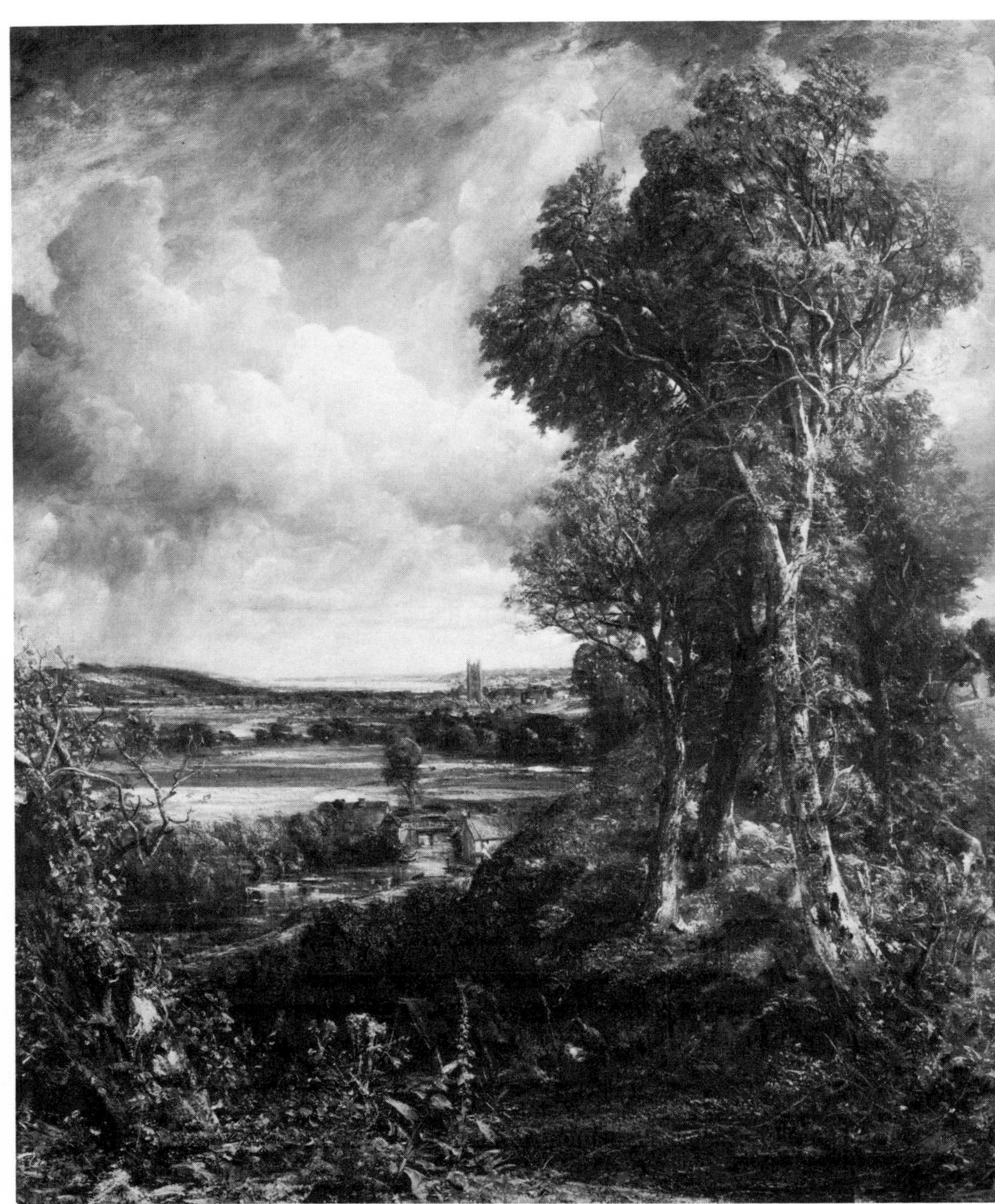

25. *Dedham Vale*, 1828. Constable

have accomplished' and those who sought 'perfection at its PRIMITIVE SOURCE, NATURE'.[14] At about the same time in Germany, Caspar David Friedrich was declaring that the artist must 'study nature after nature and not after paintings'.[15]

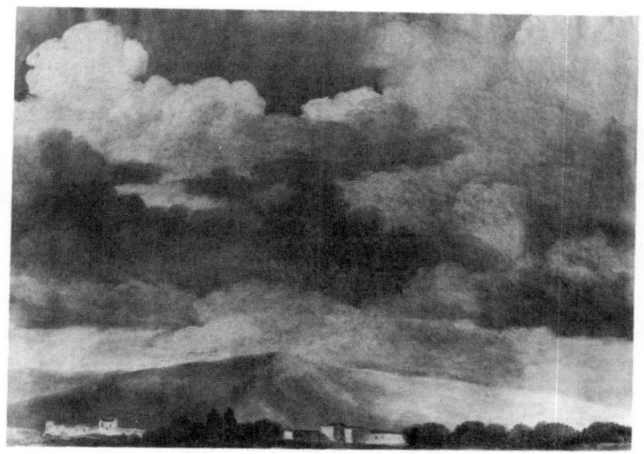

26. *Cloud Study*, c. 1780–86. P.-H. de Valenciennes

27. *Cloud Study*, 1821. Constable

Of course, the demand that artists should eschew the 'mannerism' associated with Boucher or Zuccarelli and return to nature had been a cardinal point of Neo-classical landscape theory. Thus Pierre-Henri de Valenciennes laid great stress on the importance of sketching out-of-doors in the country. Recognizing that the appearance of landscape was always changing with the movement of the sun and clouds, he recommended that artists should work quickly, never spending more than two hours on a single subject – half an hour at dawn or dusk.[16] His own studies of skies were clearly made in this way [26] and are no less convincingly true to nature than the better-known cloud paintings by Constable [27]. But these studies were not, of course, intended as ends in themselves so much as aides-mémoire for the artist when he was at work in his studio on paintings which represented nature 'such as it is' or 'such as it could be'.[17] They were, indeed, the equivalent of the figure painter's life-class drawings. Chateaubriand wrote in 1795 that 'landscape should be *drawn* from the *nude* if one wants to give it resemblance, in order to reveal, so to speak, the muscles, bones and limbs. Studies made indoors, copies after copies, will never replace work after nature.'[18]

The romantic landscape painters followed this practice, generally using their sketches from nature for parts of finished pictures rather than for complete compositions. (In French academic theory a distinction was made between the *étude* made from nature and the *esquisse* or compositional sketch.[19]) G. F. Kersting, who portrayed himself and Caspar David Friedrich on a sketching trip they made together, also recorded the other part of Friedrich's artistic life, showing him in his bare studio lit by a window which affords no

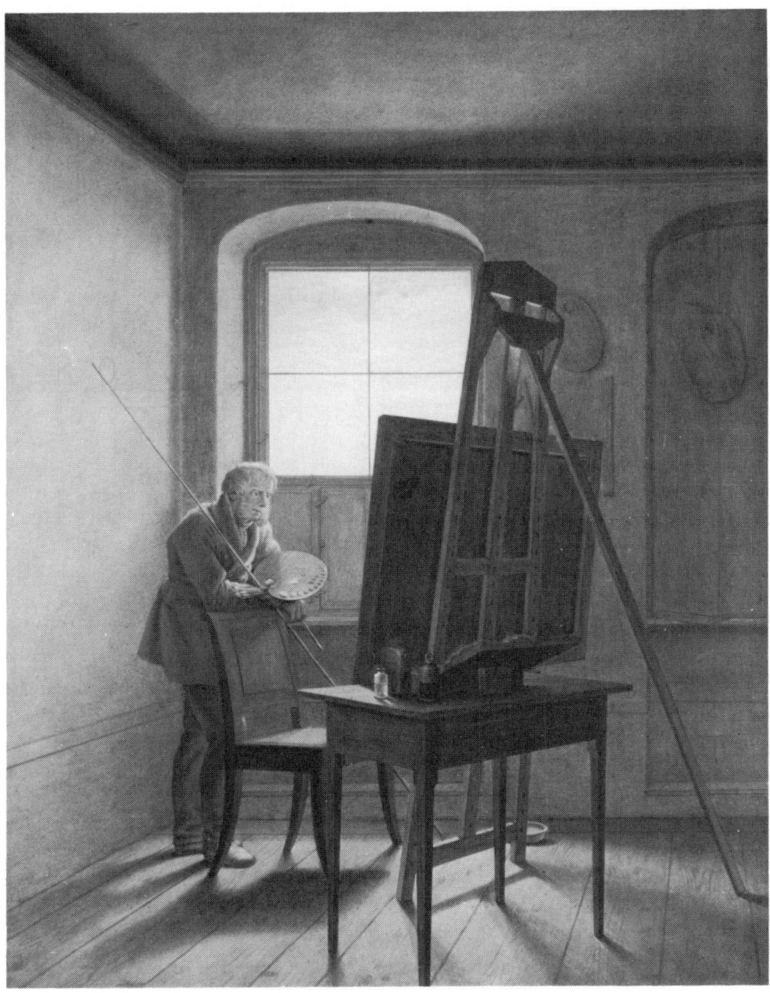

28. *Caspar David Friedrich in his Studio*, 1819. G. F. Kersting

view save that of the sky [28]. It was in this cell that Friedrich transformed the experience of nature, closing his bodily eye so that he could see with his spiritual eye and thus, as he wrote, bring to the light of day what he had seen in darkness in a work of art that 'may react upon others from the outside inwards'.[20]

This attitude may seem at variance with Constable's remark: 'Painting is a science, and should be pursued as an enquiry into the laws of nature. Why, then, should not landscape painting be considered as a branch of natural philosophy, of which pictures are but the experiments?'[21] But the great recent advances in scientific knowledge profoundly interested and moved most of the Romantics by their revelation that the universe was more, rather

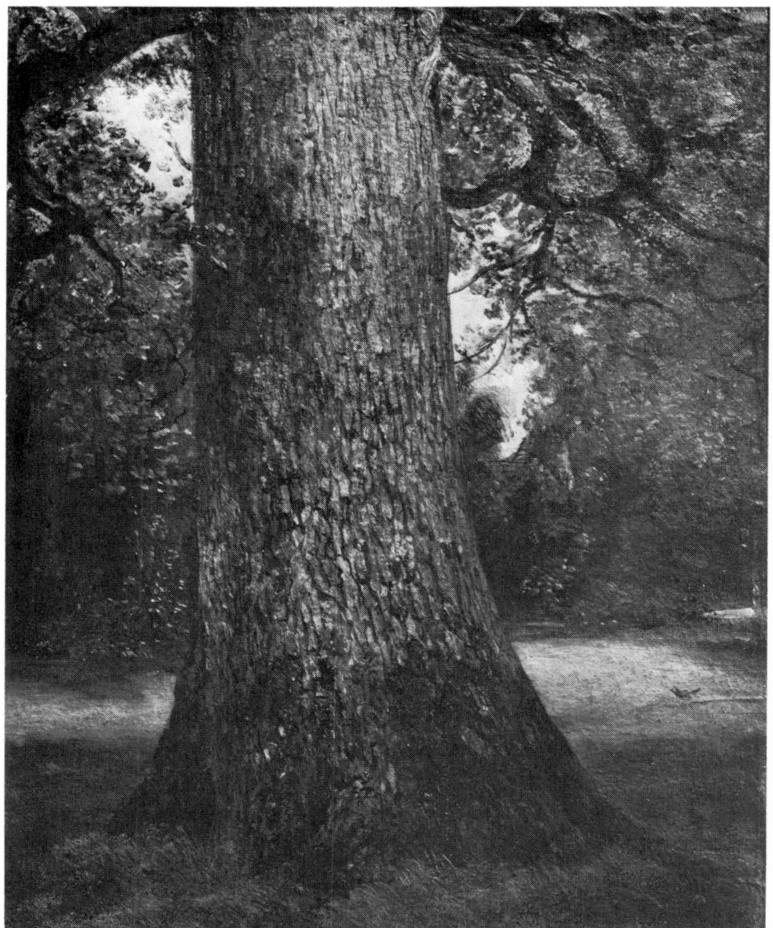

29. *Elm Tree Trunk*, *c.* 1821. Constable

than less, mysterious than had previously been supposed. Scientific observation was still consonant with religious and artistic attitudes of mind. James Jackson Jarves was to contend in *The Art Idea* (1864) that as nature is God's 'art', so science is the progressive disclosure of His soul, or that divine philosophy which, in comprehending all knowledge, must include art as one of its 'forms'. Science 'carries thought into the infinite', he wrote. Constable imagined Wilson, whom he regarded as the greatest English landscape painter, 'walking arm in arm' with Milton, the supreme Christian poet, and Linnaeus, the great naturalist – and it was probably his ambition to combine their achievements.[22] His studies from nature could satisfy the most exacting botanist, yet convey very strongly a feeling of reverential love. That of an elm tree trunk is painted with such close-up naturalism that one seems to embrace it visually [29]. Conversely, one of the most vivid accounts of a transcendental experience of nature was written by the scientist Sir Humphry Davy. 'Today, for the first time in my life I have had a distinct sympathy with nature,' he wrote in an early notebook:

> I was lying on the top of a rock to leeward; the wind was high, and everything was in motion; the branches of an oak tree were waving and murmuring in the breeze; yellow clouds, deepened by grey at the base, were rapidly floating over the western hills; the whole sky was in motion; the yellow stream below was agitated by the breeze; everything was alive, and myself part of the series of visible impressions: I should have felt pain in tearing a leaf from one of the trees.[23]

A type of landscape painting had in fact been developed in the eighteenth century for the accurate representation of subjects of scientific or historical interest – mountains, glaciers and volcanoes; classical, medieval or modern buildings. Considered as no more than topography, it was ranked very low in the hierarchy of genres. But it played a role of outstanding importance in the development of the art of landscape; and it is significant that Turner, Constable and Friedrich all began their careers with views of this type. Topographical artists were obliged to work from nature, however much they may have been influenced by the great tradition of landscape painting (often imposing a Claudean or Salvatorian pattern on their subjects). Almost by chance they discovered the potentialities of watercolour, which such artists as Paul Sandby, Francis Towne and John Robert Cozens developed into a medium of luminous subtlety, especially for the rendering of atmospheric effects, the delicately shaded green hues of the English countryside in summer or the smoky blues of distant hills. Before the end of the eighteenth century, Thomas Girtin and Turner were using it for small topographical paintings in which the ostensible subject-matter was sometimes subordinated to an harmonious evocation of nature. In Girtin's views of Kirkstall Abbey, for example, the ruined building which would previously have been considered as the only object of interest (for antiquarian reasons) becomes no more than the focal point in a rendering of light and air, low hills, trees and water.[24] The 'White

House', from which his famous view of Chelsea Embankment takes its name, is of still more purely visual significance. The little painting is a poetic evocation of sunset light, an almost abstract composition of translucent pigments [30].

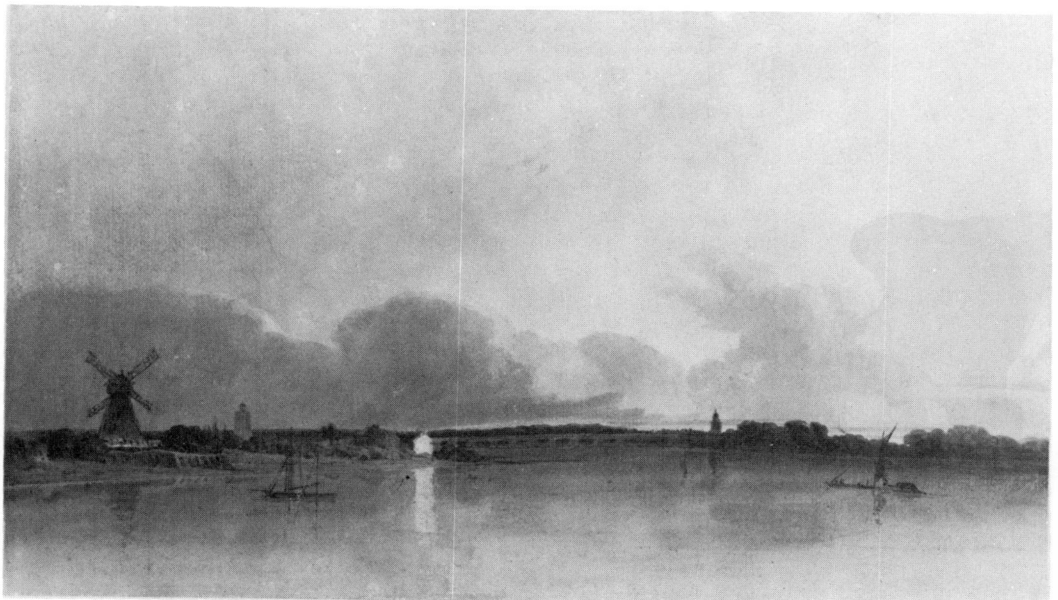

30. *The White House, Chelsea*, 1800. Girtin

In paintings of the least dramatic types of view, without any explicit literary or historical associations, early nineteenth-century artists made their most decisive break with tradition. 'A landscape which represents only animals and people occupied in the ordinary business of life generally pleases if it is an accurate imitation of nature,' wrote Pierre-Henri de Valenciennes in 1800, probably with pictures of the Dutch school in mind. But, he asked, 'does it speak to the heart like a painting of Arcadia? Does it stimulate the imagination like one of Polyphemus? Does it inspire profound reflections like the burial of Phocion?'[25] Before he died in 1819 the answers to these questions already seemed less obvious than he had supposed. Constable would surely have replied 'yes' to each of them. And the success his paintings of unspectacular East Anglian farmland enjoyed in France suggests that attitudes were changing there also. 'It is nature itself, it is a landscape seen through a window,' Jal wrote of those exhibited at the Paris Salon in 1824.[26] By 1834, the author of a French students' handbook could take it for granted

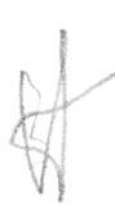

that the '*paysage portrait*' was preferable to the imaginary landscape.[27] Later, in 1842, Delacroix wrote in a letter:

You have only to come in March to a village as shabby and bare as they all are around Paris to have your theories about beauty, the ideal, choice etc. turned topsy-turvy. The meanest lane with its leafless sticks of trees, set against a flat, drab sky-line, speaks as much to the imagination as all the most famous beauty-spots. This tiny cotyledon piercing through

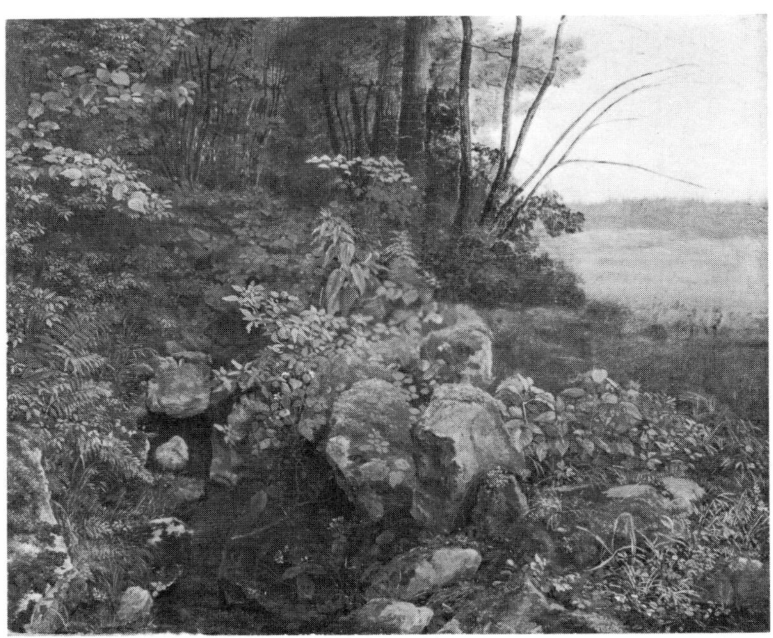

31. *Foreground Study*, *c*. 1818–20. J. A. Heinrich

the soil, this violet shedding its first scent enchant one. I love it all quite as much as those Italian pines that look like plumes and those buildings standing in a landscape like bowls arranged for dessert.[28]

This runs directly counter to eighteenth-century taste for the picturesque and the sublime. Constable referred to a view on the Sussex Downs as 'perhaps the most grand and affecting natural landscape in the world – and consequently a scene the most unfit for a picture'. He believed that 'it is the business of a painter not to contend with nature, and put this scene (a valley filled with imagery 50 miles long) on a canvas of a few inches, but to make something out of nothing, in attempting which he must almost of necessity become poetical.'[29] Elsewhere he wrote: 'My limited and abstracted art is to be found under every hedge and in every lane.'[30] The phrase

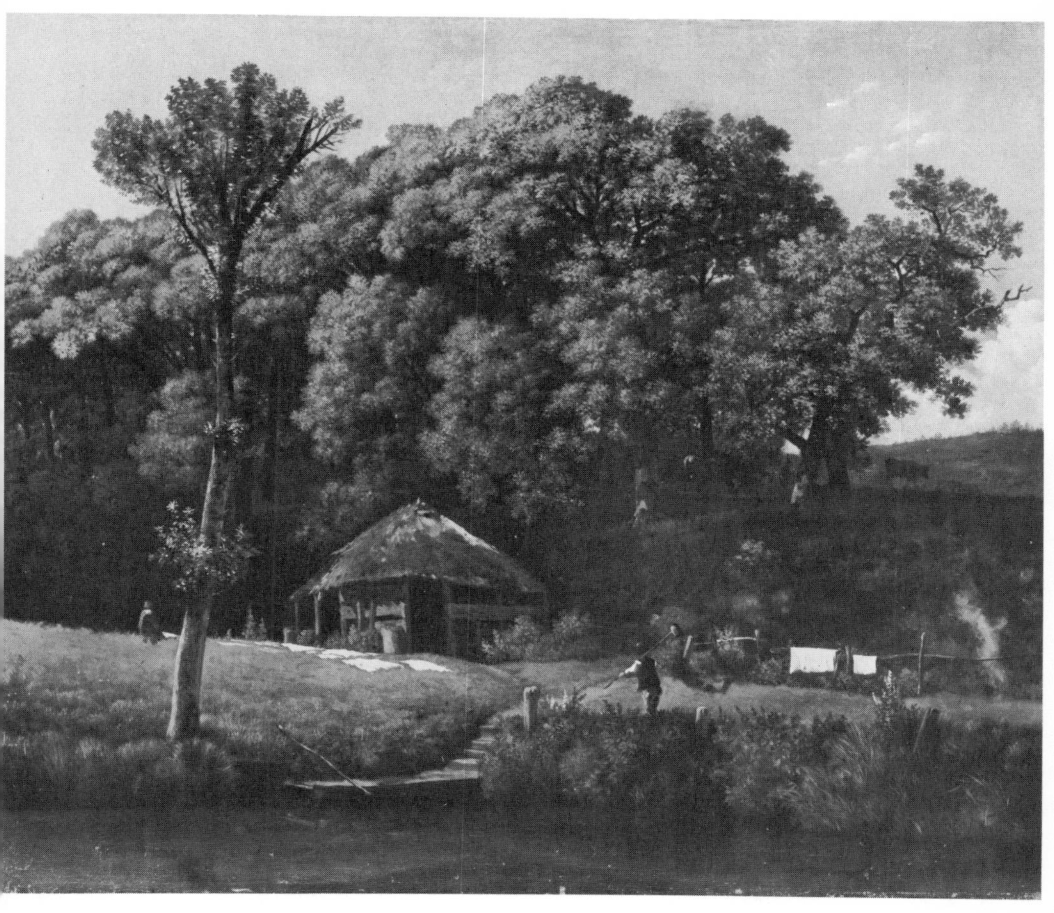

32. *Landscape in Guelderland*, *c.* 1808–10. W. J. van Troostwijk

immediately brings to mind many of his sensitive sketches of common wild flowers. And similar sketches were being painted by many other artists all over Europe at this time [31]. A few were even beginning to try to 'make something out of nothing'. In the opening years of the century, while Constable was painting his first views of the Vale of Dedham, W. J. van Troostwijk was depicting the equally unspectacular landscape of Guelderland – in one instance no more than a field with linen drying on the grass [32]. Constable's unique and revolutionary achievement was to make the flat, unassuming East Anglian scenery of his boyhood, with its canals and fields and men going about their everyday occupations, the subject of large-scale pictures [47]. He could even make visual poetry out of a dung-heap [45]. What is now called the 'Constable country' had not previously been thought worth visiting, let alone painting. In fact, Constable modified our ideas about what constitutes a beautiful landscape – in nature as well as art.

Several other English artists made paintings which, to use Coleridge's phrase, 'give the charm of novelty to things of everyday'. Turner depicted men lifting turnips on a field near Slough, and on another canvas, *Abingdon: Morning*, a herd of cows by the Thames in early light with mist still rising from the river [33]. This is reminiscent of Cuyp, but Turner eliminated the more conventional pastoral overtones to provide a glimpse of the common agricultural scene, with human figures as stolid as the cows they watch, transformed by accidents of light into a poetry no less intense for being true to life. The way in which he cut the composition at the right, through the cart which is its most clearly defined element, hints that the picture shows but a part of the working day and world.

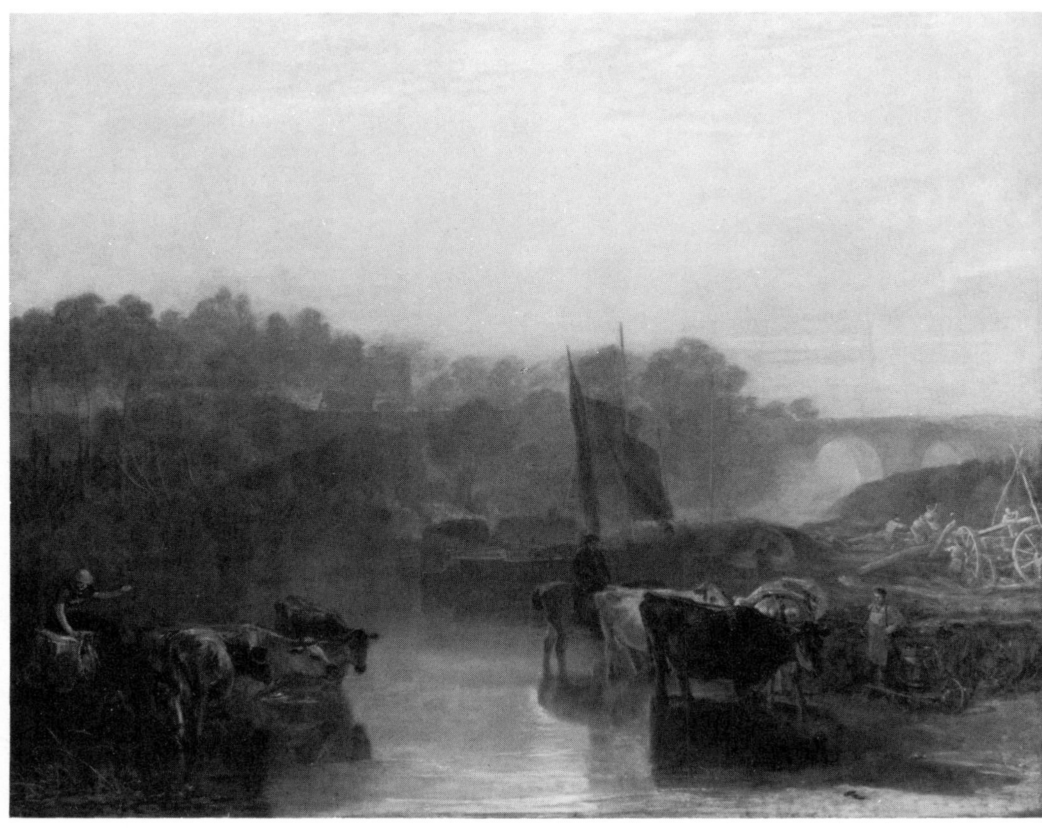

33. *Abingdon: Morning*, *c.* 1810. Turner

Only because of subsequent developments in dairy farming has it acquired extraneous nostalgic qualities. Fields of ripe corn in the undiversified flat-lands of Lincolnshire provided Peter De Wint with subject-matter for large oils as well as watercolours of daring, almost abstract simplicity. John Crome devoted one of his largest canvases to the bleak expanse of Mousehold Heath. The young William Mulready and John Linnell 'sitting down before any common object, the paling of a cottage garden, a mossy wall or an old post [would] try to imitate it minutely', and both painted views of the gravel pits at Kensington.[31] One of John Sell Cotman's most memorable watercolours is of a freshly ploughed field with a scarecrow and a single gawky farm labourer [34]. A ploughed field with a few birch trees and a lonely figure is also the subject of a painting by Caspar David Friedrich.[32] But here symbolical overtones are as persistent as they are mysterious; it is, indeed, a reminder of the

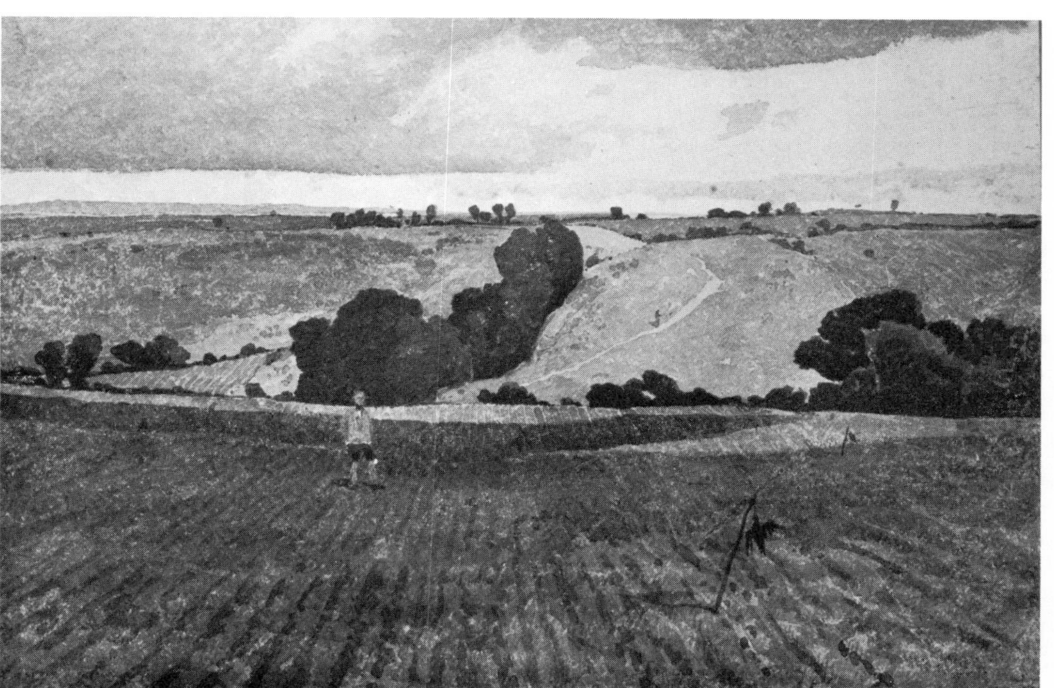

34. *The Ploughed Field*, *c.* 1807. Cotman

differences as much as of the similarities between both landscape painting and attitudes to nature in England and Germany.

Constable's and Cotman's familiar landscapes call to mind Coleridge's account of how the plan of *Lyrical Ballads* originated in the spring of 1798 as a result of conversations between him and Wordsworth

> on the two cardinal points of poetry, the power of exciting the sympathy of the reader by a faithful adherence to the truth of nature, and the power of giving the interest of novelty by the modifying colours of the imagination. The sudden charm, which accidents of light and shade, which moon-light or sun-set diffused over a known and familiar landscape, appeared to represent the practicability of combining both.[33]

In the year of the publication of *Lyrical Ballads*, 1798, Novalis had written in a notebook in uncannily similar phrases of the need to restore 'spontaneous feeling' and 'Romanticize the world': 'By endowing the commonplace with a lofty significance, the ordinary with a mysterious aspect, the familiar with the merit of the unfamiliar, the finite with the appearance of infinity, I am Romanticizing.'[34] The affinity between the two passages is striking, though hardly more so than the diversity of the writings to which they refer, *The Rime of the Ancient Mariner* and *Heinrich von Ofterdingen* or 'Goody Blake and Harry Gill' and *Hymnen an der Nacht*.

Similarities in statements by German and English writers at this period can usually be traced to a common origin. Both derived ideas about nature from the Neo-Platonic tradition which had survived in theological literature. For Calvin, external nature was the supreme evidence of the goodness of God.[35] In both countries (though not in France and Italy) the Enlightenment had been to some degree an extension of Protestantism. And when, towards the end of the eighteenth century, the young felt that Reason had failed to provide answers to questions which seemed to them more urgent than ever, it was to Protestant writers – albeit unorthodox ones like Jakob Böhme – that they turned. Hence, perhaps, the transference to nature of Protestant attitudes to God (a process which Wordsworth tried to reverse when he re-wrote *The Prelude* in old age), and the new importance given especially in Protestant countries to landscape painting as the expression of the individual's response and relationship to the rest of Creation.[36]

Philipp Otto Runge, author of the most radical of Romantic theories of landscape painting, might well have become a Lutheran pastor but for his almost 'religious' sense of vocation to be an artist, encouraged by reading Ludwig Tieck's novel *Franz Sternbalds Wanderungen* (1798). In 1801 he declared his ambition 'to convey to others, through words, signs, or whatever else might serve, something of the feeling which in my best hours animates me with a serene and stirring life'.[37] Next year he wrote in a letter to his brother Daniel:

> When the sky above me teems with innumerable stars, the wind blows through the vastness of space, the wave breaks in the immense night; when above the forest the reddish morning light appears and the sun begins to illuminate the world, the mist rises in the valley and I throw myself in grass sparkling with dew, every blade and stalk of grass teems with life, the earth awakes and stirs beneath me, and everything harmonizes in one great chord; then my soul rejoices and soars in the immeasurable space around me, there is no high or low, no time, no beginning and no end, I hear and feel the living breath of God who holds and supports the world, in whom everything lives and acts: this is our highest feeling – God![38]

Such feelings could be expressed only in landscapes. History painting had, he declared, died in the sixteenth century with the disintegration of the Catholic faith; all subsequent art, even Raphael's 'Sistine' *Madonna* with its visionary figures among clouds, had aspired towards landscape. And although no painter had as yet 'given his landscapes a true significance, or endowed them with allegorical meaning and intelligible, beautiful ideas', he envisaged a new art, *Landschafterey*, which could evoke the moral order of the universe. 'It is inevitable that this art should be the expression of the most profound religious mysticism,' he told Tieck.[39]

There are some wonderfully, sparklingly, fresh glimpses of landscape in several of Runge's paintings – a sharply focussed view of meadows near Hamburg behind the Hülsenbeck children [206], a line of tremulous grey trees against the dawn sky in the large painting of *Morning* [35]. But they are no more than glimpses. Landscape, in the normal sense of the term, played only a minor role in Runge's conception of *Landschafterey*. His aim was not so much the representation, as the integration, of plants and human figures, earth and water, light and air, in 'the great *Chime* and *Symphony* of nature'. To achieve this he had to develop a new language of visual forms, hieroglyphics like those in which God manifested his presence in the natural world.

Sometimes Runge resorted to traditional plant symbolism – the ivy clinging to the German oak, for example, in the portrait of himself, his wife and his brother linked together in mutual love and understanding [171]. The sun-flower in his picture of the Hülsenbeck children [206] – an image of the earth-bound aspiring towards divinity – seems to derive from the same Neo-Platonic source as that in Blake's poem:

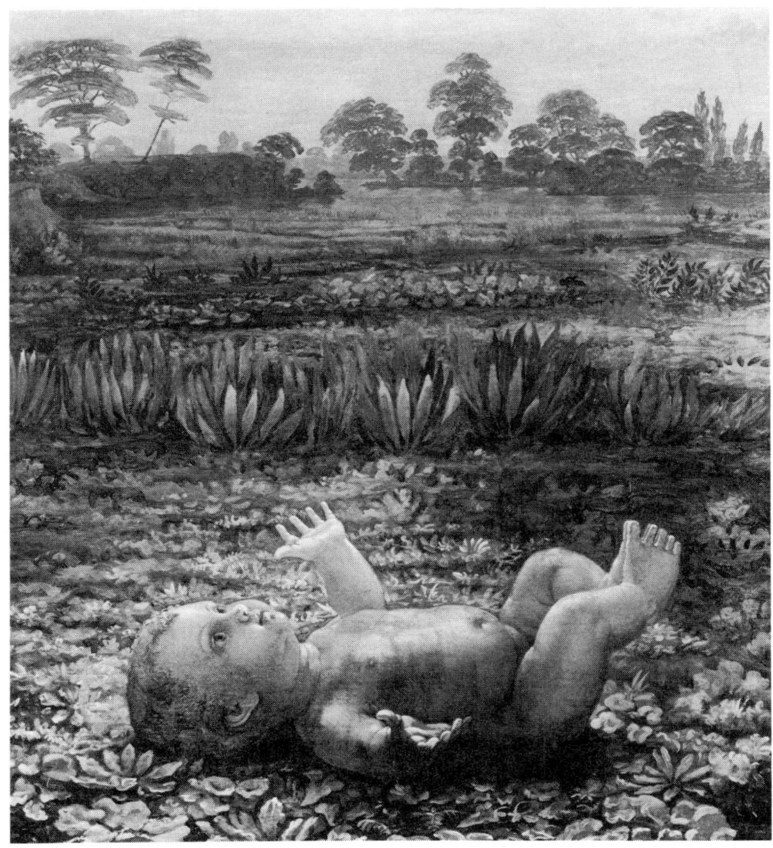

35. *Morning* (detail), 1808–9. Philipp Otto Runge

Ah, Sun-flower, weary of time,
Who countest the steps of the Sun,
Seeking after that sweet golden clime
Where the traveller's journey is done.

Where the youth pined away with desire,
And the pale Virgin shrouded with snow
Arise from their graves and aspire
Where my Sun-flower wishes to go.

The imagery is far more recondite in Runge's drawings and paintings of the times of day, *Die Zeiten*, which are mainly composed of flowers and children. But although many of his symbols have a pre-history in Baroque iconography, they are never extraneous emblems or attributes: they take their meaning from the context in which he placed them as major components of the composition.

The four large drawings of *Die Zeiten*, and the prints engraved after them, are among the most extraordinary works of art of their period, a deeply meditated attempt to resolve its contradictions and conflicts [70]. From a rational viewpoint, Goethe found them 'enough to drive one mad, beautiful and crazy at the same time'.[40] At first sight they may appear to be merely decorative, in the manner of Raphael's grotesques (or even of Dicky Doyle's whimsical fairyland on the old cover of *Punch*). But closer inspection reveals theological significance in each one: symbols indicate that *Morning* is associated with Jehovah, *Day*, *Evening* and *Night* with the Son, Father and Holy Ghost of the New Testament. Individual flowers, delicately drawn with the precise scientific knowledge of a botanical draughtsman, illustrate the transcendental beliefs of Nature Philosophy. Neo-classical linearity, the pure outlines without shading which Kant had advocated for the true representation of objects, has been converted into a vehicle for intuitive abstract ideas. But the major conflict which these drawings seek to resolve is that between mundane time – their ostensible subject – and the notion of eternity in which there is 'no beginning and no end'. Whereas previous allegories of time had been laments for the evanescence of earthly things, his are affirmations of eternal life. Perhaps he recalled, like Henry Vaughan,

> When on some *gilded Cloud*, or *flowre*
> My gazing soul would dwell an hour,
> And in those weaker glories spy
> Some shadows of eternity.[41]

Runge lived to complete only one of his four projected large paintings of *Die Zeiten* (he died in 1810 at the age of thirty-three) and he seems to have written that off as a failure, telling his brother to cut it up. His other paintings, with their non-naturalistic colours and strangely disquieting dream-like figures, were hardly seen outside a small circle of intimates. He published a book on colour theory, *Die Farbenkugel*, but the letters in which he worked out his other artistic ideas remained unprinted until 1840. And although he moved in intellectual circles in Dresden, and was friendly with Tieck and the Schlegels, the extent of his influence is very difficult to assess. There can, however, be little doubt that the aesthetic, religious and philosophical problems with which he grappled in his writings, drawings and paintings were those which most deeply concerned and perplexed his contemporaries.

The call for a painter who could give landscapes 'a true significance' was answered by Caspar David Friedrich, though not quite in the manner envisaged by Runge, and with characteristic Romantic irony and ambiguity. Friedrich and Runge had much in common.[42] Both were Protestants from pious North German homes, both came under the influence of the poet-theologian Ludwig Theobul Kosegarten. But there is one outstanding difference between them. Runge was almost as much a writer as a painter.[43] Friedrich was concerned to express in paint thoughts and emotions which could not be put into words. He was essentially a painter and his gradual retreat into himself and his own world of visual forms was perhaps the inevitable result of his inability to communicate in any other way. What he himself later said of another artist's works applies perfectly to his own: 'Just as the pious man prays without speaking a word and the Almighty hearkens unto him, so the artist with true feelings *paints* and the sensitive man understands and recognizes it.'[44] Hence the tone of intimacy and mystery, the strange and moving power of his landscapes. Crystal-clear precision of detail and an even flat surface emphasize their curiously withdrawn and laconic quality. Their simultaneously sharp focus and vague, dissolving air of unreality, their literalness combined with the heightened 'mood' of poetry make us almost painfully aware of that element of uncertainty which lies at the heart of Friedrich's work and his obsessive grappling with the problem of art and reality – with the agonizing doubts of the man of faith confronted with desacralized nature. The French sculptor David d'Angers seems to have sensed this, but in order to indicate the encompassing emotional range and intensity of Friedrich's art he could compare it only with the highest form of dramatic poetry. Friedrich is 'the only landscape painter who has yet been able to move all the faculties of my soul', he wrote in 1834: 'he has in fact created a new genre – the tragedy of landscape.'[45]

Friedrich did not, consciously, make as violent a break with tradition as that proposed by Runge. He aimed at raising landscape 'to a higher potentiality' – to use Novalis's mathematical metaphor. Although most of his paintings were inventions, they could be, and often were, taken at face value simply as topography – views of mountain ranges lit by the cool clear light of dawn; glimpses of rivers with white mists hanging on the water; trees and lakes and the church spire of a distant village; summer seascapes beneath crescent moon and evening star: windless, silent and peopled with a few lonely figures turned away from us and wholly engrossed in the mute contemplation of nature. They are all entirely credible. Yet they also have an ambivalent, almost hallucinatory quality.

Friedrich made frequent use of such easily comprehended symbols as the cross of faith [3] and the anchor of hope, ships sailing on the water of time or life [200]. The owl is a brooding presence in many works of his last unhappy years [36]. Gothic church ruins

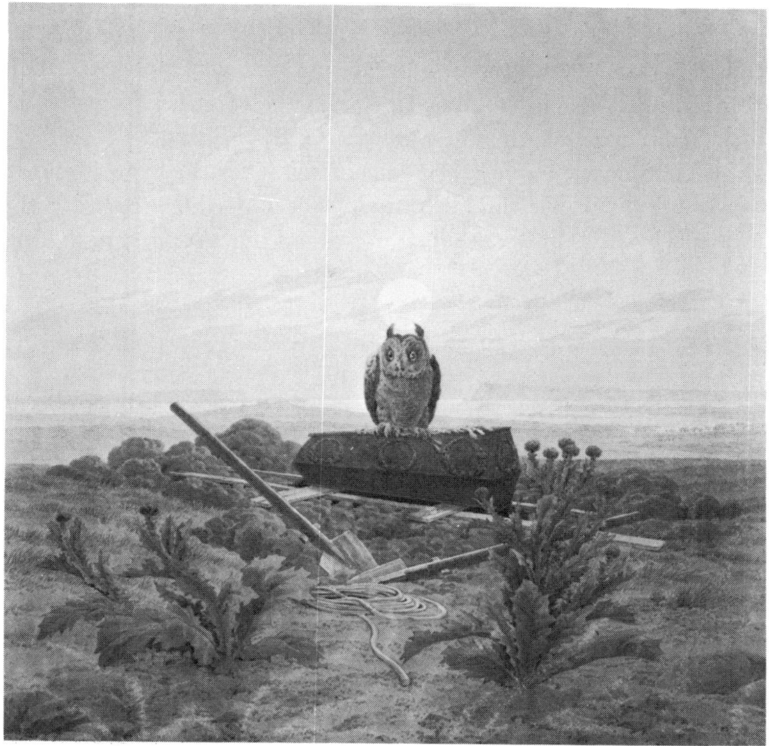

36. *Landscape with Grave, Coffin and Owl*, *c.* 1836–7. Caspar David Friedrich

manifest the decline of the Roman faith, and the trees, which echo their arches on a grander scale, the living religion of nature. He also played on the traditional emblematic associations of plants, oaks, evergreen fir trees, ivy and thistles. But it would be a mistake to seek in his work a straightforward one-to-one relationship between figurative elements and ideas. For him, as for Wackenroder and many others, all nature was the hieroglyphic language of God. 'The Divine is everywhere, even in a grain of sand,' he told Peter Cornelius; 'here I have represented it in bull-rushes.'[46]

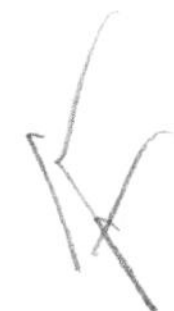

His pictures owe their extraordinary power less to emblems than to their visual subtlety, a unique manner of seeing and representing, that strange intense polarity of closeness and distance, of precise detail and sublime aura. The viewpoint is rarely that of a naturalistic painter with his feet on the ground. With Friedrich we are usually suspended in mid-air, as in *The Large Enclosure near Dresden* [37]. A man in a frock-coat surveying a mountainous prospect is depicted from a point in space at the level of his head [38]. In these and many other pictures the foreground has been cut away. On other occasions he painted the foreground in great detail, but sank an immeasurable chasm between it and the distant, almost visionary, horizon, tantalizingly out of reach, creating an uneasy mood of yearning for the unattainable. Sometimes he painted the foreground as a swelling knoll, echoing the curve of the world itself, over the brow of which the spectral tips of buildings are just glimpsed, to indicate the immensity lying on the other side, beyond our vision. The figures

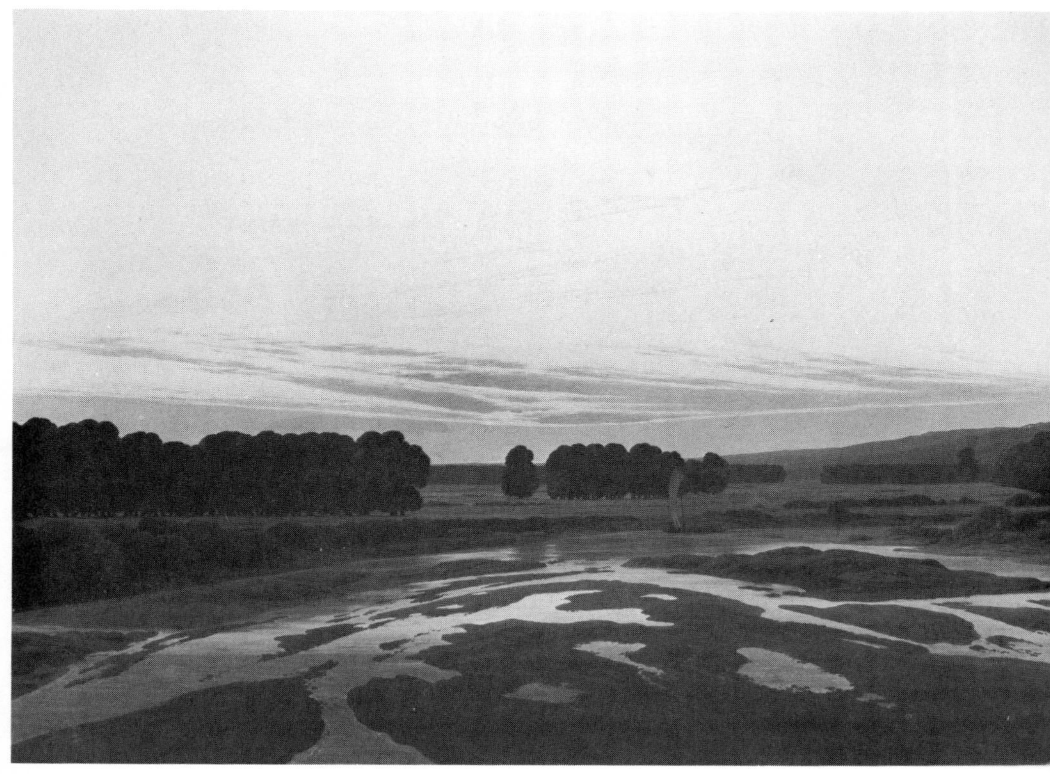

37. *The Large Enclosure near Dresden*, 1832. Caspar David Friedrich

38 (*opposite*). *The Wanderer above the Mists*, *c.* 1817–18. Caspar David Friedrich

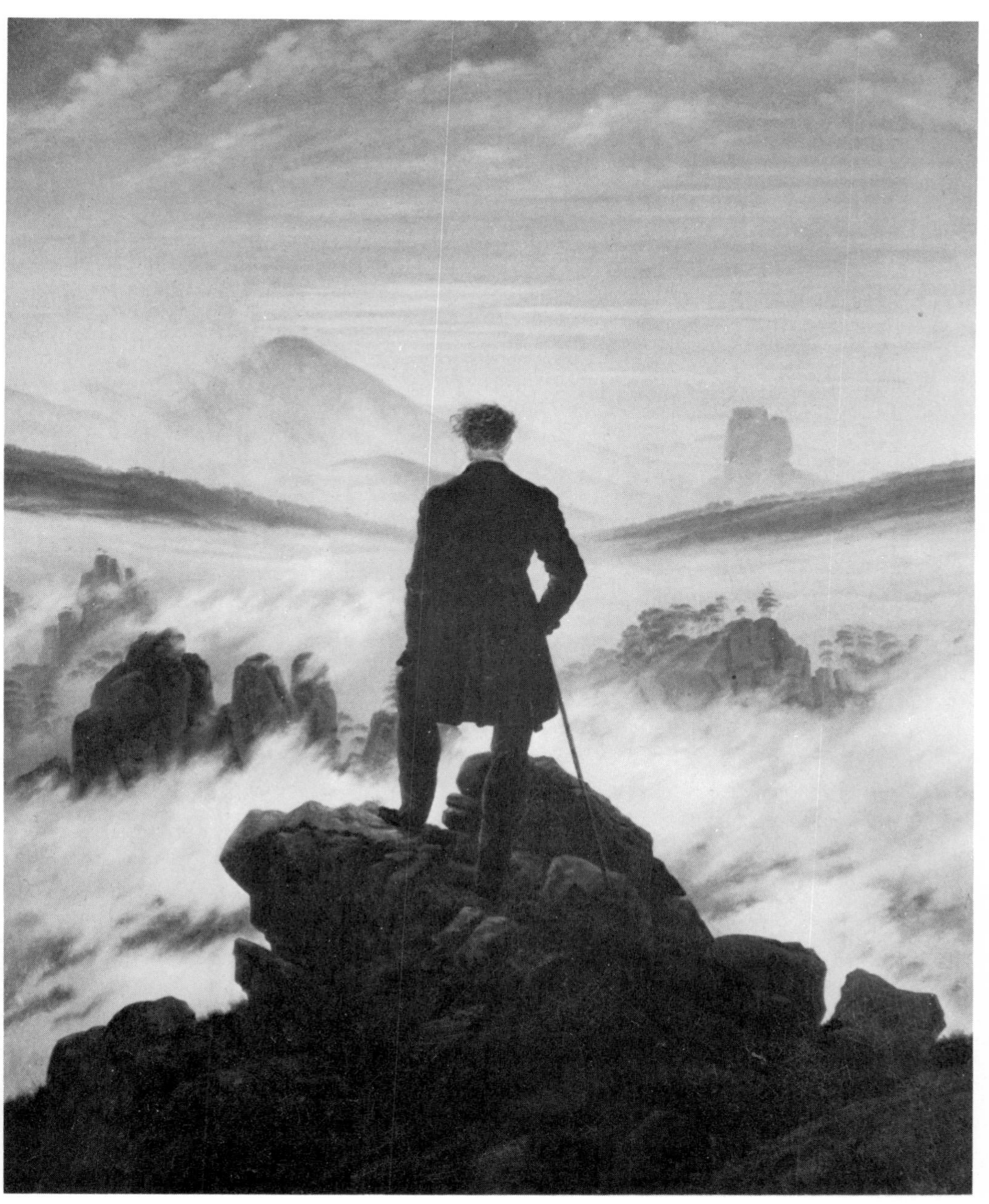

in his pictures can generally see more than we can. In *The Cliffs of Rügen*, for example, Friedrich shows himself kneeling down to peer over the vertiginous edge, measuring the depth of the drop which we can only guess [39].

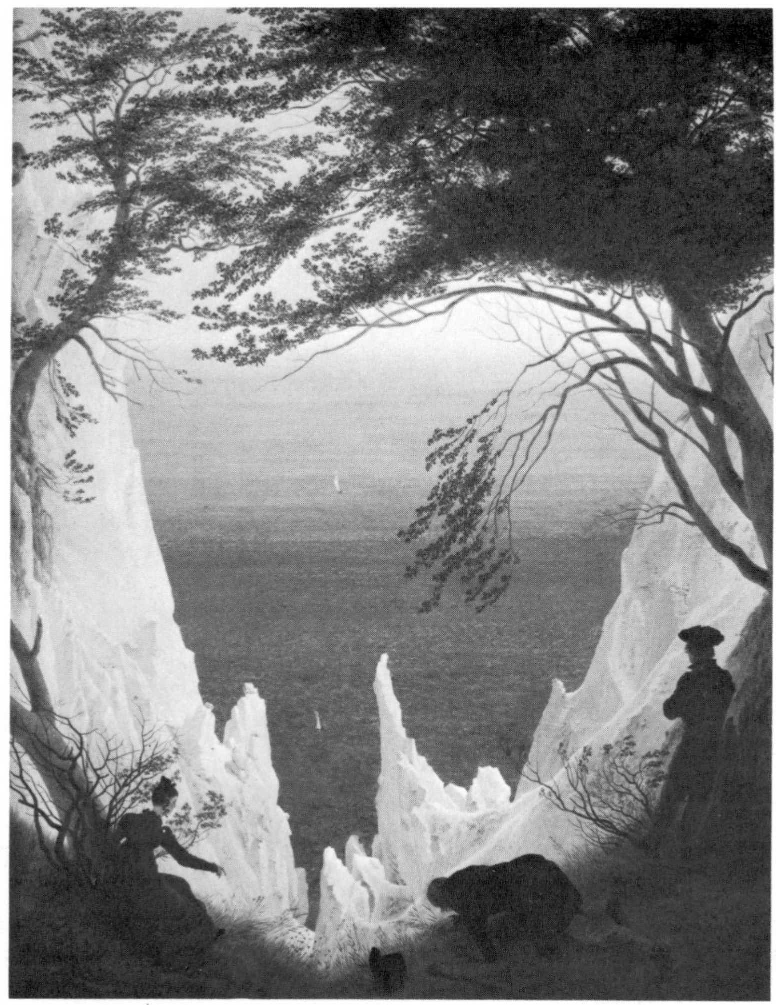

39. *The Cliffs of Rügen*, 1818–20. Caspar David Friedrich

Figures sometimes have a central symbolical significance, as in the picture of *The Four Stages of Life*,[47] or even more in *The Wanderer above the Mists* [38]. A passage in Carl Gustav Carus's *Letters on Landscape Painting* might almost seem to describe the latter:

> Stand on the peak of the mountain, contemplate the long ranges of hills, observe the courses of the rivers and all the glories offered to your view, and what feeling seizes you? It is a calm prayer, you lose yourself in unbounded space, your whole being undergoes a clarification and purification, your ego disappears, you are nothing, God is everything.[48]

Friedrich's figures are usually extraneous to the landscape – like his 'Wanderer' – neither wholly of its world nor of ours, standing on the edge of reality. Motionless, isolated, they seem to be both within and yet somehow outside nature, at once at home in it and estranged – symbols of ambiguity and alienation. Dressed in

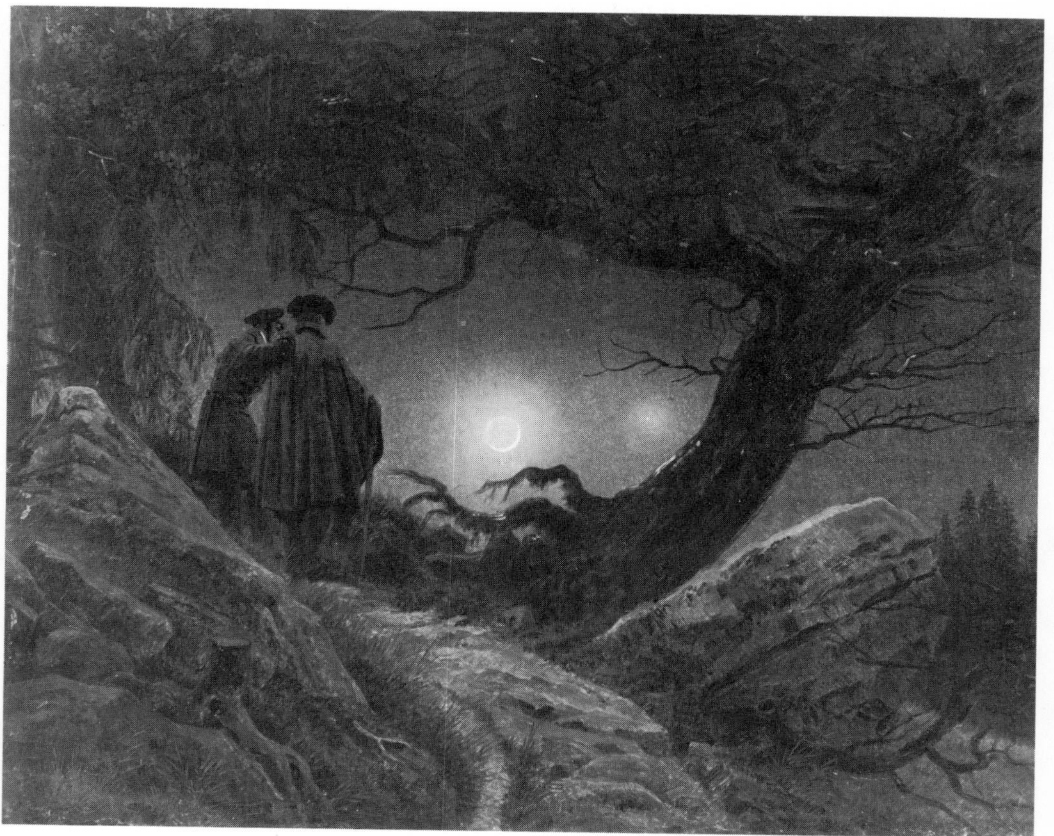

40. *Two Men Contemplating the Moon*, 1819. Caspar David Friedrich

strange, old-fashioned clothes with a hint of 'Sunday-best', they might be at prayer – or rather in self-communion, exploring realms beyond the world of sensory perception and above human understanding. Occasionally they are reminiscent of the mystics depicted in medieval miniatures, witnessing the apocalyptic visions they described. But a closer analogy, perhaps, would be with the *Sacra Conversazione*, where Saints standing in a landscape are related to the Madonna very much as Friedrich's figures are to the mountains, trees, the sea, a rainbow or the moon [40]. Art, he said, is the mediator between nature and mankind;[49] and one may wonder if he recalled the role of the Madonna as the mediatrix between God and Man.

The Lutheran faith in which Friedrich was brought up conditioned his attitude to art as well as religion. His refusal to make the art student's traditional pilgrimage to Rome may well have been prompted by his opposition to ultramontane spiritual influence. He was similarly opposed to the notion of authority, whether of the Academy or the Church. His firm faith in the inner light and his insistence on the 'private judgement' of the individual as the only valid guide to the interpretation of the Bible of nature is at once artistic and religious in a quintessentially Protestant way. 'Many have imitated him,' wrote Johann Christian Clausen Dahl, 'yet none has understood how to recreate that silent sense of the spirit of nature that was characteristic of Friedrich's art.'[50] Friedrich quarrelled with a pupil – one of the very few he had – who copied his work without understanding it. Dahl himself, a friend and colleague as much as a follower (their influence was mutual), sometimes used technical devices similar to Friedrich's, but to different effect. He was moved less by timeless moments of frozen tranquillity than by the restless movement and energy of nature, scurrying clouds and rushing waters. Imagery of Friedrich's type was often adopted by his friend Carl Gustav Carus, physician, painter and artistic theorist. But Carus's *Pilgrim in a Rocky Valley* [41] is both more literary and literal than Friedrich's figures – the very type of the Romantic 'Wanderer', the world-weary perennial seeker after higher truth who roves through so many Romantic poems and novels.

The impulse to create a new, underivative and, above all, 'serious' art of landscape, in which current attitudes to nature could be expressed, seems to have been shared by many painters who probably knew little or nothing of Friedrich. Wilhelm von Kobell, for instance, turned in the 1820s from the battle-pieces with which he had made his name, to images of perfect peace in pictures which are a cross between landscape and genre, with rather solid peasants and animals casting long dark shadows. Preoccupied with the rendering of light and space, he achieved extraordinary effects of clarity and distance, his bright clear colours providing a visual equivalent to the sharp sounds of bells and voices carried across wide valleys in the mountains. Like Friedrich, he often gave the backgrounds of his pictures an appearance of immeasurable distance by the omission of the intervening area – but quite devoid of any sense of mystical implications.

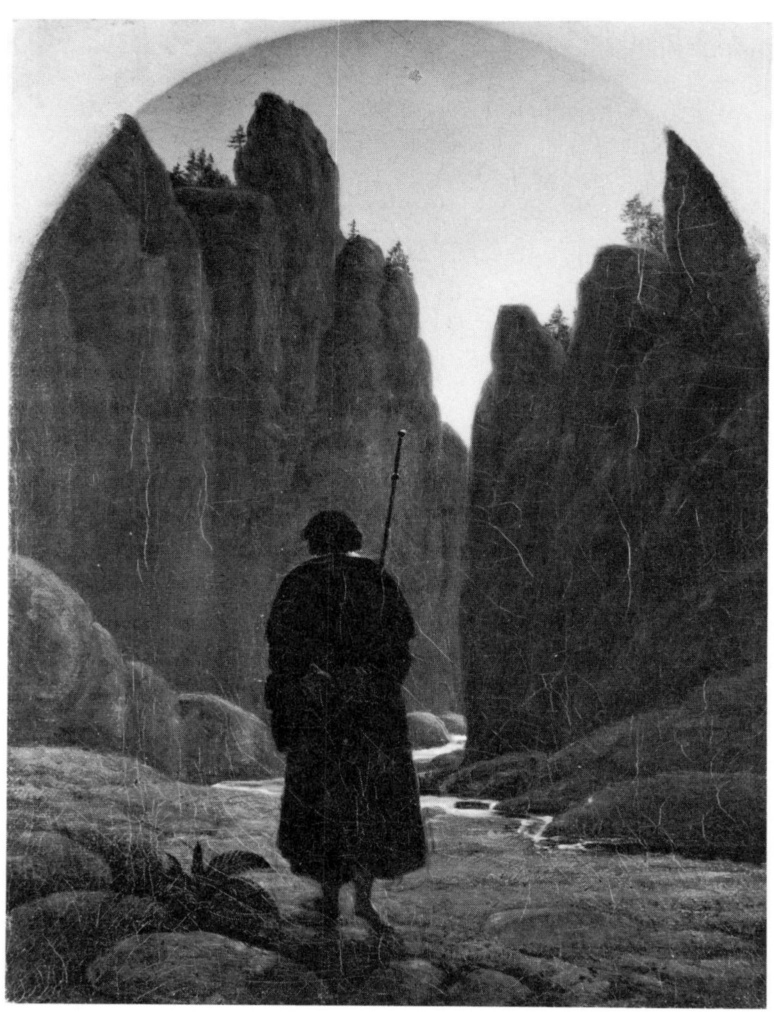

41. *Pilgrim in a Rocky Valley*, *c.* 1841. Carl Gustav Carus

Effects of breathless tranquillity reminiscent of Friedrich were achieved by several Scandinavian painters, whose work occasionally seems to carry similar symbolic meaning. Martinus Rørbye's picture of a man seated in the Campagna, beside two pieces of wood joined cross-wise, is one of the most immediately striking [42]. Christen Købke's painting of two patient women eternally waiting for a ferry-boat on a day so calm that the flag above the boat-station is hardly ruffled and smoke from a distant chimney hangs on the horizon, for example, or that of four boys on a bridge, one fishing, the others gazing at the waters below [43], may appear to be no more than realistic representations of everyday life in which cool northern sunshine is recorded with almost miraculous fidelity and sensitivity. But both are susceptible to symbolic interpretation – the

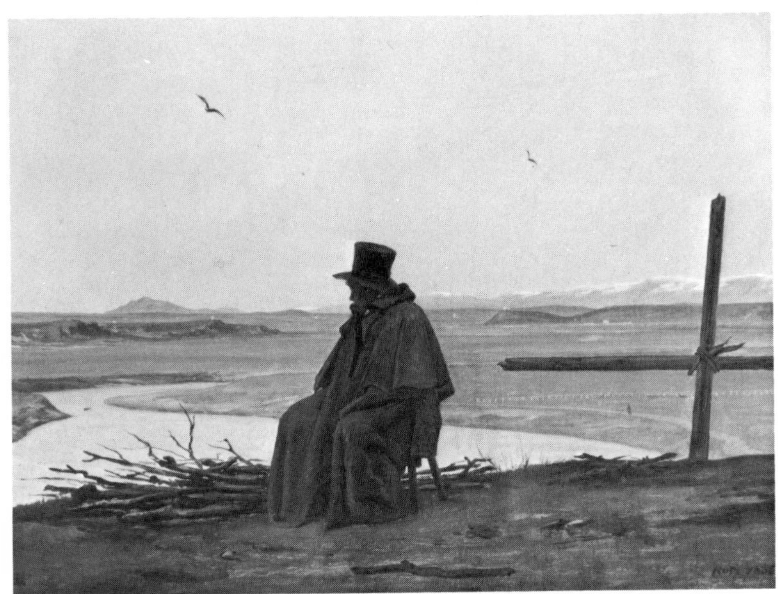

42. *The Roman Campagna*, 1835. Martinus Rørbye

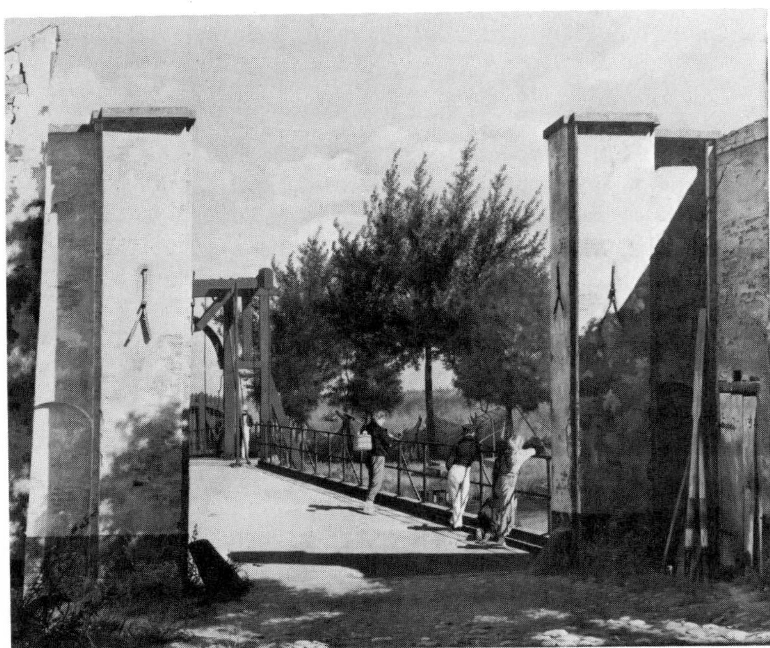

43. *The Gateway Bridge*, 1834. C. Købke

ferry-boat of death and the river of life are familiar metaphors in European literature. Such allusions are, however, made so delicately that we may wonder how far the painter himself was conscious of them.

In England, symbolic landscapes of an entirely different visionary cast were painted by Edward Calvert and Samuel Palmer, both of whom came under the spell of Blake, though not before they had begun to develop their individual styles. A childlike sense of wonder marks their first works and, although well aware of, and sometimes influenced by, earlier art, they seem to have looked at the prints of Dürer and Lucas van Leyden with the same clear bright eyes that they turned on mossed apple trees loaded with fruit, or sheep huddled round a shepherd. Calvert inscribed his woodcut *The*

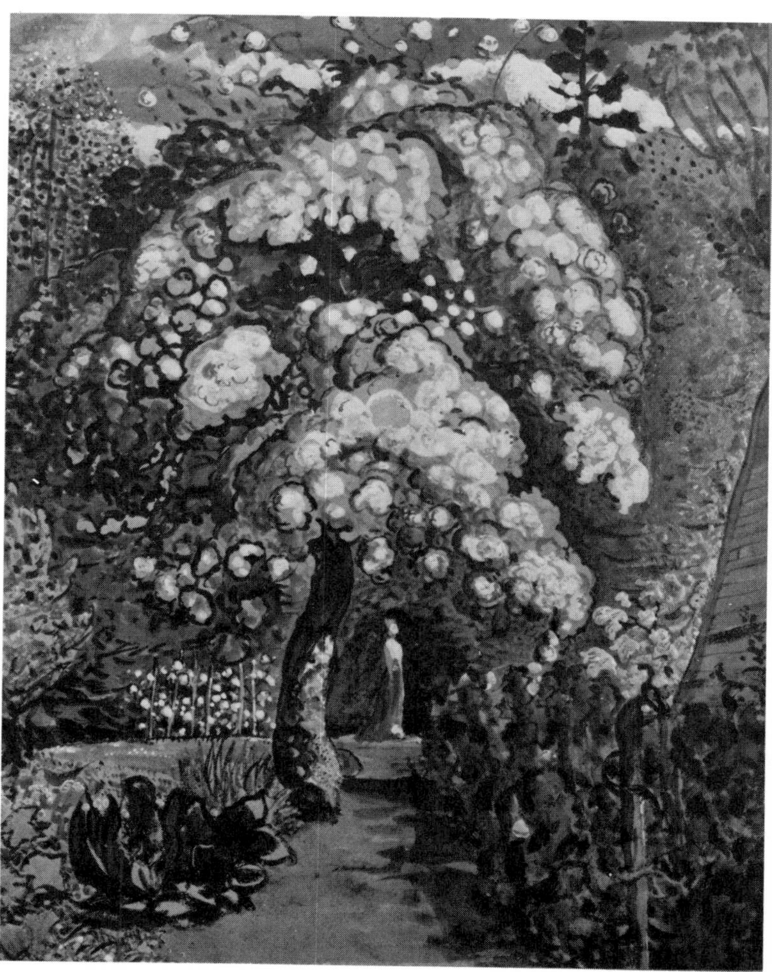

44. *In a Shoreham Garden*, *c.* 1829. Samuel Palmer

 Ploughman, published in 1827: 'Seen in the Kingdom of Heaven by vision through Jesus Christ Our Saviour.' The same words might equally well have been written by Palmer on any of the paintings and drawings of his Shoreham period (1826–32).

Palmer's watercolours of trees hung with blossom [44] and what he called 'glimpses of the perfumed and enchanted twilight of natural midsummer' are records of visions inspired by nature 'passed thro' the intense purifying separating transmuting heat of the soul's infabulous alchymy'.[51] 'Creation sometimes pours into the spiritual eye the radiance of Heaven,' he wrote in 1828:

> The green mountains that glimmer in a summer gloaming from the dusky yet bloomy east; the moon opening her golden eye, or walking in brightness among innumerable islands of light, not only thrill the optic nerve, but shed a mild, a grateful, an unearthly lustre into the inmost spirits, and seem the interchanging twilight of that peaceful country, where there is no sorrow and no night. After all, I doubt not but there must be the study of this creation, as well as art and vision; tho' I cannot think it other than the veil of heaven, through which her divine features are dimly smiling; the setting of the table before the feast; the symphony before the tune; the prologue of the drama, a dream of antepast and proscenium of eternity.[52]

But neither Palmer nor Calvert was able to preserve this visionary faculty for more than a few years. Practice in recording their visions led ineluctably to a familiarity which dimmed and finally extinguished them – as if they had been cast out of Paradise for painting the forbidden fruit.

With Constable it was all quite different. Though hardly transcendental in a mystical way, his childhood vision of nature was so brightly lit and so sharply defined in his memory that it provided him with the main source of artistic inspiration throughout his life, eventually acquiring a renovating virtue which became ever more deeply interfused with higher meaning. In sketch after sketch, and later one 'six-foot canvas' after another, he sought not merely to recapture his vision's original essence in all its innocent purity, but to re-examine it in the light of mature reflection, to use it as a touchstone against which all subsequent experience of nature and of art could be tested. 'Painting is with me but another word for feeling,' he wrote in 1821; 'and I associate "my careless boyhood" with all that lies on the banks of the Stour; those scenes made me a painter, and I am grateful; that is, I had often thought of pictures of them before I had ever touched a pencil.'[53]

In the text of *English Landscape*, which is a kind of manifesto – a work 'begun and pursued by the Author solely with a view to his own feelings, as well as his own notions of Art', Constable remarked: 'Perhaps the Author in his over-weening affection for these scenes may estimate them too highly, and may have dwelt too exclusively upon them; but interwoven as they are with his thoughts, it would have been difficult to have avoided doing so.' The young student of landscape who began by studying and painting the scenery with which he was surrounded would be 'impressed with the beauty and majesty of Nature under all her appearances, and, thus, be led to adore the hand that has, with such lavish beneficence, scattered the principles of enjoyment and happiness throughout every department of Creation'. It was with such scenes as those of his father's land and of the Stour valley, 'and he trusts with such a feeling that the Author's ideas of Landscape were formed: and he dwells on the retrospect of those happy days and years of "sweet retired solitude", passed in the calm of an undisturbed congenial study, with a fondness and delight which must ever be to him a source of happiness and contentment'.[54]

These words inevitably bring to mind that masterpiece of retrospection and introspection *The Prelude*, which Constable is unlikely to have read, for although the first version was completed by 1805 it remained unpublished until 1850.[55] However, he knew Wordsworth personally, and a remark of his when they were walking together in the country is said to have inspired a passage in a letter Constable wrote from East Bergholt in May 1819: 'Every tree seems full of blossom of some kind & the surface of the ground seems quite living – every step I take & on whatever object I turn my Eye that sublime expression of the Scripture "I am the resurrection and the life" &c seems verified about me.'[56] For him, as for Wordsworth, every season 'unfolded transitory qualities' intimating immortality. Spring blossom was not a symbol of the Resurrection so much as a revelation of eternal life. But the closest point of contact between the two is in their attitudes to their early experiences of the natural world. In 1829, or shortly after, Constable copied out the famous poem:[57]

My heart leaps up when I behold
A rainbow in the sky;
So was it when my life began;
So is it now I am a man;
So be it when I shall grow old,
        Or let me die!
The Child is father of the Man;
And I could wish my days to be
Bound each to each in natural piety.

This is the simplest statement of the idea behind *The Prelude* and, indeed, all Wordsworth's poetry: that the child's intuition of the harmony of the universe provides a clear indication that such harmony exists, but becomes of value only when contemplated and tested in maturity. Wordsworth referred to *The Prelude* (a title he seems never to have used) as a long poem on the 'growth' or 'formation' of his mind.

But the eternal and unchanging peaks of the Lake District which inspired Wordsworth had little significance for Constable, and not merely because he was brought up in different surroundings.[58] Constable's vision of universal harmony sprang from a landscape to which men contributed and from which they benefited materially

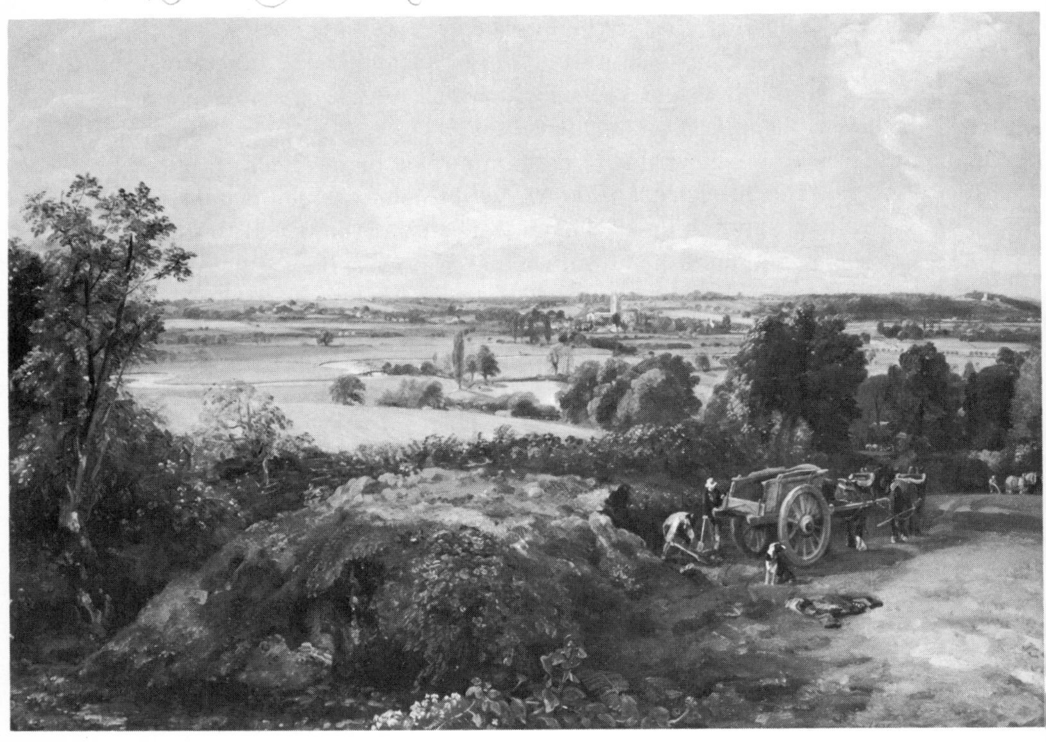

45. *View of Dedham*, 1814–15. Constable

as well as spiritually. He preferred painting man-made canals to mountain brooks, and dams to waterfalls. 'The sound of water escaping from mill-dams, etc., willows, old rotten planks, slimy posts, and brickwork, I love such things,' he wrote in 1821. 'As long as I do paint, I shall never cease to paint such places.'[59] At the time of his death he was at work on a picture of a mill with Arundel Castle in the distance (a complete reversal of the eighteenth-century topographer's order of things). In nearly all his pictures the land is worked. When a piece of common near his childhood home was 'enclosed' and a portion acquired by his brother, he showed no sentimental regret but recorded its first ploughing.[60] He was meticulous in the representation of up-to-date agricultural implements. The dung which fertilized the fields, no less than the rain that watered them, the mills in which the grain was ground, the boats on which it was transported by canal to the city – all played a part in his vision of the universal harmony. In one of his most poetic landscapes – perhaps the key work for an understanding of his philosophy of nature – men are at work on a dunghill in the foreground, with the tower of Dedham church above and beyond [45].

Each of the 'six-foot canvases' which he exhibited at the Royal Academy and on which he placed so much importance celebrates the harmony of the elements, emphasized by the reflection of the sky in water. The harmony of life, not the stasis of death. The pulse-beat of the universe can be felt in the movement of the clouds and soughing of the great trees as much as in human figures, animals, carts and barges below. He titled them laconically: *A Scene on the River Stour* (now known as *The White Horse*); *Landscape* (which his engraver Lucas unpardonably called *The Young Waltonians*); *Landscape: Noon* (*The Haywain*); *View on the Stour*; *A Boat Passing a Lock*; and again *Landscape* (*The Leaping Horse*). Each of them includes some incident which seems to link it with a particular moment of vision, when Constable experienced the 'sense of harmony'. Often it is something unexpected if not, at first sight, untoward – the haywain is not on dry land but splashing through water; the lumbering cart-horse prepares to leap over a barrier on the tow-path; the white horse is not drawing a barge but standing in one. It seems likely that these and many of Constable's other paintings are pictorial equivalents to the 'spots of time' of *The Prelude* – moments of childhood to which poet (and painter) returned with changing views in a world which was also changing.[61] Hence, perhaps, Constable's reluctance to stop working and to part with his pictures – he tended to regard them as abandoned rather than 'finished' – not because he was a 'perfectionist' but because in a world of constant 'flux' they needed constant re-adjustment. This may also help to explain his much discussed practice of painting full-size sketches for his major works [46]. These sketches probably represented the central moment in his always highly personal relationship

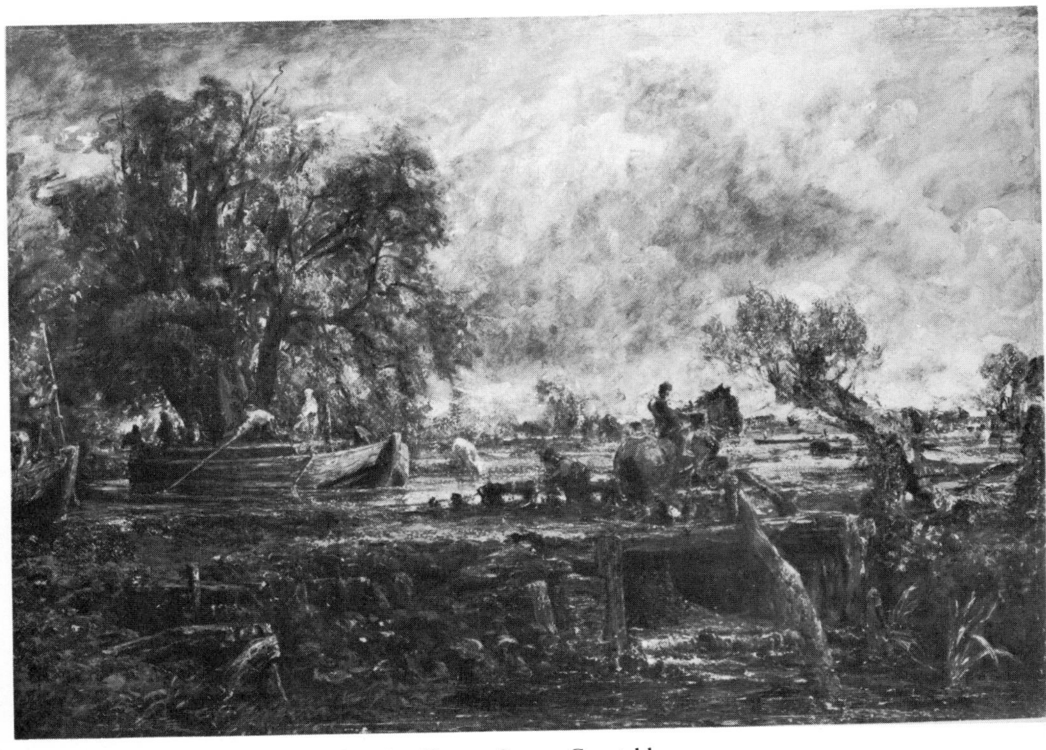

46. Sketch for *The Leaping Horse*, 1824–5. Constable

with his subject, and the finished picture his tranquil recollection of and meditation on it. In 1823 he remarked, in a different context: 'A sketch of a picture is only like seeing it in one view. It is only one thing. A sketch (of a picture) will not serve more than one state of mind & will not serve to drink at again & again – in a sketch there is nothing but one state of mind – that which you were in at the time.'[62]

To modern eyes, Constable's sketches strike first and deepest by their apparent spontaneity and truth to nature, the amazing bravura of handling, the heavily loaded brush-strokes and pigments dashed on and worked with a palette-knife, the bold massing of forms, the sparkling highlights and rich shadows.[63] The quietly contemplative finished pictures which he elaborated with such care tend to be less regarded – as does the profoundly religious feeling for the harmony of nature which they express. The tower of Dedham church, which is the focal point of so many of his compositions, is one of the most revealing, though least obvious, of the additions he made to the final version of *The Leaping Horse* [47].

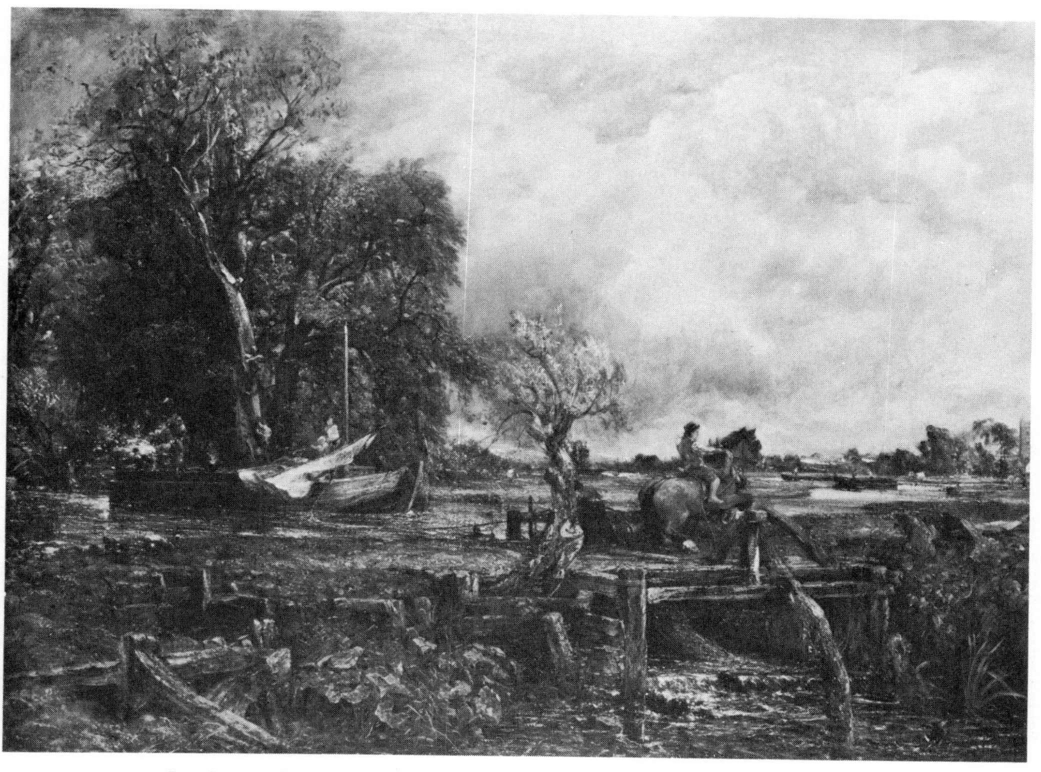

47. *Landscape* (*The Leaping Horse*), 1825. Constable

Constable first described *The Leaping Horse* as a scene 'full of the bustle . . . where four or five boats are passing with dogs, horses, boys & men & women & children, and best of all old timber – props, waterplants, willow stumps, sedges, old nets, &c &c &c'. But, shortly before sending it to the Royal Academy a few months later, he called it 'a lovely subject, of the canal kind, lively – & soothing – calm & exhilarating, fresh & blowing'. Soothing was one of his favourite words. 'My canvas soothes me into forgetfulness of the scene of turmoil and folly – and worse – of the scene around me,' he wrote in 1834. 'Every gleam of sunshine is blighted to me in the art at least. Can it therefore be wondered at that I paint continual storms: "Tempest o'er tempest roll'd" – still the "darkness" is majestic, and I have not to accuse myself of ever having prostituted the moral feeling of art.'[64] He might have said of the 'great end' of painting what Keats wrote of poetry,

> that it should be a friend
> To soothe the cares, and lift the thoughts of man.

Another of his favourite terms was 'the chiaroscuro of Nature' which he endowed with special implications, referring to 'the more abrupt and transient appearances ... which are ever occurring in the changes of external Nature', and their influence on the emotions.[65] The late watercolour of *Stonehenge*, with a louring sky relieved by a double rainbow, is one of his most dramatic illustrations of this idea [48]. But in 'chiaroscuro' he also saw the power

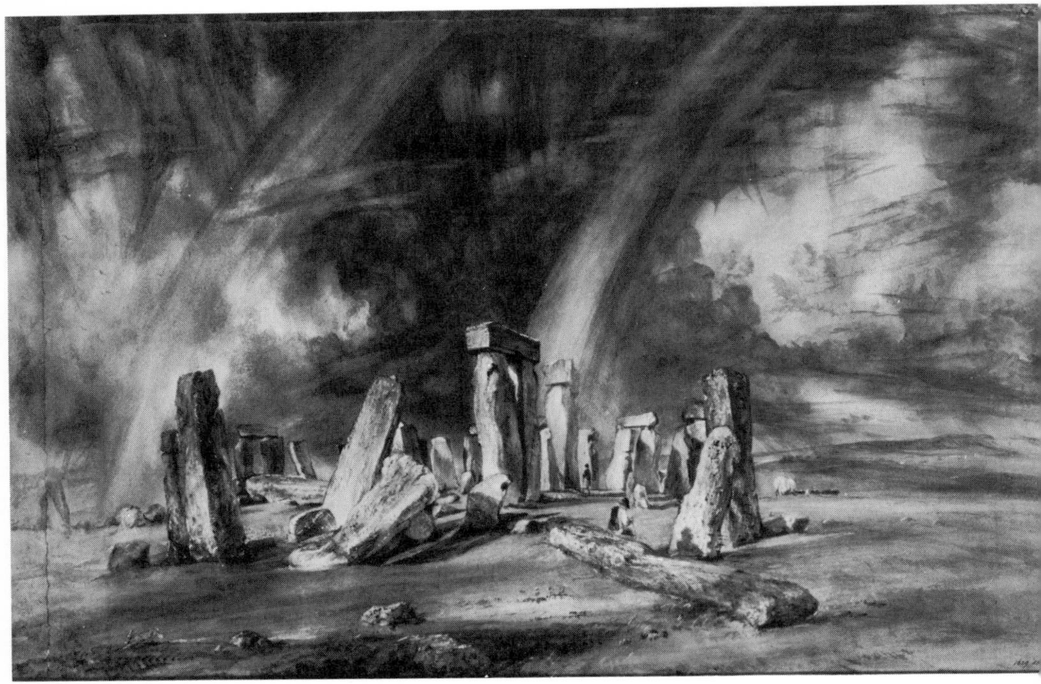

48. *Stonehenge*, 1836. Constable

of light to harmonize the visible world – 'the light of nature, the mother of all that is valuable in poetry, painting or anything else where an appeal to the soul is required'.[66] And it is in this sense that the word 'chiaroscuro' appears very prominently on the title page of *English Landscape*, the collection of prints after his paintings reproduced in mezzotint, a process by which light is created out of darkness. 'I never saw an ugly thing in my life,' he once remarked; 'for let the form of an object be what it may, – light, shade and perspective will always make it beautiful'.[67] Hence his preoccupation with the sky which is 'the source of light in nature, and governs everything'. In his paintings the sky is never 'a white sheet thrown behind the objects' but always an integral part of the landscape, 'the key note, the standard of scale, and the chief organ of sentiment'.[68]

Constable's was a total view of the visible world. Even though he focused attention on a particular place and 'spot of time', he always suggested that it was no more than a tiny section of the vast continuum. Despite his veneration for Claude, he eschewed the Claudean pictorial structure, with its neatly placed coulisses and suggestion of a closed Vale of Tempe isolated from the rest of the world. The landscapes he painted were nearly always man-made, but without any superimposed overall pattern. They are made up of innumerable parts, small-holdings in Creation as it were, united by colour, light and air. (This may perhaps reflect a deep-rooted attitude to both religion and society.[69]) Every field and tree and blade of grass seems to be equal in the love of God and of the artist. In his large view of the Vale of Dedham of 1828 [25], for instance, he abolished the Claudean framework of a sketch he had painted many years before [Fig. vii, p. 379], replacing an upright tree on the left by the trunk of a willow slanting out of the frame, and inserting beyond the tall trees on the right a distant farm-house which constitutes a little 'picture' in itself. Time and again the beginnings of new compositions are hinted at: near the edge there is nearly always some object of interest – a building, or a figure moving outwards, like the man ploughing in the landscape with a dunghill [45]. Cloud formations, which he represented complete in his sketches, are usually 'cut' in his finished paintings. Such devices might make an uncomfortably restless effect were they not counterbalanced by the harmony of colour and feeling between land and sky, so often emphasized by reflecting water. But to those familiar only with landscapes constructed on traditional lines, they gave the impression that his selection of subject-matter was almost arbitrary.

Contemporary tributes to Constable's 'naturalism' and even his own declared ambition to be a 'natural painter' are somewhat misleading. No painter has ever represented the English countryside with greater fidelity, the sparkle of dew on grass, the glint of sunshine on sappy leaves, the noble form of great elms, the myriad intricacies of the hedgerow. Yet he found the work of a contemporary 'utterly heartless' because it pretended to 'nothing but an imitation of nature ... of the coldest and meanest kind'.[70] Such straightforward illusionism he put beyond the pale of art. 'The art pleases by *reminding*, not by *deceiving*,'[71] he remarked, and his own pictures are reminders or recollections of particular scenes and the emotions they evoked. Art was no substitute for nature: the painting was independent of the scene it represented. Often he wrote of his own works simply as objects, without any reference to their content. *The Lock* 'looks most beautifully silvery, windy and delicious – it is all health & the absence of everything stagnant'.[72] Of *The Valley Farm* he remarked in 1835: 'I have got my picture into a very beautiful state; I have kept my brightness without my spottiness, and I have preserved God Almighty's daylight, which is enjoyed by all mankind, excepting the lovers of old dirty canvas, perished pictures at a thousand guineas each, cart grease, tar and snuff of candle.'[73] He might almost have been writing about a non-representational painting. When asked if a picture in his studio had been painted for 'any particular person', he replied: 'Yes, sir, it is painted for a *very particular* person, the person for whom I have all my life painted.'[74] Very few, if any, earlier artists would have made such a claim.

Turner's mature landscapes are still more obsessively personal, in a very different and often ambiguous way. He is literally at the centre of the elemental vortex of *Snow Storm – Steam Boat off a*

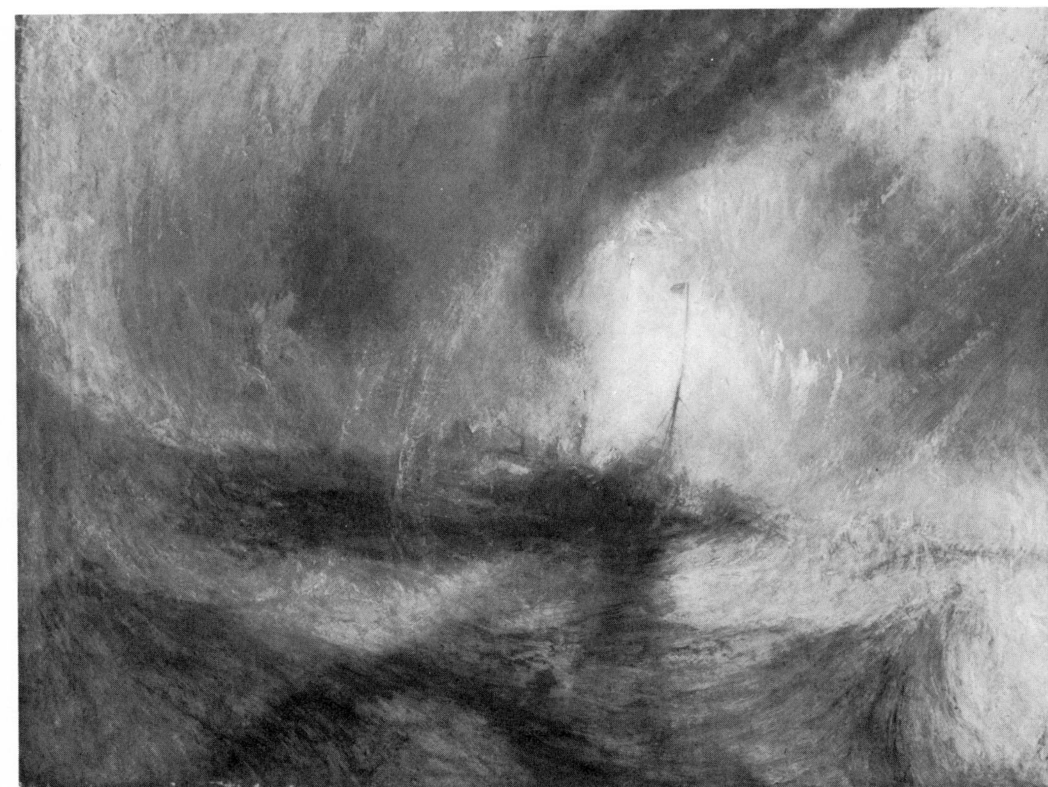

49. *Snow Storm – Steam Boat off a Harbour's Mouth*, 1842. Turner

Harbour's Mouth, of which he remarked: 'I did not paint it to be understood' [49]. Not only did he paint large canvases as well as watercolour sketches for his own eyes alone, he became increasingly reluctant to part with the pictures he exhibited and took every opportunity of buying back those he had sold. Yet he gave very little care to them when they were back in his possession.[75] Furtiveness and exhibitionism were combined in his character – withdrawal into a private, darkly pessimistic, world of imagery little comprehended by his contemporaries and, at the same time, an urge to shock, an ambition to outshine both contemporaries and old masters, an obvious glee in painting publicly on varnishing days at the Royal Academy.[76] Whereas Constable's landscapes seem to reflect both the anguish and exaltation of intense private prayer, Turner's are more like the product of passionate physical intercourse with his medium, often akin to love-making and sometimes to rape.[77]

Much of Turner's work is explicitly (and nearly all of it implicitly) concerned with the practice of painting, just as so many poems are concerned with the making of poetry, 'the intolerable wrestle with words and meanings'. This is no less obvious in his tributes to Titian, Veronese, Claude, Rembrandt, Cuyp and Ruysdael (painted rather than written art criticism) than in such elaborately titled works as *Rome from the Vatican, Raffaelle, accompanied by La Fornarina, preparing his pictures for the decoration of the Loggia* or *Bridge of Sighs, Ducal Palace and Custom House, Venice: Canaletti Painting*.[78] To some extent his poetry was simply an expression of a desire to distinguish pictorial from verbal qualities and thus sharpen his understanding of the ways in which the two arts could achieve the same aim of elevating truth.[79]

He did not, of course, attempt to produce 'pure paintings' devoid of subject or intellectual content – despite the superficial similarity of some of his later sketches to the work of abstract expressionists. Throughout his career he made use of traditional emblems to denote one level of meaning in his pictures. A hare running across the track symbolizes speed in his allegory of the forces of nature *Rain, Steam and Speed*.[80] A serpent lurks in the undergrowth of *The Bay of Baiae* as a characteristically pessimistic reminder of the evil latent in this enervatingly beautiful scene. At a deeper level ideas and images are fused. His first group of historical landscapes, conceived in 1802 or 1803, has as its main theme what John Gage calls 'the clash and metamorphosis of the elements', both expressive of and expressed by the painterly conflict of light and shade.[81] His *Apollo and Python*, in the grand tradition of Claude and Poussin, is a baroque allegory of the struggle between good and evil, and at the same time a painting 'about' chiaroscuro (which did not mean the same to him as to Constable).[82] The later, more deeply felt and complex *Regulus* [50], which records the horrifying story of how the Carthaginians cut off the eye-lids of Regulus and exposed him to the blinding rays of the sun, is an attempt to out-do Claude, a comment on the history

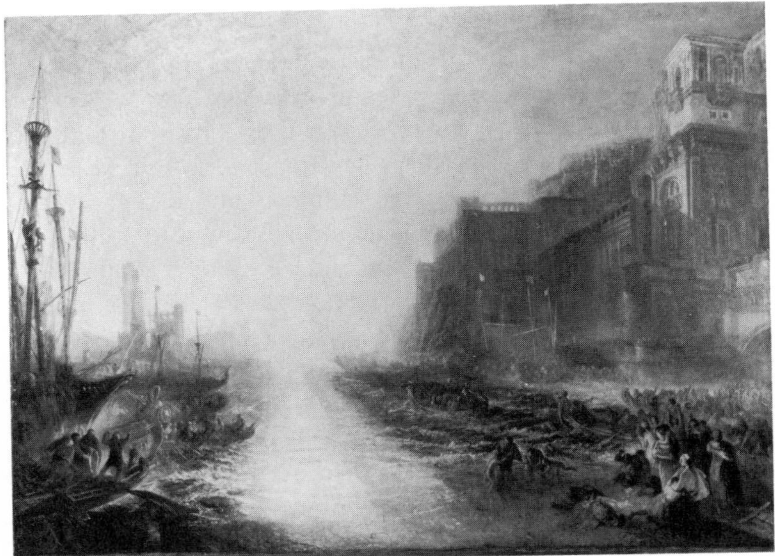

50. *Regulus*, 1828–37. Turner

of Carthage (which he associated with England at this time) and, essentially, a painting about light. 'The sun is God,' he declared shortly before his death – but a jealous God and cruel. He had remarked, in an early notebook, on the sixteenth-century Italian theorist Lomazzo's identification of light with the Deity. In Turner's work brightness signifies the life-giving force, which can also torment and destroy, a metaphor for organic and artistic creation. Darkness meant for him death and tranquillity. Criticized for the darkness of the black sails in his memorial to David Wilkie *Peace – Burial at Sea*, he replied: 'I only wish I had a colour to make them blacker.'

He seems to have been constantly preoccupied with the process of creation, and thus with the four elements from which all substances were still, in his time, supposed to derive. In one painting after another he depicted water, calm with 'liquid melting reflection', or storm-tossed, or suspended in air as mist or cloud. Some-

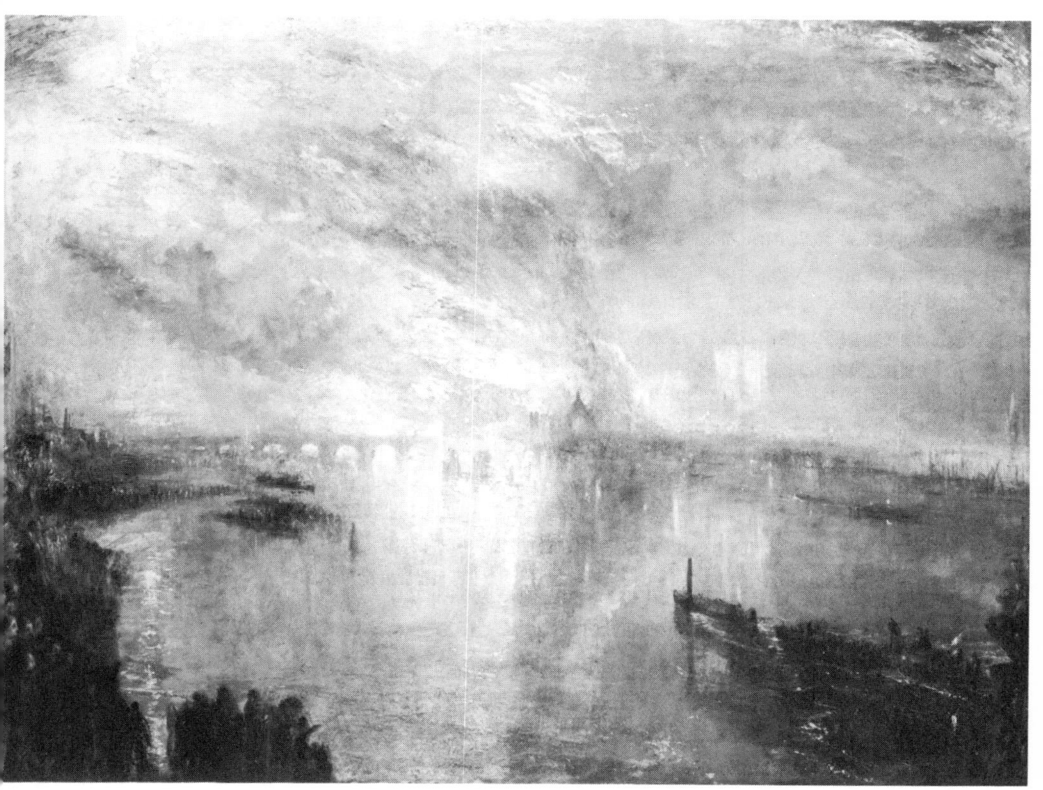

51. *The Burning of the Houses of Lords and Commons, October 16, 1834,* 1835. Turner

times he rendered fire literally, with earth, water and air in *The Burning of the Houses of Lords and Commons* [51], in conflict with ice in *Whalers (boiling blubber), entangled in flaw ice, endeavouring to extricate themselves.*[83] But fire more usually appears as light emanating from the sun, in such an idyllic painting as *Crossing the Brook*,[84] or in one as terrible as *The Slave Ship*, where water is mingled with blood (the fiery fluid) as fish and birds prey on the bodies of the jettisoned slaves [52]. Early in his career Turner planned to paint an apocalyptic subject, 'the water turned to blood', and it might be said that his whole art lies between this idea and that of one of his last works, *The Angel Standing in the Sun* [53]. It is perhaps significant that the destroying angel's wings should be so similar to the sails of a white boat in his sun-drenched view of the Venetian cemetery [54].

Earth and vegetation, the conventional material of landscape, have decreasing importance in Turner's work. Everything becomes

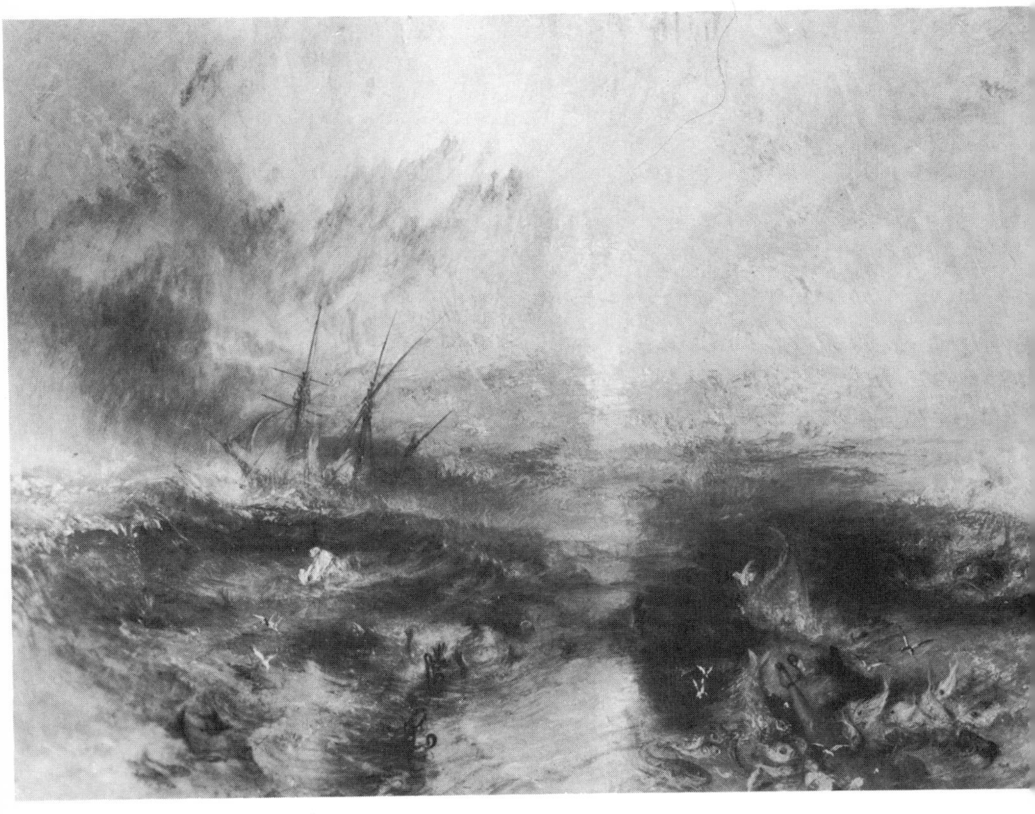

52. *The Slave Ship*, 1840. Turner

53 (*opposite above*). *The Angel Standing in the Sun*, 1846. Turner

54 (*opposite*). *Campo Santo, Venice*, 1842. Turner

transmuted into light and water. As early as 1816 Hazlitt complained that his pictures were 'too much abstractions of aerial perspective, and representations not properly of the objects of nature as of the medium through which they were seen'.[85] This is somewhat ambiguous, and it is difficult to determine whether or not he had recognized Turner's identification of the atmospheric colouring which hangs between the artist and the object with the pigments he applied to paper or canvas. Mists which transform and unite disparate objects visually, and skies coloured in shot reds and yellows by the deep radiance of the rising or setting sun, are natural paradigms of the art of painting conceived neither as the composition

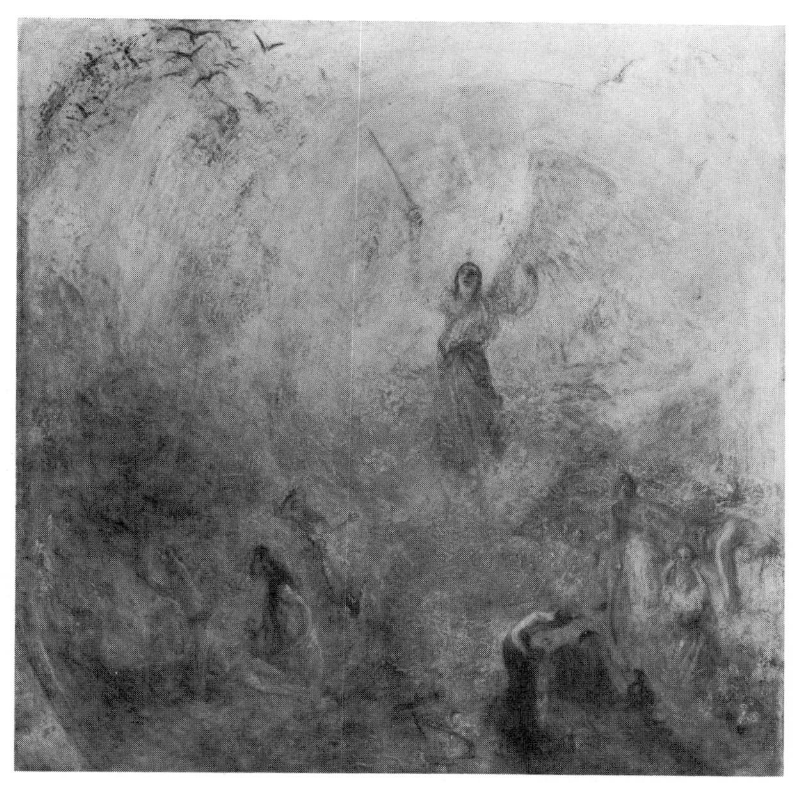

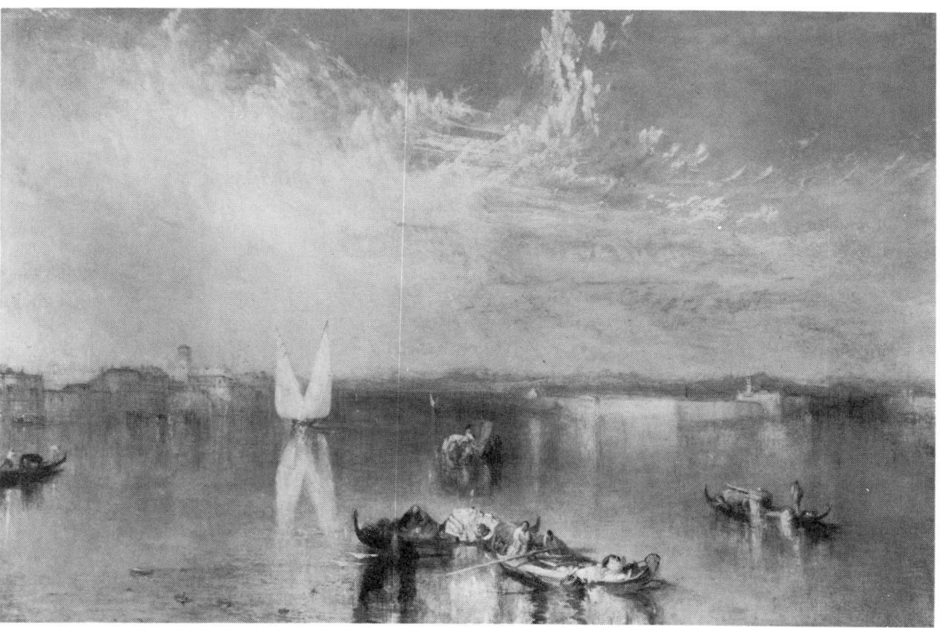

of clearly defined solid forms, nor even as the imitation of nature, but as the manipulation of opaque and translucent pigments. Turner sought to re-create rather than represent effects of light – in his own words, 'admiring Nature by the power and practicability of his Art, and judging his Art by the perceptions drawn from Nature'.[86] In his later years his vision grew still broader and less specific so that, as Lawrence Gowing has remarked, 'no single touch of paint corresponded to any specific object; the equivalence was between the whole configuration and the total subject', and the transformation it achieved seems 'like the return to a primal flux which denies the separate identity of things'.[87]

Contemplation of the enigma of light and colour seems to have drawn Turner to a kind of Neo-Platonic philosophy of life, as unorthodox as it was unsystematic, derived from the experience of painting rather than from abstract thought or books. It is a religio-scientific outlook strikingly akin to that developed by Shelley. Turner does not appear to have read Shelley's poetry until after 1838. But *The Sun of Venice Going to Sea* beautifully catches the mood of *Lines Written Among the Euganean Hills*, from which he derived his own verses printed in the Royal Academy catalogue when the picture was exhibited in 1843. *Queen Mab's Cave* of 1846 is directly related to Shelley's *Queen Mab*, and the lines used as a 'caption' for *Light and Colour* (*Goethe's Theory*) are adapted from *Prometheus Unbound*.[88] Shelley and Turner shared attitudes to mythology and science, as well as to such symbols as the serpent, the boat, the cave, water and light. And even when there is no direct connection, Turner's paintings again and again bring to mind lines like these from *The Daemon of the World*:

> If solitude hath ever led thy steps
> To the shore of the immeasurable sea,
> And thou hast lingered there
> Until the sun's broad orb
> Seemed resting on the fiery line of ocean,
> Thou must have marked the braided webs of gold
> That without motion hang
> Over the sinking sphere:
> Thou must have marked the billowy mountain clouds,
> Edged with intolerable radiancy,
> Towering like rocks of jet
> Above the burning deep:
> And yet there is a moment
> When the sun's highest point
> Peers like a star o'er ocean's western edge,
> When those far clouds of feathery purple gleam

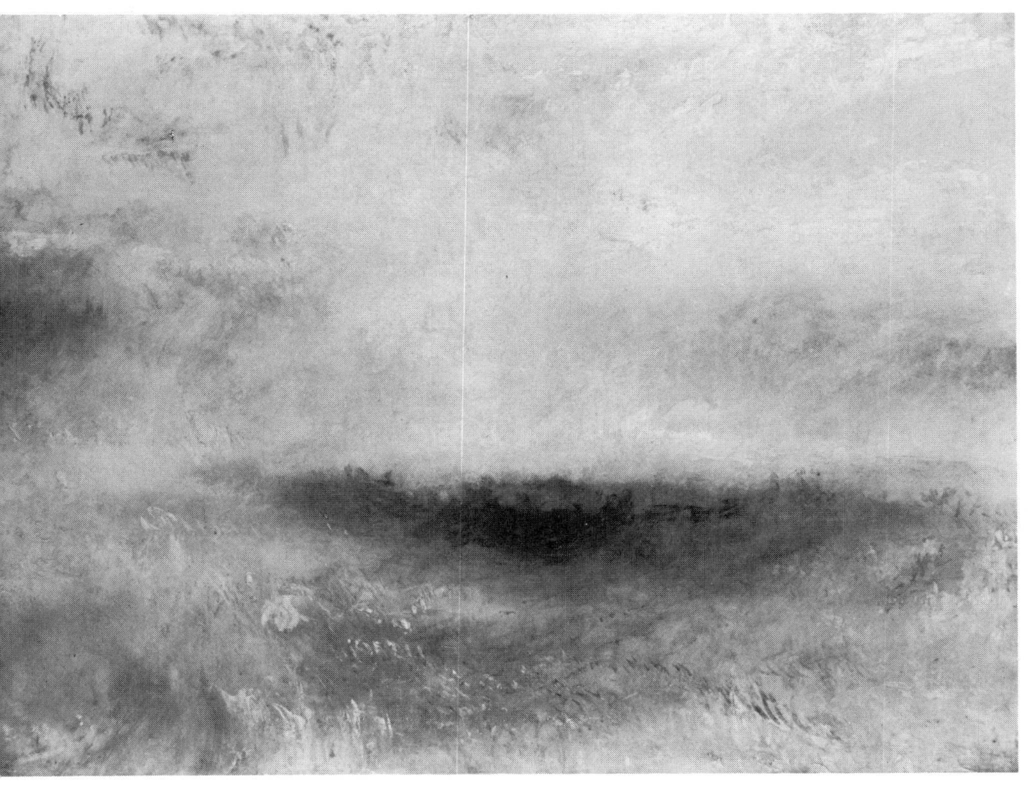

55. *Seascape*, *c.* 1840–45. Turner

> Like faery lands girt by some heavenly sea:
> Then has thy rapt imagination soared
> Where in the midst of all exciting things
> The temple of the mightiest Daemon stands.

But whereas Shelley longed to penetrate 'the painted veil . . . called life' and to be absorbed in the white radiance of eternity, Turner's concern was with the veil itself.

Turner's first biographer misquoted him as declaring: 'indistinctness is my forte' – a remark frequently repeated as evidence of Romantic delight in vagueness and of the Romantic artist's truculent contempt for criticism. What he said was, in fact: 'indistinctness is my fault' – a simple confession of the dilemma confronting a painter who sought to be true to his vision of nature, his feelings and his medium. 'It is a fault he is often accused of with justice,' wrote his friend C. R. Leslie (also the biographer of Constable) who reported the remark:

> Inferior painters, however, generally go to the other extreme, and put more into a picture than the eye really sees of nature from one point. The truth is they leave out atmosphere and chiaroscuro, the subtlest qualities of nature, but which give the greatest charm to landscape, and it is in these qualities, added to refinement of colour, that Turner excels all living painters, and very many of the old masters. He is the painter of light, air and space ...[89]

The last remarks seem to echo, in a positively favourable sense, the notorious jibe that Turner's works were 'pictures of nothing and very like'. But Leslie cannot have seen the purest and most remarkable of Turner's atmospheric paintings – the seas and skies of lambent colour, charged with mysterious energy, which defy description and can be compared only with Beethoven's last quartets [55].

It was not, of course, through such works that Turner influenced other artists. His emulators and imitators seized upon his commercially successful paintings and book illustrations. Thomas Cole, who called him 'one of the greatest landscape painters who ever lived', found, in 1830, that 'his present pictures are the strangest things imaginable', splendid in colour but no more than 'an empty amusement for the eye' which might be converted into 'an elegant entertainment of the Fancy' – as Cole himself attempted to do.[90] Two other American painters, Thomas Moran and James Hamilton, leant still more heavily on the very popular engravings after Turner's pictures. John Martin did his damnedest to rival Turner in scenes of sublime terror by making use of similar compositions, and then overcrowding them with little figures. Turner's Venetian views were not so much copied as re-orchestrated by Félix Ziem, without those notes of pessimistic despondency which give them their haunting threnodic melody. Early seascapes seem to have influenced Théodore Gudin, helping him to depict storms with great bravura and melodramatic excitement, but without Turner's tragic sense [56]. If Turner was difficult to understand, he was almost too easy to imitate – superficially.

Constable's influence, exerted mainly in France and hardly at all in England, was of a different kind. His subject-matter had little appeal for French painters, who were attracted mainly by his technique and his elevation of the simplest type of landscape to a position of unprecedented importance. Critics of the time are perhaps misleading in their statements that the younger painters were *bouleversés* when they saw *The Haywain* in the Salon of 1824.[91] The door had already been opened to those seeking an escape from academic

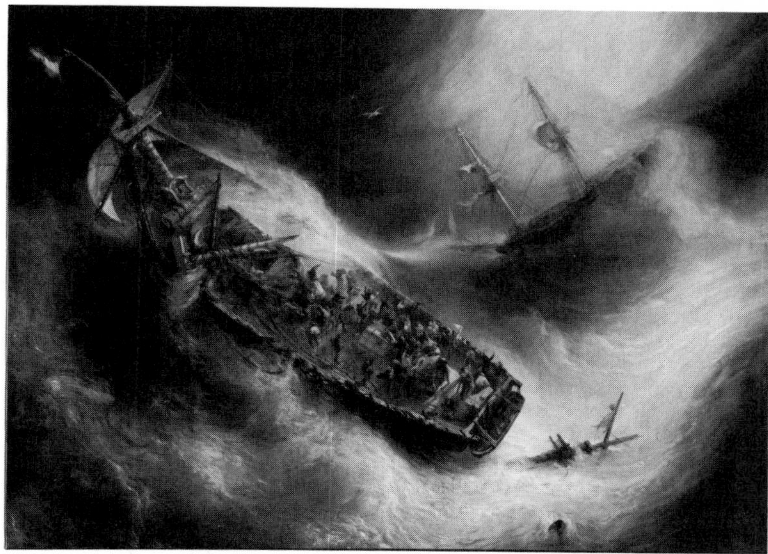

56. *The Devotion of Captain Desse*, 1830. Théodore Gudin

'*paysages de nature de convention*', and Constable did no more than push it a little wider. Paul Huet, for one, had begun to depict landscapes in a remarkably direct manner by 1822. Yet, without seeing Constable's work, he would hardly have painted as he did the large and impressive *Guardian's House in the Forest of Compiègne* [57].

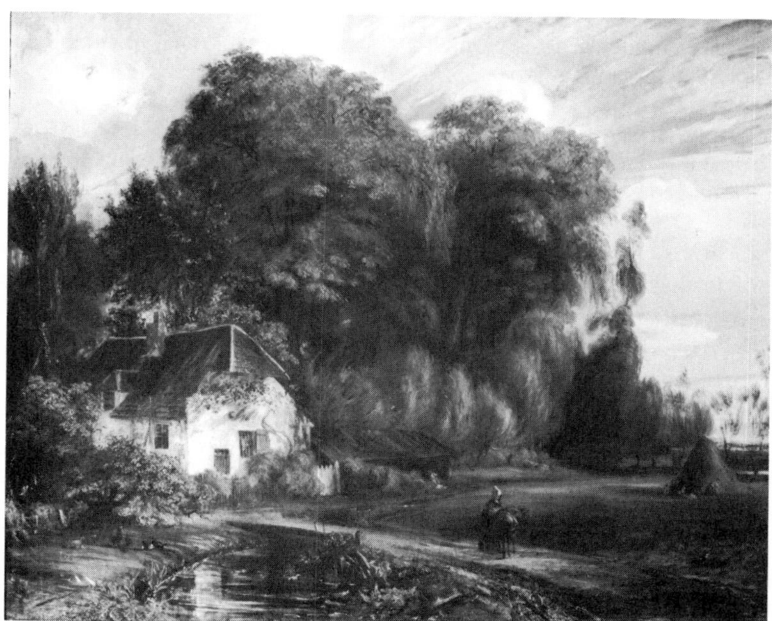

57. *Guardian's House in the Forest of Compiègne*, 1826. Paul Huet

Huet described landscape as a '*genre tout personnel*'. A landscape 'not tinctured with the colours of a man is a botched work', wrote Fromentin.[92] But the desire to convey personal emotions and beliefs was fused with an over-riding demand for truth to appearance as well as sentiment. C. G. Carus argued that the inner feelings of the artist could best be represented by the true depiction of a corresponding mood in nature.[93] Corot, whose mottos were '*conscience et confiance*' and '*la nature avant tout*', wrote that in conscientiously trying to imitate what he saw he never for an instant lost the emotion which had seized him – '*le réel est une partie de l'art ; le sentiment complète*'.[94] Such ideas completely transformed accepted notions of 'truth to nature' and 'the study of nature', about which theorists had expatiated for centuries.

The landscape painter at work *sur le motif* became a familiar figure in early nineteenth-century art. It was thus that the Nazarenes drew each other, that J. C. Erhard painted his companions on a sketching trip in the Salzkammergut [58] and that J. A. Klein portrayed himself in an etching [59]. The presence of a church spire in each of these (and many similar) works suggests, however, that the act of sketching from nature was more than a technical exercise. Sometimes the same practice, and the same attitude to the divinity in nature, were projected back into the past. In a strange visionary passage, quoted by Hazlitt, James Northcote described Claude in the Campagna:

> He led a poor little ass, which was loaded with all the implements required by a painter in his work. After advancing a few paces he stood still, and with an air of rapture seemed to contemplate the rising sun: he next fell to his knees, directed his eyes towards heaven, crossed himself, and then went on with eager looks, as if to make choice of the most advantageous spot from which to make his studies as a painter.[95]

How far this is from the Neo-classical view of Claude as the guide to the logical General Principle underlying the common face of nature! It points up the difference between Romantic and earlier attitudes to landscape. Yet the Romantics did not advocate *plein-airisme*: they seem to have needed the isolation of the studio to transform an outdoor vision into a work of art (which would always be seen indoors) and, perhaps, for the tranquil recollection of emotion.[96] They transformed old ideas about studying from nature, but sometimes so subtly that fundamental differences in attitude are masked by superficial similarities. Cloud studies had, for instance, been painted intermittently since the end of the seventeenth century (if not earlier), but suddenly assumed new importance in the early

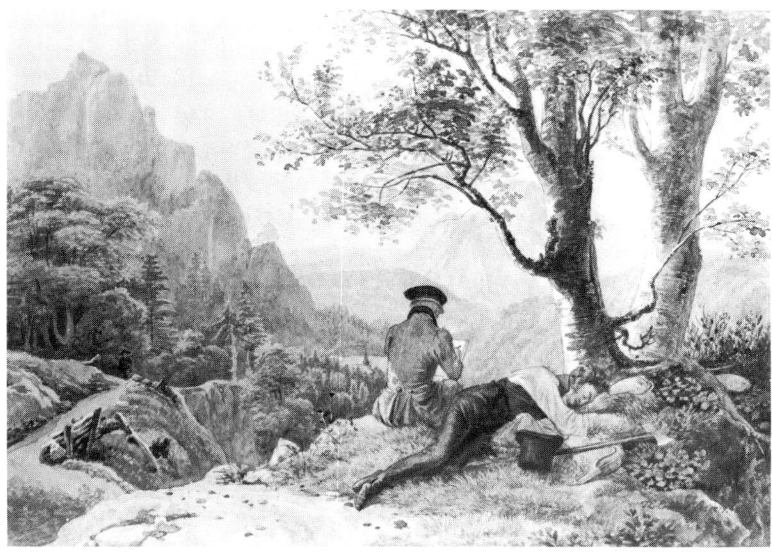

58. *In the Salzkammergut*, 1818. J. C. Erhard

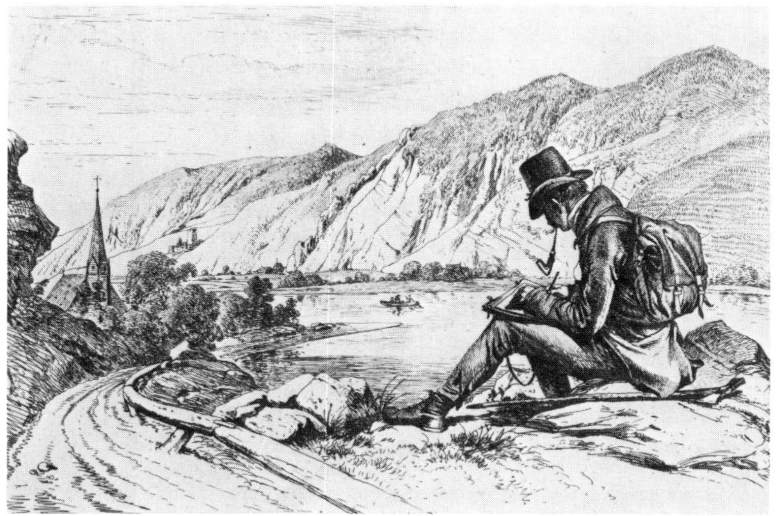

59. *The Landscape Painter on his Travels*, 1814. J. A. Klein

nineteenth. Whether this preoccupation with 'skying', as Constable called it, was technical, scientific or transcendental is difficult to determine. There can, however, be no doubt of the fascination which the constantly fleeting colours and intangible fluctuating forms of clouds exerted on artists as diverse as Constable, Turner and John Linnell in England, J. C. C. Dahl in Norway, Johann

Fischbach in Austria, C. G. Carus and Carl Blechen in Germany, F.-M. Granet and L. Riesener in France, to mention only a few of those who painted studies of them. In 1840, Adalbert Stifter, the greatest Austrian writer of his day and a more than accomplished amateur painter, described the hero of a short story gazing at warm coloured clouds from his window, suddenly overcome by the urge to 'steal' and preserve one of them, and devoting the rest of the

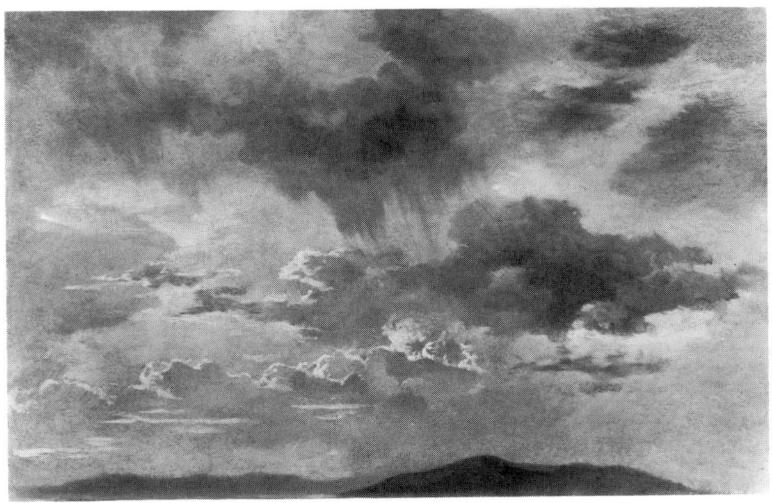

60. *Cloud Study*, *c*. 1840. Adalbert Stifter

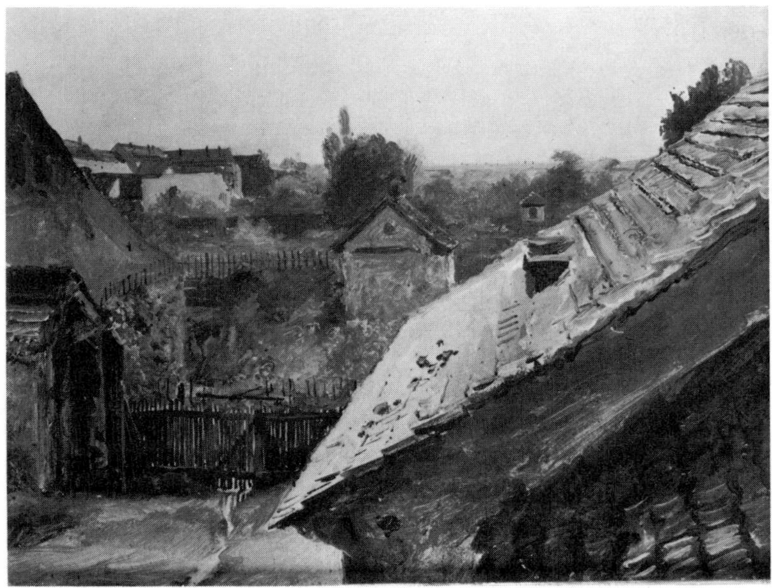

61. *View of Houses and Gardens*, *c*. 1830–37. Carl Blechen

day to atmospheric studies (*Luftstudien*) [60]. To the American painter Jasper F. Cropsey the heavens literally declared 'the glory of God' and he described cumulus clouds which as a child he had peopled with angels and to which he turned in maturity for refreshment from the cares of life – 'Grand masses of dreamy forms floating by each other, sometimes looking like magic palaces, rising higher and higher, and then toppling over in deep valleys, to rise again in ridges like snowy mountains, with lights and shadows playing amid them, as though it were a spirit world of its own'. Clouds were a natural – or supernatural – paradigm for paintings or rather for the art of painting almost in an abstract sense. Henry David Thoreau described in his journal in 1852 how he would go out each afternoon to watch the sunset 'to see what new pictures will be painted there, what new panorama exhibited, what new dissolving views ... Every day a new picture is painted and framed, held up for half an hour, in such lights as the Great Artist chooses, and then withdrawn, and the curtain falls'.[97]

The landscape seen from the window is another early nineteenth-century motif. Such pictures as the imprisoned J.-L. David's glimpse of the Luxembourg gardens, or Blechen's garret views of the outskirts of Berlin [61], were determined by the artists' peculiar circumstances and thus become possessively individual – personal effects of mind and eye. Providing an 'accidental' framework, the artificial opening in the wall helped the painter to abolish the art-

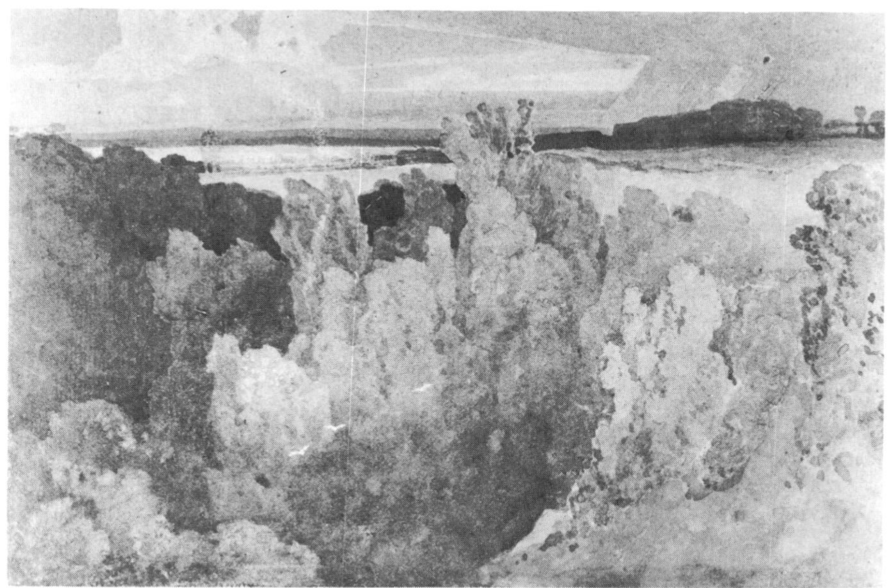

62. *Greta Woods from Brignal Banks*, *c.* 1805. Cotman

fully-natural structure of the traditional landscape and to depict a segment of the natural continuum literally from his own point of view. And many landscapes of the period seem to have been painted from windows even if they were not. Cotman's *Greta Woods* is a case in point, looking down as from some high tower on white birds floating in front of trees of delicately modulated texture, colour and form [62]. Here the balanced composition of light and shade, cut in such a way that the woods appear to stretch out indefinitely to right and left, suggests that this view is one melodious phrase in the harmony of the cosmos.

When the view from a window forms part of the picture of a room, sometimes with a figure gazing wistfully out, or with the painter's equipment neatly delineated [63], the symbolism is more obvious.[98]

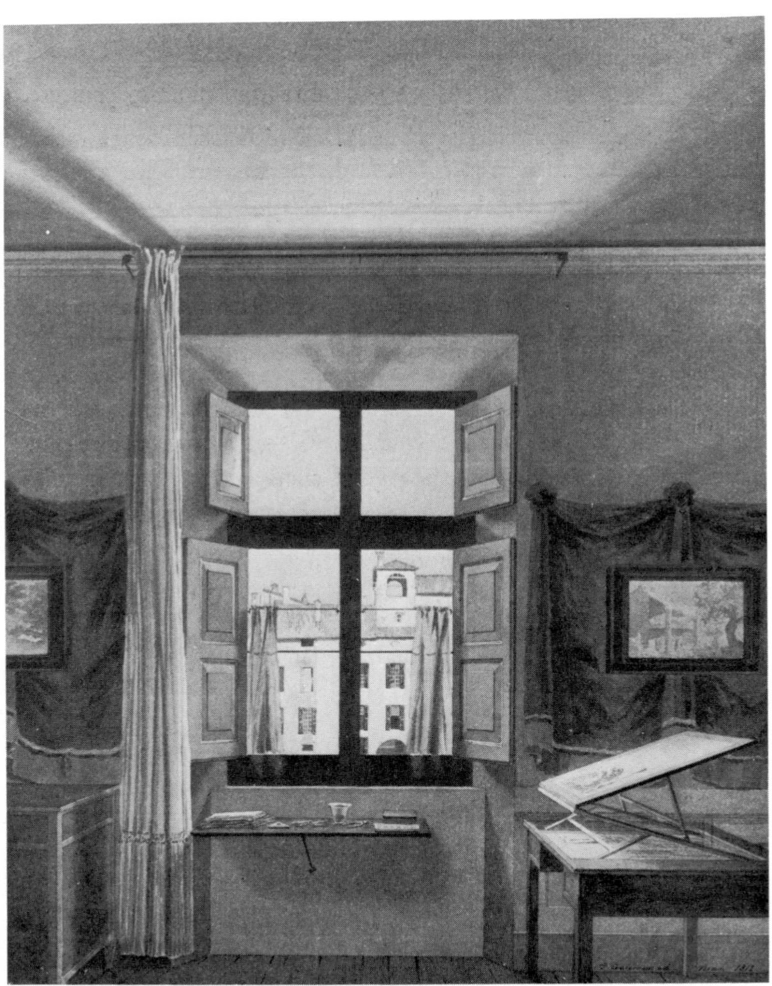

63. *The Artist's Studio in Parma*, 1812. G. B. De Gubernatis

Contrasts are implied between the internal and the external world, imagination and empirical reality, or between nature and art – in Wordsworthian terminology what the eye perceives and what it half creates. Very often these painted casements open not on to the splendours of nature, but on to city streets and enclosed gardens, and may have been intended as no more than factual records. Yet the flower garden, especially one attached to a town or suburban house, is a recurrent image in Romantic art and literature. It had the poetry of a memory of the world of nature – or of God – preserved and cherished in the midst of the city of man. In a little picture of a Viennese garden with vine pergola, hollyhocks and sunflowers by Erasmus von Engert, a woman sits knitting while she reads what must surely be a Bible [64].

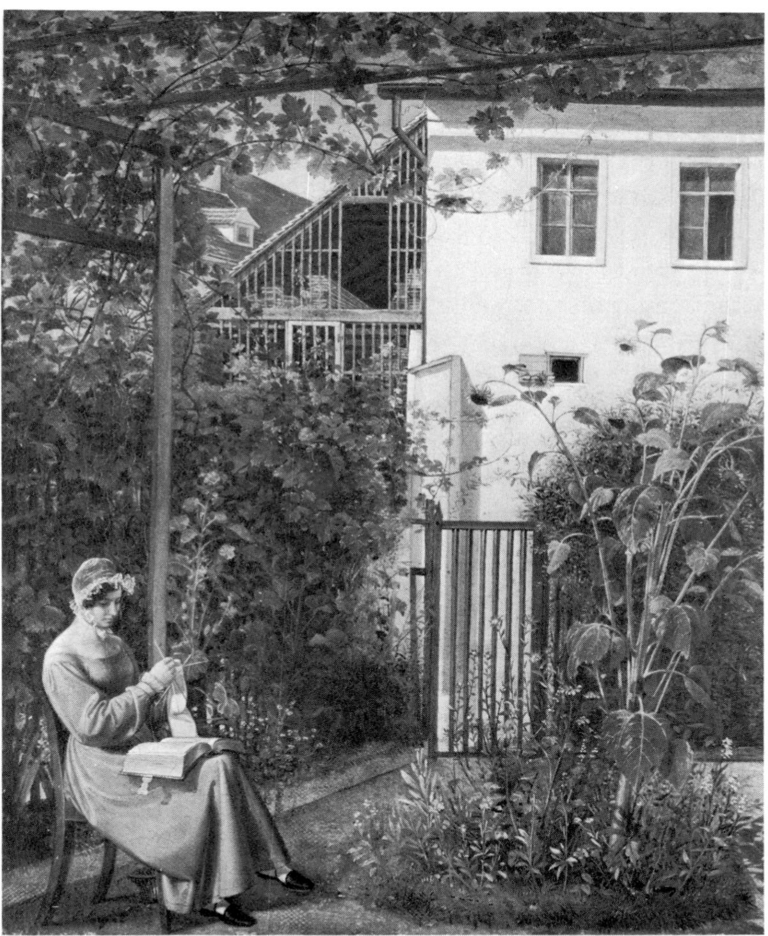

64. *A Garden in Vienna*, *c.* 1828–30. E. R. von Engert

These little portions of nature set aside for quiet contemplation, almost enshrined like relics, had an appeal quite different from that of the artfully informal landscape park with its sweeping Claudean vistas. The latter express an attitude to landscape identical with that of idealizing Neo-classical painters.[99] Opposition to them, which had been voiced satirically even in their eighteenth-century heyday, gradually became more serious. To Wordsworth, the cult of the picturesque with which they were so closely associated was a 'strong infection of the age' and he described its blasphemously presumptuous devotees

> even in pleasure pleased
> Unworthily, disliking here, and there
> Liking, by rules of mimic art transferred
> To things above all art . . .[100]

'A gentleman's park is my aversion,' Constable wrote in 1822. 'It is not beauty because it is not nature.'[101] At about the same time, Hegel, who was familiar with the *englische Gärten* of Germany, scoffed at their winding paths, irregular shrubberies, bridges over stagnant water, Gothic chapels, classical temples, Chinese houses and hermitages which could not satisfy a love of nature or of art. He preferred the formal garden, which made no pretence to be a natural landscape, but permitted human beings to be the principal objects in an external framework of natural beauty. Soon the natural wilderness was to be preserved just as it was, untouched by man, in the United States – in 1832 Arkansas Hot Springs was constituted a national reservation, in 1864 ten square miles of the Yosemite valley were granted to the State of California 'for public use, resort and recreation' and in 1872 more than two million acres in Wyoming were designated the Yellowstone National Park 'reserved and withdrawn from settlement, occupancy or sale' to be kept perpetually in its primitive 'natural condition'.[102] Nothing of the kind had ever been done before and these great American national parks for long remained a unique and wonderful phenomenon.

In Europe parks continued to be laid out with studied informality until well into the nineteenth century,[103] just as landscapes continued to be painted according to the time-honoured Dutch and Italianate formulae. Georges Michel appears to have begun imitating the Dutch pictures, so much beloved by *ancien régime* collectors, in the 1780s and to have gone on in the same way until the 1830s, often producing work of considerable merit.[104] With the general public the cults of the picturesque and sublime became ever more popular. Views of tumbledown castles and cottages, of Alpine peaks and waterfalls, jostled one another on exhibition walls throughout Europe and in the United States. They were reproduced in thousands by the new process of steel engraving: they were printed on cheap pottery table-wares. For the most part, these scenes were still represented as they had been in the eighteenth century by Caspar Wolf and others, though sometimes with the addition of symbols of the type adopted by Caspar David Friedrich. The Romantic 'Wanderer' is a recurrent figure. He stands, for instance, in the foreground of L. F. Schnorr von Carolsfeld's nightfall view of Mont Blanc – an extraordinary picture, recording the moment when the moon has risen but the snow is still almost garishly coloured by

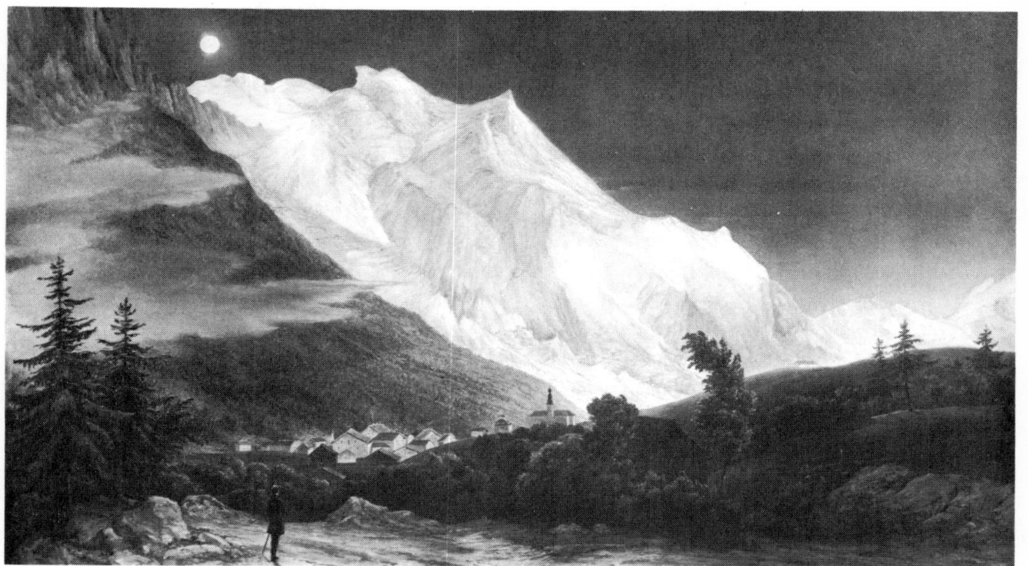

65. *Chamonix and Mont Blanc*, 1848. L. F. Schnorr von Carolsfeld

the setting sun [65]. Symbolic landscapes even appeared on porcelain plates, like that painted in Berlin with a mountain, hamlet and church, wayside cross, bridge over a stream and two figures [66].

Views of conventionally 'romantic' scenery and especially the more famous beauty-spots, for which there was a wide public demand, confronted the Romantic artist with difficulties. J.-B. Deperthes, in his conservative treatise on landscape of 1816, might claim that the infinite number of sketches made *sur place* of one site – the Temple of the Sybil at Tivoli – revealed by their variety how the physical and moral make-up of the individual influenced

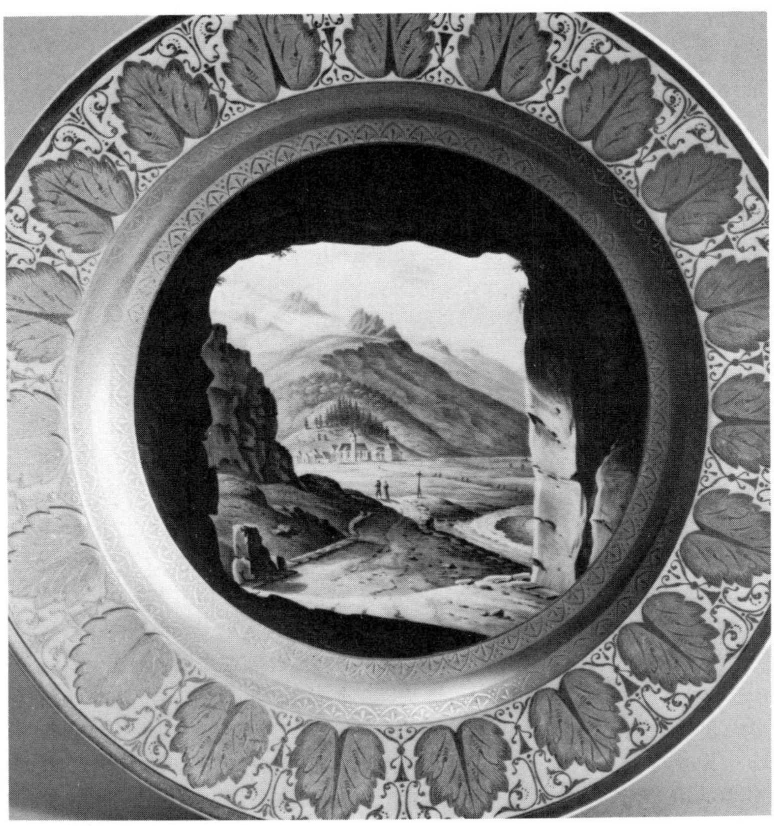

66. Berlin porcelain plate, *c.* 1817–25

his choice of viewpoint.[105] But in fact Turner was one of the few artists able to present a fresh view even of the most hackneyed subject-matter. Others who believed with the Romantics that a landscape should be the product of a personal response to nature tended to avoid scenes which had been frequently painted and described.

'I have had to tell a story that has been told before so beautifully as to make me tremble,' wrote James Ward in 1814, referring to his *Tabley Lake and Tower*, a subject previously painted by Turner and others. 'The only road left' was, he went on, 'to produce something new by a more rigid attention to truth. The effect is such as I have seen on the spot. It is a close sultry day, what is vulgarly called a Muggy or a murky day – when the air is charged or charging with Electric fluid – preparatory to a Thunder storm ...'[106] He had recently completed his masterpiece *Gordale Scar*, which is said to have been inspired by a connoisseur's assertion

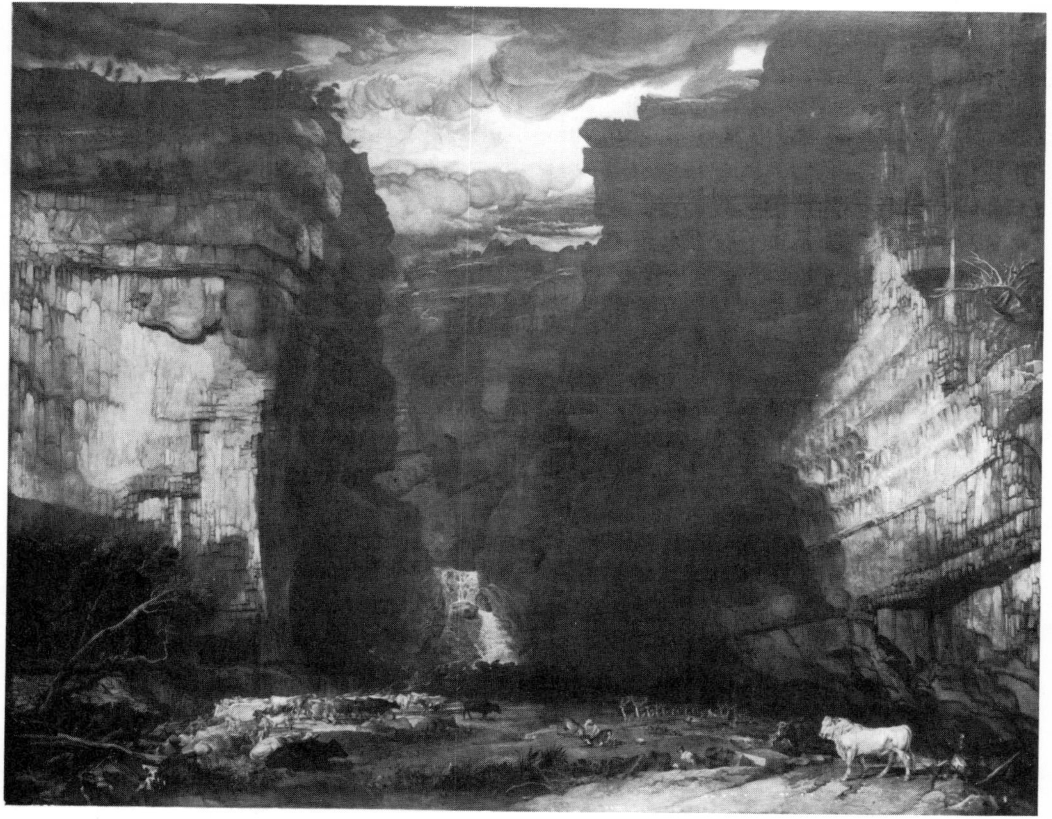

67. *Gordale Scar*, 1811–13. James Ward

that the subject could never be rendered in paint [67]. Not content with a virtuoso feat of topographical recording, he magnified the natural phenomenon by taking a worm's-eye viewpoint. This vast canvas, with its mysteriously dark focal point, its overwhelming forms and louring thunder-charged clouds, is, indeed, an apocalyptic celebration of the sublimity of nature and an expression of the ecstatic religious beliefs which were later to draw Ward into the fold of the revivalist preacher Edward Irving.

The desire for a direct approach to the 'divinity in nature' through landscape was eloquently expressed by Thomas Cole. On a visit to the Catskill Mountains in 1835 he wrote in his journal:

Before us spread the virgin waters which the prow of the sketcher had never before curled, enfolded by green woods, whose venerable masses had never figured in annuals, and overlooked by the stern mountain peaks, never beheld by Claude or Salvator, nor subjected to the canvas

> by the innumerable daubers in paint of all past time. The painter of American scenery has, indeed, privileges superior to any other. All nature here is new to art. No Tivolis, Ternis, Mont Blancs, Plinlimmons, hackneyed and worn by the daily pencils of hundreds; but primeval forests, virgin lakes and waterfalls, feasting his eye with new delights, and filling his portfolio with their features of beauty and magnificence, hallowed to his soul by their freshness from the creation, for his own favoured pencil.[107]

But this revealing passage has implications of which Cole himself was probably unaware. He had taken advantage of these 'privileges' ten years earlier, at the very beginning of his career (he was born in 1801 in Lancashire and emigrated to America in 1819), and his eerie *Lake with Dead Trees* of 1825 [68] is an unprecedented image

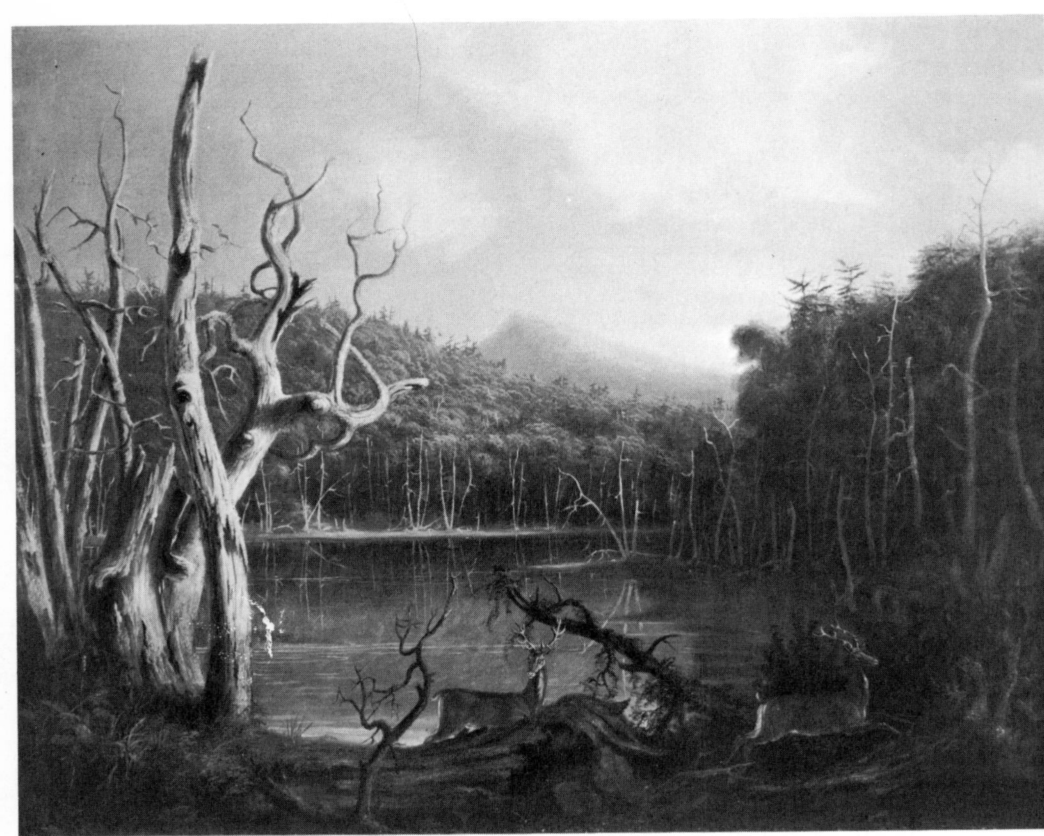

68. *Lake with Dead Trees*, 1825. Thomas Cole

of growth and decay in a virgin forest. At this time he had received little formal training: closer study of the old masters enabled him to paint with greater fluency, but also entrapped him in the patterns which regulate his later work. And it was to his didactic cycles *The Course of Empire* and *The Voyage of Life* on which he placed so much importance, and not to such much more original work as *Landscape with Dead Trees*, that he alluded when he wrote: 'Had fortune favoured me a little more than she has ... I would have followed out principles of beauty and sublimity in my works, which have been cast aside, because the result would not be marketable.'[108] The contempt for popular taste is characteristic of the Romantics. Of the inner conflict between the wish and the inability to reject visual preconceptions, and of the insufficiency of dead languages to express a new vision of Creation, Cole seems to have been less acutely aware than were his contemporaries in Europe.

Other American painters tended to seek out New World equivalents to the famous 'beauty spots' of Europe – Niagara was the most frequently painted – and all too often to fit them into time-honoured European schemata. Westward expansion revealed a new range of subjects exploited to good effect by Albert Bierstadt, Thomas Moran and Thomas Hill. The southern sub-continent also attracted artists, most notably Frederic Church who adopted an appropriately luxuriant palette and a grand rhetorical style to record *The Heart of the Andes* in 1859 and *Rainy Season in the Tropics* in 1866.[109] But although Church's pictures sometimes had a deeply personal significance for himself few of these American views of mountains and deep and gloomy woods depart very far from formulae for depicting sublime prospects established in the eighteenth century and repeated here, as in Europe, until the end of the nineteenth. It was with such pictures in mind that Asher B. Durand, the leading painter and theorist of the Hudson River School, complained that artists 'make long journeys in search of the picturesque to gain attention and win applause, when by the common roadside' they could find subjects more beautiful 'than any abortive display of the grand and striking features of nature'. The words are reminiscent of Constable: so too are the sensitively observant studies of rocks and plants which Durand painted in the 1850s. In one of his *Letters on Landscape Painting* (1855) he quoted from 'Tintern Abbey' Wordsworth's phrase 'that all which we behold is full of blessings' and a Wordsworthian atmosphere of tranquil meditation hangs over his best known work – *Kindred Spirits* of 1849 which shows Thomas Cole and the poet William Cullen Bryant communing with nature on a ledge above a ravine in the Catskill Mountains.[110] But here as in most of the pictures painted for public exhibition by the Hudson River School, there is an uneasy dichotomy between subject matter and the conventional way in which it is handled.

In his essay on Nature of 1836 Ralph Waldo Emerson wrote: 'Standing on the bare ground – my head bathed in the blithe air, and uplifted into infinite space – my mean egotism vanishes. I become a transparent eyeball; I am nothing; I see all; the currents of the Universal Being circulate through me; I am part and parcel of God.' The passage calls to mind pictures by Caspar David Friedrich rather than any American landscapes – except, perhaps, for some preternaturally calm coastal scenes by Fitz Hugh Lane who, significantly, began as a naïf painter and remained innocently immune to the influence of the Franco-Italian landscape tradition. But Americans escaped clichés more easily when painting outdoor genre scenes rather than pure landscapes. Caleb Bingham's *Fur Traders Descending the Missouri* of 1845 is a case in point, an extraordinary dreamlike evocation of hazy calm with two men and a black cat on a boat reflected with subtle distortion in still water. Another is William Sidney Mount's *Eel Spearing at Setauket*, also of 1845, a 'recollection of early days', as he originally entitled it, and the superimposition of adult vision on brightly lit memories of childhood when he had been taught to spear fish by an old Negro – a kind of Wordsworthian 'spot of time' in fact.[111]

In painting the simplest scenes – in making, as Constable put it, 'something out of nothing' – early nineteenth-century landscape painters, especially in France, made their most decisive break with tradition. Such pictures could answer the Romantic demand for landscapes expressing the artist's intimate and individual response to nature more directly and revealingly than views which were misted over with historical or literary associations, whether classical or 'romantic'. Théodore Rousseau specialized in pictures of this type – the no-man's land between the forest and the fields, one or two trees emerging from scrub, marshy plains, stagnant ponds, with few human figures and fewer habitations. There is no suggestion of aching joys and dizzy raptures in these still, austere and often elegiac works. At first sight they may even look rather dull, making one wonder why they originally provoked such extreme reactions, from the enthusiasm of Delacroix and George Sand to the hostility of the juries who refused them admission to the Salon.[112] *La Descente des Vaches dans le Jura*, an eight-foot canvas, is now so disfigured by darkened bitumen that its composition can be made out only with the aid of a preliminary sketch which seems rather tame. But when a fellow landscape painter, Jules Dupré, saw it in 1836 (exhibited in Ary Scheffer's studio because it had been refused for the Salon), he was 'transported with admiration' and said that 'he had never seen anything like it in the work of a contemporary; it seemed as unexpected and prodigious as the first appearance of Géricault's terrifying *Raft of the 'Medusa'*.[113] As Fromentin remarked, Rousseau was 'a complex artist, very much disparaged, very much vaunted, very difficult to define with moderation'.[114]

In subject-matter and technique (curiously similar to that of Constable's large sketches which he cannot have seen), few pictures could be further removed from accepted ideas of the 'classical' or 'romantic' landscapes than Rousseau's *La Descente des Vaches dans le Jura*, his large view down a dark, dank avenue of chestnut trees (Louvre), or even his sunnier and more immediately appealing paintings of the Auvergne [69]. They are often regarded as straightforward transcripts of nature and labelled 'Realist'. But that is not how he and his contemporaries saw them. He was no less preoccu-

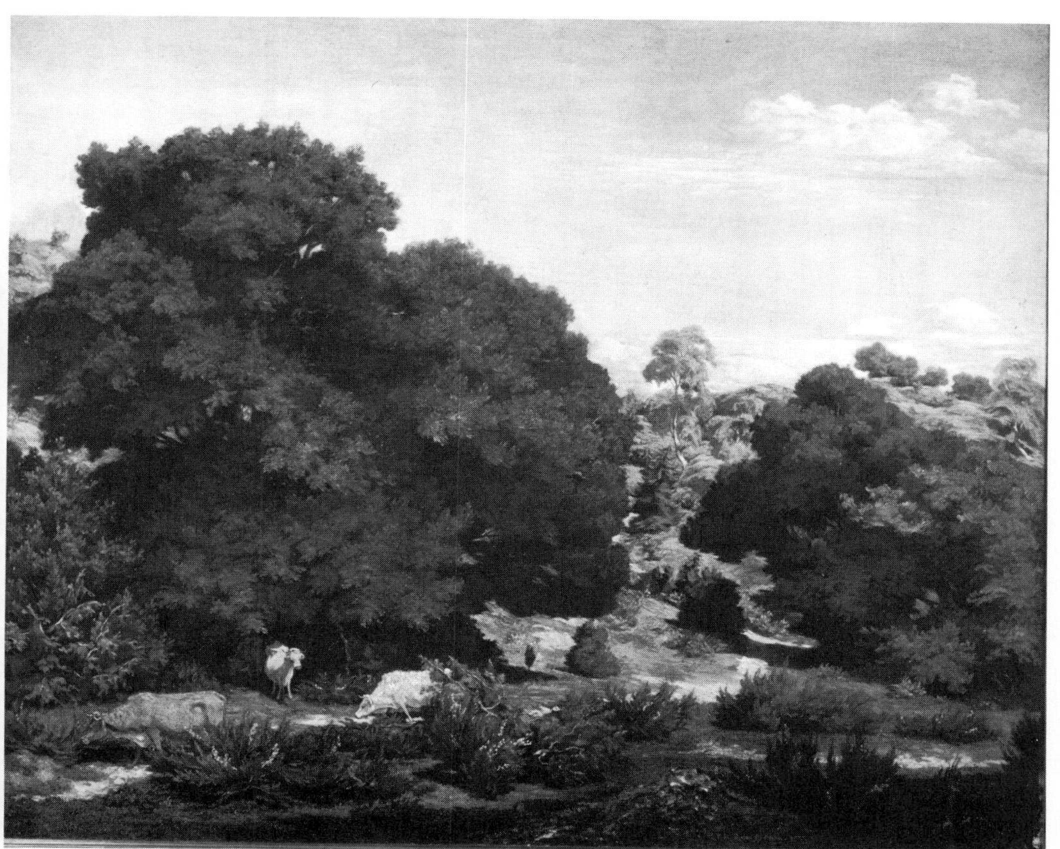

69. *Landscape in the Auvergne*, 1837. Théodore Rousseau

pied with the idea of landscape as the modern equivalent of history painting than Runge had been, and as deeply concerned with its inner significance. 'The rustle of the trees and the sprouting of the heather are for me the great subjects, those which will never change: if I can speak their language, I shall have spoken the language of all times,' he remarked.[115] And his statement that what he meant by composition was 'that which is within us entering as far as possible into the external reality of things' is reminiscent of Friedrich.[116] But Rousseau eradicated from his work symbols which the Germans had used to express their meaning and which had subsequently been reduced to empty clichés by repetition. He veered still further away than Constable from what had traditionally been considered fit subject-matter for a painter. Of the artists who transformed the idea of landscape in the first half of the nineteenth century, he was the last to appear on the scene and perhaps the most austerely uncompromising of them all in his devotion to 'the moral feeling of the art'.

By the time he died in 1868, a new generation had begun to make its presence felt and to put new interpretations on Romantic theory and practice. But in the following year, Philippe Burty quoted a passage from a story by E. T. A. Hoffmann (of 1816), as a summary of Paul Huet's attitude to his art, which could equally well be applied to Rousseau – the words are addressed to an aspiring painter:

> To seize nature in the most profound expression, in the most intimate sense, in that thought which raises all beings towards a more sublime life, is the holy mission of all the arts. Can a simple and exact copy of nature achieve this end? It is as miserable, awkward and forced as an inscription in a foreign language copied by a scribe who does not understand it and who laboriously imitates characters which are unintelligible to him. Some landscapes are no more than correct copies of an original written in a foreign tongue. The painter who is initiated in the divine secrets of art hears the voice of nature recounting its infinite mysteries through trees, plants, flowers, waters and mountains. The gift to transpose his emotions into works of art comes to him like the spirit of God.[117]

These are the ideas which first became current in about 1800, which bind together artists as diverse as Runge, Friedrich, Turner, Constable, Cotman, Huet and Rousseau, distinguishing them not only from Neo-classical and Realist painters, but also from their lame followers and innumerable purveyors of more conventionally 'romantic' landscapes.

3. Frozen Music

'Music at its most sublime must become sheer form and affect us with the serene power of antiquity,' wrote Schiller in his letters on the aesthetic education of man:

> The plastic arts, at their most perfect, must become music and move us by the immediacy of their sensuous presence. Poetry, when most fully developed, must grip us as powerfully as music does but at the same time, like the plastic arts, surround us with serene clarity. This, precisely, is the mark of the perfect style in each and every art: that it is able to remove the specific limitations of the art in question without thereby destroying its specific qualities, and through a wide use of its individual peculiarities, is able to confer on it a more general character.[1]

He was suggesting that each art should take on the quality of another. And this may, perhaps, have influenced Novalis's theory that, in their essential nature, music, the visual arts and poetry are one, and that the ultimate artistic experience would be synaesthetic: a Wagnerian *Gesamtkunstwerk* or 'total art form', in which the expressive power of all the arts would combine and blend together. In its essentially relative, not absolute, nature, this is one of the most important and most deeply Romantic concepts of the period. The true artist, it was felt, is never a poet or painter or musician only but a combination: true art is never pure – music is latent in poetry, poetry in painting and each is to be felt and experienced in the other. 'Painting, plastic art are therefore nothing but figurative music,' wrote Novalis. 'Painting, plastic art – objective music. Music – subjective music or painting.'[2] The idea was given wider currency in the dictum that 'architecture is frozen music' which originated in Germany and was diffused to the rest of Europe by Mme de Staël.[3] It was also to inspire Walter Pater's much later, but to English readers more familiar, remark that all art aspires to the condition of music.[4] Nowadays such ideas are as unfashionable with art historians as with musicologists, but they are of great significance for an understanding of Romanticism.

Music had, of course, been associated with the visual arts since time immemorial. Leonardo da Vinci, Palladio and others had all been fascinated by Pythagorean theories of musical harmony and the possibility that a building designed according to a scale of ratios based on the length of chords might echo, as it were, the celestial harmony of the spheres.[5] But their complex musical-cum-mathematical theories attracted decreasing attention after the sixteenth century. In the age of Enlightenment the relationship between music and the visual arts was approached in another way. By associating the colours of the spectrum with the notes of the octave, Newton had provided a theoretical basis for 'ocular harpsichords' and organs, which were actually constructed and aroused great interest.[6] Reminiscences of the Renaissance concept of celestial harmony (and especially Shakespeare's metaphoric use of it) lingered on in literature – as in Wordsworth's 'still, sad music of humanity'. And interest in the exact correspondence between colours and musical notes also remained alive. P. O. Runge devoted an appendix to the subject in his *Die Farbenkugel* of 1810; and in America Thomas Cole was toying with the idea of a colour pianoforte as late as 1834.[7] But the close affinity between music and painting postulated by Schiller and Novalis is of an entirely different type, anticipating Romantic notions of synaesthesia as so subtly and suggestively adumbrated by Baudelaire when describing the work of Delacroix: 'These wonderful *chords* of colour often give one ideas of melody and harmony, and the impression that one takes away from his pictures is often, as it were, a musical one.' Colour and sound were associated in the same sophisticated sense by Washington Allston when he wrote of Tintoretto and Paolo Veronese: 'They addressed themselves, not to the senses merely, as some have supposed, but rather through them to that region (if I may so speak) of the imagination which is supposed to be under the exclusive domination of music . . .'[8]

It was generally believed in the eighteenth century that music appealed to the senses and heart rather than to the intellect. To Kant it had, in the judgement of reason, less worth than the other arts because it was emotive. Music, he wrote, 'speaks by means of mere sensations without concepts, and so does not, like poetry, leave anything over for reflection, it yet moves the mind in a greater variety of ways and more intensely, although only transitorily'.[9] His attitude was very equivocal, however. He promptly went on to remark on the value of music as structure, 'expressing the aesthetical idea of a connected whole of an unspeakable wealth of thought', recognizing its absence of concepts as a positive merit. Within a very short time its emotional intensity and transitoriness were also to be extolled. '*La musique attaque plus vivement les fibres que la poésie,*' wrote C.-J. Lioult de Chêndollé in 1808; '*il y a plus de vague, quelque chose de plus indéfini, de plus aérien.*'[10] Henriette Feuerbach (sister of the materialist philosopher) claimed that music was superior to all other arts because it alone had no need for thought as an intermediary, but acted on the sensibilities as 'spirit speaking directly to spirit'.[11]

70. *Morning*, 1803. Philipp Otto Runge

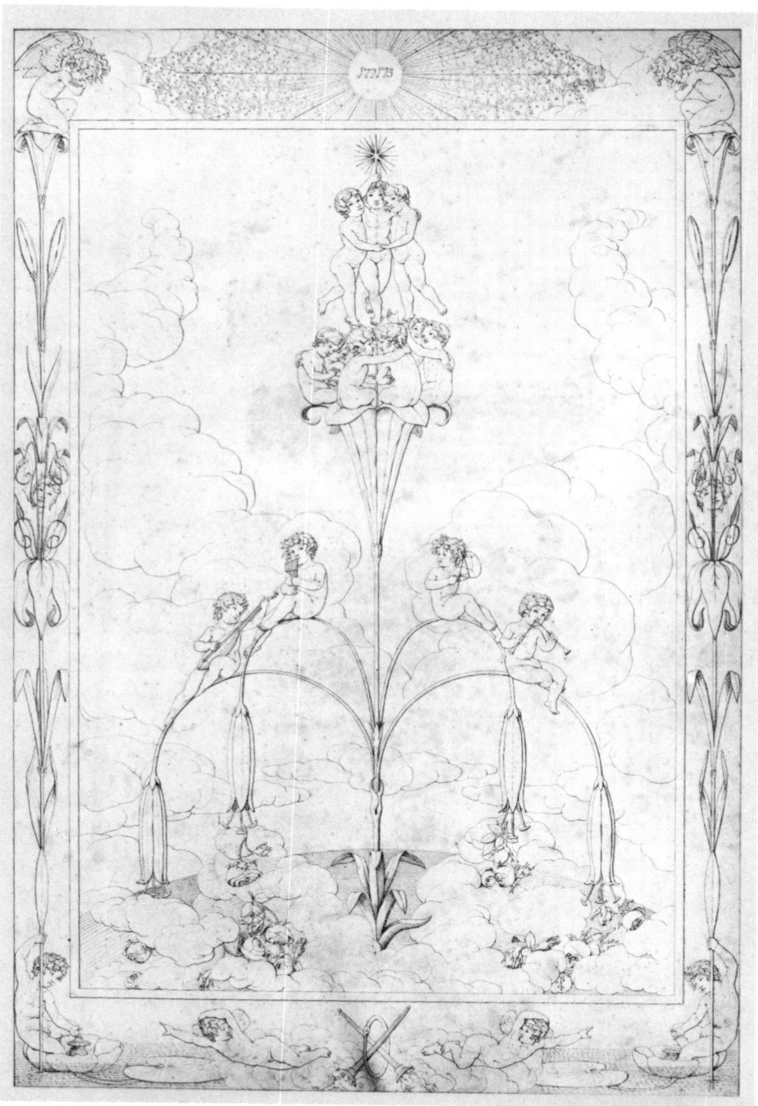

The new importance given to music by the Romantics is a manifestation of the general shift from a mimetic to an expressive aesthetic. In order to make a double assault on the soul through the senses, artists now aspired to integrate the figurative arts with music in such a way that neither would merely complement or illustrate the other. The effect of Runge's series of prints *Die Zeiten* was likened by Goethe to the music of Beethoven, which 'tries to embrace everything and in so doing always loses itself in the elemental, yet still with endless beauty in the particulars' [70]. But Runge's ambition soared beyond such analogies to the creation of 'an abstract painterly fantastic-musical poem with choirs, a composition for all the arts collectively, for which architecture should raise a unique building'.[12] The combination of visual, auditory and spiritual sensations aroused by the ritual of the Catholic Mass had come as a revelation when, a Protestant from Northern Germany, he first arrived in Dresden. He clearly wished to awaken a still stronger religious, but non-sectarian, feeling in a total work of art.

Some years later, Caspar David Friedrich sought to combine music and painting, though on a less ambitious scale. This was in a set of transparencies to be accompanied by vocal and instrumental music. The transparencies are lost, but two of Friedrich's drawings for them survive. In one, a woman is playing a harp with, behind her, the soaring windows and traceries and pinnacles of a Gothic church, into which she and the harp almost seem to merge. The strings of the harp echo the traceries – and the harp itself almost becomes one of the pinnacles – in such a way that the upward aspiring movement of the architecture evokes the rising chords of the harp, symbolizing the spirituality of music – and perhaps the 'poetry' of both art forms, for the harpist has just laid aside a small volume at which she gazes, as if for inspiration. In the other drawing [71], a young man with a mandolin is dreaming or day-dreaming among flowers which, like the flower-spirits of Runge, reach upwards towards the heavens and the sounds of angels playing on a visionary organ above. The music accompanying the transparencies, for which these were preliminary designs, was appropriately scored – a harp for the harpist, a glass harmonica for the young dreamer, guitars for a secular subject and 'distantly heard, thundery music' for that of a magic hoard in a forest. This almost anticipates the late-Romantic conception of opera as the ultimate form of *Gesamtkunstwerk* developed by Wagner, who knew Runge's *Die Zeiten* and probably his writings as well.[13] But, in practice, not even Wagner was able to fuse and unite the arts of painting and

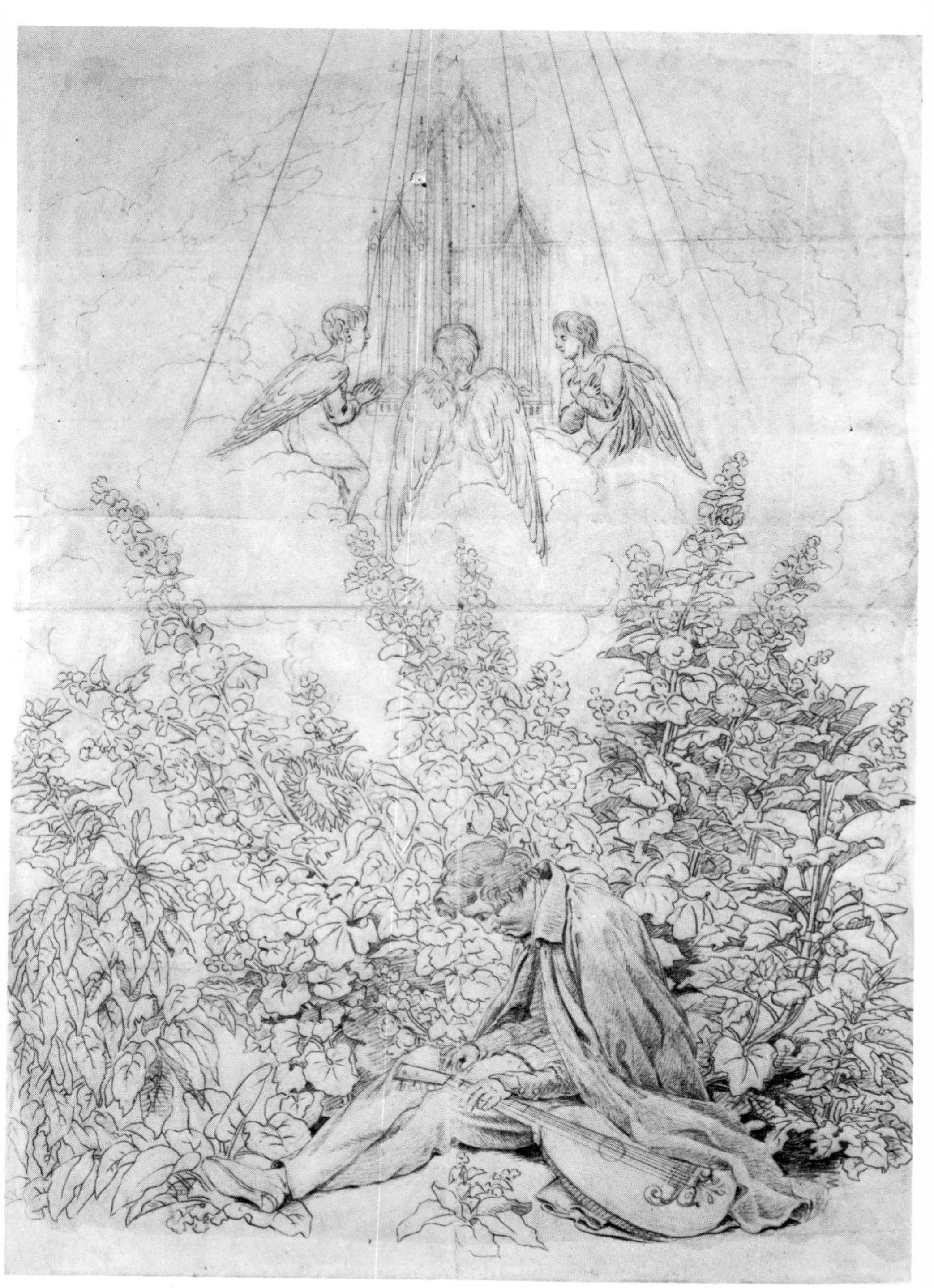

71. *The Singer's Dream*, *c.* 1830. Caspar David Friedrich

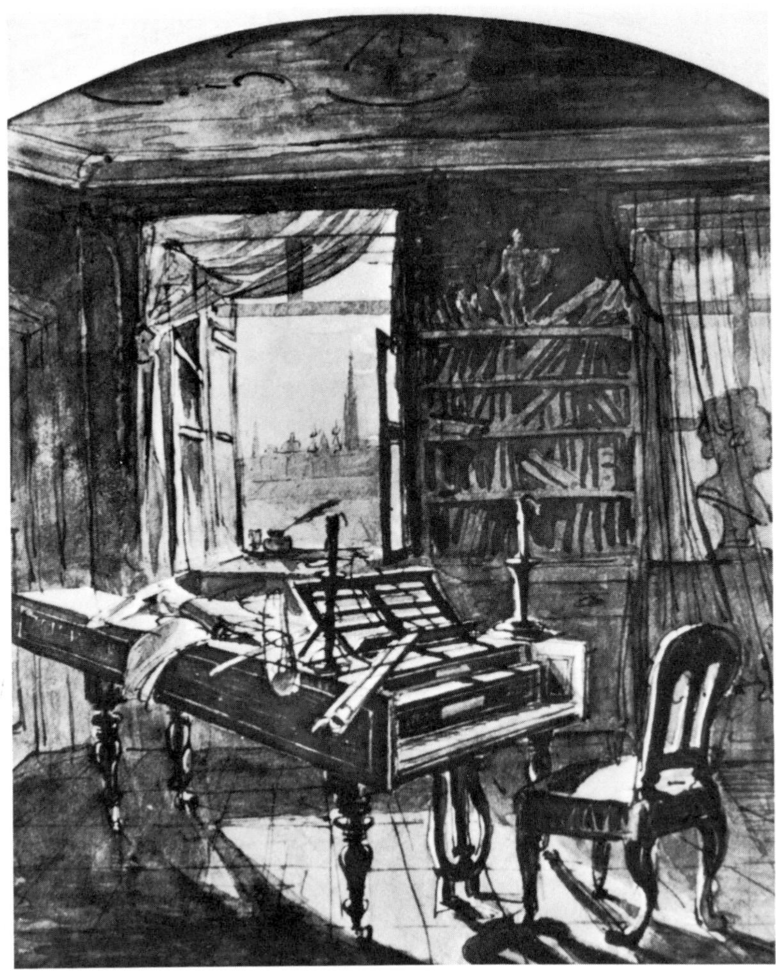

72. *Beethoven's Room*, 1827. J. N. Höchle

music any better than Runge, Friedrich or the many Romantic artists who left the sounds to the imagination in their allegories of music.

> Music, when soft voices die,
> Vibrates in the memory.

And the painters who succeeded in catching these vibrations did so by striking similar chords in pictures which could evoke a similar response. Indeed, the belief that all art was in a sense musical made any specific reference otiose, just as the notion that life was a dream discouraged explicit dream and nightmare pictures of the types which had hitherto been popular. One of the most moving tributes

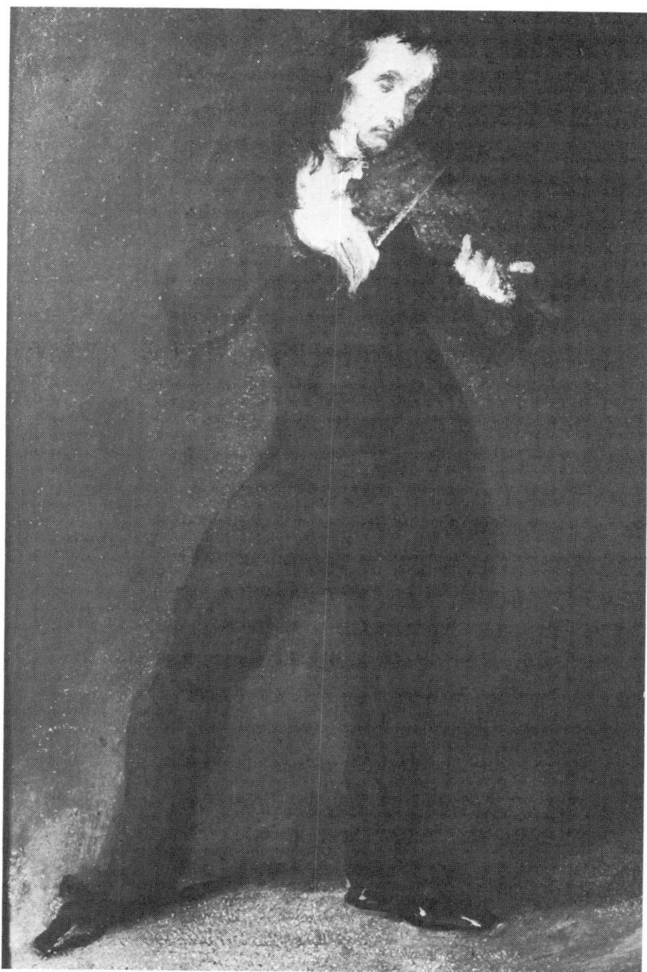

73. *Paganini*, 1831. Delacroix

to the genius of Beethoven is a drawing of his empty study immediately after his death – a silent room in which the reverberations of those last great compositions, which Beethoven had heard only in his mind's ear, still seem to linger [72].

Delacroix's portrait of Paganini is among the few paintings which explicitly and successfully render a musical sensation visually [73]. But he captured the effect not so much of the music as of the virtuoso performance, the *vibrato* of his brush-strokes echoing the glissandos and arpeggios of the maestro's bowing and fingering. This was clearly his intention. 'We must render our visions with ease,' he told his pupil Lassalle-Bordes; 'Paganini owed his astonishing execution on the violin to his daily practice of scales for one hour. It is the same exercise for us.'[14] But when he tried to express the effect of music on a listener and a performer more directly, in his portrait of George Sand and Chopin, he only just avoided the bathos of Josef Danhauser's picture of George Sand, Paganini, Rossini, Victor Hugo and others listening to a performance by Liszt, with Byron's portrait in the background.[15] Neither work succeeds in conveying the power of music to 'awaken emotion', as George Sand described it in *Consuelo* (1842–3):

> No other art can so sublimely arouse human sentiments in the innermost heart of man. No other art can paint to the eyes of the soul the splendours of nature, the delights of contemplation, the character of nations, the tumult of their passions, and the languor of their sufferings as music can. Regret, hope, terror, meditation, consternation, enthusiasm, faith, doubt, glory, tranquillity, all these and more are given to us and taken from us thanks to her genius and according to the bent of our own.[16]

A passionate and discriminating music lover, Delacroix occasionally alluded to analogies between music and painting in his journal – comparing Chopin's improvisations with painted sketches, for instance – but he showed no interest in, or even awareness of, theories of synaesthesia.[17] He praised in music the qualities he admired in painting, much as, some years later, Gautier was to write of Berlioz in terms which could be applied equally well to Delacroix:

> In this renaissance of 1830 he represented the musical Romantic idea: the breaking of old patterns, the substitution of new forms for the invariable square rhythms, the complex and skilful richness of the orchestra, the fidelity of local colour, unexpected effects of sonorousness, tumultuous and Shakespearean profundity of passion, amorous and melancholic reveries, the nostalgia and demands of the soul, undefined and mysterious sentiments which cannot be rendered in words.[18]

The differences which separate Romantic artists, writers and musicians from one another are, however, at least as clearly perceptible as their similarities. And when we turn from synaesthetic comparisons between the effect of the visual and non-visual arts to those between the particular qualities of painting, sculpture and architecture, the differences become still more pronounced. Despite frequent demands for a new type of art which would embrace all the arts, both sculpture and architecture were often excluded from definitions of Romanticism – even though architecture was described as 'frozen music', and music as the 'most romantic of the arts'.

The notion that sculpture was essentially un-Romantic – *ennuyeuse* to Baudelaire – derived from the long-established belief that it had reached an unsurpassable peak of excellence in Ancient Greece, and, also, from the supposition that it could represent only the external attributes – of strength, composure or grace – whereas painting could reveal the inner life. Logical, balanced, self-contained, static, nobly simple and calmly great, Antique sculpture was seen as the classical art *par excellence*. Greek poetry was often termed 'sculptural' in contrast to the more 'painterly' modern poetry. The nearest equivalent in painting was to be found in sixteenth-century Italy, and theorists had thus urged artists to study Raphael. But in the early nineteenth century, as attention shifted from Raphael's *Stanze* to his Madonnas (and also to the work of his predecessors) and from such classicistic statues as the Apollo Belvedere and the Medici Venus to the more severe and uncompromising marbles of the Parthenon and Aegina, so sculpture came to seem ever more remotely a thing of the past. Painting, on the other hand, especially oil painting, a product of the modern post-classical world, was still in a state of becoming, remaining to be perfected and therefore eminently suitable for representing Christian – or Romantic – ideas. This sharpened awareness of the difference between the two arts encouraged painters to abandon the cleanly modelled sculptural style of David in favour of either a flat linear manner (as developed by Ingres) or an almost Baroque bravura with rich effects of atmospheric colour (as favoured by Delacroix).

'Painting must be painting and nothing else,' wrote Friedrich Schlegel in 1803. Its one 'proper aim' was 'not life and strength alone, but the one incomprehensible union of soul, expression and individuality' which he called the 'divinity of Nature':

> Sculpture may perhaps more successfully embody the ever-springing life, the inexhaustible strength of nature, or give the simplest imitation of material forms, or the contrast of happiness and death; but painting will mistake her own peculiar province, if, instead of following the track of the old masters, she diverges from it to pursue the objects more peculiarly appertaining to sculpture, which must result only in vain delusive attempts, or in producing a feeble and sickly shadow of the antique.[19]

He later defined music and painting as arts of the 'soul and spirit', sculpture as 'the art of the highest development of organic form and corporeal and sensual beauty which reached its highest excellence in classical antiquity'.[20] These ideas were further developed by Hegel who (following Winckelmann) saw Antique sculpture as the embodiment of the classical, Greek ideal. And, he argued, sculpture could never express the Romantic ideal, which is essentially concerned with the inner life withdrawn into itself from the external world:

> Grief, agony both physical and mental, torture and penance, death and resurrection, spiritual and subjective personality, deep feeling, heart, love, and emotion, this proper content of the religious and romantic imagination is not a topic for which the abstract external shape as such in its three spatial dimensions and the material in its physical, not idealized existence could provide the really adequate form and the equally congruent material.

Only the arts of painting and music were, he said, 'adequate to express the life of the soul'.[21]

Much the same was argued in simpler terminology by Théophile Gautier. 'Of all the arts,' he wrote,

> sculpture is certainly that which lends itself least to the Romantic idea. It seems to have received its definitive form from Antiquity. Developed under an anthropomorphic religion where deified beauty could be eternalised in marble and set up on altars, it attained a perfection which would never be surpassed.

Sculptors had continued to work in the Antique style, but 'in our complicated and troubled times, this detachment from passion, from accident, from colour, this imperturbable calm' slid only too easily into the merely cold and boring – 'the antique became classic, the classic academic, and the academic *poncif*'. The 'new movement of originality and liberty' had been represented in sculpture only by those who had broken away from Antique subject-matter, notably David d'Angers, Auguste Préault, Jehan du Seigneur, Antonin Moine, Mlle de Fauveau and Barye – and they had met, according to Gautier, with critical opposition still more violent than that encountered by Romantic painters and poets.[22]

Gautier's categorization of Classical and Romantic sculpture according to subject-matter has generally been followed by later writers. But this approach is too simple. The reality is more complicated – such eminently Romantic subjects as the Norse sagas, for instance, could inspire, even as late as 1830, such wholly un-Romantic sculptural expression as Bengt Erland Fogelberg's *Wotan*, every inch a classical god apart from details of costume [74]. J. G. Schadow's famous and much earlier group of the two Prussian princesses Luise and Friederike, on the other hand, already reveals strongly Romantic tendencies [75].

In the context of late eighteenth-century portrait sculpture, Schadow's group might seem fully Neo-classical in its noble com-

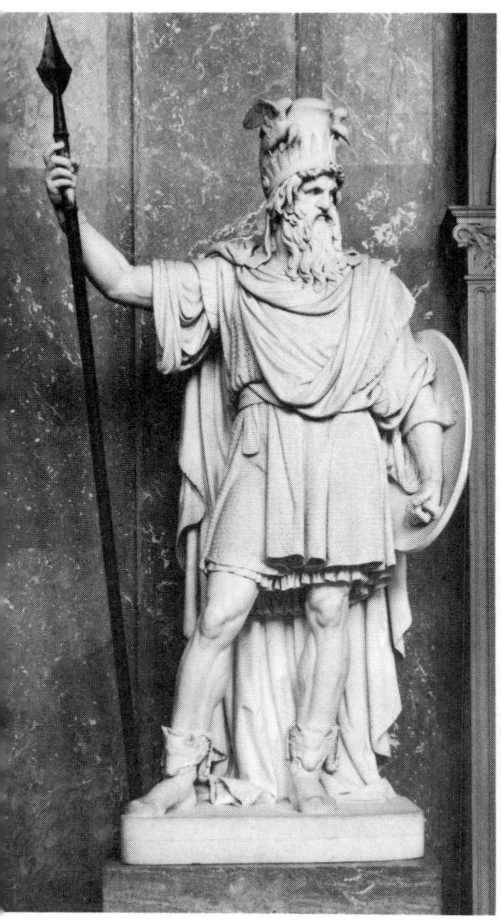

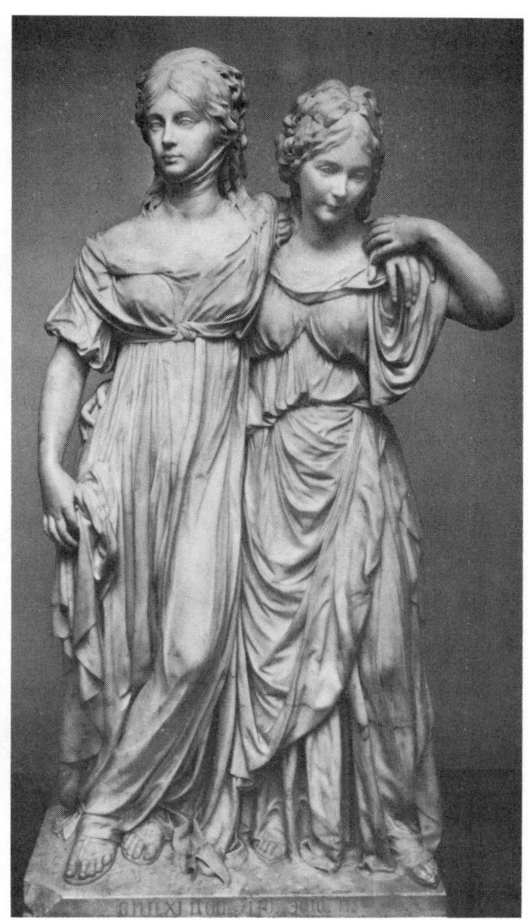

74. *Wotan*, 1830. B. E. Fogelberg
75 (*right*). *The Princesses Luise and Friederike of Prussia*, 1795–7. J. G. Schadow

posure and rejection of Rococo frivolity, in its rational (rather than schematic or merely decorative) treatment of hair and drapery, and, of course, in its obvious indebtedness to Antique prototypes. But, at the same time, it has a complexity of form and texture, an individuality of characterization and, especially, a meditative, almost apprehensive, mood of yearning which is deeply unclassical. Significantly, it may have inspired Gottlieb Schick's portrait of the Humboldt children, which Friedrich Schlegel in 1819 singled out for special praise among the works of the German painter 'who justly claims the highest place in our retrospect of the regeneration of art – he who began the struggle'.[23] However it is classified stylistically,

Schadow's group is a link in the long process of development which leads from the rejection of the Rococo and the search for a 'true style' in the mid-eighteenth century to the Romanticism of the nineteenth. The delicately naturalistic statue in which Canova portrayed Princess Leopoldina Esterhazy sketching a landscape is in many respects similar [76]. It captures that atmosphere of almost tremulous

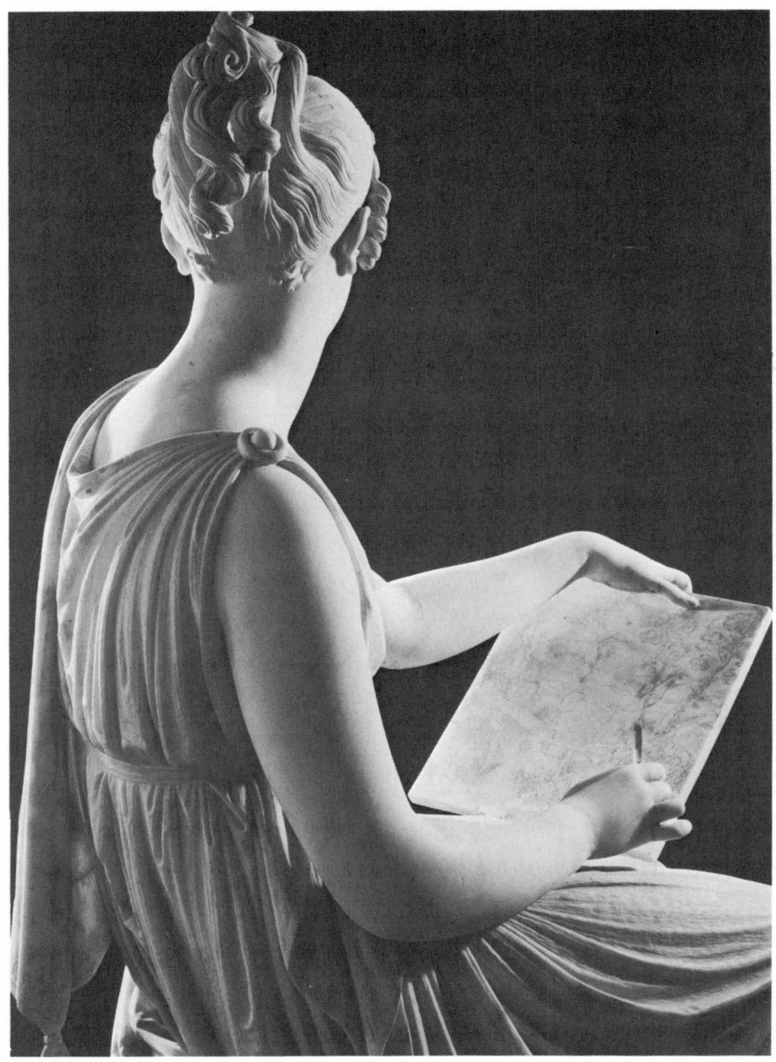

76. *Princess Leopoldina Esterhazy-Liechtenstein*, 1808–18. Canova

sensibility of – indeed it might almost be supposed to represent a character from – Goethe's novel *Wahlverwandschaften* (*Kindred Affinities*) of 1808, the very year in which the statue was begun.

The tendency towards greater naturalism in the Esterhazy statue is only one of several significant developments in Canova's work of the first two decades of the nineteenth century (and the last of his life). For as Antiquity gradually gave place in his vision to what Stendhal called '*un nouveau genre de* beau idéal, *plus rapproché de nos mœurs que de celles des Grecs*',[24] his concern with subject-matter itself was gradually overtaken by purely sculptural problems – multiple viewpoints, the complex play of subtly contrasted surface textures, and the delicate adjustment of precarious balance. In fact, some of his statues of this period have no subject (mythological or allegorical) whatsoever: his *Dancers*, for example, are simply figures in movement. None of his immediate followers went so far towards *l'art pour l'art* or was able to emulate his more daring technical achievements. They were more concerned with the sentiment than with the complex structure of his works.

Although (or perhaps because) he was popularly regarded as the greatest living artist – with kings and emperors competing for the privilege of acquiring his statues – Canova received some hostile criticism which is of interest now for the light it sheds on current attitudes to sculpture in general. His critics were curiously divided – one group holding that he was too little responsive to the concerns of his own day, the other that he lacked the bold severity of the Antique. The former line was taken by W. P. Carey when he compared two statues by Canova, *Hebe* and *Terpsichore*, with Francis Chantrey's group of the *Sleeping Children* [77], all of which

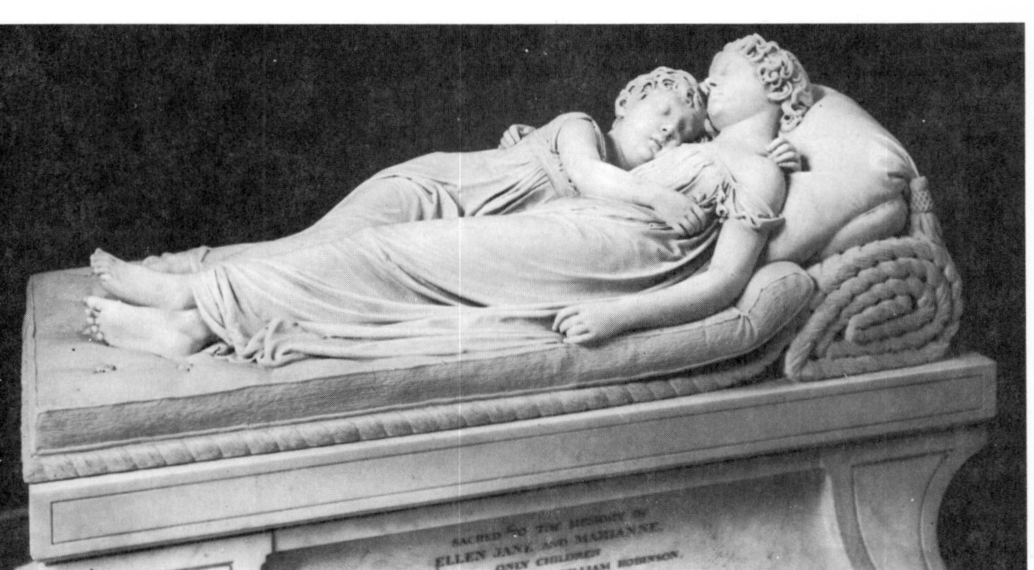

77. *The Sleeping Children*, 1817. Francis Chantrey

were exhibited at the Royal Academy in London 1817.[25] Canova's 'learned taste, deep science, and polished style' were duly appreciated and applauded, he wrote:

> But the touching graces and gentle feeling in Chantrey's two Innocents, embracing in the sleep of death, turned the tide of opinion in favour of his performance. The mournful sweetness of the conception and exquisite beauty of the execution found their way into every breast. The sentiment appealed at once to every character ...

Canova had made an unfortunate choice of subjects, Carey went on, for statues of mythological figures 'by a *living* sculptor' had only the 'recommendation of a *classic* name'. They afford 'no food for the mind, exercise no power over opinion, and are wholly foreign from the feelings and way of thinking of modern times'. Greek and Roman statues were valued 'as rare original specimens of ancient genius, which breathe the *spirit of their own time*'. But 'a *modern*', he continued, 'can have no feeling in unison with a divinity which is altogether imaginary, and whose existence at any period is the subject of his disbelief and disgust, or ridicule':

> Without an earnestness of heart, without strong passion, without enthusiasm guided by science and judgement, what is the offspring of any imitative art but a shadow – a cold form begotten mechanically; born without life; beheld with indifference and consigned by forgetfulness to the grave of oblivion?

Carey's article is an expression of widely held views, some of which may have been shared by Canova in his later years (the two statues exhibited in 1817 are variants from models of 1795 and 1809). It is also an indication of the demands which were put on sculptors in the Romantic period and which sometimes led them into the saddest excesses of sentimentality. From Chantrey's beautiful and genuinely moving group the road declines swiftly to the cemetery statuary of the mid- and late nineteenth century.[26]

The other line of criticism of Canova was initiated by a German, C. F. Fernow, who declared that his break with the Baroque tradition had been insufficiently radical, that his works were too graceful and sensuous.[27] Supporters of this view generally preferred the Danish sculptor Thorvaldsen, who was a generation younger than Canova and whose artistic relationship to him somewhat resembles that of Ingres to David. Thorvaldsen pursued certain Neo-classical tendencies further than Canova, especially those towards purity and primitivism, drawing inspiration from archaic Greek sculptures – but he abandoned others which had previously seemed as important.

Late eighteenth-century Neo-classical sculptors had striven to realize the ideal of a perfectly self-contained and self-explanatory work of art. Canova's single figures are isolated and withdrawn: those in his groups are wholly absorbed in one another. His pre-occupation with free-standing sculpture, which could present an harmonious flow of forms and textures from an infinite number of viewpoints (some of his statues were mounted on pivots so that they could be slowly rotated), led him to create figures emotionally as well as physically detached from their surroundings.

Thorvaldsen's statues, on the other hand, stand in what Julius Lange called 'an invisible landscape'. One of them, *The Lion of Lucerne* (a monument commemorating Swiss Guards killed in the French Revolution), is in fact part of a real landscape, hewn out of the living rock of a cliff [78]. The whole rock-face, indeed the

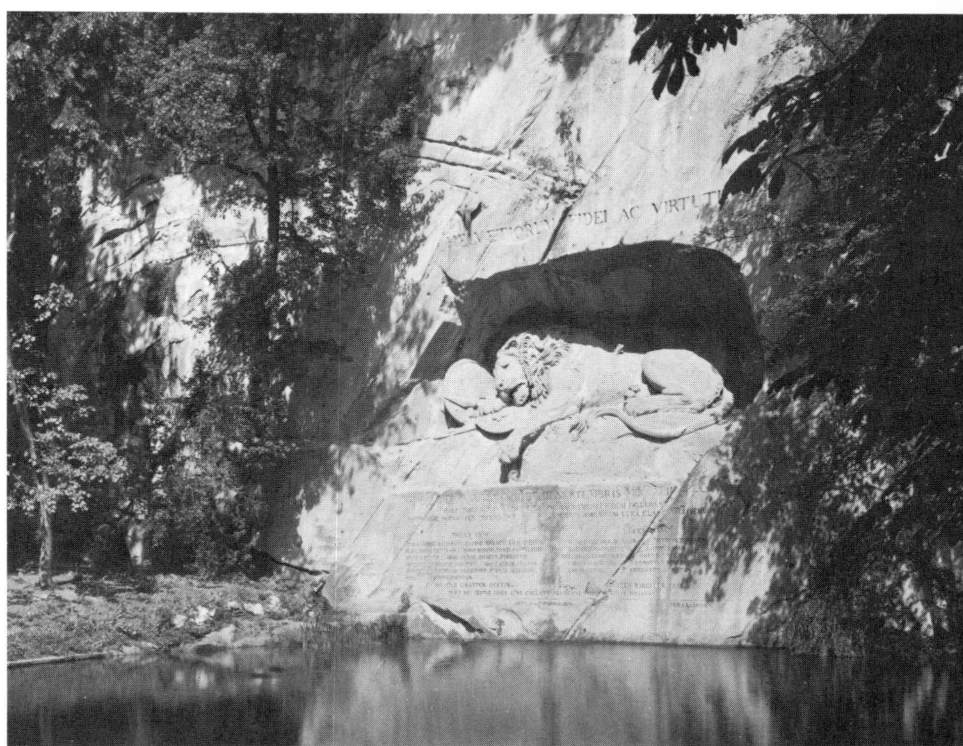

78. *The Lion of Lucerne*, 1819–21. Thorvaldsen

whole 'elemental' setting with fresh spring water below, trees on either side and small plants sprouting from fissures in the cliff, is therefore part of the work of art, forming, in fact, a new type of total 'art work'. The effect is akin to that of Caspar David Friedrich's *Hermann's Tomb* [142] and strikes a similarly primitive chord – though it is probably a coincidence that they are both 'war memorials'. This instance of sculpture physically aspiring to the condition of landscape painting is unique at this date, except for Rude's *Napoleon Awakening to Immortality* [159], which was also conceived as part of, and together with, a natural setting and one even grander than Thorvaldsen's *Lion*, for it incorporates the whole surrounding landscape with a distant view of the Jura mountains.

Most of Thorvaldsen's statues have the pictorial and literary qualities of his relief carvings, which were generally more highly praised by his contemporaries. Often they appear to form part of invisible groups, and sometimes illustrate stories which cannot be understood without external knowledge. Hegel noted this in a comparison of Pigalle's *Mercury* – represented in a 'perfectly harmless action', he said – with Thorvaldsen's statue of the same subject and Rudolph Schadow's *Girl Fastening her Sandals*.[28] Thorvaldsen's *Mercury* is, he wrote, 'depicted in a situation which is almost too complicated for sculpture' – so complicated, indeed, that Hegel misinterpreted the subject: Mercury charming Argus with his music! 'While playing his flute Mercury watches Marsyas craftily eyeing him to see how he may kill him while his hand grasps maliciously for the dagger he has concealed.' Schadow's *Girl Fastening her Sandals* is 'caught in the same occupation' as Pigalle's Mercury, 'but here the harmlessness has not the like interest linked with it when a god is represented in such naïveté. When a girl binds her sandals, or spins, there is nothing revealed but precisely this binding or spinning, and this in itself is meaningless and unimportant.' This is the reverse of Carey's argument about Canova. But in opposing both the 'pictorial' sculpture, of the type represented by Thorvaldsen's *Mercury*, and Rudolph Schadow's 'pure' sculpture – the simple representation of an ideal human form – Hegel was stressing his point that sculpture is 'classical' and cannot become the vehicle for a Romantic artist without the sacrifice of sculptural qualities.

Paradoxically, however, the Neo-classical notion of the statue as not merely free-standing but self-sufficient – a kind of Kantian *Ding an sich* (thing in itself) – was to create the conditions for the one significant or, rather, potentially significant, innovation in sculpture brought about by Romantic attitudes and ideals. Until the early nineteenth century large-scale sculpture had been almost wholly dependent on its patrons, generally the Church or State. Altars, tombs and royal or princely statues for churches, palaces or public squares were executed by sculptors 'on commission' and, very often, much more than their subjects were predetermined by their patrons. Because of the high cost of the materials, and the time involved in carving, it was virtually impossible for a sculptor to work except on commission. To the Romantic artist this dependence was, of course, abhorrent. To escape from it must have seemed essential, but impossible. Yet the means was in fact to hand: the full-scale plaster model used in the intermediate stage between the sketch and the finished work in the sculptural process.[29] This could be made inexpensively and relatively quickly. However, the first instance of a sculptor making a full-scale plaster model independently and without a commission – in other words 'on speculation' – was Thorvaldsen's heroic-scale statue of *Jason*.[30] Thorvaldsen made this in 1802 entirely on his own initiative and at his own expense. It was exhibited in Rome, seen by Thomas Hope, and a commission for its execution in marble obtained. Before long other young sculptors were producing full-scale models in the hope of attracting patrons to finance their execution in a more durable (and, of course, much more costly) medium.

This should or could have had an enormously liberating effect, freeing the sculptor's inventive spirit from the control of patrons, who now became simply purchasers or clients, accepting or rejecting what the artist created, buying modern statues in much the same way as they bought modern paintings. The sculptor was thus enabled to follow his own bent independently, even for work on the grandest scale. But the importance that the full-scale model thereby acquired opened a breach between what came to be regarded as the artistic and merely mechanical, between the creative and executive processes of sculpture. As the split widened, the sculptor tended to concentrate almost exclusively on the model, and to do no more (sometimes less) than oversee the technicians who realized it in marble or bronze – especially the latter which more accurately reproduced the original and was generally cast outside the sculptor's studio by specialist craftsmen. His role became, indeed, practically that of the musician whose works are performed by accomplished executants on instruments few of which he can himself play (Berlioz seems to have prided himself on being able to play only the guitar, recorder and drums).

The Romantics believed the essence of the work of art to be the concept in the soul of its inventor, not the score or the performance, the model or the marble, or even the painted canvas, which were merely media through which spirit spoke to spirit. At the end of

 Nathaniel Hawthorne's strange story *The Artist of the Beautiful*, the creator of a mechanical butterfly, which symbolizes the work of art, watches its destruction complacently – 'He had caught a far other butterfly than this. When the artist rose high enough to achieve the beautiful, the symbol by which he made it perceptible to mortal senses became of little value in his eyes while his spirit possessed itself in enjoyment of the reality.' The fragile model which was destroyed in the process of making a plaster or bronze cast was almost a metaphor for this concept. David d'Angers, who claimed that '*la sculpture est une religion*', likened the soul fresh from the Creator to the clay figure before it had been manhandled by plaster moulders, marble carvers or bronze founders.[31] Such ideas brought early nineteenth-century sculptors surprisingly close, in theory, to the heart of Romantic aesthetics. But the widespread belief that their art was essentially 'classical' died hard and, in fact, still survives in modern art-historical terminology. Thorvaldsen's statue of a shepherd boy [79b] is generally called Neo-classical, whereas drawings by the Nazarene painters, which are strikingly similar in feeling, are categorized as Romantic [79a and c]. Only a few daring French sculptors selected subjects and developed styles more obviously akin to those of Romantic painters.

79a. *Seated Boy*, 1821. J. Schnorr von Carolsfeld; 79b. *Shepherd Boy*, 1817–26. Thorvaldsen; 79c. *Seated Boy*, 1822. J. Schnorr von Carolsfeld

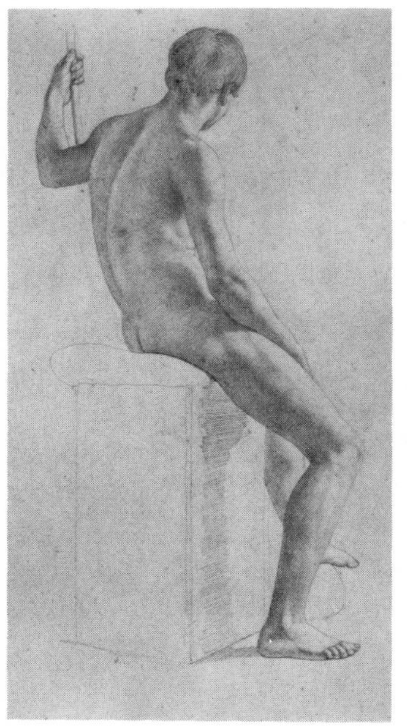

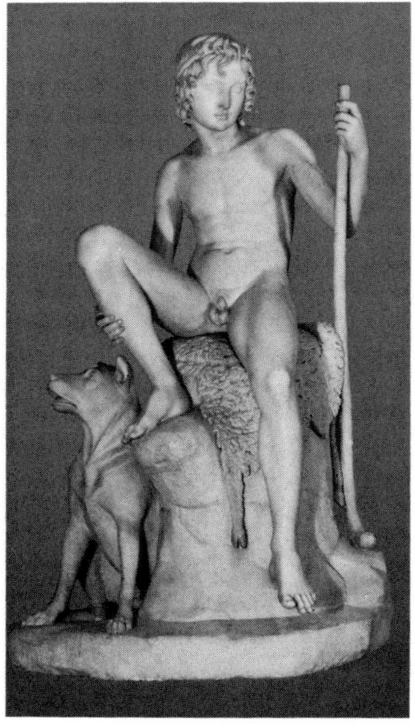

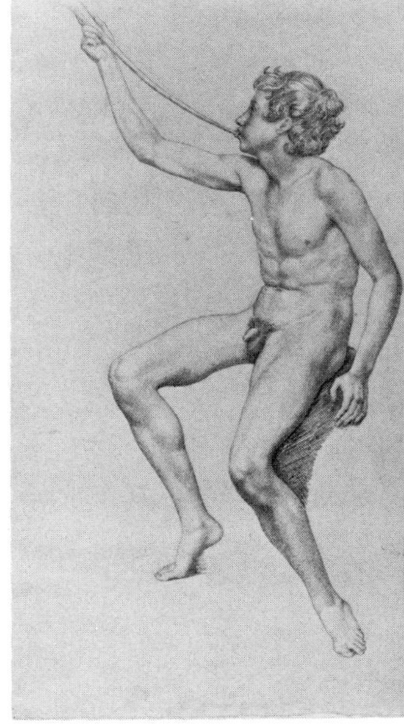

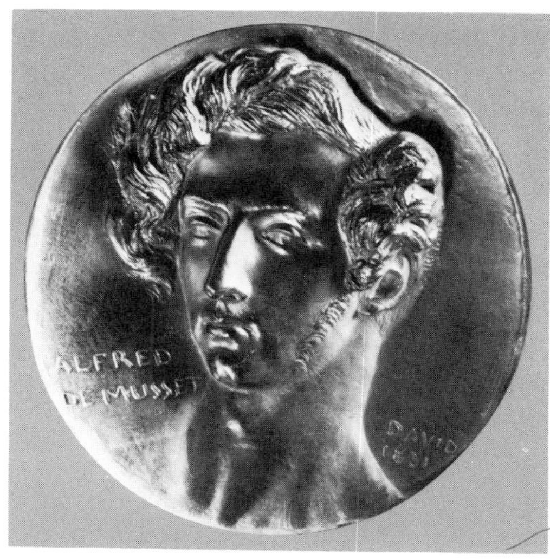

80. *Alfred de Musset*, 1831. David d'Angers

The more than 500 medallions in which David d'Angers portrayed nearly all the notabilities of his day are generally termed Romantic on account of the freedom with which they are modelled no less than because they include Géricault, Delacroix, Caspar David Friedrich, Schiller, Goethe, Chateaubriand, Hugo, de Vigny, de Musset [80], Dumas, Byron, Mickiewicz, Meyerbeer, Paganini and Rossini. His own description of how he made them could hardly

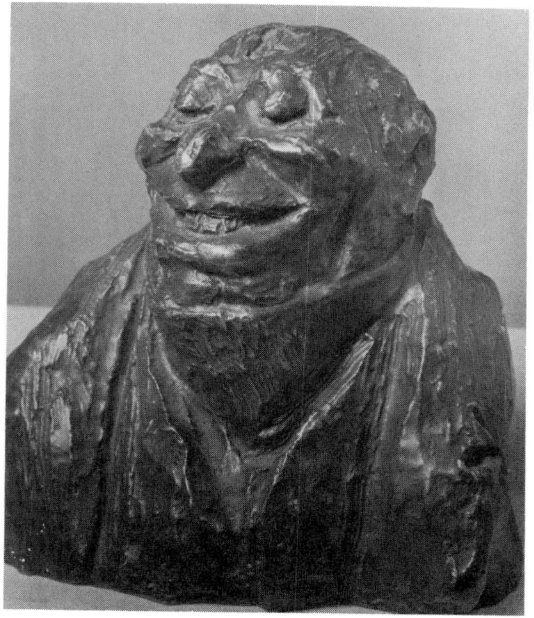

81. *Comte de Kératry*, *c*. 1832–3. Daumier

be more characteristic of the Romantic attitude towards artistic creation – 'constantly impelled by waves of irresistible emotions which left me trembling'.[32] He believed that the sculptor should represent not only the physical appearance of his subject but 'the immaterial being which ought to surround the material like an aureole'.[33] Yet there is little trace of idealization in these portraits, some of which are on the brink of caricature, close to J.-P. Dantan's statuettes and Daumier's malevolently modelled busts [81]. Comparison with the delicate late eighteenth-century relief portraits, by J.-B. Nini or James Tassie, for example, and the crisply incised medals of the Empire period reveals how radically he broke away from them.

His large-scale statues are more closely linked with the immediate past. The first, an heroic-scale figure of the Grand Condé, modelled in 1816–17 [82] and completed in marble in 1827, is related to the series of *grands hommes* commissioned by d'Angiviller for the Crown in the last decade of the *ancien régime* and including Pajou's Turenne and Houdon's Tourville. But David expressed the idea of honouring a French hero with a new sense of drama learned from the paintings of Gros. The pose of Condé is almost identical with that of Napoleon in Gros's *Battle of the Pyramids*. David gave to this figure an impetuous vitality without precedent in French sculpture. '*Ma fine, c'est comme l'orage*,' a passer-by remarked. Lady Morgan, that assiduous frequenter of *cénacles* and *salons* on her visit to Paris in 1829, probably echoed generally held views when she wrote:

> It contradicted all my preconceived opinions and tastes, as wanting the repose and stillness which are the characteristics of ancient art. In this beautiful statue there are not the sublime calm, the monumental immobility, the infectious solemnity, which makes one tread lightly and breathe low, in passing along the galleries of the Vatican ... But in its place was to be found a quality of an opposite and perhaps equal merit – living, moving, exciting, passionate humanity. The very pedestal trembles under the violent pressure of the indignant and animated form it supports.[34]

These words could be applied almost equally well to David's later nude statue of Philopoemen, the 'last of the Greeks', extracting a javelin from his thigh at the battle of Sellasia. Here, he wrote, his aim was to represent '*la lutte entre la nature physique et l'être moral*', without sacrificing the expression of pain to the beauty of forms.[35] But the more conservative critics censured him for a realism contrary to what they understood as the central principle of sculpture.

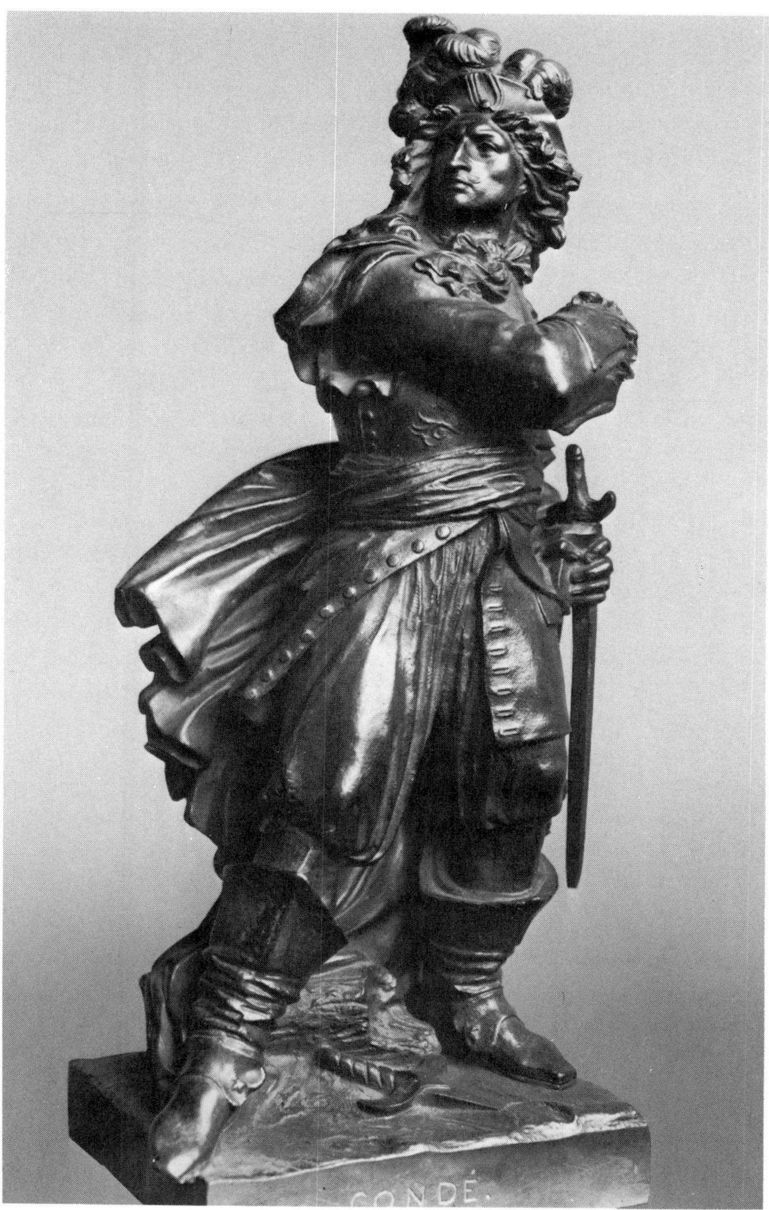

82. *Le Grand Condé*, 1827. David d'Angers

Sculptors could most easily avoid invidious comparison with the Antique by renouncing classical subject-matter and even the nude. Antoine-Louis Barye specialized in statues of animals, creating what was virtually a new genre. It became enormously popular.[36] Barye's success was immediate and even such a staunch opponent of the Romantics as Delécluze wrote of his *Tiger Devouring a Gavial* [83], when it was first exhibited in 1831: 'Life is represented with such force and passion in these two animals that we do not hesitate to call the group the strongest and best work of sculpture in the Salon.

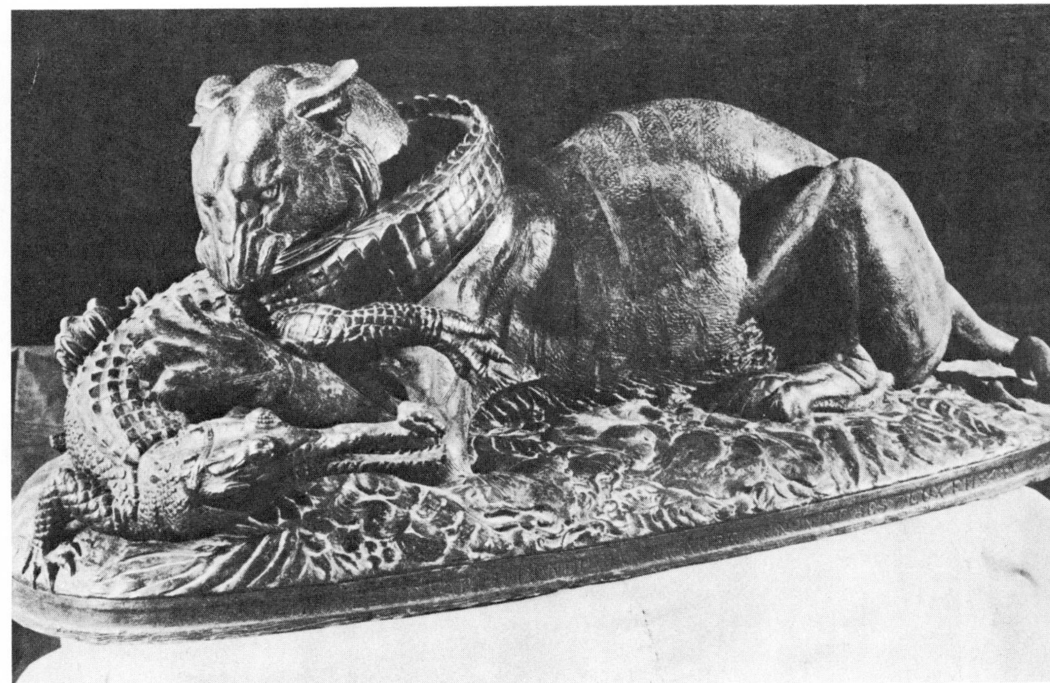

83. *Tiger Devouring a Gavial*, 1831–2. A.-L. Barye

The truth of this piece is such that, after having seen it, one is pursued by the stench of the menagerie.'[37] The Romantics were still more enthusiastic, contrasting Barye's works with the 'geometric stiffness' of the gods and nymphs officially approved by the Academy[38] – hence perhaps his exclusion from the Salon between 1837 and 1848. His response to both the beauty and the ferocity of the animal world, the strength of muscle beneath sleek pelts, and all the vital violence of nature red in tooth and claw, often recalls Delacroix who was, in fact, among his first admirers.[39]

The representation of human passions, as they were understood by the Romantics, confronted the sculptor with more difficult problems. Jehan Du Seigneur's *Orlando Furioso*, exhibited at the Salon of 1831 [84], was to be described much later, by Thoré-Burger, as a manifesto of Romanticism in sculpture – '*une sorte de préface de*

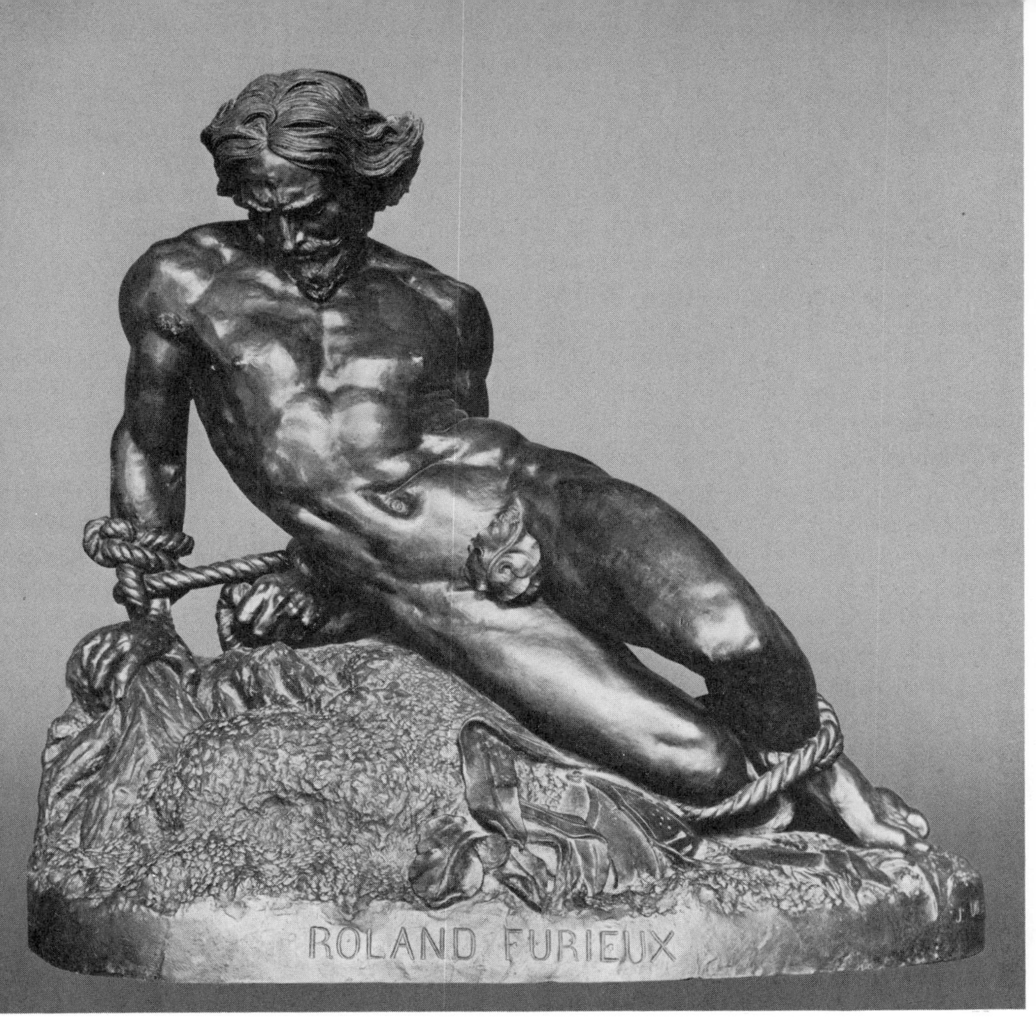

84. *Orlando Furioso*, 1830–31. J. Du Seigneur

Cromwell'.[40] But this attempt to express mental anguish within the conventions of the heroic nude aroused little enthusiasm at the time. Even the critic writing in the ostensibly pro-Romantic *L'Artiste* found it merely 'tormented'. The official world displayed indifference rather than active disapproval. Du Seigneur was not excluded from the next Salon (of 1833), where he showed a group illustrating an incident from Hugo's *Notre Dame de Paris*, but he received no commissions, and the *Orlando Furioso* was not cast until after his death.

Further transgressions of the bounds commonly set for sculpture were, however, viewed with such hostility that very few even of the plaster models have survived. Those exhibited by Auguste Préault at the Salon of 1833 were likened to exhumed corpses – a half-life-size group entitled *La Misère* (a girl dying in her mother's arms, known from a lithograph), a relief of *L'Agonie du poète Gilbert*, inspired by de Vigny, and a colossal relief of *La Famine* (both of which have perished without trace). Confronted with these works, a critic, who praised painters for breaking with the school of David, declared that the anti-academic reaction of sculptors was false and exaggerated. 'Just as the old school loved the nude, purity, and clearly defined forms, so MM. Préault and Du Seigneur adore bodies with forms barely defined, gaunt features, meagre and hideous limbs.'[41] Du Seigneur mended his ways and was soon receiving official commissions for statues of innocuous insipidity. But Préault was incorrigible. In 1834 he submitted for the Salon a group of embracing semi-nude figures entitled *Parias* (now known only from a print [Fig. viii, p. 388]) – an image of seamy sensuality which flaunted every classical rule. The jury refused it: and in the hope of discrediting Préault accepted his much more extraordinary relief *Tuerie* [85].

A disturbing confusion of agonized and shouting faces, of hands which grope and grasp, a body pierced with festering sword-thrusts and hair flowing like sea-weed, *Tuerie* is one of the most immediately

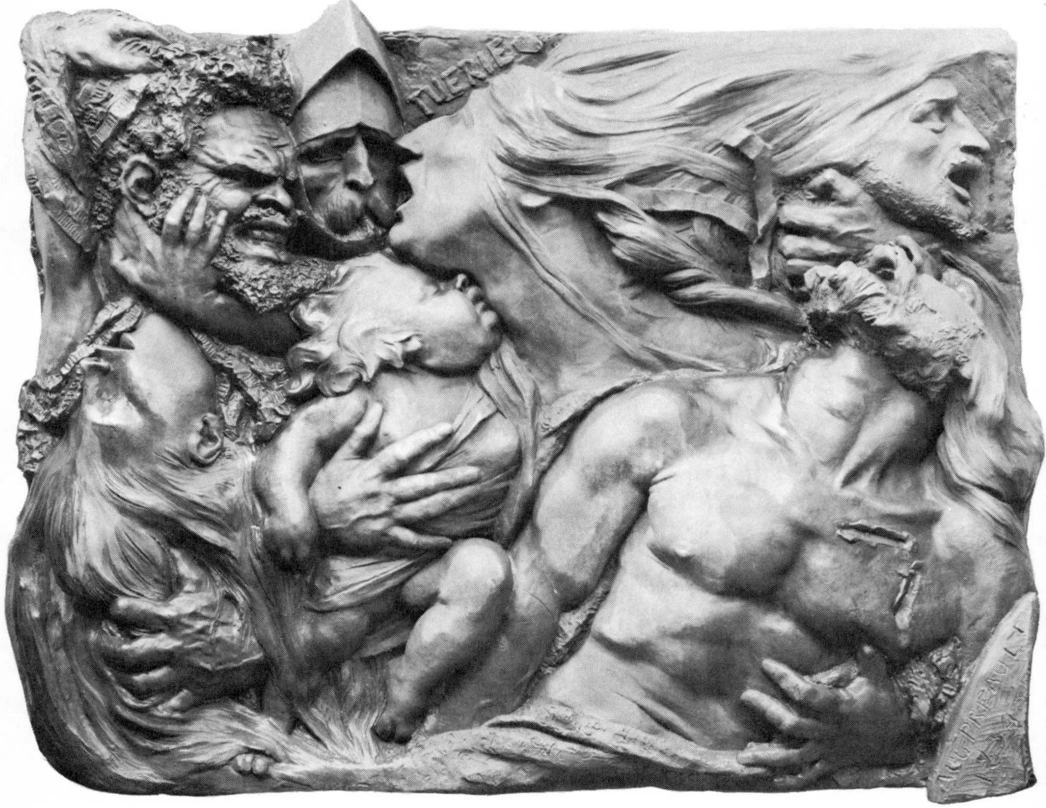

85. *Tuerie*, 1834. A. Préault

arresting and enigmatic works of nineteenth-century sculpture. There are visual reminiscences in it – two heads derive from *The Raft of the 'Medusa'* – and religious overtones in the Christ-like body on the right and the central woman and child who seem to have been torn from some Baroque Massacre of the Innocents. But there is no programme. The title *Tuerie* (slaughter) – rather than the more literary *massacre* – would seem to imply a deliberate rejection of any precise subject. Baudelaire was enthralled by the '*rêves tumultueux, même incomplètes d'Auguste Préault*';[42] yet the figures are rather too substantial for any shadowy dream kingdom. Though it might be termed the ultimate expression of the pictorial style in sculpture, it marks a departure from artistic conventions more radical than had yet been made by any painter in a work intended for public exhibition. And the firm modelling intensifies the relief's impact. The slightest movement of the eye or of the light subtly changes its appearance, clarifying some and obscuring other parts of this strangely tangible realization of the intangible – of a chaotic world of horror and suffering. Nothing could be further removed from the ideal of 'noble simplicity and calm greatness' than this complex and tormented work. Préault was, however, equally capable of evoking other emotions, the tranquillity of death after the storm of life in his relief of *Ophelia* [185] and, in a headstone he modelled for the Jewish section of the Père Lachaise cemetery [86], the silence of the tomb, of grief and of the art of sculpture

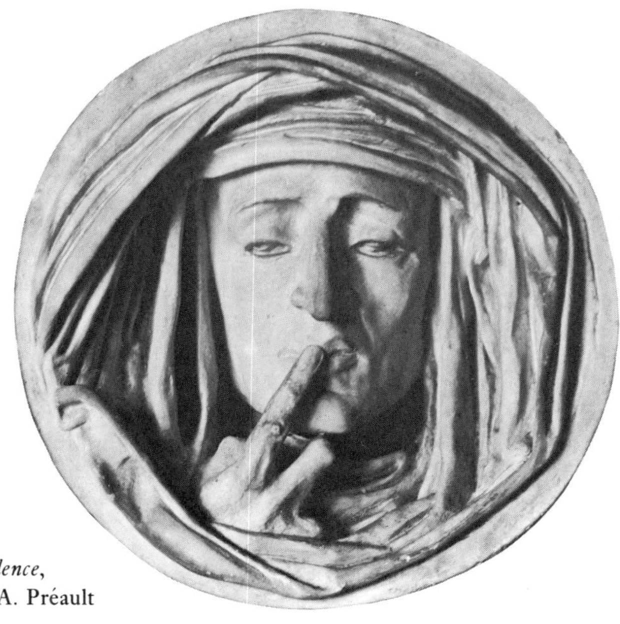

86. *Silence*, 1849. A. Préault

itself, in a relief which inspired the Parnassian poet Théodore de Banville to write:

Préault, d'un doigt fantasque
Fait trembler sur un masque
L'immortelle pâleur
*De la douleur.**

Préault wrote on a drawing of his medallion of Delacroix, '*Je ne suis pas pour le fini. Je suis pour l'Infini.*'[43] It is a succinct statement of the aims of both artists, and also of the dilemma which faced sculptors who sought to realize Romantic ideas, reducing the infinite to the finite. The example of Préault (who had great difficulty in earning a living) was not followed, and most of his contemporaries temporized by modelling 'picturesque' medieval or modern figures. But such statues could not satisfy as convinced a Romantic as the poet and novelist Pétrus Borel, who remarked in 1833:

> It is not good enough to make statues of Neapolitan dancers instead of Fauns and Bacchus, or Pepin instead of Ajax. The problem is not simply one of subject and form, the revolutionary problem is entirely spiritual; if sculpture is not expressive, if it appeals only to the grosser senses and not to the soul, it is only a craft, manual work, a boring superfluity.

Pétrus Borel classified his contemporaries not as Romantics and Classics, but as 'the thoughtful and the mindless', putting in the former category only two sculptors, Préault and Etex; four painters, Ingres, Delacroix, Paul Delaroche and Louis Boulanger; two musicians, Hector Berlioz and Giacomo Meyerbeer; and a single architect whom he misnamed 'Aimé', Chenavard.[44]

The Romantic demand for buildings which could 'appeal to the soul' – as much as music, poems or paintings – was voiced throughout Europe. 'No work of art can ever be produced by skill and understanding alone ... the inspiration of the artist has ever been, and ever must be, the source of that which confers aesthetic value on his productions,' wrote Carl Adolf Menzel in 1832:

> A piece of architecture in which there are any manifestations of genius is worked out in the same manner as a poem: invention, or the ground idea of the subject, must come first, and it is to this conception of the fancy that technical skill is afterwards applied, so as to work it up and render practicable in construction what is originally the mere apprehen-

* 'Préault, with a fantastic hand, makes the immortal pallor of grief tremble on a mask.'

sion of beauty. *This is the only true process*; by adopting the opposite course we may, indeed, be able to obtain a structure in every respect well suited for its destination, but it can never possess that mysterious charm which genius alone can bestow; nor will it ever warm the beholder to admiration, although he may not be able to deny that the builder has performed all that utility requires, or that reason ought to demand.[45]

Five years later the young John Ruskin, in his first publication, defined architecture as 'a science of feeling rather than of rule, a ministry to the mind, more than to the eye', and went on to state that 'no man can be an architect, who is not a metaphysician.[46] Like Menzel and, indeed, most other writers of the time, he made a distinction between architecture and building similar to that between poetry and verse, giving a new and paramount importance to the conception in the mind of the architect, as in that of the painter, sculptor or musician. 'In no art is there closer connection between our delight in the work and our admiration of the workman's mind,' Ruskin wrote in 1851.[47] Architecture had come to be judged not only by rational rules or functional and decorative fitness for purpose, but also by emotional and sometimes transcendental criteria.

In 1828 a German architect, Heinrich Hübsch, published a pamphlet entitled *In welchem Style sollen wir bauen?* (*In which style should we build?*).[48] Had it been phrased 'in which style shall we build?' his question might have been asked in the previous century, when a variety of historical and exotic styles were employed without, of course, doubting the essential superiority of the classical.[49] The realization that there were two distinct systems of classical architecture (trabeated Greek and arcuated Roman) and the discovery of the merits of Gothic buildings naturally weakened the authority of Vitruvius, whose treatise had formed the backbone of architectural theory ever since the Renaissance. And the shift in emphasis from the practical purpose to the emotional effect of buildings – their appeal to the heart rather than to the head – further complicated the issue, especially as different styles acquired religious, nationalistic and sometimes political overtones.

Once the Neo-classical quest for an eternally and universally valid architectural ideal had been abandoned, the old Vitruvian doctrine of decorum (the Doric order for fortresses, the Corinthian for palaces, etc.) was extended to embrace a wide range of historical and even exotic styles. Grecian was generally deemed appropriate for museums, Roman for other secular public buildings, Romanesque or Gothic for churches. Italian Renaissance styles were selected for palaces in Munich and Berlin and for clubs in London.

An Englishman who had made a fortune in India settled on the Moghul style as suitable, not for a garden pavilion (as he might have done in the eighteenth century), but for his main country residence at Sezincote. But ideas as to what was appropriate often conflicted. Ludwig I of Bavaria's determination to build a Greek Doric temple – the Walhalla near Regensburg – to enshrine busts of all the most famous Germans was much criticized. 'Why should a Greek model have been chosen for an edifice, the object, the purpose and name of which are so completely, essentially gothic? What, in Heaven's name, has the Theseum to do on the banks of the Danube?' an English writer asked; 'Surely it is not appropriate.'[50] The idea of genius was, however, associated with ancient Greece, and the architect Leo von Klenze was also well aware of the imposingly Romantic effect his building would have on the spectacular site chosen for it – as was Turner who painted it in 1842. Nearby, Klenze built a church in the neo-Romanesque *Rundbogenstil* and juxtaposed it with the Walhalla in a single view [87].

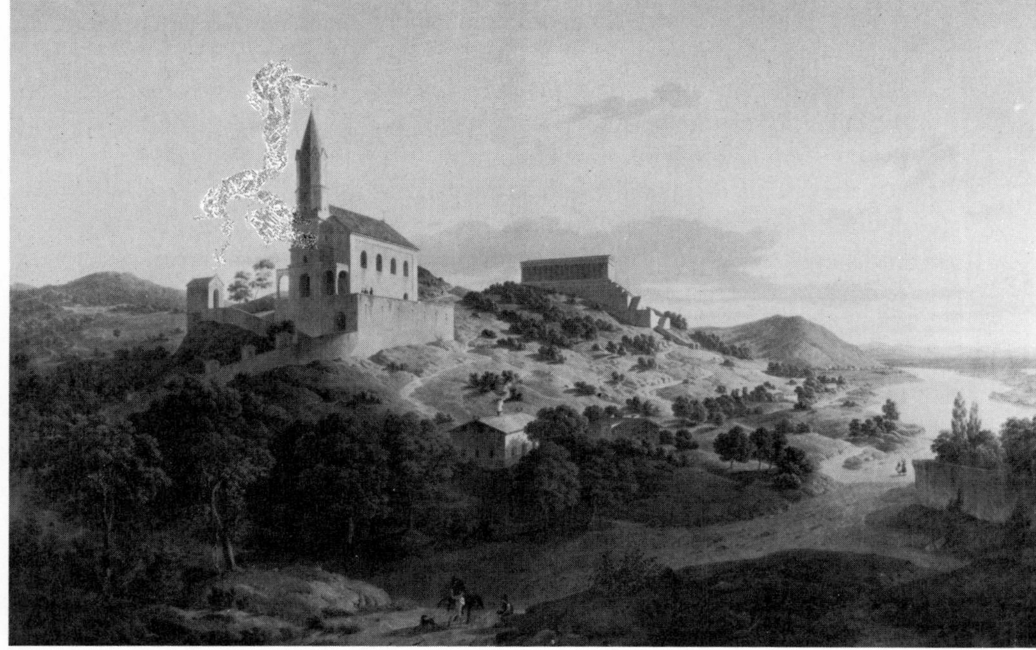

87. *The Salvatorkirche and Walhalla*, 1839. Leo von Klenze

Styles were sometimes adopted more for their scenic effect than their associations – architecture aspiring to the condition of painting. There was a general tendency to conceive streets and squares not as symmetrical, rationalized unities – by uniting several buildings into a single façade (like the rue de Rivoli or the place Vendôme in Paris) – but more loosely, naturally, almost organically, as sequences of separate, individual buildings held together merely by an underlying sense of scale and by a 'felt' artistic unity. The development of Munich under Ludwig I is the most striking, and strikingly successful, instance of this principle in planning. The Königsplatz consists of three free-standing structures in quite different (classical) styles [93], the Ludwigstrasse of a series of buildings of differing design so that all sense of order and rigidity, and hence of confinement or *Randerlebnis*, is removed.[51] Elsewhere more adventurous groupings were attempted, the most preposterous example being the structures conjured up at Devonport in 1823–4, including a Doric town hall and memorial column, two Ionic houses, a Corinthian terrace, an Egyptian library and an 'Oriental' dissenting chapel. John Foulston, the architect of this gallimaufry, called it 'an experiment (not before attempted) for producing a picturesque effect by combining in one view, the Grecian, Egyptian and a variety of the Oriental'.[52] A decade later the young Nicolai Gogol wrote:

> A town must be able to show a great diversity of masses, if it is to give pleasure to the eye. The most varied kinds of taste should be married to one another within it. Let there be set up in a single street a dark Gothic building, a building in colourful oriental style, a colossal Egyptian structure, and a Greek edifice full of pleasant harmonies. Let there here be gathered together in harmony the lightly-rounded milk-coloured cupola, the high church tower so full of the spirit of devotion, the oriental Mitra, the flat Italian roof, the Dutch roof, steep and richly decorated, the four cornered pyramid and the angular obelisk. There should be a street which would at the same time be a chronicle of the world's architectural history.[53]

But such a multicoloured prospect, 'the carnival of architecture' as Pugin called it, was seldom seriously advocated. In 1834 Gottfried Semper scoffingly described a budding architect and town-planner touring the world and filling his notebooks with designs, in the hope that he might be required to build a Parthenon-like Walhalla, a basilica in the style of Monreale, a Pompeiian boudoir, a palace like Palazzo Pitti, a Byzantine church and a Turkish bazaar (all of which had, in fact, been commissioned for Munich by Ludwig I).[54]

The imitation of styles in buildings went against Romantic theories of artistic originality and authenticity.[55] Yet it derived from the same notion of cultural pluralism – the belief that each historical and exotic style had its own individual merits and meaning – which lay behind the persistent demands for what T. L. Donaldson called in 1847 'an architecture of our period, a distinct, individual, palpable style of the nineteenth century'.[56] And the battle of styles was no carnival *bataille des fleurs* fought with trefoils and paterae, but the expression of a very serious conflict of ideas. It was, moreover, fought out on a Romantic platform. 'We do not want to revive a facsimile of the works or style of any particular individual or even period,' wrote the Gothic champion Pugin; '*but it is the devotion, majesty, and repose of Christian art, for which we are contending*; it is not a *style*, but a *principle*.'[57] Leo von Klenze, who defined architecture as the 'free development of a poetic thought', said that 'only when a style effectually has an inner vital principle can it become effective'.[58] For him a building was an organic whole, whose appeal derived from the central idea rather than the exterior. Gothic revivalists would hardly have disputed these assertions – though Klenze had Greek architecture in mind.

It is significant that the eminently Romantic notion of architecture as *erstarrte Musik* (petrified or frozen music) was first formulated, by Schelling in about 1802, with reference to Greek temples and Pythagorean theories (he associated the lyre with the triglyph).[59] Goethe kept the metaphor in this context in *Faust, Part Two*[60] and in an aphorism of 1827 where he worked out a variant, *verstummter Tonkunst* (dumb music), which he applied to St Peter's in Rome.[61] He was probably still thinking of classical-style buildings when he told Eckermann in 1829: 'I have found among my papers a sheet on which I call architecture frozen music [*erstarrte Musik*]. And really there is something in this; the state of mind produced by architecture resembles that effected by music.'[62] In this more impressionistic sense the phrase might, and very soon did, embrace all forms of architecture, including medieval.[63] Walter Pater, in his essay on Notre Dame d'Amiens (1894), was to contrast 'the mere *melody* of Greek architecture ... the sense as it were of music in the opposition of successive sounds' with the '*harmony*' of Gothic – 'the richer music generated by opposition of sounds in one and the same moment'.[64]

The speed with which the frozen-music metaphor spread across Europe (within two years it had passed by word of mouth from Berlin to London, where it was discussed by Mme de Staël and Byron[65]), and the frequency with which it was repeated, suggest that it filled a need for words to express a new idea. In its original context it could be applied not only to Greek temples but also to the stark geometrical architecture of pure forms evolved by Ledoux and Boullée in France, and by Friedrich Gilly in Prussia.[66] It acquired a different significance, however, with the development of the Romantic belief that music and Gothic architecture were the finest artistic expressions of Christendom.[67]

Both these interpretations found visual expression in the work of Karl Friedrich Schinkel, the architect most closely associated with the writers who originated the phrase.[68] His lithograph of a Gothic – or perhaps Gothic Revival? – church of 1810 is inscribed:

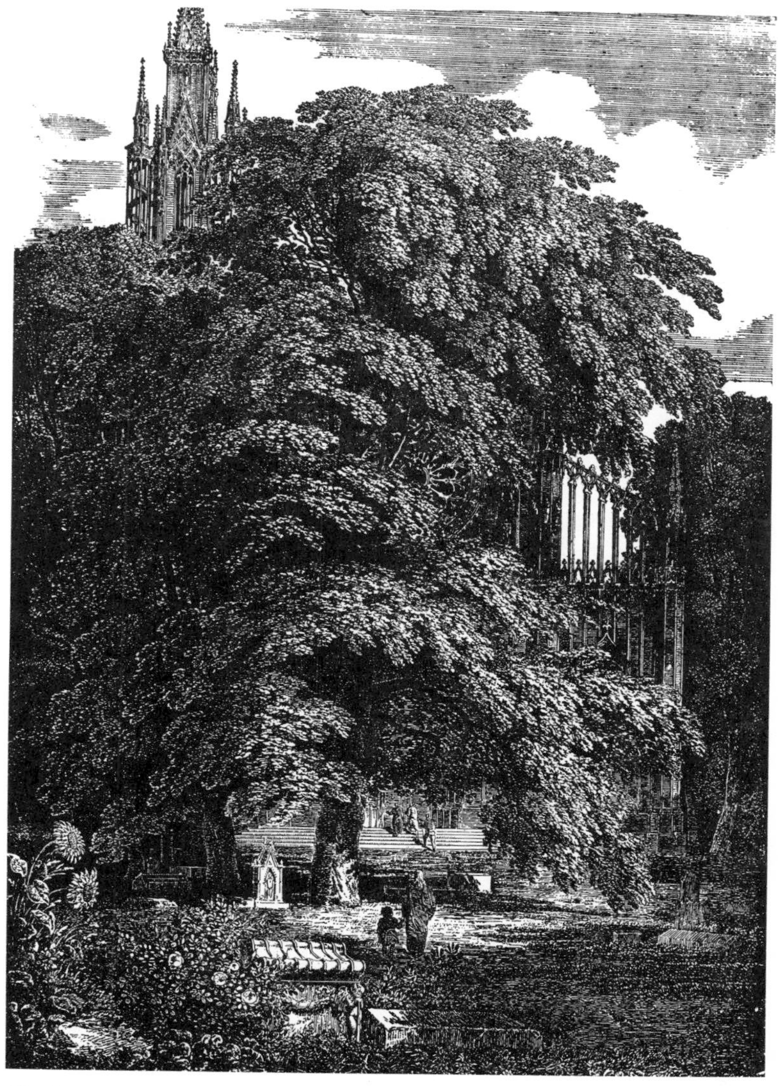

88. *The Church among Trees*, 1810. Karl Friedrich Schinkel

'An attempt to express the sweet yearning melancholy with which the heart is filled by the tones of a religious service resounding from a church' [88]. He also painted imaginary Gothic cathedrals with soaring lacy traceries and spires of an insubstantial delicacy, which

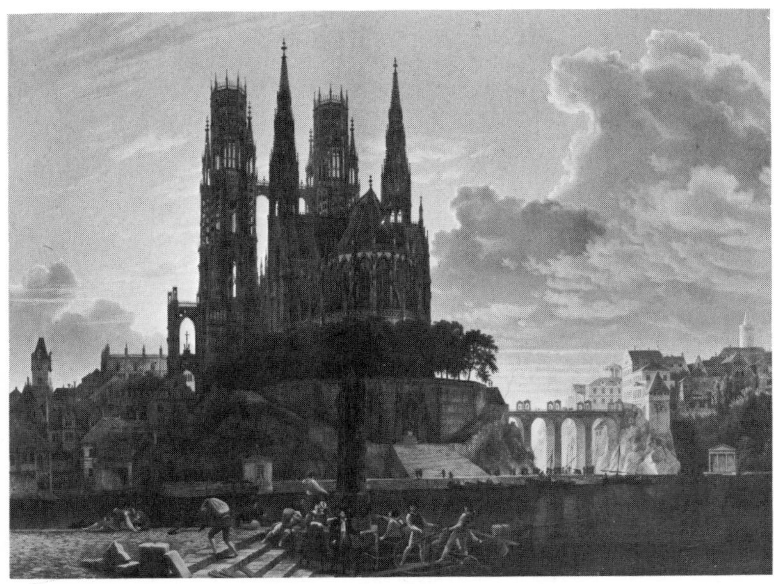

89. *Gothic Cathedral*, 1813. Karl Friedrich Schinkel

had seldom, if ever, been achieved in the Middle Ages [89]. But he stressed the connection between music and architecture most obviously in the painted decorations (now destroyed) of his great Alte Museum in Berlin. Still more significantly, round the doorway of his gaunt School of Architecture in Berlin – the almost 'styleless' Bau Akademie which is perhaps his most profoundly considered answer to the question *In welchem Style sollen wir bauen?* – he placed reliefs of Orpheus charming stones, and Amphion building Thebes with his lyre, a myth mentioned by both Schelling and Goethe when discussing 'frozen music'.

Although Schinkel employed various period styles, a remarkable consistency is felt throughout his work. From his master Gilly he acquired an understanding of the architecture of mass and geometrical form which may partly explain his precocious enthusiasm for the solid clean-lined Romanesque churches of Southern Italy, as well as his disdain for the Baroque and Rococo.[69] But he also showed from early in his career a love of such 'infinitely rich and daring' Gothic buildings as the cathedrals of Vienna and Prague.[70] 'Gothic architecture affects us by its spirit. It is daring to achieve so much with small means,' he wrote in 1810. 'Gothic buildings refuse meaningless pomp; all is deduced from an idea; hence its character of the necessary, grave, dignified and sublime.' On the other hand, 'scale and solidity in its material masses' were for him the characteristics of Antique architecture.[71] And he seems often to have attempted to synthesize the two. To his work in medieval styles he gave an almost Neo-classical volumetric clarity – not only in his neo-Romanesque churches, but also in his imaginary Gothic cathedral, which he composed out of cylinders and cones in preparatory drawings. Conversely, his dramatic management of interpenetrating spaces inside even so austerely classical a building as the Altes Museum seems to derive from his experience of Gothic. 'His frequent application of columns behind columns, and partial openings in the wall beyond them, through which the eye catches a glimpse of architectural objects in the remoter distance' was noted in 1834 by an English critic.[72] He 'well merits the appellation of *Formendichter*, applied to him by his countryman Seidel, so poetical and picturesque is his composition', wrote the same anonymous admirer.[73]

None of Schinkel's contemporaries seems to have been as profoundly concerned as he was with architectonic – as distinct from stylistic – problems. Of his immediate followers, the most successful were those who developed his *Rundbogenstil*, notably Ludwig Persius who designed the Friedenskirche at Potsdam and so brilliantly exploited the poetic lakeside site [90]. But there were many in all

90. Friedenskirche, Potsdam, 1845–8. Ludwig Persius

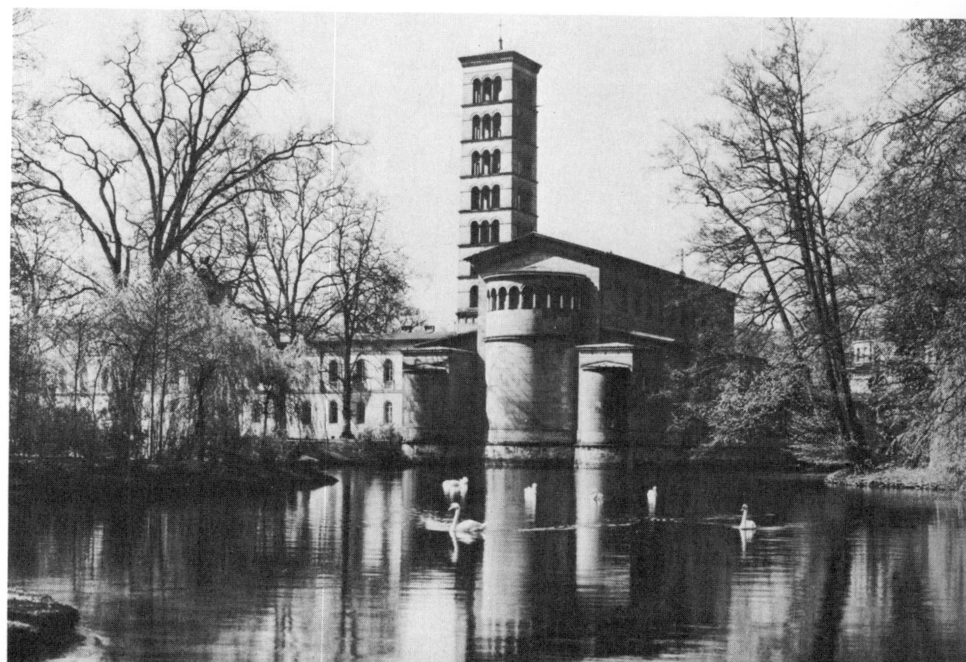

parts of Europe and also the United States who, without deserting the classical orders, moved away from Neo-classical simplicity, severity and structural rectitude. They not only made full use of the embellishments allowed by the Vitruvian rules, but gave them greater prominence to create richly modulated surfaces and profiles. Acroteria break the sky-line, cornices jut out boldly, relief carving is emphatic, columns and half-columns (rather than pilasters) are massed and extended with a kind of drum-roll rhythm. In London, John Nash gave to his Regent's Park terraces (so different from the quiet, smoothly faced eighteenth-century terraces of Bath) a spectacular Imperial Roman opulence and grandiloquence, which was

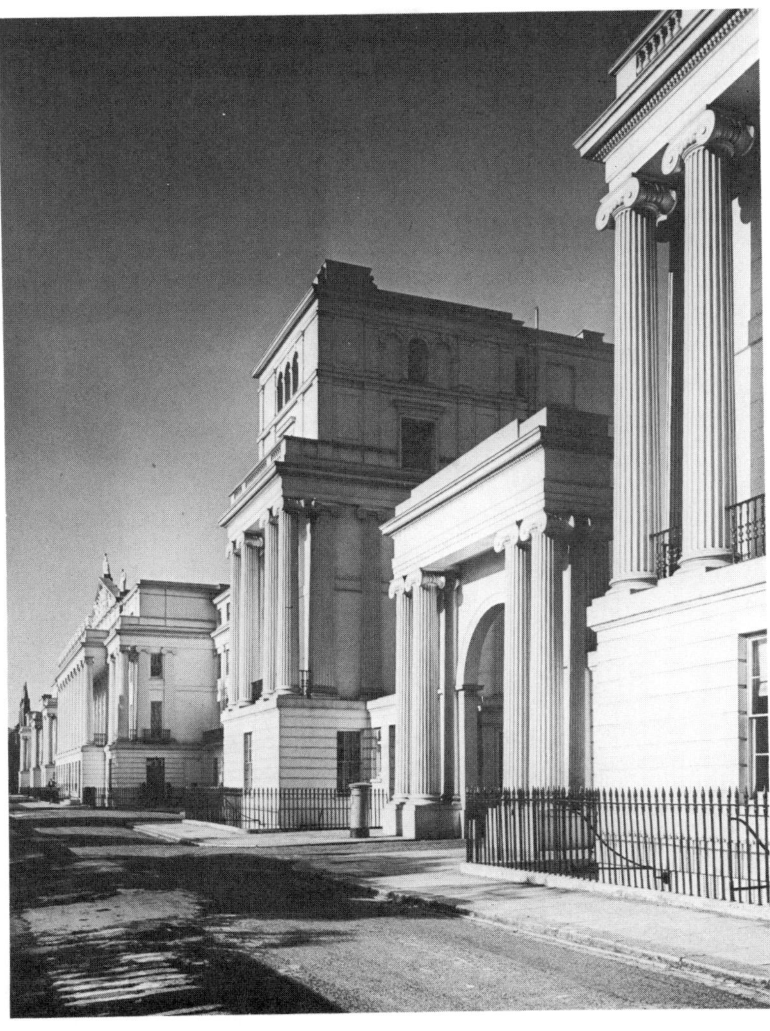

91. Cumberland Terrace, Regent's Park, London, 1826–7. John Nash and James Thomson

to remind Michelet of the paintings of John Martin [91]. Nowadays, Thomas Hamilton's project for the Royal High School in Edinburgh seems more strongly reminiscent of those images of the cataclysms of history which Martin himself called 'perspectives of feeling' [92]. Doric is here used with a new sense of drama, a new response to light and shade and movement, and those very 'accidents' of nature which Neo-classicists had discounted. The High School is, moreover, set not in a rigid urban framework of streets and houses, but on a rocky eminence among other Grecian buildings, with bare ground in between them – as ancient ruins appear on a site cleared of later constructions. The Doric National Monument

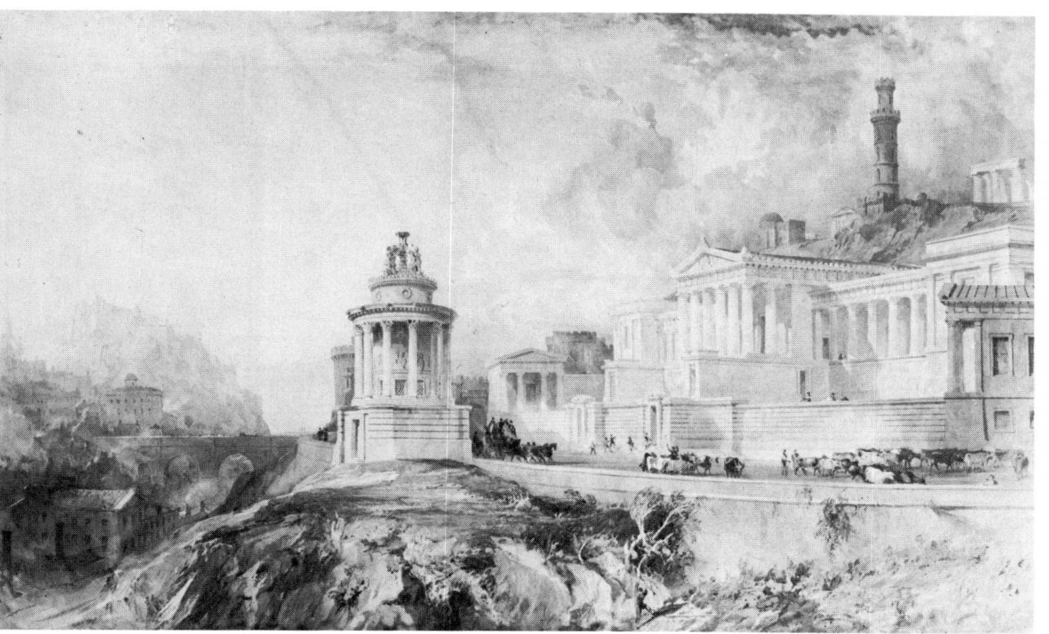

92. *The Royal High School, Edinburgh, c.* 1826–9. Thomas Hamilton

above – a precursor of Klenze's Walhalla above the Danube [87] – was never finished and so, quite fortuitously, actually looks like a ruin.

In the eighteenth century, architects learned rules of proportion and quarried details from Greek and Roman ruins. Now they tried to recreate their 'total' effect, following the writers who had gradually come to regard ruins as objects beautiful in themselves as well as sad relics of departed worth. Chateaubriand enthused over the lichens, mosses and creepers growing on the ruins of Greece and uniting art with nature. Enhanced by the passage of time, ruins spoke to the imagination. 'Modern buildings say nothing, but ruins speak,' wrote Benjamin Constant in 1808. Stendhal went further to declare that the Colosseum was more beautiful in his day than it had ever been. 'These fragments of wall darkened by time have on the soul the effect of the music of Cimarosa,' he wrote.[74]

Such emotions could not be aroused by the picturesque artificial ruins planted in so many English-style parks, in the eighteenth century. The vogue for these follies decreased as the cult of the genuine fragment of the past – emblem of transience and permanence, the fall of empires and the survival of art, mortality and immortality – grew more intense. Architects now designed complete buildings made up of Antique elements, which seem to demand that they should be notionally separated from one another and reconstructed in the spectator's imagination. Pasquale Poccianti's Cisternone of 1829–42 in Leghorn, for example, consists of the apse of a Roman bath placed behind a Tuscan colonnade, with plain blocks on either side, composing such a group of fragments of buildings of different periods and purposes as might be found on an ancient site.[75] In Munich, Klenze's Propyläen similarly combines elements in a

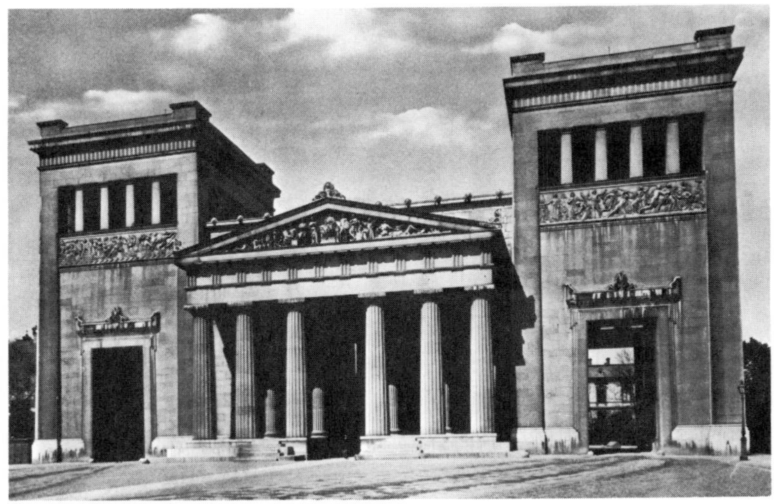

93. The Propyläen, Munich, 1848–60. Leo von Klenze

wholly unprecedented and very dramatic way [93]. In Glasgow, Alexander Thomson designed extraordinary churches, which are asymmetrical aggregates of Greek units, put together with highly developed sensitivity for the pictorial quality of the whole, and dominating their drab surroundings like ruins towering over subsequent layers of history.

But however expertly they were manipulated, the classical styles were rarely able to answer Romantic demands for an architecture to appeal to the heart. 'Do you seriously imagine, reader, that any living soul in London likes triglyphs? – or gets any hearty enjoyment out of pediments?' Ruskin fiercely demanded in 1851.[76] The noble simplicity and quiet grandeur of Greek architecture left him cold. It was quite simply monotonous, and he, too, resorted to a musical analogy, claiming that 'the true relations of monotony and change may be most simply understood by observing them in music'. That 'which is altogether monotonous is a dark and dead architecture', he declared. The vital principle of Gothic was love of change:

> It is that strange *disquietude* of the Gothic spirit that is its greatness; that restlessness of the dreaming mind, that wanders hither and thither among the niches, and flickers feverishly around the pinnacles, and frets and fades in labyrinthine knots and shadows along wall and roof, and yet is not satisfied, nor shall be satisfied. The Greek could stay in his triglyph furrow, and be at peace; but the work of the Gothic art is fretwork still, and it can neither rest in nor from its labour, but must pass on sleeplessly, until its love of change shall be pacified for ever in the change that must come alike to those that wake and them that sleep.[77]

4. *The Last Enchantments of the Middle Age*

Nineteenth-century attitudes to Gothic architecture veered between the wildest extremes of hostility and admiration, while interpretations ranged from the mechanical to the organic and eventually the transcendental. To some it was, above all, natural, recalling forests with arching branches of trees: to others it was a triumph of engineering and human ingenuity. It could be fantastic, appealing to a taste for grotesques: it was also profoundly symbolical, composed of elements every one of which, from soaring spire to leering gargoyle, had a sacramental religious significance. Some Roman Catholics saw in Gothic churches the most sublime artistic expression of Christianity. To many Protestants, as to agnostics and atheists, the same buildings evoked the darkness of medieval superstition. And Germans, Englishmen and Frenchmen all claimed Gothic to have been *par excellence* their 'national' style, while others in Europe and the United States held that it was the only valid universal architectural style evolved since Antiquity, and thus the one in which men of the nineteenth century 'should build'. But it was also seen as a European derivation from Islamic architecture and as a debasement of Roman architecture. Gothic was both praised and condemned as a manifestation of artistic liberty and of the subjection of the artist to the Church, as the expression of political absolutism, constitutional monarchy, republicanism and anarchy.

Gothic was not, of course, a discovery or even a rediscovery of the Romantics. The style seems never, in fact, to have lacked practitioners from the day when the apse of Saint-Denis Abbey was completed in 1144 to our own time (masons are still at work on the Gothic Cathedral in Washington, D.C.). In all discussions of Western architecture from the Renaissance onwards, it has been a point of reference – as an example of degradation or a standard of excellence with which buildings in other styles could be compared. And despite the fulminations of classically inspired theorists, Gothic churches continued to attract interest and admiration (sometimes of a rather unwilling kind) throughout the seventeenth and eighteenth centuries. The same could be said of medieval paintings, illuminated manuscripts, sculpture and metalwork. Nor was the literature of the Middle Ages (Dante, Chaucer, Froissart, Thomas à Kempis) ever entirely forgotten. There may have been few avid collectors and students of medieval art before the end of the eighteenth century, and their motives may have been mixed: but those who regarded the Middle Ages simply as 'a long interval of Ignorance' (the phrase is d'Alembert's) comprised an equally small, if more articulate, group.[1]

In the course of the eighteenth century, especially the second half, interest in medieval art and literature quickened. Accounts of nearly all the major cathedrals were published, usually by local antiquaries, and paintings and prints of many were diffused. Gradually an aesthetic of Gothic architecture developed. 'When an architect examines a Gothic structure by Grecian rules, he finds nothing but deformity,' Richard Hurd wrote in 1762. 'But the Gothic architecture has its own rules, by which, when it comes to be examined, it seems to have merits as well as the Grecian.'[2] Similarly, in *Von deutscher Baukunst* (1772–3), the young Goethe compared Gothic favourably with the *goût grec*, then at the height of fashion in France, and in Strasbourg Cathedral he discovered 'the deepest feelings of truth and beauty of proportion, sprung from a plain and vigorous German soul, alive on the confined, dark, priest-ridden stage of the Middle Ages'. Its tower was 'a lofty, wide-spreading tree of God, declaring with a thousand branches, a million twigs, and with leaves as numerous as the sands of the sea, the glory of the Lord, its Master'.[3]

The natural analogy was taken up by Chateaubriand in *Génie du Christianisme* (1802), with a new feeling for the beauty and impenetrable mystery of nature. But in place of Goethe's image of the single free-standing tree, he likened Gothic churches with their many carved leaves, clustered arboreal columns, cool lofty vaults, shady sanctuaries, dark aisles, secret passages and low doorways to the labyrinths of a forest.[4] In the course of thirty years much had happened to change attitudes to the Middle Ages – so much, indeed, that Goethe later renounced his youthful enthusiasm. Gothic buildings had begun to provide appropriately menacing and thrillingly gloomy settings for tales of terror, the 'horrid' novels Jane Austen was to satirize in *Northanger Abbey*. And although most of these books had a markedly anti-Catholic tendency, to Chateaubriand they suggested a religious sense which persisted even '*dans ce siècle incrédule*'. Whereas Goethe had described Strasbourg Cathedral towering above the *Pfaffenschauplatz medii aevi*, Chateaubriand was as much attracted by the foundation of religious ideals from which it rose. 'You cannot go into a Gothic church without experiencing a kind of thrill and some apprehension of the Divine,' he wrote. Looking across the gulf created by the Enlightenment and the Revolution, he saw in Gothic churches manifestations of the genius of Christendom and of '*l'ancienne France*'. It was, however, to the German Romantics – notably the Schlegel brothers and Johann Joseph von Görres – that Mme de Staël ascribed an 'entirely new' religious interpretation of medieval architecture.[5] 'We will quarrel with no man for his predilection either for the Grecian or the Gothic,' August Wilhelm Schlegel remarked in 1808. But in the latter he found an expression of the 'sublime and beneficient religion' which 'regenerated the ancient world from its state of exhaustion and debasement'. It represented an endeavour to reconcile the sensual with the spiritual, so that the impressions of the senses were hallowed by mysterious connection with higher things, and the 'forebodings or indescribable intuitions of infinity' of the soul expressed in 'types and symbols borrowed from the visible world'.[6]

The monuments of ancient Greece were rarely denigrated by the Romantics (even Ruskin paid lip-service to the Parthenon)[7] but, almost as if by sleight of hand, their merits were turned to their disadvantage. Greek architecture was rational, ordered, serene, self-sufficient, finite, a symbol of man's understanding. But, 'Grecian architecture is a thing,' Coleridge remarked; 'the Gothic is an idea.'[8] For him, Gothic architecture was 'infinity made imaginable' and he defined the infinite as that which 'is not vastness, nor immensity, nor perfection, but whatever cannot be circumscribed within the limits of actual sensuous being'.[9] Thus, Gothic was perpetually in a state of becoming, like Romantic poetry, aspiring to ideals which could never be realized in this world. And it was this sense of perpetual aspiration, of ever reaching up to God, that Schinkel stressed in his paintings of Gothic cathedrals [89]. Gothic was also a product of North European soil, like the trees of the German forests: and in his lithograph of a church surrounded by oaks Schinkel may have been alluding to this too – to its partaking in some sense in the processes of natural growth [88].

Paintings of Gothic churches often bring the organic simile to mind, but with inferences of a diversity characteristic of Romantic symbolism. Caspar David Friedrich seems to have contrasted the (to him) dead Catholic faith of ruined monasteries with the living religion of nature (or Protestantism) represented by the trees growing round them, with branches echoing Gothic arches.[10] In *The Cathedral in Winter* by his follower Ferdinand Oehme, on the other hand, candles on the high altar shed a kindly light which radiates out to the cloister where rose bushes sprout like suckers around the boles of tall columns [94]. And the devoutly Anglican Constable

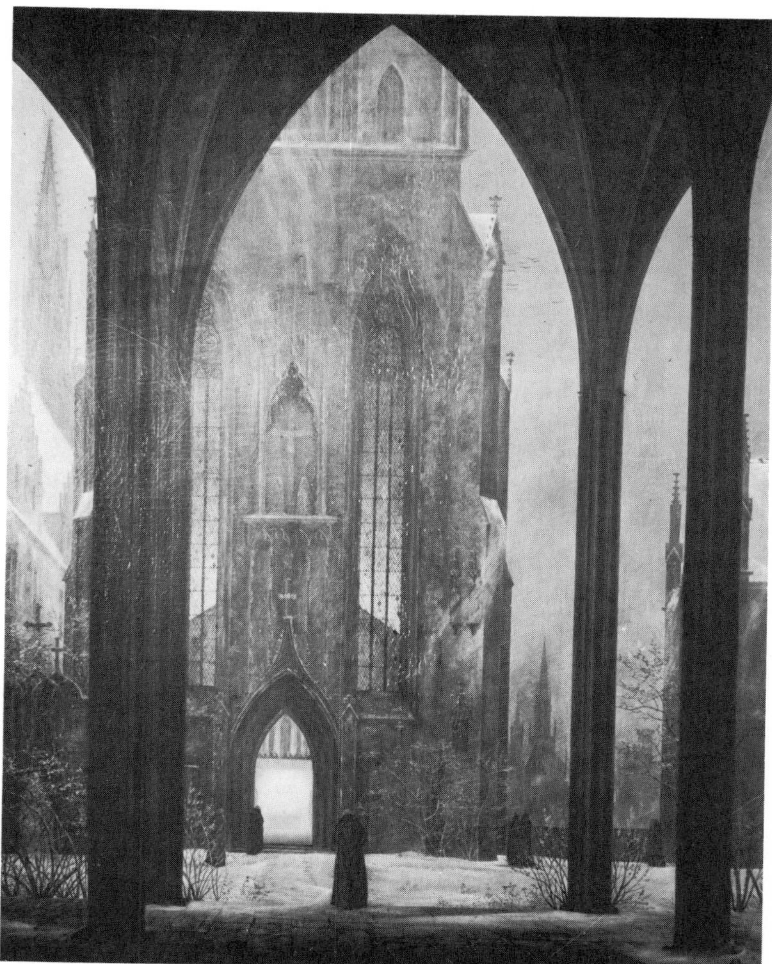

94. *The Cathedral in Winter*, 1821. E. F. Oehme

suggests perfect harmony between the spire and pinnacles of Salisbury Cathedral and the delicate tracery of trees that frames one of his views of it.[11] A similar natural metaphor is implied, whether intentionally or not, by Corot in his picture of Chartres Cathedral, with two trees reflecting the asymmetry of the western towers.[12]

But the idea of natural growth also implies that of organic decay. Hence a new attitude to medieval ruins which so often induced the melancholy mood, hovering between recollection and hope, that characterizes so much Romantic poetry. According to A. W. Schlegel, melancholy was a concomitant of Christianity: 'Such a religion must waken the vague foreboding, which slumbers in every feeling heart, into a distinct consciousness that the happiness for which we are here striving is unattainable; that no external object can ever entirely fill our souls; and that all earthly enjoyment is but

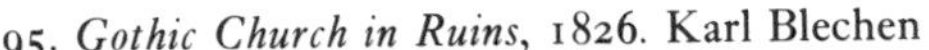

95. *Gothic Church in Ruins*, 1826. Karl Blechen

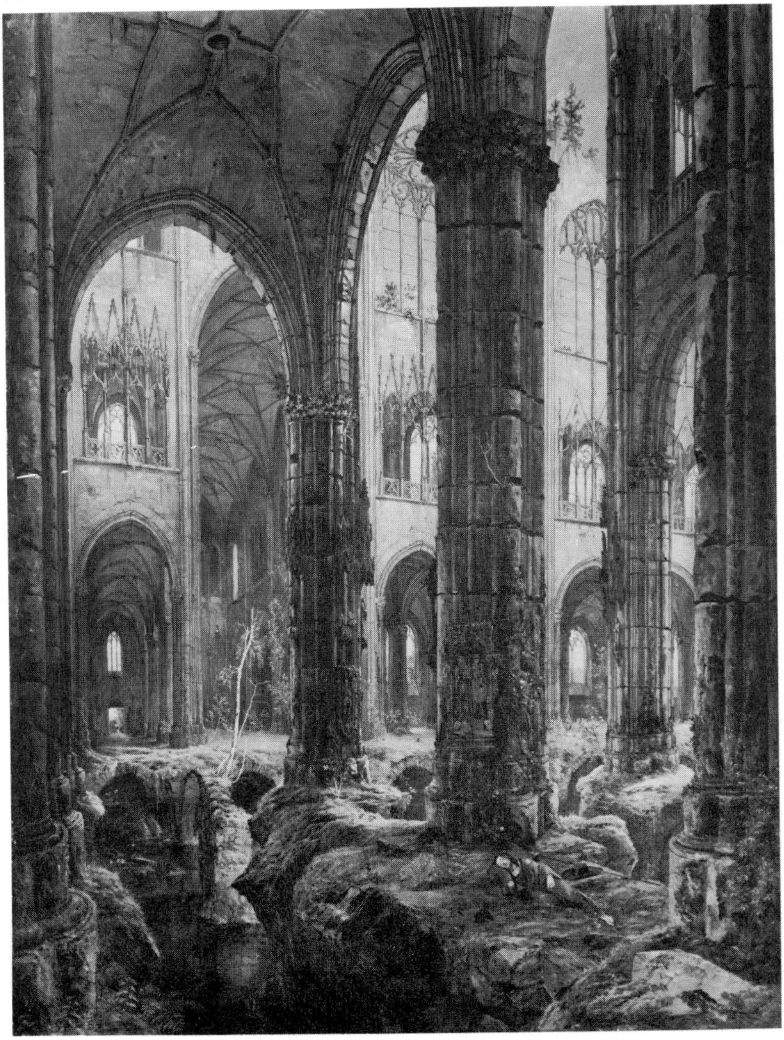

a fleeting and momentary illusion.'[13] Something of this mood is caught by Blechen's strange vision of a vast ruined church with a pilgrim – the Romantic 'Wanderer' on earth – asleep on its grass-grown floor [95]. Here Gothic is reverting to its natural state, as nature reclaims what man has tried to control and tame.

Blechen's picture also conveys a very different sense of mystery inspired by Gothic churches. Glimpses through the floor to the dark crypts below recall Victor Hugo's remark that beneath every cathedral there is another, 'low, dark, mysterious, blind and dumb':

> The vaults of an edifice forms another edifice, where one descends instead of climbing, and in which the underground stories are ranged beneath the superstructure of the monument, like those inverted forests and mountains which are seen in the reflecting water of a lake below the forests and mountains on its border.[14]

Hugo was less concerned with transcendental interpretations of Gothic than with its multifariousness, its irrationality, its dramatic contrasts of splendour and squalor, the beautiful and the grotesque. He was enthralled by the sinister aspects of the Middle Ages, the superstition and the cruelty, which he conveyed so brilliantly in his own drawings of menacing Gothic castles and towers, for in medieval architecture he found a reflection of his vision of a chaotic universe:

> *une Babel aux abords encombrés*
> *De donjons, de beffrois, de flèches élancées,*
> *D'édifices construits pour toutes les pensées;*
> *De génie et de pierre énorme entassement;*
> *Vaste amas . . .**[15]

But a church interior, especially a crypt, could also be, and often was, regarded as a haven of peace from the tumult of the everyday world. This is certainly the impression given by the paintings which François-Marius Granet – a pupil of David and a friend of Ingres – began to exhibit in 1799. Their immediate success can hardly be associated with the vogue for tales of terror: there is not a hint of 'Gothic horror' even in his picture of a corpse laid out in the undercroft of a church, with a priest and acolyte reciting prayers [96]. And the piety of the *Génie du Christianisme* can be detected only in such later works as a view of the lower church of San Francesco

* 'a Babel surrounded by keeps, belfries, spires, by buildings erected for all beliefs; an enormous mass of spirit and stone; a vast pile . . .'

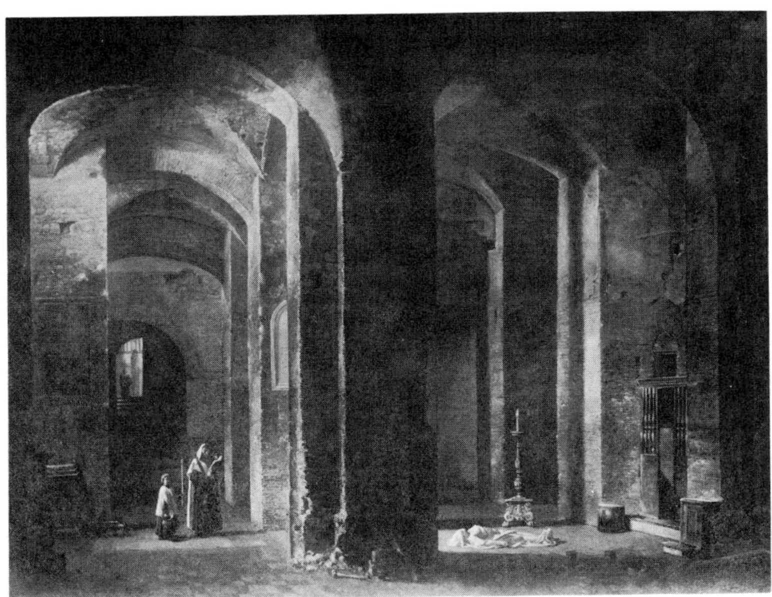

96. *Crypt of S. Martino dei Monti, Rome*, 1806. F.-M. Granet

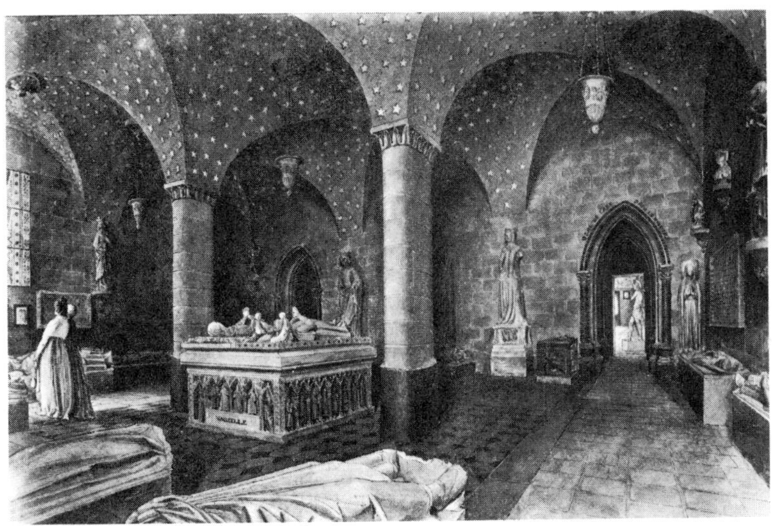

97. *Interior of the Musée des Monuments français*, *c.* 1815. J.-L. Vauzelle

at Assisi or a painting of a nun taking the veil (a spectacle which excited the indignation of Protestant travellers in Italy).[16] They probably reflected a widespread desire for quiet solitude, sometimes bordering on agoraphobia, after the events of the 1790s. That extraordinary Revolutionary creation the Musée des Monuments français may well have appealed partly for the same reason. Here, in the heart of a disturbed Paris, visitors could retreat into a still sanctuary of recumbent effigies, 'knights, ladies praying in dumb oratories' [97]. Its founder, Alexandre Lenoir, wrote that those who stood near the monument he had fabricated for Pierre Abélard and his beloved might believe they heard '*soupirs de tendresse et d'amour ... Héloise! Abélard! Abélard! Héloise!*'[17]

In England, also in the 1790s, Turner began to depict church interiors with less attention to the accuracy demanded by antiquaries than to their general effect and ambiance – the play of mass and void, beams of light cutting through the darkness of vaults and falling on details of carving and debris. The watercolour he made of the transept of Ewenny Priory in 1797 owes much to paintings by Rembrandt which he had recently seen, and to which a contemporary reviewer likened it.[18] Turner's attitude to medieval archi-

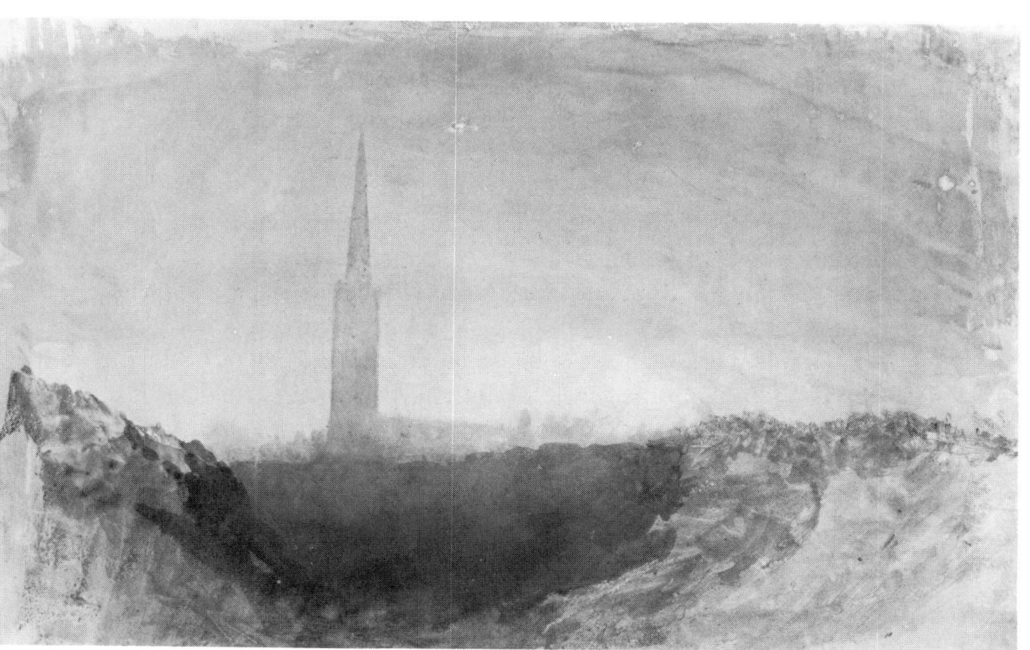

98. *A Church Steeple*, *c.* 1826. Turner

tecture, as to everything else, seems to have been purely pictorial. Yet there are few more powerful and memorable images of a spire pointing towards heaven than in his sketch of an East Anglian church [98]. Here is the Romantic 'Gothic idea' in its simplest and purest form.

The effect made on the Romantic soul by medieval architecture was much more easily and powerfully stimulated by paintings than by neo-Gothic buildings. Indeed, to Constable 'a new Gothic building' was an absurdity. 'The Gothic architecture, sculpture and painting, belong to peculiar ages,' he declared in 1836. 'We contemplate them with associations, many of which, however vague and dim, have a strong hold on our imaginations, and we feel indignant at the attempt to cheat us by any modern mimicry of their peculiarities.'[19] In 1837 Heine reported a conversation with a friend in front of Amiens Cathedral: 'He asked me why it is that we, today, are incapable of building such edifices. I answered him, "Dear Alphonse, the men of old times had convictions: we modern men have only opinions, and more than these are needed to raise cathedrals."'[20] The early nineteenth century had, indeed, produced an architecture of opinions.

Detailed study of the history of medieval buildings had fragmented the eighteenth-century notion of 'Gothic' into a multitude of chronological and regional styles – from Early Christian to English Late Perpendicular – opening the door to endless discussion about their respective merits and appropriateness for different purposes. But the opinions voiced were as often sectarian and nationalistic as aesthetic. Thus, Romanesque might be favoured by Protestants because it was untainted by memories of later medieval Catholicism, and by some of the more conservative German Catholics because it was free from the associations of liberal nationalism which clustered round Gothic. Hence the popularity of the *Rundbogenstil* in the Prussia of Friedrich Wilhelm IV and the Bavaria of Ludwig I.[21] The English equivalent, 'Lombardic', was commended for its economy, facility of execution, simplicity, durability and beauty (in that order).[22] In England and the United States, however, Gothic was generally preferred for places of Protestant worship simply because it was traditional – the style of the vast majority of Anglican cathedrals and parish churches, hallowed by the prayer and piety of many generations. The English-born but American-trained architect Richard Upjohn would consent to design Gothic churches only for Episcopalians: other denominations had to make do with the round-arched style. Here argument raged mainly around what George Gilbert Scott called 'the question of selection of a single variety of Pointed Architecture for modern use, and of which variety has the strongest claims to such selection' (he opted for English 'Decorated' of the early fourteenth century).[23] And yet, wherever an architect's choice fell, and whatever the reasons he advanced to justify it, he was liable to be criticized for building a mere sham. Constable spoke for many when he condemned the Gothic Revival as a 'vain endeavour to reanimate deceased art, in which the utmost that can be accomplished will be to reproduce a body without a soul'.[24] His words are a reminder that modern objections to nineteenth-century architecture and to the compulsive obtrusion of questions of style are as much a product of Romantic ideas as are the buildings themselves. In the eighteenth century it would never have occurred to anyone to question the principle of imitation in architecture – nor had buildings been expected to have souls.

Antiquarianism and Romanticism, demands for archaeological accuracy and for spontaneous artistic originality, for authenticity and above all sincerity, the claims of the letter and the spirit of Gothic, all clash in the nineteenth-century church. The architects of the numerous churches built in England during the first three decades of the century (mainly after 1815) evaded the conflict by assembling elements from medieval buildings or, sometimes, by merely dressing geometrically regular forms with neat, sparse Gothic details. These churches, which retain a certain eighteenth-century elegance attractive to modern eyes (St Peter's parish church in Brighton, by Charles Barry, for example), appalled serious-minded contemporaries, and none more so than A. W. N. Pugin, to whom they were burlesques of Gothic – 'showy worldly expedients, adapted only for those who live by splendid deception'.[25]

'The present age has no vernacular style of architecture,' a critic complained in 1839. 'Architecture is become a language. We learn a number of dead styles as we do a number of dead languages.'[26] But to Pugin, Gothic was as much a living language as the Latin of the Mass, and a Gothic church not merely an agent for arousing nostalgic memories of the pious Middle Ages but a statement of eternal truths which had been obscured by the Renaissance, the Protestant Reformation and, he later came to think, the Counter-Reformation as well. Brought up as a Protestant (his mother was an Irvingite), he began his career precociously by designing furniture in a slightly solidified version of the eighteenth-century 'Gothick taste'. His conversion to the Roman Church and to the true principles of Gothic architecture came simultaneously. With all the zeal of a convert, he set about the task of reclaiming the unregenerate in books which were inspired – so he proclaimed in the first of them in 1836 – 'by no other feelings but that of advancing the cause of truth over that of error'.[27] He felt acutely 'the fallen condition of the arts' and the need for 'sincerity'.

Pugin was exceptionally well informed about English medieval buildings, and he had begun to make drawings of them for his father when still a child. He was aware of the writings of French and German Romantics – of Chateaubriand, Montalembert and (if only indirectly) the Schlegels.[28] He seems also to have read eighteenth-century architectural theorists, from whom he derived his eminently rational 'two great rules ... 1st, that there should be no features about a building which are not necessary for convenience, construction, or propriety; 2nd, that all ornament should consist of enrichment of the essential construction of a building'.[29] His contention that these principles had been, and could be, carried out only in 'Pointed or Christian Architecture' was, however, original.

Accepting the generally held belief that Greek architecture derived from the post and lintel construction of a hut (the 'first principle' of Neo-classicists), he argued that it was 'essentially wooden' and therefore false. Gothic was the perfect expression of construction in stone, both true to its materials and natural in a new sense (the overworked analogies with forest glades being conveniently forgotten in his theory).[30] He thus freed honestly constructed Gothic Revival churches from the stigma of the sham and, in effect, from his own identification of Christian architecture with medieval Catholicism. By a shift in emphasis from styles to principles, from the integrity and imaginative faculty of the architect to the nature and potentialities of his media, Pugin provided an architectonic (and not merely picturesque) solution to the conflict between antiquarianism and Romanticism. He also provided a theory later used to justify functionalist practices which would have horrified him.

But Pugin was himself as much interested in ornament as in structure and the 'glorious' (a favourite word of his) impression made by a church as a setting for 'the most solemn rites of Christian worship' – with bejewelled chalices and monstrances, cloth-of-gold copes and chasubles gleaming through clouds of incense, and the solemn, moving music of Gregorian chant. The vestments and liturgical vessels made to his design and the coloured plates in his *Glossary of Ecclesiastical Ornament* (1844), his most substantial book, give as clear an indication of his aspirations as his churches. Of the twenty-five churches, all designed in five years, which he assembled in the engraved frontispiece to his *Apology for the Revival of Christian Architecture* (1843), few were completed according to his wishes and none entirely satisfied him [99]. 'I have never had the chance of producing a single fine ecclesiastical building, except

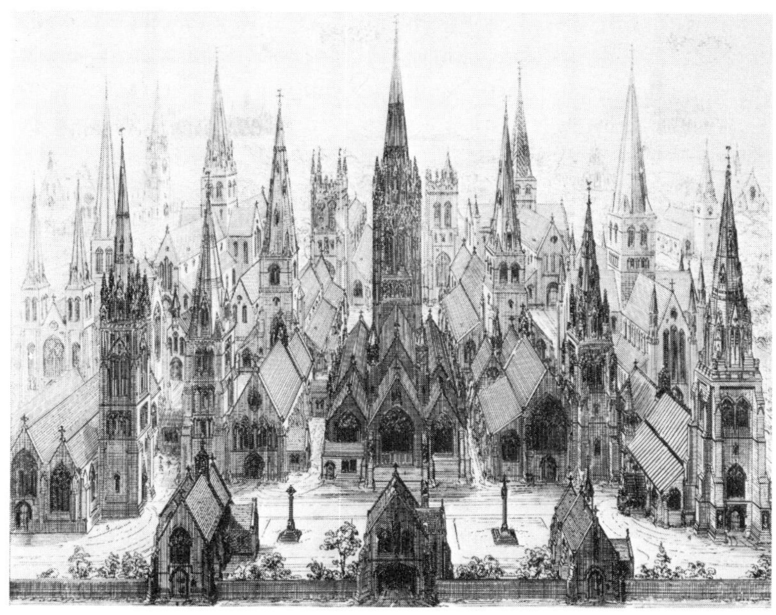

99. *The Present Revival of Christian Architecture*, 1843. Pugin

100. St Augustine's Church, Ramsgate, 1845–50. Pugin

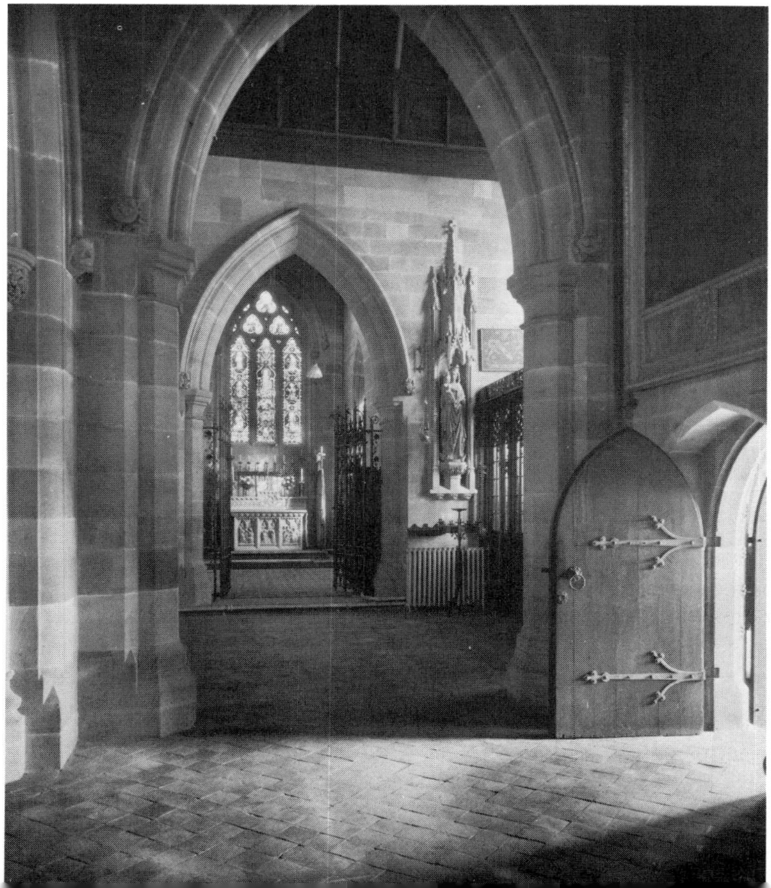

 my own church, where I am both paymaster and architect,' he wrote in 1850.[31] And this exception, St Augustine's, Ramsgate, is one of the most impressive churches of the century – a free essay in the fourteenth-century Gothic of East Kent, robustly built of local materials, richly textured and planned with a feeling for the mystery of warmly lit interior spaces [100]. Otherwise he was able to indulge his love for the intricacy and prodigality of medieval decoration only in secular buildings, most notably the House of Lords at Westminster [114].

After Pugin's early death, the battle for true principles was carried on in the second half of the century most auspiciously by the Anglican architects William Butterfield, William Burges and George Edmund Street, who made a more daring use of the Gothic language of architectural forms and more boldly exploited dramatic contrasts of mass and void, texture and colour. Sometimes, indeed, their churches bring to mind Coleridge's remark that 'the Gothic architecture impresses the beholder with a sense of self-annihilation, he becomes, as it were, a part of the work contemplated. An endless complexity and variety are united into one whole, the plan of which is not distinct from the execution. A Gothic Cathedral is the petrification of our religion.'[32]

In 1841 Pugin remarked that artists had begun to revive the principles of painting as he hoped to restore those of architecture. Friedrich Overbeck, 'that prince of Christian painters', he wrote, 'has raised up a school of mystical and religious artists who are fast putting to utter shame the natural and sensual school of art in which the modern followers of Paganism have so long degraded the representation of sacred personages and events.'[33] This movement had, in fact, begun thirty years earlier – before Pugin was born – when Overbeck, Franz Pforr and four other young artists established the Brotherhood of St Luke in Vienna. But there is a close affinity between their aims and his, as there is between the device they adopted in 1809 and the frontispiece to Pugin's *True Principles* of 1841 [101a and b] – both showing a religious artist at work in a room shut off from the everyday world, and both alluding to truth (the former in the W for *Wahrheit* on the keystone of the arch).

Franz Pforr's *Entry of Rudolf of Habsburg into Basle in 1273*, begun in Vienna in 1808 and completed in Rome two years later, is perhaps the first large picture of a medieval subject painted in a self-consciously archaic manner [102]. But the reasons for the choice of both subject-matter and style are complex. A childhood love for tales of chivalry – illustrated in his earliest drawings – had

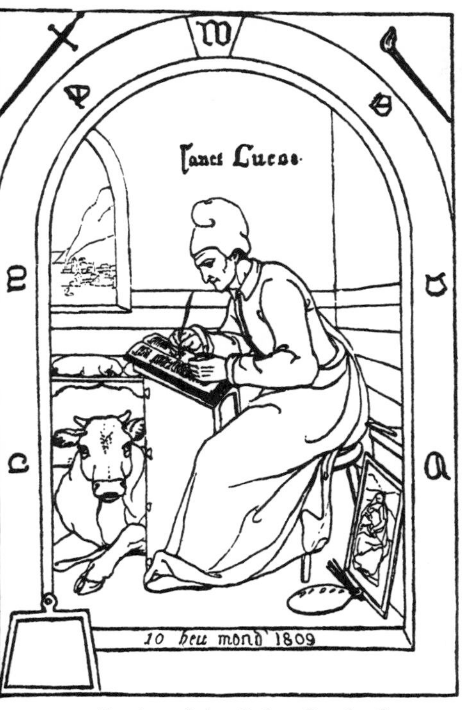

101a. Device of the *Lukas-Bund*, 1809. F. Overbeck

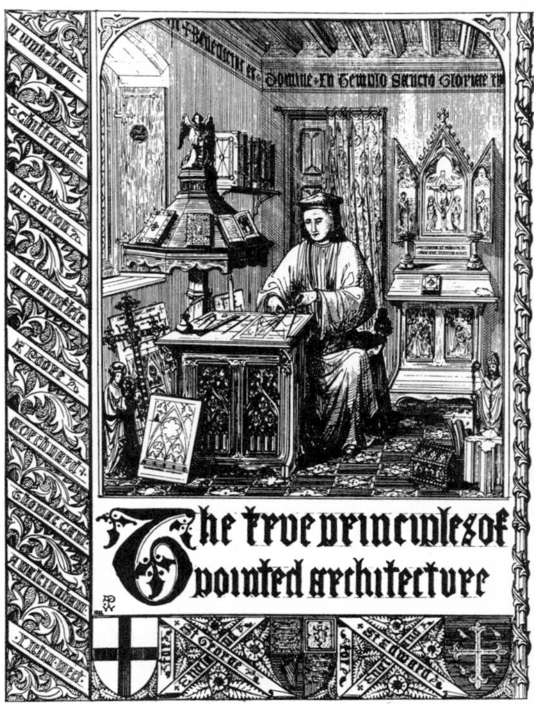

101b. Frontispiece to *The True Principles of Pointed or Christian Architecture*, 1841. Pugin

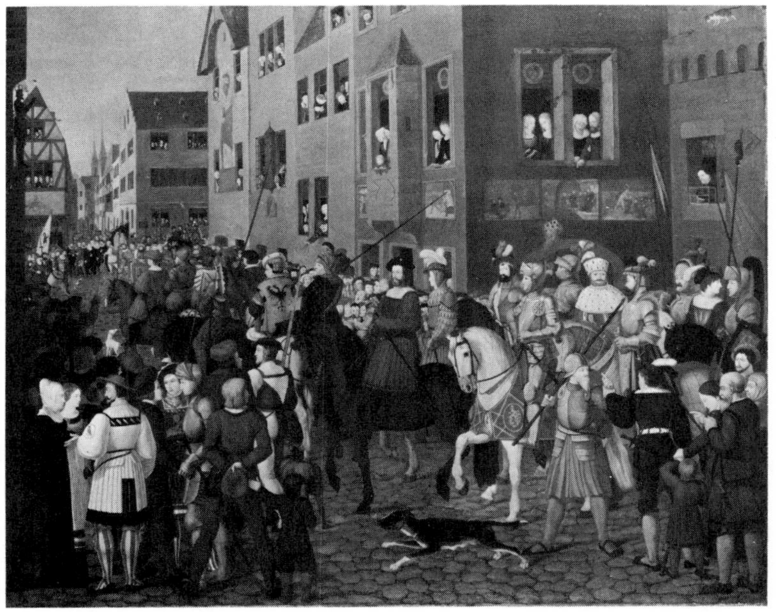

102. *The Entry of Rudolf of Habsburg into Basle, 1273*, 1808–10. Franz Pforr

 matured into a more sober passion. 'My inclination tends towards the Middle Ages when the dignity of man was still fully apparent,' Pforr wrote in 1810:

> It showed itself clearly and distinctly on the battlefield as well as in the council chamber, on the market place as in the family circle. The spirit of these times is so beautiful and so little used by artists. The fantastic is often interwoven with the real, seldom without a moral, and all is pervaded by a contemplative atmosphere which is so suitable for art.[34]

Whether he had developed this view independently, or under the influence of the Schlegels, Tieck or Chateaubriand, he had found in the Middle Ages a world far more appealing than that of Napoleonic Europe – and one which he could freely enter and inhabit.[35] Thus Overbeck portrayed him 'in a surrounding in which he would perhaps feel happiest' – in a vine-grown Gothic porch, with a virginal figure knitting as she reads and a medieval church beyond [103].

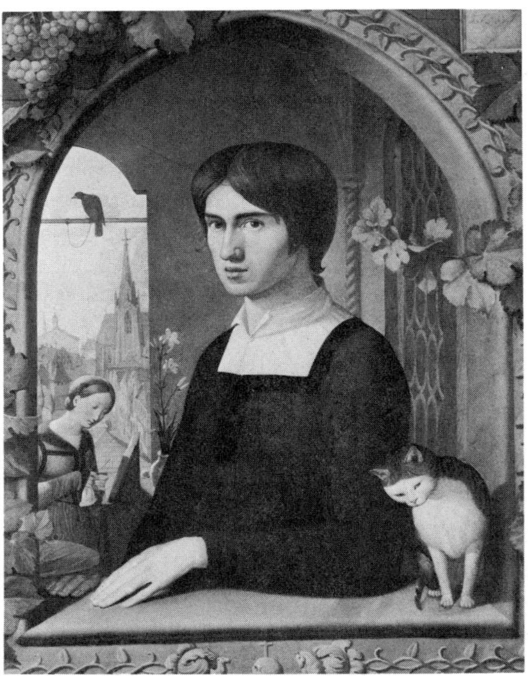

103. *Franz Pforr*, 1810. F. Overbeck.

It was probably Overbeck who played the dominant role in the stylistic development of the two artists, conditioned by religious (Protestant) and aesthetic (Neo-classical) beliefs.[36] Visiting the art gallery in Vienna, they were shocked by the sensuality of the generally admired works by Correggio, Titian and the seventeenth-century Bolognese masters, detecting 'a cold heart hiding behind daring brush-strokes and beautiful colours'.[37] 'Noble simplicity' (Pforr used Winckelmann's phrase) was apparent to them only in the paintings by Raphael, Perugino and, especially, the old German artists in whom Pforr found artistic inspiration, as well as details of costume, for the flattened perspective, stiffly posed figures and naïve brightness of clear colour of *The Entry of Rudolf of Habsburg into Basle* [102].

In fact Overbeck and Pforr simply re-phrased Neo-classical theory in Christian terms, demanding not merely purity but

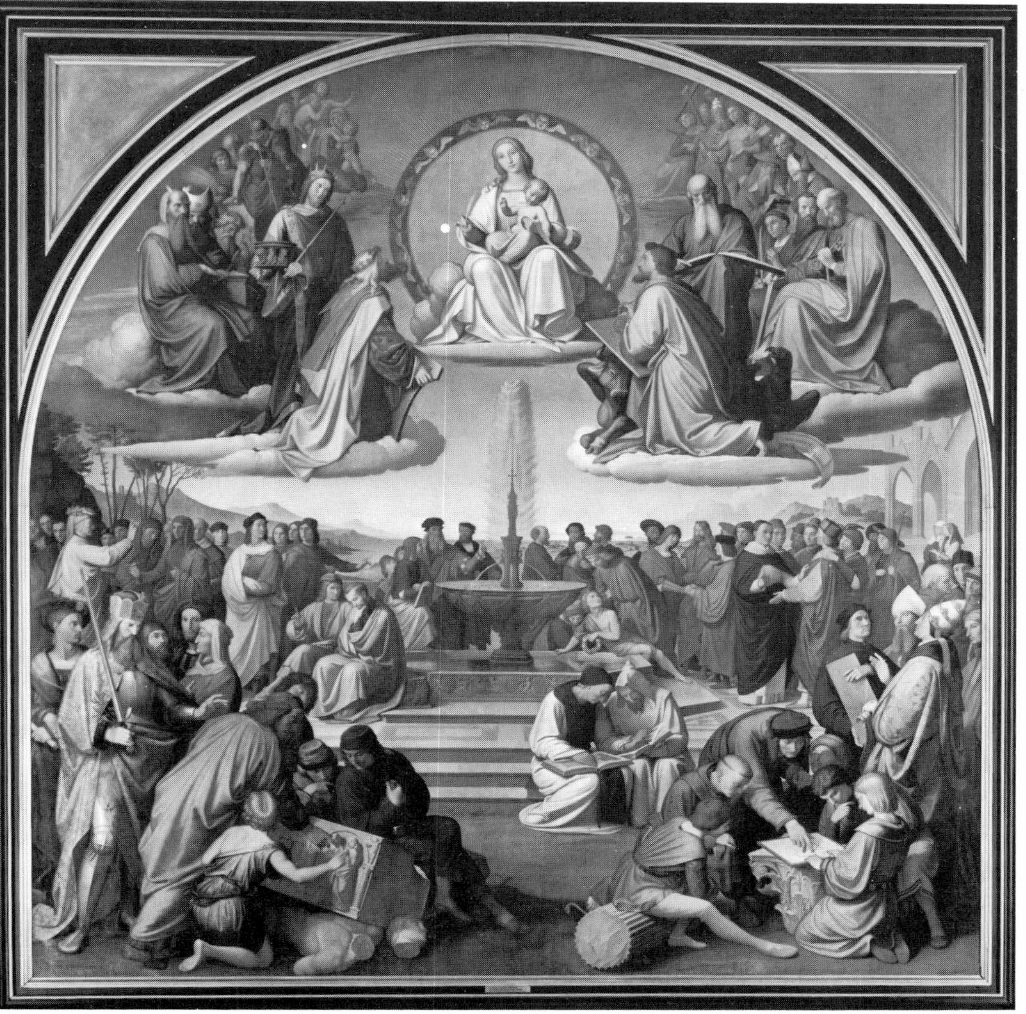

104. *The Triumph of Religion in the Arts*, 1831–40. F. Overbeck

chastity, the simplicity of child-like faith, meditative tranquillity, devoutness, and subjects which expressed Christian truth and morality. With the Schlegels they believed that painting was essentially Christian and spiritual, sculpture pagan and physical. By returning to the styles of the fifteenth and early sixteenth centuries, they hoped to revive the art of painting in its most highly developed form before, as they believed, artists had been corrupted by admiration for Antique marbles. This radical revision of the history of art according to Vasari, and all subsequent writers, is the message of Overbeck's *Triumph of Religion in the Arts* [104], where Antiquity, represented by a smashed statue and an overturned Corinthian column, is ignored by a throng of artists including Dürer, Lucas van Leyden, Memling, Fra Angelico and even Brunelleschi, Mantegna and Raphael – though Nicola Pisano studies the palaeo-Christian sarcophagus which enables him to create a 'superior' art of sculpture. In the background there is a symbolically unfinished Gothic cathedral. Long before he began this vast work in 1831, Overbeck had been converted to the Roman Church and become the centre of the predominantly Catholic-convert group of German artists in Rome nicknamed the Nazarenes (on account of their long hair and beards). But he retained a kind of Protestant horror of paganism, post-Raphaelite art and, it seems, post-Reformation Catholicism, which gave his work an inter-denominational appeal.[38] (Another version of *The Triumph of Religion in the Arts* was commissioned for the Orthodox Alexander II of Russia, and a large preliminary drawing was bought by the Prince Consort as a Christmas present for Queen Victoria.)

Overbeck and Pforr were but the first of many painters who sought to revive styles which we call Early Renaissance but they regarded as late medieval.[39] Even before he had come into direct contact with the Nazarenes, Julius Schnorr von Carolsfeld painted his *Visitation* with a delicacy and slightly self-conscious *gaucherie* inspired by Italo-Flemish work of the fifteenth century [105]. In the 1820s Italian painters and sculptors began to revive the late *quattrocento* styles which were to be exploited by the so-called *Puristi* in the next two decades.[40] French artists seeking to recapture the pristine purity of Christian art included Hippolyte Flandrin, a pupil of Ingres who had carefully studied the earlier Italian masters.[41] Victor Orsel, founder of the 'mystical' school of Lyon, composed his allegory *Good and Evil* in the form of a stained-glass window, incorporating little scenes of virtuous and vicious knights in the style of *quattrocento* predella panels [106].

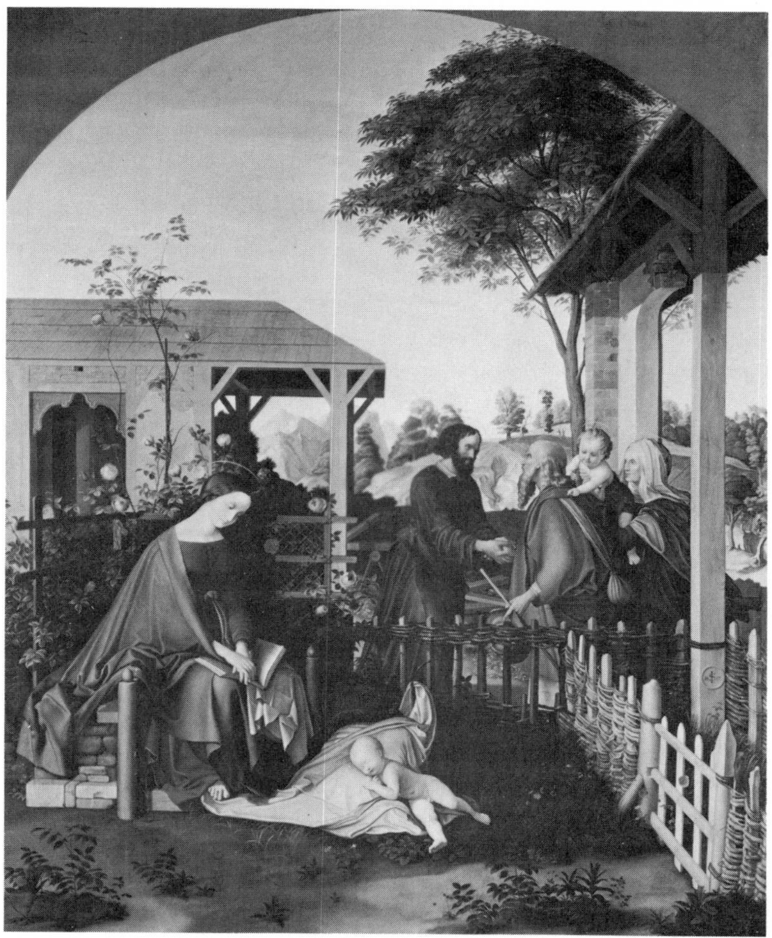

105. *The Family of St John the Baptist Visiting the Holy Family*, 1817. J. Schnorr von Carolsfeld

British artists were urged by Lord Lindsay to draw inspiration from 'Christianity and the Romano-Teutonic tradition', to seek out 'neglected relics of an earlier, a simpler, and a more believing age – talk to the spirit that dwells within them in its own universal language, and listen reverently for a reply'.[42] In creating an art to rival that of the fifteenth century, 'Germany has done much already – England may do much, possibly more', he wrote in 1848. But it may have been merely a coincidence that in September of the same year the Pre-Raphaelite Brotherhood was founded in London by

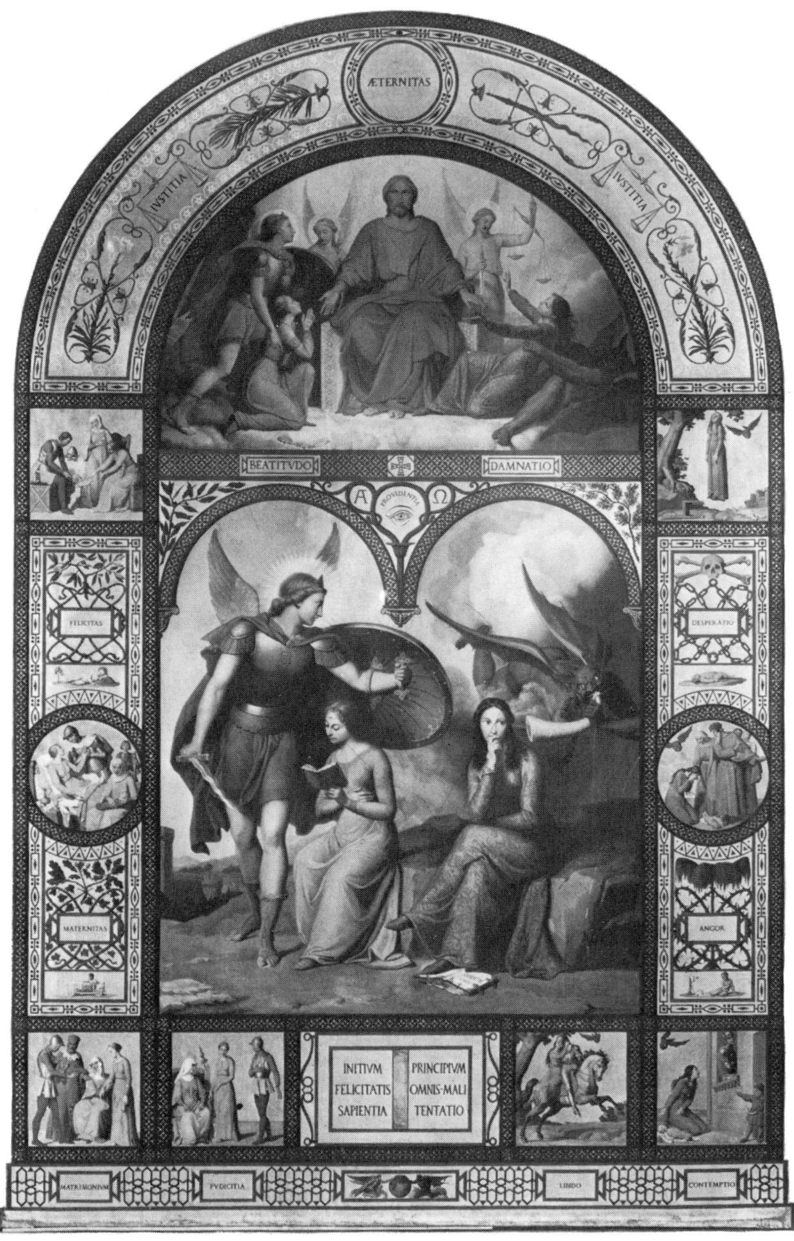

106. *Good and Evil*, 1823–32. Victor Orsel

William Holman Hunt, Dante Gabriel Rossetti, John Everett Millais and four other painters. They were, so they later recorded, motivated not by admiration for the early painters so much as hostility towards 'the stereotyped tricks of the decadent schools' and 'all that was conventional in contemporary art'.[43] The young Rossetti even 'denounced the science' of perspective, 'and objected strongly to each result of its application, declaring that what it proved to be wrong was obviously better'. This is borne out by his first exhibited painting *The Girlhood of the Virgin* with its naïvely rendered naturalistic detail.[44] Here, too, medievalism is limited to furnishings: the figures, especially that of Joachim, are curiously modern.

Initially, the Pre-Raphaelites were less concerned than the Nazarenes with Christian art. Of the first three paintings they exhibited in 1849 only Rossetti's was of a religious subject. Millais's contribution was *Isabella*, illustrating a story from Bocaccio as seen in the Romantic mirror of Keats's poem, rendered with a naïveté of sharp colour contrasts, flat modelling and absence of aerial perspective which heightens the psychological tension.[45] Hunt showed *Rienzi vowing to obtain justice for the death of his young brother, slain in a skirmish between the Colonna and Orsini factions* [107]. He took the subject (to which Wagner had already devoted an opera) from a novel by Lord Lytton, but with a characteristically deeper purpose

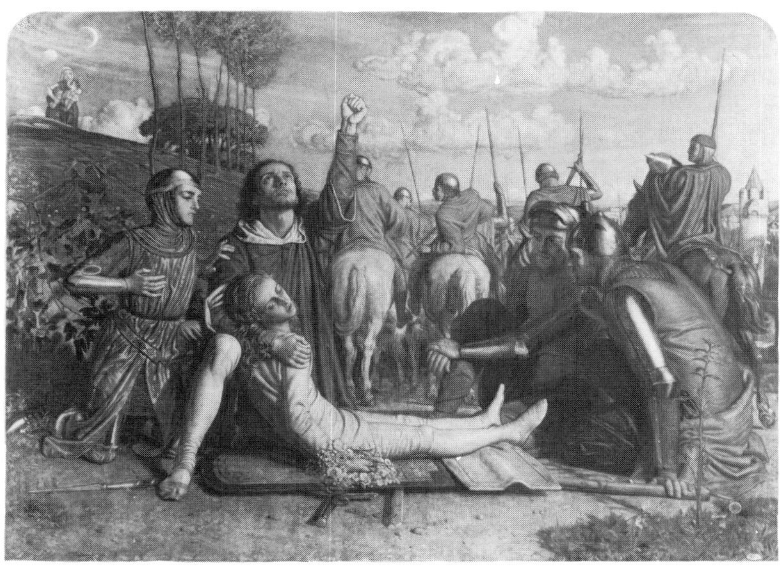

107. *Rienzi Vowing to Obtain Justice*, 1849. W. Holman Hunt

than that of merely illustrating a colourful story. 'Like most young men I was stirred by the spirit of freedom of the passing revolutionary time,' he recorded. 'The appeal to heaven against tyranny exercised over the poor and helpless seemed well fitted for pictorial treatment. "How long, O Lord!" many bleeding souls were crying at that time.' His picture and that by Millais are in fact related to a long secular tradition, or rather two interwoven traditions, of political and poetic medievalism – 'lost causes and the last enchantments of the Middle Age' – which had been revised rather than revived by the Romantics.

Ever since the Middle Ages, tales of chivalry, of valiant knights and fair ladies, battles and tourneys, had maintained an extraordinary popularity little affected by classical theories of literature. They charmed adults as well as children at all levels of society, from the 'common people of England', who thrilled to the ballad of *Chevy-Chase*, and French villagers, who bought from pedlars the romances of the *Bibliothèque Bleue*, to the sophisticated, who continued to read *The Faerie Queene* or Tasso's *Gerusalemme Liberata*.[46] But at the higher cultural level the vision of the age of chivalry was kept bright mainly by two works of affectionate mockery, *Orlando Furioso* and *Don Quixote*, both of which had provided subjects for artists throughout the eighteenth century. There can, indeed, be little doubt that Ariosto and Cervantes were largely responsible for the whimsical note evident in so much Gothicry, even though more serious attitudes to the Middle Ages may often be detected behind the *papier mâché* tracery.[47]

The Middle Ages were naturally attractive to the descendants of old families, and not least to the crowned heads of Europe. The age of chivalry might, on the other hand, be regarded as one of aristocratic rather than absolutist rule. This was the view cherished in France by members of the *noblesse de l'épée*, whose privileges had been curtailed by Louis XIV and whose power had been eroded by the parvenu *noblesse de la robe*.[48] It was rather different in England, where Whig oligarchs saw the barons of the Middle Ages as champions of British liberty – and those whose claims to Norman descent were tenuous (Horace Walpole, for instance) could find spiritual ancestors in the opponents of King John.[49] But the motives of creators of Gothic Revival buildings were often mixed. Fonthill [108] is a case in point, envisaged in 1777–8 as a faery palace, built as an ivory tower from which William Beckford could look down on the society which had ostracized him (begun 1796, completed 1807, toppled down 1825), and encrusted with heraldry as a reminder that the owner 'has the very singular distinction of an immediate and lineal descent from all those barons (of whom any issue are remaining), who extorted, at the point of their swords, from a reluctant and tyrannical sovereign, the Magna Charta, that great

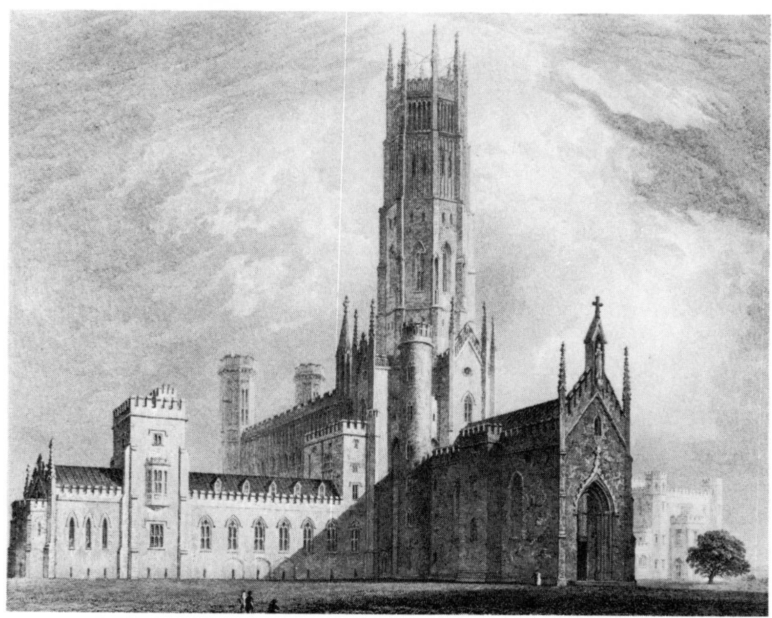

108. *View of Fonthill Abbey*, 1823. After John Martin

foundation of our liberties'.[50] A Gothic Revival building also became, in the course of the eighteenth century, an all but essential – architecturally natural – feature of the English landscape-garden, with which it was exported to France and to Germany where it promptly lost its oligarchic associations.[51]

The French Revolution, which united royalty and nobility in adversity, brought absolutist and aristocratic interpretations of chivalry closer together. Medievalism thus acquired an anti-Jacobin tone. In the 1790s the Landgrave Wilhelm IX von Hessen raised in his park at Wilhelmshöhe a remarkably deceptive sham castle [109], with nearby the elegant pavilions of a tournament field where he and his courtiers, attended by servants in medieval costume, could retreat from the realities of Revolutionary Europe into a fairy-tale world. At about the same time the Emperor Franz II of Austria conjured up a somewhat similar castle called the Franzensburg [110], also with a tournament field, at Laxenburg, outside Vienna.

The Franzensburg was a kind of museum of the Middle Ages (curiously similar to the Musée des Monuments français [97] in Paris, assembled in very different circumstances), partly composed of fragments of medieval buildings, including a whole thirteenth-century chapel transported from Klosterneuburg, and filled with

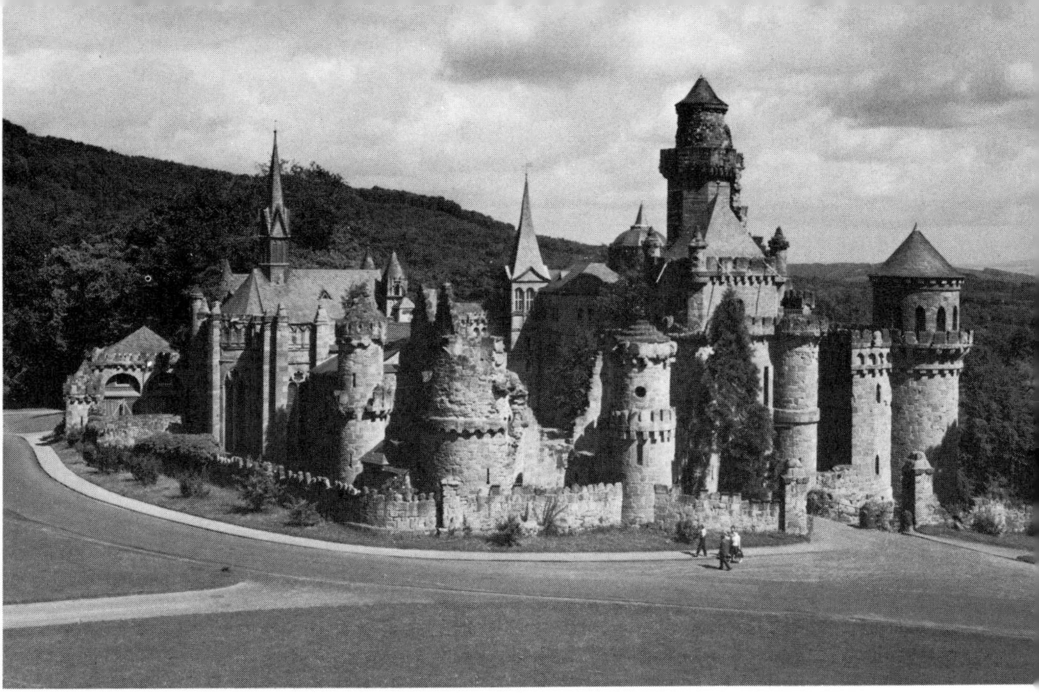

109. The Löwenburg, Kassel, 1790–99. H. C. Jussow

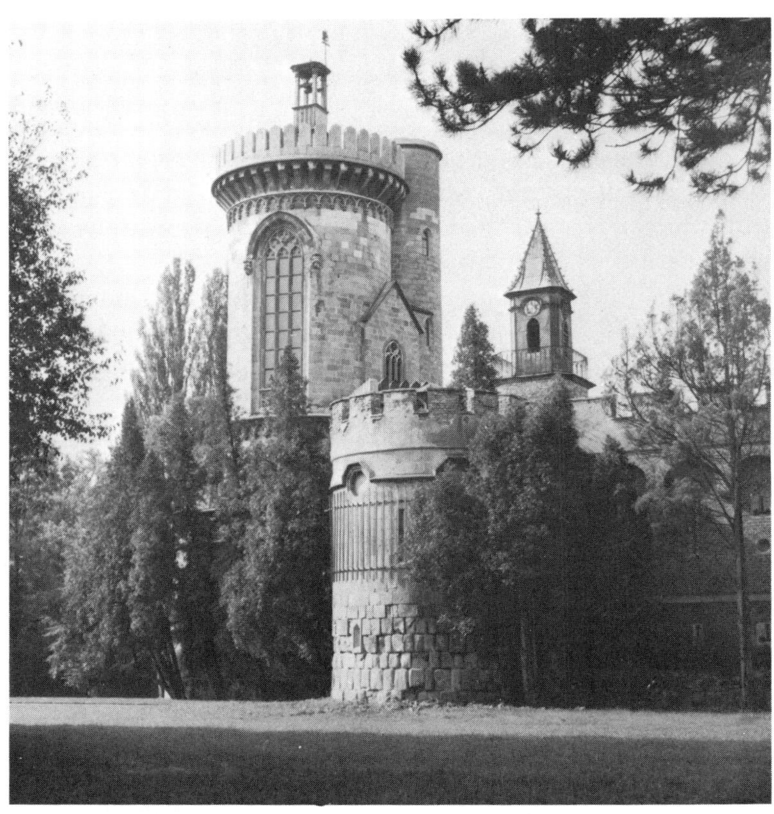

110. Franzensburg, near Vienna, 1798–1801. F. Jäger

paintings, sculpture, stained glass and weapons. It even incorporated a dungeon with instruments of torture and a life-size figure of a prisoner rattling chains. Nor was this simply a touch of Gothic horror: to Vittorio Barzoni, an Italian anti-Jacobin, it brought to mind the Westphalian courts whose arbitrary powers were reduced by the Emperor Maximilian I.[52] And it was partly as a memorial to Maximilian I, the 'last of the knights', a devotee of medieval romances and a great promoter of pageants and tournaments, that Franz II conceived his castle. It was also, of course, a celebration of the glory of the house of Habsburg, an evocation of the age of chivalry and a monument to legitimacy and enlightened despotism. A few years later, Germans struggling to throw off the Napoleonic yoke were to find in Gothic architecture an emblem of national unity. Thus, in 1815, Heinrich Olivier commemorated the signature of the Holy Alliance in a painting of Franz II, the Emperor of Russia, and the King of Prussia *cap à pie* in armour, standing in a flamboyant Gothic church [111].

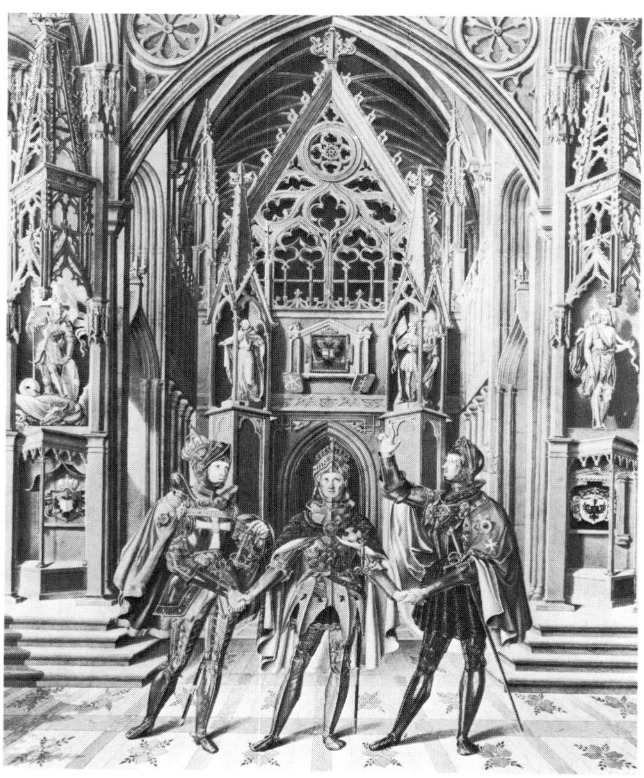

111. *The Holy Alliance*, 1815. H. Olivier

In the France of Louis XVI, painters had quite often depicted morally improving subjects from French medieval history, composed rather in the manner of seventeenth-century religious pictures, though simplified, solidified and with historically correct details of costume and setting (the Salon of 1773 included no fewer than nine scenes from the life of St Louis[53]). This style was revived in the last years of the Empire in paintings of medieval and Renaissance subjects commissioned for the sacristy of Saint-Denis, including J.-J.-F. Le Barbier's *St Louis Taking the Oriflamme* which was clearly intended to allude to Napoleon when begun in 1811 but could easily be associated with the recently restored Louis XVIII when exhibited in 1814.[54] Under the Restoration and the July Monarchy, painters worked in much the same manner on altarpieces for Parisian churches and large scenes from French history for the Galéries historiques at Versailles – sometimes suggesting that they had learned and forgotten as little as the Bourbons themselves.

In architecture, the restored Bourbons continued to favour the Neo-classical style, which they had sponsored before the Revolution, even for the Chapelle expiatoire in Paris designed by P.-F.-L. Fontaine as a memorial to Louis XVI and Marie Antoinette. But in Italy, the King of Sardinia, Carlo Felice, harked back to the Middle Ages in his conception of monarchy and ordered the reconstruction of the burial place of his ancestors, the Abbey of Hautecombe in Savoy, in a kind of hyper-Gothic, thickly encrusted with sculpture and bristling with crocketed pinnacles – creating an interior far more elaborate than that which had been desecrated during the Revolution. A similarly rich style was adopted in 1842 to enlarge and encase the classical mortuary chapel of the Orléans family at Dreux, with stained-glass windows after Ingres and Delacroix. The connection between monarchy and medievalism was, perhaps, more notably expressed in the extraordinary series of royal castles of the nineteenth century[55]: Windsor, above all, which was transformed into a magnificently picturesque composition between 1824 and 1837 by Sir Jeffrey Wyatville (nephew of the architect of Fonthill) [112]; Pena, near Cintra, conjured up in the 1840s for the German consort of the Queen of Portugal; the louring Château de Pierrefonds, re-built by Viollet Le Duc for Napoleon III from 1858 until work was interrupted in 1870; and, distinctly *fin de race*, the manic-obsessive Neuschwanstein, soaring above the Alpsee, begun in 1869 for Ludwig II of Bavaria and not entirely finished before he was certified insane in 1886 [113].

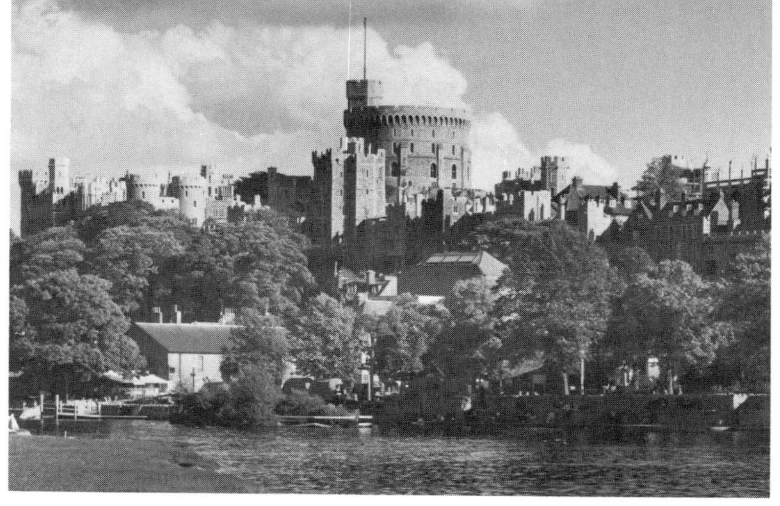

112. Windsor Castle, remodelled 1824–37. Jeffrey Wyatville

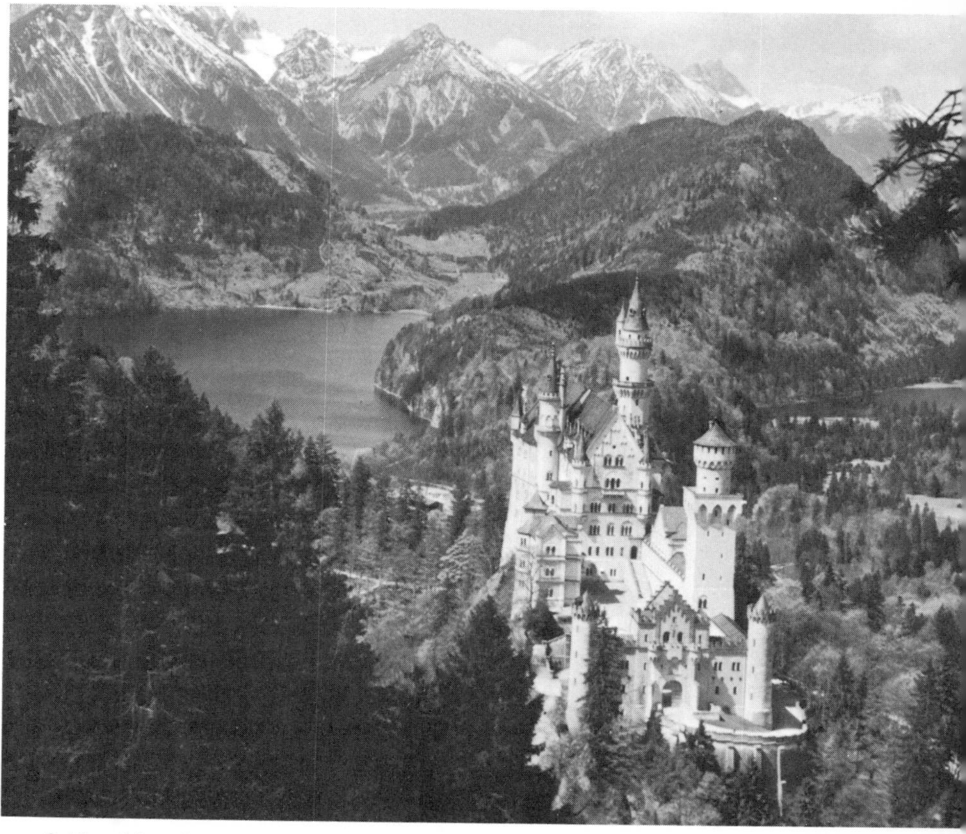

113. Schloss Neuschwanstein, 1869–86. C. Jank, E. Riedel, G. Dollmann

Yet the old association of the age of chivalry, and consequently Gothic architecture, with opposition to absolutism was not forgotten. Ludovic Vitet in 1831 claimed that the '*style ogivale*' expressed the aims of the July Revolution – its principle was liberty, it embodied the spirit of association and the community of national feelings. '*Elle est bourgeoise*,' he wrote.[56] To the liberal philosopher Edgar Quinet it represented the unification of the diversity of mankind.[57] Gothic was said to have been the creation of master-masons emancipated from the strict rules of the monastic orders, the style evolving in the French cities which rose against the feudal establishment and began to develop their own municipal councils.[58] It even freed from servility the many craftsmen who carved capitals and roof-bosses and choir stalls.[59]

Such ideas may have played a part in determining the British Parliament to rebuild the burnt-out New Palace of Westminster in the Gothic style [114]. Yet Pugin, who designed the details to which the Houses of Parliament owe most of their visual effect, was almost

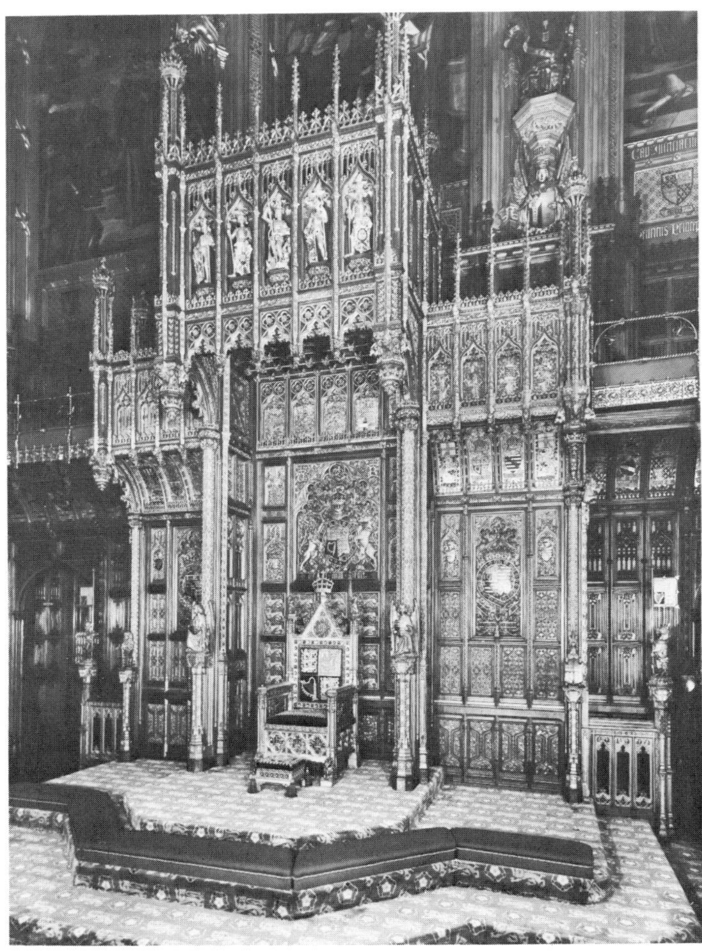

114. The House of Lords, Throne Room, London, *c*. 1846. Pugin

exclusively concerned with the religious significance of 'Pointed or Christian architecture'. And within the British parliamentary system medievalism was associated less closely with liberal than with conservative sentiments. The Gothic Revival and the Catholic revival (both Anglican and Roman) were brought close together in Disraeli's Young England movement, which was inspired partly by reactionary instincts and partly by a desire to revivify spiritual values in a world increasingly dominated by Benthamite utilitarianism. It has been aptly described as the Oxford movement translated from religion to politics.[60] Daniel Maclise's portrait of the Roman Catholic baronet Sir Francis Sykes and his family in medieval costume catches the mood beautifully [115]. They seem to be on their way to the most preposterous manifestation of medievalism of these years, the famous 'Eglinton Tournament' organized by the Earl of

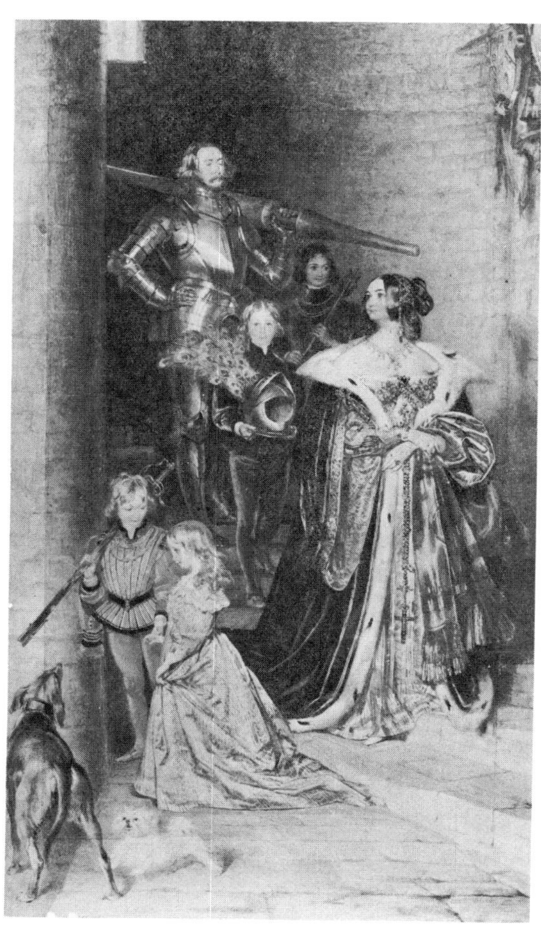

115. *Sir Francis Sykes and his Family*, 1837. Daniel Maclise

Eglinton at his castle in Scotland, in which Disraeli was later to discern symbols of great truths and higher purposes. 'Had it not been for the revival of Church principles this glorious pageant would never have occurred,' a character remarks in *Endymion*. 'But it is a pageant only to the uninitiated.'[61]

But even to the initiated the main appeal of such a spectacle was probably picturesque and poetic. Even Chateaubriand, so anxious to explain the religious significance of the age of chivalry, described it as the only poetic period in the history of France, '*l'âge de la féerie et des enchantements*'.[62] And it is unlikely that many of those who built neo-Gothic houses and filled them with furniture and knick-knacks in the same taste (very popular with the middle classes in France, England and America[63]) were much concerned with religious or political overtones. Whoever chose this style 'adopts that which poets and painters have always admired', an English architect, Francis Goodwin, wrote in 1835.[64] But the design for a 'Gothic Villa' which he illustrated is of a type which perpetuated eighteenth-century notions and met with increasing hostility from those who had absorbed Romantic beliefs about painting and poetry as well as about the Middle Ages. To Pugin, such a building was an example of the miserable degradation of 'our national and Catholic architecture' to a style adopted 'not on consistent principle, not on authority, not as the expression of our faith, our government, or country, but as one of the disguises of the day, to be put on and off at pleasure, and used occasionally as circumstances or private caprice may suggest'.[65] No one was better qualified to judge, for he had in his unregenerate youth adopted Gothic for furniture and metalwork in just this way.

Pugin's early designs, which carry eighteenth-century interpretations of Gothic into the 1820s, are somewhat similar in their crocketed and traceried elegance to the furnishings [116] which were created in France at the same time – and also aroused critical hostility. 'Nothing was less like the Middle Ages than the troubadour style clocks which flourished about 1825,' Gautier later remarked. 'It is one of the great merits of the Romantic school that it radically disembarrassed the arts of them.'[66] Such objects expressed the sentimental attitude charmingly summed up in a print after A.-E. Fragonard, entitled *The Romance* [117]. There was, however, a more serious side to *style troubadour* paintings, the first of which, Fleury Richard's *Valentine de Milan*, appeared in the Salon of 1802 – the year of *Génie du Christianisme*.[67]

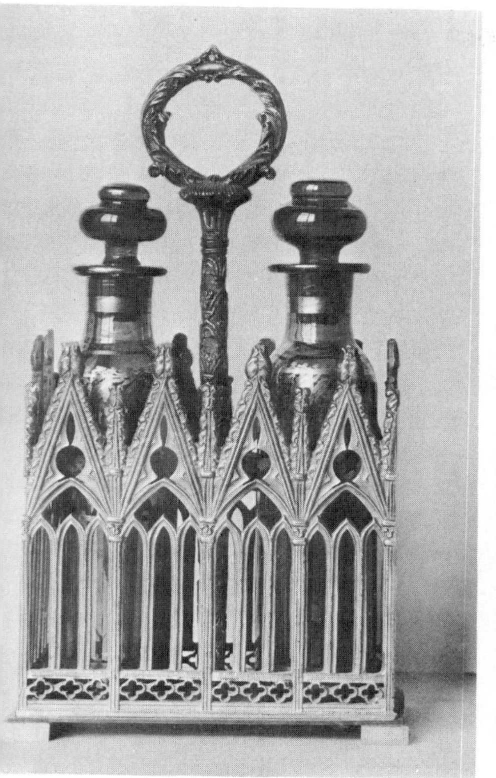

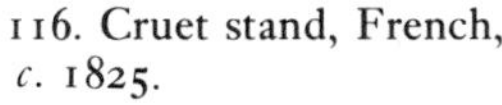

116. Cruet stand, French, *c.* 1825.

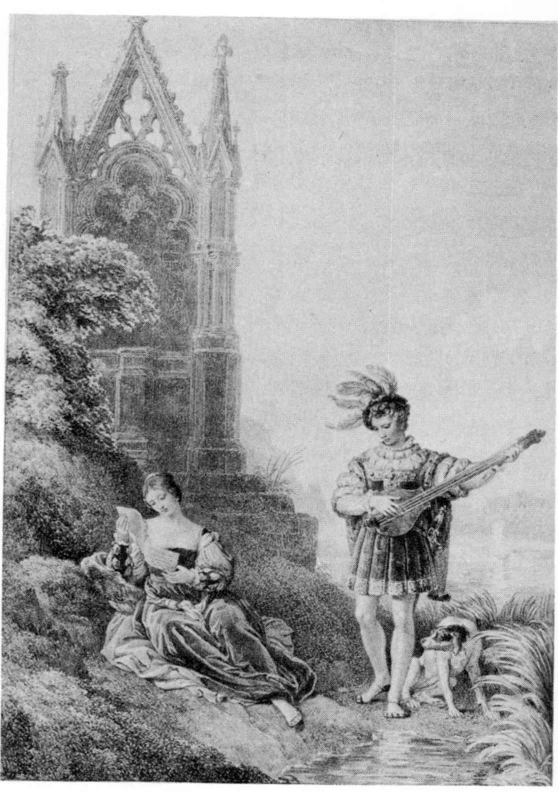

117. *The Romance*, 1824. F.-S. Delpech after A.-E. Fragonard

In composition as in sentiment, these pictures hark back to prints illustrating the Comte de Tressan's revisions and translations of *chansons de geste*, published in the 1780s. They are, moreover, painted in the manner of Dutch seventeenth-century cabinet pieces, which appealed so strongly to *ci-devant* taste. Most of them represent touching anecdotes from literature or French history, of the sixteenth century as well as the Middle Ages, with due regard for accuracy of details of costume and architecture, sometimes derived from exhibits in the Musée des Monuments français. And like that institution they probably played a part in furthering the growth of historical consciousness. Widely diffused in engravings, they provided the basic pattern for pictures of similar themes produced in all European countries and America throughout the nineteenth century. But the waxwork view of the Middle Ages which they presented could hardly satisfy those who had read the original texts with Romantic sensibility.

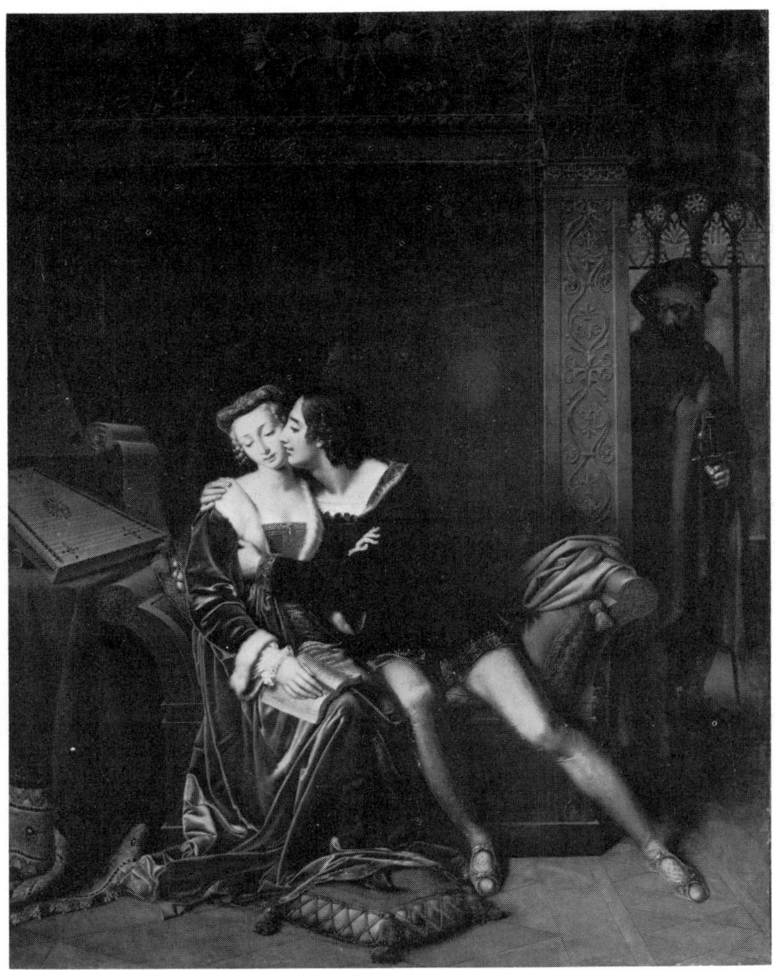

118. *Paolo and Francesca*, 1812. M.-P. Coupin de la Couperie

Les amours funestes de Françoise de Rimini (*Paolo and Francesca*) by Marie-Philippe Coupin de la Couperie, shown at the Salon of 1812 and bought by Josephine, is a well-marked specimen of the genre – sentimental rather than passionate, neatly painted with attention to individual details [118]. Ingres may well have seen a print after this picture before he painted for Caroline Murat (Josephine's sister-in-law) the first of his five renderings of the same subject, though he found artistic inspiration in a wide range of other sources as well. But he matched the medieval subject with an appropriately 'primitive' style (Netherlandish rather than Italianate), emphasized by smoothness of finish and acidic sharpness of colour

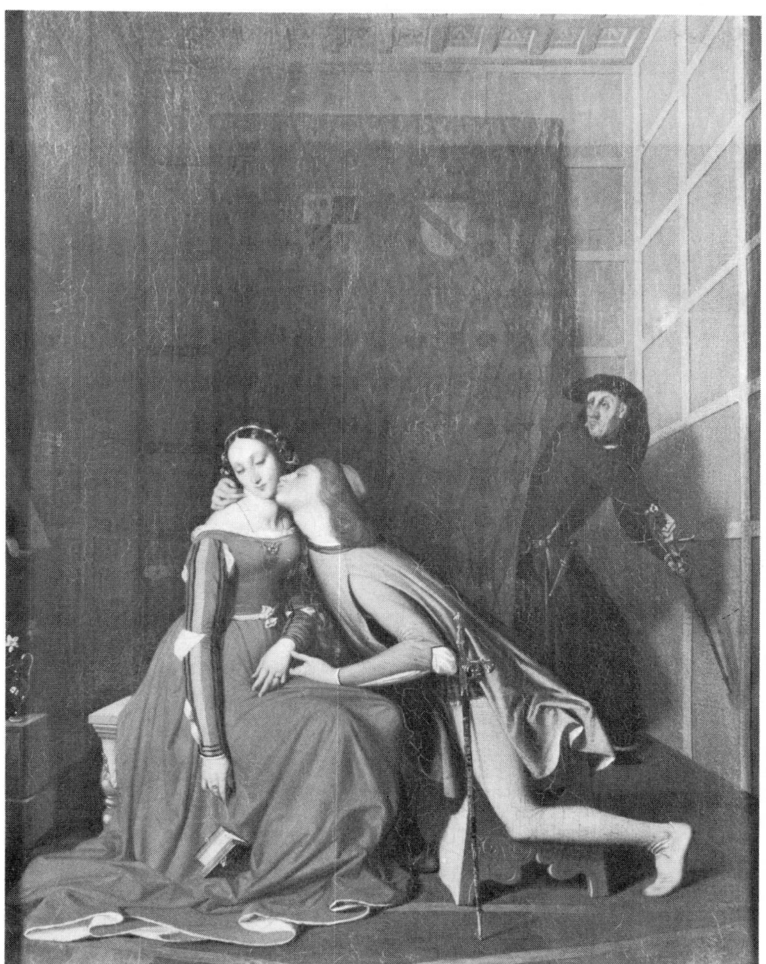

119. *Paolo and Francesca*, 1819. Ingres

contrasts. In his more successful second version, of 1819, he heightened the dramatic tension by imprisoning, almost entombing, the lovers in a box-like room from which they can be released only by the rapier which Gianciotto Malatesta draws at the very moment when the book falls from Francesca's hand and Paolo strains forward to embrace her [119]. 'Bold lover, never, never, canst thou kiss, though winning near thy goal!' – the costume piece has acquired poetic intensity as a characteristically Romantic meditation on love, death, time and art.

For another painting, *Roger Freeing Angelica* [120], Ingres took from *Orlando Furioso* an incident frequently illustrated since the sixteenth century. He differed from his predecessors by clothing Roger in correct *quattrocento* armour (derived from funerary monuments in Rome where he was living at the time) and, still more, by investing the scene with an almost aberrant sensuality wholly foreign to Ariosto. Angelica's slippery, soft, ivory nakedness, contrasted with the metal-clad Roger, her chained wrists and compliantly yielding pose, belong, rather, to the world of de Sade. Yet

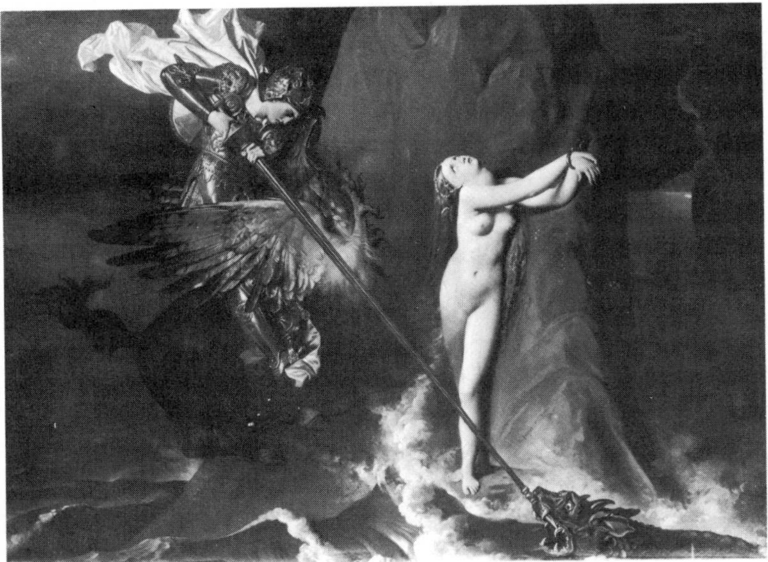

120. *Roger Freeing Angelica*, 1819. Ingres

the few critics who noticed the picture in the Paris Salon of 1819 (in which Géricault's *Raft of the 'Medusa'* was also shown) were shocked only by its stylistic primitivism. One complained that it recalled verses – '*plus niais que naïf*' – of the 'new troubadours' who attempted to imitate the old Provençal poets. By a strange coincidence, in the same year, Keats transformed a romance from the Comte de Tressan's collection into the opulently sensuous English Romantic poetry of *The Eve of St Agnes* – with due reference to

> an ancient ditty long since mute,
> In Provence call'd, 'La belle dame sans mercy'.

It was, however, more than a coincidence that between 1818 and 1827 the Nazarenes in Rome were frescoing rooms in the casino of the Marchese Carlo Massimo with scenes from Dante, Ariosto and Tasso, though in choice of subjects as well as in style they revealed their predominantly religious view of the Middle Ages. The Dante room is dominated by Philipp Veit's ceiling fresco of the *Paradiso*, a subject ignored by painters since the early Renaissance, and here rendered in the manner of Fra Angelico. In the Ariosto and Tasso rooms the glamour of chivalry takes second place to Christian symbolism. The love of Angelica and Medoro is illustrated in purely spiritual terms. And one may doubt if any nudes more chaste than Overbeck's Olindo and Sofronia had been depicted since the fifteenth century. (Even as a student Overbeck refused to draw from the female nude model, saying, 'I would rather draw less accurately than forfeit certain feelings which are the artist's greatest treasures.'[68]) They certainly make as striking a contrast with those in Delacroix's later picture of the same subject as with Ingres's Angelica.[69]

'In looking through Montfaucon I have convinced myself that the ancient history of France, of the time of St Louis and others, is a new mine to exploit,' Ingres wrote in an early notebook. 'A history painter who took possession of this century would be able to turn it to good account, as fine as possible from the artistic point of view and much more interesting for contemporaries to whom Achilles and Agamemnon, beautiful as they are, appeal less to the heart than St Louis, Philippe de Valois, Louis le Jeune and many others.'[70] With such ideas in mind he made careful studies of medieval armour, and in 1821 painted *The Entry of the future Charles V into Paris* in the style of a fifteenth-century miniaturist.[71]

Delacroix, of course, exploited the Middle Ages in a different way. Throughout his career he produced small pictures of medieval historical and literary subjects (also a watercolour of Paolo and Francesca[72]) which initially owed much to the *style troubadour*, though he gave less attention to details of costume than to effects of colour, and much less to sentiment than to violence. Rapine, battle, murder and sudden death are his themes. When he drew inspiration from Scott's medieval novels he characteristically chose to represent the assassination of the Bishop of Liège from *Quentin Durward* and the abduction of Rebecca from *Ivanhoe.*[73] Commissioned to paint the death of Charles le Téméraire at the Battle of Nancy, he remarked in 1828 that the subject was '*tout-à-fait dans ce qui me plaît à faire*'.[74] Next year a picture of the Battle of Poitiers was commissioned from him by the Duchesse de Berry.[75] Later he devoted two of his largest canvases to medieval subjects, *The Battle of Taillebourg, 1242* and *The Entry of the Crusaders into Constantinople, 1204* [121], both on commission from the Crown.

'*Voilà enfin une bataille véritable!*' Louis Batissier wrote of *The Battle of Taillebourg* when it was first exhibited in 1837. 'Here they fight, kill, wound, die, triumph: it is a terrible pell-mell of swords, pennants, horses, soldiers, officers, Frenchmen and Englishmen.'[76] It is one of fifteen vast pictures painted for the Galérie des Batailles at Versailles – a series intended to reawaken the sense of patriotic pride in a nation '*qui s'ennuie*' under the July Monarchy. The *Entry*

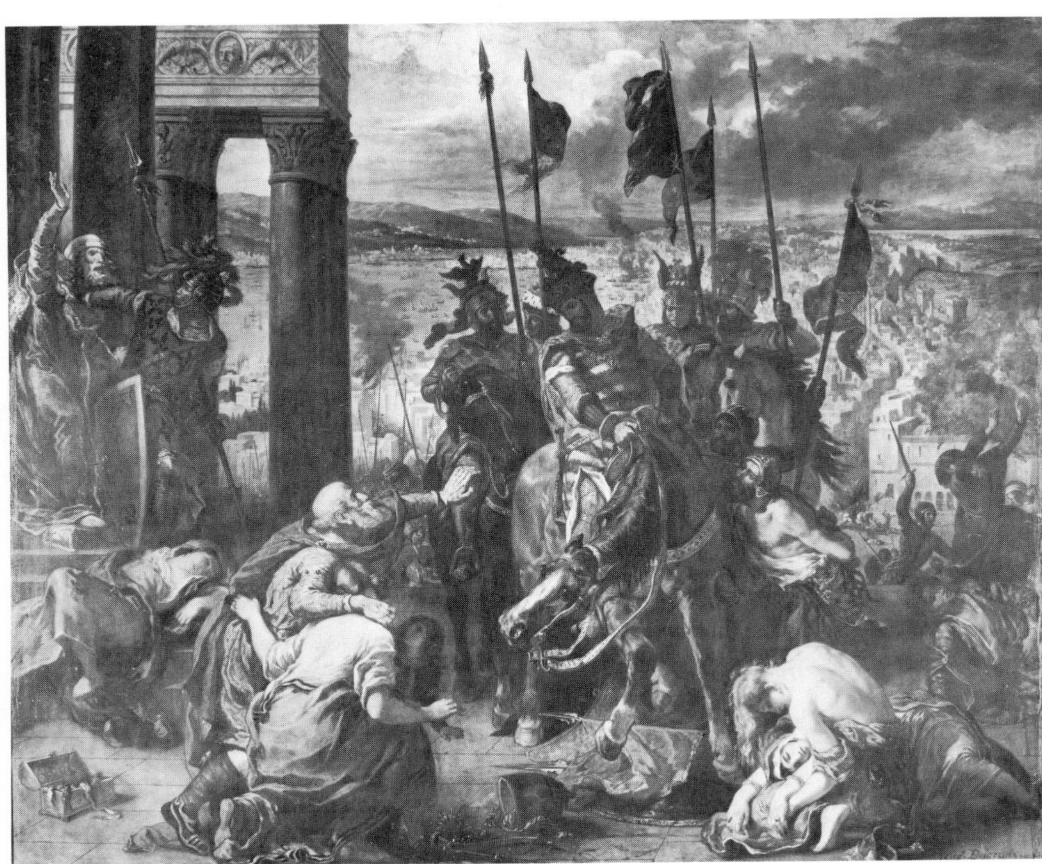

121. *Entry of the Crusaders into Constantinople, 1204*, 1840. Delacroix

into Constantinople, though it represents one of the more discreditable episodes in medieval history (which not even the Pope of the day had been able to justify), was painted for the Salles des Croisades, also at Versailles – a suite of rooms panelled with large and small pictures recording French participation in the Crusades, and one of the few great Romantic decorative complexes to have been realized. But Delacroix seems to have taken little interest in the didactic aim of the series or even the historical significance of the subject. 'What makes the picture so deeply moving is its tempestuous and gloomy harmony,' Baudelaire wrote. 'Everywhere the fluttering and waving of flags, unfurling and snapping their bright folds in the transparent atmosphere! Everywhere the restless, stirring crowd, the tumult of arms, the ceremonial splendour of the clothes, and a rhetorical truth of gesture amid the great occasions of life!' It is an image of another more violent and cruel, but also more poetic and colourful, world, in which details of costume and even the anatomy of figures are made subservient to an overwhelming pictorial harmony. Achille Ricourt, founder of *L'Artiste* and an admirer of Delacroix, was asked if one area of brilliant colour represented a man's back or chest – '*Ni l'un ni l'autre, c'est de la peinture*'.[77]

5. *The Sense of the Past*

The visions of the Middle Ages summoned up in the early nineteenth century are segments of a new panorama of world history, outlined by an earlier generation of historians, but coloured and elaborated with telling effect by the Romantics. For medievalism played a more important role in 'pre-Romanticism' than in Romanticism itself. Even medieval subject-matter was used less frequently by Romantic painters and writers than is commonly supposed. The case of Sir Walter Scott is revealing. After some youthful excursions into medievalism of a distinctly eighteenth-century cast – translating German *Sturm und Drang* literature, collecting Border ballads, writing poetry in the tradition of Ariosto and Spenser – he began in 1814 to write the Waverley novels on which his fame now rests. The first nine are set in the eighteenth or late seventeenth centuries. Not until 1819, with *Ivanhoe*, did he set one on the Middle Ages. And *Ivanhoe*, as one of his new type of novel, recounting the adventures of an ordinary man caught up in the current of historical events, is very different from the Gothic romances which had previously been so popular.[1] Despite some anachronisms, *Ivanhoe* is a far more conscientious attempt to depict a distant period than any earlier work of fiction (though not, of course, as exhaustively 'researched' as mid-nineteenth-century historical novels by George Eliot, Charles Reade and others were to be[2]). Scott's studies of recent history – he was born only twenty-six years after the 1745 rebellion and knew personally many men who had been engaged in it – had taught both him and his readers a vital lesson in historical and cultural relativism: that the past differed from the present in a great deal more than the clothes people wore and the buildings they inhabited.

G. M. Trevelyan attributed 'almost wholly to the Waverley novels' the difference in historical outlook between Gibbon and Macaulay – Gibbon who wrote as if every Roman emperor, every Gothic chieftain and every hermit of the Thebaid was a man of the eighteenth century, and Macaulay who never failed to stress the difference between the mentality of his own time and that about which he was writing. This may be an exaggeration. As any reader of Meineke's *Historism* will appreciate, there was a great deal of 'straight' historical writing between Gibbon and Macaulay which helped shape the new historical consciousness. But without Scott and the several other historical novelists indebted to him (Hugo, Mérimée and de Vigny in France, Manzoni in Italy, Fenimore Cooper in America), history would hardly have become so widespread a subject of popular interest as it did in the nineteenth century. For although the philosophical historians of the eighteenth century, with their 'enlightened' tolerance, had gradually come to regard manners and beliefs different from their own with greater sympathy, and sometimes as alternatives rather than aberrations, they lacked the imaginative empathy, the ability to identify, demanded by the Romantics. This was what Barthold Georg Niebuhr meant when he complained in 1814 that neither Hume nor Gibbon had given any indication of 'what human hearts felt'.[3]

But it is seldom sufficiently stressed how great, perhaps crucial, a part in the development of the Western historical sense was played not so much by historians and historical novelists as by history itself. The French Revolution sharpened the historical sense in a way that no other event had ever done. No other event had ever seemed so cataclysmic. Creating between the present and immediate past a gulf which was seen to widen with every year that went by from 1789 to 1815, it quickened awareness of the passage of time. All previous history, especially the earlier revolutions of seventeenth-century England, were suddenly set in a dramatic new perspective. To some extent it democratized history by making apparent the influence of political events on ordinary people – and vice versa. It also revealed unexpected complexities in the relationship between ideas and acts, events and opinions. Macaulay was well aware of this. 'Was there', he asked in 1835,

> was there one observer to whom the French Revolution, or revolutions in general, appeared in exactly the same light on the day when the Bastille fell, on the day when the Girondists were dragged to the scaffold, the day when the Directory shipped off their principal opponents for Guiana, or the day when the Legislative Body was driven from its hall at the point of the bayonet?

He declared that 'a man who held exactly the same opinion about the Revolution in 1789, in 1798, in 1804, in 1814, and in 1834, would have been either a divinely inspired prophet or an obstinate fool'.

 And, significantly enough, this comes from the review of a book about the English Revolution of 1688.[4]

But if the French Revolution illuminated some aspects of past history it clouded and sometimes distorted others. The search for causes, which began in 1790, fostered a belief in determinism, with which historians approached other historical problems. This was to be closely allied with the notion of the *Zeitgeist*, partly derived from that of the *ancien régime* – terms first used in the 1790s, it may be noted. And the fact that the Revolution occurred towards the end of a century gave apparent and specious support to what was later to be called periodization. No previous transition from one century to another had been so clearly marked. Certainly, the idea of belonging to a particular century seems first to have become widespread in the nineteenth. Almost prophetically, the young Hegel entitled his first publication ... *towards a Readier Examination of the Condition of Philosophy at the Beginning of the Nineteenth Century* (Jena, 1801).

The transition from the eighteenth to the nineteenth century could be not merely sensed but seen at every level of society and throughout the whole of Europe, if nowhere more conspicuously than in France. It affected even dress and hairstyles. The upper ranks of French society had for long been acutely fashion-conscious. But their almost annual modifications of costume and coiffure, seldom amounting to much more than the addition or omission of a

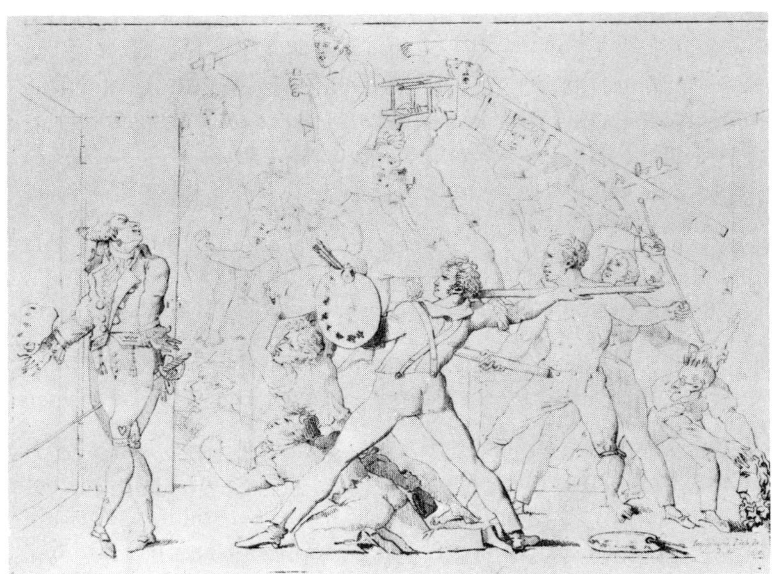

122. *J.-L. David's Studio*, *c.* 1805. P.-N. Bergeret

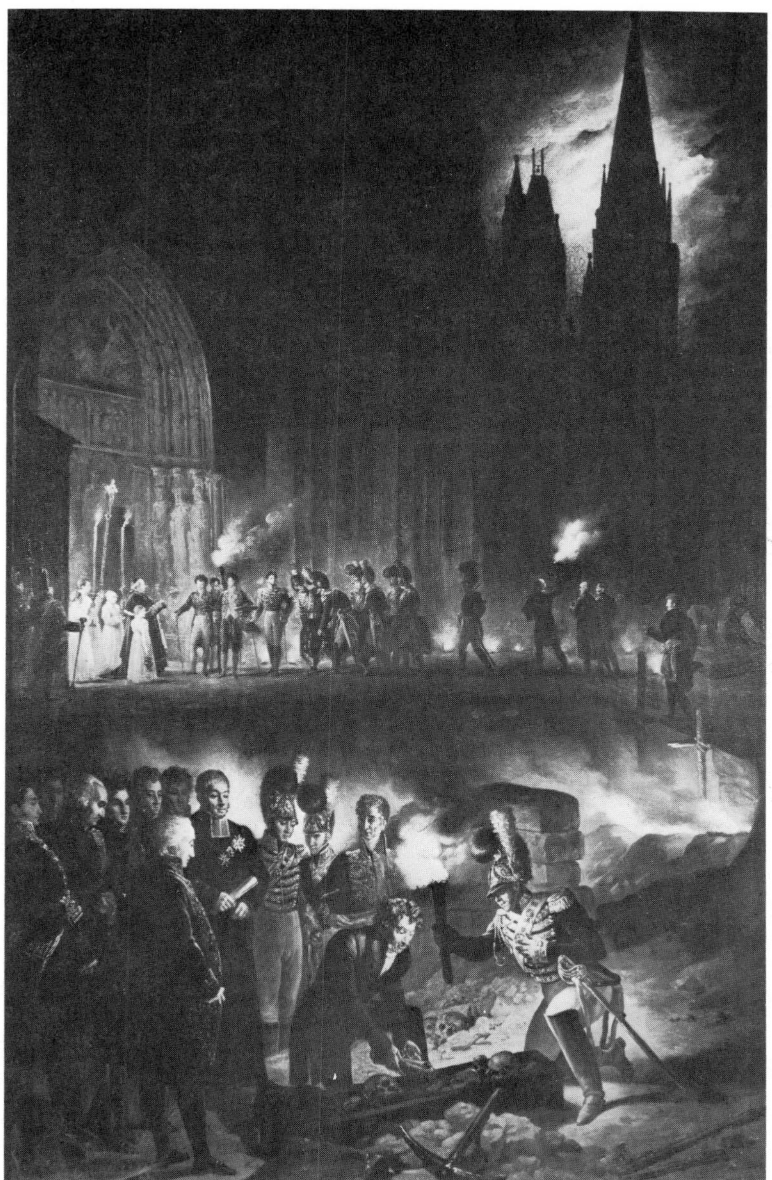

123. *The Exhumation at Saint-Denis*, 1822. F.-J. Heim

furbelow or ribbon, were such as to be barely perceptible outside a charmed circle. The changes which took place between 1790 and 1810 were immediately obvious and far more widespread. By the beginning of the nineteenth century in France, the fashionable dress of the pre-Revolutionary period was not merely out of date but had become emblematical of an entire way of life which had passed away. In caricatures the royalist is immediately recognizable by his wig and knee-breeches. P.-N. Bergeret in about 1805 drew David and his pupils wearing skin-tight trousers and taking up the stance of Romulus and Tatius as they confront a painter whose perruque, costume and pose mark him as a representative of Rococo art and *ci-devant* attitudes [122]. To supporters of legitimacy, conversely, natural hair and trousers were badges of Jacobinism. The revival of eighteenth-century clothes and powdered hair or wigs for 'court dress' by the restored monarchs in 1815 was an attempt to disguise the fact that an irrevocable change had taken place.

Soon after 1815 in France, men of all political complexions found themselves looking back wistfully to recent periods which had

124. *Le Soldat Laboureur*, 1820. E.-J.-H. Vernet

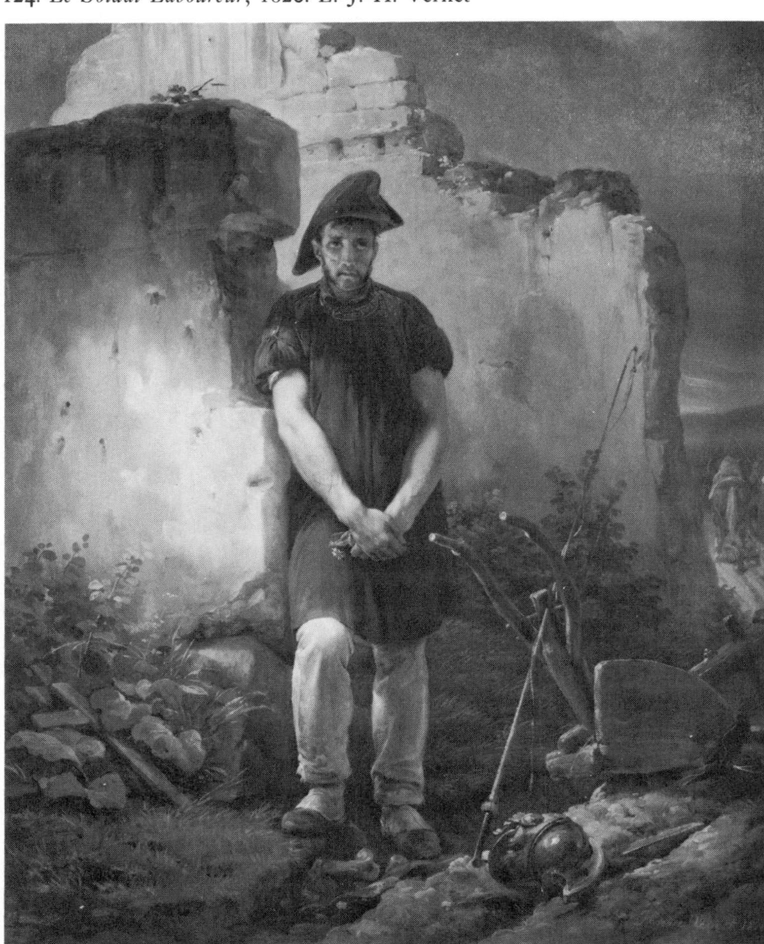

already come to seem tantalizingly out of reach – aristocrats to the *ancien régime* with its elegance, opulence, security and privileges (the abuses were the best part, one of them remarked), Republicans to the dawn of liberty which had so soon been overclouded, Bonapartists to the years of glory. Both the closeness and the remoteness of the world before the Revolution is expressed in F.-J. Heim's extraordinary picture of the ceremonial, almost sacramental, exhumation in 1817 of the bones of the kings of France, which had been so unceremoniously thrown out of the royal tombs at Saint-Denis in 1793 [123]. The presiding figure is that curious link between two centuries and three régimes, the Marquis de Dreux-Brézé (*maître des cérémonies* when the States General assembled in 1789 and when Louis-Philippe entered the Chamber of Deputies on 3 August

125. *The Swiss Guard at the Louvre*, 1819. Géricault

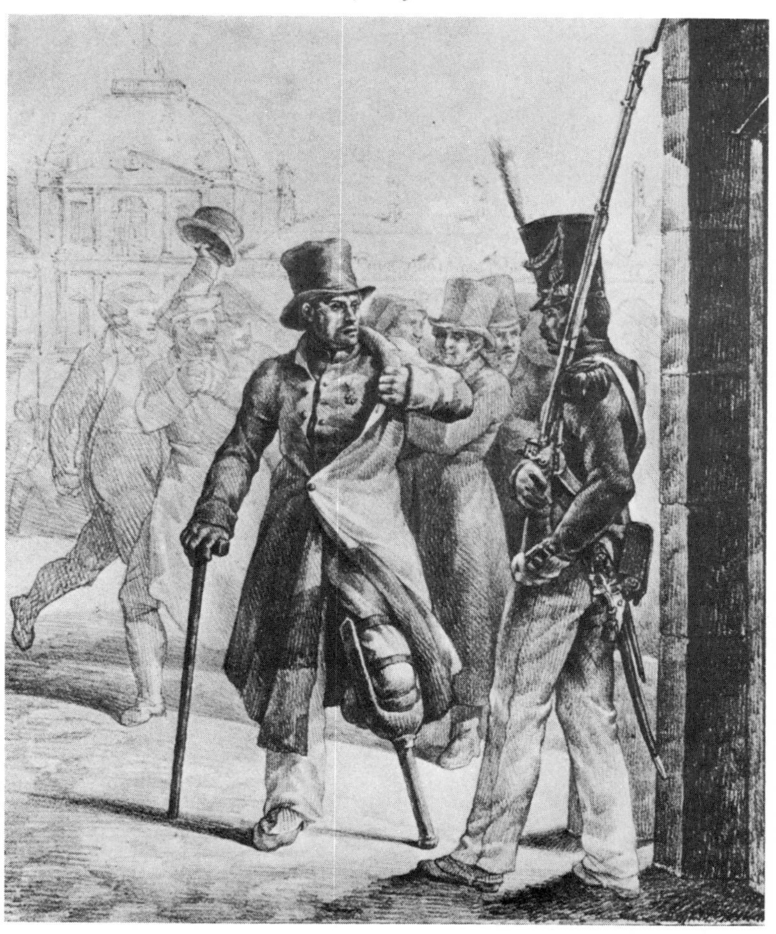

1830). But, between the group piously gathering Bourbon relics in the foreground and the Gothic Abbaye Royale de Saint-Denis, there is the ditch dug by the Revolutionary vandals. Another, and much more disturbing picture, Horace Vernet's *Le Soldat Laboureur* of 1820, shows how relics of a still more recent period might accidentally come to the surface [124]. A discharged soldier who has turned to work on the land at Waterloo meditates on a French helmet unearthed by his ploughshare – an image of the Romantic heroism of the defeated, of the thrill of war and the monotony of peace, as well as of the peremptory swiftness of time. The same sense of contrast between present and recent past, and a still stronger pathos invest a lithograph by Géricault (probably assisted by Vernet) of a ragged maimed veteran displaying his Napoleonic medal and commanding an officious Suisse outside the Louvre to present arms.

The authorities of the Restoration were well aware of how, and how effectively, visual images could revive memories of Revolutionary idealism and Napoleonic heroism. Vernet's pictures of the first Republican victory, *The Battle of Jemappes*, and the last Napoleonic stand, *The Defence of the Barrière de Clichy*, were both excluded from the 1822 Salon (though his more sentimental military scenes won official approval and two were acquired by the Duc de Berry).[5] But artists went on painting Revolutionary scenes even though they had no chance of being shown at the Salon. In 1825 the young Ary Scheffer recorded the departure of the Republican volunteers in 1792 – *Allons, enfants de la Patrie!* [126]. And prints

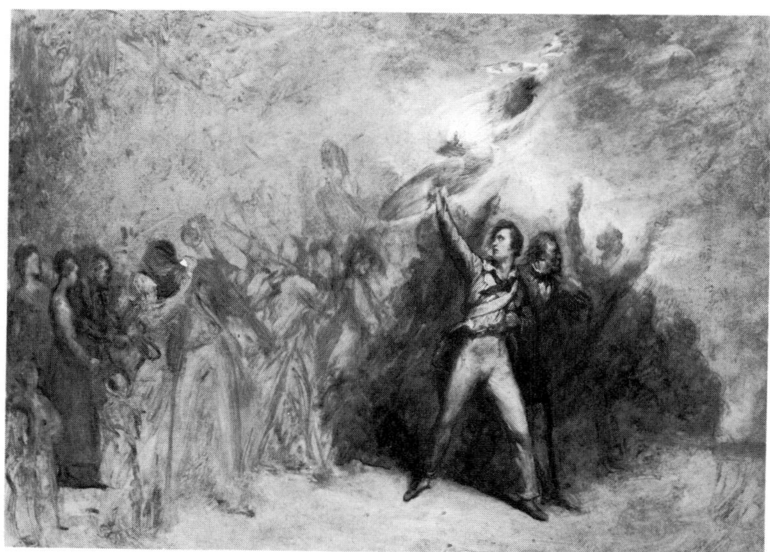

126. *Allons, enfants de la Patrie!*, 1825. Ary Scheffer

of veterans from the Grande Armée, by Charlet and others, were very widely circulated, contributing to the formation of the Napoleonic legend. Attempts to create a counter-image were less successful, though they produced one masterpiece in Pierre-Narcisse Guérin's picture of the dashingly handsome young Vendean general Henri de la Rochejaquelin, with the white Bourbon banner behind him and the insignia of the Sacred Heart on his chest [127]. This

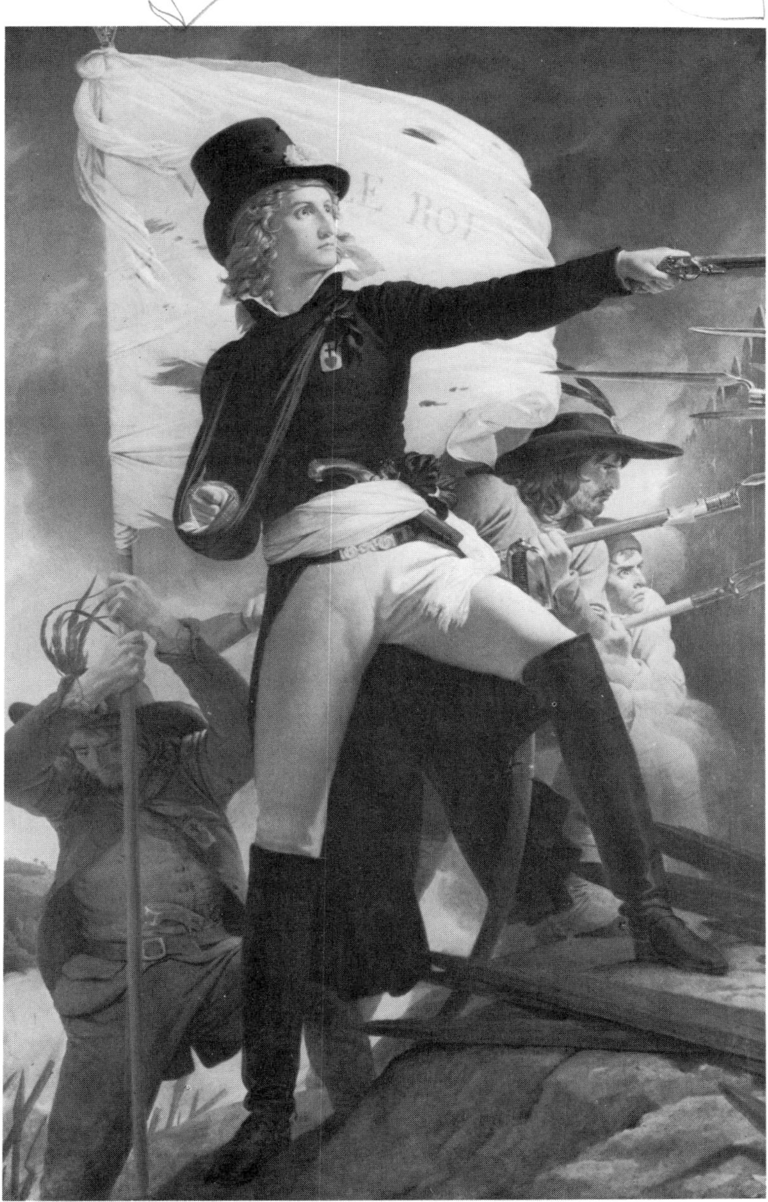

127. *Henri de la Rochejaquelin*, 1817. P.-N. Guérin

is, indeed, a Royalist answer to David's Revolutionary martyr icons and Gros's Empire portraits, composed in the same artistic language as the latter.

The practice of commenting on current topics by means of pictures set in more distant times (usually Antiquity) had, of course, been established before the end of the eighteenth century and much exploited during the Revolution and under the Empire. This tradition doubtless inspired the official sponsors of a competition, held in 1830, for three paintings to decorate the debating chamber of the Palais Bourbon: Mirabeau refusing the royal prorogation of the States General on 23 June 1789 (an instance of justified resistance to the abuse of the royal prerogative), Boissy d'Anglas facing the mob which invaded the Convention of 20 May 1795 (equally justified resistance to demagogic brute force) and Louis-Philippe taking the oath on 10 August 1830 (the happy ending). But none of the painters succeeded in expressing the political point very effectively (Delacroix's *Boissy d'Anglas* might be read as a glorification of anarchic violence[6]). In the interim a somewhat different attitude to history had manifested itself, a tendency to seek parallels (relevant but neutral morally) rather than precedents and moral exemplars in the past. Hence, perhaps, the popularity of paintings of Henri IV who, just over two centuries before, had brought peace to France by uniting Catholics and Protestants. One of the more popular stories about him was that of how the Spanish Ambassador found him playing with his children – the King as father in a distinctly homely bourgeois sense [128]. He was also celebrated as the

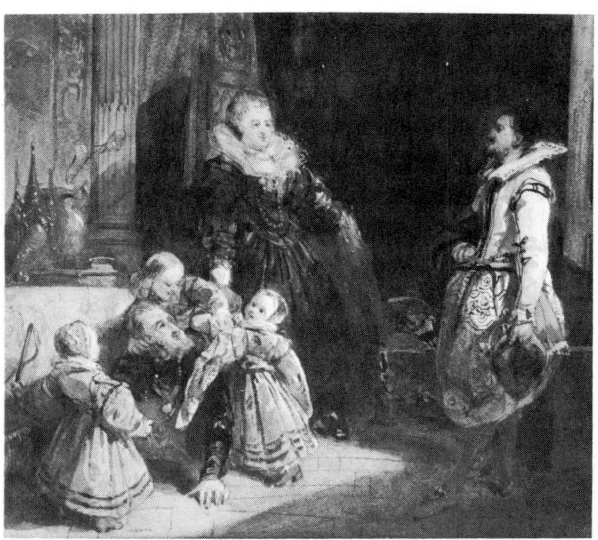

128. *Henry IV and the Spanish Ambassador*, *c.* 1827. R. P. Bonington

attractive gallant who shared the amiable weaknesses of his compatriots, and was thus depicted dallying with Gabrielle d'Estrées. Only when artists painted his death did they run into trouble – for he was commonly (though erroneously) supposed to have been assassinated by Jesuits, whose return to France in 1815 was widely unpopular.[7]

Paintings of Mary Queen of Scots which began to appear in the Salons of the Empire may have owed some of their appeal – like Schiller's tragedy – to the cult of another decapitated queen, Marie Antoinette. On the other hand, Bergeret's *Anne Boleyn Receiving the Death Sentence* had, perhaps, a special meaning for sympathizers with the divorced Empress Josephine. Contemporary allusions were seldom specific, and it is now hard to tell how often they were intended or merely read into pictures. Delaroche's *Cromwell Uncovering the Coffin of Charles I*, shown at the Salon of 1831, is a case in point. 'It cannot be denied that in exhibiting this picture Delaroche seems to have intended to challenge historical parallels,' Heine wrote. 'If one begins with a parallel between Louis XVI and Charles I, one naturally proceeds to draw another between Cromwell and Napoleon.'[8] The names of Charles X and Louis-Philippe can hardly have failed to spring to mind also. English history was very popular in France at this period, and immediately after the July Revolution, a writer in the *Globe* compared almost year by year and personality by personality the history of England between 1660 and 1688 with that of France between 1815 and 1830.[9]

This tendency to seek parallels in the past may seem to run counter to the growing awareness that people of other periods felt, thought and acted in different ways and were thus to be judged by the standards of their own rather than later times. Yet, in practice, the two attitudes complemented one another, inspiring historical studies which made subtle play with the similarities and dissimilarities between past and present. Whether writing about the French Revolution or a twelfth-century Abbot of Bury St Edmunds, Carlyle was mainly concerned with the 'condition of England' of his own day.

'We all have our eyes fixed on our chronicles, as if, having reached maturity and moved on to greater things, we had stopped a moment to take acount of our youth and its errors.'[10] So wrote Alfred de Vigny in the preface to *Cinq Mars* (1826), in which he suggested that the ills of France had all spread from Richelieu's attack on the power of the nobility. An incident in this novel provided Delaroche with the subject for one of his most successful pictures – the aged and ailing Richelieu in his state barge, towing the boat in which the young and healthy conspirators, Cinq Mars and de Thou, travel to their death on the scaffold [129]. It was exhibited together with

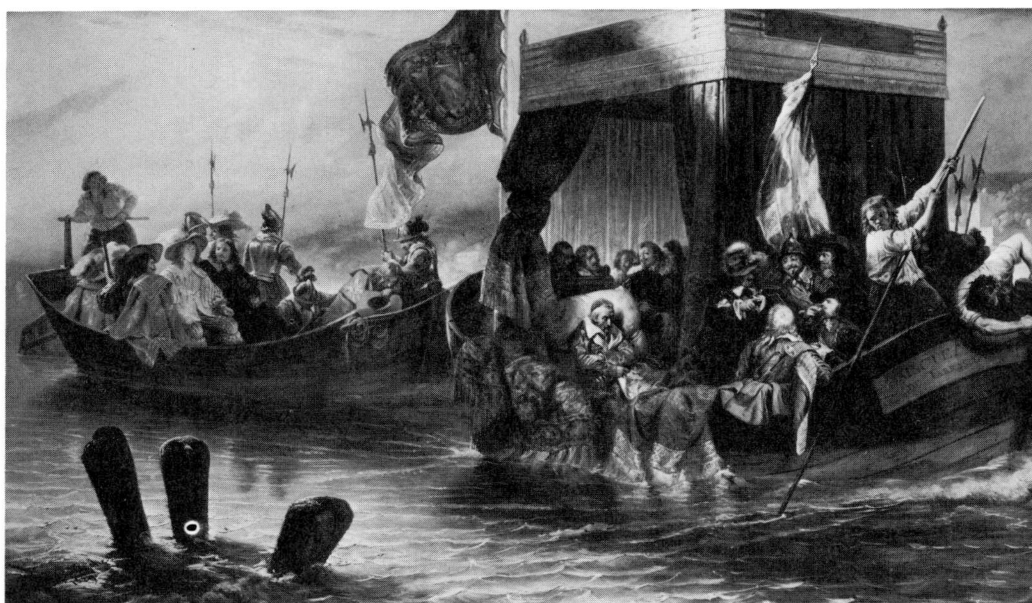

129. *Cardinal de Richelieu*, 1829. Paul Delaroche

The Death of Mazarin in 1831, when a critic in *L'Artiste* commented on the 'very happy idea of M. Delaroche to resume in two pictures the long struggle of the French aristocracy against the establishment of absolute power, a struggle which finally presented the monarchy alone against the people in a combat of social interests, and led to the great revolution in which it perished'.[11]

The popularity of pictures of this type, which enjoyed world-wide diffusion in prints, derives from that of the historical anecdote, valued for its power to highlight a moment in the past, and appealing to the heart as much as to the mind. Ludovic Vitet, for instance, used a pictorial analogy to explain the episodic construction of his dramatic sequence (it cannot be called a play) *Les Barricades*, published in 1826:

> I imagined that I was walking through Paris in May 1588 on the stormy day of the Barricades . . . and every time that a picturesque scene, a picture of manners, a trait of character, presented itself, I tried to retain the image by sketching a scene. One feels that only a series of portraits could come from this, or as a painter would say, of *studies*, of *sketches* which cannot aspire to any merit other than that of resemblance.

Prosper Mérimée (a friend of Vitet) remarked of his similar work about the peasants' revolt in 1358, *La Jaquerie: Scènes féodales* (1828), 'I believe I have lightened rather than darkened the colours of my picture.' It was, he wrote, an attempt 'to give an impression of the horrifying *mores* of the fourteenth century'.[12] And this could, of course, be better achieved by the anecdote than the general survey or narrative. 'The only things I like in history are anecdotes, and of them I prefer those in which I think I have found a true painting of the manners and characters of a given epoch,' he declared in the preface to his novel *Chronique du règne de Charles IX* (1829).[13]

The political implications which are so clear in these works by Vitet and Mérimée[14] are, however, hard to seek in the majority of paintings of historical subjects – *The Death of Queen Elizabeth* or *The Princes in the Tower* by Delaroche, for example. As illustrations of how people in the past had felt, they all made a strong appeal to sentiment. The historical authenticity of details suggested that the sentiments were equally true. But beneath the smooth surface there lurk the smouldering desires and brooding fears of the Romantics. Sexual frustration, religious doubt, social insecurity are themes which can hardly be ignored in such pictures. The same could be said of the 'grand' or 'Romantic' operas, nearly all of which had fairly remote historical settings (chronologically, the Middle Ages or sixteenth century and, geographically, the outposts of Europe in Sicily, Spain and Scotland were favoured). They were perhaps the most popular expressions of Romanticism in music, especially in Italy where Verdi – himself active in the Risorgimento – gave to stories of the type previously selected by Gaetano Donizetti and Vincenzo Bellini a thrillingly vibrant nationalist significance, as well as a greater melodic richness to enhance the psychological drama.

Sometimes, of course, early nineteenth-century paintings of historical subjects reveal little more than a vague yearning for 'good old times'. This is evident in scenes from eighteenth-century novels (*The Vicar of Wakefield* and a bowdlerized version of *Tristram Shandy* were favourites), which became popular in England around 1830. In the United States the colonial epoch acquired a 'quaint' charm exploited in John Quidor's illustrations to Washington Irving. Pictures of eighteenth-century subjects which began to appear in France at the same time may have had political overtones. Of Achille Devéria's *Ball Given to King Christian VII of Denmark in the Palais Royal in 1768*, shown at the Salon of 1831, Victor Schoelcher commented approvingly: 'It is the portrait of a whole epoch . . . this glittering society of the mid-eighteenth century which so gaily led the monarchy to its end.'[15] The Rococo had raised its curly head some years earlier, but theorists still maintained Neo-classical objections to a style which was now regarded as the expression of a doomed, degenerate age (and perhaps most frequently revived in the figurative arts for appropriately erotic subjects). Jean Gigoux's *Mme Dubarry and Louis XV* of 1833 was thus criticized as an attempt to exploit 'the period called *rococo* or *Pompadour* which is certainly the least approachable; a period essentially yet superficially witty, lively, libertine and courtly', that could be represented only by the 'graceful brush of the inimitable Watteau'.[16]

The history of taste in interior decoration and the decorative arts in these years is instructive. For more than a decade after 1815 the Empire style survived throughout continental Europe, simplified in Germany (where it merged into Biedermeier), but elsewhere growing heavier and coarser with the years. It seems to have persisted because of its association with the 'true style' of Neo-classical theory. In England, however, silversmiths began to develop a neo-Rococo manner shortly after 1800, influenced, no doubt, by the fine eighteenth-century plate brought over by émigrés and also, perhaps, by a desire to avoid the Antique Revival manner that could be associated with Jacobinism. Their lead was followed by makers of porcelain, who imitated the richer products of the Sèvres factory before turning to exuberantly Rococo wares, and eventually by designers of furniture and wall decorations. In 1829, for instance, interiors of the Duke of Wellington's Apsley House in London were embellished by Benjamin Dean Wyatt in a Régence manner then termed 'Louis XIV'.[17] In so far as there was any dominant style of the 1820s and '30s, it was a cumbrous neo-Rococo. Balzac, the true founder of the psychology of taste in furniture (and himself a collector of eighteenth-century pieces), was well aware of this. In *La Cousine Bette*, set in the year 1838, the upstart Célestin Crevel has his apartment decorated by an architect who had been at the height of fashion under the Restoration and now 'created his white and gold drawing-room hung with red damask, for the thousandth time . . . The candlesticks, the sconces, the fender, the chandelier, the clock, were highly ornamented, in pseudo-Rococo style.'[18]

It was against this style that the more thoughtful designers reacted by turning back to the sixteenth century and, rather less frequently, the Middle Ages. After the appearance of a French translation of Benvenuto Cellini's autobiography in 1822, a sixteenth-century style, with abundance of writhing human figures and strapwork, became increasingly popular for work in precious metals and, as the taste spread to the less wealthy, in cheaper materials including electro-plate. This neo-Mannerist style seems to have been originated in France by Jacques-Henri Fauconnier and Karl Wagner, followed by François-Désiré Froment-Meurice, who was extravagantly praised by both Balzac and Victor Hugo. Their works were free essays in the styles of the virtuoso Italian and German goldsmiths. But copies, not to say fakes, of sixteenth-century ceramics – Italian maiolica, French Sainte-Porchaire pottery (fancifully called 'Henri II ware'), and Palissy's snake- and lizard-encrusted dishes – had come on the market by the 1850s. (A reprint of Bernard Palissy's writings in 1844 helped to put him on a level with Cellini.) At the same time, deceptive imitations of French eighteenth-century *ébénisterie* were made. And in England, from the later 1830s, neo-medieval furniture and metalwork were produced, largely under Pugin's influence and in a style of earnest historical revivalism very different from the frivolous Gothic Revival manner which had survived from the previous century.

Ancient Greek and Roman objects were also imitated. Eighteenth-century designers and craftsmen had shown a remarkable reluctance to copy the furnishings of classical antiquity. The design of that most elegant of chairs, the Greek *klismos*, though well known from vase paintings and marble sculptures, was very rarely adopted by eighteenth-century furniture makers. Wedgwood and the many potters who followed his lead seldom reproduced both the colour schemes and the forms of what were then called 'Etruscan vases'. But, in the early nineteenth century, the *klismos* became a household commonplace, the bronze furniture found at Pompeii was faithfully copied (with only such slight modifications as the castration of the over-excited satyrs supporting a famous table). Black- and red-figure vases were made, not necessarily to deceive (many were proudly marked by their makers). From about 1815 Pio Fortunato Castellani confected highly praised imitations of Greek and Etruscan jewellery in Rome.

Whether they were in Antique, Medieval, Renaissance or eighteenth-century styles, these objects generally reveal close study of prototypes, which were illustrated in an increasing number of books and more easily accessible than ever before in museums. The motives of those who acquired them were probably mixed. The cult of hand-craftsmanship, which gathered adherents with the progress of industrialized production, doubtless played a part. But revivalist ornaments and furnishings seem to have been valued mainly (like the objects from which they derived) as examples of different styles, each of which had its own merits both intrinsically and as expressions of an historical period. They reflected the new relativist attitude to history in the same way as did novels, plays, operas, paintings of historical scenes, and nearly all the more prominent buildings erected in Europe at the time – Grecian temple-museums, neo-Romanesque and neo-Gothic churches, neo-Renaissance palaces, Elizabethan-style country houses or François I-style châteaux.

The buildings and decorative objects most generally and obviously associated with Romanticism are those in neo-Gothic styles, and the historical paintings those of medieval or sixteenth-century subjects. But the attitude to history which they reveal is no less clearly evident in paintings of Greek and Roman subjects and buildings in Antique styles. Indeed, the discovery that the term Antiquity signified not one ideal style, albeit subject to the process of growth, maturity and decline, but a number of different styles on a par with one another, contributed to the development of the new historical consciousness. Its effect is nowhere more clearly seen than in reactions to Herculaneum and Pompeii.

The discovery of the two cities (in 1738 and 1748), nowadays regarded as the greatest archaeological events of the eighteenth century, aroused rather less enthusiasm at the time than might be expected. Of the thousands of works of art disinterred, none entered the canon of Antique masterpieces.[19] Few of the sculptures were ranked with, let alone above, those found in Rome at the same period. It was the quantity rather than the quality of the paintings that impressed.[20] Some artists, notably David, found in them inspiration for their linear style. But it was generally believed that, as they dated from the decadence of Antique art, they should be imitated only in so far as they reflected earlier and purer work. Motifs were, of course, picked up by decorators and designers, but they were used mainly in grotesques of the type already established by Raphael and others in the sixteenth century. On the strange architectural paintings, which we nowadays associate with Pompeii, they turned a blind or a disdainful eye.[21]

Not until the 1790s did Pompeiian paintings with isolated figures or other motifs on dark backgrounds become popular. The earliest recorded example of the imitation of the essentially Pompeiian type of architectural painting, with its curious elisions and false perspectives, are those in Klenze's Maxpalais in Munich of 1828–30 and the Queen's salon of the Königsbau in the Munich Residenz of

1830–35.[22] By this time the idea of a Pompeiian style was firmly established. Still later, in the 1840s, Gärtner built for Ludwig I of Bavaria at Aschaffenburg a complete Pompeiian house, as faithful to the prototypes beneath Vesuvius in its architecture as in its decoration [130]. In 1860 Prince Napoleon had a Pompeiian house built for him in Paris – with furniture by Rossigneux and table silver by Christofle all carefully copied from first-century pieces. Its interior is recorded in a painting by Gustave Boulanger, which shows Gautier, the actress Rachel and others dressed in Roman costume and rehearsing a play that was performed there [131]. As the repre-

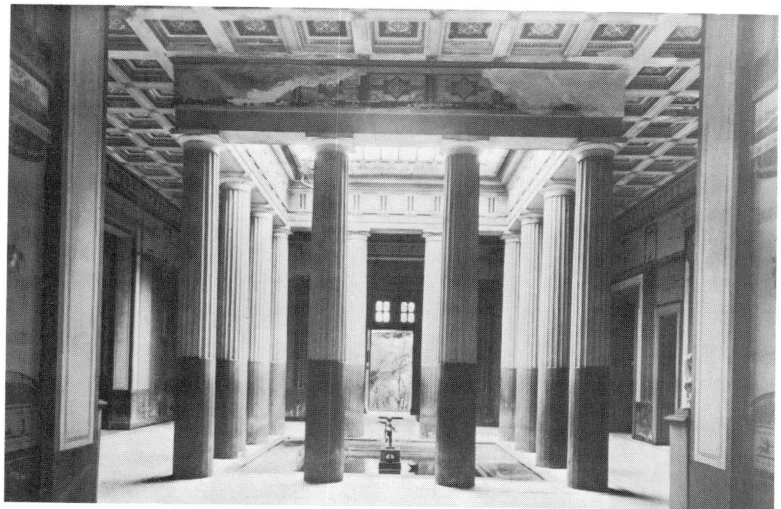

130. The Pompeiian House, Aschaffenburg, 1841–6. F. von Gärtner

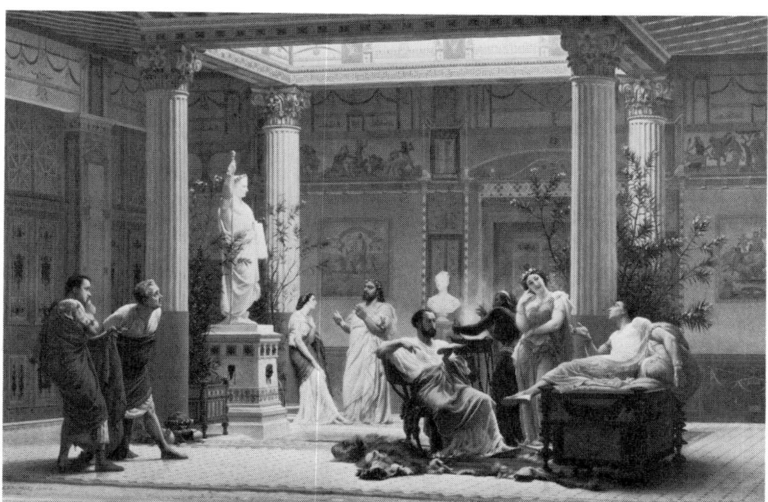

131. *Prince Napoleon's Pompeiian House*, 1861. G. Boulanger

sentation, not of a Pompeiian scene, but of a mid-nineteenth-century attempt to recreate one, this picture has more levels of literary meaning than of artistic significance. The same might be said of H.-A.-J. Moulin's statue *A Discovery at Pompeii* – a svelte and improbably boyish excavator in a dancing posture, derived from the Antique, holding a modern spade in one hand and brandishing in the other an Antique statuette of a corpulent satyr [132].

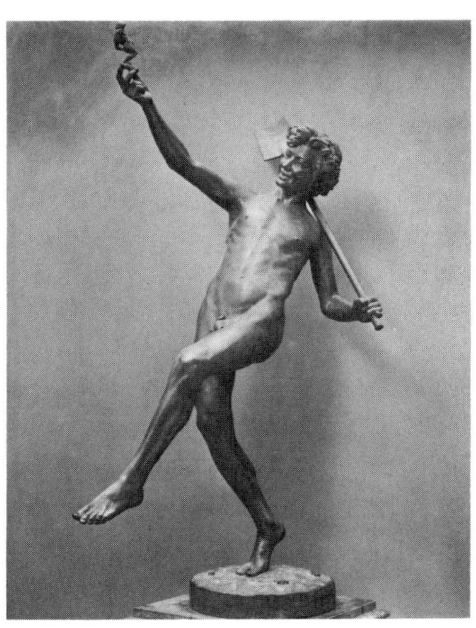

132. *A Discovery at Pompeii*, 1863. H.-A.-J. Moulin

In these years, too, a new attitude to the physical rediscovery of the past was being applied at Pompeii itself. Whereas the site had at first been regarded as no more than a mine from which precious objects might be extracted, it was now seen as an historical terrain to be explored and mapped out in detail, with as much regard for broken pots and fallen stones as works of art. The distinction is similar to that between the Neo-classical artist's selection from Antiquity and the Romantic's attempt to retrieve a moment of the past. Both looked back, but in different ways and for different purposes. Attention had shifted from the eternal to the transient; from the merits of works of art which might assist in the creation or re-creation of the 'true style', to the clues which buildings, paintings, statues, domestic utensils, petrified foodstuffs, and calcinated figures of men and dogs might provide for the re-creation of the past which would extend knowledge of how people lived and felt in the first century: and especially on that day in A.D. 79 when the Stabian cities were engulfed in lava.

This change in attitude had taken place gradually in the first half of the nineteenth century. Official reports on the discoveries, published by the Accademia Ercolanense between 1755 and 1792, were devoted exclusively to objects and included no plans of buildings. Views of the more spectacular ruins which had been uncovered appeared elsewhere. But no accurate plans were made available until 1812, when Mazois began to publish his great folios under the patronage of Queen Caroline (sister of Napoleon and wife of Murat).[23] She and her advisers – Mazois and the Comte de Clarac – also wished to restore three houses at Pompeii, leaving their wall-paintings, furnishings and utensils *in situ*, to demonstrate how members of different social classes had lived. The fall of Napoleon and change of régime prevented this; but in the years after 1815 repeated protests were made against the removal of all objects, and even wall-paintings, from the site to the museum. And although the new approach was primarily scientific, it also owed much to the Romantic love of ruins in general, and the poetic poignancy of this particular site, beautifully evoked by Leopardi in *La Ginestra*:

Questi campi cosparsi
Di ceneri infeconde, e ricoperti
Dell' impietrata lava,
Che sotto i passi al peregrin risona ...
Fur liete ville e colti,
E biondeggiâr di spiche, e risonaro
Di muggito d'armenti;
Fur giardini e palagi,
Agli ozi de' potenti
Gradito ospizio; e fur città famose
Che coi torrenti suoi l'altero monte
Dall' ignea bocca fulminando opprese
*Con gli abitanti insieme ...**

In the eighteenth century, the destruction of the Stabian cities had been recorded by several artists, but picturesquely, from distant viewpoints. The first 'close-up' of the horror of the cataclysm seems

* 'These fields scattered with unfertile ashes and covered with stony lava which resounds under the travellers' feet ... were gay hamlets and farms, golden with corn and echoing with the lowing of cattle; were gardens and palaces, delightful resorts for the leisure of the rich; and were famous cities which, together with all their inhabitants, were blasted by the fiery breath of the haughty mountain.'

to have been that painted by Pierre-Henri de Valenciennes in 1813 [133], and this owes more to Pliny and the tradition of Renaissance classicism than to recent excavations (the two-storied house with pedimented windows is a striking anachronism). Two ceilings in

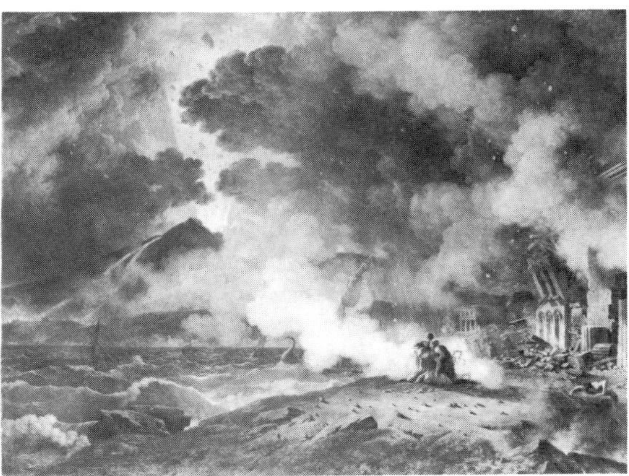

133. *The Eruption of Vesuvius, 24th August 79 A.D.*, 1813. P.-H. de Valenciennes

the Louvre depict the event allegorically, one by F.-J. Heim (1826) with a suggestion of divine vengeance, the other by F.-E. Picot (1828) with an oblique reference to the works of art which had been miraculously preserved. In 1827 Joseph Franque exhibited a painting *A Scene During the Eruption of Vesuvius*, inspired by the discovery of the skeletons of three women and a child who had apparently died when trying to escape from the city.[24] Also in 1827, the last day of Pompeii provided the subject for an opera by Pacini. And this, together with recent excavations, moved the Russian K. P. Bryullov to paint his huge, once very well known and popular *Last Day of Pompeii* [134]. Lord Lytton's famous novel, which followed in 1834, was written with this picture in mind, though he also drew on Sir William Gell's writings on Pompeii. The latter enabled him to describe accurately the streets of the city and its various buildings, including the 'house of the tragic poet', which he assigned to his unappealing hero, Glaucus. In turn, Lytton inspired Randolph Rogers's statue of Nydia, the blind girl in his novel (a work so popular in America that more than fifty replicas were carved) and, probably, a large painting by the American artist James Hamilton (Brooklyn Museum). A somewhat more sophisticated response to the excavations was provided by Gautier's charming ghost story, *Arria Marcella*, inspired by the imprint of a woman's corpse on a piece of lava in the Naples Museum.

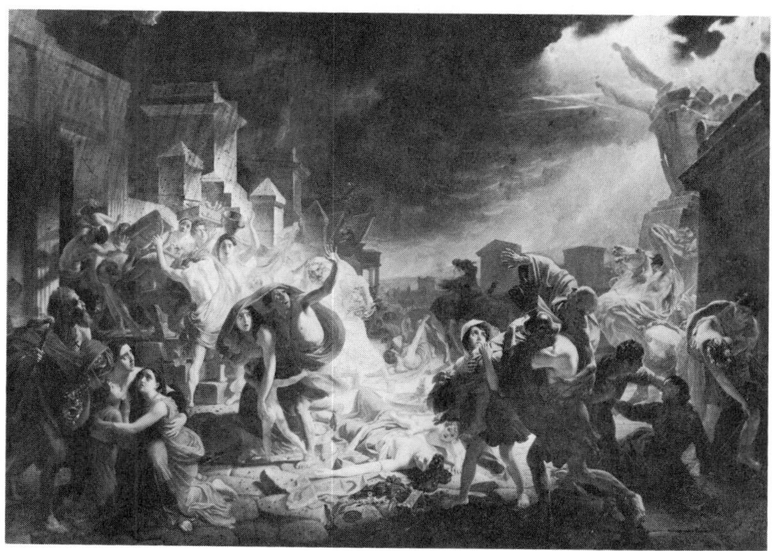

134. *The Last Day of Pompeii*, 1830–33. K. P. Bryullov

These pictures are images of catastrophic destruction of a peculiarly early nineteenth-century type. But Pompeii yielded evidence of life as well as death – of life more feverish if less noble, more colourful if less pure, than had previously been imagined. The obscurantism, superstition, viciousness and cruelty of the ancient world were only too clearly displayed. New light was also shed on ancient architecture, revealing that even the larger houses lacked

135. *Antiochus and Stratonice*, 1840. Ingres

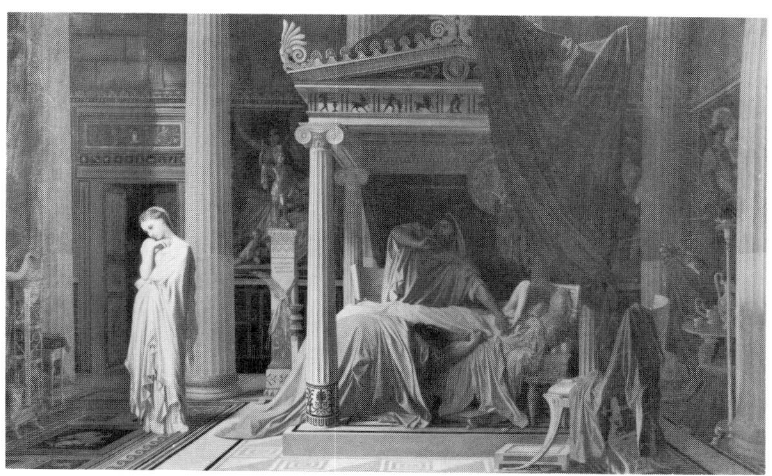

strict symmetry, that they were not precisely rectilinear, that they were garishly painted and often decorated with erotic pictures and obscene symbols. It was also found that the solemn Doric columns of Paestum had originally been coated with gaily painted plaster and that the Parthenon itself had been brightly coloured. The late eighteenth-century vision of Antiquity as a world of purity, nobility and elegance came to seem not merely marmoreally cold, but inaccurate. Artists were bound to take cognizance of these discoveries. Ingres rendered Greek architecture in bright polychromy [135]; Chassériau made use of an archaeological reconstruction of the baths at Pompeii and of furniture in the Naples museum for his *Tepidarium* of 1853 (Louvre).

In the historically permissive climate of the time, this change made Antiquity seem more rather than less attractive, if also more distant from the modern world. It had affected attitudes to literature before the visual arts. Herder, in the eighteenth century, found the origin of poetry not in neatly constructed verses but in the Dionysian ecstasy, the dithyrambus – 'a delirious rapture of the Bacchantes who, struck by the lightning of wine, sang with foaming mouths of the birth and deeds of its inventor'.[25] There is little trace of noble simplicity and calm greatness here; but this was the vision of the ancient world which was to inspire Hölderlin in Germany, Keats and Shelley in England, Leopardi in Italy. As an Italian remarked in 1824, 'The Romantic style is closer than the modern classical style to that of the ancient classics.'[26] It was no longer the rationality of the ancient world that was to be compared with the modern but its mystery, its vitality and sensuality – 'the laurel, the palms and the paean, the breasts of the nymph in the brake'.

Thus, Delacroix accused Ingres and most self-styled classicists of misinterpreting ancient art: 'What characterizes the Antique is the wise fullness of forms combined with the feeling of life, the breadth of scheme and the grace of the whole.'[27] He applied the same criteria to buildings: 'Modern monuments are always executed by rule and compass, in the strictest manner and down to the last corner; those of Antiquity are made by feeling, at any rate so far as details are concerned.'[28] The sensual Prud'hon understood ancient art better than the austerely cerebral David, he thought, and David better than Ingres with his '*goût mêlé d'antique et de raphaëlisme bâtard*'.[29] In Delacroix's view, Titian and Rubens were the painters who had most faithfully recaptured 'the spirit of antiquity and not the imitation of its exterior forms'.[30] And this perception deeply influenced his own paintings of classical themes. There

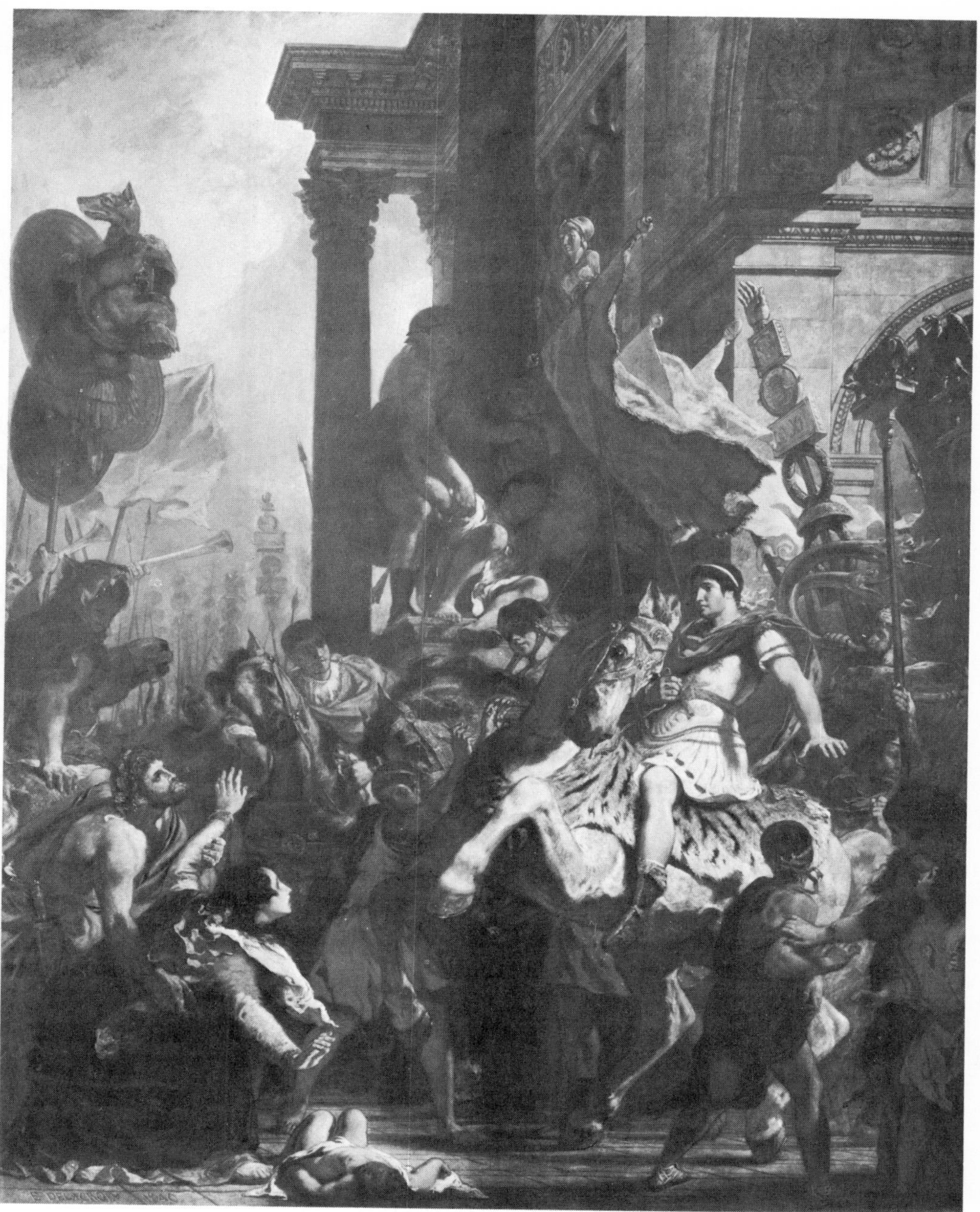

136. *The Justice of Trajan*, 1840. Delacroix

is a full-blooded richness and vibrant dramatic force in his *Justice of Trajan* [136], which owes debts equally to Antique sculpture, to Rubens and the Venetians. He took the subject not from a Roman

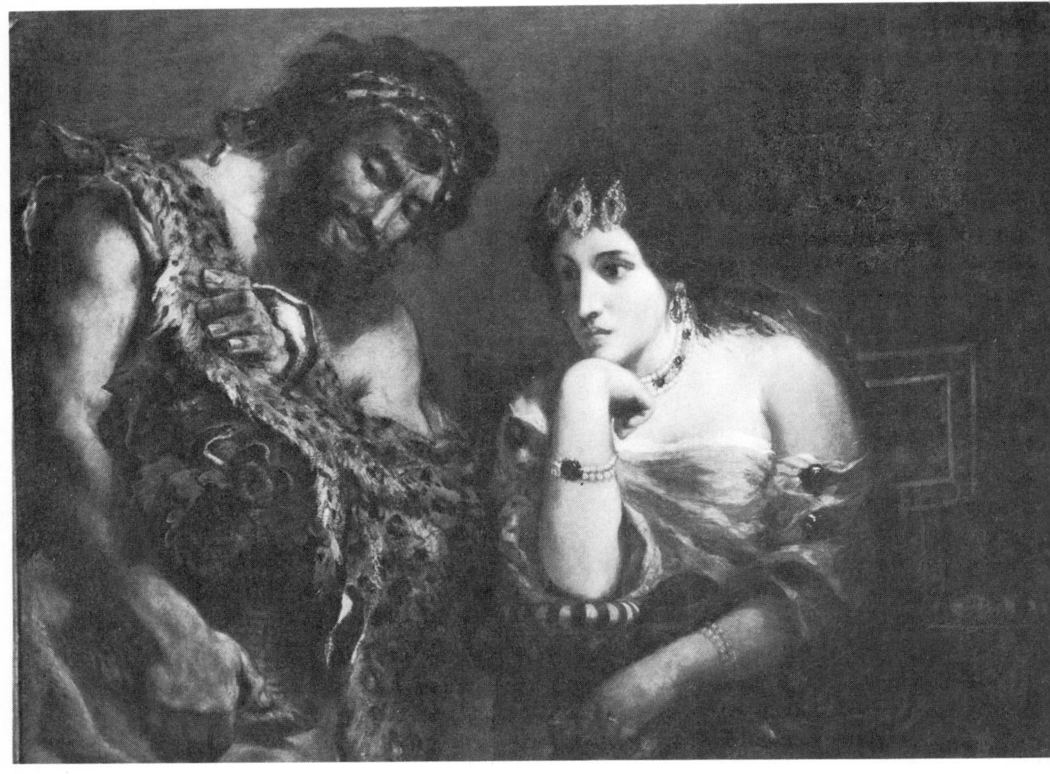

137. *Cleopatra and the Clown*, 1838. Delacroix

historian but from Dante, just as he went not to Plutarch but to Shakespeare for the barbarity, the irrationality, the psychological complexity and tragic intensity of *Cleopatra and the Clown* [137], as if to illustrate his belief that the ancient world could be recreated only when seen through a modern sensibility – modern in the Baudelairean sense of the word.

Delacroix's view of Greco-Roman civilization was characteristically ambiguous. He depicted its dawn and dusk in the hemicycles at either end of the library of the Palais Bourbon – *Orpheus Bringing the Arts and Civilization to the Ancient Greeks* and *Attila and his Barbarian Hordes Over-running Italy* [138] – and in between, on the pendentives of five cupolas, a series of scenes referring to the natural sciences, philosophy, law, theology and poetry. This is no complacently optimistic conspectus of human progress. The most memorable figure in the room is that of Attila, and the pendentives include the death of Archimedes, the suicide of Seneca, and the elder Pliny watching the eruption of Vesuvius in which he was to

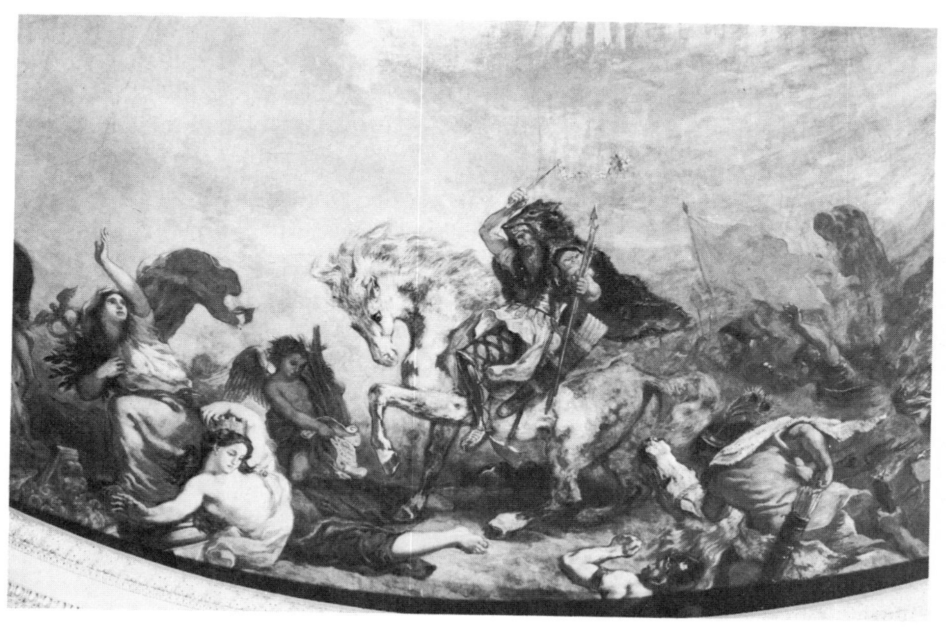

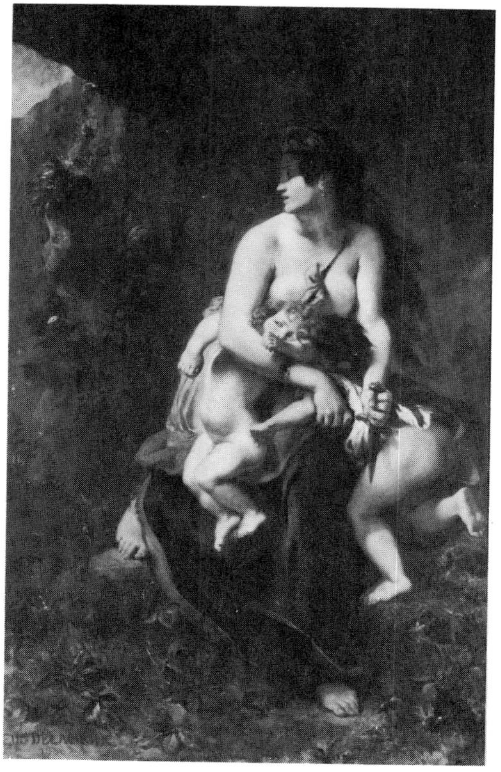

138 (*above*). *Attila Over-running Italy*, 1843–7. Delacroix

139. *Medea*, 1838. Delacroix

perish. Did Delacroix select these subjects in order to stress the frailty of civilized values? In another pendentive he painted the exiled Ovid among the Scythians (which he repeated in one of his most poetic works),[31] contrasting the civilized and the natural man, without comment. For here, as in the Attila hemicycle, the subject is also, perhaps predominantly, simply the conflict of two physical types – a conflict which, like that of forms and colours, can be resolved only in paint. Perhaps the greatest and most moving of his paintings of classical subjects is *Medea* [139], a kind of savage antithesis to the Christian image of Charity and one in which he united voluptuous beauty and insensate violence, animal vigour and terror, the smouldering fury of the rejected wife, and the demented mother's revulsion from her children. This is no illustration of a text in a dead language but, so to speak, a translation of Euripides into Romantic poetry and the language of modern experience.

6. *The Cause of Liberty*

'*Pas trop de politique!*' Auguste Jal sarcastically remarked at the beginning of his book on the Salon of 1827. 'As if anything was not political at present; anything except the conduct of our statesmen . . . Romanticism in painting is political; it is the echo of the cannon shot of 1789.'[1] In fact, Romanticism came to be associated with Revolution in France only because so many Romantics were driven into opposition by the government of Charles X (immediately after 1815 most of the more progressive writers had supported the Restoration). But politics in the modern dialectic sense – as the struggle between left and right, progress and reaction, rather than the interplay of factions in monarchic and oligarchic states, or an abstract matter of theory – was a product of the French Revolution. It was then that the essential questions were first posed in clearly defined terms. And the association of *avant-garde* art and politics began effectively with David's involvement in the Revolution. So also, it may be added, did the tendency to read into works of art political messages which may or may not have been intended by their authors. For it was at this moment that the quintessentially Romantic notion of the artist projecting his individual – philosophical, religious and political – view of the world was first put about. *Weltanschauung* is one of the neologisms of the period.

The issues were seldom as straightforward as historians are sometimes inclined to suggest. There were many shades of opinion in the political spectrum, and opinions were often modified by events. Even those artists who painted explicitly political pictures often found themselves faced with a dilemma by the conflict of ideals – and none more than the greatest of them, Goya. *The Disasters of War* has been likened by André Malraux to 'the sketchbook of a Communist after the occupation of his country by Russian troops'.[2] The sense of urgency, of personal commitment, of anguished disillusion is certainly felt, overwhelmingly so, indeed. But consistency of political attitude is more than a little difficult to trace in Goya's total *œuvre*. The story of his *Allegory of Madrid* is disconcertingly eloquent of this. It was painted in 1810, as an allegorical portrait of Joseph Bonaparte, whom Napoleon had set on the Spanish throne. After the liberation of Madrid from the French in 1812, Goya substituted the word *Constitución* for Joseph's head, only to put it back a few months later when the French retook the city, to replace *Constitución* again in 1813, and finally to cover it with a portrait of Ferdinand VII in 1814![3] Also in 1814, he painted his masterpiece *The Third of May* [12] as one of two pictures intended, so he wrote at the time, 'to perpetuate with his brush the most notable and heroic actions or events of our glorious revolution against the tyrant of Europe'. But it would be preposterous to interpret this profoundly moving image simply as an expression of reactionary Bourbon politics, or even of Spanish nationalism. Like the *Disasters of War* etchings and the paintings associated with them, it transcends the merely topical, poignantly focusing on deeper, more generally experienced ordeals, dilemmas, perplexities and burdens of the human condition, especially that conflict between two concepts of liberty which had been brought to a head by the French Revolution and has vexed the Western world ever since. It might almost illustrate a remark from Benjamin Constant's *De l'esprit de conquête* of 1813: 'Human beings are sacrificed to abstractions: a holocaust of individuals is offered up to "the people".'[4]

Constant was one of the first writers to distinguish clearly between 'negative' liberty, or freedom from oppression, and 'positive' liberty, or freedom to lead one prescribed way of life. The first French Republican army had been called into existence by the need for defence from external coercion. But within a very short time this demand for negative liberty was converted into a claim for the positive liberty to impose on France and elsewhere Republican government – '*la despotisme de la liberté*', as Marat approvingly called it. During the following years *Liberté, égalité et fraternité* were often to appear incompatible with individual freedom, especially in the countries that were over-run as the French armies spread across Europe. And this was not to be without consequence for the arts, especially in Germany where liberty was closely associated with nationalism.

It was, of course, in late eighteenth-century Germany, with Herder and Fichte, that the notion of a *Volksgeist* which controls, or ought to control, a nation's culture first developed. This provided the writers of the *Sturm und Drang* movement with a theoretical basis for their attempt to liberate German arts from French influence. Opposition to the literary classicism of Boileau might, however, be extended to classicism in general. To many Germans the ancient world was admirable but alien. 'Greek figures and Greek gods no longer correspond to the form of the human species; they are as foreign to us as the Greek sounds and names in our poetry,' wrote Georg Forster in 1790.[5] '*Wir sind keine Griechen mehr*,' wrote P. O. Runge in 1802.[6] *Sturm und Drang* also had a social aspect, as an expression of opposition to the aristocratic – and still predominantly Francophile – culture of the princely courts. For this reason the majority of German intellectuals had welcomed the French Revolution and, initially, the eastward advance of the Republican army. Napoleon's dismantling of the cumbrous Holy Roman Empire and its reassembly into larger units, together with

140. *At the Advance Post*, 1815. G. F. Kersting

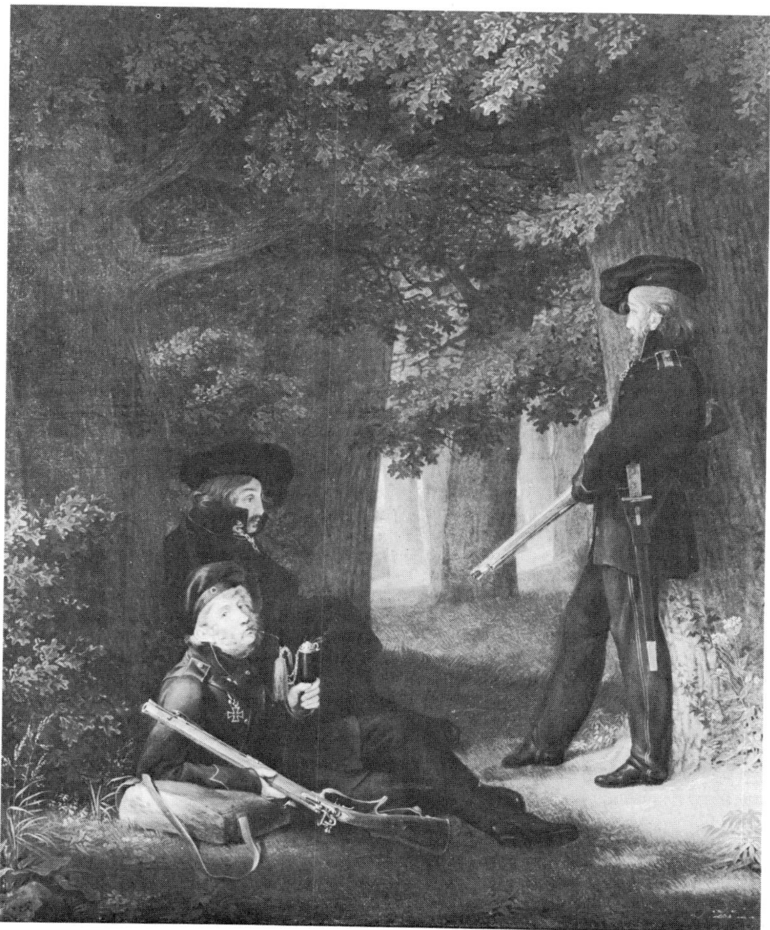

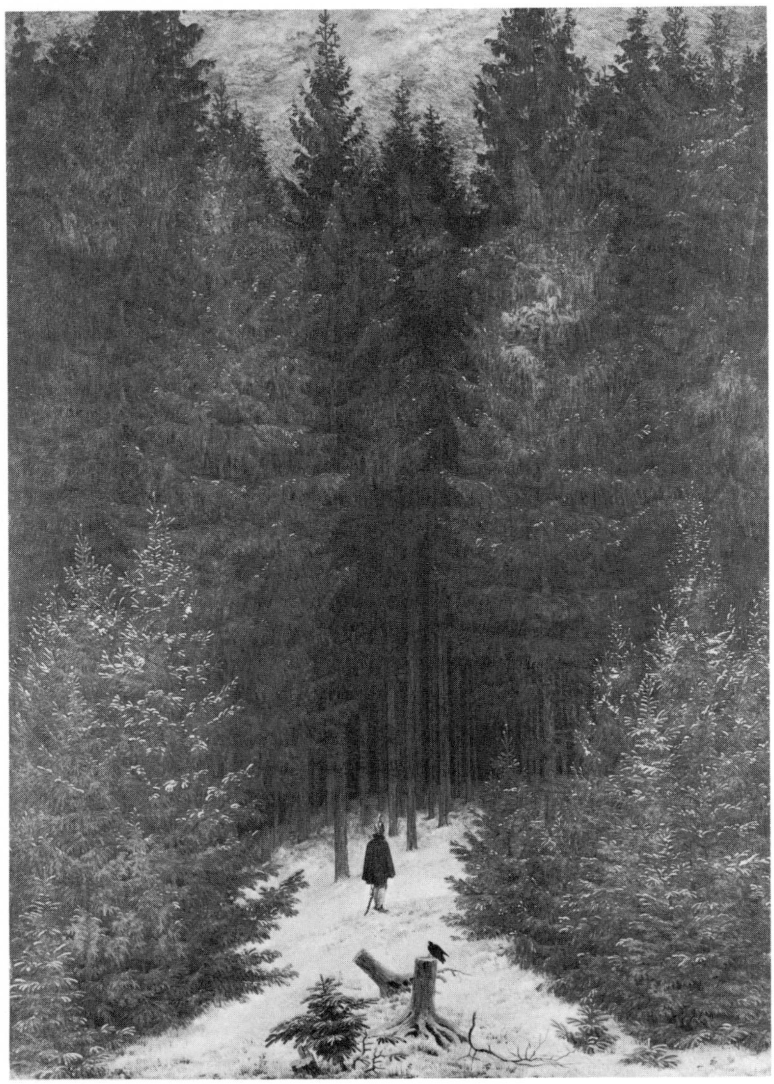

141. *The 'Chasseur' in the Forest*, 1814. Caspar David Friedrich

the institution of the *code Napoléon* east of the Rhine, was also widely welcomed. But, as French authority grew increasingly oppressive, Francophobia and nationalism acquired a new militancy. Both nationalist and liberal hopes came to be focussed on Prussia, where the state was reorganized after 1806 on more nearly democratic lines – 'We must do from above what the French did from below,' Hardenberg had told the King. The Battle of Leipzig in 1813, when the Prussians routed the French, was the first victory for the new

German nationalism, which began as a quest for negative liberty but was soon converted into a 'positive' demand.

The high-minded spirit of German nationalism at the time of the War of Liberation – the *Freiheitskrieg* as it was called – is beautifully conveyed in a painting, by Caspar David Friedrich's friend G. F. Kersting, of three *Lützower* – members of a regiment of volunteers which included several notable writers and artists, Joseph von Eichendorf, Fouqué, Karl Immermann, Theodor Körner, Philipp Veit and Kersting himself [140]. They are dressed in what was supposed to be the old German fashion, with floppy hats; they have

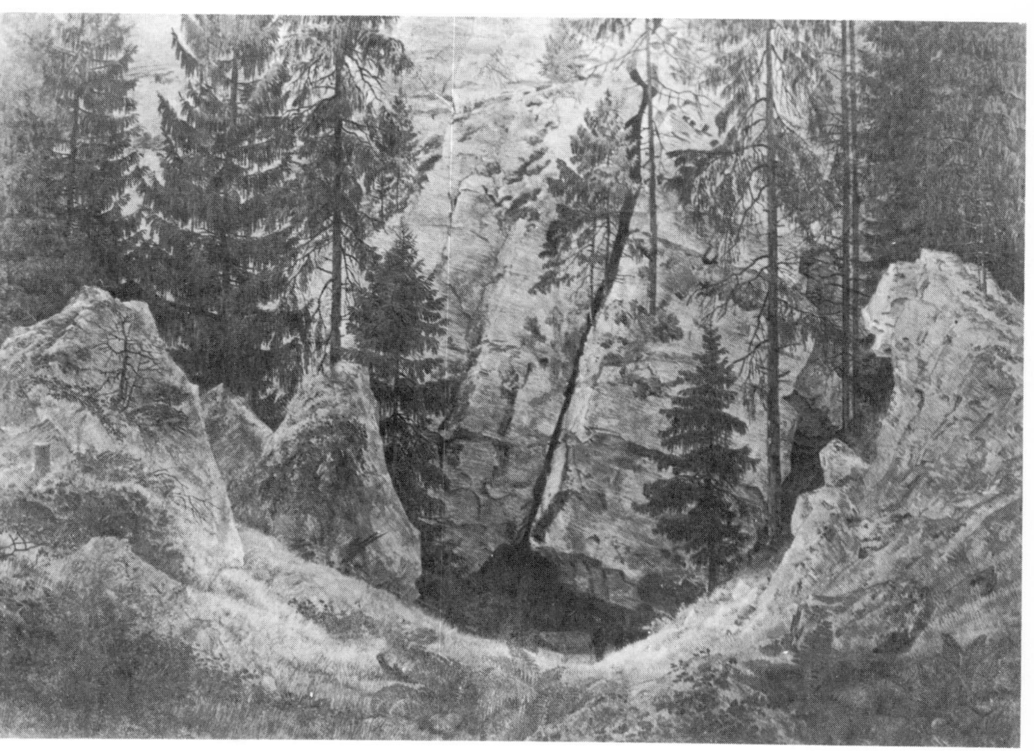

142. *Hermann's Tomb*, *c.* 1813–14. Caspar David Friedrich

long Teutonically blond hair and moustaches (one of them wears a beard), and are placed in a symbolically German oak wood. In another picture by Kersting, a girl makes a wreath of oak leaves for men who had fallen in the war.[7] Caspar David Friedrich expressed his response to the war rather more subtly. Yet the meaning of *The 'Chasseur' in the Forest* [141] was easily recognized by a reviewer when it was first exhibited in 1814: 'A raven perching on an old branch sings the death song of a French Chasseur who is wandering alone through the snow-covered evergreen forest.'[8] At the same period Friedrich painted more than one evocation of an imaginary tomb of Hermann or Arminius – the ancient Teutonic leader whose fight against the Romans was seen as an historical parallel for the German war of liberation from the French – containing one of his most moving images, that of a lonely sarcophagus set in a cleft of the living rock of ages at the heart of the German fatherland [142].

In these years Friedrich's nationalism was coloured with liberalism. Writing to Ernst Moritz Arndt in March 1814 about a projected monument to Scharnhorst, who had been killed in the Battle of Leipzig, he remarked: 'So long as we remain the menials of princes nothing great of this kind will be seen. Where the people have no voice, the people will not be allowed to be conscious of and honour themselves.'[9] His pessimism was soon to be justified by the repression of the liberal movement after 1815. *Hutten's Tomb* [143], probably of 1823, alludes to the new political situation, showing a ruined Gothic chapel with a headless statue of Faith on one wall, and a man in *altdeutsche* costume (like the uniforms of the *Lützower*)

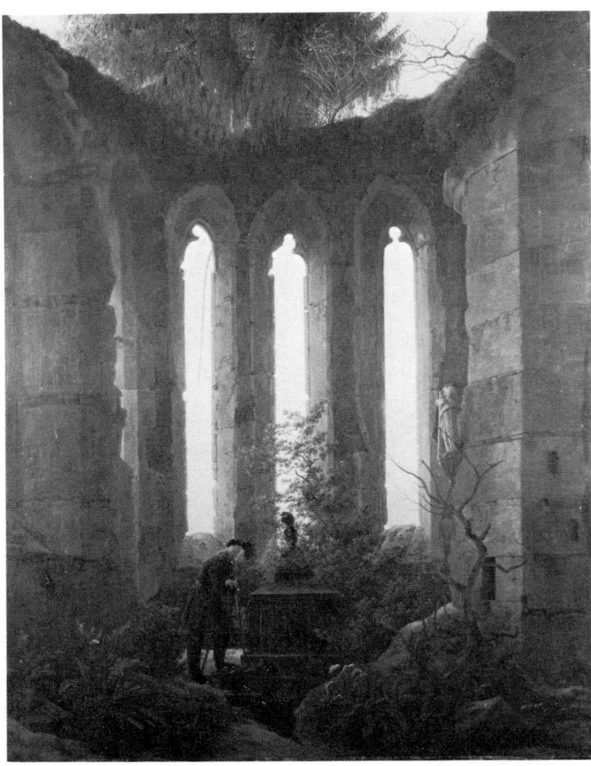

143. *Ulrich von Hutten's Tomb*, 1823–4. Caspar David Friedrich

meditating on the tomb of Ulrich von Hutten. Hutten, the humanist and supporter of Luther, had called for the creation of a strong centralized German state, but joined the abortive revolt of the Imperial Knights in 1523 and died an exile in Switzerland. The tercentenary of Hutten's death had coincided with the tenth anniversary of the War of Liberation, and Friedrich inscribed on the sarcophagus the names of several men of liberal outlook who had fought in it but were subsequently rendered powerless or driven into exile: *Jahn 1813*, *Arndt 1813*, *Stein 1813*, *Görres 1821*. It is the most clearly allegorical of Friedrich's paintings and probably the last to carry an explicit political message. He was to portray himself more than once in the *altdeutsche* hat and cloak, regarded by the authorities as the costume of a *Demagoge*.[10] But this may well have had, for him, artistic rather than political significance, as a symbol of his demand for freedom of expression and the creation of an autonomous German style.

Memories of the *Freiheitskrieg* were, however, cherished by the reactionary legitimists it had restored to power as well as by liberals. Of the several war memorials, the most prominent is that above Kelheim on the Danube, built between 1842 and 1863 to the design of Leo von Klenze and at the expense of Ludwig I of Bavaria, who had also raised the Doric Walhalla above Regensburg as a monument to German genius [87]. The gaunt mass of the Befreiungshalle [144] distantly recalls the mausoleum of Theodoric at Ravenna. In this overpowering building, with its richly coloured marble interior

144. The Befreiungshalle, Kelheim, 1842–63. Leo von Klenze

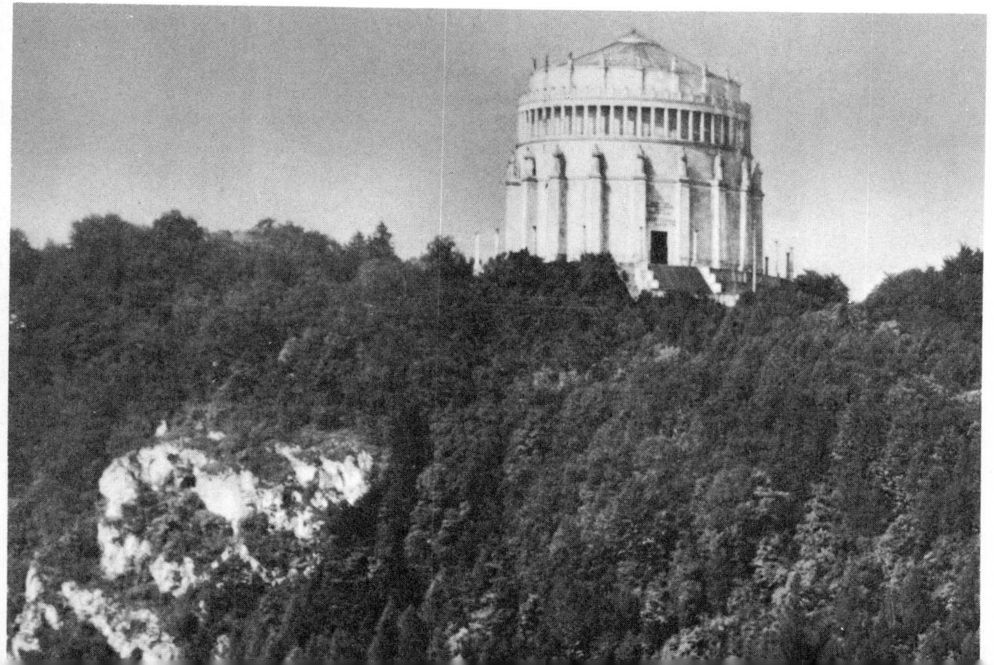

ringed round by gigantic white statues of goddesses of victory, there is certainly no hint of the spirit of liberalism. Nor, apart from the inscriptions and the insistently Aryan features of the muscular goddesses, is there much that is specifically Germanic. Ludwig was as hostile to German unification as to liberalism, and seems to have confined nationalism strictly to the cultural domain. It was, perhaps, for this reason that, although he commissioned for Munich buildings in a wide variety of styles, he showed relatively little interest in Gothic, which had become elsewhere a kind of emblem of German unification.

The Prussian national monument to the War of Liberation, on the Kreuzberg in Berlin, was erected in 1821 in a prickly Gothic style (anticipating the later and larger Scott memorial in Edinburgh and Albert Memorial in London), and constructed – almost prophetically – of cast iron [145]. It was designed by Schinkel who,

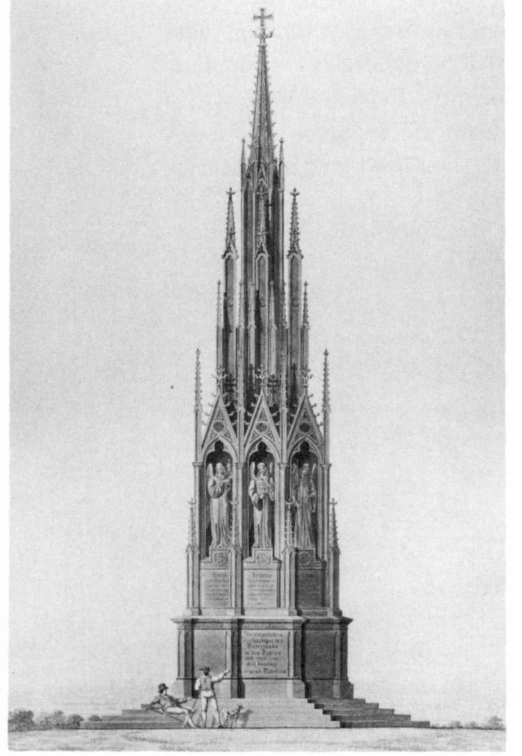

145. *Freiheitskrieg Memorial, Berlin*, 1818–21.
Karl Friedrich Schinkel

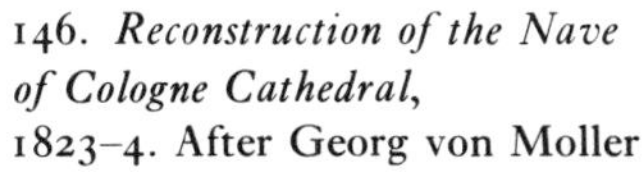

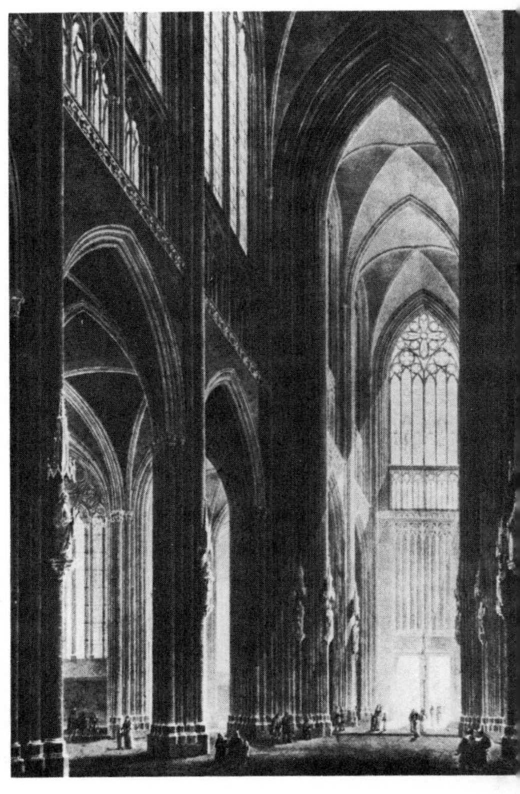

146. *Reconstruction of the Nave of Cologne Cathedral*,
1823–4. After Georg von Moller

a few years earlier, had strongly recommended for political and aesthetic reasons the restoration and completion of Cologne Cathedral, which became the focal point of German cultural nationalism. But although Schinkel directed the work of restoration, the moving spirit was Sulpiz Boisserée [146], who had already played an important role in the development of Romantic aesthetics by assembling a large and remarkable collection of early German paintings and by introducing Friedrich Schlegel to the study of Gothic architecture. Under the Empire Boisserée had tried to interest Napoleon in his project for the completion of the Cathedral, and in 1814 he lost no time in turning to the Crown Prince of Prussia (later Friedrich Wilhelm IV). He also found a propagandist in the prominent Catholic revivalist Joseph Görres, who suggested that the Cathedral should be completed as a monument to the *Freiheitskrieg*. 'Long shall Germany live in shame and humiliation, a prey to inner conflict and alien arrogance, until her people return to the ideals from which they were seduced by selfish ambition, and until true religion and loyalty, unity of purpose and self-denial shall again render them capable of erecting such a building as this,' he wrote in 1814.[11] The completed Cathedral would, he said, become a symbol of a new Reich – though one rather different from that envisaged by the Prussian authorities, who drove Görres into exile when he published a mildly liberal-Catholic pamphlet, *Germany and Revolution*.

By 1842, however, when official backing was finally given to the project for completing the Cathedral and the foundation stone of the nave was laid, the connections between freedom, nationalism and Gothic architecture had acquired new shades of meaning. One journalist declared: 'The Cathedral is the greatest of Germany's bulwarks, which she will guard or perish, and which will fall only when the blood of the last Teuton has mingled with the waves of Father Rhine.'[12] Görres marked the occasion with a book in which he represented the Gothic style both as a German invention exported to the rest of Europe – though this belief had been discredited long before – and as the symbol of the metaphysical yearnings and aspiring spirit of the German soul which, with the development of the pointed arch, liberated itself from the geometric restraint of the Romanesque. Here, the cultural nationalism of Herder and the Romantics, and the demand for freedom from alien dominion which had inspired the *Freiheitskrieger*, have already taken on implications which were to grow more sinister in the following years.

The same process can be seen in representations of the aboriginal Germans. In his first major work Carl Blechen painted the Sem-

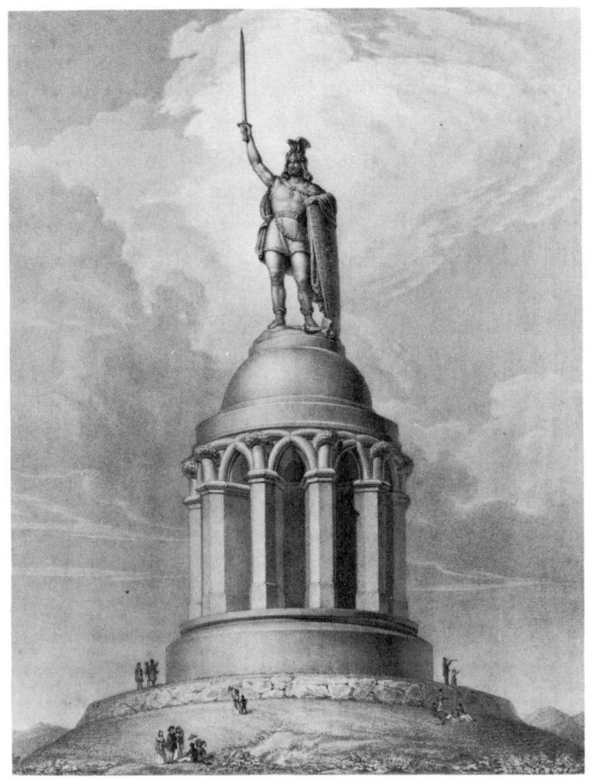

147. *Monument to Hermann by E. J. Bandel*, 1819–75. J. Giere

nones – a powerful Germanic tribe described by Tacitus – enjoying the freedom of pastoral life on the Müggelberge.[13] But the warrior Hermann, whose imaginary tomb had been depicted with such primitive evocativeness by Friedrich [142], was soon enrolled as the emblem of a militant type of nationalism – as in Ernst von Bandel's statue, begun in 1819, though not finally raised on the Teutoburg near Detmold until 1875 [147]. Among later heroes of German nationalism, Dürer had, of course, been prominent ever since Wackenroder presented him as the Teutonic counterpart of Raphael, worthy of the same esteem and reverence. In the early nineteenth century he came to be regarded almost religiously as the patron of German artists [198]. The leaders of the Protestant Reformation provided more potent symbols of liberal nationalism. Carl Friedrich Lessing's *Hussite Sermon* of 1836, showing a Hussite preaching in the open air to a group which includes all social classes, with a church burning in the background, even though it had been commissioned by the

King of Prussia was interpreted as a call for national, religious and social freedom [148]. 'And how significant this subject is for the present day when the same battle against the church for spiritual freedom is being fought in other ways and brought to its conclusion,'

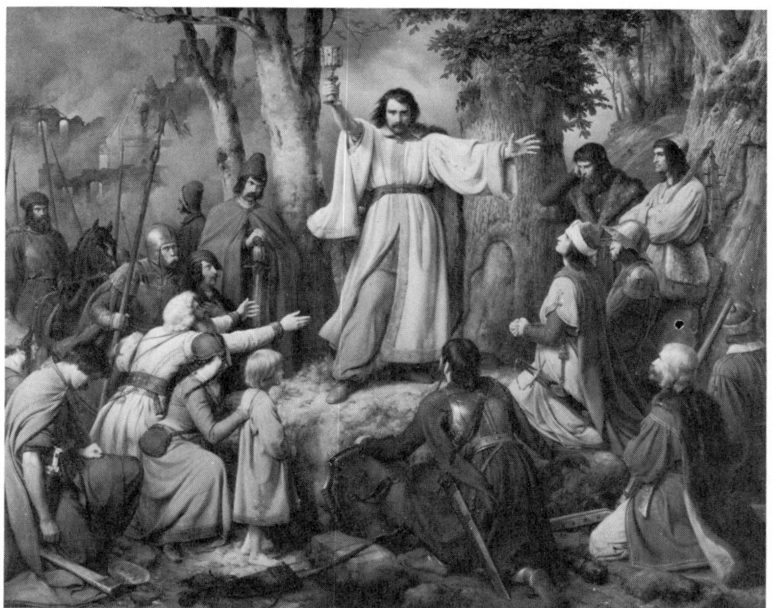

148. *The Hussite Sermon*, 1836. C. F. Lessing

a writer in the radical *Rheinische Zeitung* declared in 1842. Another contemporary likened its effect to that of a rapturous, fully orchestrated performance of the Lutheran chorale *Ein feste Burg ist unser Gott* – or of the *Marseillaise*. But he wrote with the benefit of hindsight, after 1848, when Lessing had been actively engaged in the revolution in Düsseldorf.

In Italy, supporters of the Risorgimento similarly made use of historical parallels for novels and the plots of operas as well as paintings. One such subject was the victory of the Lombard League over the Emperor Frederick Barbarossa at the Battle of Legnano in 1176, depicted by several artists including the politician and novelist Massimo d'Azeglio,[14] before Verdi wrote his opera *La Battaglia di Legnano*, first performed in 1849.[15] The Sicilian Vespers of 1282, still more popular with painters, also provided a plot for Verdi. Significantly, a picture of this subject was commissioned from Francesco Hayez by the Milanese Conte Francesco Teodoro Arese immediately after his release from the Spielberg, where he had been imprisoned for his part in the abortive uprising of 1821, the first attempt to liberate Lombardy from Austrian rule. Hayez also painted a very striking full-length portrait showing Arese in his cell in the Spielberg [149]. No such explicitly dissident picture could,

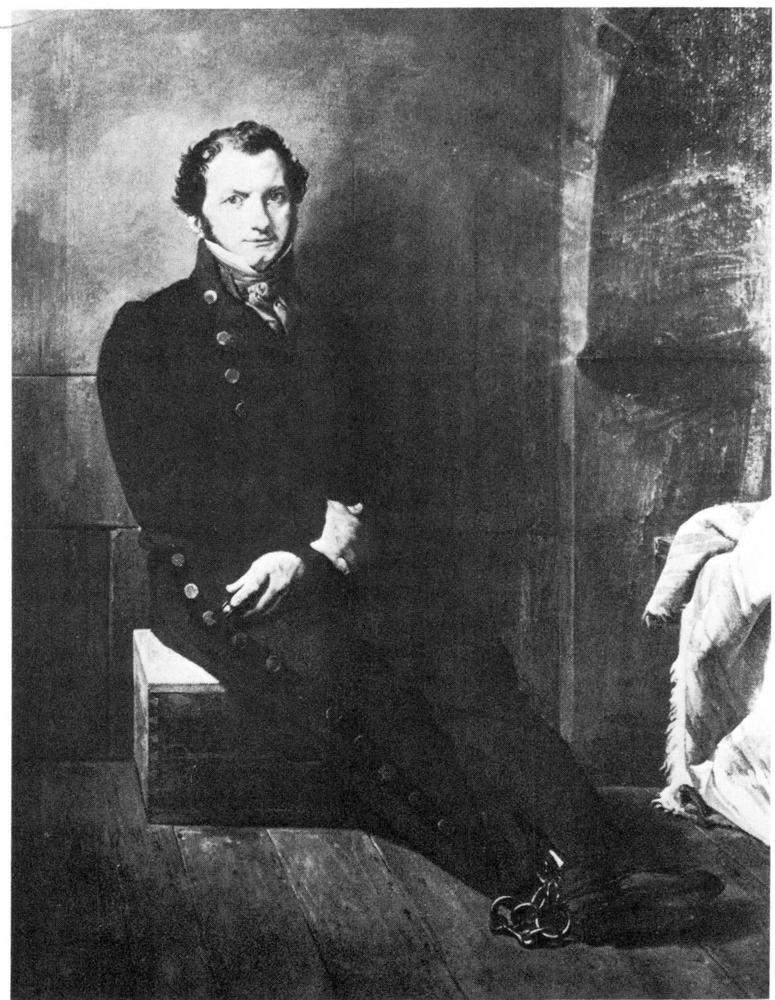

149. *Count Arese in Prison*, *c.* 1827. Francesco Hayez

of course, be publicly exhibited in Italy at this time. Artists who wished to protest at foreign domination were bound to seek parallels in other periods or other countries. Thus, Hayez depicted the plight of the Christians who were condemned to exile or virtual slavery when the British authorities handed over the Albanian city of Parga to Ali Pasha in 1819.[16] And other Italians were to record the heroism of modern Greeks fighting for their liberty.[17]

The contrast, poignant in its melancholy, between ancient and modern Greece had long been a theme for sententious moralizing In the mid-eighteenth century the liberation of the country was described as a 'glorious cause/The cause of Liberty, the Cause of Nations', though this was no more than a velleity.[18] Byron saw little hope of improvement when he lamented the subjugation of 'fair Greece sad relic of departed worth' in the second canto of *Childe Harold* (1812), and not until he wrote the third canto of *Don Juan* in 1820 did he so much as dream 'that Greece might still be free'. But these poems and a steadily increasing quantity of travel literature, including Chateaubriand's *Itinéraire de Paris à Jérusalem* (1811), helped to stimulate sympathy for the Greek cause when the War of Independence finally broke out in earnest in 1821. And Byron's active participation and death at Missolonghi, in 1824, transformed it into a Romantic crusade. Despite, or perhaps because of, the initial indifference of the West European powers (Metternich hoped that the revolt would burn itself out 'beyond the pales of civilization'), Philhellenism became an intellectual cult. 'The Greeks occupy the thoughts of everyone,' Delécluze wrote in his journal in 1826; 'at any rate of everyone who is opposed to monarchical and ultramontane ideas.'[19]

Although England played a major part in the Philhellenic movement, few English artists seem to have alluded to it – the most notable exceptions being Turner, Thomas Barker of Bath and Charles Lock Eastlake.[20] The Greek cause was far more popular with French painters, though for reasons which seem to have been artistic as much as political. 'I have had enough of ancient Greeks; it is the modern Greeks who interest me,' wrote Jal in his account of the Salon of 1824:

> Hector, Achilles, Agamemnon bore me with their sublimities; Georges Colocotroni, Odysseus, Jorgaki, those are the names which reverberate in my heart. I have wept enough over the eternal misfortunes of the eternal Ilium; Ipsara! your recent misfortunes arouse my soul. What are the soldiers of King Priam to me? The Keflis, the Anatolians preoccupy me.[21]

A supporter of Géricault and Delacroix, Jal prefaced these remarks with the statement that 'Romanticism runs at full flood in society, and as painting is also the expression of society, painting is becoming Romantic': he concluded them with a glowing account of *The Massacres of Chios* [15].

In Paris, in 1826, there were charity concerts in aid of the Greeks. There was also an exhibition '*au profit des Grecs*' at the Galérie Lebrun, supported by most of the leading artists. Delacroix showed what was later to become the most famous image of the war [150], which has often been mistitled *Greece Expiring on the Ruins of Missolonghi*, though it was called at the time, and Delacroix himself

150. *Greece on the Ruins of Missolonghi*, 1826. Delacroix

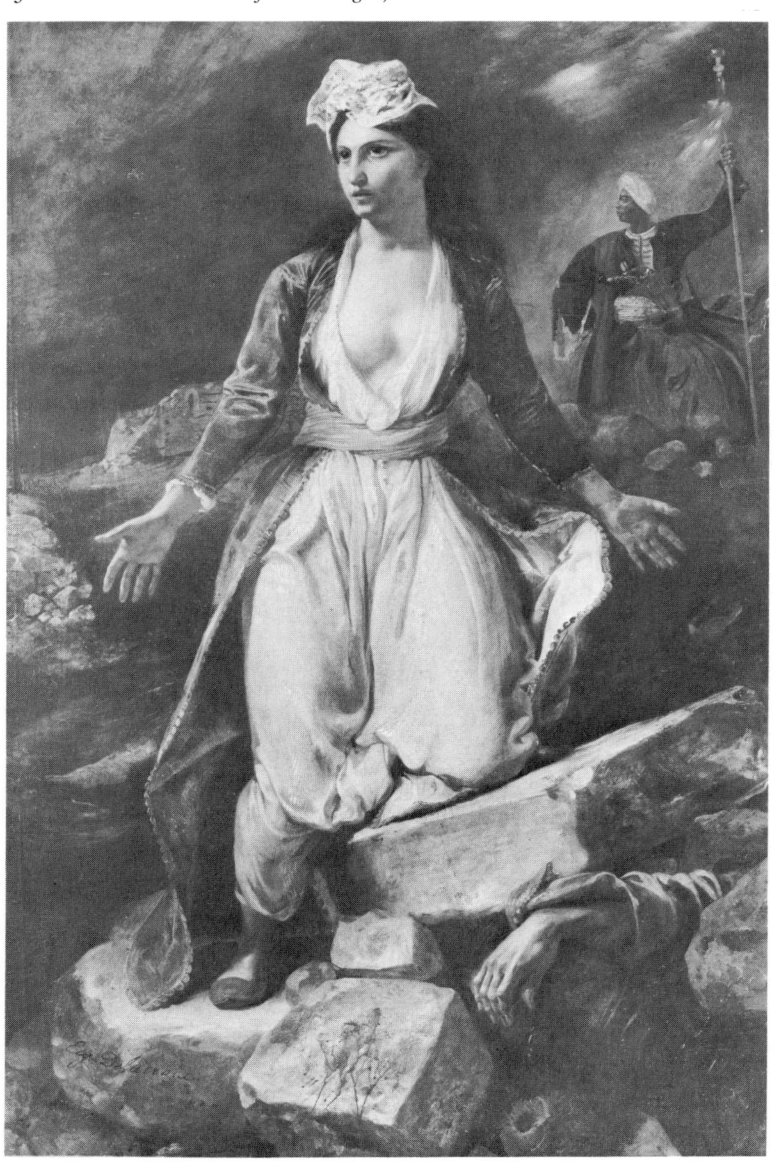

always named it, *Greece on the Ruins of Missolonghi.* The central figure is, in fact, appealing for help with an open-armed gesture, palpitating with life, and personifying the triumph of the spirit of liberty over disaster (represented by the pile of masonry and a dead hand), in a way which brings to mind Wordsworth's sonnet to Toussaint L'Ouverture of 1807:

Thou hast left behind
Powers that will work for thee: air, earth, and skies;
There's not a breathing of the common wind
That will forget thee; thou hast great allies;
Thy friends are exultations, agonies,
And love, and man's unconquerable mind.

At the Salon of 1827 Delacroix showed a picture of a skirmish between Greeks and Turks, and the same exhibition included several modern Greek subjects by other artists[22] – most notably, perhaps, Ary Scheffer's *The Women of Souli* [151].

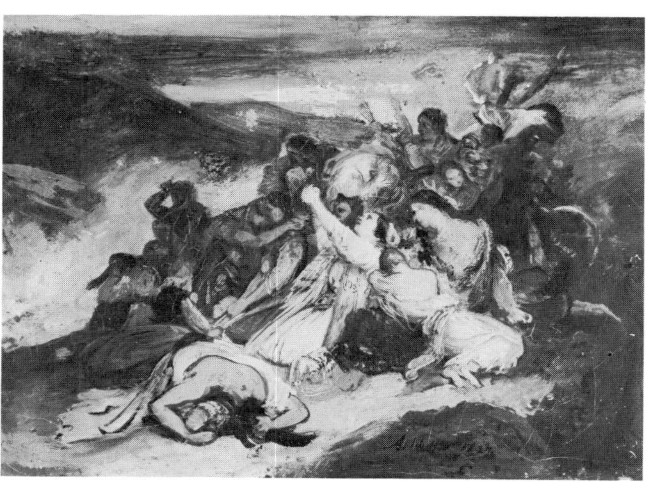

151. *The Women of Souli*, 1823. Ary Scheffer

The Polish uprising of 1830–31 inspired almost as much sympathy in Western Europe as the Greek war had done. In Edinburgh, David Scott recorded one of its episodes in a painting of extraordinary cumbrous power and an oppressive melancholy which even recalls Goya – the Russian troops burying their dead during a ceasefire granted by the Poles [152]. The German Dietrich Monten depicted the tragic end of the revolt in a painting entitled *Finis Poloniae* [153]. And in France, Léon Cogniet painted a desolate Pol-

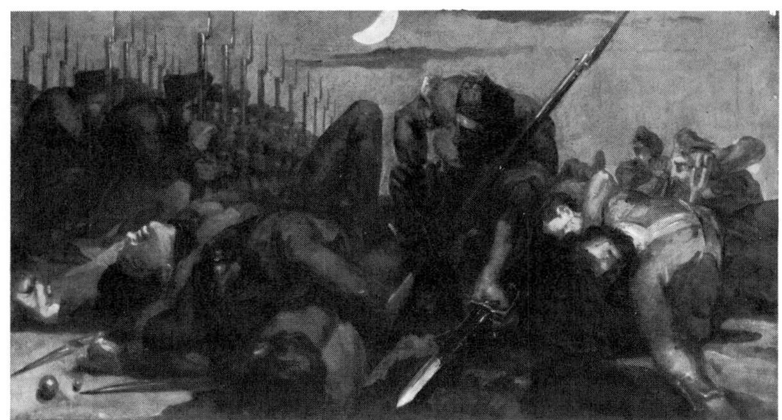

152. *Russians Burying their Dead*, 1832. David Scott

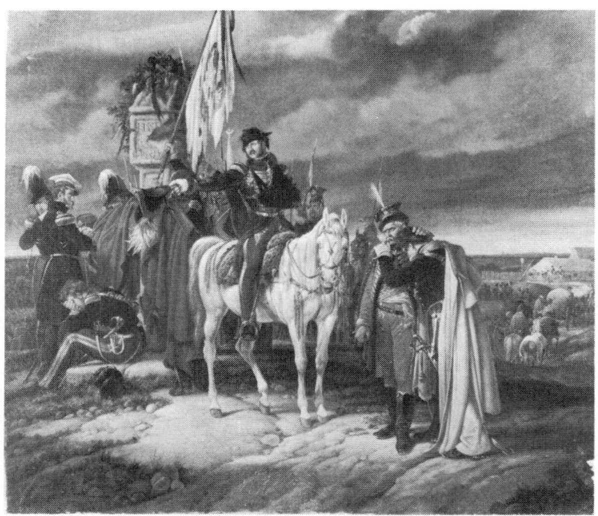

153. *Finis Poloniae*, 1832. D. Monten

ish army officer (probably the patriot and poet Alexandre Rypiński) with Warsaw in flames behind him [154] – a work with a curious after-history, for it was copied on a larger scale in 1852 by Cogniet's pupil Henryk Rodakowski to represent a hero of the equally unsuccessful Hungarian uprising of 1848. But the Polish insurrection aroused less interest than the Greek war among artists, who found in the latter not only an expression of nationalism and liberalism but a gigantically magnified reflection of their own struggle for liberty from academic rules and, ironically, the ancient Greeks. Thus political and artistic ideas and ideals were often fused. In an article which Delacroix read with approval, the liberal Ludovic Vitet was to ascribe to the Greek war the complete revaluation of classical Greek art and literature.[23]

Events in Poland were also inevitably overshadowed in the minds of French artists by the success and failure of the July Revolution in Paris. Here again it was Delacroix who left the most famous art-

154. *The Polish Officer*, *c.* 1831, Léon Cogniet

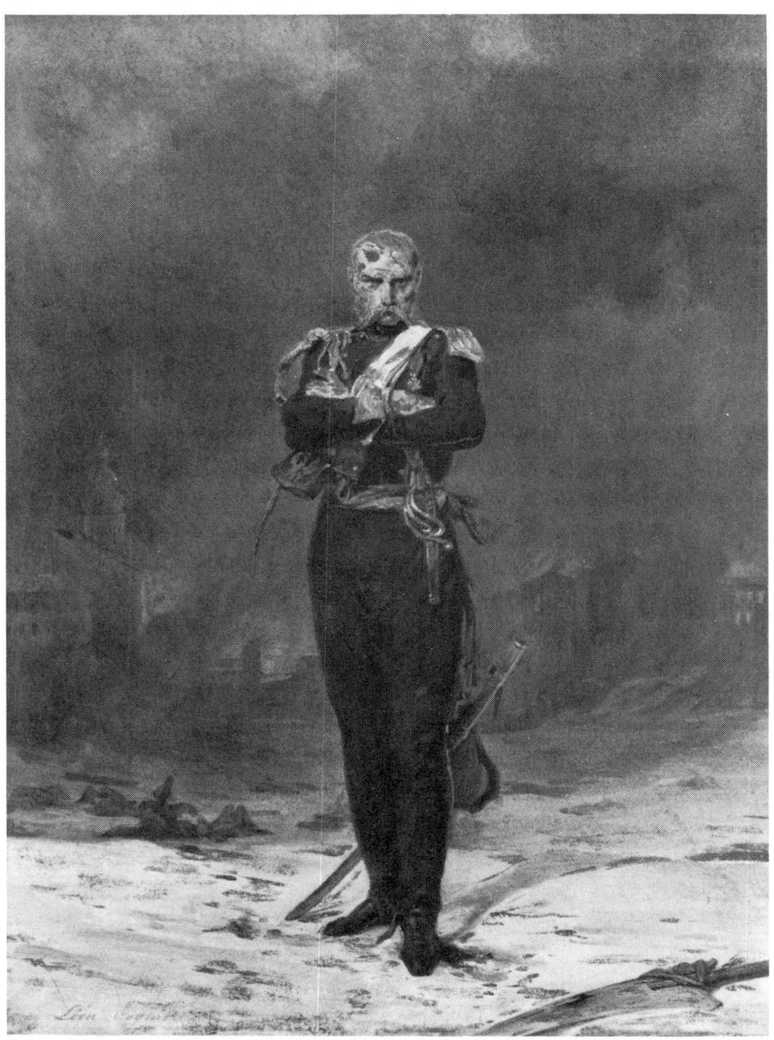

istic record – perhaps the best known visual image of revolution ever created – *The 28th July: Liberty Leading the People* [155]. This enigmatic combination of allegory and real life, history painting and reportage, was not very favourably received when shown at the Salon of 1831. It was bought by the state, but judged too inflammatory to be exhibited for more than a short while (it was displayed

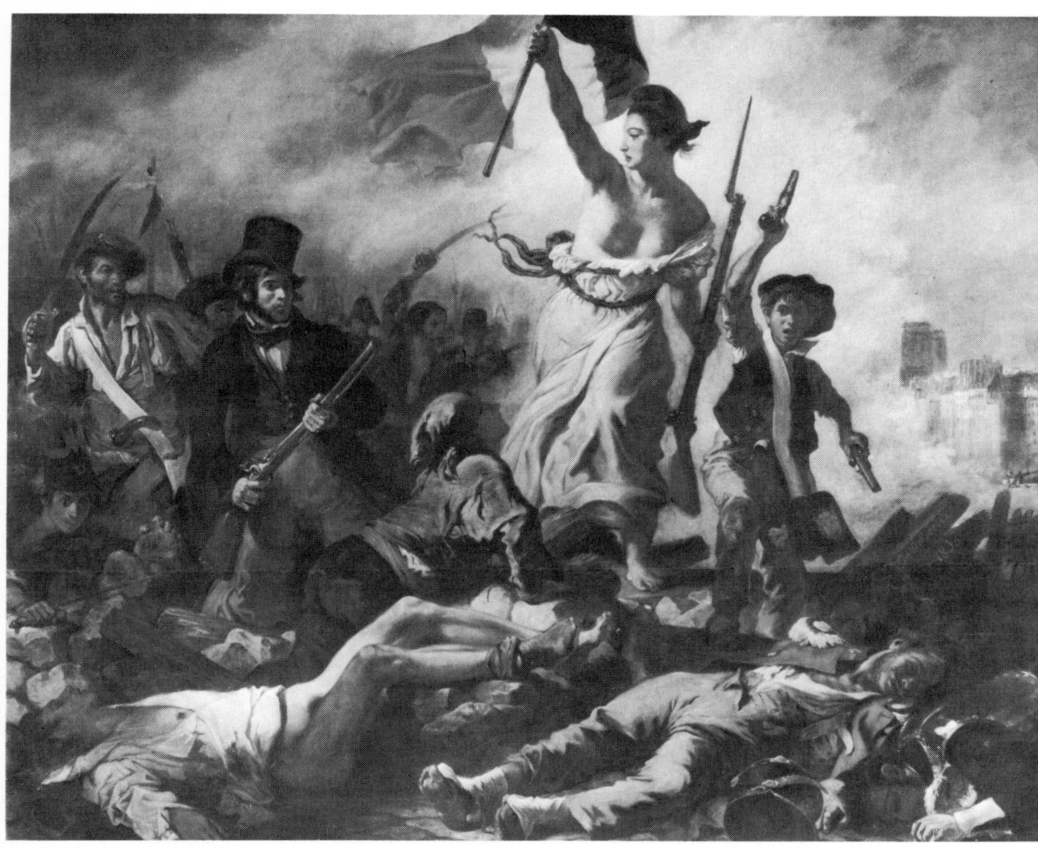

155. *The 28th July: Liberty Leading the People*, 1830. Delacroix

again after the 1848 Revolution, and also in 1855, but only for a few weeks, and it was not made permanently available to the public until after 1861). Though more idealized than other representations of the July days – Lecomte's picture of the barricade in the rue de Rohan, for example, or Charlet's powerful lithographs of militant workers [156] – it is more vivid and also more disturbing. Liberty, bayoneted-rifle in one hand, Tricolour in the other, is flanked by a *gamin* brandishing pistols, a bourgeois in a high hat and a prole-

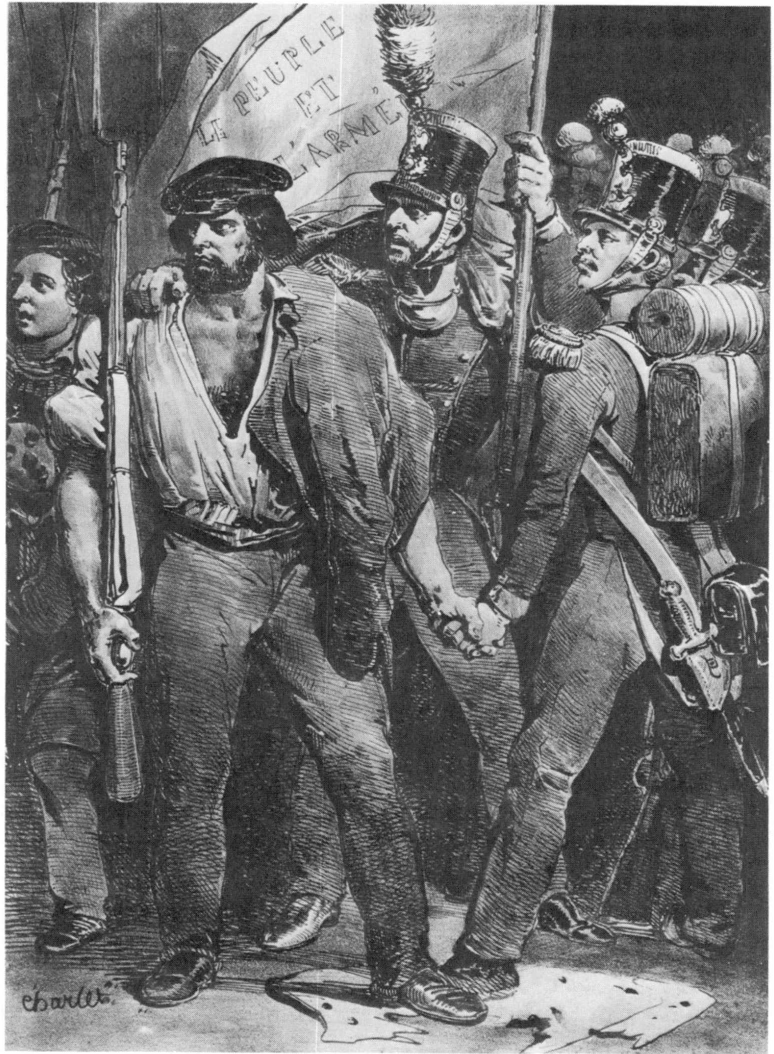

156. *Aux Armes Citoyens!*, 1830. N.-T. Charlet

tarian holding a sabre, as she advances inexorably towards the spectator, from whom she turns her head to rally her followers. Despite a physical similarity with *Greece on the Ruins of Missolonghi*, she represents not a negative but, and very much so, a positive concept of liberty. And the life-size corpses in the foreground, one so strongly reminiscent of *The Raft of the 'Medusa'*, suggest that Delacroix, who was certainly no demagogue, was as well aware as Benjamin Constant of the way in which individuals can be sacrificed to political ideals. The picture seems to represent an unresolved conflict between the personal and artistic freedom Delacroix demanded and the political libertarianism which he came increasingly to fear. It was a conflict which, whether consciously or not, was faced by every Romantic, and it was eventually to drive many of them into retreat towards the citadel of art for art's sake.

Artistic and political liberty were, however, very commonly associated with one another in the years around 1830. And as liberty was identified with nature so frequently in literature and, especially, political oratory, one is bound to ask if any of the 'free' landscapes which broke away from the classical tradition to represent '*la nature telle qu'elle est*' had political connotations as well.[24] Most of them clearly had none – Corot's Italian landscapes for instance.[25] Paul Huet's large *Sun Setting Behind an Old Abbey in a Wood* might be more susceptible to a politico-allegorical interpretation – the twilight of the House of Bourbon – were it not for the lines from a sentimentally nostalgic poem by Victor Hugo printed in the Salon catalogue.[26] There can, however, be no doubt of the political commitment of this '*paysagiste patriote*', as Daumier called Huet: he had been a Carbonaro at the age of seventeen and fought beside Alexandre Dumas on the barricades in 1830. Many years later, he was to recall that towards the end of the Restoration an '*irrésistible élan de liberté*' had inspired all the arts, including that of landscape painting.[27] And his *Amnesty* of 1832 is an explicit and moving

157. *Amnesty 1832*, 1832. Paul Huet

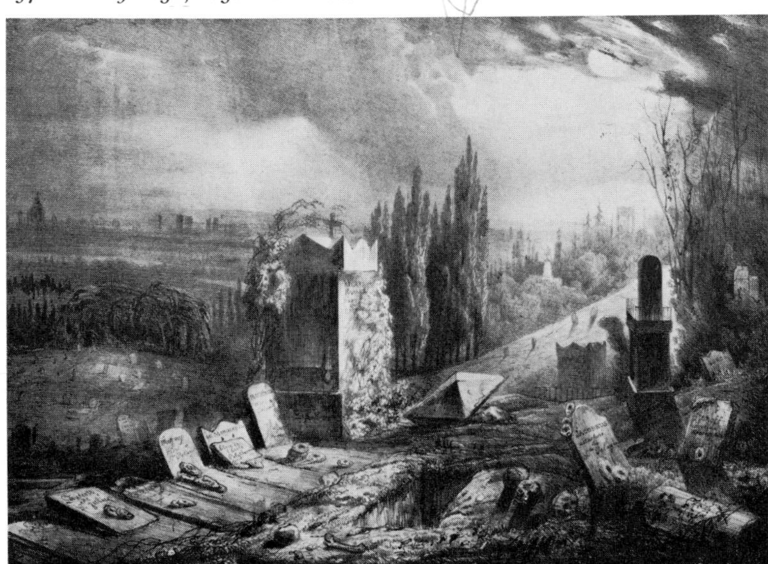

protest against the first acts of Orléanist repression – an elegiac view of a cemetery with monuments to Republicans who had been executed or died in prison [157]. At this troubled moment political feelings could hardly be excluded from landscapes which expressed an artist's view of the world, in the widest sense, and not merely the nebulous '*état de l'âme*' of Amiel's much later phrase.[28] But such feelings were not necessarily liberal, of course. In England, Constable painted Salisbury Cathedral in 1831 with his fears for the Anglican Establishment, then threatened by Reform agitation, very much in his mind – literally and metaphorically 'the church under a cloud', as his friend Archdeacon Fisher said.

It was sometimes suggested, even by the Romantics themselves, that the Romantic cult of energy had helped to create a mood of revolutionary violence. '*On recueille dans les rues les fruits qu'on a semés dans les livres*,' wrote Ximénès Doudan in 1832.[29] Perhaps for this reason the Salon juries after 1831 tended to be harsher in their reaction to stylistic dissidence than to subject-matter (figurative paintings by Delacroix, landscapes by Théodore Rousseau, some of Barye's sculptures of ferocious animals were among the works refused). But works of art alluding to or even depicting events of the first Revolution and the Empire, banned under the Restoration, were now frequently shown – though Louis-Philippe intervened personally in 1833 to exclude Chenavard's painting of the signature of the death warrant of Louis XVI, which the jury had accepted. Indeed, the authorities of the July Monarchy did their best to exploit and turn to their own advantage nostalgic memories of Republican and Napoleonic *gloire*. The Arc de Triomphe de l'Etoile, begun in 1806, was completed and adorned with vast reliefs, the most notable of which, *The Departure of the Volunteers* (popularly known as *La Marseillaise*) by François Rude, perfectly catches the heroic spirit of the army of 1792 as seen from the vantage point of 1833 [158]. This strongly emotive sculpture is, however, cast in Antique language, which probably made it more acceptable to the authorities than Delacroix's *Liberty*: the figures are without *culottes* only for the sake of heroic nudity. Rude later executed a more realistic testament to his Republican sentiments in the monument to Godefroy Cavaignac, who had been partly responsible for throwing up the barricades in 1830.[30] That he should at the same time (1847) have modelled a statue of Napoleon embarrassed his Republican biographer, writing in 1856. But in the 1840s Napoleon was seen as the heir to the Revolution, and also as a Romantic hero, greater in defeat than in success, and the archetype of artistic genius striving

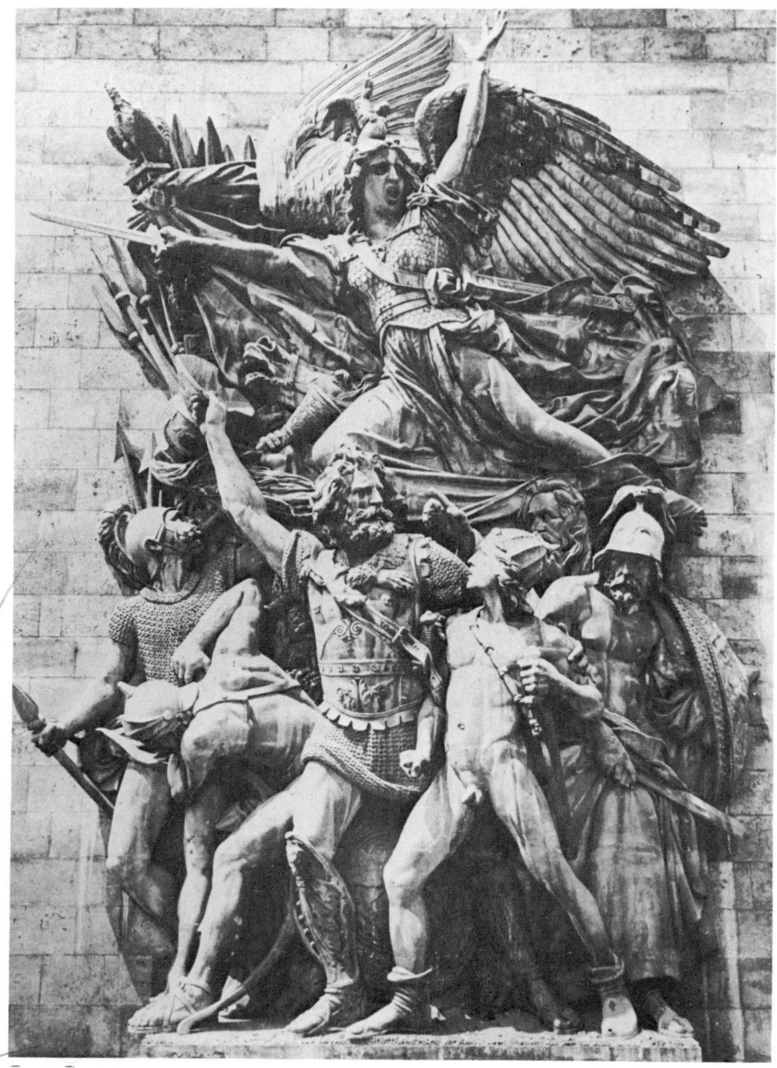

158. *The Departure of the Volunteers 1792*, 1833–6. François Rude

for liberation. It was in this form that Rude represented him 'waking to immortality' on his death-bed on St Helena [159]. This extraordinary statue, set neither in a church nor a city square but in the open country near Dijon, facing towards the mountains of the Jura and the Alps, is among the most striking manifestations of Romantic ideas in politics and art, and at the same time a reminder of their uneasy relationship. For it is perhaps the most impressive of the many images which nourished the Napoleonic legend, soon to acquire a very different significance.

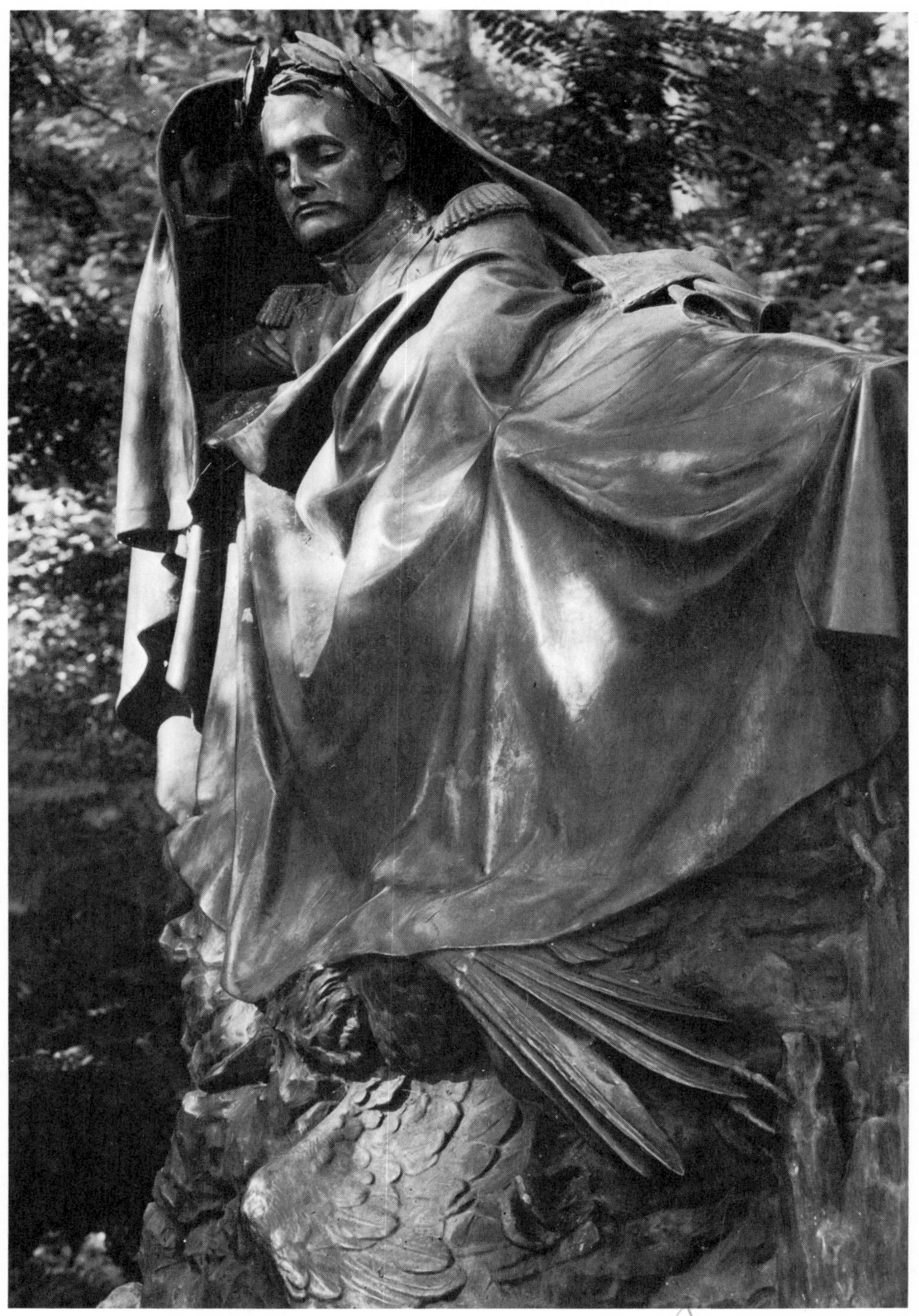

159. *Napoleon Waking to Immortality*, 1847. François Rude

Pierre-Jean David d'Angers was another earnestly engaged Republican sculptor, destined to be exiled from France during the Second Empire. 'Political ideas have always been the motive force of my artistic life,' he wrote in 1839.[31] In 1827 he had lent his support to the Greek cause by modelling a statue of *A Greek Girl at the Tomb of Marco Botzaris*, which he later had carved in marble and presented to the Greek government.[32] He carved Revolutionary subjects for the Arc de Triomphe in Marseille in 1834; presented a distinctly liberal interpretation of constitutional monarchy on the pediment of the Panthéon in Paris in 1837; and made of the Gutenberg monument for Strasbourg a declaration of his faith in enlightenment through the printed word (with one relief panel devoted to the abolition of slavery). His statue *The Young Bara*, shown at the Salon of 1839, is a kind of double monument to the Republican youth killed by Vendean counter-revolutionaries and to David, who had immortalized him and his heroic death.[33] These were all public works, but he expressed his political sympathies still more clearly in his bronze medallions and the comments he wrote on their subjects. They included nearly all the famous figures of the Revolution: Robespierre, '*homme admirable ... moeurs douces*'; Barère, '*ce grand homme*'; Carnot, '*l'homme le plus admirable de son époque*'; Saint-Just, '*pauvre jeune homme!*'; Babeuf, Marat, and so on. He recorded the victims of Restoration repression, the four Sergeants of La Rochelle, and the champions of liberty: the Abbé Gregoire, Michelet, Edgar Quinet, Louis Blanc, Filippo Buonarotti and Blanqui. And although he sometimes portrayed men whose political views differed from his own, none could be regarded as an enemy of liberty. 'We artists are factual historians and party questions should not concern us,' he remarked. He had marble and bronze for genius, virtue and heroic courage, but none 'for tyrants and the Rothschilds'.[34]

Among artists, David d'Angers was unusual in his interest in politicians and political theorists. The Romantic cult of liberty was more often centred on figures of an entirely different type who represented a different concept of liberty: bandits, brigands and outlaws. The Italian bandits who recur in the art, literature and music of the period had, of course, made earlier appearances in art, those which animate Salvator Rosa's rocky landscapes being the most famous. (To judge from their cuirasses and helmets, they represent *Landsknechte* and other unemployed mercenaries who ravaged the Italian countryside in the sixteenth and early seventeenth centuries.) Salvator also made these savage figures the subject of 'picturesque' etchings which were imitated towards the end of the eighteenth century, most notably by John Hamilton Mortimer in England.[35] In the early nineteenth century, artists who specialized in painting bandits depicted them in modern costume and carrying modern fire-arms, though belonging to an older, literary rather than pictorial, tradition – that of the outlaw.

Robin Hood had been a folk hero in England since the Middle Ages, as the central figure in a cycle of comic and adventurous tales (less remote and aristocratic than those about King Arthur and his knights), and also, perhaps, as a symbol of resistance to injustice. He made a sudden reappearance in Walter Scott's *Ivanhoe* (1819) and Thomas Love Peacock's *Maid Marian* (1822) – a book which Peacock described in a letter to Shelley as 'a comic romance of the twelfth century, which I shall make the vehicle of much oblique satire on all the oppressions that are done under the sun'.[36] Scott depicted his Highland counterpart in *Rob Roy* (1817), a novel which provided subjects for several French painters under the Restoration.[37]

In Germany, Schiller had created a similar character, Karl von Moor, as the tragic hero of his famous play *Die Räuber* (1781).[38] And here the myth of the bandit as revolutionary appears to have begun. For whatever Schiller's intention may have been, this play was given a political significance in the 1790s and cited when – much to his surprise – he was made an honorary citizen of the French Republic. Shortly afterwards bandits were to play a real-life political part, but on the other side, employed by the legitimists as guerrillas to harass the Napoleonic armies in southern Italy and Spain. Their activities might be given a nationalist interpretation associated with the cause of liberty, but they could not resume their role as political revolutionaries until after 1815 when, in Italy, they came into conflict with the troops of the Papal States and Bourbon Kingdom.

It is, of course, highly improbable that any bandits had been politically motivated either during the Empire period or afterwards. It was possible, nevertheless, to see them as victims of an unjust social system. Their defiance of authority might seem to symbolize opposition to the Restoration. And they were often invested with the freedom-loving characters of a Robin Hood or Karl von Moor. Thus, the Swiss artist Léopold Robert, who painted those who had been rounded up by the police and imprisoned, wrote from Rome in 1822: 'Ever since I arrived here I have been struck by these Italian figures, by their manners and their picturesque and savage clothes. I hoped to render them with all possible truth, and above all with

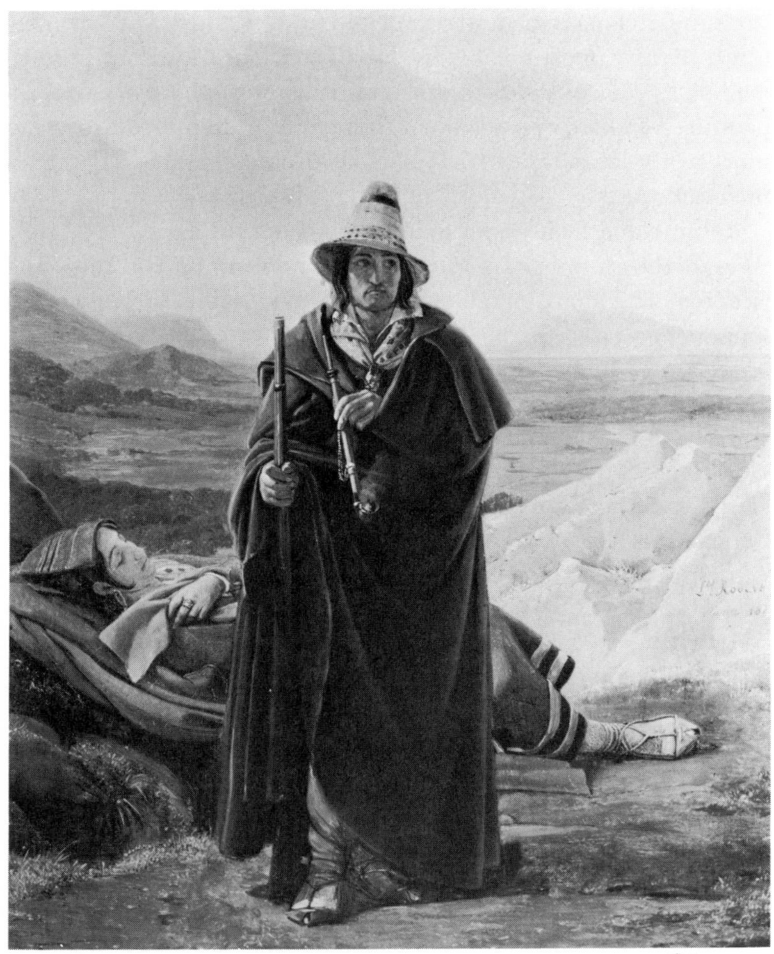

160. *Bandit on the Watch*, 1825. Léopold Robert

that simplicity and nobility which one marks in this people and which they inherit from their ancestors' [160]. Feuillet de Conches described Maria Grazia, who was painted by several artists while her husband languished in the Castel' di Sant' Angelo, as 'the true type of brigand's wife; of superb stature and form, her head crowned with the most magnificent tresses, strong, proud, fearless, with a commanding eye and gesture resembling the "Liberty" of Barbier's dithyramb ...' (the poem which inspired Delacroix while painting *Liberty on the Barricades*).[39]

In the vast brigand literature of the early nineteenth century, the bandit is generally described as a fugitive from injustice, rather than from justice, obliged to take to the hills and survive as best he can, preserving his code of honour (often the cause of his proscription) while rejecting the conventional morality of the society from which he was excluded. Thus he was depicted as a type of Romantic hero, passionate and melancholy, rugged as the untamed landscape into which he was so skilled at disappearing. He was associated with the Romantic cults of wild country, of the persecuted and social outcast, of the political dissident, of anyone who displayed independence of spirit. The enormous appetite of the public for paintings of bandits at this period is symptomatic, and since none of the great Romantic artists indulged it, those by Léopold Robert, Victor Schnetz and Horace Vernet were extravagantly praised (by Stendhal and Delacroix among others). To satisfy the demands of his patrons and admirers Robert painted no fewer than fourteen variants of his *Sleeping Brigand*.[40]

Although these painters departed from the outworn Salvator Rosa convention, they merely rejected an old formula for a new one, no more credible and still further divorced from reality than their pictures of happy peasants and dancing Neapolitan fishermen (which also enjoyed great popularity[41]). What had at first seemed realistic and daring (in comparison with paintings of Antique heroes) soon came to look contrived. Léopold Robert's work has some historical importance in the current of Romanticism which was to merge into Realism. But out of this context his bandits can hardly be taken seriously. Painted in a somewhat dry academic manner, they are not strong enough to carry the weight of the notion of freedom that they imply. The fascination which bandits exerted on the Romantics – '*ces brigands de la pensée*' as Philothée O'Neddy was to call them[42] – found true expression only in literature and in music: in Mérimée's *Colombe* (1841) and *Carmen* (1843), Auber's charming opera *Fra Diavolo* (1830), and especially Berlioz's *Lélio* (1831) and *Harold en Italie* (1834).

Berlioz, above all, was a devotee of the Romantic brigand cult. When he was at the French Academy in Rome, he and the sculptor Etex set out one day hoping to fall in with a band of brigands and share their life. Somewhat earlier he had been inspired by the Greek war and composed a *scena* entitled *La Révolution grecque*: later he was to go through a Saint-Simonian Socialist phase. But it was for personal rather than national independence, for artistic rather than democratic liberty that he strove. Thus he looked back on his student years in Rome as if he really had been a bandit in the Campagna:

> Poignant memories of days of freedom now vanished! Freedom of the heart, of the mind, of the soul, of everything. Freedom to do nothing, not even to think; freedom to forget time, to despise ambition, to laugh at fame, to dismiss love; freedom to go north, south, east or west, to sleep in the open, to live on little, to wander at large, without premeditation, to dream, to drowse away whole days immobile in the breath of the *sirocco*.[43]

And he described the July Revolution almost as if it had been a vast operatic spectacle:

> I shall never forget how Paris looked during those famous days: the wild excitement of the whores, the grim resignation of the Swiss Royal guards, the strange pride of the working class in being, as they said, masters of Paris and taking nothing; the young men bragging of fantastic exploits . . . And the music that there was then, the songs, the harsh voices resounding through the streets – nobody who did not hear it can have any idea of what it was like![44]

It was not so much the departure of the Bourbons and the advent of Louis-Philippe, as the passions, the tumultuous violence, the thrill of Revolution that caught the imagination of Berlioz and, one feels, of Delacroix too.

Natural rebels, artists tend to support the great liberal movements of their day. But concepts of political and artistic liberty are not identical and may sometimes be contradictory. The Romantic artist was primarily concerned with his own liberty – his freedom to express his genius, as much as his emancipation from the dictates of academies and the whims of patrons. Paradoxically, however, he achieved this less frequently in representations of subjects with political meanings than in those which had none – a scene of his own choice from literature or history, a portrait, a landscape or even a still-life. The Romantic artist stood at the centre of his world as a creative and destructive force. And if his obsession with his own work and personality and uniqueness was eventually to drive him to take refuge in the doctrine of *l'art pour l'art*, it was also productive of great Romantic masterpieces, some of which celebrate the cause of political as well as artistic liberty.

7. *Artist's Life*

The Romantic conception of the artist – with all that it implies of 'vocation', 'artistic temperament' and struggling 'misunderstood genius' – is now so widely accepted that it is easy to forget its relatively recent origin. Some earlier artists had, of course, been nonconformist or eccentric in their way of life.[1] And some, especially Neo-classical artists, had been impelled by a sense of mission so earnest that their personal statements can occasionally be misconstrued in a Romantic sense. 'I belong not to the Berlin Academy but to Humanity which has a right to demand of me the highest possible development of my faculties,' Asmus Jakob Carstens wrote in 1796 to the Prussian minister who had cancelled the grant on which he was living in Rome:

> I shall continue with all my strength to justify myself to the world through my works. Thus I renounce all those benefits, preferring poverty, an uncertain future, and perhaps an infirm and helpless old age, with my body already showing signs of illness, in order to fulfil my duty to humanity and my vocation to art. My capabilities were entrusted to me by God. I must be a faithful steward so that when He says: 'Give a reckoning of thy stewardship', I shall not have to say: 'Lord, the talent with which you entrusted me I have buried in Berlin'.[2]

What Carstens was asserting was not his liberty to follow his own particular artistic bent, wherever that might eventually lead him, but his resolve to progress along the 'true road' marked out by Neo-classical theorists. Very soon, however, Romantics were claiming the right to go their own way unhelped and unhindered – in order to develop their individual sensibilities and to express their innermost feelings without regard to, and often in defiance of, theoretical rules and social conventions. In 1810 Blake 'demanded' not only the freedom to depict his world of imagination but the encouragement which he believed to be his due. If art lovers refused to support him 'theirs is the loss, not mine, & theirs is the Contempt of Posterity', he wrote.[3]

The word 'artist' had signified in the eighteenth century 'the professor of an art, generally an art manual', and 'a skilful man, not a novice'.[4] This is very far from what Friedrich Schlegel had in mind when he remarked that artists were to the rest of mankind what human beings were to the rest of creation.[5] Artists had gradually come to regard themselves as people set apart, rather like the Calvinist 'elect'. In 1798 the twenty-one-year-old Philipp Otto Runge attributed to God the love of art which impelled him to leave the Hamburg shipping firm, to which he had been apprenticed, and to become a painter. Two decades later a sense of destiny might replace the deity. Berlioz recorded in his memoirs how, as a medical student in Paris, he attended a performance of Gluck's *Iphigénie in Tauride* and 'vowed as I left the Opéra that in spite of father, mother, uncles, aunts, grand-parents, friends, I would be a musician. I actually wrote off then and there to my father, acquainting him with the imperious and irresistible nature of my vocation and entreating him not to oppose it uselessly'.[6]

Such a decision – and there were many other young aspiring musicians, poets and artists who confronted their parents in a similar fashion – was a relatively new phenomenon. It is important to remember that Bach, Haydn, Mozart and even Beethoven and Schubert had no choice as to their careers: they were never given the opportunity to do anything but become musicians. Similarly, the careers of most eighteenth-century and earlier painters and sculptors had been determined by their families. But Runge, Géricault, Delacroix, Constable, Wilkie – to mention only some of the more famous – followed the call of art against the initial opposition of their families and relations. The entry of such rebels into the artistic community had a stimulating effect. For if few of them had the financial independence which enabled Géricault to paint *The Raft of the 'Medusa'* without any prospect of finding a purchaser for it, they all inherited from their middle-class background an independence of spirit and disdain for servility which they passed on to their fellow artists, and which helped them to confront both private patrons and the general public with a new sense of independence.[7] For the same reason they came to distrust popular taste, especially that of the middle class. 'It is said *vox populi vox dei*: I never believed it,' Beethoven remarked. 'The painter who seeks popularity in art closes the door on his own genius', wrote Washington Allston.[8]

Art had ceased to be a trade or a profession: it had become a vocation. And the scorn with which ascetics of former ages had regarded worldly priests was now turned by dedicated artists on their weaker brethren who ingratiated themselves with the public by painting decorative pictures or composing 'popular' music. In 1806 Beethoven wrote to the man who had commissioned his *Irish Melodies*: 'I will take care to make the composition easy and pleasing,' adding, however, 'so far as I can and so far as is consistent with that elevation and originality of style which, as you yourself say, favourably characterizes my work and from which I will never stoop.'[9] Barely thirty years earlier, it may be recalled, Haydn and Mozart had been ranked as liveried servants. A revolution had taken place in the relationship between artists and patrons. Painters (who had rarely been as badly treated as musicians) and the purchasers of their work tended increasingly to see one another, if not quite as equals, at any rate in some kind of mutual relationship 'giving benefit for benefit'.[10] Some artists even went so far as to turn the tables on their clients by adopting the attitude which Dr Johnson had attributed to the patron: they treated the public with insolence and expected to be paid with flattery as well as cash.

The artist's new consciousness of himself and of his uniqueness found its most explicit expression in self-portraits. The spirit of self-assured independence which marks the self-portraits of Géricault and Delacroix is equally apparent in those by artists less closely associated with the Romantic movement. In 1804 Ingres, still a young rebel in David's studio and criticized for his 'bizarre' behaviour, depicted himself with an almost arrogant turn of the head and fire in the eyes, very much the typical young artist of the time with an overcoat slung over his shoulder, working on the portrait of a friend. This was not the image which the aged Monsieur Ingres later wished to perpetuate, however, and he subsequently removed the unfinished portrait and replaced the untidy overcoat with a smart velvet-trimmed cloak – though he did nothing to soften the indignant look.[11] Another of David's pupils, and one who was to remain truer to his tenets, A.-D. Abel de Pujol, portrayed himself in 1806 wearing a Roman toga, but with hypersensitive features and the piercing gaze as of one possessed, which gave him the uncanny appearance of a Romantic physically emerging out of his Neo-classical background [161].

Most Romantic self-portraits are characterized by a gentler mood of introspection, with dreamy eyes and melancholy in the corners of the mouth [162, 163]. Independence was indicated less by an attitude of defiance than by an easy, almost indolent, pose, denoting freedom from formality. In the eighteenth century successful artists had

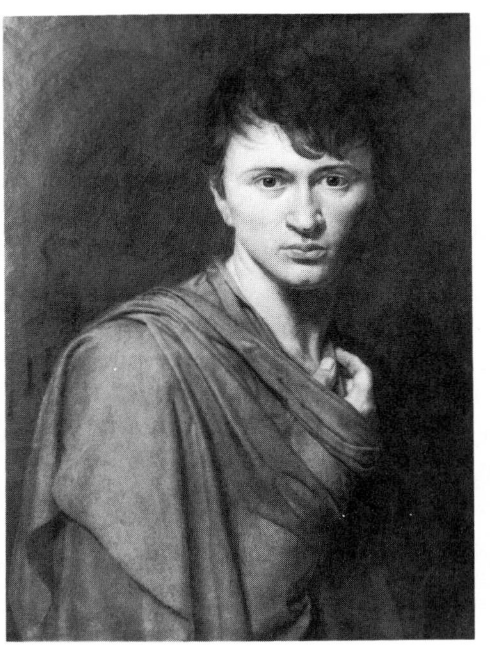

161. *Self-Portrait*, 1806. Abel de Pujol

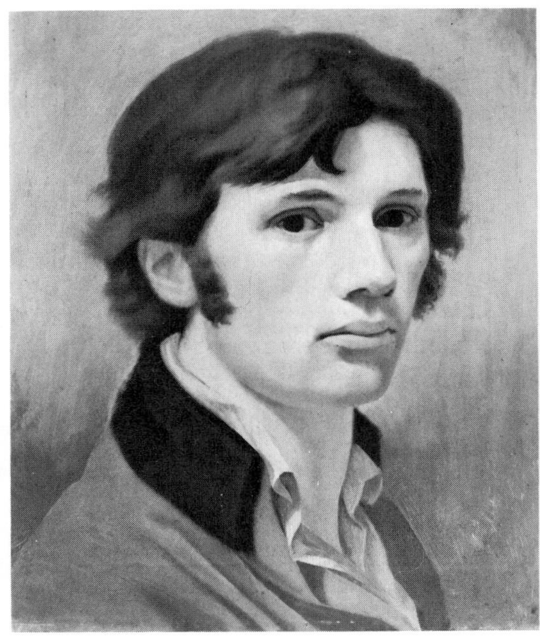

162. *Self-Portrait*, 1802. Philipp Otto Runge

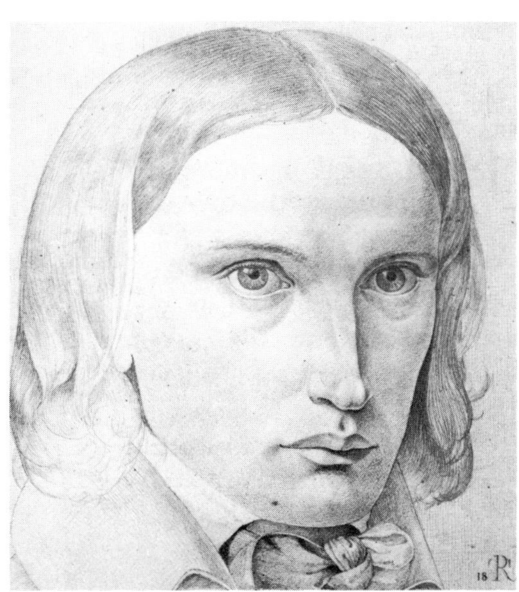

163. *Self-Portrait*, 1817. M. T. Rehbenitz

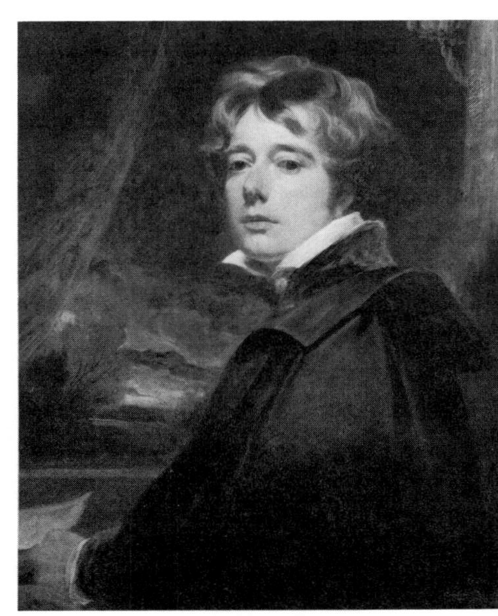

164. *Self-Portrait*, 1818. G. H. Harlow

loved to depict themselves as gentlemen wearing their richest clothes and the stars and ribbons of orders they had been awarded by royal patrons. Such pride in worldly success was now thought to demean the true artist, to whom the highest honours (much as they might secretly be coveted) were but a poor recompense for the immortality he could bestow on those he portrayed. The Romantics also tended to reject another type of earlier self-portrait, which had presented the artist as craftsman. Very rarely did they show themselves in paint-stained working clothes. They preferred to appear, with lightly tousled hair, Byronic open-necked shirts or loosely tied cravats, good though never showy clothes negligently worn, as men of intellect and sensibility, members of the republic of arts and letters [164].

Writers and musicians were portrayed in exactly the same way, standing apart from the world, as if above conventional social distinctions. Girodet painted a windswept Chateaubriand musing on the ruins of Rome, writer rather than vicomte, mystic rather than diplomatist – though Napoleon thought he looked like a conspirator who had come down the chimney [165]. Joseph Severn recorded Shelley meditating in the Baths of Caracalla, and Keats almost drowsing over a book by the open window of his house in Hampstead [166]. A solitary Wordsworth, 'he of the cloud, the cataract,

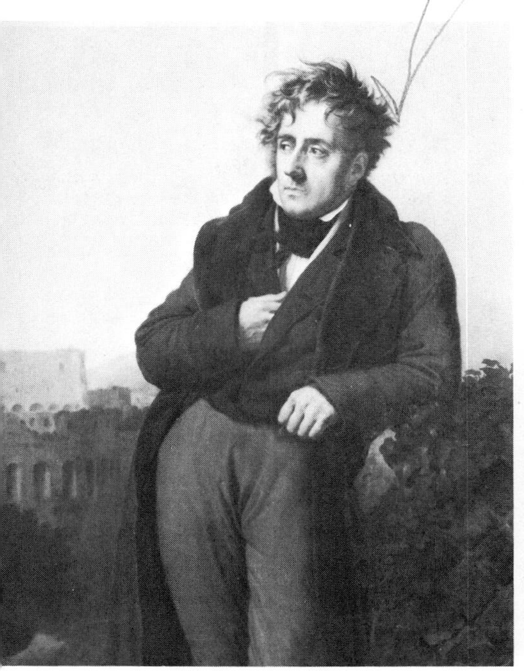

165. *Chateaubriand*, 1809.
A.-L. Girodet de Roucy-Trioson

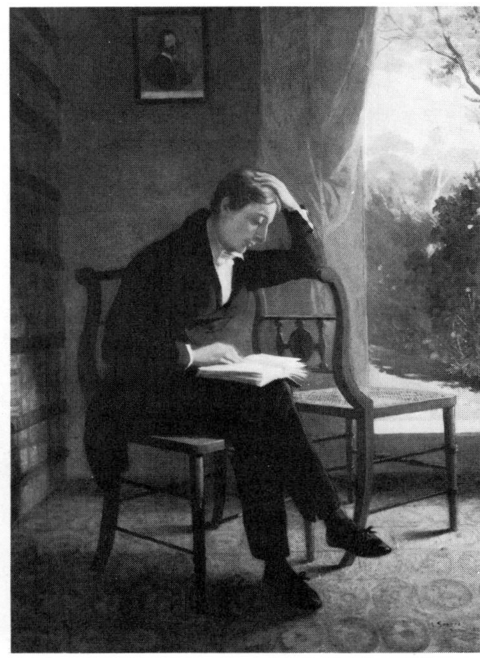

166. *Keats*, 1821.
J. Severn

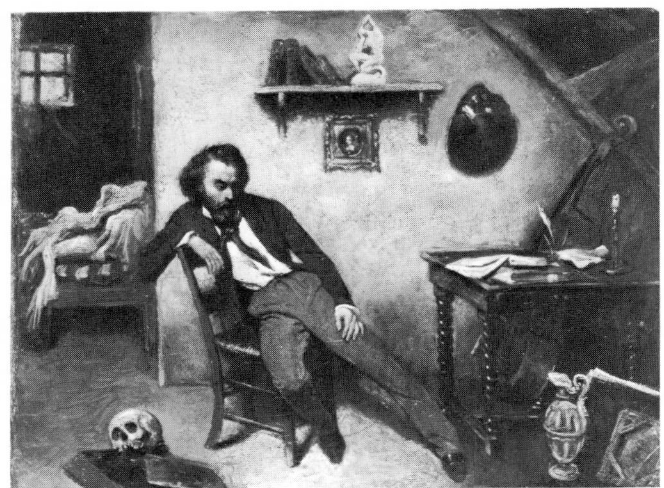

167. *Alfred de Musset in his Mansarde*, 1840. A.-C. Mélicourt-Lefebvre

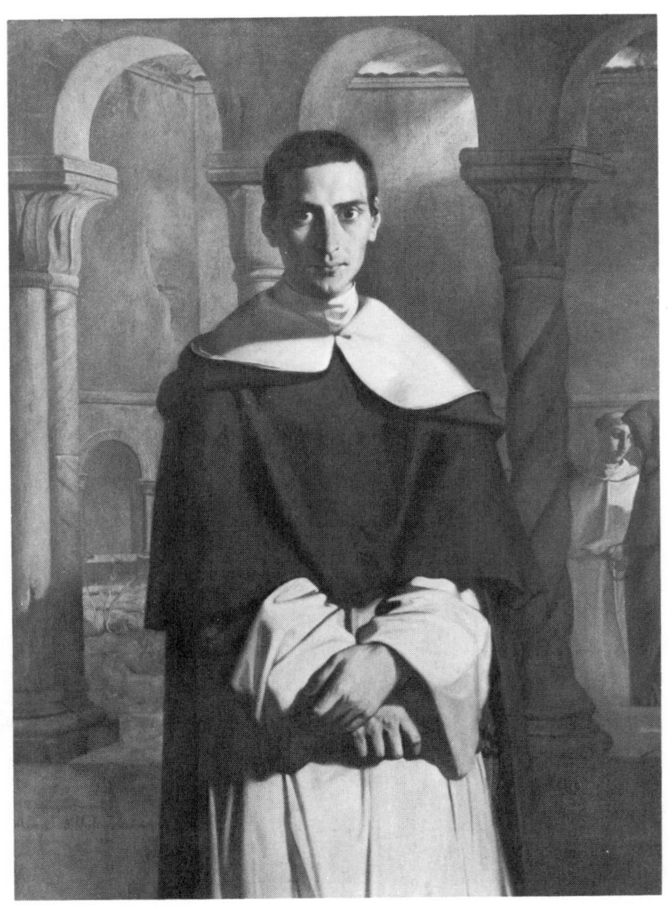

168. *Lacordaire O.P.*, 1840. T. Chassériau

the lake', one of the 'great spirits' sojourning on earth, broods over Helvellyn in what is perhaps B. R. Haydon's most memorable picture.[12] Alfred de Musset was depicted alone in his garret '*à l'âge où l'on croit à l'amour*' [167]. Chassériau portrayed the liberal theologian Lacordaire not as the champion of God and Liberty – the motto of *L'Avenir* in which he wrote – but as a being both physically and spiritually withdrawn from everyday life in his monastery [168].

The informal portrait was not, of course, an invention of the Romantics: nor was melancholy sensibility. But the most notable early nineteenth-century portraits suggest a more intimate community of understanding between artist and sitter than had hitherto been usual – of 'soul speaking to soul' as Delacroix's friend Mme Cavé put it.[13] This *rapport* is as clearly apparent in Bryullov's portrait of the journalist Nestor Vasilevich Kukolnik [169] as in that

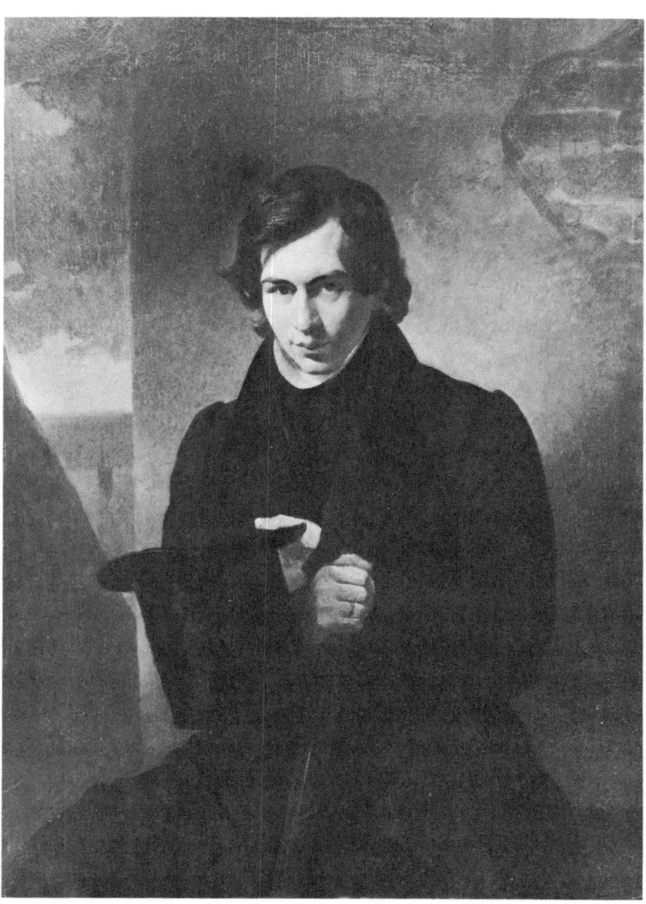

169. *Nestor Vasilevich Kukolnik*, 1836. A. P. Bryullov

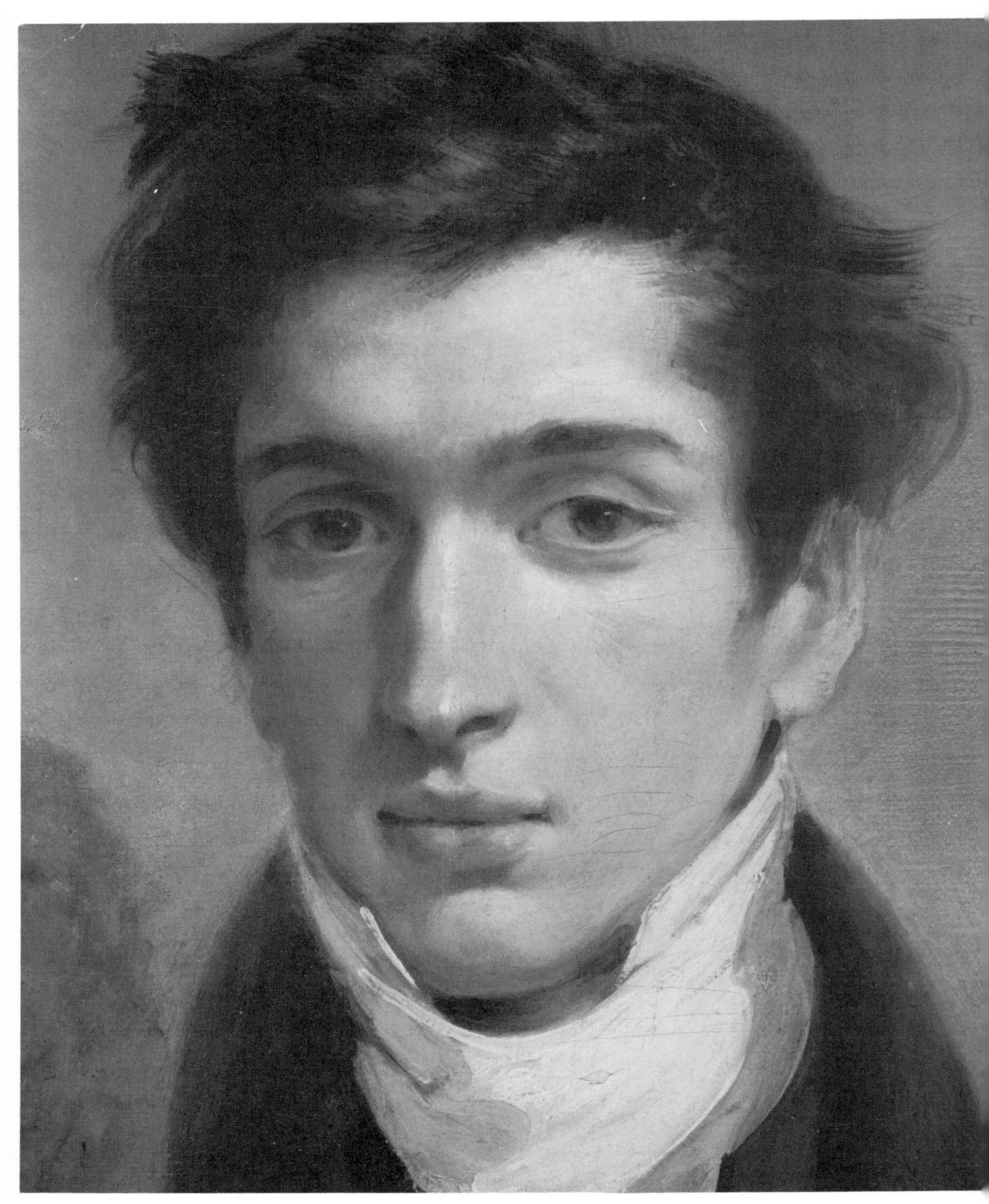

170. *Baron Schwiter* (detail), 1826–30. Delacroix

by Delacroix of his friend and fellow artist Baron Schwiter [170]. Such paintings seem to reflect the belief that art was not a luxury to be enjoyed by the rich (as in the early eighteenth century), but the rightful possession of an aristocracy of sentiment. Art was a divine language to be understood only by the few, Wackenroder and Tieck declared. Runge called it a secret *Familiengespräch*, incomprehensible outside the family circle,[14] and in *Wir Drei* he depicted himself with his wife and brother, bound together in their understanding of it by ties still stronger than those of birth and marriage [171]. The artist who sets his 'thoughts' before the general

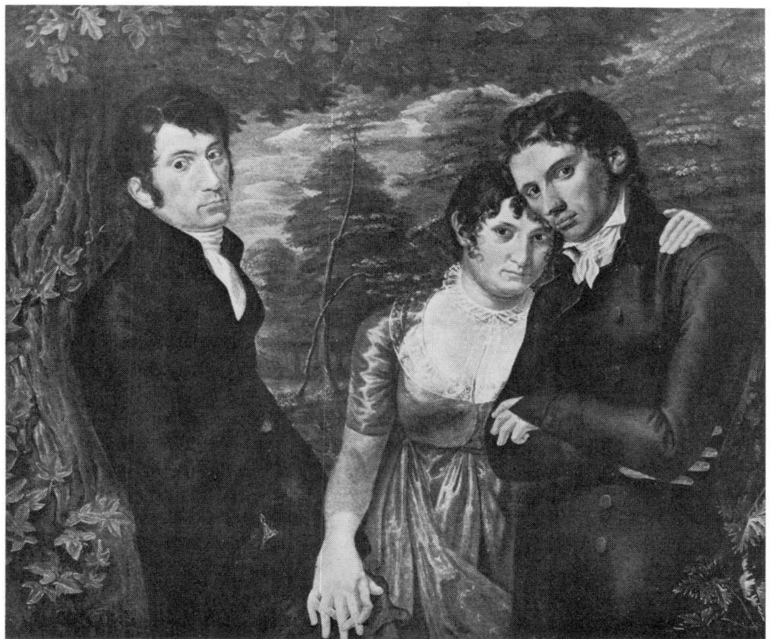

171. *Wir Drei*, 1804. Philipp Otto Runge

public is indifferent to their praise or blame: 'He did not wish to speak their language,' Prosper Marilhat told a fellow landscape painter in 1837.[15] The same belief persuaded Liszt that his symphonic poems, which needed a full orchestra and a large auditorium, were intended for only a few sensitive souls. 'They do not at all claim everyday popularity,' he wrote.[16]

'There are only two classes of men on earth, that which feels enthusiasm, and that which scorns it,' says Corinne in Mme de Staël's novel. And it was Mme de Staël who coined the word *vulgarité* to characterize the attitudes and tastes of the insensitive multitude (the 'lower class' of feeling rather than of rank and riches). In Germany, where the universities played such an important part in the development of Romantic thought, the students' slang term for a townsman, *Philister*, came to be applied to all who stood outside the charmed circle (even in the feline world if we are to believe E. T. A. Hoffmann's *Lebensansichten des Katers Murr*). The word caught on and was introduced in the 1820s to England, where Matthew Arnold was to give it still wider currency and a somewhat deeper meaning after the mid-century. In his essay on Heine, Arnold claimed that 'Philistine must originally have meant, in the minds of those who invented the nickname, a strong, dogged, unenlightened opponent of the chosen people, of the children of light.' But he wrote this with the benefit of hindsight. The word originally indicated passive indifference and lack of comprehension rather than open antagonism: that came later, beginning to emerge only with the widening of the rift between artists and the general public – and even then mainly in the minds of the former.

The artist must 'possess a force of character that seems hardly compatible with its delicacy', Hawthorne declared: 'he must keep faith in himself while the incredulous world assails him with its utter disbelief, he must stand up against mankind and be his sole disciple, both as respects his genius and the objects to which it is directed'. For, whether or not it was a figment of the Romantic imagination, many artists sincerely believed in the public's hostility to art, music and literature. They identified as its spokesmen any opponents of innovation (many of whom were highly cultivated and just as much opposed to bourgeois taste). And they associated with them any artist who won popular success. Yet, despite its intellectual snobbery, this notion of a militant Philistia was not without certain beneficial side-effects. It fostered those little coteries in which new ideas were incubated – at Jena, at Heidelberg, in the *cénacles* of Paris, in Milan, in Hampstead and in the Lake District. So far as the visual arts are concerned, there were the *Barbus* or *Penseurs* in David's studio, the *Lukasbund* in Vienna, the Nazarenes and the Italian *Puristi* in Rome, and later, in England, the Pre-Raphaelite Brotherhood. Though created in opposition to the official academies, they often resembled (sometimes intentionally) the societies formed by artists before the academies were established and, inevitably, tended to substitute one kind of dogmatism for another. But there were a great many informal groups, based on friendship and a healthy dose of mutual admiration, which enabled individuals to develop their independence in the face of a real or imaginary hostile world. One such was constituted by the several artists, including Géricault, who frequented Horace Vernet's studio in the early years of the Restoration.

Vernet's own picture of his studio shows it crowded with young artists and discharged Napoleonic soldiers – also a number of animals [172]. The painter is fencing with one of his pupils, another pupil Eugène Lami blows a horn, A.-A. Montfort (Géricault's friend and disciple) is stripped to the waist for boxing, only J.-N. Robert-Fleury, already qualified as a painter of brigands, works at

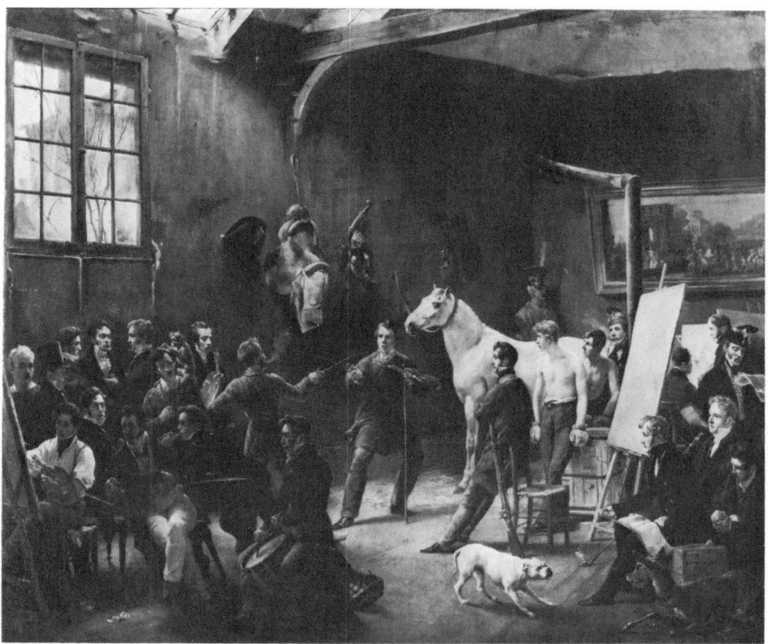

172. *The Artist's Studio*, *c.* 1820. Horace Vernet

an easel. It is an image of a free and unconventional way of life that might well arouse the envy, and also the suspicion, of the desk-bound bourgeois. These men look like Carbonari in training for a physical assault on the establishment, perpetrators of *machines infernales* rather than *grandes machines*. A more sedate conception of the artist's life was presented by the soulful portraits which the Germans in Rome never tired of painting and drawing of one another [103, 163]. With their northern clothes and long hair, they proclaimed their nationality and their membership of an artistic community distinct from the rest of society. But the sense of apartness was sometimes transformed into one of alienation, as in Buonaventura Genelli's strange cycle of prints *Aus dem Leben eines Künstlers*

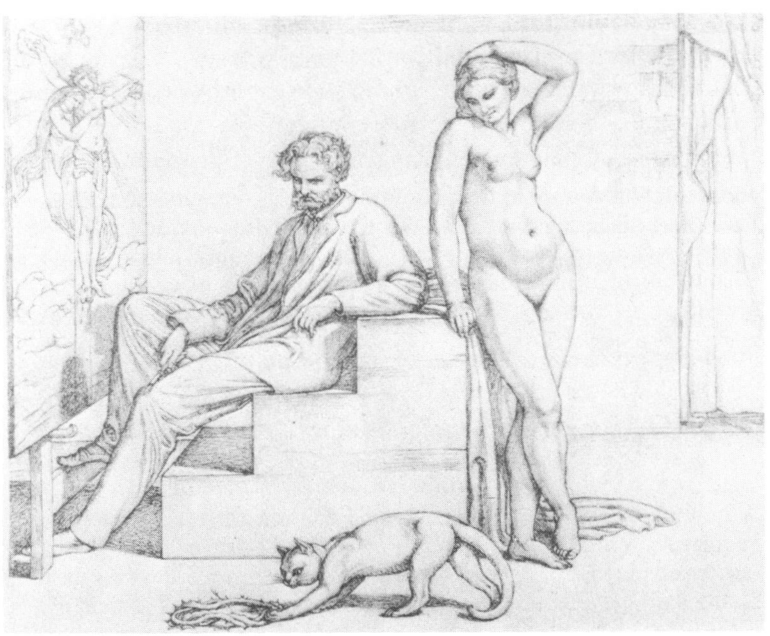

173. *Mysterium*, 1868. Buonaventura Genelli

[173] or Géricault's haunting portrait of a young artist [174] – that image of the isolated sufferer from the *mal de siècle*.

'*L'indépendence a pour conséquence l'isolement*,' wrote Benjamin Constant in *Adolphe* (1816). Many years later Delacroix transcribed the sentence in his journal. He also copied out Michelangelo's statement: 'I go my lonely way along paths which no man has made for me.'[17] Before the nineteenth century loneliness had generally been regarded as a misfortune, but the Romantics made a cult of it. This sets Sénancour's musings among the lakes and mountains of Switzerland and in the dark depths of the forest of Fontainebleau – a voice sobbing in the wilderness – some way apart from the much more complex *Confessions* of Rousseau. Chateaubriand believed the greatest passions to be dependent on loneliness, and 'he who carries them into the desert returns them to their kingdom'; while Kierkegaard declared: 'My sorrow is my knight's castle. It rests like an eagle's nest upon the summit of a mountain and towers high above the clouds. None can storm it.' Loneliness and unhappiness were the inevitable companions of genius, according to Heine:

> Even though it encounter no malignant enmity from without, genius will be sure to find within itself an enemy ready to bring calamity upon it. This is why the history of great men is always a martyrology: when

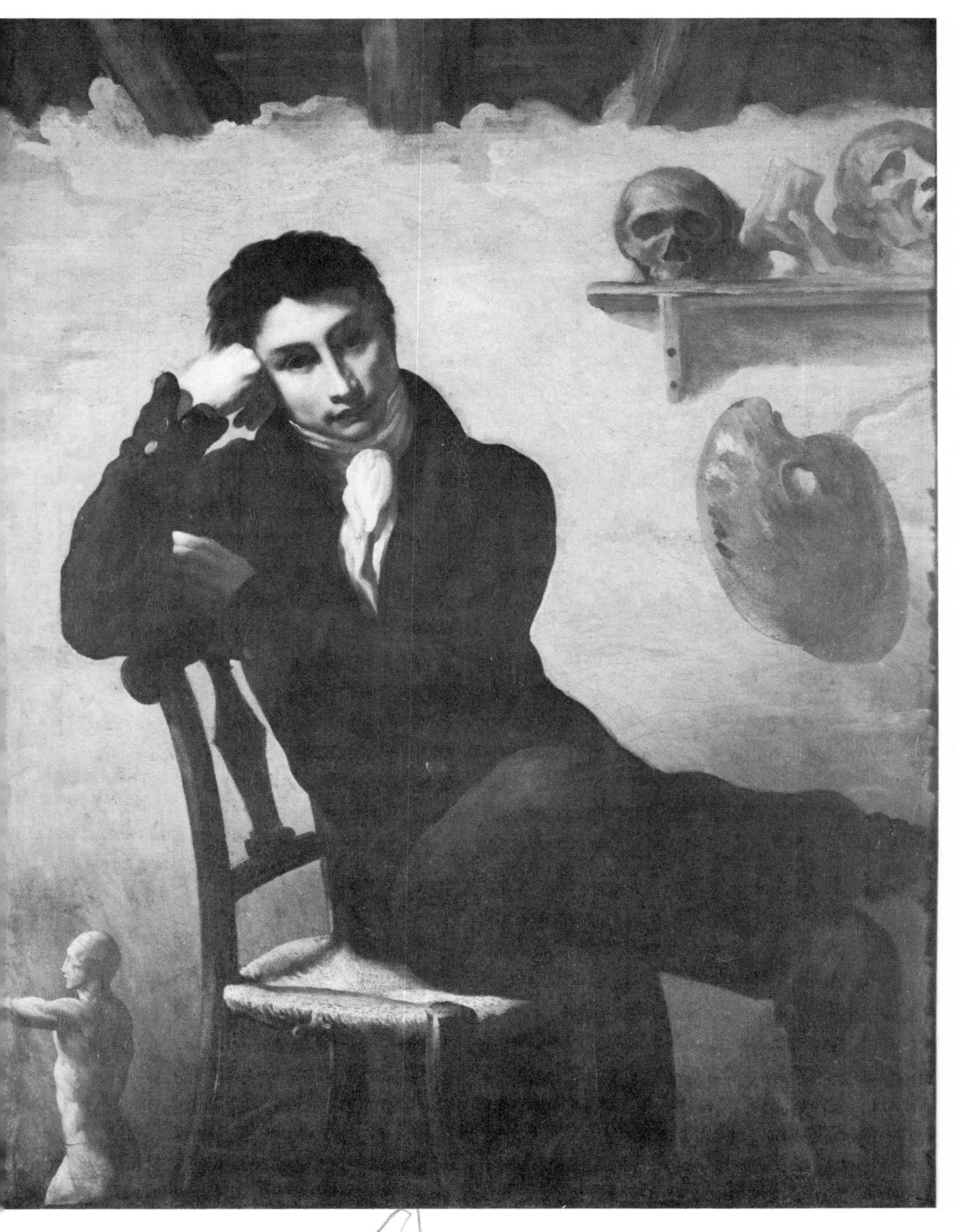

174. *Portrait of a Young Man*, *c*. 1818–19. Géricault

they are not sufferers for the great human race, they suffer for their own greatness, for the grand manner of their being, for their hatred of philistinism, for the discomfort they feel among the pretentious commonplaces, the mean trivialities of their surroundings – a discomfort that readily leads them to extravagances . . .[18]

This is, of course, a myth invented by the Romantics – a myth as insidious as it was beguiling in its implications, and one which still survives today.

A late nineteenth-century art critic, Lemonnier, wrote of Delacroix: 'Lonely upon a rock, high above all the noise of the universe, his is the egoism of the gods. Let none require of him that he should descend into the world of men.'[19] The image recalls Napoleon on St Helena, especially as he was depicted in the 1830s and '40s. But there is also a hint of religious analogy, of the artist on the mountain like Moses or Christ, the intermediary between God and man – an idea which, with Caspar David Friedrich, became quite explicit [38]. It was, however, with Michelangelo that Delacroix seems sometimes to have associated himself – identified would be too strong a word for his reverential attitude. '*Penser au grand Michel-Ange*,' he wrote in 1824; '*cherche la solitude*.' The article he wrote in 1830, describing Michelangelo as a victim of misunderstanding, a wild genius despised by the mediocre, is indeed an essay in self-revelation and to some extent self-justification. In the course of it he described how the image of the great artistic genius would appear before him 'late at night at the moment when, frightened by his own creations, he was the first to experience the secret terror which he had sought to awaken in the souls of others'.[20] Two decades later he seems to have recalled this passage when painting a darkly pensive Michelangelo seated in his studio at the feet of his statue of Moses and beside his 'Medici' Madonna [175]. This profound meditation on the mystery of art and the solitude of genius has an almost religious quality which links it with Delacroix's several paintings of Christ in the Garden of Olives: it is a kind of Agony in the Studio.

But Delacroix's *Michelangelo* is also related, if only distantly, to the innumerable illustrations of scenes from the lives of artists which were so enormously popular in the first half of the nineteenth century in Germany, Italy and especially France.[21] They were welcomed by a public with a love of historical anecdote and an increasing interest in the history of art, made possible by the contemporary expansion of museums as well as by the proliferation of books and art periodicals. But they are most significant as expressions of the artist's obsession with himself and his own predicament. The genre

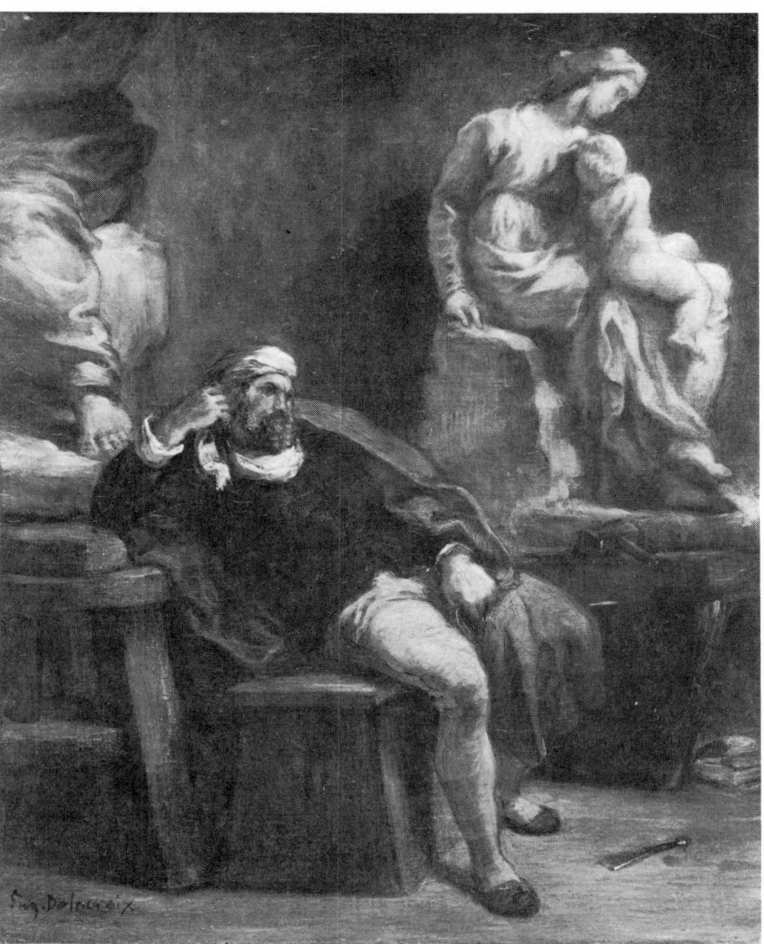

175. *Michelangelo in his Studio*, 1850. Delacroix

became established shortly after the Restoration. For although scenes from artists' lives had been painted earlier, they were usually in the tradition of history pictures, especially death-bed scenes. The death of Leonardo in the arms of François I, for example, had been depicted by Angelica Kauffmann in 1778 and François-Guillaume Ménageot in 1781, and *The Honours Rendered to Raphael after his Death* made the name of Pierre-Nolasque Bergeret in 1806.[22] Under the Restoration the focus shifted from posthumous honours to scenes which indicated the respect formerly accorded to living artists – the Emperor Charles V picking up Titian's paintbrush, for example, or Queen Christina telling Guercino that she wished to touch the hand that had created so much beauty.[23] Many of them

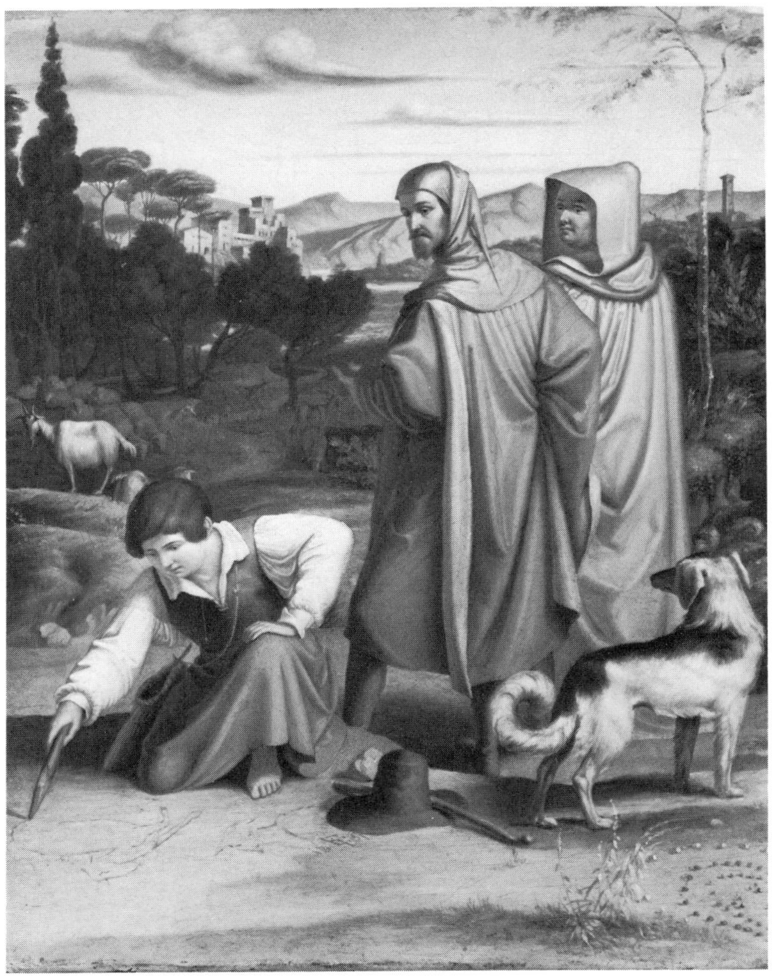

176. *Giotto as a Shepherd Boy*, *c.* 1831–5. E. Förster

are the work of artists who enjoyed greater success with the general public than with critics, and it is tempting to suspect that in some instances they were a riposte to the Romantics who equated popular success with artistic failure.

Several fundamental Romantic notions about art were, however, made explicit in paintings of this kind. Artistic vocation, for example, is the subject of E. J. Förster's *Giotto as a Shepherd Boy*, which might equally well be entitled 'the calling of Giotto' [176]. The influence of both religion and nature on the young artist is suggested by William Dyce's charming *Titian Preparing for his*

First Essay in Colour [177]. In Germany, the spiritual character of artistic inspiration was illustrated by Raphael's vision or dream of the Virgin.[24] The more sensuous aspects of his personality attracted French artists: A. E. Fragonard showed him gently adjusting the attitude of a pretty and distinctly flesh-and-blood model who poses for a picture of the Madonna, Ingres depicted him on no fewer than

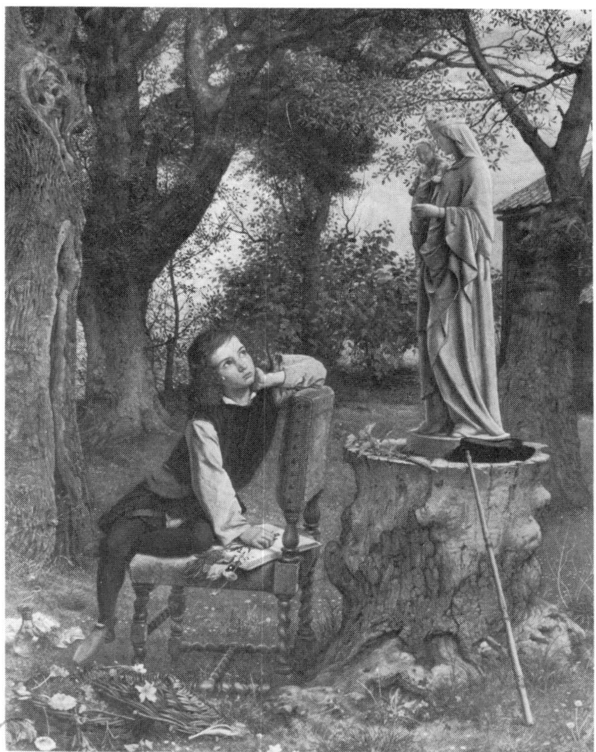

177. *Titian Preparing for his First Essay in Colour*, 1856–7. W. Dyce

five occasions in the arms of his mistress la Fornarina. Stories about Raphael's amorous inclinations, which became so popular in the early nineteenth century, may perhaps have been thought to justify the sexual irregularity associated with the lives of artists or to exalt free love over legalized concubinage (i.e. marriage to the Cardinal of Bibiena's niece). But it was as an example of artistic spontaneity that the young Delacroix imagined 'Raphael in the arms of his mistress, turning from la Fornarina to paint his Saint Cecilia, creating his sublime pictures and compositions as others breathe and speak, moved by an easy, effortless inspiration'.[25] A few years later he was to record in his journal the many *dolce chiavature* he enjoyed with his own models.

Ingres's *Aretino in Tintoretto's Studio* represents the artist getting the better of a captious critic and mean patron – a subject which may well have been close to his own heart when he first painted it in 1815.[26] But generally these pictures reveal the relationship between patron and painter to have been happy enough to comfort those who bought them. Art collectors of the period liked to identify themselves with the great patrons of the past. For the same reasons, the misfortunes associated with an artistic career were rarely depicted. Ribot's scary picture of 1867, showing Alonso Cano being tortured (in an unsuccessful attempt to make him confess to the murder of his wife), is the most notable exception, and it comes significantly late in the genre. Such subjects as Tintoretto painting his dead daughter or the deaths of Masaccio and Correggio have only a generalized pathos. Impoverished and neglected artists hardly appear in these paintings at all, and it seems that painters had as little desire to commemorate as collectors to be reminded of them. For symbols of misunderstood genius, the painter turned away from his own profession to such figures as Tasso, Thomas Chatterton or Christopher Columbus.[27]

'*Hélas!*' wrote Victor Hugo in 1846, 'I have seen darkness prevail and Christ, Socrates, Jean Huss, Columbus manacled.'[28] The story of Columbus returning to Spain in chains after his third voyage of discovery was one upon which several nineteenth-century artists seized, the most popular and histrionic representation being that by Gustaaf Wappers [178]. Columbus dying, neglected by the court he had served so well, was another subject nicely calculated to appeal to nineteenth-century sentiment. Thus Claudius Jacquand painted 'Christopher Columbus feeling the approach of death, shows his son the chains with which he had once been bound and asks for them to be buried with him in his coffin'. The chains appear in many images of Columbus, and the author of a monument to his memory called them 'the symbol of his martyrdom' – a fine example of the sanctification of genius which accompanied the secularization of religion.

Several pictures were devoted to a less obviously painful incident, but one which illustrated the vicissitudes suffered by men of genius – the unsuccessful attempt made by Columbus in 1486 to convince the junta of learned men at Salamanca of the feasibility of his scheme to reach the Indies by sailing westwards. Here the unimaginative pedants regard him with looks of bewilderment, incredulity

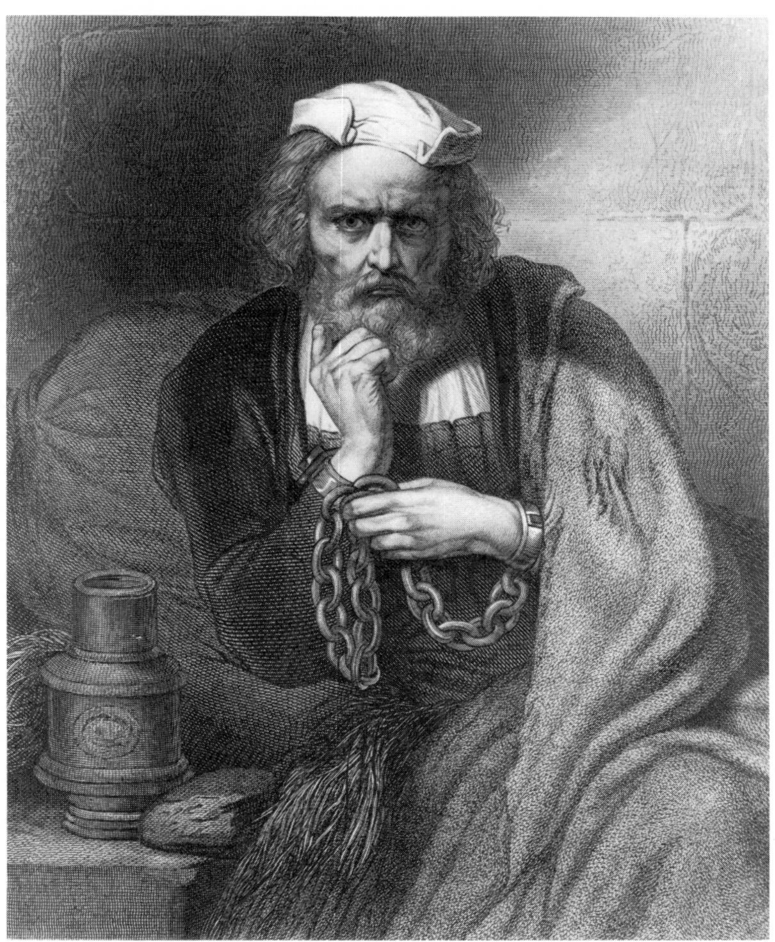

178. *Columbus in Chains*, 1846. After Gustaaf Wappers

or derision. There were, of course, happy incidents in the life of Columbus – his reception at La Rábida, where he first found a man capable of understanding him (painted by Delacroix and Wilkie among others), the 'egg trick' with which he discomfited the supercilious grandees who remarked that many people could accomplish what he had done. But the whole Columbus saga was shot through with 'romantic' pathos, which gives a melancholy undertone even to the many paintings (by Delacroix, Eugène Devéria, Joseph-Nicolas Robert-Fleury and others) of his triumphant reception by Ferdinand and Isabella after his return from his first voyage. The explorer who had ventured into a totally new world, the visionary who had seen beyond the ken of men of common sense, misunderstood by his contemporaries but receiving from posterity his just reward, Columbus became for Romantics in the nineteenth century the archetypal man of genius.

Torquato Tasso provided a symbol of a different kind – and one that combined the image of the free spirit unnaturally confined with that of the martyr for love. His works had been read and illustrated by artists ever since their first appearance. But in the late eighteenth century attention began to shift from the poetry to the poet, whose life came to be seen as 'one of the most interesting in the world'.[29] Goethe's play about him, begun in the 1770s and completed in 1789, was partly responsible, though it is devoted to a moment in Tasso's career before his incarceration in the madhouse, and is concerned less with his love for the Duke of Ferrara's sister than with the conflict between the worlds of imagination and common sense. Reflecting Goethe's own desire for balance and tranquillity after the years of storm and stress (there are similarities between its hero and Werther), it ends with the emotional Tasso's moving address to the solid, practical man, Antonio:

Ich fasse dich mit beiden Armen an!
So klammert sich der Schiffer endlich noch
*am Felsen fest, an dem er scheitern sollte.**

Mme de Staël, who introduced the play to French and English readers, presented Tasso as a more conspicuously Romantic figure: 'brave as his knights, in love, loved, persecuted, crowned, and dying of grief while still young on the eve of his triumph, he is a superb example of all the splendours and all the misfortunes of a great talent.'[30] She complained, indeed, of a Germanic coldness and too great a tendency to metaphysical philosophizing in Goethe's hero.

In Tasso's adventurous and amorous life, the 'Troubadour-style' painters found several sympathetic subjects: Louis Ducis showed him visiting his sister in Naples, reading his poetry to the Princess Leonora, and in the madhouse visited by Montaigne. F.-M. Granet also illustrated Montaigne's visit in a picture where the impression of imprisoned light, given by so many of his interiors, acquires greater significance from the subject-matter [179]. The source for the story is the essay in which Montaigne cited Tasso as an example of how great wits are ruined by their own strength and vivacity, remarking: 'I was even more piqued than sorry to see him at Ferrara

*'I cling to thee with both arms! Thus does the mariner clasp the firm rock on which he has run aground.'

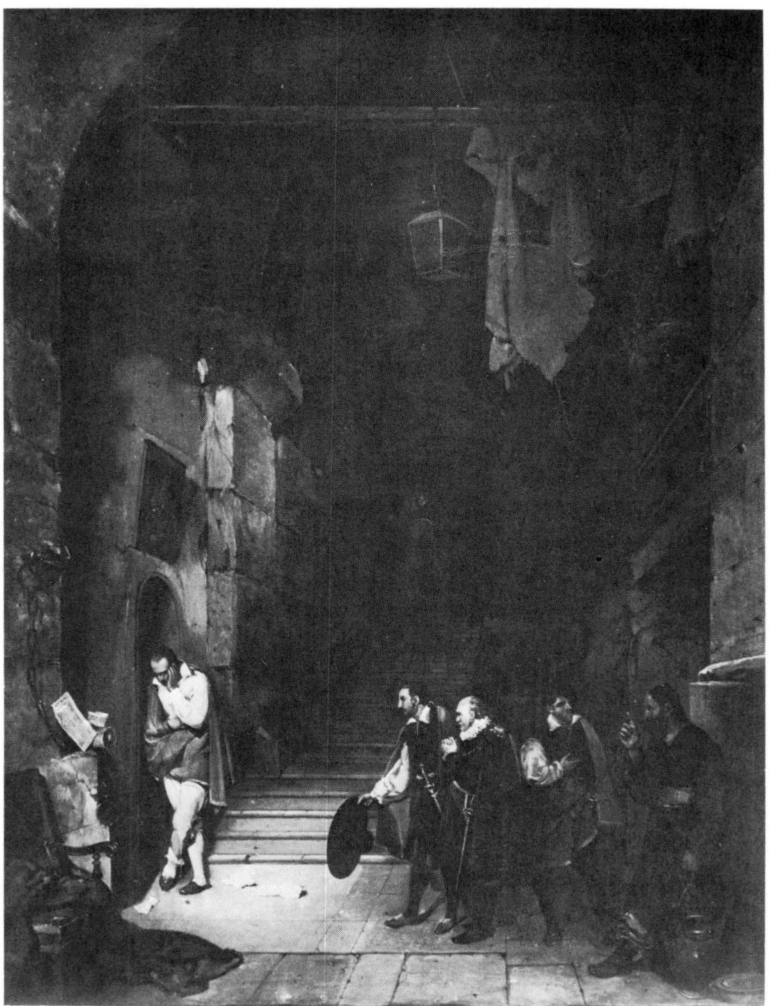

179. *Montaigne Visiting Tasso in Prison*, 1820. F.-M. Granet

in so pitiful a condition, out-living himself and his works ...' But this is the voice of Goethe's Antonio, the response of the prosaically sane to the poetically deranged.

To the Romantics, the mere fact of Tasso's imprisonment was a source of wonder and indignation, of which there is a strong hint in Granet's painting. Byron wrote of Ferrara: 'But, as misfortune has a greater interest for posterity, and little or none for the contemporary, the cell where Tasso was confined in the hospital of St Anna attracts a more fixed attention than the residence or the monument of Ariosto – at least it had this effect on me.'[31] He was clearly thinking of himself and the poet or artist in general, as much as of Tasso, when he wrote the opening lines of his 'Lament':

> Long years! – It tries the thrilling frame to bear
> And eagle-spirit of a Child of Song –
> Long years of outrage, calumny, and wrong;
> Imputed madness, prison'd solitude,
> And the mind's canker in its savage mood,
> When the impatient thirst of light and air
> Parches the heart ...

Shelley, who believed that his father had wished to have him shut up in a madhouse, also began to write a poetic drama about Tasso.

'How indignant one feels,' Delacroix wrote in 1819 to J.-B. Pierret (partly responsible for a translation of *La Gerusalemme Liberata* which had just appeared),

> with those shameful patrons who oppressed [Tasso] under the pretext of protecting him against his enemies, and who deprived him of his beloved manuscripts! What tears of rage and indignation he must have shed on seeing that in order to make sure of keeping them from him, his patrons declared him mad and incapable of creating! How many times must he have struck his head against those shameful iron bars, thinking of the baseness of men and blaming for her lack of affection the woman he had immortalized through his love! What a slow fever was to consume him! How his days must have dragged by, with the added pain of seeing them wasted in a lunatic's cell! One weeps for him; one moves restlessly in one's chair while reading his story; one's eyes gleam threateningly, one clenches one's teeth involuntarily.[32]

He planned to paint a picture of Tasso's imprisonment, with life-size figures, in 1822. And although the two he completed in 1824 and 1839 are small in scale they have an emotional grandeur and depth of anguish which set them apart even among his works. They are far more disturbing than most madhouse scenes, for the one depicts an eminently sane poet surrounded by prosaic lunatics, and the other, onlookers from the common world peering through the bars at the man whose genius they can comprehend only as insanity [180]. Dark in tone and with no soothingly sensuous passages – such as relieve the tension in *The Massacres of Chios* or *The Death of Sardanapalus* – these images of the artist mocked and rejected like Christ convey a sense of despair born of impotent rage and relieved only by a flickering spark of hope in the spirit's power to endure.

Tasso's story was so strongly etched in the minds of the Romantics that some of them came to believe that men of genius were doomed to share his fate ('*Tout génie est martyr*,' wrote Lamar-

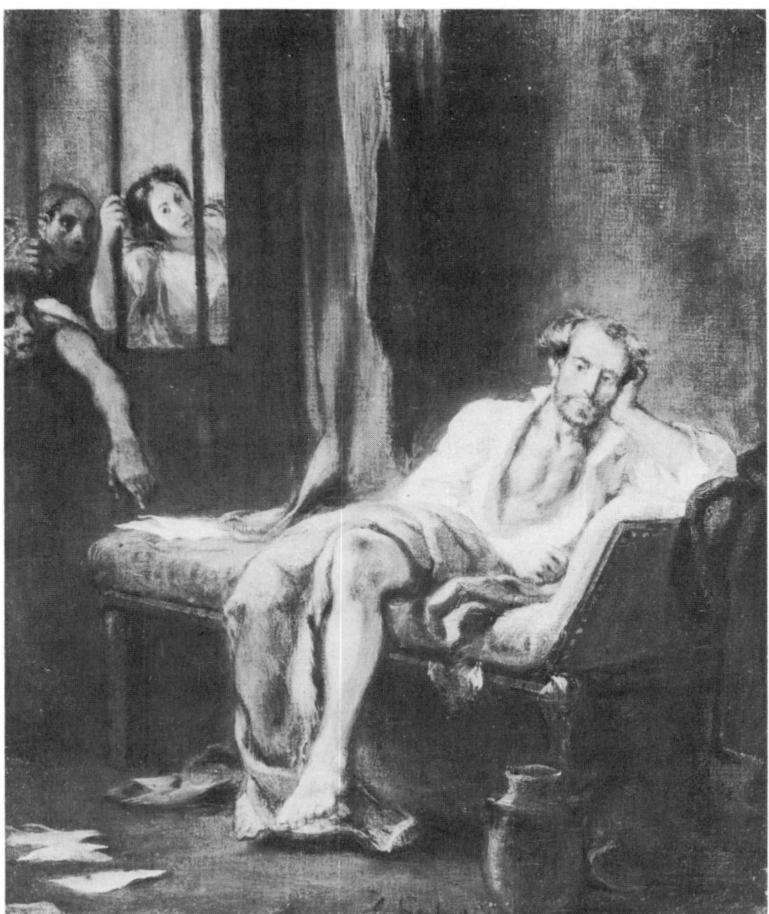

180. *Tasso in the Madhouse*, 1839. Delacroix

tine) – and not only metaphorically. Thus Louis Boulanger depicted Paganini 'like Tasso, sadly seated in a dungeon, alone, with his great thoughts, sublime, shining in the shadows'.[33] And in a published letter about this image, he remarked that the great virtuoso's pale brow marked with sorrow had made him wonder 'if a fatal destiny had not pressed its iron hand on that burning soul to make it pay for receiving too many gifts and shining more brightly than others; or if some bitter memory had not darkened that severe head'.

Of the historical and fictitious characters with whom the Romantics, and especially the painters, identified themselves – Dante (the exile and the lover of the unattainable Beatrice, as well as the poet of the *Divine Comedy*), Faust, Hamlet, to mention those who recur most frequently – none provided a more telling image than Don Quixote. And to this enigmatic figure they gave an entirely new significance. *Don Quixote* had been constantly reprinted, translated and imitated ever since its first appearance, and few works of modern literature provided more subjects for eighteenth-century painters – most notably C.-A. Coypel and C.-J. Natoire, who did cartoons for whole series of tapestries which were particularly popular in royal circles. But to judge from such illustrations, as well as numerous written comments, *Don Quixote* was generally regarded as a collection of comic tales about the hapless knight – whose misfortunes aroused nothing but mirth – interspersed with pastoral episodes appealing to sentiment.[34] The eighteenth-century reader appears to have laughed where we sigh, and to have sighed where we yawn – or skip. Deeper levels of meaning and feeling were first detected by the Romantics – by A. W. Schlegel, Bouterwek, and Sismondi who, in 1813, dubbed *Don Quixote* '*le livre le plus triste qui ait jamais été écrit*'.[35]

> Of all tales, 'tis the saddest – and more sad
> Because it makes us smile

wrote Byron.[36] Chateaubriand saw it as the work of a man forced to laugh in order to forget the sadness of life.[37] For Alfred de Vigny, the Don symbolized the elevated spirit who is always scorned and ostracized. And Balzac transferred the characteristics of the creation to his creator, describing Cervantes and Dante in exile, 'Milton in a hovel', 'Poussin unknown', and Napoleon on St Helena as 'images of the divine spectacle presented by Christ on the cross, dying so that he may be reborn, putting off his mortal remains so that he may reign in heaven'.[38]

Still more obviously, at a lower level, the Don seemed to personify the Romantic in his own and the public estimation, as the lover of medieval romances, the man of imagination who creates and inhabits a world of enchanted castles, the knight errant seeking to re-establish spiritual values in a materialistic age. He and the gluttonous, money-grubbing Sancho Panza, with all his worldly-wise proverbs, correspond almost exactly to the two types of men in Restoration France according to Alfred de Musset, as already mentioned. But the knight and his companion were also aspects of the same personality. 'Everyone is Don Quixote at some time, and everyone Sancho,' wrote Sainte-Beuve. 'This unsteady alliance between enthusiastic idealism and positive *terre à terre* good sense is found more or less in everyone. It is not even a question of age: one goes to sleep as Don Quixote and wakes up as Sancho Panza.'[39]

Between 1820 and 1824 no fewer than five illustrated editions of *Don Quixote* were published in Paris alone, and many more were to appear in subsequent years. Hardly a single notable artist in France at this period – apart from the deep-dyed *classiques* – failed to paint or draw an episode from the novel. Bonington borrowed the attitude of Rembrandt's philosopher for the great anti-rationalist, seated by a window and poring over old folios [181]. Some years

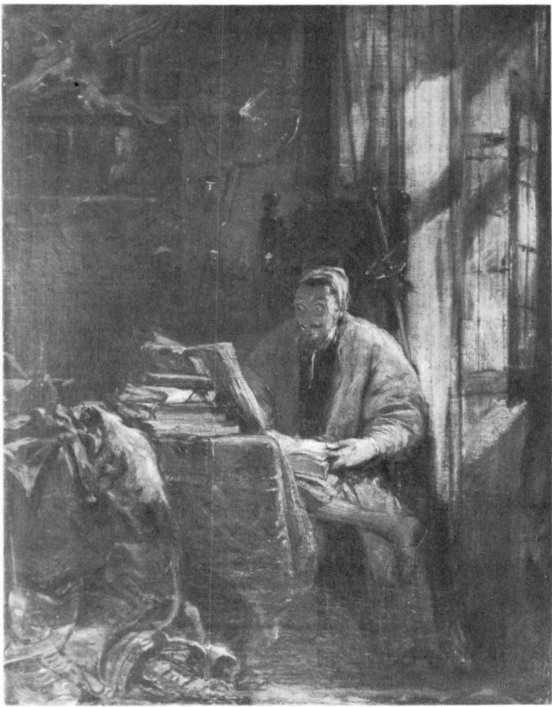

181. *Don Quixote in his Study*, *c.* 1825. R. P. Bonington

later Célestin Nanteuil showed him with one hand on a book, a sword uplifted in the other and armour littering the floor.[40] Delacroix also set him in his library, but with his housekeeper and the parish priest inspecting the volumes which, in their view, had turned his brain (a scene which does not exactly appear in the novel).[41] In the best of Gustave Doré's many illustrations, the Don figures as a knight errant of imagination, riding through a barren landscape beneath a sky in which clouds take the form of towers, castles and giants.[42]

The duality which Sainte-Beuve noted in the Don and Sancho had been recognized somewhat earlier by Thoré, in a watercolour which Decamps exhibited at the Salon of 1835. The same modest work inspired the novelist Jules Janin to write: 'Oh! what happiness to share the dream of Don Quixote the great, Don Quixote the hero, the magnanimous, the sublime child, the noblest, the worthiest, the wisest of men, in a word all that possessed the sweetest, the most honourable, the holiest of fools.'[43] A painting by E.-J. Pigal in the same Salon contrasted the ascetic Don and his carnal companion still more sharply.[44] But the artist who most deeply understood and responded to the subject was Honoré Daumier. Though his caricatures might suggest that he had as little in common with the Romantic knight as with his money-loving squire, he gave them in painting after painting a poignancy achieved by no other illustrator of the novel. Usually he showed them as separate, almost antagonistic, figures. But in the most notable of his pictures [182] the two are brought together with their mounts – Rosinante and the ass – compressed into one form as if to indicate the dualism and conflict within a single personality.

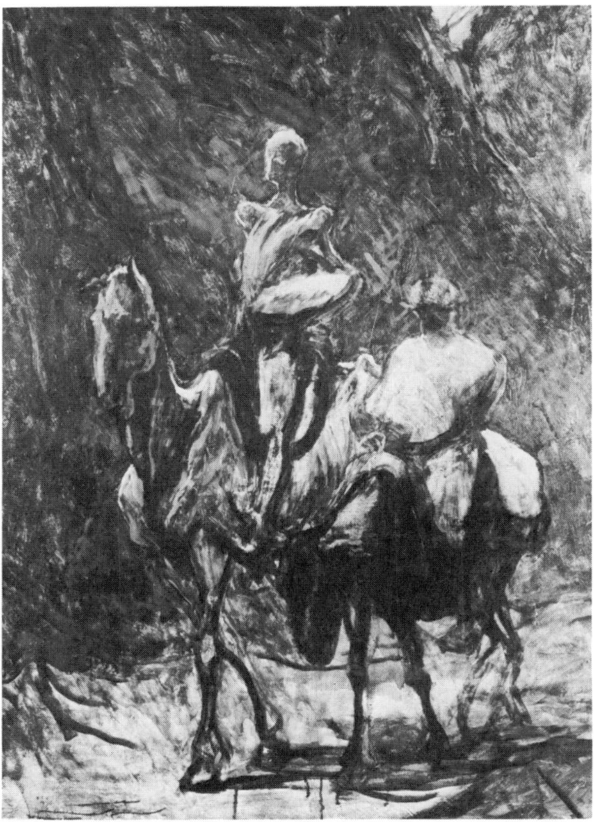

182. *Don Quixote and Sancho Panza*, *c.* 1865. Daumier

The emergence of Don Quixote as the paradigmatic Romantic poet or artist, in communion with eternal truths inaccessible to everyday materialist common sense, coincides with the development of new attitudes to the demented and insane. Until the eighteenth century, and in some parts of Europe even later, lunacy had generally been regarded as demonic possession, an affliction which might be exorcized but could not be cured by human means: it was a judgement of God. The Enlightenment introduced a more scientific and humane approach and already, before the beginning of the nineteenth century, a few physicians had made empirical studies of madness on which later theories and curative methods were to be based. But public madhouses remained to all intents and purposes prisons, and their inmates were treated as criminals rather than patients. Their appearance may be judged from Goya's painting of the madhouse at Saragossa, to which his attention had probably been drawn by Meléndez Valdés, an enlightened lawyer concerned with the problem of prison reform [183].

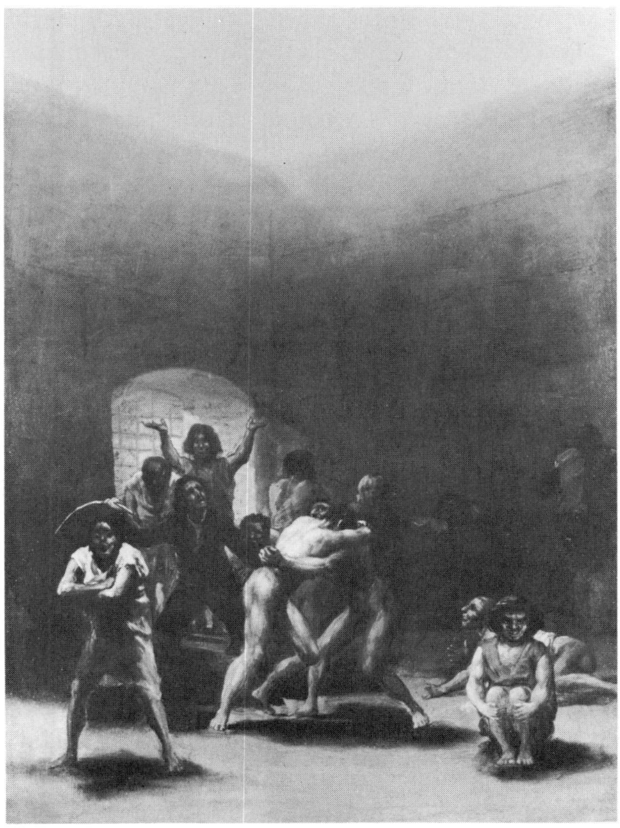

183. *The Yard of a Madhouse*, 1793. Goya

Goya described this picture as 'the yard of a madhouse and two naked madmen fighting, with the man in charge beating them, and others wearing sackcloth'. But he included it in a series which he ironically entitled '*varias diversiones populares*' – popular sports – and it acquires deeper significance from its conjunction with pictures of actors, bull-fighters, robbers, and a marionette seller. According to his own account he painted them 'in order to use my imagination which has been painfully preoccupied with my illness and misfortunes', and included in them 'observations of subjects normally outside the scope of commissioned work in which there is no room for the inventive powers and inspiration of the imagination'. The series as a whole explores without comment the worlds of make-believe and reality, the imagination and the understanding. His own attitude is more than ever inscrutable, especially in the madhouse scene where the only sane man is the keeper with a whip, surrounded by brutalized, staring idiots.

Goya's madmen conform in vacuous face and exaggerated gesture to a long-established tradition for the representation of the insane which survived well into the nineteenth century, even in images which reflect Romantic ideas – for example, a striking drawing of lunatics huddled round a poetically pensive figure by Wilhelm von Kaulbach, and the view of the courtyard of a lunatic asylum which Buonaventura Genelli included in his series of scenes from the life of an artist.[45] Géricault's portraits of monomaniacs are quite different, at once more true to life and more subtle in their implications. Commissioned by Dr Georget, an official at the Parisian Salpêtrière which housed both criminals and lunatics, they were probably intended to illustrate case-histories. Georget believed that insanity was caused by stresses which society imposed on the individual and that it was particularly common in free countries 'among people agitated by factions and parties, subject to the violent political movements which overturn all the elements of society, and to the revolutions which compromise all interests'.[46] The malady proliferates, he wrote, in circumstances which 'stimulate the mind, activate the spirit and bring into play all the passions of man'. The old woman with a mania for gambling and the victim of kleptomania [184] portrayed with such penetrating insight by Géricault are 'cases' of the deranged and disorientated – people who have pursued beyond the bounds of reason that lust for enrichment which characterized society under the Restoration, just as Géricault's 'old man with delusions of military command' is a demented counterpart of Napoleon's marshals. In depicting these haunted, haggard, yet

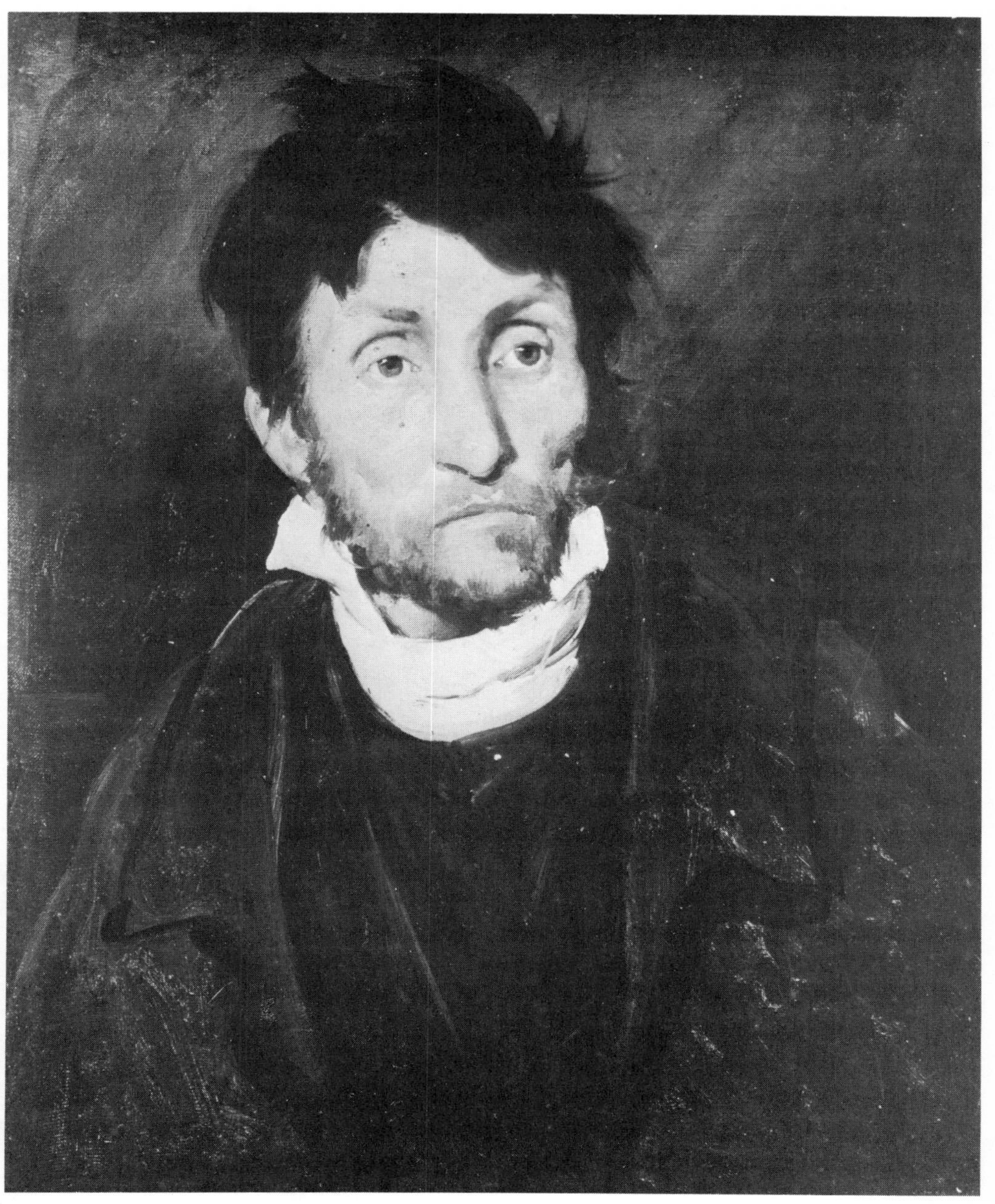

184. *The Kleptomaniac*, 1822–3. Géricault

always curiously gentle, sensitive faces, which retain an inalienable human dignity, Géricault transcended the scientific origin and purpose of the commission in such a way as to suggest a bond of peculiar sympathy. He probably first met Dr Georget when, after completing *The Raft of the 'Medusa'* (which, of course, includes men driven out of their senses by hunger, thirst and exposure), he is said to have experienced symptoms of mental disorder and to have attempted suicide in a fit of depression. But he must also have been aware of the metaphorical identification of the madman with the inspired artist which was given such emphasis and a new significance by the Romantics.

The tenuousness of the barrier between sanity and insanity provides the main theme for many of E. T. A. Hoffmann's stories and novels, whose main characters are usually musicians or artists: Kapelmeister Kreisler (a distorted self-portrait); the man who believes himself to be the composer Gluck; the goldsmith who is compelled to murder those who acquire his works; the mysterious painter of *Die Jesuiterkirche in G.*[47] But Romantic painters seem to have turned a blind – or perhaps simply a terrified – eye to mad (as to impoverished) artists, preferring as an image of insanity 'poor Ophelia divided from herself and her fair judgement'. Delacroix and others depicted *Ophelia's Song* in such a way as to suggest that this scene in *Hamlet* provided a prototype for those episodes in Romantic operas – by Bellini or Donizetti – in which the crazed heroine's coloratura arias, devoid of literal meaning, attain the ecstasy of pure music. Ophelia's death, graphically described in Gertrude's famous speech, provided a still more inspiring subject for paintings, most notably by Delacroix (who did three), and also

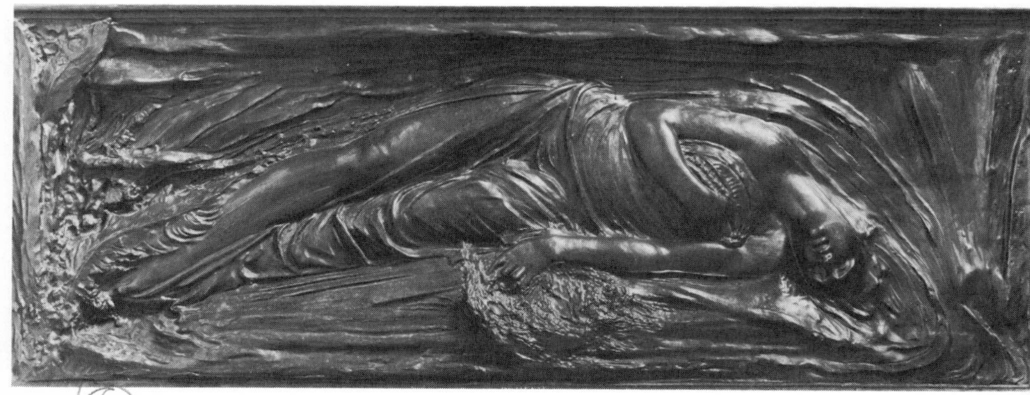

185. *Ophelia*, 1843–76. Auguste Préault

for a sculpture by Auguste Préault [185]. For here a number of dominant Romantic themes might be united – the beauty of nature, forlorn love, madness and death.

Hamlet had an almost overwhelming appeal for the Romantics, who read in its ambiguities a precocious statement of their own view of a disordered universe. '*Romantische Melodie*' the young Friedrich Schlegel called it in 1793, remarking that 'no poem is so Romantic and so musical' – a notion that helped him to form his definition of Romanticism.[48] Chateaubriand described it as

> that tragedy of maniacs, that Royal Bedlam in which every character is either crazy or criminal, in which feigned madness is added to real madness, and in which the grave itself furnishes the stage with the skull of a fool ... that Odeon of shadows and spectres where we hear nothing but reveries, the challenge of sentinels, the screeching of the night-bird and the roaring of the sea

and in which the account of Ophelia's death is 'like the spell of an enchantment'.[49] According to Victor Hugo, 'Unhealthy as he is, Hamlet expresses a permanent condition of man. He represents the discomfort of the soul in a life unsuited to it.' And in his analysis of Hamlet's personality, Hamlet becomes a kind of character sketch for the Romantic artist or poet – with a large element of self-portraiture:

> He is tormented by that possible life, interwoven of reality and dream, concerning which we are all anxious. Somnambulism is diffused through all his actions. One might almost consider his brain as a formation: there is a layer of suffering, a layer of thought, then a layer of dream. It is through this layer of dream that he feels, comprehends, learns, perceives, drinks, eats, frets, mocks, weeps and reasons. There is between life and him a transparency – the wall of dreams; one sees beyond it, but one cannot step over it ... Apart from men, Hamlet has still within him an undefined something which represents them all. *Agnosco fratrem.* If at certain hours we felt our own pulse, we should be conscious of his fever. His strange reality is our own reality, after all.[50]

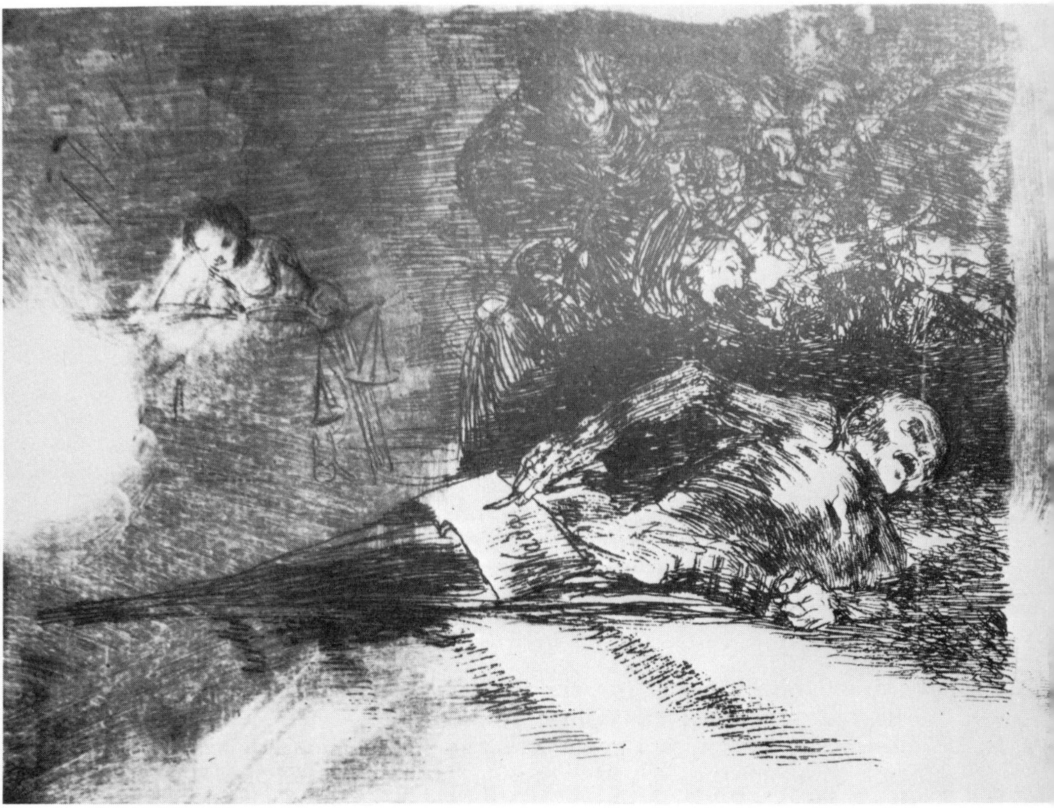

186. *Nada. Ello dirá*, *c.* 1812–20. Goya.

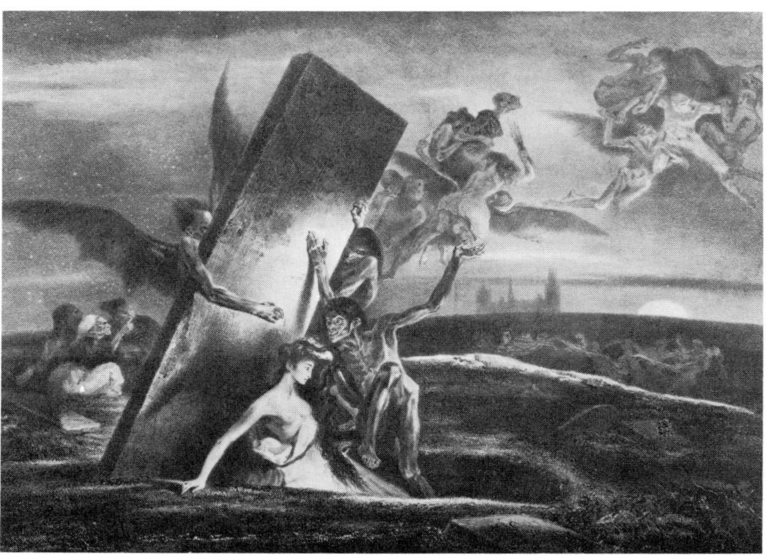

187. *The Phantoms*, 1829. L. Boulanger

8. *The Mysterious Way*

One of the prints in Goya's *Los Desastres de la Guerra* (probably etched between 1812 and 1820 though not published until 1864) shows a half-buried corpse holding a piece of paper inscribed *Nada* – nothing [186]. In comparison with this deeply disturbing work, such other Romantic graveyard scenes as Louis Boulanger's illustration to Victor Hugo's *Les Fantômes* look little more than exercises in making the flesh creep [187]. Its precise significance is, however, hard to determine. An old story (first printed in 1854) recounts that the Bishop of Granada on a visit to Goya noticed a painting of a similar subject and remarked: 'Nothing! Nothing! What a sublime conception: Vanity of vanities, all is vanity.' And Goya is said to have commented: 'Ah, poor Lord Bishop, how he misunderstands me! My ghost really implies that he has been to eternity and found nothing there.'[1] But does it? In the print the background is no gaping void: on one side a figure holding scales – presumably a reference to the Last Judgement – may be dimly descried, and on the other the darkness is crowded with howling faces which suggest the presence beyond the grave of a mysterious 'something' of terrifying intangibility. There is certainly no suggestion of Schopenhauer's '*das leere Nichts*' or of a desire for 'the renunciation of the will-to-live' with which it has been associated. Like so many of Goya's works, this print has a savagely ironical ambiguity which undermines our complacency. It presents no doctrine – either of immortality or of extinction. It simply confronts a problem which lies beyond the bounds of human understanding and can be resolved only by individual self-communing.

The same might be said of *Die Nachtwachen des Bonaventura* (published in 1804–5 by an author who still eludes identification), a strange book peopled with phantoms and echoing with diabolical laughter, which often calls to mind *Los Desastres de la Guerra* and *Los Proverbios* (though Goya can hardly have known or even have heard of it). Ending with the words spoken by the narrator as he scatters his father's dust in the air, 'and the echo in the charnel house cries for the last time "*Nothing*"', it appears to be a manifesto of nihilism and declaration of the utter meaninglessness of life. But it is also a satire on false sentiments, and that necessarily implies belief in those that are true. By merciless parody it exposes the smug optimism and facile rationalizing of such products of the English 'graveyard school' as Young's *Night Thoughts* and Hervey's *Meditations among the Tombs* and *Contemplations on the Night*.[2] The contrast between it and these once (to modern taste almost incredibly) popular and internationally famous prolusions is in many ways similar to that between Goya's anguished print and the many moonlight graveyard pictures, like P.-J. de Loutherbourg's *Visitor to an Ancient Churchyard* [188], which were calculated to appeal to the late

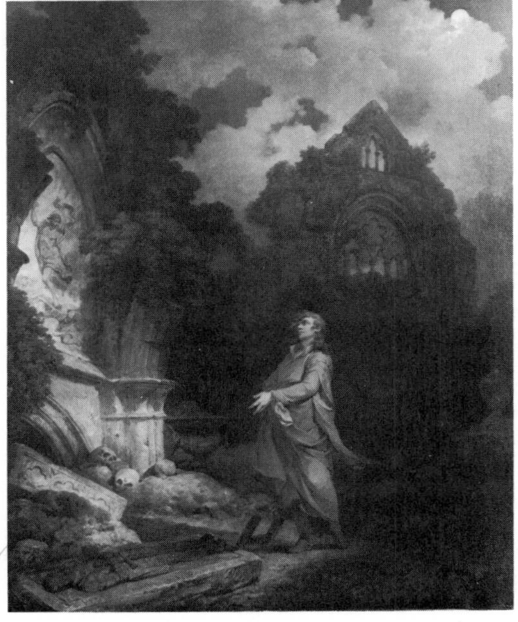

188. *Visitor to an Ancient Churchyard*, 1790. P.-J. de Loutherbourg

eighteenth-century man of sensibility. Goya explored depths of feeling more profound with an imagination far beyond the range of Loutherbourg, not to mention the merely fashionably Romantic Boulanger.

Images which call Goya to mind also appear in a vision of the Last Judgement by the German master of Romantic irony Jean Paul (who surely influenced 'Bonaventura'). In it he described corpses rising from their graves to ask Christ: 'Is there no God?':

> He answered, 'There is none.' At this the dead quivered and trembled ... the quivering ran through all the shadows, so that one by one the shudder shook them into nothingness. And Christ spoke on saying, 'I have traversed the worlds, I have risen to the suns, with the milky ways I have passed athwart the great waste spaces of the sky; there is no God. And I descended to where the very shadow cast by being dies out and ends, and I gazed out into the gulf beyond, and cried "Father where art Thou?" But answer came there none, save the eternal storm which rages on, controlled by none; and towards the West, above the chasm, a gleaming rainbow hung, but there was no sun to give it birth, and so it sank and fell by drops into the gulf. And then I looked up to the boundless universe for the Divine eye, behold it glared at me from out of a socket, empty and bottomless. Over the face of chaos brooded Eternity, chewing it for ever, again and yet again ...' The pale and colourless shades flickered away into nothingness, as frosty fog dissolves before warm breath, and all grew void. Then the dead children ... cried, 'Jesus, have we no Father?' He answered with streaming tears, 'We are orphans all, both I and ye. We have no Father.'[3]

Jean Paul's declared aim was to shock his readers into belief, and a similar ambivalence of intention hangs over many Romantic expressions of faith and doubt. Hippolyte Flandrin's astonishingly stark *Pietà*, for instance, conveys such a sense of inconsolable grief and desolation that it might seem to express the artist's conviction

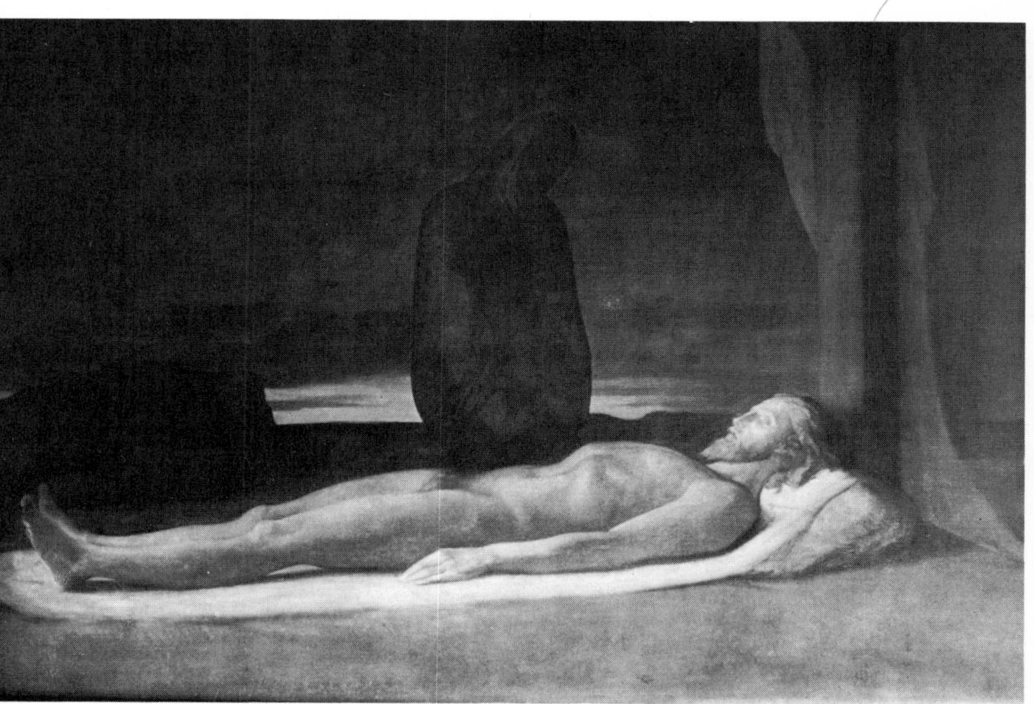

189. *Pietà*, 1842. H. Flandrin

of the finality of death and impossibility of resurrection [189]. He was, however, a pious Roman Catholic. Perhaps the Bishop of Granada was not altogether mistaken in his interpretation of the *Nada* print. Yet much of its power derives from the way in which Goya left the question open.

For Jean Paul, God was an emotional necessity, very different from the mechanistic prime mover – the 'God who winds up our sundials' of Lichtenberg's aphorism – conjured up as a rational necessity and then exorcised by thinkers of the Enlightenment. Atheism was for him the ultimate in loneliness and he likened the non-believer to 'the great Egyptian sphinx of stone half buried in the sands', gazing on a universe which has become 'the cold mask of formless eternity'.[4] It is surely a coincidence, though an interesting one, that Shelley (who knew no German) should have written a few years later in 'Ozymandias' of the shattered statue round whose

> colossal wreck, boundless and bare
> The lone and level sands stretch far away.

Shelley hoped for the extinction which Jean Paul feared. 'I could lie down like a tired child,' he declared in the uncannily prophetic 'Stanzas Written in Dejection',

> Till death like sleep might steal on me,
> And I might feel in the warm air
> My cheek grow cold, and hear the sea
> Breathe o'er my dying brain its last monotony.

But he developed a kind of mystical atheism strikingly unlike eighteenth-century scepticism. His longing to lose identity and be absorbed into the infinite – into the winds that breathe through the universe – brings him at times close to Schelling, and also to Novalis who called *Selbsttödung* (the annihilation of self, though the word carries a suggestion of *Selbstmord* or suicide) 'the true philosophical act … the real beginning of all philosophy'.[5]

In their different ways, Goya, 'Bonaventura', Jean Paul, Shelley, Schelling and Novalis all reflect the subtle complexity of the relationship between Romanticism and the Enlightenment. None of them can be described as an opponent of enlightened thought. They all shared its abhorrence of superstition, injustice and intolerance. But they rejected what they considered to be the more superficial, because so predominantly cerebral, tendencies of eighteenth-century scepticism, particularly those associated with Voltaire – what Novalis called the transformation of 'the infinite, creative music of the universe into the monotonous clatter of a boundless mill, which, turned by the stream of chance, and swimming thereon, was a mill of itself, without architect and miller, properly a genuine *perpetuum mobile*, a real self-grinding mill'.[6]

Some philosophical justification for the new attitude had been provided by the greatest thinker of the eighteenth century, Immanuel Kant, for in the *Critique of Pure Reason* (1781) he declared that the arguments by which he demonstrated the inability of human reason to assert the existence of a supreme being were 'necessarily sufficient to demonstrate also the invalidity of any counter-assertion'. This contention has been debated ever since, but there can be no doubt of its importance in the development of Romantic thought. Kant was himself a religious man, if one of a new non-sectarian type who sought for a universal truth underlying all the creeds while eschewing any form of public or even private worship. But he was deeply aware that the Idea of God could be apprehended only by a personal act of faith. We may feel in this a reflection of the Protestantism which so sharply divides the Enlightenment in Germany and England from that of France, where dogmatic Catholicism was attacked and replaced by a no less dogmatic scepticism. For Kant's very definition of Enlightenment is in some respects almost a rephrasing of the Reformers' declared will to free themselves from the authority of Rome and to work out their salvation guided by their own interpretation of scripture and their inner light. In *Was ist Aufklärung* (1784) he wrote:

> Enlightenment is man's exodus from his self-incurred tutelage. Tutelage is the inability to use one's understanding without the guidance of another person. This tutelage is self-incurred if its cause lies not in any weakness of the understanding, but in indecision and lack of courage to use the mind without the guidance of another. 'Dare to know' (*sapere aude*)! Have the courage of your own understanding; this is the motto of the Enlightenment.[7]

Kant said that he had to 'abolish knowledge to make room for faith'. By so doing he brought about yet another of those distinctions which are so characteristic of Romantic thought: that between what the Germans call *Verstand* and *Vernunft* and Coleridge 'understanding' and 'reason' (which Wordsworth identified with imagination). Kant's delimitation of the bounds of human understanding opened the door to speculation about what lay beyond and, albeit unwittingly, to the revival of mysticism – especially the Protestant nature-mysticism of Jakob Böhme, which exerted such a strong influence on the German Romantics and on Blake. It might be said that 'dare to feel', have the courage of your own intuition, was the motto of the Romantics. That the development of these ideas coincided with the growing conviction that the work of art – poem, painting or musical composition – could and should arouse emotions and explore beliefs which went beyond the understanding was of crucial importance for the Romantic fusion, and sometimes confusion, of art and religion.

Writing of Kant and mechanistic deism, Heine remarked: 'Do you not hear the bells ringing? Kneel down. They are taking the sacraments to a dying god.'[8] But ironically the bells he heard, or could have heard, from his Paris window when he wrote this in 1834 were, in fact, ringing in the greatest religious revival since the sixteenth century. The new emphasis placed on an act of faith as the only means of solving the riddle of existence was the counterpart of that anguished doubt which characterized the spiritual life of so much of the nineteenth century. Intimately associated with the yearning for reconciliation with God or with nature, the search for faith and its achievement and loss became a dominant theme in Romantic art and literature. Heine himself had sought without finding. Alfred de Musset lamented:

> *Je ne crois pas, ô Christ, à ta parole sainte:*
> *Je suis venu trop tard dans un monde trop vieux.*

In their agonies of doubt, some found consolation in human, sensual love, which regained for them an almost medieval religious sanctity. Others resorted to the new religion of art. Nature philosophy provided a related means of easing the burden of the mystery. But many took refuge in the established churches, if seldom without considerable heart-searching before and after conversion. As a contemporary noted, Lamartine's poetry springs to life only when he expresses the '*angoisses du scepticisme*'.[9]

There was, however, another aspect to the anti-rationalism and religious revival of the early nineteenth century: the widespread belief that the *philosophes* had been directly responsible for the French Revolution and the collapse of established order throughout continental Europe. In the *Génie du Christianisme*, published in 1802, Chateaubriand only alluded to the 'abyss' into which scepticism had plunged France; but his paean in praise of the beauty of Christianity, in contrast with paganism, made his point abundantly clear. And the book owed much of its immediate success to its appearance at the very moment when Napoleon was re-establishing the Church in France as a counter-revolutionary measure.

Similarly, in England after Waterloo, religion was given stronger official support and the state re-emerged as a patron of religious art and architecture. For the building of new churches, those bulwarks against revolution, the English Parliament voted considerable sums – a million pounds in 1818 and a further half million in 1824, to provide for 214 new buildings – which were augmented by numerous private contributions. These 'Commissioners' Churches' are capacious and distinctly austere, usually neo-Gothic but sometimes neo-Grecian, and are to be found in the suburbs of many English towns. There was less need for new churches in unindustrialized France, but those desecrated during the Revolution called for prompt attention. And the Crown, the Prefect of the Seine and other authorities under the Restoration commissioned a vast number of altarpieces to replace those which had been destroyed. So many of them appeared in the Salon of 1819 that one critic suggested that a holy-water stoup should be placed by the door so that visitors might cross themselves on entering.[10] (It was in this company, it should be remembered, that Géricault's *Raft of the 'Medusa'* was first exhibited.) These commissions provided welcome opportunities for artists to work on the grand scale, and a few of the pictures were masterpieces, notably Delacroix's *Christ in the Garden of Olives*.[11] Prud'hon's *Crucifixion*, with Christ's body bathed in a cold nacreous light, his face in mysterious darkness, with the shadowy forms of the holy women crouched in despairing grief at his feet, is at once dramatic and deeply moving, perhaps the most notable religious picture to have been painted in France since the seventeenth century [190]. Its outstanding quality was recognized and acclaimed at the time, and in a most revealing fashion. For although commissioned for the Cathedral of Metz, it was diverted to the Louvre, as if it were too good to be wasted on a church, and a copy was sent to Metz. This might suggest an underlying cynicism in the official religious revival: it certainly provides a comment on the relationship between art and religion.

It is a justification, or perhaps a consequence, of the Romantic demand for sincerity and integrity that so many of the most moving religious works of art and architecture of the period were executed outside, if not in direct opposition to, state-sponsored religion. Nearly all the most notable churches built in England during the first half of the nineteenth century were products either of the

 Roman Catholic revival, which attacked the Anglican establishment from without, or of the Tractarian movement, which sought its regeneration from within. For Pugin (a Roman Catholic convert),

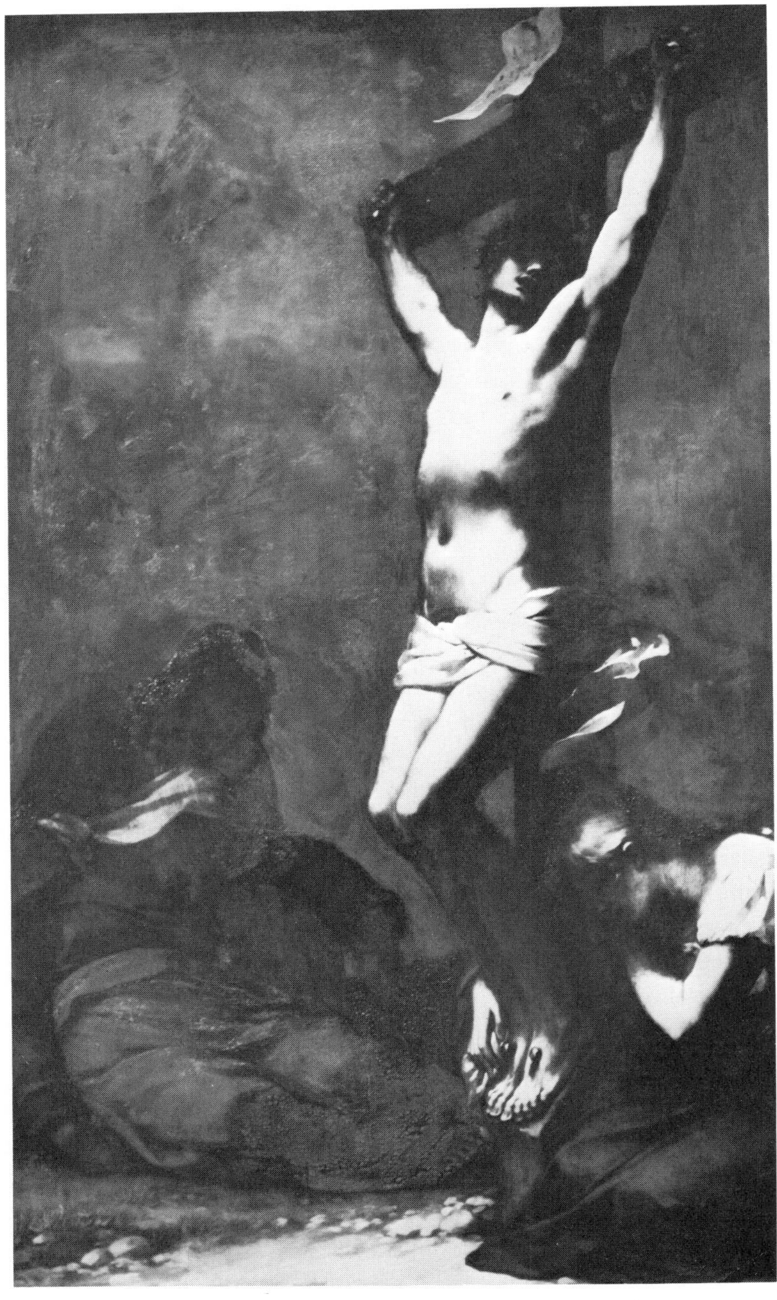

190. *Crucifixion*, 1822. P.-P. Prud'hon

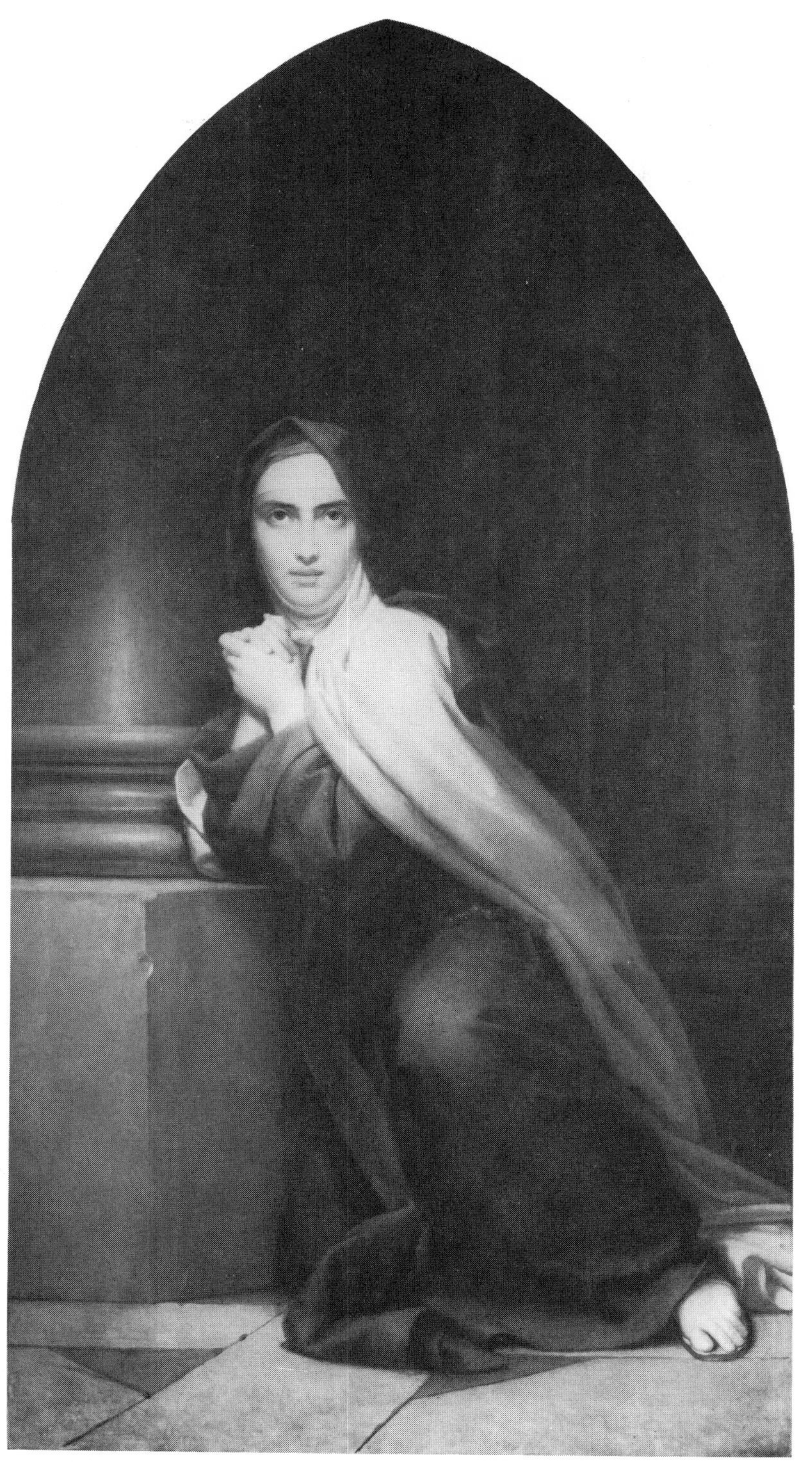

191. *Saint Theresa*, 1828. F. Gérard

'the mass of paltry churches erected under the auspices of the commissioners' were 'a disgrace to the age'. He believed that it was 'the faith, the zeal, and, above all, the unity, of our ancestors, that enabled them to conceive and raise those wonderful fabrics that still remain to excite our wonder and admiration'.[12]

In the new climate of tolerance – generated by the Enlightenment but given fresh significance by the Romantics – the intensity and integrity of religious faith came to acquire greater importance (to all save the guardians of the established churches) than its orthodoxy or heterodoxy, its truth or falseness judged by external standards. Hence the Romantics rejected not only what they regarded as the shallow scepticism of the eighteenth century but also that half-belief in casual creeds which marked conventional church-going – 'the religion of the Philistines' in Novalis's phrase, 'which functions merely as an opiate' (the origin, probably, of Marx's more famous dictum).[13] This may account, to some extent, for the prodigious popularity enjoyed by pictures of praying figures, of monks and nuns and especially the Italian peasants, of whose simple heartfelt piety there could be no question.[14] Even the more formal altarpieces tend to depict acts of devotion – none more effectively than Gérard's rapt and hauntingly intense *Saint Theresa*, an extraordinarily powerful image of total self-submission and abnegation probably inspired by the *Génie du Christianisme* and painted for the chapel of a charitable institution founded by Chateaubriand's wife [191]. But artists were also drawn to those who had been persecuted for their heretical beliefs. In Spain, Goya had satirized the Inquisition from an enlightened standpoint. And after its demise his follower Eugenio Lucas made a speciality of spine-chilling pictures of its operations – scenes which are a cross between visions of hell and images of martyrdom with the traditional roles reversed, members of the Holy Office taking the place of devils or pagan persecutors, and the Jew or Protestant emerging as the saintly victim.[15] From an only slightly different point of view Delaroche showed the Bishop of Winchester interrogating Joan of Arc, and Granet *The Interrogation of Savonarola*, contrasting the unimaginative and uninspired powers of established religion with the visionaries who occupied so important a place in the Romantic pantheon.[16]

The Romantics believed with St Paul that 'the letter killeth but the spirit giveth life' – and none more fervently than the greatest English visionary poet and arch-non-conformist William Blake. This was the text he inscribed under the first plate of his *Illustrations to the Book of Job*. Reinterpreting the most puzzling and poetic of

Old Testament books according to his own lights, he represented Job as the perfect and upright man, who erred by following the Mosaic law literally, but without passion. Significantly, Job is identical in features with Jehovah – his higher nature and the God he has created in his own likeness [192]. In the first plate, Job and

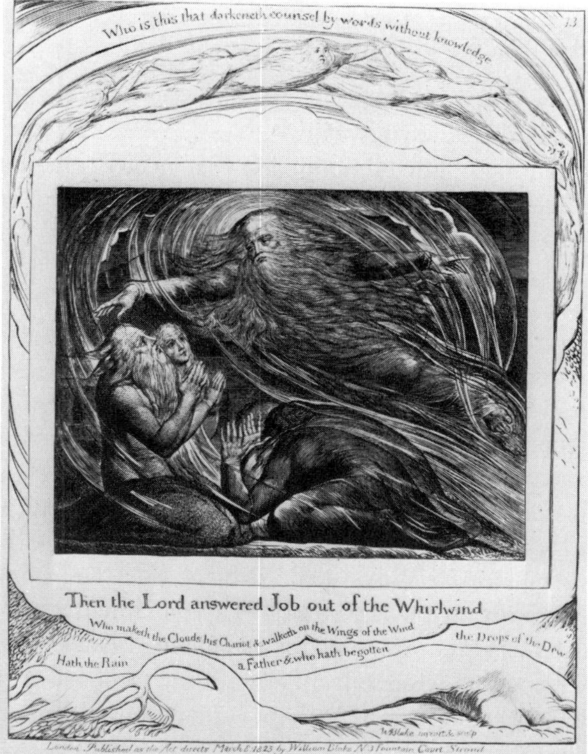

192. *Then the Lord answered Job out of the Whirlwind*, 1825. Blake

his family sanctimoniously observe the Sabbath with their musical instruments of praise hung up for the day: in the last, after suffering chastisement, they sing and play on harps and horns. Blake rejected the arid self-righteous cheerlessness of organized religion (Job's comforters are Pharisees) with its denial of the joys of the body as well as the imagination. Much earlier, in *Songs of Experience*, he had written:

I went to the Garden of Love,
And saw what I never had seen:
A Chapel was built in the midst,
Where I used to play on the green.

And the gates of the Chapel were shut,
And 'Thou shalt not' writ over the door;
So I turn'd to the Garden of Love
That so many sweet flowers bore;

And I saw it was filled with graves,
And tomb-stones where flowers should be;
And priests in black gowns were walking their rounds,
And binding with briars my joys and desires.

Now he showed how Satan 'smote Job with sore boils' for condemning his physical love for his wife.

Blake identified 'The Abomination that maketh desolate' with 'State Religion, which is the source of all Cruelty'. This he wrote in 1798, in a margin of *An Apology for the Bible in a Series of Letters addressed to Thomas Paine* by Richard Watson, Bishop of Llandaff: it is one of a series of annotations which help to clarify Blake's attitude to both religion and the Enlightenment.[17] The book in question was prompted by Paine's *Age of Reason* and other works which, the Bishop said, were 'circulated, with great and pernicious industry, amongst the unlearned part of the community, especially in large manufacturing towns'; and he hoped that his 'Defence of Revealed Religion might, if generally distributed, be efficacious in stopping that torrent of infidelity which endangers alike the future happiness of individuals, and the present safety of *all Christian States*'. Underlining the last words, Blake commented: 'Paine has not attacked Christianity. Watson has defended Antichrist.' At the end of the book he wrote: 'It appears to me now that Tom Paine is a better Christian than the Bishop' – though that is not to suggest that he found Paine's rationalism entirely satisfying.

Blake accepted much of Enlightenment thought: he subscribed to its demand for tolerance and social justice, welcoming the Revolutions in America and France. But, like other Romantics, he found that the thinkers of the Enlightenment had failed to answer some vital questions and left a void at the centre of their system. As art and life were for him identical, his attitude to Neo-classical artistic theory was the same: he accepted its demands for high seriousness, universality and purity, but rejected its subjection of the imagination to the reason. The God-given faculty of imagination should control the fallible human understanding and not *vice versa*. When Reynolds wrote in his seventh *Discourse* that 'in the midst of the highest flights of fancy or imagination, reason ought to preside from first to last', Blake commented: 'If this is True, it is a devilish Foolish Thing to be an Artist.'[18] In the same set of annotations,

Blake tells us that his objections to Reynolds were the same as those to Bacon's *Advancement of Learning*, Locke's *Essay on Human Understanding* and Burke's treatise on *The Sublime and Beautiful* ('founded on the Opinions of Newton and Locke'), which he had read 'when very Young': 'They mock Inspiration & Vision. Inspiration & Vision was then, & now is, & I hope will always Remain, my Element, my Eternal Dwelling Place.'

Blake is so much greater than the sum of his works that any attempt to isolate aspects of his art or thought is futile. The great anti-systematizer cannot be reduced to a system. And it is irrelevant to complain with T. S. Eliot that his philosophy resembles 'an ingenious piece of home-made furniture' put together from 'odds and ends about the house'. His art and writings (which cannot be understood independently of one another) are expressions of a burning need, not to rationalize, still less to synthesize, but to reconcile the conflicts of his own mind which mirrored those of the universe – his imagination with his understanding, his ideal of man with his experience of men, and, above all, his knowledge of God with both the jealous Jehovah of the Old Testament and the mechanistic prime mover, Mr Nobodaddy. Apparent inconsistencies result partly from the exploratory nature of his thought, but largely from the comparative way in which he sets side by side the visual and verbal image, the visions of different moments, opinions moulded by the course of events. When he had written and illuminated his *Songs of Experience* he always bound them up with *Songs of Innocence*. The notion of a single ideal by which all things might be rationally judged was illusory: 'One law for the Lion & Ox is Oppression.'

Blake's attitude to Reason found expression in three large colour prints of about 1795 [193]. Hecate with owl and ass and book of necromancy, a winged creature (reminiscent of Goya's monsters) hovering in the air, seems to represent superstition. The slouching form of Nebuchadnezzar, one of his most terrifyingly memorable images, shows the man who has abandoned Reason for bestial sensuality. The third is of Newton, and places Reason in a different context. In *Europe*, which dates from the same years, he refers to 'a mighty Spirit ... nam'd Newton' who prepared the way for the overthrow of tyranny in the French Revolution:

> he seiz'd the trump & blow'd the enormous blast!
> Yellow as leaves of Autumn, the myriads of angelic hosts
> Fell thro' the wintry skies seeking their graves,
> Rattling their hollow bones in howling and lamentation.

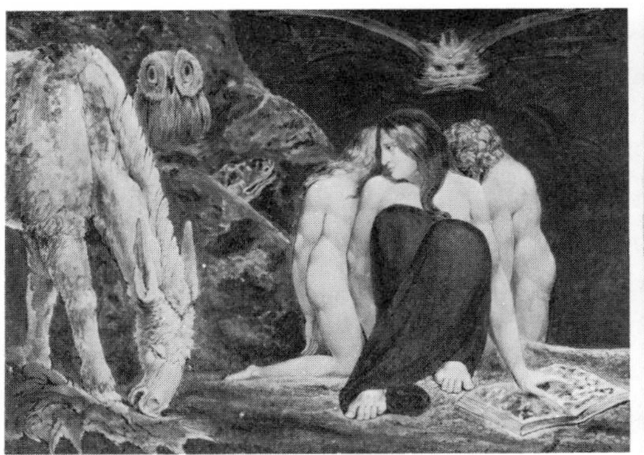
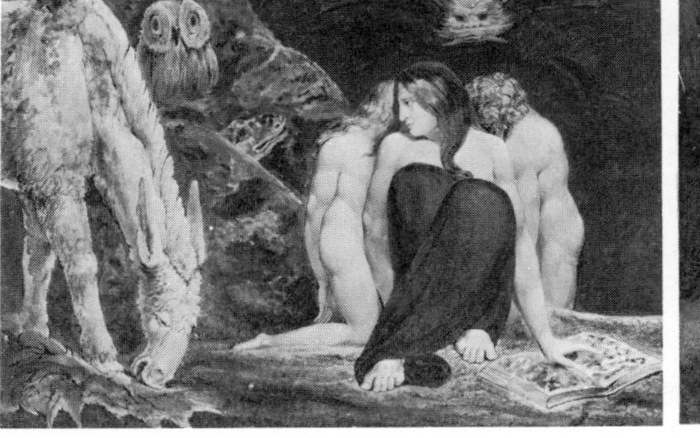

193a. *Hecate*, 1795. Blake

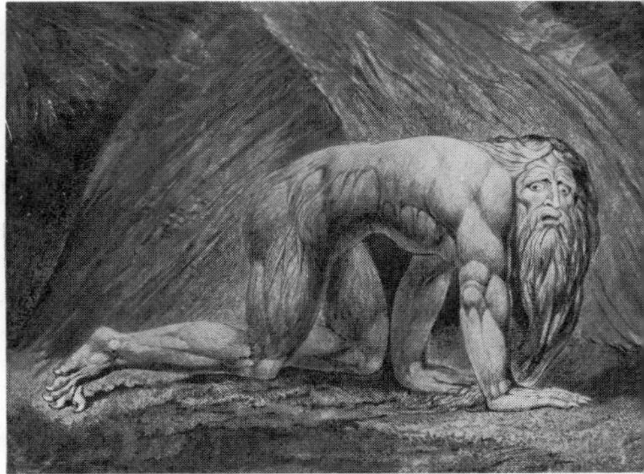

193b. *Nebuchadnezzar*, 1795. Blake

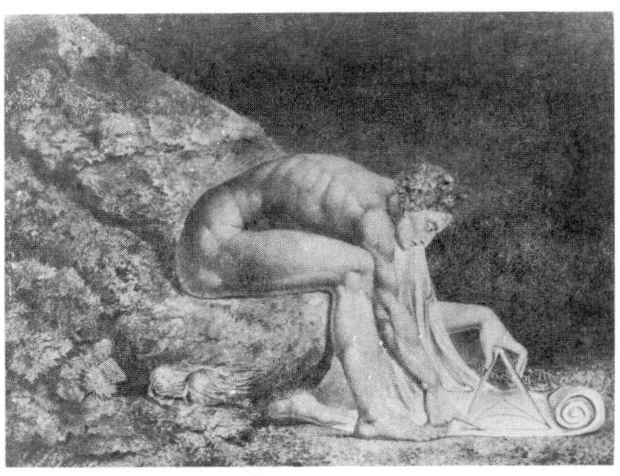

193c. *Newton*, 1795. Blake

But in the print, Newton, a figure of flawless classical beauty derived from Blake's artistic hero Michelangelo, is immersed in the waters of materialism, turned in on himself as he studies geometrical ratios. The dividers he holds in his hand are those held in the frontispiece of *Europe* by Urizen, who is at once Jehovah and the god of the deists, inexorably cruel and sublimely beautiful [194]. Elsewhere Blake describes how Urizen wept as he delivered the 'Philosophy of Five Senses' into 'the hands of Newton and Locke'. The sixth sense mattered to Blake far more than the others. Hence his distaste for 'Pretended Copiers of Nature, from Rembrandt to Reynolds' who – so he believed – were content to reproduce only what could be comprehended through the five senses, and to whom nature thus became 'nothing but blots and blurs'.

'The Nature of my Work is Visionary or Imaginative,' Blake wrote in 1810:

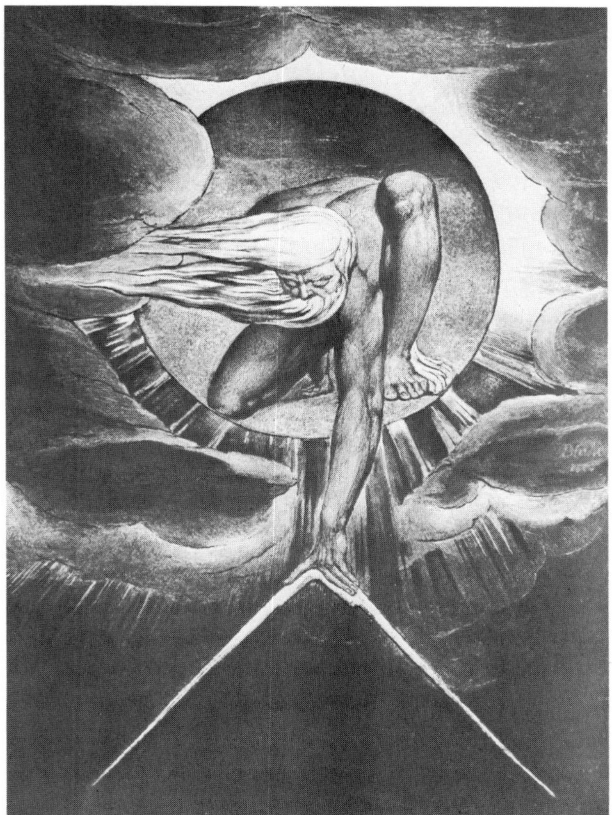

194. Frontispiece to *Europe: A Prophecy*, 1794. Blake

This world of imagination is the world of Eternity; it is the divine bosom into which we shall all go after the death of the Vegetated body. This world of Imagination is Infinite & Eternal, whereas the world of Generation, or Vegetation, is Finite & Temporal. There exist in that Eternal World the Permanent Realities of Every Thing which we see reflected in this Vegetable Glass of Nature.[19]

This approaches Neo-Platonism, though of a highly individual kind, for Blake believed that he had stood apart in Plato's cave and seen not just the shadows but the very substances and the light behind them.

'What', it will be Question'd, 'When the Sun rises do you not see a round disc of fire somewhat like a Guinea?' O no, no, I see an Innumerable company of the Heavenly host crying 'Holy, Holy, Holy is the Lord God Almighty'. I question not my Corporeal or Vegetative Eye any more than I would question a window concerning a Sight. I look thro' it & not with it.[20]

The language, pictorial as well as verbal, in which Blake recorded his visions, was derived from an astoundingly wide knowledge of books and works of art, especially prints. Its main sources have been exhaustively studied, yet the visions themselves remain as mysterious as ever.[21] The greatest of his images have qualities altogether beyond the reach of most of his sources in medieval sculpture and manuscript illumination or engravings after sixteenth-century paintings. They have a strangely persuasive vitality. 'It's God,' says Robert Frost's Eve, 'I'd know him from Blake's painting anywhere.' If his drawing and composition were sometimes weak and the phraseology of his poems often confused, there is never any doubt of the reality for him of the visions that inspired them, as transcendental experiences in which he broke through the barriers of the five senses. They carry total conviction.

As painter and poet, Blake found salvation in a Christ whom he could identify with 'imagination'. But there were times when his faith faltered, his visions forsook him and he could see no more than cruelty in man and chaos in the 'vegetable glass of Nature'. In 1804 he wrote to William Hayley: 'O Glory! and O Delight! I have entirely reduced that spectrous Fiend to his station, whose annoyance has been the ruin of my labours for the last passed twenty years of my life.' Suddenly, he continued, 'I was again enlightened with the light I enjoyed in my youth, and which has for exactly twenty years been closed from me as by a door and by window shutters.'[22]

Since so much of Blake's best work was executed in the middle of the preceding two decades – from 1789 when he published *Songs of Innocence* to about 1795 when he published *Europe* and the large colour prints – this letter has puzzled many who have associated 'the light' with artistic and poetic inspiration.[23] But was he not, perhaps, referring to the light of faith – in God and Man – which he had enjoyed in his youth? If so, the 'spectrous fiend' was doubt. And, indeed, his great works of the later 1780s and 1790s seem to be the product of an internal struggle between the two. Doubt may almost have extinguished faith in the later 1790s, when he was rarely able to rise above the level of his illustrations to Gray's *Odes* and James Hervey's platitudinous meditations. Significant exceptions include the paintings in which Urizen/Jehovah answers a terrified Job out of the whirlwind, and an angel supports a faltering Christ in the Garden of Olives.[24] The light restored to Blake in 1804 was occasionally to be dimmed: three years later he recorded a moment of complete despair. But he gradually achieved a mood of calm conviction. There was even a note of complacency in some of his later writings. He told George Richmond that the visions forsook him for weeks together, and then he turned to his wife: 'What do we do then, Kate?' 'We kneel down and pray, Mr Blake.' An inability to pray – like that which afflicted the Ancient Mariner – may have been responsible for the anguished tension of his earlier works.[25]

The Agony in the Garden, illustrated by Blake in his years of deepest depression, had a particular fascination for the Romantics. It provided the subject for a poem in which Alfred de Vigny (influenced by Jean Paul's vision of the Last Judgement[26]) expressed the agonizing doubt that haunted his generation. For here Christ's prayer is answered by silence:

Une terreur profonde, une angoisse infinie
Redoublent sa torture et sa lente agonie.
Il regarde longtemps, longtemps cherche sans voir.
Comme un marbre de deuil tout le ciel était noir;
La terre sans clartés, sans astre et sans aurore,
Et sans clartés de l'âme ainsi qu'elle est encore,
Frémissait. – Dans le bois il entendit des pas,
*Et puis il vit rôder la torche de Judas.**

This interpretation of the Gospel story cannot be extended to Romantic depictions of the subject. Yet it is perhaps significant that the most deeply moving of Goya's religious paintings should be *The Agony in the Garden* [195], in which the figure of Christ strongly resembles the kneeling man on the frontispiece to *Los Desastres de la Guerra* – the series which includes the *Nada* plate. Little is known for certain of Goya's religious outlook. He attacked the abuses of the Church, yet his mood is far removed from that of eighteenth-century sceptics, with their belief in the perfectibility of man and dismissal of what lay beyond empiricism. No theologian was more acutely aware of man's fallen state, no mystic more preoccupied by unseen presences. *The Agony in the Garden* has been described as a product of 'the religious hour' in Goya's life; but it has a tension suggesting a passionate desire for, rather than the achievement of, faith. The very lack of certainty about Goya's religion, and the wide variety of ways in which his religious works can be interpreted, may indeed reflect the conflict between Christianity and rationalism in

* 'A profound terror, an infinite anguish increased his slow agony. He looked for long, for long sought without seeing. The sky was black as mourning marble; the earth shuddered without light, without stars and without dawn, and without the light of the soul, such as it is, still. In the woods he heard footsteps and then saw, prowling, the torch of Judas.'

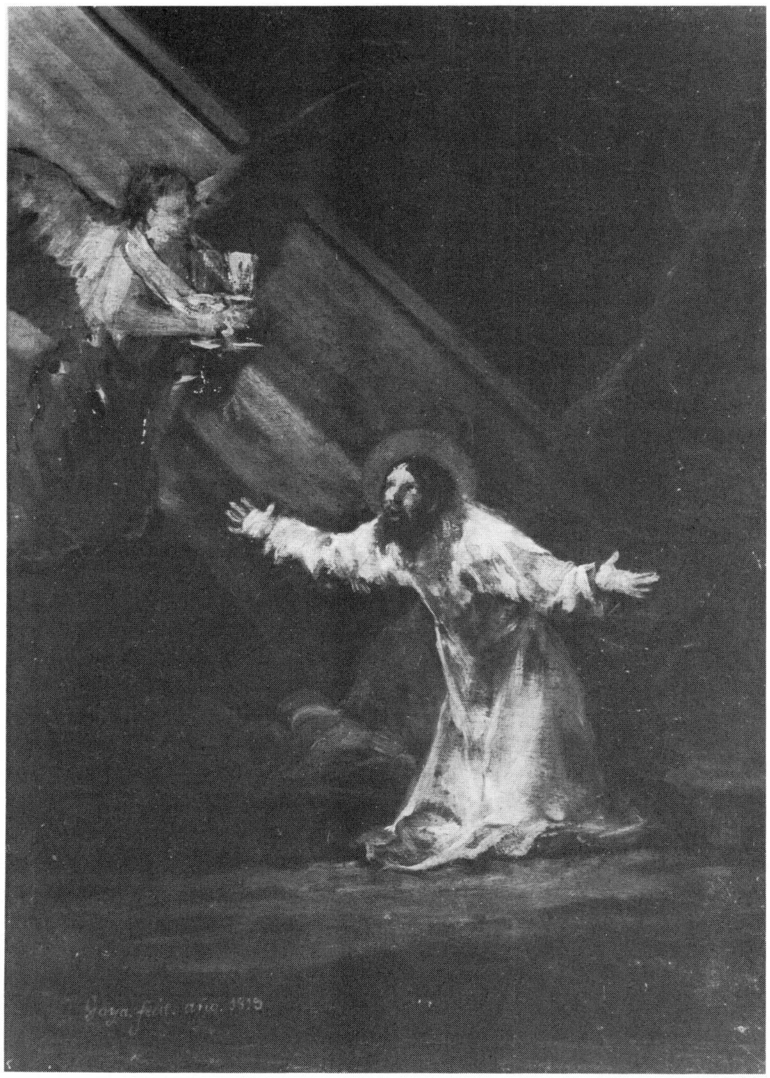

195. *The Agony in the Garden*, 1819. Goya

his own mind – a conflict he could resolve only in the creation of works of art which explored uncharted worlds of faith, feeling and imagination. And in many he achieved that penetration of the barriers of understanding which was held to be the main aim of music and poetry, as well as painting, by all the Romantics, however orthodox or heterodox their creeds.

‘The origin and character of all modern poetry can be derived so easily from Christianity,’ wrote Jean Paul in 1804, ‘that one might just as well call Romantic poetry Christian.’[27] The same could be said of painting. This was the point made by Runge when he contrasted the ‘Sistine’ *Madonna* with a head of Jupiter to show how the modern sense of love and life came into being with Christianity. The virtues of the Beatitudes were, he recognized, peculiarly Christian, and set a gulf between the ancient and modern worlds. The Romantics’ keen awareness of this made any proposition for regeneration by way of a return to Antiquity (as advocated by Winckelmann) seem altogether impossible. But modern (i.e. Romantic) artists should strive for a similar spiritual unity. Friedrich Schlegel held that every effort to revive the arts would be vain until ‘the prosaic mist engendered by imitations of the antique’ was dispelled and ‘we summon to our aid, if not religion, at least the idea of it, by means of a system of Christian philosophy founded on religion’.[28]

The development of these ideas had momentous consequences for the visual arts. At the most elementary level, they confronted sculptors with an awkward dilemma. ‘I know that when I am dead,’ Thorvaldsen sadly remarked,

> they will say that my Christian figures are Greeks – and rightly, for without the Greek school it is impossible to work in a correct and intelligible way. And my Greek figures will be said to be Christians – and again correctly, for I have never been able to allow myself to work with thoughts other than those which constitute all my aspirations. Without these principles I would never have been able to create my Apostles or my Christ.[29]

And the works in question abundantly demonstrate his point. It is not merely that his *Christ* owes an obvious debt to Antiquity [196] but that such an ostensibly ‘pagan’ figure as his shepherd boy has in both body and face a dreamy melancholy – more than gravity and less than sadness – wholly foreign to the ancient world [79b]. The Christ is a more perplexing figure. Stark white and very much larger than life, he looms out of shadows in a dark niche above the altar of the Vor Frue Kirke in Copenhagen, unapproachably remote, wrapt in his own inscrutable thoughts. Thorvaldsen seems to have derived inspiration from the most primitive and least sensuous ancient statues known to him (the marbles from Aegina which he ‘restored’ for the King of Bavaria), and also perhaps from Gothic sculpture and Dürer’s northern images of the Man of Sorrows. And

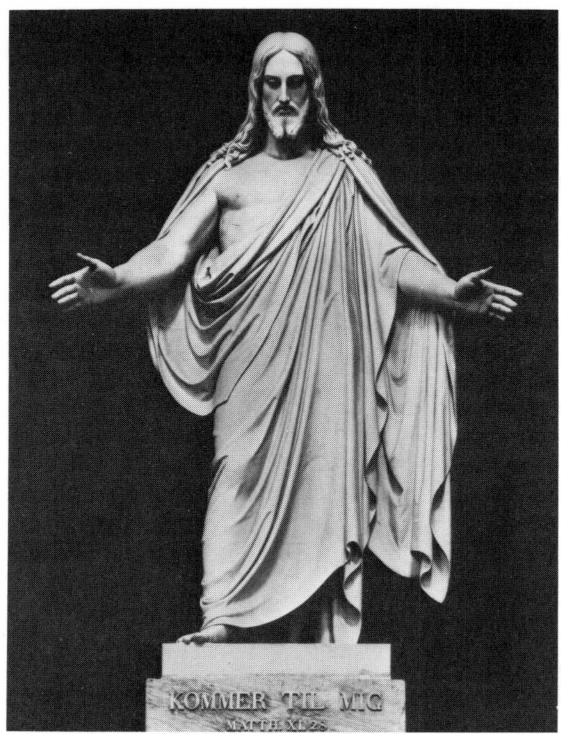

196. *Christ*, 1821–39. Thorvaldsen

this may account to some extent for the statue's ambivalence, the unresolved conflict between form and feeling in the open-armed gesture, which recalls the text 'Suffer the little children to come unto me', and the impassive, almost indifferent expression of the beautiful, coolly chiselled face, which increasingly dominates the figure as one approaches the altar, and brings to mind Swinburne's lines on the 'pale Galilean' at whose breath the sensual pagan world turned grey [196a].

The demand for a Christian art encouraged some sculptors, and many more painters, to seek its true principles in works of the fifteenth century, executed before the Western Church had been divided by schism and, as they believed, before pagan antiquity had begun to reassert its baneful influence. But the Nazarenes and artists of similar tendency in France, Italy and England were from the start criticized for evading rather than confronting the problems which faced early nineteenth-century Europe. 'What pleases us about the older pictures is above all their pious simplicity,' Caspar David Friedrich observed. 'However, we do not want to become simple as

196a. Detail of 196

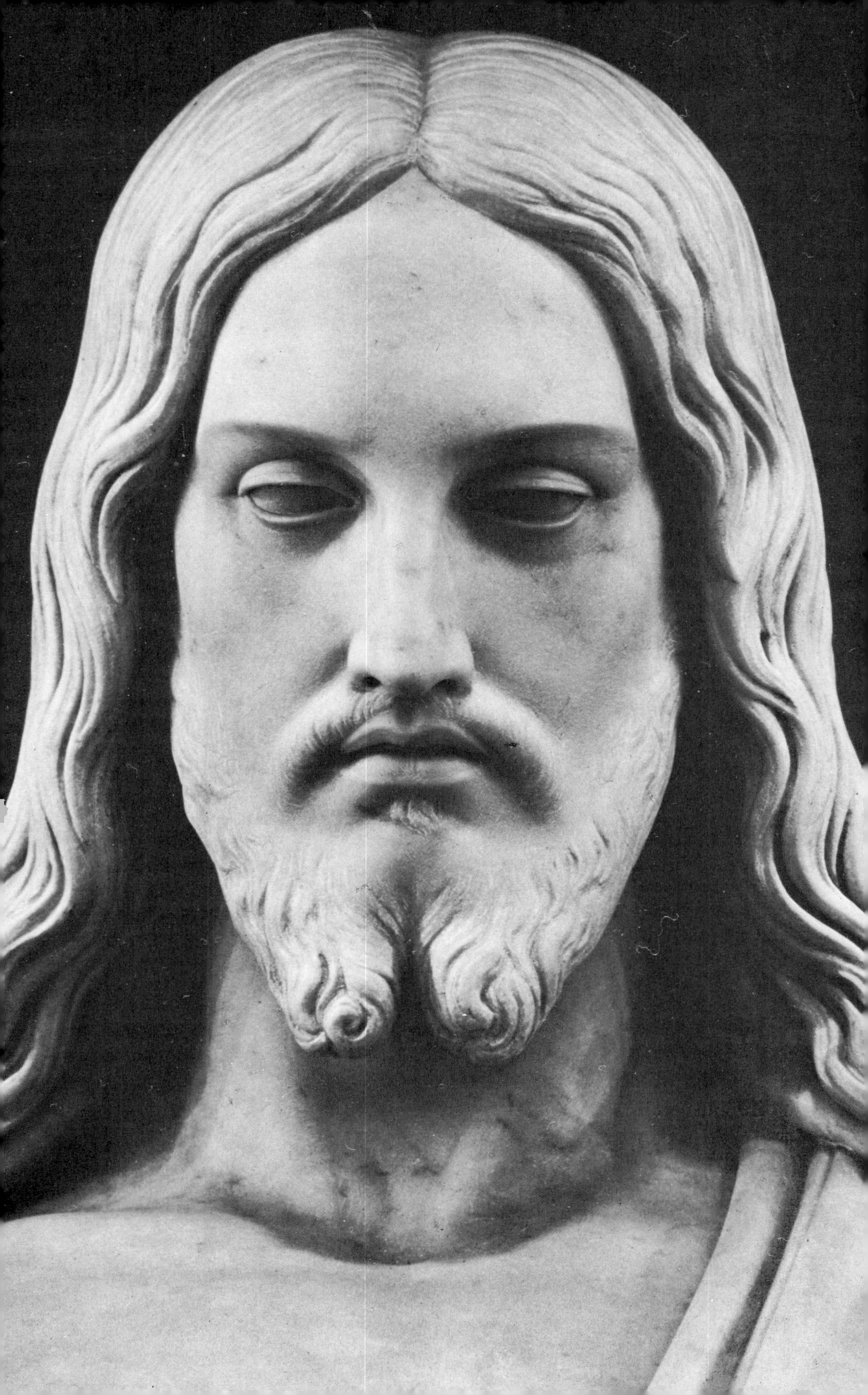

many have done, and ape their faults, but rather to become pious and emulate their virtues.'[30] He was, of course, referring to the German 'Nazarene' artists who had renounced their homeland and their Protestant faith for Rome. The Nazarenes were particularly attacked for their sectarianism – nearly all were converts to Catholicism – for their substitution of church membership for religion, and of dogma for a faith that was strenuously achieved and arduously maintained. It was not long before Tennyson was to declare that

> there is more faith in honest doubt,
> Believe me, than in all the creeds.

The work of the Nazarenes, and the many followers who diluted and sweetened their style, came to be regarded as no more than effusions of religiosity.

New notions of the nature of religious belief, and of the potentiality of paintings to explore feelings beyond the world of sensual perception, contributed to the dual process by which religious art was gradually secularized during the early nineteenth century; and conversely, and still more strikingly, a great deal of what had previously been regarded as secular art was given an unmistakable religious significance. As we have already seen, Caspar David Friedrich himself found a means of expressing his intensely personal faith in landscapes, in which Christian imagery sometimes indicates the direction of his thought. Constable also found landscape the only satisfactory medium for the expression of his quasi-religious belief in cosmic harmony. Asher B. Durand in America declared that a landscape painting 'will be great in proportion as it declares the glory of God'. Even the representation of a nude figure might take on a religious connotation for those who believed with Novalis that 'The body of Man is the only temple in the world. Nothing is holier than this high form. Bending before man is a reverence done to this Revelation in the flesh. We touch heaven when we lay our hand on a human body' (to quote the aphorism that was translated by Carlyle and widely diffused in England[31]). The remark calls to mind the life drawings of the Nazarenes [79] – so much less self-conscious than their archaizing paintings – and the many nudes which populate the mystical works of Blake.

As a result, the barrier separating religious from secular art was blurred if not altogether erased. Delacroix, who has been described as 'the only great religious painter of the nineteenth century'[32] (though he seems to have been an agnostic), clearly made no distinction between his Christian and pagan pictures. Nor did his

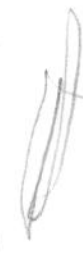

patrons. Some of his paintings of religious subjects were, it is true, commissioned for churches, though invariably by the secular rather than the ecclesiastical authorities. But he executed the majority without commissions and sold them to collectors who hung them in their living rooms. In 1842, for example, he painted an *Education of the Virgin* for George Sand, who supplied the canvas (originally intended for a new pair of corsets) and read novels to him as he worked, while her son Maurice began to make a copy of it for the church at Nohant. Delacroix's sombre *Deposition from the Cross* was bought by the Comte de Geloës, who hung it in his Paris house where Delacroix saw it from time to time when he went there for dinner. At the Salon of 1847 he sold to a Belgian collector a *Crucifixion* [197] and an *Odalisque*, the one as spiritually tormented as

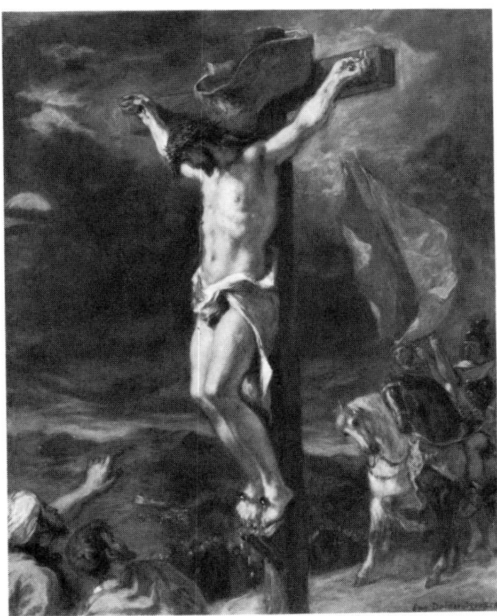

197. *The Crucifixion*, 1846. Delacroix

the other was voluptuously fleshy. This may not surprise us nowadays. And, of course, religious paintings by old masters had often been transferred from churches to secular buildings (the Madonnas of Raphael and the altarpieces of Correggio, for example). But, before the nineteenth century, scenes from the Passion had rarely, if ever, been bought from contemporary painters as works of art rather than as devotional images.

Romanticism was decried by T. E. Hulme as 'spilt religion', and there is some truth in the jibe. Art was often identified with religion, especially by those who were not orthodox Christians. '*Die Kunst selbst ist Religion*,' Schinkel declared.[33] And the equation was qualified rather than denied by the devout Runge when he wrote: 'Religion is not art. Religion is the highest gift of God, it can only become lovelier and more clearly understood through art.'[34] This seems to be the message of the Catholic Overbeck's *Triumph of Religion in the Arts*, which represents the mystical union of painters, sculptors, architects and patrons who glorified the Church [104]. But, with its allusions to Raphael's *Disputa* and *School of Athens*, it is also a tribute to the Romantic artist and his exalted vision of himself, as he comes to occupy a place beside, if not indeed to supersede, the theologian and philosopher as guide to the realms beyond human understanding. Artists might even usurp the role of saints. In a print after Franz Pforr, modelled on a fifteenth-century *Sacra Conversazione*, Raphael and Dürer kneel by a throne on which a personification of Art has taken the place of the Virgin as mediatrix

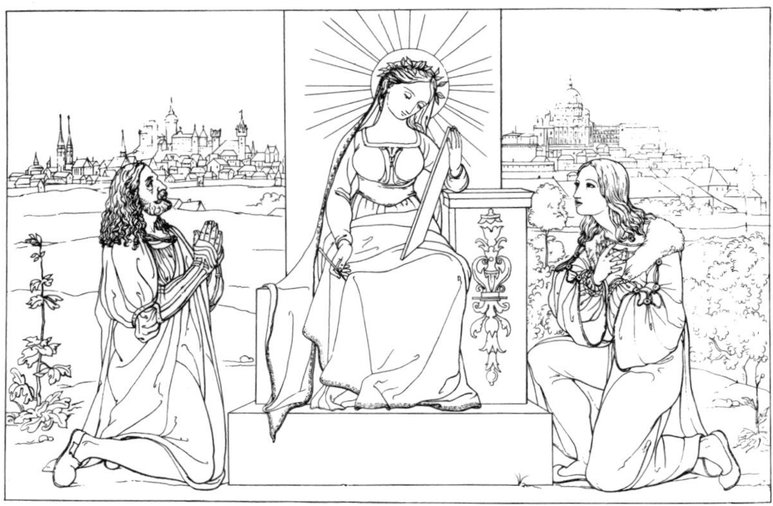

198. *Dürer and Raphael at the Throne of Art*, 1832–5.
G. C. Hoff after Franz Pforr

between Man and God [198]. Dürer himself fills the Virgin's role in a strange drawing of his apotheosis, which Konrad Eberhard based on the traditional scheme of the Assumption and Coronation – in the lower register, mourners stand round Dürer's tomb in the Nuremberg cemetery, above, Christ places a crown on his head.[35]

The cults of the Virgin and of Art were also fused in the large altarpiece which the 'pagan' Ingres painted for the Cathedral of his native Montauban [199]. Its subject, Louis XIII placing himself and France under the protection of the Virgin, was dictated to Ingres who accepted it reluctantly. But he made of it a glorification of art – or rather of the art of Raphael. For at first sight the King seems to be offering his crown and sceptre to a combination of the 'Sistine' *Madonna* and the *Madonna* of Foligno, and this impression

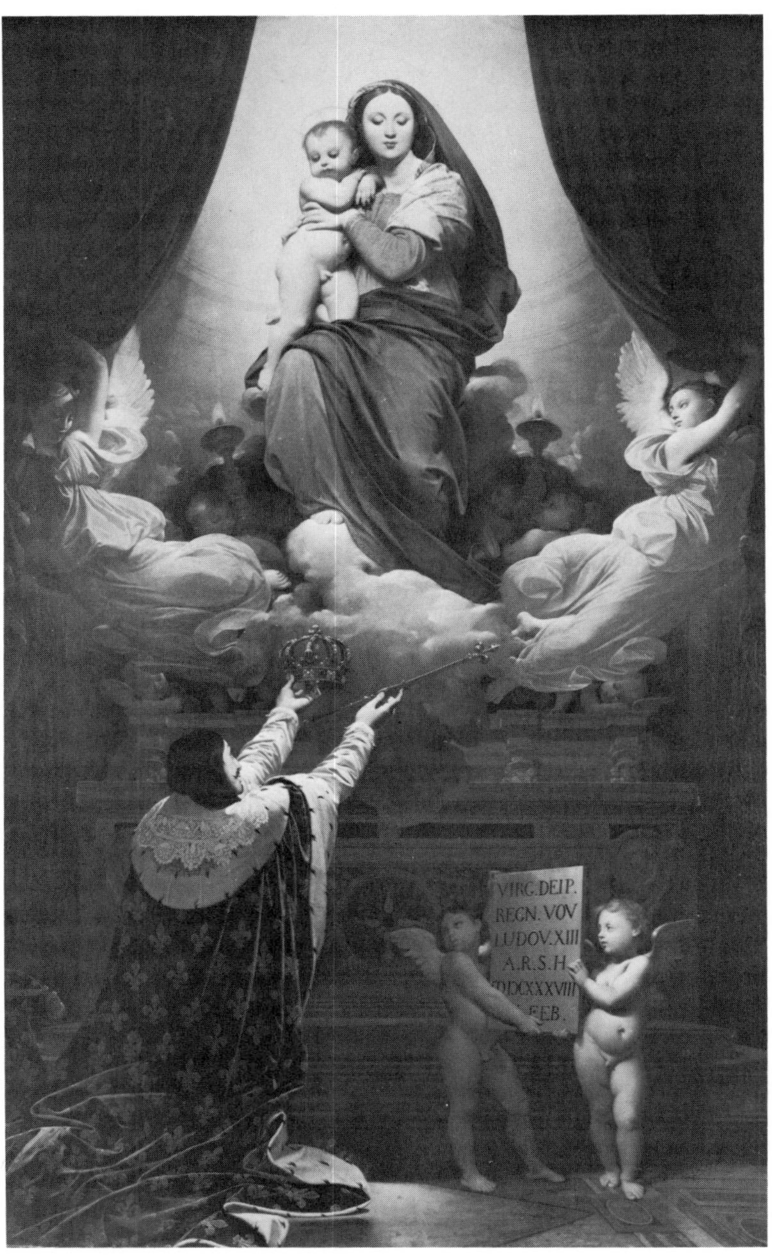

199. *The Vow of Louis XIII*, 1824. Ingres

is strengthened by the contrast between the meticulous, almost illusionistic, way in which his robes of lace and ermine, velvet and gold thread are rendered and the generalized idealism of the Virgin and angels. By emphasizing the dichotomy, Ingres converted the ostensible religious subject of the painting into one which lay much closer to his heart and was primarily artistic, though with spiritual (philosophical rather than theological) overtones – the conflict between the real and the ideal, the worlds of sensual perception and imagination.

Yet the Virgin in this painting is no disembodied spirit – nor are the angels who so shocked the good clerics of Montauban that they covered their sex with gilt vine leaves. She closely corresponds with the ideal described by Ingres's friend Quatremère de Quincy, in the life of Raphael he published in 1824 – the very year in which *The Vow of Louis XIII* was completed:

> There are subjects and objects the *ideal* of which has no affinity with the *beautiful* in the Greek divinities. The ideal of a Venus, a Juno, or a Minerva, cannot be that of a Holy Virgin. The general idea of the Virgin is a combination of divinity and humanity, of nobleness and of modesty, of virgin simplicity and maternal affection. It would be as inappropriate to give the style, the features, or the dress of the Virgin, the grandeur of form and the general character of the antique statues, as it is to represent her, which many have done, under the commonplace and vulgar image of an ordinary mother or nurse, with an ordinary child.[36]

Although he had been the sternest supporter of classical doctrine in France, the former friend of David and of Canova, whose biography he was to write, Quatremère here reveals how he, as much as Chateaubriand or Friedrich Schlegel, had come to appreciate the essential difference between the ideals of ancient and Christian art. He also reminds one of the Romantic ideal of Woman, and of the links between religion and physical love as well as art.

* * *

Ingres made a clear distinction between the untouchable beauty of his Madonnas and the seductive charms of his other female figures – the congealed sensuality of such erotic fantasies as the defenceless Angelica chained to a rock [120] or the plump women in the sensual circle of *Le bain turc*, born slaves to animal passions.[37] Even the fashionable ladies he portrayed are decked out in jewels and silks which seem to be emblems of marital subjection as much as social status. And the cunningly placed looking-glass which so often reflects the back of the sitter's head in his portraits clearly implies that such beautiful objects must, like Antique statues, be seen in the round to be fully appreciated. Such pictures might suggest that he rejected out of hand emergent ideas about women as equal partners with men, rather than as mere agents of intellectual stimulation and sexual gratification, not to mention Romantic notions of love. Yet he had, early in his career, provided one of the most explicit formulations of the Romantic fusion of the cults of love, religion and art in his image of Raphael and the Fornarina. And it was a theme to which he returned intermittently throughout his career partly, perhaps, to resolve a conflict in his own mind about the relationship between the four elements in the composition: the artist, his mistress, the realistic portrait, and the idealized religious painting (the *Madonna della Sedia* or the *Transfiguration*).[38] He was at work on the last version of the subject in 1860, but abandoned it, completing two years later *Le bain turc* on which he proudly inscribed his age – eighty-two – as if to boast of the persistence of his creative potency and sensual receptivity.

The obvious links between procreation and creation, both artistic and divine, were strengthened by the Romantics' belief that art and love were mysteries akin to those of religion. Novalis confessed that he felt 'not love but religion' for Sophie von Kühn, whom he was to identify with the Virgin Mary in a poem written after her death. Some forty years later, Natalie Yakolov wrote to Alexander Herzen of her love for him in phrases which had by then become commonplace: 'You know this paradise of the soul . . . But for me this is the first time that the light illuminates my soul. I worship. I pray. I love.'[39] While such ideas prevailed, it is hardly surprising that the artist's self-portrait with his wife and child should often resemble a Holy Family.[40] And other secular images are suffused with a sense of religious hush – as is the extraordinary small masterpiece in which Caspar David Friedrich commemorated his marriage to Caroline Bommer, in the prow of a ship together, hand in hand, as they are borne along on the full tide of their love towards the heavenly city of their private longings [200].

The Romantics rejected, no less censoriously than the Neo-classicists, what they regarded as a frivolous attitude to love, displayed in the paintings of Boucher or such a novel as *Les liaisons dangereuses*. But they did not, of course, condemn the erotic. Even when exalting an unattainable ideal and yearning for a union which might never be consummated, they dwelt on physical love as much as cerebral

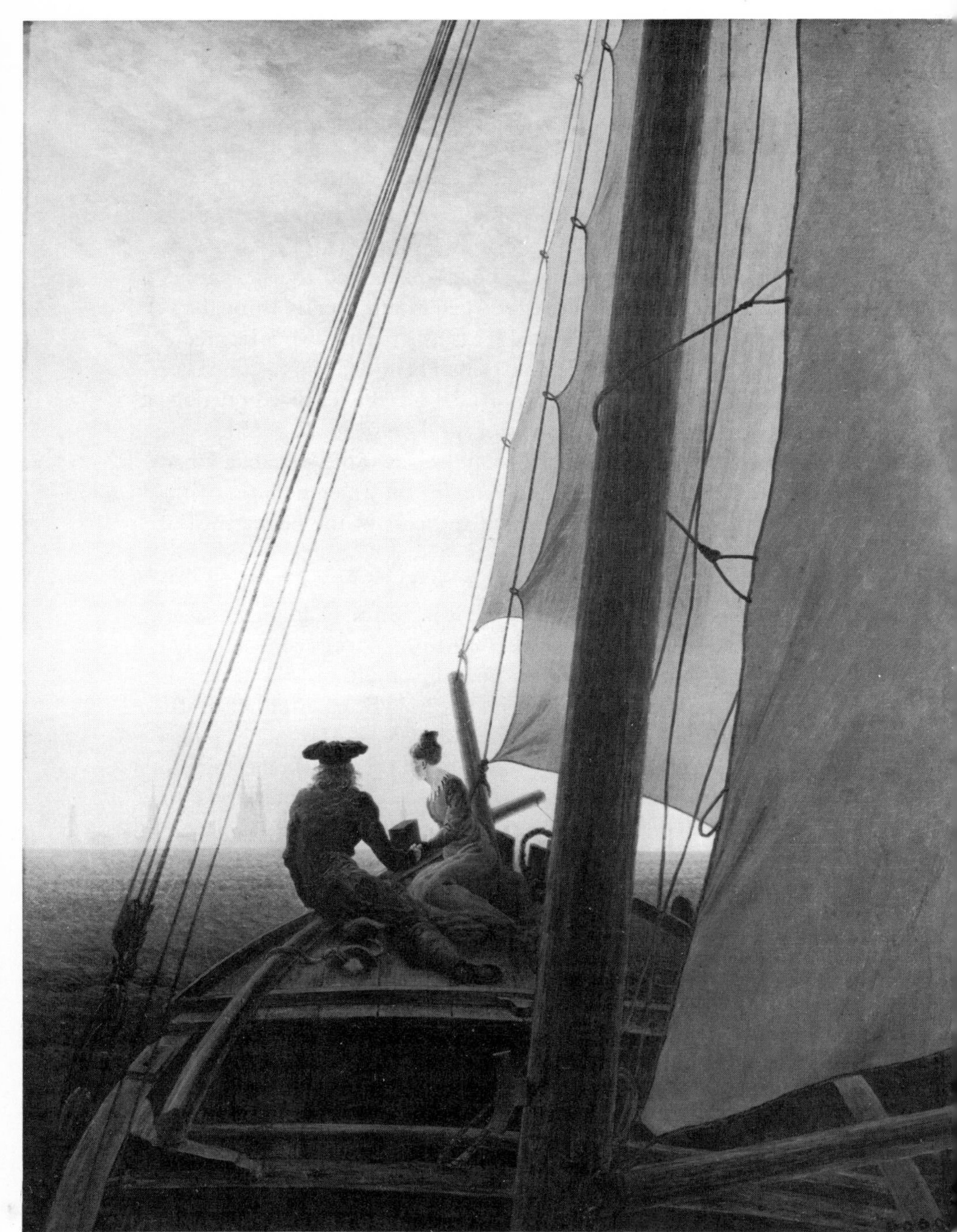

200. *On the Sailing Ship*, *c.* 1818–19. Caspar David Friedrich

passion. The 'more happy, happy love' which Keats ascribed to the figures on the Grecian Urn is a sensual pleasure of eternal duration, without orgasmic termination and aftermath:

For ever warm and still to be enjoy'd
For ever panting and for ever young;
All breathing human passions far above,
That leaves a heart high-sorrowful and cloy'd
A burning forehead, and a parching tongue.

Romantics extolled the perfect union of bodies and souls in a love at once physical and spiritual – what Mme de Staël's Corinne called 'the supreme power of the heart, mysterious enthusiasm that encloses in itself all poetry, all heroism, all religion'. It was as much to be distinguished from what generally passed for love as was poetry from mere verse, the higher reason from the understanding, or church-going from religion. Hence the new distinction between true marriage and 'licensed concubinage'.[41] One of George Sand's heroes remarks, in words which echo through nineteenth-century fiction: 'What constitutes adultery is not the hour which a woman gives to her lover, but the night which she afterwards spends with her husband.'

Similarities have often been noted between medieval and Romantic cults of love, both of which invested the relationship between the sexes with a mystical aura. They may, indeed, account for some of the popularity enjoyed by the ballads of the troubadours and the *chansons de geste* in the early nineteenth century. Significantly, however, the incidents in medieval literature which seem to have held most appeal for the Romantics were those describing the infraction of the code of courtly love – the story of Launcelot and Guinevere and its echo in that of Paolo and Francesca. In 1786 Fuseli had depicted Paolo and Francesca sporting in amorous dalliance.[42] But the scene was purified of its wantonness in Flaxman's eminently chaste line engraving, which seems to have provided the prototype for paintings by Ingres [119], a tremulously innocent sculpture by Alexander Munro [201], and also a curious little religious-amorous picture by Johann Evangelist Scheffer von Leonardshoff, entitled *Andachtsstunde* (prayer-time).[43] Flaxman also showed the lovers in hell, lamenting their sin with gestures recalling those of Adam and Eve expelled from Eden. But this could hardly satisfy a Romantic interpretation of Dante's *Amor, che a nullo amato amar perdono* (love which excuses no loved one from loving). In a painting of 1818 by Fuseli, they fly through the air in attitudes of

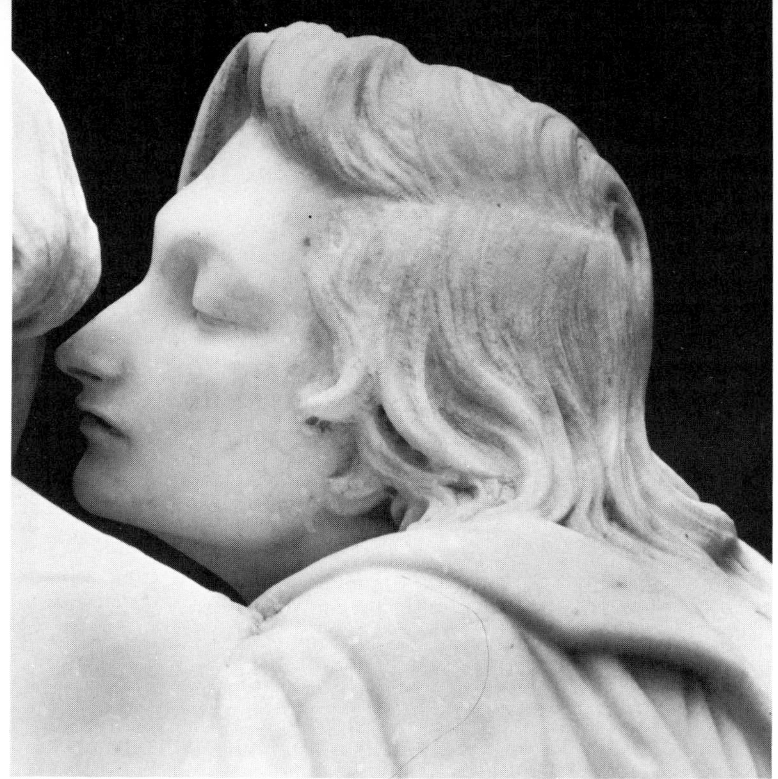

201. *Paolo and Francesca* (detail), 1852. A. Munro

ecstasy. But it was left to Blake to convert the whirlwind of lovers into a circle of bliss, with Paolo and Francesca eternally united in a ring of bright light – not sinners but victims of Urizen's arbitrary

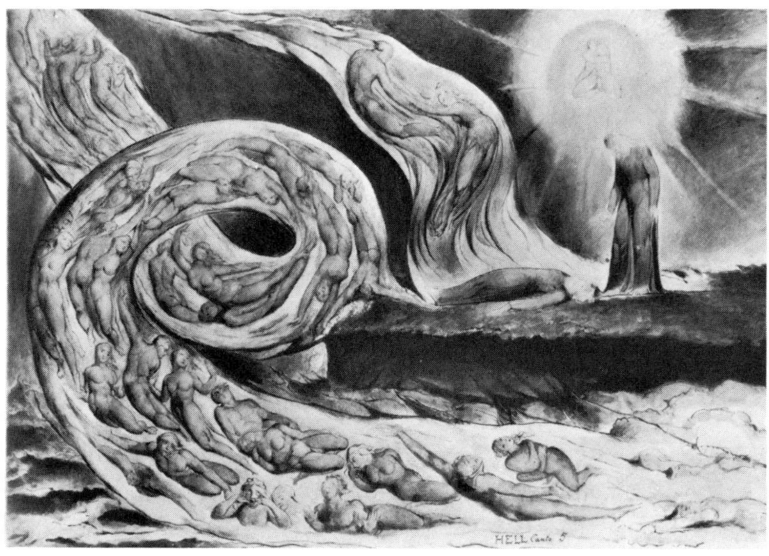

202. *The Whirlwind of Lovers: Paolo and Francesca*, *c.* 1824–6. Blake

moral code [202]. In paintings by Ary Scheffer, who had a similar contempt for conventional morality, Paolo and Francesca again float free in space. And this metaphor for sexual ecstasy was to appear again and again in Romantic art, in works ranging from the sublime to the ridiculous [203] and, ultimately, of course, in the ultra-Romantic Wagnerian *Liebestod*.

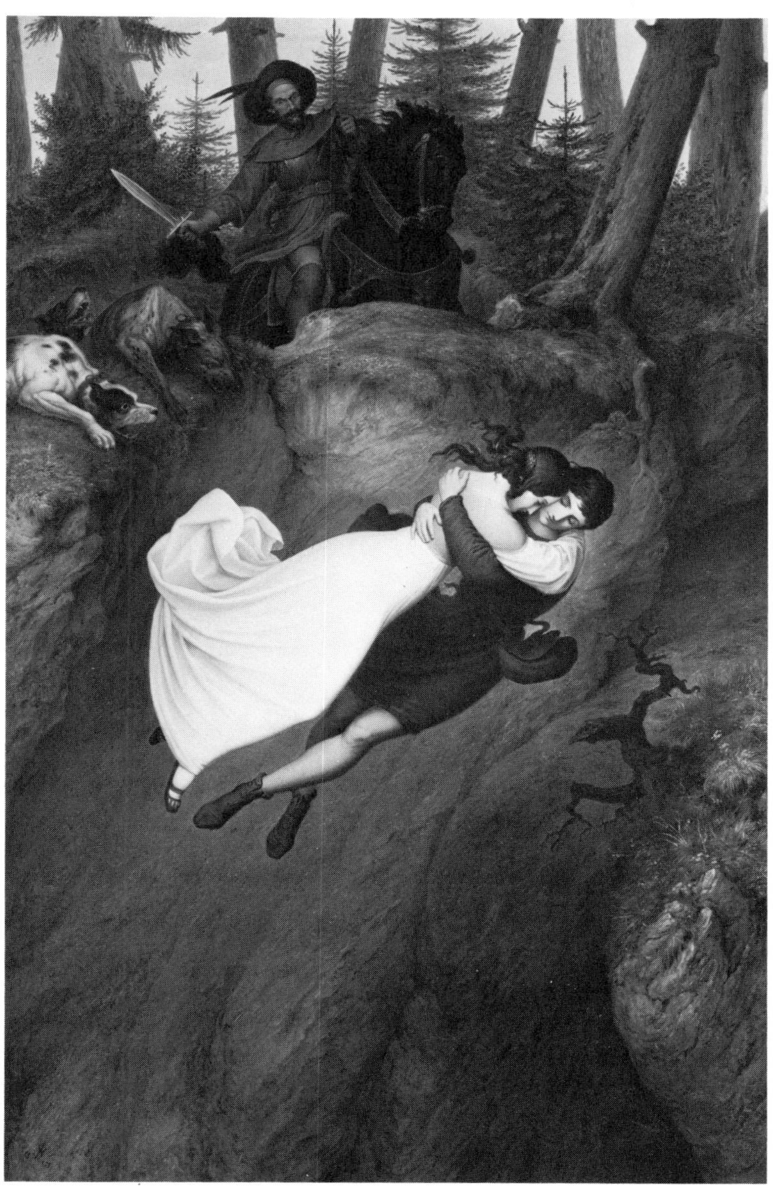

203. *The Leap from the Rocks*, 1833. L. Schnorr von Carolsfeld

That so many Romantics depicted lovers as doomed or dying – if not, like Paolo and Francesca, already dead – is a reflection of the morbid idea that no completely perfect union could be achieved this side of the grave. Chassériau painted the drowning Leander opening his arms in an embracing gesture to Hero, and the star-crossed Romeo and Juliet not on the balcony but in the charnel house. The Romantic notion that love, like art, was the constant pursuit of an ideal which might be approached but never attained (the theme of so many of E. T. A. Hoffmann's stories) seems to have been the inspiration of another painting by Chassériau – though a scene of metamorphosis rather than death – in which Daphne eludes the grasp of Apollo as she turns into a tree.[44] Here, Apollo, with his lyre, is the image of both artist and lover, clutching at the ideal which forever eludes him, while his kneeling posture and the halo round his head imply a religious connotation.

Love and death in an atmosphere of violence and sensual licence became an intoxication in Delacroix's *Sardanapalus* [19], the most voluptuous of all his paintings, pulsating with colour, flashing with light which glances off gold and pearls and precious stones. The sinewy virility of the black slave who kills the horse, and the beautiful passionate bodies of the women in attitudes of frenzied exhaustion or of a pain which is almost rapture, give an orgiastic appearance to this scene of carnage. Illustrating

> the pleasure that winces and stings,
> The delight that consumes the desire,
> The desire that outruns the delight,

it might well have appealed to Swinburne. This almost indecent exposure of throbbing sensuality shocked the sensibilities of the critics who first saw it in 1827. They much preferred the *Agony in the Garden*, with its ethereally beautiful angels, which Delacroix showed in the same Salon. For Delacroix, love and art were more easily and closely identified with sexuality than with religion. Yet *The Death of Sardanapalus*, which recalls Baroque scenes of martyrdom, has religious overtones too, though of a new kind. When the pyre has been lit beneath the king's throne-bed, the whole world of sensuous beauty which he has created around himself will dissolve in flames and smoke. The picture may thus be seen as a manifesto of the Romantic belief in the artist as creator and destroyer – of both life and art.

The relationship between sexuality and religion could be expressed in many different ways. In 'happy copulation, bliss on bliss', Blake saw a means of reuniting the divided parts of man's nature and regaining the harmony enjoyed before the Fall. For him, the union of bodies in perfect love was the mundane parallel to the union of the soul with God. Similarly, the yearning for reconciliation with nature might find expression in images of physical passion. One of the seekers after truth in Novalis's philosophical novel *Die Lehrlinge zu Sais* declares:

When that mighty emotion for which language has no other name than love and voluptuousness expands within him like a powerful all-dissolving vapour and, trembling in sweet terror he sinks into the dark alluring womb of nature, his poor individuality consumes itself in the overwhelming waves of desire, and nothing remains but a focus of immeasurable procreative force, an engulfing whirlpool in the great ocean.[45]

The passage brings to mind paintings by Turner – those encircling, whirling vortices of vaporous pigment, whose sexual implications become quite explicit when they are set beside his hardly less mysterious watercolours of copulating couples.

* * *

Of all the images which seized the Romantic imagination few are more revealing than that of Mazeppa, the rational being bound unwillingly to an uncontrollable force of nature. Géricault, Delacroix, Horace Vernet [204], Louis Boulanger, Chassériau and many others illustrated the story of the Polish page who, as punishment for an intrigue with a noble lady, was tied naked to the back of a wild horse

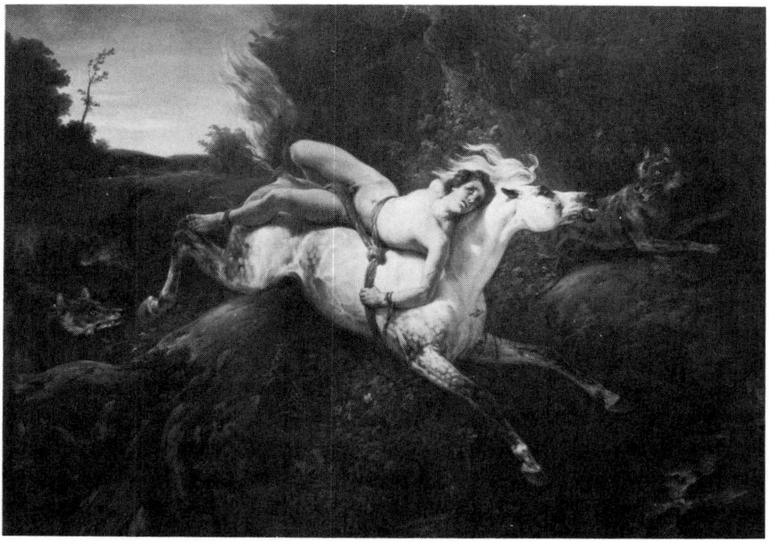

204. *Mazeppa and the Wolves*, 1826. H. Vernet

which galloped off through rivers and forests until it died of exhaustion.[46] It was first told by Voltaire as an aside in his *Histoire de Charles XII*, where it might well have remained had Byron not made it the subject of a poem in which he elevated the love story to the level of a grand romantic passion, significantly similar to that of Paolo and Francesca, and described in detail the victim's sufferings as he is carried through the wild landscape, pursued by wolves. Byron egocentrically identified himself with Mazeppa, as a martyr for love driven into exile. A different interpretation was put on the poem by Victor Hugo who, with reference to the illustrations by his friend Louis Boulanger, saw it as an allegory of the artist painfully transported by his genius:

> *il traverse d'un vol, sur les ailes de flamme*
> *Tous les champs du possible et les mondes de l'âme,*
> *Boit au fleuve éternel,*
> *Dans la nuit orageuse ou la nuit étoilée,*
> *Sa chevelure aux crins des comètes mêlée*
> *Flamboie au front du ciel ...**[47]

But the wild horse might alternatively symbolize the blind force of physical passion, to which the hapless Mazeppa is bound as a poetically just punishment. Delacroix, who illustrated the Mazeppa theme in the 1820s, later found far more telling images for the violent release of animal instincts in the spectacle of wild beasts savaging each other. Here, in their purest, crudest, form were the impetuous spontaneity, the heedless energy and the unselfconscious surrender to instinctive feelings which Romantics demanded – in art as in life.

After a visit to the Natural History Museum in Paris in 1847, Delacroix asked himself why he had been so deeply stirred by the wild animals he saw there, by the tigers, panthers, jaguars, lions especially. They had taken him outside the world of his everyday thoughts, reminding him of the need 'to jolt oneself from time to time, to put one's head out of doors, to try to read in Creation which has nothing in common with our cities and the works of man'.[48] This had, in fact, been the lesson he had learned fifteen years

* 'On wings of flame he flies over the fields of the possible and the worlds of the soul, drinks at the eternal river, in the starlit or stormy night; his hair, mingled with the tails of comets, flames on the brow of the sky ...'

before on his journey through Morocco which had given his whole art such an amazingly productive jolt, revealing a world of vibrant colour and passion to which his memory was to return again and again for reanimating refreshment (his last painting of a skirmish with Arabs and horses dates from the year of his death). Europeans had, of course, been fascinated for centuries by the exotic – the world outside which could provide a piquant contrast to the familiar scene – but the Romantics recognized in its external strangeness expressions of their own interior selves.[49] It is perhaps significant that nearly all Delacroix's paintings of animals have a North African setting.

The fascination of the animal world – the 'life of sensations rather than of thoughts' for which Keats longed – complemented rather than contradicted Romantic preoccupations with what lay spiritually beyond. For before Darwin's theory of the origin of species (based on a distinctly Romantic notion of conflict) replaced the ancient belief in a 'great chain of being' which extended from the angels by way of men and beasts to inanimate nature, animals were regarded not so much as sub-human as other-than-human. Denizens of another world, they lived according to their own laws, possessing their own integrity. And, of course, they represented natural forces in the most unequivocal way.

At the beginning of his essay *Über naive und sentimentalische Dichtung* (1795–6), Schiller linked animals and plants with children, peasants and primitive people, all inspiring a kind of love and 'respectful emotion' simply because they were natural. Thirty years earlier Rousseau had revolutionized thought on education by contending that the natural instincts of children should be encouraged and developed, rather than suppressed as manifestations of original sin; and this had even affected the way they were dressed – no longer as small adults but in clothes which permitted freedom for boisterous movement. But Schiller went further. Children '*are* what we *were*,' he wrote; 'they are what we should again become. We were nature like them and our culture must, by way of reason and liberty, lead us back to nature.' For him, the child represented the potentiality which the adult failed to realize. There is perhaps a reflection of these ideas in Philipp Otto Runge's portraits of children, who are depicted at eye-level, not from the superior height of grown-ups. In one instance, indeed, a child standing on a chair looks down on us almost condescendingly, with an innocent – or all too know-

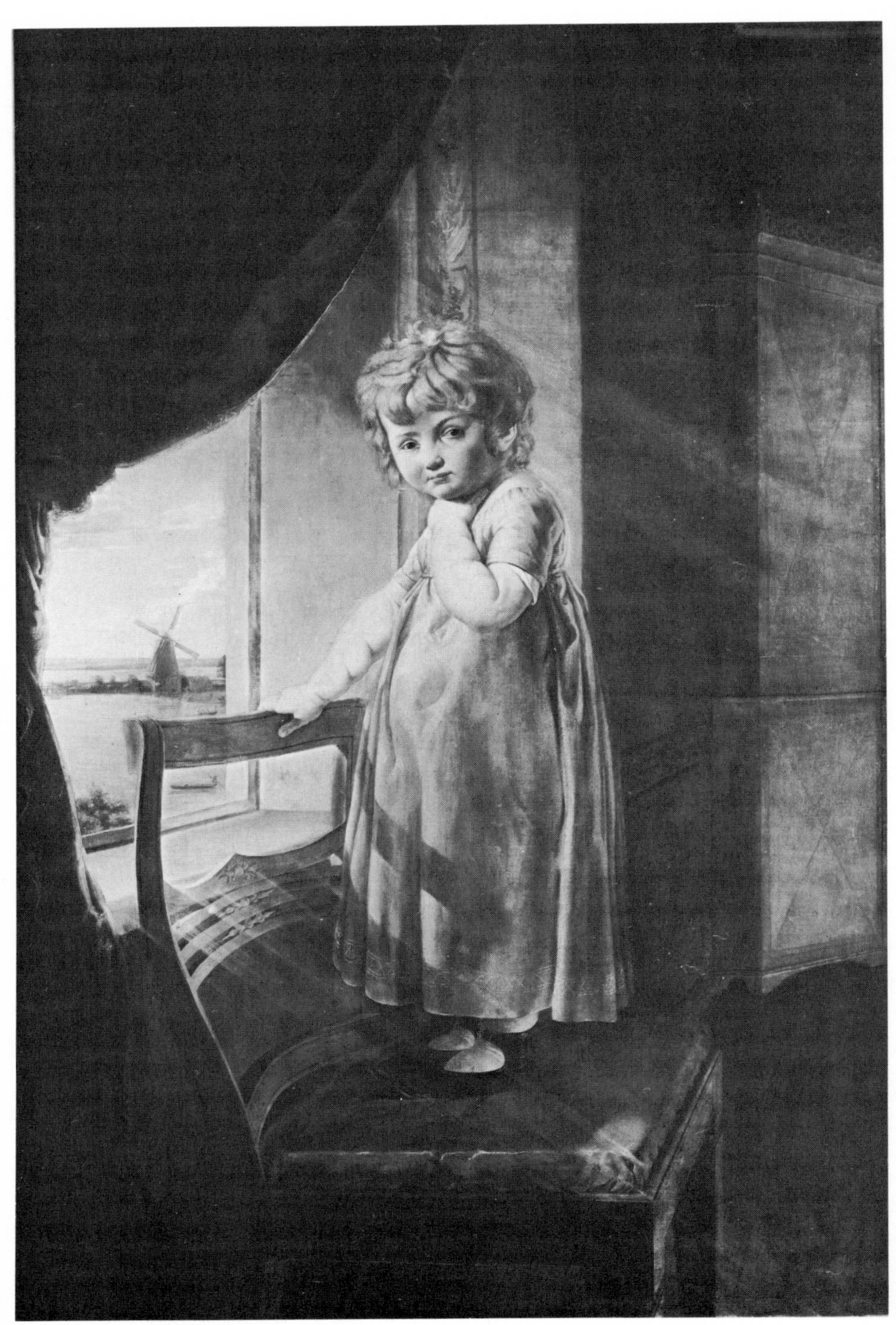

205. *Luise Perthes*, 1805. Philipp Otto Runge

ing? – glance of mutual understanding and forgiveness [205]. His picture of the *Hülsenbeck Children* [206] might illustrate what Schiller called 'the idea of the child's pure and free force, of its integrity and infinity'. It also reminds one of Emerson's much later remark that, as the minds of children are whole, 'their eye is as yet unconquered and when we look into their faces we are disconcerted'.

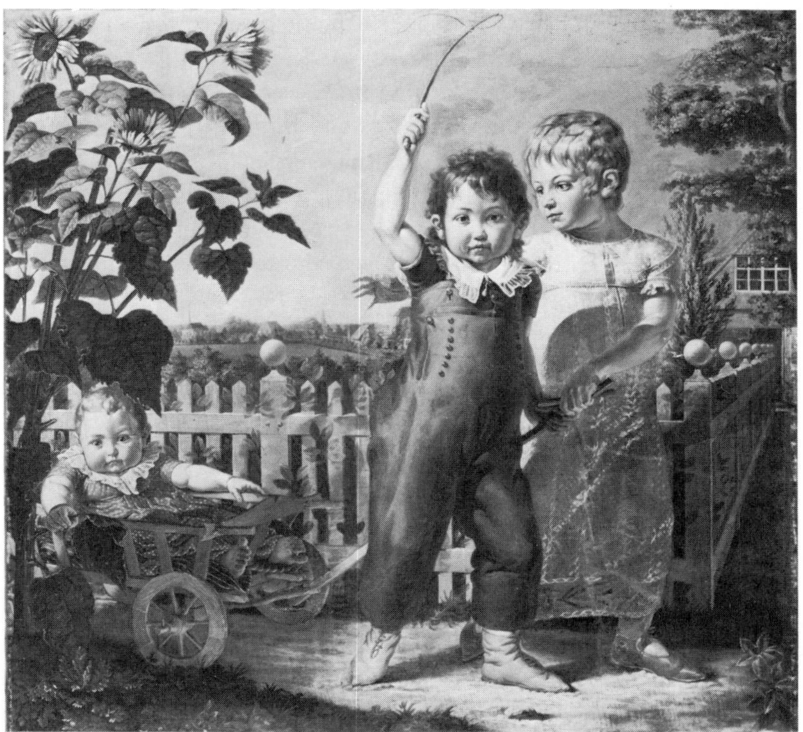

206. *The Hülsenbeck Children*, 1805. Philipp Otto Runge

Runge believed that 'we must become children again to reach perfection', and said that people failed to understand his works because they refused to look at them as children would.[50] At about the same time, Wordsworth was developing his almost mystical cult of the child as a link with the natural and the supernatural world beyond human understanding:

> Heaven lies about us in our infancy!
> Shades of the prison house begin to close
> Upon the growing boy,
> But He beholds the light, and whence it flows,
> He sees it in his joy;

The Youth who daily further from the east
Must travel, still is Nature's Priest,
And by the vision splendid
Is on his way attended;
At length the Man perceives it die away,
And fade into the light of common day.

It was widely believed that 'few adult persons can see nature', as Emerson wrote in 1836. 'The lover of nature is he whose inward and outward senses are still truly adjusted to each other; who has retained the spirit of infancy even into the era of manhood.'

In this context both the wanderers and the children who figure in so many Romantic landscape paintings, especially those by Constable and Caspar David Friedrich, take on a deeper significance. But many other painters attempted to regain the lost paradise of childhood by recapturing a naive view of the brightness and beauty of nature. Thus, the Nazarenes went back to what they regarded as the infancy of art in order to cleanse their vision of artifice and to represent a world of unpolluted innocence. Christ's admonition 'except ye be converted and become as little children ye shall not enter the kingdom of heaven' was applied to art as well as religion.[51]

Exploration of the child's world gave a new importance to folk legends and fairy-tales, which were taken more seriously than ever before, collected, edited, rewritten, imitated, dramatized, set to music and, of course, illustrated. Novalis claimed for *Märchen* which 'poeticize poetry' the first place among literary genres, seeing in them a reflection of man's past state and a representation of the goal towards which he ought to strive.[52] For the German Romantics, fairy-tales were also expressions of the *Volksseele*, and the artist who illustrated them returned to the uncontaminated origins of his culture as well as to the naïve fantasies of his individual childhood. The cult of *Märchen* was an almost exclusively Germanic phenomenon, but one which influenced Coleridge, who defended fairy-tales by saying that they had taught him to distrust the evidence of the senses and to regulate his words by conceptions, not by sight. They were mentally valuable, he said, for their implausibility stretched the intelligence, inducing contemplative 'love of the great and the *whole*'.[53]

It was similarly suggested that dreams, in which the adult mind was liberated from the shackles of commonsense, might provide glimpses of the eternal realities. 'In them we must often see and acknowledge memories of a state of mind which has gone before,' wrote Gotthilf Heinrich von Schubert, a doctor of medicine and a philosopher (strongly influenced by Schelling), who was preoccupied with all the apparently irrational phenomena discovered, but inadequately explained, by scientific investigators of the previous century. 'The road behind us is dark,' he remarked in his *Ansichten von der Nachtseite der Naturwissenschaft* (*Views on the Dark Side of Natural Science*) of 1806: 'Only occasionally is it lit up by dreams of a remarkable clarity and intensity, dreams which appear to be related to each other but which have no connection with present everyday existence.'[54]

Such ideas were widespread. Shelley, for instance, who seems to have had no direct contact with Schubert or his writings, wrote in his lines on Mont Blanc in 1816:

Some say that gleams of a remoter world
Visit the soul in sleep, – that death is slumber,
And that its shapes the busy thoughts outnumber
Of those who wake and live. – I look on high;
Has some unknown omnipotence unfurled
The veil of life and death? or do I lie
In dream, and does the mightier world of sleep
Spread far around and inaccessibly
Its circles? For the very spirit fails,
Driven like a homeless cloud from steep to steep
That vanishes among the viewless gales!
Far, far above piercing the infinite sky,
Mont Blanc appears, – still, snowy and serene ...

His poem of 1817 'Marianne's Dream' consists of a succession of landscape images often reminiscent of Turner's paintings, but also incorporating symbols of the type used by Caspar David Friedrich:

The sky was blue as the summer sea,
The depths were cloudless overhead,
The air was calm as it could be,
There was no sight or sound of dread,
But that black Anchor floating still
Over the piny eastern hill.

This is, no doubt, a coincidence. But Schubert specifically linked the dream, the landscape and the child in a description of four paintings by Friedrich (whom he knew personally), which he included in his *Ansichten von der Nachtseite der Naturwissenschaft*.[55] Referring to the first of a cycle of pictures illustrating the seasons of the year, the times of day and the stages of human life, he wrote:

We do not know what profound charm lies over the beginning of childhood. It may be that it is glorified by an echo of the unknown dream whence we came or by that reflection of the divine which hovers in its purest form above the quiet and the childlike. When we wake from that dream we find ourselves in the morning glow of an everlasting spring day and no trace of bygone autumn tinges its bright green. We awake among flowers by the clear source of life, where the eternal sky is mirrored in its virgin purity. The wind does not strive yet beyond the brink of the nearby hills. We seek and understand in nature the flowers only, and we still perceive life as an image of playful, innocent lambs. There the first ray of that longing which guides us from the cradle to the grave touches an early unfolding mind and, unaware of the endless distance which separates us from the eternal source of light, the child's arms open wide to grasp what he believes to be within his reach. But his first steps already are an error and from the lovely hill of childish dreams where we perceived the first rising rays, we hurry downward into the deep bustle of life, where another twilight surrounds us.

There are, however, rather surprisingly few explicit pictures of dreams in early nineteenth-century art.[56] Nor are there many graphic records of waking visions apart from Blake's weird drawings of the man who built the pyramids, the man who taught him painting in dreams, the ghost of the flea, King John and other historical characters who 'visited' him.[57] The majority of Blake's works seek 'to connect the visible and invisible world', as Fuseli remarked, 'to lead the eye from the milder light of time to the radiance of eternity'.[58] And, in a similar way, a very large proportion of Romantic paintings, drawings and even sculptures have an hallucinatory, dreamlike or sometimes nightmarish quality: the preternaturally still landscapes by Caspar David Friedrich, with their sense of suspended time; Runge's extraordinary compositions of children and vast flowers; Goya's perplexing and terrifying *Caprichos*, *Proverbios* and 'black paintings'; Samuel Palmer's water-colours lit 'with such a mystic and dreamy glimmer as penetrates and kindles the inmost soul' (which he saw in Blake's little woodcut illustrations to Virgil); Turner's sunset seascapes with strange monsters emerging from the waves; Préault's tortured *Tuerie*. Schelling defined aesthetic activity as an interplay of conscious and unconscious mind beyond the reach of rational analysis.[59] And the study of dreams and other irrational phenomena was not so much reflected in as paralleled by the creation of works of art which attempted to break through the barrier of the five senses and explore the relationship between the worlds of the psyche and the soma, visionary perception and physical reality.

'*Nach innen geht der geheimnisvolle Weg*,' wrote Novalis – the mysterious way leads inwards.[60] In E. T. A. Hoffmann's novel *Lebensan-*

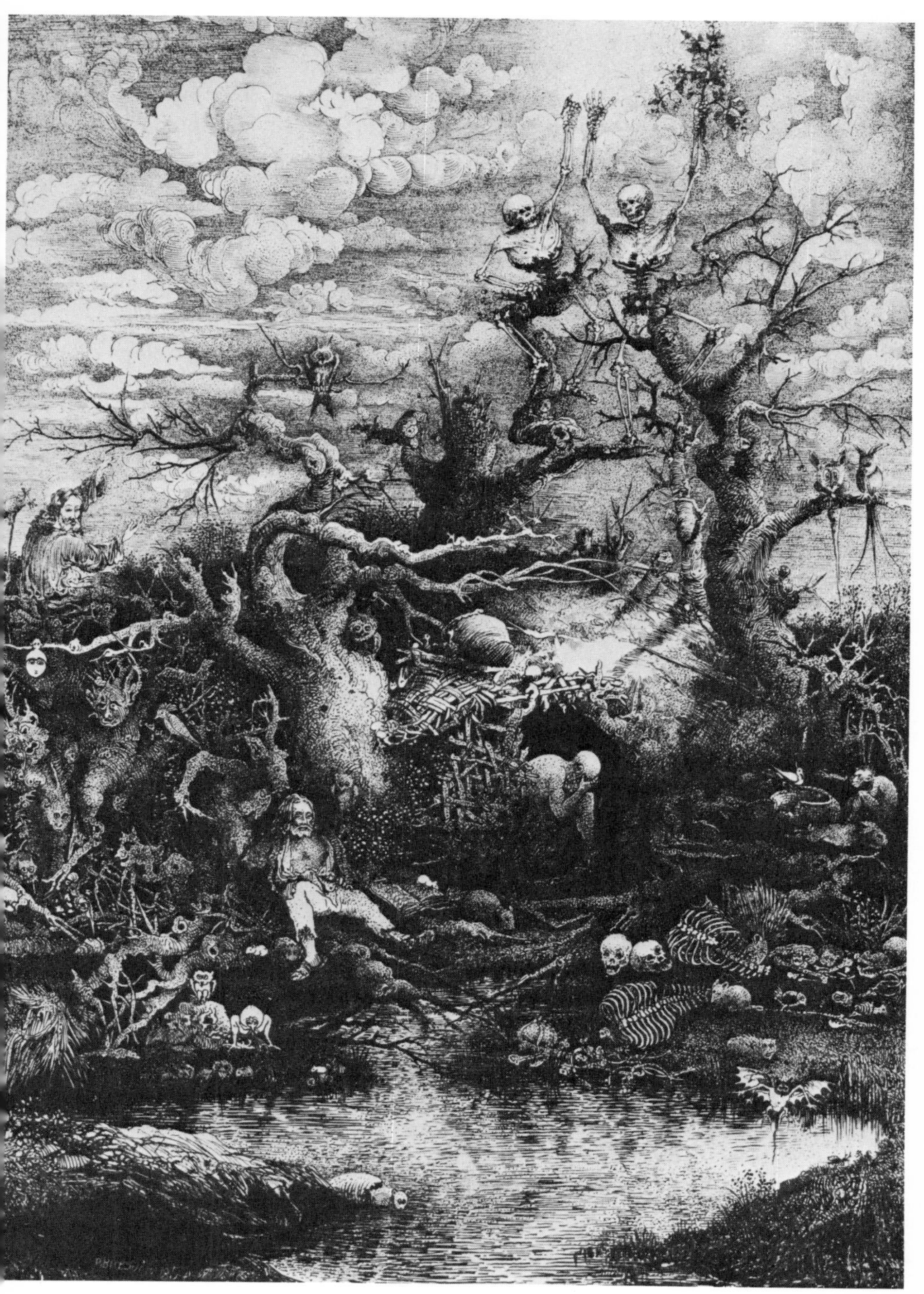

207. *Comédie de la Mort*, 1854. R. Bresdin

sichten des Katers Murr, the Abbot of Kanzheim declares: 'The most divine, most glorious miracles occur in the innermost recesses of the human soul and it is the duty of man to proclaim these miracles to the world in whatever form he can, be it in words, in sound, or in paint.' This is the optimistic Christian view which Hoffmann contrasts with the crazed Kreisler's vision of a disordered and perhaps meaningless universe. The depths of the soul might reveal glimpses not of heaven but of hell – Delacroix's molochistic images of destruction or Rodolphe Bresdin's obsessively detailed *Comédie de la Mort*, with its skulls and skeletons and grinning reptilian monsters among gnarled willows and a beggar dying by a stagnant pond [207]. There is a description of Bresdin's print in Huysmans's *À Rebours* – a reminder that the mysterious way could lead to the ivory tower, or to what Julian Schmidt called (in a history of Romanticism of 1848) 'the outstanding point of true egoism, utterly detached from the substantial world, madness itself which is the imagination wholly free from reality'.[61]

9. *Epilogue*

The influence of Romanticism has been so profound and pervasive that no account can encompass it. To some degree all subsequent Western art derives from it, just as all European history since 1789 has been to some extent a consequence of the French Revolution. Romantic ideas about artistic creativity, originality, individuality, authenticity and integrity, the Romantic conception of the meaning and purpose of works of art and the role of the artist continue to dominate aesthetic thought. So deeply are they embedded in our attitudes and ways of thinking that we are rarely aware of them. They emerge where least expected. Even the notion of an *avant-garde* marching ahead of popular taste is Romantic in origin.

In the immediate aftermath of the Romantic revolution, there was a self-conscious reaction on the part of the so-called Realists, who took as their battle cry *il faut être de son temps* (itself a Romantic idea[1]). Later in the century, the Symbolists acknowledged the Romantics as their precursors.[2] But Symbolism was an extension of only those aspects of Romantic art that had been renounced by the Realists in their rejection of *l'art pour l'art*.[3] The confrontation between the Symbolists and Realists merely brought out into the open a conflict which had smouldered inside the artistic personalities of many individualists, of Géricault (so much admired by the Realists) and Caspar David Friedrich (revived by the Symbolists) for example. But whereas the Romantics had sought to explore the relationship between reason and imagination, between perception and idea, between what they saw and what they felt, their successors tended to concentrate either on visual appearances or on the interior vision.

From the beginning, opposition had been directed more frequently to the trappings popularly associated with the Romantics than to their essential ideas. Indeed, many of the most effective attacks on such externals were made by the Romantics themselves – Ludwig Tieck's and Walter Scott's satirical accounts of the Gothic horror novel, Alfred de Musset's *Lettres de Dupuis et Cotonet*. The degeneration of Romantic notions of love into a cult of lachrymose sentimentality, and the devaluation of Romantic symbols into the clichés of commercial painters were similarly mocked by the Romantics themselves, as in Peter Hasenclever's picture of a tearful young woman seated beside copies of Goethe's *Werther* and a trashy novelette, a vase of roses and forget-me-nots, and a letter beginning *Innigstgeliebte Fanny*, while gazing through a window at a moonlit landscape.[4]

In another painting, of a studio in the Düsseldorf Academy where he was then a student, Hasenclever satirized the German artistic 'establishment' of the 1830s from a Romantic viewpoint [208]. At first sight this might seem to be no more than a glimpse of the *vie bohème*, but every detail is charged with meaning. Pieces of armour

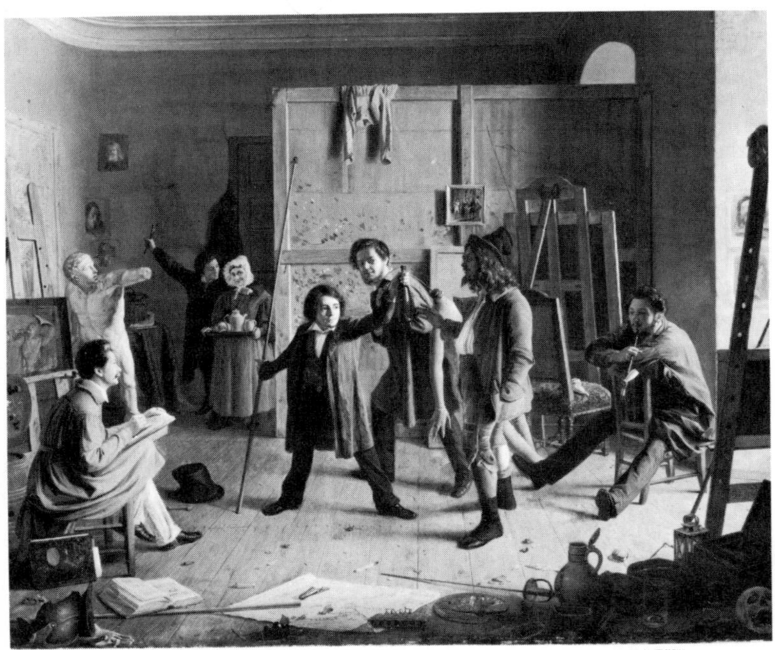

208. *Studio Scene*, 1836. J. P. Hasenclever

and a sword, essential ingredients of the historical costume-piece, lie on the floor together with the optical apparatus which assisted painters to obtain illusionistic effects; the model of a human foot on a plinth symbolizes academic concentration on the parts of the body; the Antique class is represented by a plaster Borghese Warrior, whose gesture is aped by the artist Anton Greven who holds in his other hand a preposterously long marlstick; in the centre,

Hasenclever himself drags away a lay-figure, arms and legs a-dangle; another painter, Joseph Wilms, with long hair and a beard, poses in the costume of a bandit; a gigantic canvas intended for a *grande machine* serves merely as a screen; there is a map of Düsseldorf on which only the Academy, the pawn-shop and places of amusement are marked; and to indicate the *gemütlich* bourgeois atmosphere of the Academy, an old maid-servant with a neat white cap is bringing in a tray of coffee. Hasenclever went beyond the usual Romantic objections to academies, as institutions for stifling artistic individuality, to protest at an art out of touch with the realities of life. He was later to become a Communist, play a part in the Revolution of 1848, and have his work discussed and commended by both Marx and Engels.

The type of painting satirized by Hasenclever was, of course, a favourite with the general public not only in Europe but also in the United States where the Düsseldorf school had an almost overwhelming influence on artists. A remarkable number of Americans went to study in Düsseldorf – Albert Bierstadt, George Caleb Bingham, Eastman Johnson, Emanuel Gottlieb Leutze, Worthington Whittredge, Richard Caton Woodville – and paintings by the Düsseldorf professors were exhibited in a special gallery in New York from 1849 to 1862.[5] But the technical facility which the Americans acquired from the Germans came increasingly to seem superficial, and they soon turned their attention to France. Thus, after a wearisome spell at the Düsseldorf academy, William Morris Hunt discovered Jean-Francois Millet whose 'subjects were real people who had work to do'. Millet's 'fields were fields in which men and animals worked; where both laid down their lives; where the bones of the animals were ground up to nourish the soil, and the eternal wheel of existence went on'.[6]

'This is realism,' Gustave Courbet wrote in 1855 of the great painting of his studio, remarking that it included 'a poor weather-beaten old man, a ninety-year-old Republican veteran of '93 ... looking at a heap of "romantic" cast-offs at his feet' [209]. Thus he announced his break with his own Romantic past. The discarded sombrero and guitar on the floor are similar to those in a portrait he had painted of himself in troubadour guise eleven years earlier. Courbet's studio crowded with figures, both bourgeois and proletarian, and showing the artist in relation to society (he is literally backed by friends and supporters, including Baudelaire, Pierre-Joseph Proudhon, Champfleury, Max Buchon and the collector Alfred Bruyas), has little in common with the solitary cells in which

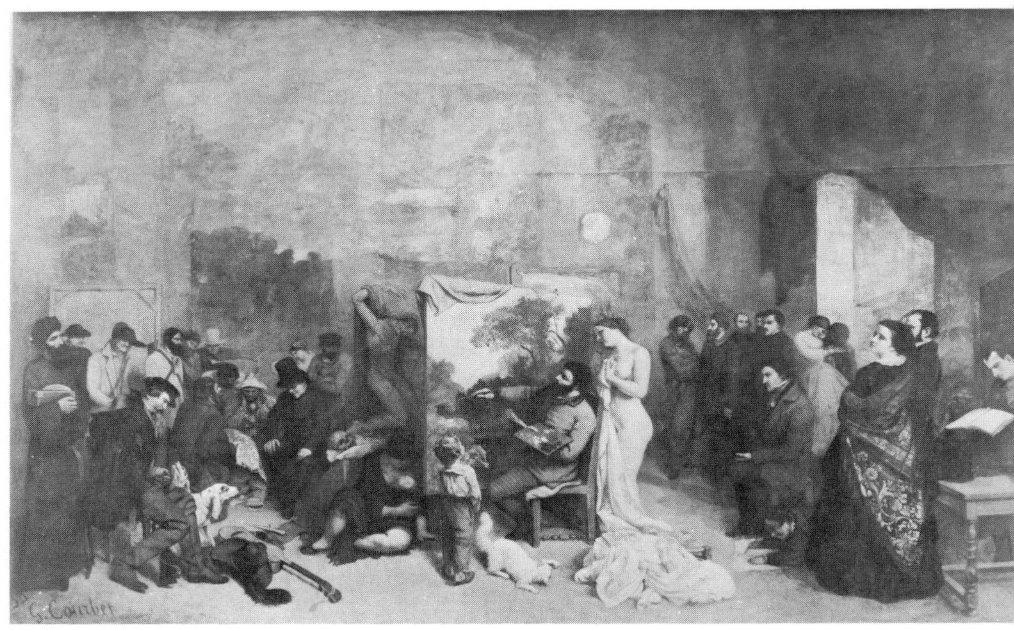

209. *The Studio of the Painter*, 1854–5. Courbet

genius is condemned and confined as in paintings by Géricault [174] or Delacroix [175]. It is more like the studio of another politically engaged artist, Horace Vernet [172], though the atmosphere of turbulence has been quelled and a tone of almost religious hush now prevails.

The Studio reveals that although Courbet had thrown off the trappings of Romanticism, he clung tenaciously to the more important Romantic beliefs. It is a piece of autobiography – an *allégorie réelle déterminant une phase de sept années de ma vie artistique*, he called it – and thus a manifesto of individualism as much as of Realism, the most intensely personal of all the great monumental paintings from *The Raft of the 'Medusa'* to *Guernica*. Some of the symbols are of a conventional type, but appear to have had for him a special significance. The nude artist's model presumably stands for naked truth; a lay-figure of St Sebastian for dead religious and academic art. Two children, one a peasant boy in sabots gazing enraptured at the picture on the easel, the other lying on the floor and sketching, reflect Romantic beliefs about the clear, uncorrupted eye of childhood, the naïve vision. And the central place in the vast composition is given to the key form of Romantic expression in the visual arts: a landscape, and what is more significant, one which depicts the artist's childhood home in the Franche Comté.

The room in which Courbet paints is stark and almost unfurnished, an *atelier* in the sense of a workshop as well as an artist's studio. It makes a very striking contrast with the thickly carpeted

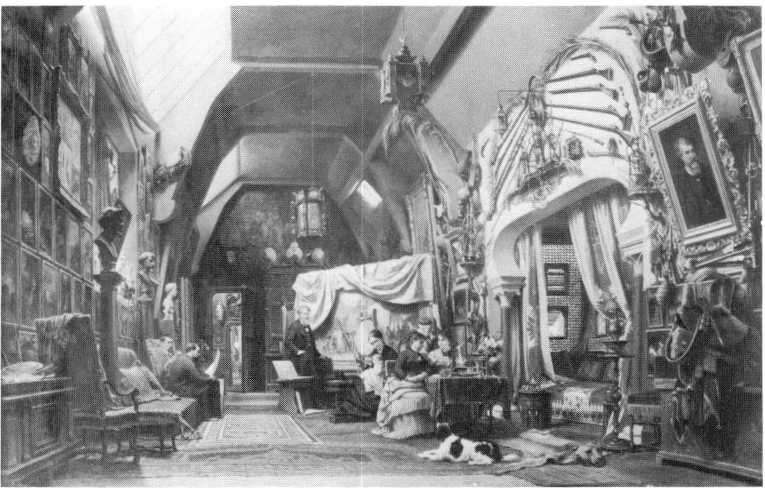

210. *The Studio of Eugène Giraud*, *c.* 1860. Charles Giraud

and well-upholstered, eminently *haut bourgeois* studio of such a contemporary as the mondaine painter Eugène Giraud, Chevalier of the Légion d'Honneur in 1851, Officier in 1866, protégé and friend of Princess Mathilde [210]. A painter of landscapes, portraits, historical pieces, Spanish and Italian scenes and exotic North African subjects, Giraud not only clung to, but exploited, the trappings of Romanticism. They are displayed like trophies on his walls. And he made a fortune, benefiting from Romanticism much as financiers profited from the political Revolutions of 1830 and 1848.[7]

The insistence of the Romantics on individuality and originality precluded the creation of a single Romantic style, leading inevitably both to the creation and to the rejection of divergent styles, giving to Western art a new restless dynamism. The word 'Romantic' came increasingly to be attached to what was rejected. But the ideas which had inspired the great Romantic artists, writers and musicians survived as potent as ever though reformulated in slightly different terms. The Romantic revolution which began in the 1790s was like the battle which 'men fight and lose' in William Morris's *A Dream of John Ball*; 'and the thing they fought for comes about in spite of their defeat, and when it comes turns out not to be what they meant, and other men have to fight for what they meant under another name'.

Notes

ABBREVIATIONS USED IN THE NOTES AND CATALOGUE OF ILLUSTRATIONS

Baudelaire: Charles Baudelaire, *Curiosités esthétiques, L'art romantique . . .*, ed. H. Lemaitre (Classiques Garnier), Paris, 1962.

Börsch-Supan / Jähnig: Helmut Börsch-Supan and K. W. Jähnig, *Caspar David Friedrich*, Munich, 1973.

R. Bray: René Bray, *Chronologie du Romantisme*, Paris, 1932.

Constable's Correspondence: *John Constable's Correspondence*, ed. R. B. Beckett, 6 Vols., Ipswich (Suffolk Records Society), 1962–70; vol. VII as John Constable, *Further Documents and Correspondence*, ed. L. Parris, C. Shields and I. Fleming-Williams, London and Ipswich, 1975.

Constable's Discourses: *John Constable's Discourses*, ed. R. B. Beckett, Ipswich, 1970.

Constable Exhibition: L. Parris, I. Fleming-Williams and C. Shields, *Constable*, exh. cat., Tate Gallery, London, 1976.

Delacroix Exhibition: Maurice Serrulaz, *Mémorial de l'Exposition Eugène Delacroix*, Paris, 1963.

Delacroix: Journal: *Journal de Eugène Delacroix*, ed. André Joubin, Paris, 1932.

Delécluze: M.-E.-J. Delécluze, *Louis David, son école et son temps*, Paris, 1855.

H. Eichner: Hans Eichner, ed., *'Romantic' and Its Cognates: The European History of a Word*, Toronto, 1972.

A. J. Finberg: A. J. Finberg, *The Life of J. M. W. Turner R.A.* (1939), rev. Hilda F. Finberg, Oxford, 1961.

French Painting 1774–1830: *French Painting 1774–1830: The Age of Revolution*, exh. cat., Detroit Institute of Arts, Metropolitan Museum of Art, New York and (as *De David à Delacroix*) Grand Palais, Paris, 1974–5.

Hegel / Knox: G. W. F. Hegel, *Aesthetics*, tr. T. M. Knox, Oxford 1975.

S. Hinz: Sigrid Hinz, *Caspar David Friedrich in Briefen und Bekenntnissen*, Berlin, 1968.

Keynes: Geoffrey Keynes, ed., *The Complete Writings of William Blake*, London, 1957.

La peinture romantique anglaise: *La peinture romantique anglaise et les préraphaélites*, exh. cat., Petit Palais, Paris, 1972.

C. R. Leslie: C. R. Leslie, *Memoirs of the Life of John Constable* (1845), ed. J. Mayne, London, 1951.

J. Lindsay: Jack Lindsay, *Turner: His Life and Work* (1966), St Albans, 1973.

Novalis: Novalis, *Schriften*, ed. P. Kluckhohn and R. Samuel, Stuttgart, 1960–75.

Runge: Philipp Otto Runge, *Hinterlassene Schriften*, Hamburg, 1840.

Ruskin: *The Works of John Ruskin*, ed. E. T. Cook and A. Wedderburn, London, 1903–12.

F. Schlegel, *Kritische Schriften*: Friedrich Schlegel, *Kritische Schriften*, ed. W. Rasch, Munich, 1964.

1. Arthur O. Lovejoy, 'On the Discrimination of Romanticisms' (1923) in *Essays in the History of Ideas*, Baltimore, 1948, pp. 228–53. Lovejoy later adopted a less restrictive attitude to Romanticism, cf. his *The Great Chain of Being* (1936), New York, 1960, pp. 288–314.

2. F. R. de Toreinx (alias Rontiex), *Histoire du Romantisme en France*, Paris, 1829, p. 16.

3. Letter of 5 March 1857 to F.-B. de Mercey, printed in *Réunion des Sociétés des Beaux Arts des Départements*, 9e session, 1885, p. 351. Commenting on de Mercey's book, *Études sur les Beaux-Arts* (Paris, 1855), Schnetz regretted that it included so little on 'le mouvement révolutionnaire artistique qui s'opéra en France de 1814 à 1825' and went on to say: 'J'étais dans la mêlée à cette époque, et j'ai pu suivre toutes ses phases; ce mouvement n'a pas été une insurrection, ni l'effet d'un parti pris; il s'est autant produit par la pente naturelle des idées. Je dirai plus, ce mouvement avait été commencé par M. David lui-même, par l'enseignement quotidien qu'il donnait à ses élèves dans les dernier temps de son séjour à Paris.' As justification for the last statement, he enclosed a copy of a letter written to him by David from Brussels in 1825, including the remark: 'Je dis plus, bouchez-vous les oreilles aux propos gigantesques des partisans de l'antique, dont je suis un associé, mon goût dans tous les temps m'y portait naturellement; vous, le vôtre, n'est pas inférieur quand on sait le traiter comme vous ...'

1. FOR LACK OF A BETTER NAME (*pages 21–55*)

1. The first is that by Friedrich Schlegel in *Athenäum*, 1798, Fragmente 116, beginning: 'Die romantische Poesie ist eine progressive Universalpoesie ...', F. Schlegel, *Kritische Schriften*, pp. 38–9.

2. *La Muse française*, II (1824), p. 301; cit. André Maurois, *Victor Hugo*, London, 1956, p. 107.

3. Preface to *Nouvelles Odes*, Paris, 1824; see R. Bray, p. 100. A similar remark had been made in the editorial preface to the first volume of *Tablettes romantiques* (continued as *Annales romantiques*), Paris, 1823, v: 'Tout dans ce siècle est devenu matière à discussion: les crimes, les vertus, le mauvais, le beau. La littérature, comme la politique et la religion, a eu ses fanatiques. Pour réussir à s'entendre plus difficilement, on a inventé une dénomination nouvelle, un genre nouveau, le genre romantique. On l'a opposé au classique. Mais n'oublions pas qu'il n'y a que deux sortes de littérature, la bonne et la mauvaise ...' In the same periodical Charles Nodier (pp. 6–14) proposed that a distinction be drawn between the *romantiques* and 'une école innommée ... que j'appellerai cependant, si l'on veut, l'école *frénétique*'. Hugo was among the contributors to *Tablettes romantiques*.

4. For Goethe's attitude, see R. Benz, *Goethe und die romantische Kunst*, Munich, 1940, and Gerhard S. Kallienke, *Das Verhältnis von Goethe und Runge*, Hamburg, 1972. Byron's attitude was well known: in 1818 Pietro Giordani remarked that he refused to discuss his own work, poetry in general and 'peggio poi de' *romantici*, ch'egli abomina !! (e sai che essi l'hanno costituito lor patriarca, anzi idolo)', *Epistolario di Pietro Giordani*, ed. A. Gusalli, Milan, 1865, iv, p. 203.

5. Stendhal identified Romanticism with contemporaneity, writing in *Racine et Shakespeare* (1823): 'Le *romantisme* est l'art de présenter aux peuples les oeuvres littéraires qui, dans l'état actuel de leurs habitudes et de leurs croyances, sont susceptibles de leur donner le plus plaisir possible. Le *classicisme*, au contraire, leur présente la littérature qui donnait le plus grand plaisir à leurs arrière-grands-pères' (ed. R. Fayolle, Paris, 1970, p. 71). For Pushkin, see John Mersereau Jr, 'Pushkin's Concept of Romanticism' in *Studies in Romanticism*, III, 1963–4, pp. 24–41.

6. Théophile Silvestre, *Les Artistes français, études d'après nature* (1855), Paris, 1878, p. 118. Delacroix read and approved the chapter about himself: see *Delacroix: Journal*, II, p. 163. In a letter of 8 June 1855 he remarked of the 'Romantic school': 'Les écoles, les coteries, ne sont autre chose que des associations de médiocrités . . .' (*Correspondance générale d'Eugène Delacroix*, ed. A. Joubin, Paris, 1836–8, III, p. 265.) For his claim to be a pure classic, see P. Jamot, *Le Romantisme et l'art*, Paris, 1928, p. 101.

7. *Journal de Delécluze 1824–1828*, ed. R. Baschet, Paris, 1948, p. 124. A caricature of 1824 expresses the anti-Romantic conception of '*le Romantisme*' as a deformed ogre trampling on '*les classiques*, and '*bon sens*' [Fig. iii. Photo: Bibliothèque Nationale, Paris].

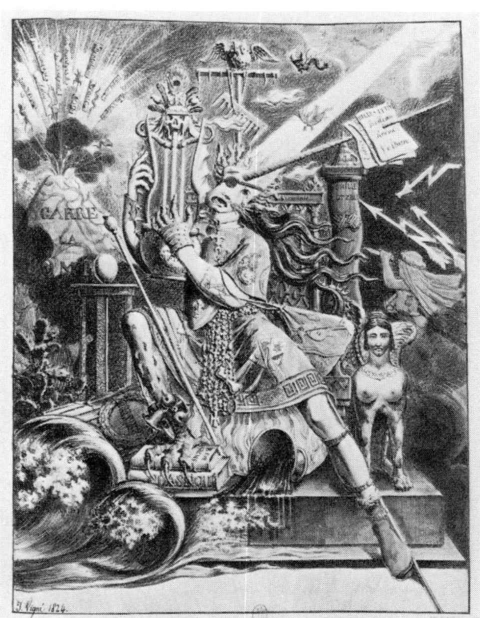

Figure iii. *Le Romantisme ou le Monstre littéraire*, 1824. J. Vigné

8. P. Valéry, *Mauvaises pensées*, Paris, 1942, p. 35.

9. H. Eichner, p. 150.

10. Anonymous reviewer of Salon of 1827, cit. M. Z. Shroder in H. Eichner, p. 150.

11. Jacques Barzun, *Classic, Romantic and Modern* (1943), New York, 1961, pp. 155–68, quotes numerous instances of modern usage of the word 'romantic' but assigns to them a wilfully wide range of meanings.

12. *Il Conciliatore*, 13 September 1818, p. 14. The words *all nonsense* are printed in English in the original text. In the same periodical Ermes Visconti defined Romanticism negatively (3 November 1818): 'Romanticism does not consist in constantly telling stories of witches or goblins and miracles worthy of the *prato fiorito*, or in moaning and shaking in cemeteries . . . Romanticism does not consist in the melancholy and gloomy . . . The Romantic style does not aim at blindly exalting mediaeval times . . . The theories of the so-called innovators are not a means of escaping from rules; they only exempt one from the incumbrance of pedantry.' For the ideas of the founders of *Il Conciliatore* in Milan, see G. A. Borgese, *Storia della critica romantica in Italia*, Naples, 1905.

13. The fullest account of the history of the word is in H. Eichner.

14. O. Strunk, *Source Readings in Music History*, London, 1952, p. 777. See also Ronald Taylor, *Hoffmann*, London, 1963, p. 50. Hoffmann's more important writings on music (short stories and reviews) are collected in a Goldmann gelbe Taschenbuch, E. T. A. Hoffmann, *Musikalische Novellen und Schriften*, Munich, n.d.

15. For Préault see E. Chesneau, *Peintres et statuaires romantiques*, Paris, 1880, p. 142. For Allston see Barbara Novak, *American Painting of the Nineteenth Century*, New York and London, 1969, p. 291.

16. In a lecture of 1807 Schelling paid tribute to 'Winckelmann's splendid institution of a new theory ... he re-established the whole operative function of the soul in art and raised it from ignoble dependence into realms of spiritual liberty ...': see Herbert Read, *The True Voice of Feeling*, London, 1953, p. 327. A similar point was made by Hegel, *Vorlesungen über die Ästhetik* (1835), ed. R. Bubner, Stuttgart, 1971, pp. 117–18.

17. Eva Reitharovà and Werner Sumowski, 'Beiträge zu Caspar David Friedrich' in *Pantheon*, XXXV, 1977, pp. 43–6.

18. Jacob van Ruisdael's *Jewish Cemetery*, *c.* 1660, in the Dresden Gallery had been highly praised by Goethe. It has sometimes been described as a proto-Romantic picture. For an interpretation in the context of seventeenth-century iconography, see Ioury Kouznetsov, 'Sur le symbolisme dans les paysages de Jacob van Ruisdael' in *Bulletin du Musée National de Varsovie*, XIV, 1973, pp. 31–41.

19. The phrases are quoted by Marjorie Hope Nicolson, *Mountain Gloom and Mountain Glory*, Ithaca, N.Y., 1959, p. 2.

20. 'Über den Grund unseres Glaubens an eine göttliche Weltregierung' in *Philosophisches Journal*: the German text is printed with a commentary in Ronald Taylor, *The Romantic Tradition in Germany: An Anthology*, London, 1970, pp. 111–26.

21. Novalis, I, p. 318.

22. Ramdohr's book *Charis* had been mocked in the Schlegels' periodical: see H. Lippuner, *Wackenroder/Tieck und die bildende Kunst*, Zürich, 1965, p. 213.

23. Friedrich's text was revised for publication by C. A. Semler, the author of a treatise on landscape painting as a vehicle for emotional expression, *Untersuchungen über die höchste Vollkommenheit in den Werken der Landschaftsmalerei*, Dresden, 1800.

24. For the description of the frame (printed between the description and interpretation of the picture), see Catalogue of Illustrations, no. 1.

25. S. Hinz, p. 96.

26. S. Hinz, pp. 82–134. The key to his outlook is probably the statement (Hinz, p. 86) 'Des Künstlers Gefühl ist sein Gesetz', strikingly similar to a remark in Friedrich Schlegel's 1798 definition of Romantic poetry (*Kritische Schriften*, p. 39): 'die Willkur des Dichters kein Gesetz über sich leide.'

27. A. J. Finberg, p. 126. The painting is in the Museum of Fine Arts, Boston, Mass.

28. One by Friedrich Leopold Count Stolberg (*Travels through Germany* ..., London, 1796) provoked J. H. Fuseli to comment: 'To see the simple object before us unite with immensity overpowers, no doubt, every mind; but why "the manifest omnipotence of God" should be more perceptible to a philosopher in the thunders and foaming clouds of a cataract than in the whisper of a gentle breeze is not easily discovered': see Ernest Lee Tuveson, *The Imagination as a Means of Grace*, Berkeley and Los Angeles, 1960, p. 175.

29. A. J. Finberg, p. 117.

30. ibid., p. 126.

31. *Winter* (the first section of *The Seasons* to be published), London, 1729, lines, 414–24. For Turner and James Thomson, see Jack Lindsay, *Turner* (1966), St Albans, 1973;

Anne Livermore, 'J. M. W. Turner's unknown verse-book' in *The Connoisseur Year Book*, 1957, pp. 78–86; Jerrold Ziff, 'J. M. W. Turner on Poetry and Painting' in *Studies in Romanticism*, III, 1964, pp. 193–215. For Thomson's attitude to nature, see John Barrell, *The Idea of Landscape and the Sense of Place*, Cambridge, 1972. For Loutherbourg's painting, see *Philippe Jacques de Loutherbourg*, exh. cat., Iveagh Bequest, Kenwood, 1973, no. 39.

32. The tone of *Winter* is set by its opening invocation:

> 'See, WINTER comes, to rule the varied year,
> Sullen and sad, with all his rising strain;
> Vapours, and Clouds, and Storms. Be these my theme,
> These that excite the soul to solemn thought,
> And heavenly musing. Welcome, kindred glooms!
> Congenial horrors, hail!'

33. W. H. Pyne, *Wine and Walnuts*, London, 1823: see W. Thornbury, *The Life of J. M. W. Turner*, R.A., London, 1862, I, pp. 159–60.

34. *The Life, Letters and Writings of Charles Lamb*, ed. P. Fitzgerald, London, 1895, IV, p. 205.

35. Panoramas or dioramas without noises off and other effects enjoyed great popular success throughout the nineteenth century but tended to be regarded by artists as mechanical performances. John Constable wrote in 1803: 'great principles are neither expected nor looked for in this mode of describing nature' (C. R. Leslie, p. 17).

36. *Turner: Imagination and Reality*, exh. cat., Museum of Modern Art, New York, 1966, p. 10.

37. In France Napoleon was often associated with Hannibal: see Carl Körner, *Die Funktion der Beaux-Arts in Frankreich 1795–1815*, Stuttgart, 1976, pp. 102, 257–8. But in England this association was not always intended as a compliment, e.g. J. C. Eustace, *A Classical Tour through Italy An. MDCCCII* (1813), London, 1817, IV, p. 122.

38. In officially inspired French writings of the Empire, Napoleon is generally called a 'pacificateur' rather than a 'vainqueur'. As early as 1797 he declared in the proclamation issued at Bassano: 'Le directoire exécutif n'a rien épargné pour donner la Paix à l'Europe': see Carl Körner, op. cit., pp. 133–41.

39. The first battle-pieces by Gros were the subject of political as much as artistic controversy: see Jean Lacambre in *French Painting 1774–1830*, no. 88. The *Bataille d'Aboukir* (Musée de Versailles) was commissioned by Murat, who occupies the central place in it. The anonymous author of *La Critique des critiques du Sallon* [sic] *de 1806* (Paris, 1807, p. 37) replied to those who had compared Gros unfavourably with Le Brun: '. . . les batailles de le Brun sont remplies de figures purement *académiques*, il a des poses et des attitudes *de prédilection*; celles de M. Gros sont sensiblement plus conformes à la nature'. In colour, 'Le Brun est lourde, terne, monotone, généralement tirait sur le brique; celle de M. Gros est chaude, transparente, variée. Cet artiste semble, pour cette partie de l'art, tenir le milieu entre Rubens et Paul Véronese.'

40. Delécluze, p. 295.

41. ibid., p. 246.

42. *L'Artiste*, I, 1831, p. 211.

43. A. de Musset, *Œuvres complètes en prose*, ed. M. Allem and P. Courant, Paris, 1960, p. 958. The quotation is from a review (27 October 1830) of a charity exhibition (for those wounded in the July Revolution), where Gros's Napoleonic paintings which had been inaccessible to the general public since 1815 were once again put on show. *Napoleon in the Plague House at Jaffa* [Fig. iv, page 330] is now in the Louvre.

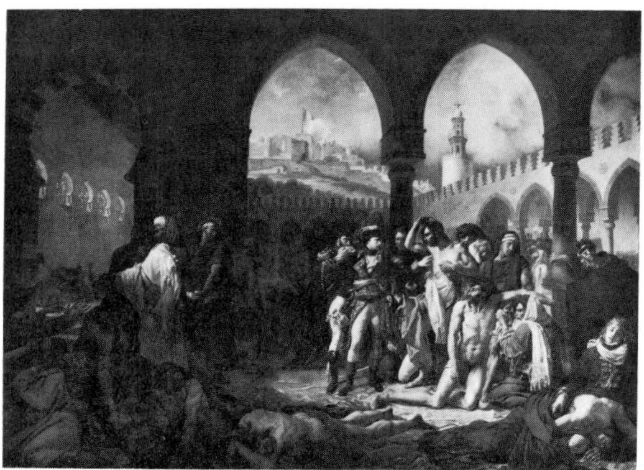

Figure iv. *Napoleon in the Plague House at Jaffa*, 1804. A.-J. Gros (*see note 43*)

44. e.g., *Napoleon on the Battlefield of Eylau* by Charles Meynier, in *French Painting 1774–1830*, no. 128.

45. Columns set up in various parts of France, by a Consular order of 1800, inscribed with the names of soldiers who had fallen in battle, seem to be the first 'war memorials' in the modern sense of the term: see Carl Körner, op. cit., pp. 47–8.

46. L. Aragon, *La semaine sainte*, Paris, 1958, p. 94.

47. A. de Musset, op. cit., p. 74.

48. The pictures were condemned by the few critics who bothered to mention them: see *Ingres*, exh. cat., Petit Palais, Paris, 1967–8, nos. 70, 107. This may account for Ingres's hostility to Géricault: see P. Courthion, *Ingres raconté par lui même et par ses amis*, Paris, 1947, I, pp. 110–11. In the Salon of 1822 Delacroix's *Barque of Dante* was to receive wide-spread critical attention while Ingres's *L'Entrée à Paris du Dauphin, futur Charles V* (now Wadsworth Atheneum, Hartford, Conn.) was completely ignored.

49. Article signed *F.*, in *Journal des Artistes*, III, 22 November 1829, p. 321. Although this periodical was generally anti-Romantic it published a series of articles by Eugène Sue criticizing the *classiques*.

50. L. Véron, *Memoires d'un Bourgeois de Paris*, Paris, 1856, I, p. 271; cit. L. Eitner, *Géricault's 'Raft of the Medusa'*, London and New York, 1972, p. 34.

51. Delécluze, p. 382.

52. *Delacroix: Journal*, II, p. 1, 2 January 1853.

53. Reported by George Sand; cit. G. P. Mras, *Eugène Delacroix's Theory of Art*, Princeton, 1966, pp. 127–8.

54. When Delacroix formulates his ideas about colour his words often echo seventeenth- and eighteenth-century writings: G. P. Mras, op. cit., pp. 119–28, describes the background of his ideas in earlier theory. For the best analysis of his development as a colourist (with valuable comments on the possible influence of scientific colour theories of his own time), see Lee Johnson, *Delacroix*, New York, 1963, pp. 64–80.

55. *Delacroix: Journal*, I, p. 50.

56. Published under the pseudonym F. R. de Toreinx, this long (more than 400 pages) and not strikingly original work deserves more attention than it has so far received, if mainly because it is the first history of French Romanticism and takes account of literature, music

and painting. (Few copies have survived, but there is one in the Bibliothèque Nationale, Paris.) Following Stendhal, Rontiex equated Romanticism with contemporaneity: 'Le romantisme est justement ce qu'on ne peut définir. C'est une modification quelle qu'elle soit, que les arts d'imagination subissent. C'est une forme nouvelle substituée aux anciennes, trop récente encore pour être usée, qui deviendra classique comme les autres en viellissant ...' (p. 16). On the origin of the movement he wrote: 'Ce fut en l'année 1801 que l'enfant naquit en France. Chateaubriand fut son père. Les cinq volumes du *Génie du Christianisme* furent les linges dans lesquels on l'enveloppe. Depuis cette époque il a bien fois changé d'habit, mais il ne faut point oublier sa layette' (p. 6). Mme de Staël was 'la marraine du romantisme' (p. 180), Goethe 'le patriarche des romantiques', Walter Scott the 'romancier romantique par excellence' (p. 58), Victor Hugo 'le véritable type du romantisme' (p. 373). Rontiex cited as the most notable painters Horace Vernet, Gros, Gérard, Staub, Cogniet and Hersent. He attacked Delacroix's *Massacres of Chios* (p. 128) and also declared: 'M. Delacroix est romantique sans doute, car il innove; mais il est certes encore plus mauvais et plus ridicule que les classiques mêmes quand ils ne veulent pas que l'on donne des armures aux individus qui se battent, ni qu'on pleure, ni qu'on meure sans une pose académique ...' (p. 410). A review of Toreinx was published in *Journal des Artistes*, III, 1829, pp. 411–13.

57. A. Jal, *Esquisses, croquis, pochades, ou tout ce qu'on voudra sur le salon de 1827*, Paris, 1828, p. 114. A lithograph of Delacroix's *Christ in the Garden of Olives* was printed as the frontispiece to this volume.

58. *Le Nain Jaune*, 20 December 1814, xxvii–xxxi.

59. Cit. H. Girard, *Émile Deschamps: Un bourgeois dilettante à l'époque romantique*, Paris, 1921, p. 111. The nationalistic line was a commonplace: a writer in the *Journal des Débats* in 1817 referred to the 'guerre entre les romantiques allemands et les classiques français', and a writer in *Le Constitutionnel* of 1818 solemnly declared: 'Notre honneur national littéraire tiént à la conservation des unités grecques'! (R. Bray, p. 21.) The idea that Romanticism was un-French may stem partly from the anti-French comments in *Sturm und Drang* of a generation earlier.

60. R. Bray, p. 126.

61. P. van Tieghem, *Le romantisme dans la littérature européenne* (1948), Paris, 1969, p. 173.

62. Amaury-Duval, *L'Atelier d'Ingres* (1878), Paris, 1924, p. 66.

63. *Revue française*; cit. Norman Schlenoff, *Ingres, ses sources littéraires*, Paris, 1956, pp. 178–9.

64. Alfred de Vigny, *Les Consultations du docteur Noir* ... (1832), ed. F. Germain, Paris, 1970, p. 193. Homer had, however, been regarded as a persecuted genius as early as 1789: see Jon Whitely, 'Homer Abandoned: A French Neo-classical theme' in F. Haskell, ed., *The Artist and the Writer in France, Essays in Honour of Jean Seznec*, Oxford, 1974, p. 46.

65. Lady Morgan, *France in 1829–30*, London, 1831, I, p. 109.

66. T. Thoré, *Salons*, Paris, 1868, p. 240; cit. P. Grate, *Deux Critiques d'art de l'époque romantique*, Stockholm, 1959, p. 54: Ingres is 'l'artiste le plus romantique du dix-neuvième siècle, si le romantisme est l'amour exclusif de la forme, l'indifférence absolue sur tous les mystères de la vie humaine, le scepticisme en philosophie et en politique, le détachement égoiste de tous les sentiments communs et solidaires'.

67. Baudelaire, p. 103.

2. THE MORALITY OF LANDSCAPE (*pages 56–118*)

1. For English attitudes to mountain scenery in the eighteenth century, see M. Hope Nicolson, *Mountain Gloom and Mountain Glory*, Ithaca, N.Y., 1959.

2. The most famous description of the country around Tintern was in William Gilpin's very popular *Observations on the River Wye* (1782), 5th edn, London, 1800, pp. 45–55. Two Italian visitors described the landscape and the Abbey in somewhat similar terms: Luigi Angiolini in *Lettere sull' Inghilterra* (1788) and Carlo Gastone della Torre Rezzonico in *Giornale del Viaggio d'Inghilterra negli anni 1787 e 1788* (1824): see Renzo Negri, *Gusto e Poesia delle Rovine in Italia*, Milan, 1965, pp. 114–17.

3. Hippolyte Taine in *Histoire de la littérature anglaise*, Paris, 1864–9, appears to have been the first writer to describe Wordsworth as a member of the 'English romantic school': see George Whalley in H. Eichner, pp. 214, 246.

4. W. B. von Ramdohr, *Charis*, Leipzig, 1793, II, p. 125. He also refers to a third category: 'Es giebt endlich bloss lachende belebte Gegenden, dergleichen die Niederländer viel gemahlt haben, flache Gegenden mit viel Staffage u.s.w.' This system of categorization exactly follows that derived in the Renaissance from the three types of drama – satiric, tragic and comic: see E. H. Gombrich, 'The Renaissance Theory of Art and the Rise of Landscape' (1953) in his *Norm and Form*, London, 1966, pp. 107–21. Ramdohr's recognition of Allart van Everdingen as the originator of a type of wild northern landscape was probably based on a fine example of his work in the Dresden gallery. He may also have been influenced by Christian Ludwig von Hagedorn (a close friend of Winckelmann and a Neo-classical theorist of some importance) who wrote in *Reflexions sur la peinture* (1762), tr. Huber, Leipzig, 1775, I, p. 138: 'Une contrée sauvage n'est pas belle; mais la nature de cette contrée peut intéresser par sa nouveauté & en même temps avoir pour l'effet de belles parties qu'on ne trouve point dans des cantons agréables ... Les aspects les plus affreux du nord n'ont été plus stériles pour l'esprit d'un *Aldert van Everdingen*, que les cascades agréables de Tivoli pour le génie d'un *Salvator Rosa*: au moyen de la subordination, le tronc hérissé d'un chêne renversé par l'ouragan, ne déparera pas le paysage d'un *Gaspre Poussin*.'

5. J. J. Rousseau, *Discours sur l'origine et les fondemens de l'inégalité parmi les hommes* (1754) in *Œuvres complètes* (Bibl. de la Pléiade), Paris, 1969, III, p. 170. In this passage he was referring to the 'savages' of America, but the pastoral way of life was more usually associated with Europe. Thus Charles Batteux on pastoral poetry in *Les Beaux Arts réduits à un même principe*, Paris, 1773, p. 306: 'C'est la simplicité des moeurs, la naïveté, l'esprit naturel, le mouvement doux & paisible des passions. C'est l'amour fidèle & tendre des Bergers, qui donne des soins, & non des inquiétudes, qui exerce assez le coeur, & ne fatigue point. Enfin, c'est ce bonheur attaché à la franchise, & au repos d'une vie qui ne connoît ni l'ambition, ni le luxe, ni les emportemens, ni le remords ...'

6. *Constable's Discourses*, p. 55.

7. His *Liber Studiorum*, the series of aquatints published in parts 1807–19, was a deliberate attempt to rival Claude's *Liber Veritatis*, and the various subjects were categorized as Historical, Mountainous, Pastoral, Elevated Pastoral, Marine and Architectural, slightly enlarging the traditional system of classification: see E. H. Gombrich, op. cit., p. 21.

8. A. J. Finberg, p. 220.

9. C. R. Leslie, pp. 202–3. Much earlier, in 1810, John Williams had written: 'The genius of Mr. Turner is that he has formed a manner of his own; if it partakes of the style of any preceding painter it is Cuyp, whose aerial perspective Mr. Turner seems in some sort to copy; yet it is but doing common justice to our countryman to notice that he is in almost every other respect superior to Cuyp' (A. J. Finberg, p. 168).

10. C. R. Leslie, p. 279. See also E. H. Gombrich, *Art and Illusion*, London and New York, 1960, pp. 174–8.

11. There were four copies after Jacob van Ruisdael in Constable's studio at the time of his death: see *Shock of Recognition*, exh. cat. Tate Gallery, London, 1970–71, no. 2.

12. C. R. Leslie, p. 276, quotes Constable writing: 'There should be a moral feeling in the art, as well as everything else.' His comment on pictures as drawing-room furniture is in *Constable's Discourses*, pp. 57–8.

13. C. R. Leslie, p. 97, quoting a letter of 1822. William Hazlitt held a similar opinion, writing in an article of 1814 (the basis for that on 'Fine Arts' in the 1824 edn of *Encyclopaedia Britannica*): 'A constant reference to the best models of art necessarily tends to enervate the mind, to intercept our view of nature, and to distract the attention by a variety of unattainable excellence. An intimate acquaintance with the works of the celebrated masters may indeed add to the indolent refinements of taste, but will never produce one work of original genius, one great artist . . . It is a little extraordinary that if the real sources of perfection are to be sought in Schools, in Models, and Public Institutions, that wherever schools, models and public institutions have existed, there the arts should regularly disappear, – that the effect should never follow from the cause' (*Collected Works*, London, 1903, IX, p. 408).

14. Introduction to *Various Subjects of Landscape*, 1833: see *Constable's Discourses*, p. 10.

15. S. Hinz, p. 85.

16. P. H. Valenciennes, *Élémens de perspective pratique à l'usage des Artistes suivis de Réflexions et Conseils à un élève sur la Peinture, et particulièrement sur le genre du paysage*, Paris, 1799–1800, p. 384.

17. ibid, p. 380. Valenciennes described two ways 'd'envisager la Nature', both calling for artistic selection and manipulation: 'La première est celle qui nous fait voir la Nature telle qu'elle est, et la fait représenter le plus fidèlement qu'il est possible. Dans cette manière on éloigne tels objets qui ne paroissent pas assez intéressans; on en rapproche tels autres qui se conviennent, quoi qu'ils se trouvent très-éloignés; on cherche des accords et des contrastes; enfin l'Artiste choisit telle ou telle vue, parce qu'elle lui semble plus agréable et plus pittoresque. La seconde est celle qui nous fait voir la Nature telle qu'elle pourroit être, et telle que l'imagination ornée la représente aux yeux de l'homme de génie qui a beaucoup vu, bien comparée, analysé et réfléchi sur le choix qu'il faut en faire . . .'

18. François-René de Chateaubriand, 'Lettre sur l'art du dessin dans les paysages' written in London, 1795, and first published in *Mélanges et poésies*, Paris, 1828, p. 5. He described how landscapes were drawn indoors: 'Il sembleroit que l'étude du paysage ne consiste que dans l'étude des coups de crayon ou de pinceau; que tout l'art se réduit à assembler certains traits, de manière à ce qu'il en résulte des apparences d'arbres, de maisons, d'animaux et d'autres objets. Le paysagiste qui dessine ainsi ne ressemble pas mal à une femme qui fait la dentelle, qui passe de petits bâtons les uns sur les autres, en causant et en regardant ailleurs . . .' W. H. Pyne (*Library of Fine Arts*, 1832) gave a similar account of the practice of such fashionable drawing masters as Jean Pillement, Joseph Goupy and J. B. Chatelaine; see Paul H. Walton, *The Drawings of John Ruskin*, Oxford, 1972, pp. 2–3.

19. The distinction was made in the Diderot-d'Alembert *Encyclopédie* (1756), where the *étude* was described as a painting or drawing of a separate feature, such as a head, hand, piece of drapery or portion of landscape, and an *esquisse* as the 'first draft' of a pictorial work, whether traced, drawn or painted. But by the mid-nineteenth century the authoritative *Dictionnaire de l'Académie des Beaux Arts* (1858) stated that an *étude* might be a work of art in its own right, independently of any intention to use it elsewhere: see Albert Boime, *The Academy and French Painting in the Nineteenth Century*, London and New York, 1971, pp. 149–50. Failure to distinguish between these terms has sometimes led to confusion about the aesthetics of the sketch.

20. S. Hinz, p. 92. Kersting's drawing of Friedrich and himself on a sketching tour is in the Kupferstichkabinett, Staatliche Museen, Berlin.

21. C. R. Leslie, p. 323, with comment on a similar passage in George Turnbull, *A Treatise on Ancient Painting*, London, 1740.

22. ibid., p. 101; see also L. Parris and C. Shields, *Constable: The Art of Nature*, exh. cat., Tate Gallery, London, 1971, p. 8.

23. John Davy, *Memoirs of the Life of Sir Humphry Davy*, London, 1839: see Geoffrey Grigson, *The Romantics*, London, 1942, p. 128.

24. British Museum and Victoria and Albert Museum, London.

25. P. H. Valenciennes, op. cit., p. 631.

26. A. Jal, *L'Artiste et le philosophe, entretiens critiques sur le salon de 1824*, Paris, 1824, p. 292. He added: 'Mais le procédé qui mène à cette expression de la vérité est tout près de *la manière*.'

27. Thénot, *Cours complète de paysage*, Paris, 1834.

28. Eugène Delacroix, *Selected Letters*, tr. and ed. Jean Stewart, London, 1971, pp. 236–7.

29. *Constable's Correspondence*, VI, p. 172.

30. ibid., III, p. 59.

31. See L. Parris, *Landscape in Britain c. 1750–1850*, exh. cat., Tate Gallery, London, 1973, nos. 240, 244, 260, 272.

32. Kunsthalle, Hamburg, 1053.

33. S. T. Coleridge, *Biographia Literaria*, London, 1817, ch. xiv; reprinted in *Lyrical Ballads*, ed. G. Sampson, London, 1914, p. xxiii.

34. Novalis, II, p. 545.

35. M. Hope Nicolson, op. cit., comments on the different attitudes to nature derived from the Bible (which particularly influenced Protestants) and from classical writers. In his last lecture Constable quoted Martin Luther: 'When I behold the beautiful azure vault of Heaven, besprinkled with constellations of shining orbs, the prospect fills my mind, and I feel the highest gratification at such a glorious display of Omnipotence' (*Constable's Discourses*, p. 73).

36. Chateaubriand's attitudes to nature and religion differed from those of his English and German contemporaries, as Ximénès Doudan noted (*Des révolutions du goût*, *c.* 1855, ed. H. Moncel, Paris, 1924, p. 31): 'Dans un siècle incrédule, Rousseau voit enfin le beauté de ces monts, de ces eaux que Saint Bernard avait regardées d'un œil méprisant, et M. de Chateaubriand semble avoir gardé quelque chose du scepticisme de son temps quand, pour ramener les hommes au Dieu qu'ils avaient quitté, il replace les autels des chrétiens au milieu des pompes de la nature.'

37. Runge, I, p. 3.

38. ibid., p. 9.

39. ibid., pp. 6–7, 27.

40. Remark made in 1811 to Sulpiz Boisserée, who recorded it in a letter to his brother first printed in S. Boisserée, *Briefwechsel/Tagebücher*, Stuttgart, 1862, I, p. 114. For Runge's relationship with Goethe, see Jörg Traeger, *Philipp Otto Runge und sein Werk*, Munich, 1975.

41. From the poem entitled 'The Retreate' in *Silex Scintillans*, London, 1650. Vaughan was influenced by the writings of Jakob Böhme, as Runge was to be a century and a half later.

42. The question as to whether Runge influenced Friedrich or vice versa has been much debated: for the best summary of their relationship, see Jörg Traeger, op. cit., pp. 180–85.

43. In addition to his many letters, full descriptions of his own drawings and paintings, and his treatise on *Die Farbenkugel*, Runge wrote poems and also two *Kindermärchen* (in

Hamburg dialect), which were included in the Grimm brothers' collection of fairy-tales and thus went round the world.

44. S. Hinz, p. 127.

45. Letter to Victor Pavie from Dresden, 6 December 1834: see H. Jouin, *David d'Angers et ses relations littéraires*, Paris, 1890, pp. 87–8. For other comments on Friedrich by David d'Angers, see H. Jouin, *David d'Angers, sa vie, son œuvre, ses écrits et ses contemporains*, Paris, 1878, I, p. 298 and L. Cerf, *Souvenirs de David d'Angers sur ses contemporains*, Paris, 1928, pp. 99–107.

46. S. Hinz, p. 220. For literal allegorical interpretations of Friedrich's work, see Börsch-Supan/Jähnig, and timely correctives in the article by Charles Rosen in *The New York Review of Books*, XX, 1 November 1973, pp. 12–17.

47. Museum für bildenden Künste, Leipzig; Börsch-Supan/Jähnig, no. 411. For a social interpretation of this work, see Peter Märker, 'Caspar David Friedrich zur Zeit der Restauration' in Berthold Hinz et al., *Bürgerliche Revolution und Romantik. Natur und Gesellschaft bei Caspar David Friedrich*, Giessen, 1976, pp. 48–50.

48. *Briefe über Landschaftsmalerei*, Leipzig, 1835, p. 29.

49. S. Hinz, p. 91. The remark is reminiscent of a passage in a lecture by Schelling of 1807, quoted in Herbert Read, *The True Voice of Feeling*, London, 1953, p. 324: 'Plastic art, therefore, manifestly occupies the position of an active link between the soul and nature, and can only be comprehended in the living centre between the two of them.' Art is described as the 'Vermitterlin der Religion' by Friedrich's friend C. G. Carus in *Briefe über Landschaftsmalerei*, Leipzig, 1835, p. 25.

50. S. Hinz, p. 218.

51. *The Letters of Samuel Palmer*, ed. Raymond Lister, Oxford, 1974, I, p. 16.

52. ibid., p. 50.

53. *Constable's Correspondence*, VI, pp. 77–8. He cited *The White Horse* (now Frick Collection, New York) as one of the 'strongest instances' of such pictures.

54. *Constable's Discourses*, p. 13.

55. He could, however, have read the great invocation, 'Wisdom and Spirit of the Universe' (*The Prelude*, I, lines 428–37), published in Coleridge's periodical *The Friend* in 1809 and included in the 1815 edition of Wordsworth's *Poems*. Several of Constable's phrases in *English Landscape* seem to echo these lines:

'Wisdom and Spirit of the universe!
Thou Soul that art the eternity of thought,
That giv'st to forms and images a breath
And everlasting motion, not in vain
By day or starlight thus from my first dawn
Of childhood didst thou intertwine for me
The passions that build up our human soul;
Not with the mean and vulgar works of man,
But with high objects, with enduring things –
With Life and Nature ...'

For the most interesting comparative study of Constable and Wordsworth (to which I am much indebted, especially for the notion of 'spots of time'), see Karl Krober, 'Constable and Wordsworth: The Ecological Moment in Romantic Art' in *Journal of the Warburg and Courtauld Institutes*, XXXIV, 1971, pp. 377–86 and *Romantic Landscape Vision: Constable and Wordsworth*, Madison, Wisconsin, 1975.

56. *Constable's Correspondence*, VII, p. 56.

57. L. Parris and C. Shields, *Constable: The Art of Nature*, exh. cat., Tate Gallery, London, 1971, no. 39.

58. C. R. Leslie, p. 18, remarked with reference to Constable's visit to the Lake District in 1806: 'I have heard him say that the solitude of mountains oppressed his spirits. His nature was peculiarly social and could not feel satisfied with scenery, however grand in itself, that did not abound in human associations. He required villages, churches, farmhouses and cottages . . .' For some of the Lake District drawings, see Constable Exhibition, nos. 69–80.

59. *Constable's Correspondence*, VI, p. 78.

60. I. Fleming-Williams, 'A Runover Dungle and a Possible Date for *Spring*' in *Burlington Magazine*, CXIV, 1972, pp. 390–93. Constable's unquestioning acceptance of the enclosure of common land makes a striking contrast with the hostility of the poet John Clare: for the latter, see John Barrell, *The Idea of Landscape and the Sense of Place*, Cambridge, 1972.

61. *The Prelude*, XI, lines 258–389 of the 1805 text, beginning:

> 'There are in our existence spots of time,
> Which with distinct pre-eminence retain
> A vivifying virtue, whence depressed
> By false opinion and contentious thought,
> Or aught of heavier or more deadly weight,
> In trivial occupations, and the round
> Of ordinary intercourse, our minds
> Are nourished and invisibly repaired.'

62. *Constable's Correspondence*, VI, p. 142.

63. The most extreme statement of preference for the sketches is that by Roger Fry, *French, Flemish and British Art*, London, 1951, pp. 204–12. For him, Constable's 'habit of making' his finished paintings was 'entirely bad. They are almost always compromises with his real idea. He watered that down, filling it out with redundant statements of detail which merely satisfy an idle curiosity and inevitably obscure the essential theme.'

64. *Constable's Correspondence*, III, pp. 121–2. In 1821 he wrote of a landscape then ascribed to Nicolas Poussin: 'It cannot surely be saying too much when I assert that his landscape is full of religious and moral feeling, and shows how much of his own nature God has implanted in the mind of man.' In 1828 he caustically commented on un-named Royal Academicians (probably with Etty in mind) that they 'stickle for the "elevated & noble" walks of art – i.e. preferring the *shaggy posteriors of a Satyr* to the *moral feeling of landscape*' (*Constable's Correspondence*, VI, p. 74 and III, p. 19).

65. Introduction to *English Landscape*, *Constable's Discourses*, p. 9.

66. C. R. Leslie, p. 121.

67. ibid., p. 280. The remark is perhaps an echo of Boileau's 'Il n'est point de serpent ni monstre odieux/ Qui par l'art imité ne puisse plaire aux yeux' (*L'Art poètique*, III, lines 1–2). Emerson wrote that there was 'no object so foul that intense light will not make beautiful', cit., Barbara Novak, *American Painting of the Nineteenth Century*, New York and London, 1969, p. 123.

68. Letter to John Fisher, 23 October 1821: 'I have often been advised to consider my sky as "*a white sheet thrown behind the objects*". Certainly, if the sky is obtrusive, as mine are, it is bad; but if it is evaded, as mine are not, it is worse; it must and always shall with me make an effectual part of the composition. It will be difficult to name a class of landscape in which the sky is not the key note, the standard of scale, and the chief organ of sentiment.

You may conceive, then, what a 'white sheet' would do for me, impressed as I am with these notions and they cannot be erroneous. The sky is the source of light in nature, and governs everything; even our common observations on the weather of every day are altogether suggested by it. The difficulty of skies in painting is very great, both as to composition and execution; because, with all their brilliancy, they ought not to come forward, or, indeed, be hardly thought of more than extreme distances are; but this does not apply to phenomena or accidental effects of sky, because they always attract particularly' (*Constable's Correspondence*, VI, p. 77).

69. In religion he was an orthodox Anglican and presumably held the Protestant belief in the individual's relationship with God. In politics he was by nature conservative, a Tory, though perhaps less concerned with the rights of the great landlords than with those of the yeoman landholders. He opposed the Reform Bill as a 'tremendous attack on the constitution of the country' which would 'give the government into the hands of the rabble and dregs of the people, and the devil's agents on earth, the agitators' (October, 1831; *Constable's Correspondence*, III, p. 49). Two buildings which recur in his paintings seem to symbolize his attitudes to Church and State – the tower of Dedham Parish Church and the house in which Willy Lot, a small farmer, lived throughout Constable's life.

70. To C. R. Leslie, 20 January 1833. The artist in question was F. R. Lee.

71. C. R. Leslie, p. 106.

72. *Constable's Correspondence*, VI, p. 197.

73. C. R. Leslie, p. 240.

74. ibid., p. 239.

75. On the condition of the pictures in his gallery in 1846, see A. J. Finberg, p. 414.

76. For Turner's activities on varnishing days, see John Gage, *Colour in Turner*, London, 1969, pp. 165–72.

77. The engraver David Lucas, in a marginal annotation to C. R. Leslie, remarked of Constable's *Dedham Vale: Morning* (now coll. Major Sir Richard Proby Bt), 'He has often told me that this picture cost him more anxiety than any work of his before or since that period in which it was painted, that he had even said his prayers before it' (*Constable's Correspondence*, VII, p. 55). Adrian Stokes, *Painting and the Inner World*, London, 1963, pp. 49–84, persuasively suggests a sexual significance in the 'clumps and clefts' which recur in Turner's paintings.

78. Both pictures are now in the Tate Gallery, London.

79. Jerrold Ziff, 'J. M. W. Turner on Poetry and Painting' in *Studies in Romanticism*, III, 1964, pp. 193–215, shows that Turner's interest in poetics and first attempts to write poetry date from the time of his appointment as Professor of Perspective at the Royal Academy in 1807.

80. See John Gage, *Turner: Rain, Steam and Speed*, London, 1972, pp. 19–22.

81. John Gage, *Colour in Turner*, London, 1969, p. 139.

82. ibid., pp. 139–40. The painting is in the Tate Gallery, London.

83. Tate Gallery, London.

84. Tate Gallery, London.

85. A. J. Finberg, p. 241. Hazlitt's critique, published in the *Examiner*, ends with the often quoted remark: 'All is without form and void. Someone said of his landscapes that they were *pictures of nothing, and very like.*'

86. A. J. Finberg, p. 230.

87. Lawrence Gowing, *Turner: Imagination and Reality*, New York, 1966, p. 16.

88. *The Sun of Venice Going to Sea* and *Light and Colour* (*Goethe's Theory*) are in the Tate Gallery, *Queen Mab's Cave* in the National Gallery, London. Turner's kinship with

Shelley was noted by E. T. Cook, *A Popular Handbook to the National Gallery*, London, 1893, pp. 381, 404, and has more recently been discussed by John Gage, *Colour in Turner*, London, 1969, pp. 145–7.

89. Adele M. Holcomb, '"Indistinctness is my fault": A Letter about Turner from C. R. Leslie to James Lenox' in *Burlington Magazine*, CXIV, 1972, pp. 557–8.

90. L. L. Noble, *The Life and Works of Thomas Cole* (1853), ed. E. S. Vesell, Cambridge, Mass., 1964, p. 86.

91. For comments on Constable in the French press see Pontus Grate, *Deux Critiques d'art de l'époque romantique*, Stockholm, 1959, pp. 36–8. P.-A. Coupin wrote 'qu'une foule de jeunes gens se sont précipités sur les traces des Anglais et se sont empressés, pendant le cours même de l'Exposition, de faire des paysages et des vues, où ils ont cherché, avant tout, à être vrais et simples ...' A writer in *Figaro*, 1828, declared: 'c'est à Constable que nous devons les premiers essais d'une peinture qui choquait, par la rudesse de sa vérité, des yeux fascinés par une nature de convention, mais qui déjà dénotait une recherche scrupuleuse de tous les accidens du paysage. Un grand nombre de nos artistes ont marchés sur les traces des Anglais ...' Many years later, in 1858, Delacroix described Constable and Turner as reformers who broke out of the rut of traditional landscape painting, and from whose example the French school greatly profited (E. Delacroix, *Correspondance Générale*, ed. A. Joubin, Paris, 1938, IV, p. 60). Nevertheless, 'true and simple' landscapes had previously been painted with great success by French artists, most notably David's *Vue du Jardin du Luxembourg* (Louvre), but also by Louis Gauffier (*c.* 1796), Turpin de Crissé (1806) and J.-L. Demarne (1814): see *French Painting 1774–1830*, nos. 65, 177, 46. These are, however, all small-scale works. The establishment of a Rome prize for *paysage historique* had firmly stressed Academic preference for the classical landscape.

92. L. Rosenthal, *Du Romantisme au réalisme*, Paris, 1914, p. 273.

93. E. Heller, *The Artist's Journey into the Interior*, London, 1965, p. 79.

94. P. Courthion, *Corot raconté par lui-même et par ses amis*, Geneva, 1946, pp. 86, 95–6.

95. The passage was printed in *The Picture Galleries of England* (1824), ascribed by Hazlitt to 'an eminent master' (William Hazlitt, *The Collected Works*, London, 1903, IX, p. 66). For other early nineteenth-century English references to Claude, see Claire Pace, 'Claude the Enchanted' in *Burlington Magazine*, CXI, 1969, pp. 733–40.

96. C. R. Leslie (pp. 59, 73) mentions only two pictures (as distinct from sketches) painted by Constable 'entirely in the open air': *Boat Building* (Victoria and Albert Museum) and *Hampstead Heath: the House called 'The Salt Box' in the Distance* (Tate Gallery). Paul Huet wrote: 'L'émotion devant la nature est quelquelfois un obstacle à l'étude; pour ma part j'ai, devant ses grands spectacles, éprouvé de si vives impressions qu'il m'était impossible de tracer une ligne; le lendemain seulement, le souvenir encore vibrant, je pouvais retrouver la scène que j'avais vue la veille' (René-Paul Huet, *Paul Huet (1803–1869) d'après ses notes, sa correspondance, ses contemporains*, Paris, 1911, p. 77). A similar attitude towards the sketch was expressed by Thomas Cole in 1835: 'In speaking of sketching from nature I believe I have before mentioned that mine are *generally* mere outlines & I have found that for *me* the mode I have adopted is the best – others may pursue a different course to advantage. My desire & endeavour is always to get the objects of nature, sky, rocks, trees, &c – as strongly impressed on my mind as possible & by looking intently on an object for twenty minutes I can go to my room & paint it with much more truth, than I could if I employed several hours on the spot. By this means I become more intimately acquainted with the characteristics of the spirit of Nature than I could otherwise do. I think that a vivid picture of any object in the mind's eye is worth a hundred finished sketches made on the spot – which are never more than half true – for the glare of light destroys the true

effect of colour & the tones of Nature are too refined to be obtained without repeated painting & glazings. And by my method I learn better what Nature *is* and painting *ought to be* – get the philosophy of Nature & Art – whereas a finished sketch may be done without obtaining either one or the other – and is in great measure a mere mechanical operation' (H. S. Merritt in *Baltimore Museum of Art Annual*, II, 1967, p. 79).

97. Wash drawings of clouds have been attributed to Claude and there are slightly later documented examples by Willem van de Velde (1633–1707); but the earliest recorded study of clouds in oils appears to be by A.-F. Desportes: see *Paysages de François Desportes (1661–1743)*, exh. cat., Musée Nationale de Compiègne, 1961, no. 2. For the comments on clouds by Cropsey and Thoreau see Kynaston McShine, ed., *The Natural Paradise: Painting in America 1800–1950*, New York, 1976, pp. 87–9.

98. See L. Eitner, 'The Open Window and the Storm Tossed Boat' in *Art Bulletin*, XXXVII, 1955, pp. 281–90. Numerous paintings and drawings of open windows, ranging in date from the fifteenth to the twentieth century, are assembled by J. A. Schmoll gen. Eisenwerth, 'Festerbilder' in L. Grote, ed., *Beitrage zur Motivkunde des 19. Jahrhunderts*, Munich, 1970, pp. 13–165. For a semi-satirical image by Jules David (1844) of a top-hatted artist drawing from a Parisian garret window, see P. Grate, op. cit., p. 191.

99. The English-type garden was styled 'romanesque' by C.-H. Watelet in 1774: see H. Eichner, p. 86. But the word 'romantic' and its cognates had for long been applied in a different sense to formal Italian Renaissance gardens which were associated with Tasso's garden of Armida.

100. *The Prelude*, 1805, XI, lines 153–6.

101. *Constable's Correspondence*, VI, p. 98, with reference to Fonthill. Constable had, of course, painted views of more than one gentleman's park, notably Malvern Hall (National Gallery, London). But he also painted two views of his father's flower garden with its neatly tended beds (Ipswich Borough Council).

102. G. W. F. Hegel, *Vorlesung über die Ästhetik* (1835), ed. R. Bubner, Stuttgart, 1971, p. 351. The description seems to have been lifted from F. H. Jacobi, *Woldemar*, Königsberg, 1794, p. 83 – a passage also cited by Tieck: see G. H. Danton, *The Nature Sense in the Writings of Ludwig Tieck*, New York, 1907, p. 18. For the preservation of the natural wilderness in America see Roderick Nash, *Wilderness and the American Mind* (1967), New Haven, 1973.

103. There is no adequate international history of nineteenth-century garden design. For the British Isles alone, see Geoffrey Taylor, *The Victorian Flower Garden*, London, 1952, and Miles Hadfield, *Gardening in Britain*, London, 1960, pp. 241–430. The general tendency seems to have been towards fragmentation of the grandiose eighteenth-century lay-out and greater concentration on the individuality of plants and the simulation of landscapes to which they were indigenous. This led to the creation of 'rock gardens' at Hoole House, Cheshire (modelled on the Valley of Chamonix) in 1838 and at Redleaf, Sussex, the home of the notable patron of artists William Wells, in 1839. From the late 1830s, the formal gardens of Renaissance Italy and seventeenth-century France were also imitated – the outstanding example of the former type being Shrubland, near Ipswich, designed by Sir Charles Barry shortly after 1848.

104. Too few of Georges Michel's paintings are dated to provide the basis for a study of his stylistic development. A storm scene of 1794–5 (Musée des Beaux Arts, Nantes) is an accomplished essay in the manner of Ruisdael: see Jacques Foucard in *French Painting 1774–1830*, no. 131. Michel is known to have made copies of landscapes by Ruisdael, Hobbema, Rembrandt and other Dutch painters for the dealer Lebrun *c.* 1800.

105. J.-B. Deperthes, *Théorie du Paysage*, Paris, 1818, pp. 160–61.

106. Douglas Hall, 'The Tabley House Papers' in *Walpole Society*, XXXVIII, 1962, p. 95.

107. L. L. Noble, op. cit., p. 148.

108. ibid., p. 220.

109. The two paintings are in the Metropolitan Museum, New York, and the California Palace of the Legion of Honor, San Francisco.

110. New York Public Library. For Durand see James Thomas Flexner, *That Wilder Image*, 1962, New York, 1970, pp. 52–65 and Barbara Novak, *American Painting of the Nineteenth Century*, New York and London, 1969, pp. 80–91.

111. Bingham's painting is in the Metropolitan Museum, New York; Mount's is in the New York Historical Association, Cooperstown, New York; both are reproduced in B. Novak, op. cit., pp. 104–5.

112. It is sometimes said that Rousseau was totally excluded from the Salon through the period of the July Monarchy, but he exhibited in 1834 (winning a third-class medal), 1835 and 1838 though only one picture by him was shown on each occasion and his larger works were refused – *La Descente des Vaches dans le Jura* in 1836 and *L'Allée des châtaigniers* in 1841. Even his contemporaries found his exclusion hard to explain and in 1867 Philippe Burty referred to *L'Allée des châtaigniers* as a 'tableau composé si largement, dessiné avec tant de recherche, peint si sobrement, exprimant avec tant de vérité le site, la saison et l'heure du jour, qu'on y chercherait vainement la moindre menace contre les institutions sociales les plus ombrageuses' (E. Chesneau, *Peintres et statuaires romantiques*, Paris, 1880, pp. 276–7). Alfred Sensier, *Souvenirs sur Th. Rousseau*, Paris, 1872, p. 34, states that Rousseau was little concerned with politics, although he made sketches for a picture of the funeral of General Lamarque, the event which set off the Republican insurrection of June 1832. He ascribed Rousseau's exclusion from the Salon to his friendship with a group of writers who attacked the Institut, of whose members the juries were at this period composed.

113. A. Sensier, op. cit., p. 79. *La Descente des Vaches dans le Jura* and the sketch for it are in Musée Mesdag, The Hague.

114. E. Fromentin, *The Masters of Past Time* (1876), tr. A. Boyle, ed. H. Gerson, London, 1948, p. 154.

115. A. Terasse, *L'Univers de Théodore Rousseau*, Paris, 1976, p. 7.

116. A. Sensier, op. cit., p. 278.

117. Quoted by Philippe Burty, *Paul Huet*, Paris, 1869, p. 17. The passage comes from E. T. A. Hoffmann's story *Die Jesuitenkirche in G.*, first published in *Nachtstücke I* (1816), in *Ausgewählte Schriften*, Berlin, 1827, II, p. 128.

3. FROZEN MUSIC (*pages 119–55*)

1. Friedrich Schiller, *On the Aesthetic Education of Man* (1795), ed. and tr. E. M. Wilkinson and L. A. Willoughby, Oxford, 1967, p. 155. This passage seems to anticipate the Romantic idea of an 'essential art' transcending subject-matter and material. But Schiller was mainly concerned with the liberation of the mind from the bias inherent in a material or a type of art, in order to restore or enforce spontaneity or receptivity in perception: see Michael Podro, *The Manifold in Perception*, Oxford, 1972, p. 58.

2. *Das Allgemeine Brouillon* (1798–9), in Novalis, III, p. 109.

3. For the 'architecture is frozen music' topos, see Erika von Erhardt-Siebold, 'Harmony of the Senses in English, German and French Romanticism' in *Publications of the Modern Language Association of America*, XLVII, 1932, pp. 577–92; and, especially, Eva Börsch-Supan, 'Die Bedeutung der Musik im Werke Karl Friedrich Schinkels' in *Zeitschrift für Kunstgeschichte*, XXXIV, 1971, p. 276–80. The German wording was originally 'erstarrte

Musik', literally 'congealed music', used by Schelling in a lecture given in Berlin 1802–3 (though not published until 1859). The general idea seems to have been current in and around Berlin, and Friedrich Schlegel described architecture as 'eine musikalische Plastik' in a notebook *c.* 1800. The phrase 'gefrorene Musik' was first used satirically in a Berlin periodical of 1803. In 1804 Mme de Staël in London asked Henry Crabb Robinson: 'What does Schelling mean when he says that architecture is frozen music?' These were the words in which the idea entered the English language and was given wider currency by Byron, who wrote in a note to *The Bride of Abydos* (1813): 'Someone has said that the perfection of architecture is frozen music – the perfection of beauty to my mind always presented the idea of living music.'

4. Walter Pater, *The Renaissance* (1877), London, 1910, p. 135. Pater was, however, qualifying rather than repeating the earlier phrase and began the essay 'The School of Giorgione' in which the remark occurs by stating: 'It is a mistake of much popular criticism to regard poetry, music, and painting – all the various products of art – as but translations into different languages of one and the same fixed quantity of imaginative thought, supplemented by certain technical qualities of colour, in painting; of sound, in music; of rhythmical words, in poetry.'

5. See Rudolf Wittkower, *Architectural Principles in the Age of Humanism*, London, 1952, pp. 89–140.

6. The most famous was that made by Louis-Bertrand Castel in 1735.

7. L. L. Noble, op. cit., p. 141. The construction of a 'Farbenklavier' had, however, been dismissed as 'eine unglückliche Idee' in W. H. Wackenroder and L. Tieck, *Phantasien über die Kunst* (1799), ed. K. O. Conrady, Leck/Schleswig, 1968, p. 189. The idea was reduced to the level of kitsch in the twentieth century by the cinema organ and Walt Disney's *Fantasia*.

8. Baudelaire, p. 238, in a review of the Exposition Universelle, 1855. In a reprint of this review (also 1855) Baudelaire added another sentence and a stanza from his poem 'Les Phares': 'Un poète a essayé d'exprimer ces sensations subtiles dans des vers dont la sincérité peut faire passer la bizarrerie:

> Delacroix, lac de sang, hanté des mauvais anges,
> Ombragé par un bois de sapins toujours vert,
> Où, sous un ciel chagrin, des fanfares étranges
> Passent comme un soupir étouffé de Weber.'

For Allston's remark see E. P. Richardson, *Washington Allston* (1948), New York, 1967, p. 60.

9. Immanuel Kant, *Kritik der Urteilskraft*, Berlin, 1790, p. 218 (tr. J. H. Bernard, 1951).

10. C.-J. Lioult de Chêndollé, *Extraits de journal*: see F. Baldensperger, *Sensibilité musicale et romantisme*, Paris, 1925, p. 80. The remark was made in 1808 with reference to Boccherini, a composer who would not nowadays be thought Romantic.

11. See André Cœuroq, *Musique et littérature*, Paris, 1923, pp. 11–48.

12. Runge, II, p. 202. For his ideas about music, see Jörg Traeger, op. cit., p. 131.

13. Jörg Traeger, op. cit., p. 178.

14. A. Robaut, *L'Œuvre complet de E. Delacroix*, Paris, 1885, p. 106.

15. Delacroix's double portrait of 1838 remained on his hands until his death and the two heads were subsequently cut from it (now in the Louvre and Ordrupgaard Museum, Copenhagen): see Delacroix Exhibition, nos. 274–5. J. Danhauser's painting is repr. in *Berlioz and the Romantic Imagination*, exh. cat., Victoria and Albert Museum, London, 1969, no. 276.

16. H. G. Schenk, *The Mind of the European Romantics*, London, 1966, pp. 202–3.

17. *Delacroix: Journal*, II, p. 22.

18. Théophile Gautier, *Histoire du Romantisme* (1870), Paris, 1874, p. 260. Berlioz was not, however, interested in Delacroix's paintings and Delacroix actively disliked the music of Berlioz: see Amaury-Duval, *L'Atelier d'Ingres* (1878), Paris, 1924, p. 94.

19. *Kritische Friedrich-Schlegel-Ausgabe*, ed. Hans Eichner, Paderborn, 1959, IV, p. 77.

20. ibid., X, p. 233, from *Philosophie des Lebens* (1827).

21. Hegel/Knox, II, p. 788. Hegel was, however, able to put a Romantic interpretation on the earlier works of Greek sculpture: see ibid., p. 724.

22. Théophile Gautier, op. cit., pp. 29, 245. His account of the critical hostility to David d'Angers and Barye was, of course, exaggerated. His remark: 'Pour nos époques compliquées et troublées, ce détachement de la passion, de l'accident, de la couleur, ce calme immuable, arrivent aisément à la froideur et à l'ennuï', was perhaps influenced by the section in Baudelaire's *Salon de 1846* entitled: 'Pourquoi la sculpture est ennuyeuse'. Delacroix made the same point in his essay of 1857 *Des variations du beau* (*Œuvres littéraires*, Paris, 1923, I, p. 48): 'On peut dire de la peinture comme de la musique, qu'elle est essentiellement un art moderne... Le paganisme donnait au sculpteur une ample carrière... Le christianisme, au contraire, appelle la vie au dedans: les aspirations de l'âme, le renoncement des sens, sont difficiles à exprimer par le marbre et la pierre: c'est, au contraire, le rôle de la peinture de donner presque tout à l'expression.'

23. Friedrich Schlegel, 'On the German Paintings exhibited at Rome in 1819' in *Aesthetic and Miscellaneous Works*, tr. E. J. Millington, London, 1849, p. 290. The portrait of the Humboldt children (destroyed in World War II) is repr. Gustav Pauli, *Die Kunst des Klassizismus und der Romantik*, Berlin, 1925, p. 339.

24. H. Beyle, 'Salon de 1824' in Stendhal, *Mélanges d'art et de littérature*, Paris, 1927, p. 232. In view of Stendhal's identification of Romanticism with contemporaneity, this was tantamount to calling Canova a Romantic.

25. *New Monthly Magazine*, IX, 1818, p. 297. W. P. Carey, an art dealer and critic, was an early friend and supporter of Chantrey. Canova's *Hebe* was modelled in 1795 and the version shown at the Royal Academy completed in marble for Lord Cawdor before July 1816: it is now at Chatsworth House (see *The Age of Neo-classicism*, exh. cat., Royal Academy, London, 1972, no. 317). The *Terpsichore*, completed for Simon Clarke, is the second of two versions of a statue modelled in 1808: now in the Cleveland Museum of Art (see Henry Hawley in *The Bulletin of the Cleveland Museum of Art*, LVI, 1969, pp. 287–305).

26. e.g., *The Babes in the Wood* by Thomas Crawford, 1851, and *Le Nid* by Onésyme Croisy, repr. Maurice Rheims, *La Sculpture au XIXe siècle*, Paris, 1972, pp. 343, 388.

27. C. F. Fernow, *Über den Bildhauer Canova und dessen Werke*, Zürich, 1806.

28. Hegel/Knox, I, p. 213. The statue of Mercury is in Thorvaldsens Museum, Copenhagen. Rudolf Schadow's *Sandalenbinderin* is in the Nationalgalerie, Berlin.

29. Full-scale models had been made by sculptors since the Renaissance, though it is difficult to determine to what extent this was a general practice. Canova invariably made full-scale models in clay, which were then cast in plaster in order to preserve them: see H. Honour, 'Canova's Studio Practice' in *Burlington Magazine*, CXIV, 1972, pp. 149–59, 214–49. For a different account of Canova's practice, see two publications by H. W. Janson (to which I am indebted for several points), 'German Neoclassic Sculpture in International Perspective' in *Yale University Art Gallery Bulletin*, XXXIII, 1972, pp. 4–22, and introduction to *Tradition and Revisions: Themes from the History of Sculpture*, exh. cat., Cleveland Museum of Art, 1975. Professor Janson states that Canova made and exhibited 'his major uncommissioned pieces in plaster' in the hope of attracting buyers who 'would have replicas

made in marble or bronze'. In this way he 'redefined' sculpture. However, no specific instance of this is cited by Professor Janson, nor do I know of any. In fact, Canova seems never to have worked in this manner, if only because he was never short of commissions.

30. For the fullest account of this statue, see Herbert von Einem, *Thorvaldsens 'Jason': Versuch einer historischen Würdigung*, Munich, 1974. It was completed in marble in 1828 and is now in the Thorvaldsens Museum, Copenhagen.

31. Henri Jouin, *David d'Angers, sa vie, son œuvre, ses écrits et ses contemporains*, Paris, 1878, I, pp. 513–14. The difference between the model and the finished work was seen in another light by Hegel, who regarded sculpture as essentially 'classical': 'In the days of great artistic dexterity artists either worked their marble without having models in clay, or if they did have such, went to work far more freely and unconstrainedly than happens in our own day when, to speak the strict truth, the artist provides only copies in marble of originals, called models, previously worked in clay' (Hegel/Knox, II, p. 772).

32. Henri Jouin, op. cit., I, p. 206.

33. Letter of 4 August 1842, in which David went on to remark: 'Le statuaire, dès l'instant qu'il prend le ciseau pour représenter un grand homme, sent que c'est une apothéose qu'il va faire, un poème avec une seule figure qu'il va tracer' (Henri Jouin, *David d'Angers et ses relations littéraires*, Paris, 1890, p. 207). This is close to Edgar Quinet, *Considérations philosophiques sur l'art*, Strasbourg, 1839, p. 10, ending: 'En un mot, toute sculpture est une apothéose.' David had modelled a medallion portrait of Quinet in 1838 and seems to have known him personally. But Quinet reverted to the Romantic commonplace in describing sculpture as 'art païen, c'est par la paganisme qu'il a atteint toute sa hauteur: il conçoit l'homme au même point de vue que l'épopée. Au contraire, la peinture conserve toutes les circonstances du temps et du lieu... L'individualité conquise et consacrée par le christianisme, a créé chez les modernes le règne de la peinture'.

34. Lady Morgan, *France in 1829–30*, London, 1831, I, p. 302. David modelled a bust and a medallion portrait of Lady Morgan.

35. Henri Jouin, op. cit., 1878, I, p. 320. The marble statue of Philopoemen is in the Louvre.

36. Animal sculptures had, of course, been carved since ancient times, and in the late eighteenth century a whole room in the Museo Pio-Clementino of the Vatican was devoted to Antique specimens (extensively restored by Francesco Antonio Franzoni). From the Renaissance onwards, figures of animals were modelled, carved in marble and cast in bronze by numerous sculptors, but the specialist in such work – the *animalier* – seems to have appeared for the first time in the nineteenth century, in the wake of Barye.

37. Charles Saunier, *Barye*, Paris, 1925, p. 16.

38. Alexandre Decamps in *L'Artiste*, 1834: see C. Saunier, op. cit., p. 21. See also Gérard Hubert, 'Barye et la critique de son temps' in *La Revue des Arts*, VI, 1956, pp. 223–30.

39. Delacroix's early enthusiasms waned, and late in life he remarked that Barye was 'mesquin dans ses lions' (*Journal*, III, p. 15).

40. H. Martin et al., *Jean Du Seigneur Statuaire*, Paris, 1866, p. 18.

41. *L'Artiste*, V, 1833, p. 141.

42. Baudelaire, p. 394.

43. Luc Benoist, *La Sculpture romantique*, Paris, *c.* 1930, p. 73. Several references in *Delacroix: Journal* testify to his friendship for Préault, though he wrote on 16 June 1854 of the 'pauvre Préault qui fait des *Ophélia* et autres excentricités anglaises et romantiques' (II, p. 201).

44. Pétrus Borel, 'Des artistes penseurs et des artistes creux' in *L'Artiste*, V, 1833, pp. 253–9. The statues of Neapolitan dancers to which he refers are probably those by Fran-

cisque Duret (Louvre). He praised *Caïn et sa famille après son crime* by Antoine Etex (now Musée des Beaux Arts, Lyon) and the plaster groups of *La Mendicité* and *La Misère* by Préault, '... des sujets poignant toute âme chrétienne, toute âme que l'égoïsme n'a pas encore pétrifiée'. Borel's reference to the architect whom he calls Aimé Chenavard is puzzling. Aimé Chenavard was an ornamentalist and artistic adviser to the Sèvres porcelain factory. But Antoine Chenavard, a pupil of Durand, was professor of architecture at the Lyon academy 1823–61: see L. Hautecoeur, *Histoire de l'Architecture classique en France*, Paris, 1955, VI. Neither Aimé nor Antoine appears to have been related to the better-known painter Paul-Marc-Joseph Chenavard.

45. C. A. Menzel, *Versuch einer Darstellung des jetzigen Zustandes der Baukunst*, Berlin, 1832, quoted in *Foreign Quarterly Review*, XIV, 1834, p. 96.

46. *The Poetry of Architecture* (1837–8) in Ruskin, I, p. 5. Ruskin was to search in vain for living architects who came up to his standards. 'There are no architects at present,' he remarked late in life.

47. *The Stones of Venice*, Ruskin, IX, p. 64.

48. See Nikolaus Pevsner, *Some Architectural Writers of the Nineteenth Century*, Oxford, 1972, pp. 64–6, and Klaus Döhmer, '*In welchem Style sollen wir bauen?*': *Architekturtheorie zwischen Klassizismus und Jugendstil*, Munich, 1976.

49. The most remarkable manifestation of late eighteenth-century interest in the variety of architectural styles is Joseph Friedrich Freiherr zu Racknitz, *Darstellung und Geschichte des Geschmacks der vorzüglichsten Völker*, Leipzig, 1796, which accounts not only for Greek, Roman and Gothic architecture, the French Louis XIV, Louis XV and Louis XVI styles (with hostile comments on the latter), Egyptian, Chinese and Moorish, but also Mexican, Tahitian and, for good measure, the 'Kamtschadalisher Geschmack' (the huts of Kamtchatka). The idea that Gothic was particularly appropriate for churches seems first to have been enunciated by John Carter 1774–6: see George Germann, *Gothic Revival*, London, 1972, p. 56. But A. W. N. Pugin was characteristically to contest the eighteenth-century attitude: 'Our national and Catholic architecture ... is considered suitable for some purposes, – MELANCHOLY, and *therefore fit for religious* buildings!!!' (*An Apology for the Revival of Christian Architecture in England*, London, 1843, p. 2).

50. Mrs Jameson, *Visits and Sketches at Home and Abroad*, London, 1834, II, p. 52. For other comments on the choice of style, see Klaus Döhmer, op. cit., pp. 104–5. Similar objections had been made to the erection of a replica of the Parthenon on Calton Hill, Edinburgh, as a National Monument 'of the Triumphs of the late War by Sea and Land': see *Quarterly Review*, XXVII, 1822, pp. 327–36.

51. See Heinrich Beenken, *Schöpferische Bauideen der deutschen Romantik*, Mainz, 1952, with the interesting suggestion that the design of the Ludwigstrasse may owe something to painted panoramas.

52. J. Mordaunt Crook, *The Greek Revival*, London, 1972, p. 110.

53. Werner Hofmann, *Art in the Nineteenth Century*, London, 1961, p. 196.

54. Klaus Lankheit, *Révolution et Restauration*, Paris, 1966, p. 69. Almost contemporaneously Alfred de Musset wrote in *La Confession d'un enfant du siècle* (1836): 'Notre siècle n'a point de formes. Nous n'avons imprimé le cachet de notre temps ni à nos maisons, ni à nos jardins, ni à quoi que soit.... les appartements des riches sont des cabinets des curiosités: l'antique, le gothique, le goût de la Renaissance, celui de Louis XIII, tout est pêle-mêle. Enfin nous avons de tous les siècles, hors du nôtre, chose qui n'a jamais été vue à une autre époque: l'éclectisme est notre goût; nous prenons tout ce que nous trouvons, ceci pour sa beauté, cela pour sa commodité, telle autre chose pour son antiquité, telle autre pour sa laideur même; en sorte que nous ne vivons que de débris, comme si la fin du monde

était proche' (A. de Musset, *Œuvres complètes en prose*, ed. M. Allem and P. Courant, Paris, 1960, p. 89).

55. On the frequent demands for originality in architecture in Germany, see Klaus Döhmer, op. cit.; for England, Roger A. Kindler, 'Periodical Criticism 1815–40: Originality in Architecture' in *Architectural History*, XVII, 1974, pp. 22–37. Morse Peckham, *The Triumph of Romanticism*, Columbia, South Carolina, 1970, pp. 123–44, suggests that the architect asserted his individuality by his personal reconstruction of the past.

56. Nikolaus Pevsner, op. cit., p. 82.

57. A. W. N. Pugin, op. cit., p. 2.

58. O. Hederer, *Leo von Klenze*, Munich, 1964, pp. 14–16. Klenze tried to maintain eighteenth-century faith in one true style, claiming that there was only one *Baukunst* – that perfected in ancient Greece – all other styles were merely *Bauarten*. But his conception of Greek architecture embraced the *Rundbogenstil*.

59. Eva Börsch-Supan, op. cit., p. 278. The association of Doric with music became a commonplace. In an essay of 1843 on American architecture, Horatio Greenough remarked that the Greek temple 'loses its harmony if a note be dropped in the execution' (*Form and Function*, ed. H. A. Small, Berkeley and Los Angeles, 1958, p. 56).

60. Eva Börsch-Supan, op. cit., p. 279. The passage comes in a speech of the Astrologer:

> 'Hail now a spirit-masterpiece; for, lo,
> The clouds resolve in music as they go.
> From airy tones flows strength that none may see,
> For, as they move, all, all is melody;
> It sets the pillared shafts, the triglyphs ringing,
> We seem to hear the whole huge temple singing.'
>
> *Faust*, *Part Two*, tr. Philip Wayne, Harmondsworth, 1959, p. 85.

61. *Reflexion*, p. 1133: see Eva Börsch-Supan, op. cit., pp. 276–7. Mme de Staël, in *Corinne*, remarked of St Peter's: 'La vue d'un tel monument est comme une musique continuelle et fixée': see Erika von Erhardt-Siebold, op. cit., p. 587. Later Berlioz wrote of St Peter's: 'Attracted by the light, my eyes would look upwards to Michelangelo's glorious dome and my thoughts accomplish an abrupt transformation ... I passed in an instant to the music of the spheres, the quiring seraphim, goodness and serenity, and the infinite peace of heaven' (*Memoirs*, tr. David Cairns, London, 1970, p. 199).

62. Eva Börsch-Supan, op. cit., p. 293.

63. Joseph von Eichendorff in 1844 said that the medieval castle of Marienburg made him realize the meaning of the phrase 'gefrorene Musik', which he misattributed to 'Schlegel': see Eva Börsch-Supan, op. cit., p. 261.

64. Walter Pater, *Miscellaneous Studies*, London, 1895, pp. 95–6. He curiously reverses the attitude to melody and harmony expressed by Rousseau in 1753: 'The pleasure of harmony is only a pleasure of pure sensation, and the enjoyment of the senses is always brief, satiety and boredom soon follow; but the pleasure of melody and of song is a pleasure of interest which appeals to the heart': see J. Starobinski, *Jean-Jacques Rousseau: La Trasparance et l'obstacle*, Paris, 1958, p. 110.

65. Erika von Erhardt-Siebold, op. cit., pp. 587–8.

66. Wackenroder, who played a major part in the development of Romantic ideas about music, was an admirer of the architecture of Friedrich Gilly. 'Das ist ein Künstler!! So ein verzehrender Enthusiasmus für alte griechische Simplizität! – Ich habe einige sehr glückliche Stunden ästhetischer Unterhaltung mit ihm gehabt. Ein göttliche Mensch,' he

wrote to Tieck in 1793: see Heinz Lippuner, *Wackenroder/Tieck und die bildende Kunst*, Zürich, 1965, p. 96.

67. 'Musikalisch und lyrisch ist das Christenthum,' wrote Moritz von Arndt in 1815, and promptly went on to describe the musical effect of Gothic architecture: see G. Eimer, *Caspar David Friedrich und die Gotik*, Hamburg, 1963, p. 34.

68. Eva Börsch-Supan, op. cit., indicates several passages in Schinkel's notebooks which are paraphrases from Schelling's lectures. He was no less indebted to F. and A. W. Schlegel, and most of all to Goethe.

69. In 1803 he described the Zwinger at Dresden as 'Voll erstaunlicher Muschel- und Blumenpracht im schlechtesten Stil'. In 1804 he wrote from Naples to a Berlin publisher, proposing a book of architectural drawings which would include early medieval buildings in Sicily: see *Karl Friedrich Schinkel aus Tagebüchern und Briefen*, Munich and Vienna, 1967, pp. 18, 38–9.

70. ibid., pp. 20–21.

71. Nikolaus Pevsner, op. cit., p. 62. Schinkel also remarked in 1810, 'Antique architecture is vain and pompous,' but this was presumably with reference to Rome rather than Greece. Much later, and in a different context – the basic theory of architecture – he was to declare: 'To build Greek is to build right ... The Principle of Greek architecture is to render construction beautiful, and this must remain the principle of its continuation.'

72. *Foreign Quarterly Review*, XIV, 1834, p. 105.

73. ibid., VII, 1831, p. 457. The same anonymous writer published another eulogy of Schinkel in the same periodical, XXVIII, 1842, pp. 460–61. Both he and Schinkel were violently attacked by Joseph Gwilt, *Elements of Architectural Criticism*, London, 1837, pp. 79–98.

74. Roland Mortier, *La poétique des ruines en France*, Geneva, 1974, pp. 177, 201, 205. This is the best available account of the cult of ruins from the Renaissance to the nineteenth century, with special reference to France. Renzo Negri, *Gusto e poesia delle rovine in Italia fra il sette e l'ottocento*, Milan, 1965, is also valuable. The development of the idea that ruins might be more beautiful than the original buildings of which they were the remains coincides with the emergence of new attitudes to the restoration of Antique sculpture. In 1815 Canova advised that the Elgin marbles should not be restored. In the early years of the nineteenth century the practice of removing sculpture from ancient sites also began to arouse opposition, beginning with protests at Lord Elgin's activities in Athens.

75. Repr. E. Lavagnino, *L'Arte Moderna*, Turin, 1961, p. 100.

76. *The Stones of Venice*, Ruskin, IX, p. 69.

77. ibid., X, p. 214. It is interesting to compare this passage with the remark of an architect, F. Debret, in 1824: 'Bien que je suis loin de regarder cette architecture [Gothic] comme classique et que je ne la considère au contraire que comme le délire d'une imagination ardente, qui semble avoir réalisé des songes, je suis cependant forcé d'admirer ses monuments comme des productions que la génie d'un peuple essentiellement poète peut seul enfanter' (see L. Hautecoeur, op. cit., VI, p. 285).

4. THE LAST ENCHANTMENTS OF THE MIDDLE AGE (*pages 156–91*)

1. For the hostile attitudes of the *philosophes*, see Peter Gay, *The Enlightenment: An Interpretation. The Rise of Modern Paganism*, New York, 1966, pp. 207–12.

2. Richard Hurd, *Letters on Chivalry and Romance* (1762); but the comparison between *The Faerie Queene* and classical epics, Roman and Gothic architecture had been made as early as 1715 by John Hughes: see Paul Frankl, *The Gothic*, Princeton, 1960, p. 373. Hurd was mainly concerned with literature; for the origin of his ideas see R. Wellek, *A History*

of Modern Criticism: The Later Eighteenth Century, London, 1955, pp. 121–2. The idea of the incompatible merits of Greek and Gothic architecture was later expressed by Wilhelm Heinrich Wackenroder, *Herzensergiessungen eines Kunstliebenden Klosterbruders* (Berlin, 1797): 'Warum verdammt ihr den Indianer nicht, dass er indianisch und nicht unsere Sprache redet? – Und doch wollt ihr das Mittelalter verdammen, dass es nicht solche Tempel baute wie Griechenland' (*Sämtliche Schriften*, ed. C. Grützmacher and S. Claus, Munich, 1968, p. 44). Wackenroder was not, however, an enthusiastic admirer of Gothic architecture: see Heinz Lippuner, *Wackenroder/Tieck und die bildende Kunst*, Zürich, 1965, pp. 91–102.

3. Goethe, *Kunsttheoretische Schriften und Übersetzungen* (Berliner Ausgabe, XIX), Berlin, 1973, pp. 29–38. Commentaries are numerous: see Nikolaus Pevsner, 'Goethe e l'architettura' in *Palladio*, IV, 1951, pp. 174–9.

4. *Génie du Christianisme* (1802), ed. P. Reboul, Paris, 1966, I, p. 399. A remarkably similar passage is in S. T. Coleridge, *Philosophical Lectures*: '... a cathedral like that of York, Milan or Strasbourg with all its many chapels, its pillared stems and leaf-work, as if some sacred grove of Hertha, the mysterious deity of their pagan ancestry, had been awed into stone at the approach of the true divinity and thus dignified by permanence into a symbol of the everlasting gospel' (J. Rykwert, *On Adam's House in Paradise*, New York, 1972, p. 88). The woodland simile was also used by Wordsworth in *The Excursion* (1814), V, lines 148–51.

5. *De l'Allemagne* (1813), ed. S. Balayé, Paris, 1968, II, p. 79, quoting a passage in which Görres used the forest simile: 'On se croirait au milieu d'une forêt dont la mort a pétrifié les branches et les feuilles, de manière qu'elles ne pouvent ni se balancer, ni s'agiter, quand les siècles comme le vent des nuits s'engouffrent sous les voûtes prolongées.'

6. A. W. Schlegel, *A Course of Lectures on Dramatic Art and Literature*, tr. J. Black, London, 1846, pp. 23–7.

7. Ruskin usually indicated that his hostility was towards only *neo*-Greek architecture. There was, however, a tendency to judge ancient Greek buildings by criteria derived from Gothic. Hence the interest aroused by the optical refinements of the Parthenon (to which Ruskin referred with admiration), revealing that it was not composed of 'dead' flat surfaces: see Peter Collins, *Changing Ideals in Modern Architecture*, London, 1965, p. 92.

8. In a letter to the American painter Washington Allston: see James Early, *Romanticism and American Architecture*, New York, 1965, p. 86.

9. *Specimens of the Table Talk of Samuel Taylor Coleridge* (1835), Oxford, 1917, p. 248 and *Coleridge's Miscellaneous Criticism*, ed. T. M. Rayner, Cambridge, Mass., 1936, p. 7.

10. *Klosterfriedhof in Schnee*, formerly Nationalgalerie, Berlin, destroyed 1945: see Börsch-Supan/Jähnig, pp. 351–2.

11. *Salisbury Cathedral from the Bishop's Grounds*, 1823, Victoria and Albert Museum.

12. Louvre. For an interpretation of this picture, see Donat de Chapeaurouge, 'Die "Kathedrale" als modernes Bildthema' in *Jahrbuch der Hamburger Kunstsammlungen*, XVIII, 1973, pp. 162–3.

13. A. W. Schlegel, op. cit., loc. cit.

14. *Notre-Dame de Paris* (1831), ed. M.-F. Guyard, Paris, 1976, pp. 367–8.

15. *Des Rayons et des ombres* (1840): see Georges Poulet, *Etudes sur le temps humain* (1952), Paris, 1976, II, p. 199.

16. Late in life Granet was to draw illustrations to *Les Martyrs* and paint *Eudore dans les catacombes* (1846, Musée Granet, Aix en Provence): see E. Ripert, *François-Marius Granet*, Paris, 1937, pp. 149, 167, 235. Chateaubriand celebrated the virtues of celibacy in *Génie du christianisme*. For Protestant horror at the spectacle of a nun taking the veil, see J. R. Hale, *The Italian Journal of Samuel Rogers*, London, 1956, pp. 104–6.

17. Alexandre Lenoir, *Musée Impérial des monumens français*, Paris, 1810, p. 185. The monument was composed of pieces of medieval sculpture which Lenoir put together over what he believed to be the bones of Abelard and Héloise.

18. A. J. Finberg, pp. 42–3.

19. *Constable's Discourses*, p. 70.

20. Heinrich Heine, *Werke und Briefe*, ed. G. Erler, Berlin, 1962, VI, p. 68.

21. Michael Bringmann, *Studien zur neuromanischen Architektur in Deutschland*, Heidelberg, 1968, though concerned mainly with the late nineteenth century, includes a brief account of the earlier *Rundbogenstil* churches (pp. 17–35).

22. John Shaw, 1839: see B. F. L. Clarke, *Church Builders of the Nineteenth Century*, London, 1938, p. 43.

23. George Gilbert Scott, *A Plea for the Faithful Restoration of our Ancient Churches*, London, 1850, p. 72. Scott argued (p. 76) 'that since the indigenous architecture had fallen into decay and become extinct, we had been wandering for three centuries in mistaken paths, and on now at last discovering our error, we find ourselves in the anomalous position of having no style of architecture of our own ... our best course was, therefore, to retrace our steps, till we should find the point in the old path from which we had deviated, and that this was to be looked for in the architecture which had been the natural production of our religion and race: not at the period immediately preceding its extinction, but at that of the highest development.'

24. *Constable's Discourses*, p. 70. Delacroix was also hostile to the Gothic Revival: see *Delacroix: Journal*, I, p. 348.

25. A. W. N. Pugin, *The True Principles of Pointed or Christian Architecture*, London, 1841, p. 45.

26. *The British Critic*: see B. F. L. Clarke, op. cit., p. 32.

27. A. W. N. Pugin, *Contrasts*, London, 1836, p. 35.

28. See Phoebe Stanton, 'The Sources of Pugin's *Contrasts*' in J. Summerson, ed., *Concerning Architecture: Essays on Architectural Writers and Writing presented to Nikolaus Pevsner*, London, 1968, pp. 120–39; and Nikolaus Pevsner, *Some Architectural Writers of the Nineteenth Century*, Oxford, 1972, pp. 103–22.

29. A. W. N. Pugin, *The True Principles ...*, p. 1.

30. Gothic architects had, of course, been admired (not least in the eighteenth century) for their engineering ability. The 'functional' or rational quality of Gothic had also been praised: see Peter Collins, op. cit., pp. 208-17. I know of no statement of the moral superiority of Gothic to Greek architecture on the basis of truth to materials before that made by Pugin in 1841. But Pugin was a polemicist rather than a theorist, and he may have been doing no more than stealing a weapon from the Grecians' armoury. Viollet le Duc's more closely argued theory of the rationalism of Gothic certainly had greater influence.

31. John Newman, *North East and East Kent* (N. Pevsner, ed., *The Buildings of England*, XXXIX), Harmondsworth, 1969, p. 406.

32. Quoted James Barr, *Anglican Church Architecture*, Oxford, 1846, p. 202.

33. *Contrasts*, 2nd edn, London, 1841, p. 12.

34. Keith Andrews, *The Nazarenes*, Oxford, 1964, p. 25.

35. Pforr's remarks are also curiously akin to passages in Novalis, *Die Christenheit oder Europa*, written in 1799 and submitted to *Athenaeum* but not printed until 1826.

36. Overbeck's father, a Mayor of Lubeck, had befriended Asmus Jakob Carstens, which suggests that he appreciated Neo-classical art. Carstens's independent attitude to the Berlin Academy (see p. 245) may have influenced the young Overbeck. But Overbeck's reluctance

to submit to the teaching of the Academy in (ultra-Catholic) Vienna may well have been inspired by his middle-class status and his Protestantism. His dislike for the sensuality of High Renaissance painting seems to be as much Protestant as Neo-classical.

37. Keith Andrews, op. cit., p. 8. Distrust of colour had been expressed also by Schiller: see Nikolaus Pevsner, *Academies of Art Past and Present* (1940), New York, 1973, p. 147.

38. It is often suggested that Overbeck had always been a Catholic at heart, but his outlook seems to me close to that of members of the Oxford Movement who refused to go over to Rome – more like that of Keble than J. H. Newman, for instance.

39. Artists had previously drawn inspiration from the 'Primitives': see Robert Rosenblum, *Transformations in Late Eighteenth Century Art*, Princeton, 1967, p. 165.

40. Gaspero Martellini in Florence began to paint pictures of the Virgin and Child in a Tuscan early *cinquecento* style in 1820 (see Sandra Pinto, *Collezioni della Galleria d'arte moderna di Palazzo Pitti, Ottocento, parte prima*, Florence, 1972, p. 78). In 1825 Tommaso Minardi, a protégé of Canova, painted for the Noviziato dei Gesuiti, Rome, *San Stanislao morente* in an Umbrian *quattrocento* style. Slightly later in the Veneto, Placido Fabris turned from copying Venetian masters to painting Bellinesque pictures (see *The Connoisseur*, CXLVIII, 1961, p. 195). Among sculptors, Canova evoked the style of Ghiberti in the metopes for the church at Possagno 1820–22. Pietro Tenerani, a pupil of Thorvaldsen, later revived the style of Andrea Bregno. The term *purismo* – originally used in the mid-eighteenth century to describe the aims of writers who sought to purify the Italian language of foreign words – seems first to have been applied to the figurative arts in the late 1830s, generally in a derogatory sense. To reply to critics, Antonio Bianchini published a somewhat defensive manifesto *Del purismo nelle arti*, Rome, 1843, countersigned by Overbeck, Minardi and Tenerani. (The text of this rare pamphlet and other documents relating to the dispute between *puristi* and *anti-puristi* is reprinted in Paola Barocchi, *Testimonianze e polemiche figurative in Italia: l'Ottocento*, Messina and Florence, 1972, pp. 175–228.) In 1845 Giuseppe La Farina wrote: 'lo studio prediletto della maggior parte dei giovani sono Giotto, l'Angelico, il Ghirlandaio, il Perugino ed altri di quei secoli puristici; ma sventuratamente molti d'essi volendo servilmente imitare non produssero che delle caricature' (P. Contrucci et al., *Monumenti del Giardino Puccini*, Pistoia, 1845, p. 100). The *puristi* did not, however, constitute a closely related group of artists; for those associated with this tendency, see E. Lavagnino, *L'Arte moderna*, Turin, 1961, pp. 295–389. For one of the most interesting of the painters, Luigi Mussini, see Carlo Del Bravo, 'Sul seguito toscano di Ingres' in *Colloque Ingres*, Montauban, 1969, pp. 29–38, and Sandra Pinto, op. cit., pp. 80–81, 211.

41. Flandrin does not seem to have known Overbeck's work until he went to Rome in 1833. Of *The Triumph of Religion in the Arts* he wrote in 1833: 'Je trouve cela beau et bien pensé; mais pour le rendre, Overbeck emploie des moyens que ne sont pas à lui. Il se sert tout à fait de l'enveloppe des vieux maîtres ... Il veut se servir de la peinture pour écrire ses idées, plus le moyen sera vrai et correct, mieux elles seront rendues' (Henri Delaborde, *Lettres et pensées d'Hippolyte Flandrin*, Paris, 1865, p. 205).

42. Lord Lindsay, *Sketches of the History of Christian Art* (1849), London, 1885, II, p. 392. Although Sir Thomas Lawrence acquired Overbeck's cartoon for *The Seven Lean Years* in 1819, and Julius Schnorr von Carolsfeld stated in 1825 that English visitors to Rome were eager to buy his drawings (see Keith Andrews, op. cit., p. 69), there seem to be few printed records of the Nazarenes in English before the 1840s. The interest taken in them in the 1840s may have been stimulated by the suggestion that German artists should paint frescoes for the Houses of Parliament.

43. W. Holman Hunt, *Pre-Raphaelitism and the Pre-Raphaelite Brotherhood*, London, 1905, I, p. 107. His references to the Nazarenes were generally hostile – e.g., they 'affected

without sincerity the naïveté of Perugino and the early Flemings' (op. cit., p. 142) – possibly because the Pre-Raphaelites had often been compared with them. In 1850 a writer in the *Athenaeum* called the Pre-Raphaelites 'a body of young painters, untravelled, without experience and below these Germans in intelligence ...'

44. W. Holman Hunt, op. cit., I, p. 118. *The Girlhood of the Virgin* is in the Tate Gallery.

45. *Isabella* is in the Walker Art Gallery, Liverpool.

46. 'The old song of *Chevy-Chase* is the favourite ballad of the common people of England,' Addison wrote (*Spectator*, 70, 21 May 1711). Tales of Robin Hood were equally popular and kept another vision of the Middle Ages alive throughout the seventeenth and eighteenth centuries. In France such medieval romances as *L'Histoire de Pierre de Provence et la belle Maguelonne*, *Les Quatre fils Aymon*, *Huon de Bordeaux* and *Robert le Diable* were printed and reprinted often with their original illustrations from the fifteenth century to the 1820s. Many were included in the *Bibliothèque bleue* printed at Troyes and circulated by pedlars: see Alexandre Assier, *La Bibliothèque Bleue*, Paris, 1874, and Pierre Brochon, *Le Livre de colportage en France depuis le XVIe siècle*, Paris, 1954. The Comtesse d'Auneuil, *Les Chevaliers errans*, Paris, 1709, is an imitation of this type of romantic tale. In Spain, medieval romances held their popularity uninterruptedly throughout the centuries. The sixteenth-century epics of chivalry (by Ariosto, Tasso and Spenser) were probably read only by the more highly educated, but all were reprinted from time to time. It was to justify a well-established taste that Richard Hurd wrote his *Letters on Chivalry and Romance*, London, 1762.

47. The most famous of English eighteenth-century medievalists, Horace Walpole, seems however to have been influenced mainly by romances, fairy-tales and chronicles. His attitude was at first whimsical – in a letter to H. S. Conway of 24 October 1746 he complained that recent poems 'have not half the imagination of romances, and are dull without any agreeable absurdity'. In a letter of 11 August 1748 he had been reading Hall's *Chronicle* to some friends: 'We came to a paragraph, which I must transcribe, for though it means nothing in the world, it is so ridiculously worded in the old English that it made us laugh for three days.' In a revealing letter to the Rev. William Cole, 9 March 1765, he described the origins of *The Castle of Otranto*, mentioned his desire to buy some 'ancient wooden chairs ... all of various patterns, and carved and turned in the most uncouth and whimsical forms', and outlined his plans for a bower in the garden of Strawberry Hill – 'Though I write romances, I cannot tell how to build all that belongs to them. Madame Danois, in the Fairy Tales, used to tapestry them with jonquils ...' Mme Danois was the Comtesse d'Auneuil (see note 46). On 4 May 1781 Walpole told Cole: 'I am a composition of Antony Wood and Madame Danois, and I know not what trumpery writers.' Yet on 12 August 1769 he had described, also to Cole, his plan for a serious history of medieval architecture.

48. The conflict between the Crown and the ancient nobility stimulated research on the history of medieval France. The Comte de Boulainvilliers, *Histoire de l'ancien gouvernement de la France*, Paris, 1727, described how the Frankish nobility, from whom he claimed descent, had originally been responsible for electing kings. This idea was taken up by Montesquieu, *De l'esprit des lois*, 1748. Medieval institutions were extolled by J.-B. de La Curne de Sainte-Palaye, *Mémoires sur l'ancienne chevalerie* (read to the Académie des Inscriptions 1744–6, published 1753). The great collector of medieval objects and drawings of them, François-Roger de Gaignières, who was clearly royalist in his sympathies, inspired Bernard de Montfaucon's illustrated *Monuments de la Monarchie française* (Paris, 1729–30) – though both seem to have been in touch with the Benedictine historians whose interests were, of course, mainly ecclesiastical.

49. The several aspects of the Middle Ages which appealed in mid-eighteenth-century England – genealogy, pageantry, chivalry, 'good old days' – are all recorded in a stanza of a poem on the 'ruined' tower built to Sanderson Miller's design in 1747:

'When Henry stemmed Iernes' stormy flood
And bound to Britain's yoke her savage brood,
When by true courage and false zeal impelled
Richard encamped on Salem's palmy field,
On Towers like these Earl, Baron, Vavasour,
Hung high their banners floating in the air.
Free, hardy, proud they braved their Feudal Lord
And tried their rights by ordeal of the sword.
Now the full board with Xmas plenty crowned,
Now ravaged and oppressed the country round.
Yet Freedom's cause once raised the civil broil
And Magna Carta closed the glorious toil.'

L. Dickins and M. Stanton, *An Eighteenth Century Correspondence*. London, 1910, p. 273.

50. John Rutter, *Delineations of Fonthill and its Abbey*, London, 1823, p. 28. This book was written with the approval and help of Beckford.

51. The Gotisches Haus at Wörlitz, begun in 1773, appears to be the earliest and is set in the first large-scale English-style park in Germany. It was built for the Anglophile Prince (later Duke) Leopold Friedrich Franz von Anhalt-Dessau, who filled it with a collection of medieval and sixteenth-century objects including Rogier van der Weyden's portrait of a lady now in the National Gallery of Art, Washington. For the most recent account, see Marie Luise Harksen, *Führer durch das Museum Gotisches Haus in Wörlitz*, Wörlitz, 1975. In France the Jardin de Betz, laid out in the English style by the Duc d'Harcourt from 1780 for the Princesse de Monaco, included an extraordinary collection of neo-Gothic ruins, towers, a *colonne de Tancrède*, statues, tombs and a large *donjon*, several of which were adorned with inscriptions composed by the medievalist historian La Curne de Sainte-Palaye. The park was fully described in a poem published in 1792 by the Abbé Cérutti (better known as a propagandist for the Third Estate at the outbreak of the Revolution): see René Lanson, *Le goût du Moyen Age en France au XVIIIe siècle*, Paris, 1926, p. 40 and pl. xix.

52. Vittorio Barzoni, *Descrizioni*, Milan, 1815, pp. 160–61. Barzoni states that his account of Laxenburg was written in 1803.

53. H. Jacoubet, *Le comte de Tressan et les origines du genre troubadour*, Paris, 1923, p. 130.

54. Listed in the catalogue of the Salon of 1812 but not finished in time to be shown. It was illustrated and described in C. P. Landon, *Salon de 1814* (Annales du Musée), Paris, 1814, 11. It is still in the sacristy of Saint-Denis, see J. Bottineau, 'Le décor de tableaux à la sacristie de l'ancienne abbatiale de Saint-Denis' in *Bulletin de la Société de l'histoire de l'art français*, 1973, pp. 254–81. The important part played in the development of paintings of historical subjects in the nineteenth century by this and similar works commissioned under Napoleon is stressed by Francis Haskell, 'The Manufacture of the Past in Nineteenth Century Painting' in *Past & Present* 53, 1971, pp. 109–19.

55. For a valuable account of such castles, see Heinz Biehn, *Residenzen der Romantik*, Munich, 1970.

56. L. Vitet, *Rapport à M. le Ministre de l'Intérieur sur les monumens, les bibliothèques, les archives et les musées ...*, Paris, 1831, p. 12. For an account of Ludovic Vitet, see introduction to Maurice Parturier, *Lettres de Mérimée à Ludovic Vitet*, Paris, 1934. Vitet was appointed Inspector-General of Historical Monuments immediately after the July Revolution.

57. E. Quinet, *Considérations philosophiques sur l'art*, Strasbourg, 1839, p. 9.

58. Alexandre de Laborde, *Les monumens de la France classés chronologiquement*, Paris, 1816, I, p. 38, attributed the early development of Gothic to the Crusaders, but not as a result of the influence of Islamic architecture: 'Éclairés par les connaissances de tout genre qu'il recurent en Italie, à Constantinople, et dans toutes les villes de l'orient, les croisés revinrent avec un esprit général de réforme et un vif desir d'amélioration. Tout allors s'épura à-la-fois; et une sorte de goût plus raffiné s'introduisait dans les idées comme dans les usages, un changement heureux s'opéra sans effort dans tout ce qui tient aux agréments de l'ordre social. La langue s'épura, les préjugés s'adoucirent, le fanatisme même se modéra. On sent que les arts ne durent point rester en arrière.' This notion appears to have been further developed in the late 1820s (though Paul Frankl, op. cit., pp. 523–4 dates it to the 1840s) by Vitet and others including Victor Hugo: 'Mais les croisades arrivent. C'est un grand mouvement populaire; et tout grand mouvement populaire, quels qu'en soient la cause et le but, dégage toujours de son dernier précipité l'esprit de liberté. Des nouveautés vont se faire jour. Voici que s'ouvre la période orageuse des Jacqueries, des Pragueries, et des Ligues. L'autorité s'ébranle, l'unité se bifurque. La féodalité demande à partager avec la théocratie, en attendant le peuple qui surviendra inévitablement et qui se fera, comme toujours, la part du lion. *Quia nominor leo*. La seigneurie perce donc sous le sacerdoce, la commune sous la seigneurie. La face de l'Europe est changée. Eh bien! la face de l'architecture est changée aussi (*Notre Dame de Paris*, edn cit., p. 213). These ideas were later taken up by Viollet le Duc. In Italy, Pietro Estense Selvatico, *Scritti d'arte*, Florence, 1859, pp. 314–5, remarked: 'Uscita dal monastero, l'architettura diventa uno stato come tutti le altre arti ... Emancipata l'arte dai vincoli ieratici e dalle leggi fisse che nel chiostro la reggevano, aggiunge la emulazione allo studio: le tradizioni, non inceppanti più l'intelletto, si fanno stimolo alla immaginazione, sicchè essa progredisce a rapidità prodigiosa, manifestandosi energica e libera nell' individuo, anzichè nella casta ...' Walter Pater, in his essay on Notre Dame d'Amiens of 1894 (*Miscellaneous Studies*, London, 1899, pp. 91–3), assumed that the Gothic style emerged when 'towns in eastern and Northern France rose against the feudal establishment, and developed severally the local and municipal life of the commune'. He contrasted the 'new, revolutionary Gothic manner' with the 'derivative and traditional, Roman or Romanesque, style, the imperial style, of the great monastic churches'.

59. Charles Barry said he 'hoped to raise up a school of carvers guided, but not servilely confined, by the examples of Gothic antiquity': see Kenneth Clark, *The Gothic Revival* (1928), London, 1950, p. 160.

60. Robert Blake, *Disraeli* (1966), London, 1967, p. 171.

61. Benjamin Disraeli, *Endymion* (1881), London, 1927 (Bradenham edn), p. 259. Disraeli had not attended the tournament and his account seems to derive from memories of what he heard at the time.

62. *Génie du Christianisme*, edn cit., II, p. 177. Tournaments provided attractive subjects for artists at this period, e.g., Pierre Révoil (a notable collector of medieval objects and the founder of the Lyon school), Musée des Beaux Arts, Lyon; and Carl Philipp Fohr (protégé of an historian of the Middle Ages, Philipp Dieffenbach): see *Carl Philipp Fohr 1795–1818*, exh. cat., Kurpfälzische Museum, Heidelberg, 1968, no. 23.

63. For English furnishings in the Gothic taste, see Duncan Simpson, *Gothick*, exh. cat., Royal Pavilion, Brighton, 1975; for American, Katherine S. Howe and David B. Warren,

The Gothic Revival Style in America, 1830–1870, exh. cat., Museum of Fine Arts, Houston, 1976.

64. Francis Goodwin, *Domestic Architecture* (1835), London, 1850, I, p. 12.

65. A. W. N. Pugin, *An Apology* ..., p. 2.

66. Théophile Gautier, *Histoire du romantisme*, Paris, 1874, p. 58. Troubadour-style furnishings (and pictures) had previously been attacked by Charles Forbes René de Montalembert, article of 1837 in his *Du vandalisme et du Catholicisme dans l'art*, Paris, 1839, p. 181; also by Viollet le Duc, *Dictionnaire raisonné du mobilier français*, Paris 1858, p. 425.

67. The painting (now lost) was illustrated in C. P. Landon, *Annales du Musée*, IV, Paris, 1803, p. 14. At least two engravings were published, and one may have influenced Franz Pforr's drawing for an *Allegory of Friendship* (repr. Keith Andrews, op. cit., pl. 19a). For an account of the Empire phase of the troubadour style, see Suzanne Lodge, 'Lenoir, Josephine and the Troubadour Style' in *Neoclassicismo: Atti del convegno internazionale promosso dal Comité International d'Histoire de l'art*, Genoa, 1973, pp. 64–76.

68. Keith Andrews, op. cit., p. 7 and, for the Casino Massimo frescoes, pp. 46–54. See also *Die Nazarener*, exh. cat., Städelschen Kunstinstitut, Frankfurt am Main, 1977, B26.

69. Bayerische Staatsgemäldesammlung, Munich; Delacroix Exhibition, no. 481.

70. Boyer d'Agen, *Ingres d'après une correspondance inédite*, Paris, 1909, p. 485. As Ingres goes on to say, 'Il faut avouer que l'amour de la religion, qui animait ces vieux temps guerriers, donnait aux tableaux un air mystique, simple et grand ...', it seems likely that the passage was written during his first period in Rome and was influenced by the Nazarenes. His further remarks suggest that painting medieval subjects may have played a more important part in the development of his style than is generally allowed: 'J'en conclus qu'il me faut prendre cette route comme la bonne et me contenter d'explorer les Grecs, sans lesquels il n'y a pas de vrai salut, de les amalgamer pour ainsi dire à ce nouveau genre. C'est comme cela que je peux devenir un novateur spirituel, adroit, et donner à mes ouvrages ce beau caractère inconnu jusqu' ici et qui n'existe que dans les ouvrages de Raphaël. J'ai la conviction que, si Raphaël avait eu des tableaux grecs à peindre, ils nous intéressait beaucoup moins: j'ose dire qu'avec l'idée toute parfaite que nous avons des Grecs par leurs monuments, il aurait pu nous rendre difficiles sur les résultats. Donc, peignons des tableaux français, des Duguescelin, des Bayard, et tant d'autres.'

71. Wadsworth Atheneum, Hartford, Conn.: see Robert Rosenblum, *Jean-Auguste-Dominique Ingres*, London, 1967, pp. 116–19; *Ingres*, exh. cat., Petit Palais, Paris, 1968, no. 121.

72. Delacroix Exhibition, no. 60.

73. *L'Assassinat de l'éveque de Liège* (1829) is in the Louvre, *L'Enlèvement de Rebecca* (1846) Metropolitan Museum, New York; Delacroix Exhibition, nos. 136, 352. The latter subject was also painted by Léon Cogniet, 1828, Wallace Collection, London.

74. Musée des Beaux Arts, Nancy; Delacroix Exhibition, no. 196.

75. Louvre; Delacroix Exhibition, no. 122. As the July Revolution intervened between the commissioning and the completion of the picture the Duchesse de Berry refused to pay for it.

76. Musée de Versailles; Delacroix Exhibition, no. 229. There is no equivalent to the patriotically didactic Galerie des Batailles in any other country. But pictures of medieval battles painted elsewhere sometimes had a nationalistic programme. Amos Cassoli, for example, won a competition for a patriotic painting held by the short-lived revolutionary government in Florence in 1859 with *The Battle of Legnano* (Galleria d'Arte Moderna, Florence).

77. Jean Gigoux, *Causeries sur les artistes de mon temps*, Paris, 1885, pp. 71–2.

1. For Scott's attitude to the Gothic novel, see his article in *Quarterly Review* (1810), in *Miscellaneous Prose Works*, Edinburgh, 1833, XVIII, p. 162. Ludwig Tieck included in *Peter Lebrecht* (1795) an amusing parody of the beginning of a Gothic novel with a list of its main ingredients – though he had begun his own career by writing such fiction: see J. Trainer, *Ludwig Tieck: from Gothic to Romantic*, The Hague, 1964, p. 41.

2. See Morse Peckham, *Romanticism and Behavior*, Columbia, S. Carolina, 1976, p. 53.

3. Friedrich Meinecke, *Historism* (1959), tr. J. E. Anderson, London, 1972, p. 184.

4. Review of Sir James Mackintosh's *History of the Revolution in England* in *Edinburgh Review*, July, 1835, Lord Macaulay, *Essays and Lays of Ancient Rome*, London, 1909, pp. 318, 320.

5. *Bataille de Jemappes*, painted for the Duke of Orleans (Louis-Philippe), is now in the National Gallery, London, *Barrière de Clichy*, in the Louvre. *Le trompette blessé* and *Le chien du régiment*, bought by the Duc de Berry in 1819, are both in the Wallace Collection, London.

6. Musée de Bordeaux, sketch Smith College Museum of Art, Northampton, Mass.; Delacroix Exhibition, nos. 142, 143. The work is strongly reminiscent of *L'Assassinat de l'évêque de Liège*, 1829 (Louvre), Delacroix Exhibition, no. 136.

7. P.-N. Bergeret, *Lettres d'un artiste sur l'état des arts*, Paris, 1848, p. 132.

8. *Heine in Art and Letters*, tr. E. A. Sharp, London, 1895, p. 74. A writer in *L'Artiste*, III, 1831, p. 28, suggested that Delaroche had not been awarded the Légion d'Honneur because of the implications of Cromwell. The picture is now in the Musée des Beaux Arts, Nîmes; smaller versions are in the Kunsthalle, Hamburg, and Hermitage Museum, Leningrad. For very interesting comments on the work, see Francis Haskell, 'The Manufacture of the Past in Nineteenth Century Painting' in *Past & Present* 53, 1971, pp. 109–19.

9. *Le Globe*, 2 August 1830, p. 646. For French reactions to the 1688 Revolution in the previous century, see Jean-Marie Goulemot, *Discours, histoire, et révolutions*, Paris, 1975.

10. Georg Lukács, *The Historical Novel*, tr. H. and S. Mitchell (1962), Harmondsworth, 1969, p. 84.

11. *L'Artiste*, I, 1831, p. 186.

12. A. W. Raitt, *Prosper Mérimée*, London, 1970, p. 87.

13. Prosper Mérimée, *Romans et Nouvelles*, ed. M. Parturier, Paris, 1967, I, p. 11.

14. When Vitet reissued *Les Barricades* under a new title, *La Ligue, scènes historiques*, he inserted in the preface, dated 20 May 1830, a defence of the freedom of the press and also the statement that the Ligue was 'au fond, un mouvement de liberté'.

15. *L'Artiste*, I, 1831, p. 209.

16. *L'Artiste*, V, 1833, p. 119.

17. John Hardy, 'The Building and Decoration of Apsley House' in *Apollo*, XCVII, 1973, pp. 170–79.

18. *La Cousine Bette* in *La Comédie Humaine*, ed. M. Bouteron, Paris, 1950, VI, p. 234. For a general account of early nineteenth-century French taste in eighteenth-century furniture and paintings, see O. Simches, *Le Romantisme et le goût esthétique du XVIIIe siècle*, Paris, 1964; and Carol Duncan, *The Pursuit of Pleasure: The Rococo Revival in French Romantic Art*, New York, 1976.

19. The Dancing Satyr, the 'Narcissus' and the paintings in the Villa of the Mysteries might well have qualified but were not unearthed until later.

20. The 'Aldobrandini Marriage', which had been found in Rome in 1606, held its place as the most notable example of Antique painting until the end of the eighteenth century

– 'the best relique of those remote ages that has yet been found', as Sir Joshua Reynolds called it in 1772 (*Discourses on Art*, ed. R. R. Wark, San Marino, California, 1959, p. 87).

21. This type of painting neatly illustrated a passage in which Vitruvius (*De architectura*, VII, 5) had condemned the fashionable decorations of his time.

22. Early examples of the type of wall-painting with a single figure on a dark background are in the Villa Hamilton at Wörlitz, 1795 (Adolph Gartmann, *Der Wörlitzer Park*, Berlin, 1913); and a room from Palais Geymüller-Caprara, now in the Historische Museum der Stadt Wien, Vienna (Peter Pötschner. 'Das Pompejanische Zimmer der Herr Geymüller ...' in *Alte und moderne Kunst* 54–5, 1962, pp. 21–8). In France, a writer in *Journal des artistes*, 1831, remarked that paintings in this style were in 'un goût de decoration nouveau pour nous' (Jon Whiteley, *The Revival in Painting of Themes inspired by Antiquity in Mid-Nineteenth Century France*, Ph.D. thesis, Oxford, 1972). For the first imitations of the Pompeiian type of architectural painting, see Peter Werner, *Pompeji und der Wanddekoration der Goethezeit*, Munich, 1970.

23. François Mazois, *Les ruines de Pompéi*, Paris, 1812–38. In the preface to the first volume (p. 4) he stressed the importance of Pompeii as a complete city lacking only its inhabitants: 'Ici c'est un temple avec toutes ses dépendances, là un portique, plus loin des théâtres, puis le prétoir, et des temples encore; de longues rues bien pavées, ornées de trottoirs et de fontaines, présentent, de chaque côté des bâtiments consacres au public, des habitations particulières, des boutiques, et des palais ...'

24. Now in the Philadelphia Museum of Art. The painting was identified as that shown in the Salon of 1827 by Prof. Francis Haskell and Dr Jon Whiteley (see *Paintings and Sculptures 1770–1830*, exh. cat., Heim Gallery, London, September 1972, no. 21). The discovery of the skeletons was recorded by Mazois, op. cit., pp. 31–2: 'Trois de ces squelettes, comme le prouvent les ornements qu'ils conservoient encore, appartenoient à des femmes: désespérant de pouvoir échapper à la pluie brûlante, épuisées sans doute par la fatigue et la terreur, elles s'étoient assises contre un pilier d'un portique, et elles y rendirent le dernier soupir en s'embrassant étroitement: les frêles ossements d'un enfant nouveau né étoient auprès des leurs, et probablement ces infortunées ne formoient qu'une même famille.'

25. Christa Karoli, *Ideal und Krise, enthusiastichen Künstlertums in der deutschen Romantik*, Bonn, 1968, p. 7.

26. Montani, in *Antologia*, XIV, 1824: see G. A. Borgese, *Storia della critica romantica in Italia*, Naples, 1905, p. 93.

27. Essay on Prud'hon (1846) in E. Delacroix, *Œuvres littéraires*, Paris, 1923, II, p. 143.

28. T. Silvestre, *Les Artistes français* (1855–6), Paris, 1878, p. 95.

29. *Delacroix: Journal*, III, p. 310.

30. ibid., pp. 57–8.

31. National Gallery, London, signed and dated 1859.

6. THE CAUSE OF LIBERTY (*pages 217–44*)

1. A. Jal, *Esquisses, croquis, pochades ou Tout ce qu'on voudra sur le Salon de 1827*, Paris, 1828, pp. iii–iv. For the use of political terminology in art criticism, especially in nineteenth-century France, see Francis Haskell, 'Art and the Language of Politics' in *Journal of European Studies*, IV, 1974, pp. 215–32.

2. A. Malraux, *Saturn: An Essay on Goya*, London, 1957, p. 110.

3. The picture was to suffer further transformations: in 1842 the portrait of Ferdinand VII was painted over with the inscription, *El Libro de la Constitución*: shortly afterwards an attempt was made to recover Goya's original portrait of Joseph, but little remained and the words DOS DE MAYO were inscribed in its place.

4. Isaiah Berlin, *Four Essays on Liberty*, Oxford, 1969, p. ix. For the distinction between negative and positive liberty, *passim*.

5. *Ansichten vom Niederrhein* (1791), in *Forsters Werke*, Berlin and Weimar, 1968, II, p. 99.

6. Runge, I, p. 6.

7. *Die Kranzwinderin* in Staatliche Museen Preussischer Kulturbesitz, Nationalgalerie, Berlin.

8. Börsch-Supan/Jähnig, no. 207.

9. S. Hinz, p. 25. This is the only explicitly political statement in Friedrich's writings.

10. On the revolutionary significance of *altdeutsche Tracht*, see Peter Märker, 'Caspar David Friedrich zur Zeit des Restauration' in B. Hinz et al., *Bürgerliche Revolution und Romantik*, Giessen, 1976, pp. 43–72.

11. W. D. Robson-Scott, *The Literary Background of the Gothic Revival in Germany*, Oxford, 1965, p. 288.

12. ibid., p. 293.

13. Repr. Gertrud Heider, *Carl Blechen*, Leipzig, 1970, p. 44. The picture, formerly in the Nationalgalerie, Berlin, was destroyed in the war.

14. *Romanticismo Storico*, exh. cat., Palazzo Pitti, Florence, 1973–4, no. 11. For a general account of d'Azeglio, see Ronald Marshall, *Massimo d'Azeglio An Artist in Politics*, Oxford, 1966; for his work as a painter, *Massimo d'Azeglio*, exh. cat., Galleria Civica d'Arte Moderna, Turin, 1966.

15. Verdi was anticipated by A. Buzzi, whose *La Lega Lombarda* was first performed in Paris in 1846: see F. Nicolodi in *Romanticismo Storico*, pp. 241–2.

16. Hayez painted three versions of *The Sicilian Vespers* and also three versions of the *Refugees of Parga*: see S. Coradeschi, *L'Opera completa di Hayez*, Milan, 1971, nos. 49, 151. His source for the latter was a poem by the Milanese liberal Giovanni Berchet. The picture was extolled by Giuseppe Mazzini: see *Romanticismo Storico*, no. 2.

17. *Marco Botzari uccide un Turco* by Michele Bisi (Pinacoteca Tosio Martinengo, Brescia); *Un Greco con pistola alla mano* by Cesare Poggi (exh. Accademia delle Belle Arti, Milan, 1830); a curious allegory *Costantino Ipsilanti ed Amasia* (exh. Milan 1834) and a painting of the oath of Byron at the tomb of Botzaris (Museo Civico, Treviso) by Lodovico Lipparini. G. Mosconi's comments on *L'Uscita dei Greci da Missolungi* reveals how Risorgimentist interpretations might be put on pictures of Greek subjects – 'tutte quelle altre forti passioni di cui è capace un popolo che per difendere la libertà della patria non teme di far crollare le mure delle proprie città e sacrificare gli averi e le vite per abbattere l'empia tirannide de' suoi oppressori ...' (*Ricoglitore Italiano e straniero*, II, 1834, p. 326.)

18. In Samuel Johnson's modern Greek tragedy *Irene*: see Terence Spencer, *Fair Greece Sad Relic*, London, 1954, p. 253.

19. *Journal de Delécluze 1824–1828*, ed. R. Baschet, Paris, 1948, p. 345. There were some exceptions among the legitimists: Ludwig I encouraged Munich university students who began to form a German legion to fight in Greece, but he was sharply reprimanded by Metternich: see Wolf Seidl, *Bayern in Griechenland*, Munich, 1965, p. 38.

20. Jack Lindsay, *Turner* (1966), London, 1973, p. 184, suggests that Turner referred to the national restoration of Greece in two paintings he exhibited in 1816, *The Temple of Panellius Restored* and *View of the Temple of Jupiter Panellius with the Greek national dance of the Romaika*. C. L. Eastlake painted *Lord Byron's Dream*, 1827 (Tate Gallery). In 1825 Thomas Barker depicted *The Massacres of Chios* on a wall of his house in Bath (I am indebted to Francis Haskell for this information).

21. A. Jal, *L'Artiste et le philosophe, entretiens critiques sur le salon de 1824*, Paris, 1824, p. 13.

22. Delacroix's painting is in the Oskar Reinhart Collection, Römerholz, Winterthur. Other paintings of modern Greek subjects included *Marc Botzaris rentre à Missolonghi* by Eugène Devéria (Salon of 1827); *Sujet grec moderne: Après le massacre de Samothrace* by Auguste Vinchon (Salon of 1827, now Louvre); *Greek Pirates Attacking a Turkish Vessel* by Eugène Isabey (1827, Cleveland Museum of Art); *Grec mourant* and *Un officier grec blessé sous les murs de Missolongi* by C. Bonnefond (see E.-C. Martin-Daussigny, *Éloge de C. Bonnefond*, Lyon, 1861, pp. 5, 17); *Byron à Missolonghi* and *Mort de Lord Byron* by J.-D. Odevaere (Rijksmuseum, Amsterdam, and Musée des Beaux Arts, Bruges); *Prise de Missolonghi* by P.-R. Vigneron (Musée, Bagnères-de-Bigorre); *L'amiral Canaris au tombeau de Thémistocle* by C.-E. Leprince (1830); *Jeune Grec* by Léopold Robert (1830; see C. Clément, *Léopold Robert*, Paris, 1875, p. 308). Sculptures on similar themes included *Jeune Grec pleurant sur le tombeau de Lord Byron* by E. Chaponnière (1827); *Un jeune Grec moderne mourant sur les ruines de l'ancienne Grèce* by Antoine Etex (1827; see A. Etex, *Souvenirs d'un artiste*, Paris, 1877, p. 35); and a statue by David d'Angers, see below. In 1831 a panorama of the Battle of Navarino by Langlois was shown in Paris. In 1827 the wallpaper manufacturer Zuber issued a set of panoramic papers entitled: *Les vues de la Grèce moderne ou le Combat des Grecs* (see *Trois siècles de papiers peints*, exh. cat., Musée des Arts Décoratifs, Paris, 1967, no. 244).

23. 'Pindar et l'art grec' (1860) in *Études sur l'histoire de l'art*, Paris, 1864, pp. 13–19; and see *Delacroix: Journal*, III, p. 260.

24. See Hans Wolf Jäger, *Politische Metaphorik im Jakobinismus und im Vormärz*, Stuttgart, 1971, pp. 34–51, 86–91. It is possible that the vogue for English painting in Restoration France was connected with the notion of England as a land of political liberty; if so, the 'natural' landscape in the English style may have had a significance doubly underlined. Classical landscapes, on the other hand, seem to have been associated not only with the Académie but also with the Restoration authorities who instituted a prize for such pictures: see René-Paul Huet, *Paul Huet (1803–69) d'après ses notes, sa correspondance, ses contemporains*, Paris, 1911, p. 91. A reviewer of the first Salon of the July Monarchy wrote in *L'Artiste*, II, 1831, p. 1: 'Une révolution s'est opéré dans la peinture de paysage comme dans les autres branches de l'art. Ces paysages de nature de convention, ces respectables paysages bien balayés, bien épousseté, sans ronces et sans épines, à lignes bien composées, bien guindées, bien cadencées, ont disparus à peu près du Salon. C'est la nature, la nature telle quelle est, que le paysagiste s'essaie à rendre aujourd'hui, et chaque œuvre, au lieu d'être jetée dans un moule toujours analogue, marqué de la contrefaçon du cachet de Poussin, porte l'emprunte individuelle du talent du peintre ...'

25. Corot was notoriously apolitical and in 1848, when the popular agitations against the King and Ministry were mentioned to him, remarked, 'Alors décidément on n'est pas tout à fait content d'eux?' (P. Courthion, *Corot raconté par lui-même et par ses amis*, Geneva, 1946, p. 130).

26. Now in the Musée, Valence; repr. P. Grate, op. cit., p. 83. This large work, of about the same size as Constable's 'six-foot canvases', has a sunset sky painted in thick impasto which seems to owe a debt to Turner, probably transmitted by Bonington whom Huet knew personally. But Gustave Planche remarked that Huet's view of Rouen 'peut lutter avec les Turner' while the *Old Abbey* could be compared with the works of 'notre Claude Lorraine' (*Revue des Deux Mondes*, 2nd series, I, 1831, p. 494). The lines by Victor Hugo printed in the *livret* are from 'Rêves', dated June 1828 (*Odes et ballades*, V, ode 25):

'Trouvez-moi, trouvez-moi
Quelque asile sauvage,
Quelque abri d'autrefois.

Trouvez-le moi bien sombre,
Bien calme, bien dormant,
Couvert d'arbres sans nombre,
Dans le silence de l'ombre,
Caché profondément.'

27. For Daumier's description of Huet and Louis Cabat (another painter of natural landscapes influenced by the English school) as patriotic, i.e. Republican, painters, see Catalogue of Illustrations, no. 157. Paul Huet's political affiliations are described by his son René-Paul Huet, op. cit., p. 34. After 1832 he became reconciled to the Orléanist régime and in 1848 enlisted as a volunteer to fight against the insurrection, but Louis Napoleon's coup d'état revived his Republicanism to which he remained faithful for his remaining years. In a letter of 2 September 1868 defending the art of landscape painting, he wrote: 'Vers la fin de la Restauration, la jeunesse semblait sortir d'un long épuisement; entraînée par un irrésistible élan de liberté, elle courait à toutes les sources de la vie, vers le beau et vers le bien. Il y eut comme un tourbillon lumineux, la colonne de feu de l'intelligence. Philosophie, histoire, politique, on voulait tout embrasser, tout envahir. L'art ne fut pas oublié, ce fut sur ce flot que fut porté le pauvre paysage; la poésie toute élégiaque, caractère essentiel de ce temps, lui tendait la main' (E. Chesneau, op. cit., pp. 53–4). It is perhaps significant that in the 1850s he returned to a subject projected in the 1820s, *L'inondation de Saint-Cloud* (Louvre), especially in view of Jules Michelet's association of this work with Géricault's *Raft of the 'Medusa'* (see René-Paul Huet, op. cit., p. 490).

28. This famous remark, usually quoted out of context, follows the description of a garden in autumn dated 31 October 1852: 'Un paysage quelconque est un état de l'âme, et qui lit dans tous deux est émerveillé de retrouver la similitude dans chaque détail' (Henri-Frédéric Amiel, *Fragments d'un journal intime*, ed. B. Bouvier, Geneva and Paris, 1922, I, p. 86).

29. Ximénès Doudan, *Des révolutions du goût*, ed. H. Moncel, Paris, 1924, p. xxviii.

30. Cemetery of Montmartre, Paris: see Linda Nochlin, *Realism*, Harmondsworth, 1971, p. 65.

31. H. Jouin, *David d'Angers et ses relations littéraires*, Paris, 1890, p. 155.

32. The plaster is in the Musée des Beaux Arts, Angers. The marble which David gave to the Greek government had been mutilated before 1853 when he visited Greece. It was later restored in France.

33. The statue of Bara (plaster, Musée des Beaux Arts, Angers) is based on J.-L. David's unfinished painting, Musée Calvet, Avignon. The pediment of the Panthéon was commissioned from David in 1830 by Guizot, then Minister of the Interior, and the sketch model completed 1832. As some figures represented on it had fallen from official favour (e.g. La Fayette), he was asked to substitute others in 1834 but refused: see Henri Jouin, *David d'Angers, sa vie, son œuvre*, Paris, 1878, I, p. 335.

34. Letter of 1854: see *David d'Angers*, exh. cat., Hôtel de la Monnaie, Paris, 1966, p. 26. The remark was made to justify his early monument to the Vendéan leader the Marquis de Bonchamp. David was careful to represent Napoleon as 'General Bonaparte', not as Emperor; he refused to model a bust of Talleyrand and to execute a monument to Joachim Murat because, he said, 'il m'est impossible d'oublier que cet homme a tourné ses armes contre la patrie' (Henri Jouin, op. cit., 1878, I, pp. 386–7).

35. See *John Hamilton Mortimer ARA 1740–1779*, exh. cat, Towner Art Gallery, Eastbourne, and Iveagh Bequest, Kenwood, 1968.

36. Richard Garnett, introduction to *Maid Marian*, London, 1891, p. 7; in the event, comedy prevailed over satire in this tale. In *Ivanhoe*, Scott represented Robin Hood as an

opponent of 'the tyrannical exercise of the forest rights and other oppressive laws by which so many English yeomen were driven into a state of rebellion' (vol. II, ch. xviii). Similar attitudes were ascribed to Salvator Rosa's brigands by Lady Morgan in her very popular *Life and Times of Salvator Rosa* (London, 1824, I, pp. 108–18), and, although she admitted that his early biographers had barely alluded to his life among them, provided a very picturesque account of it none the less.

37. e.g., Camille Roqueplan's *Mort de l'espion Morris*, Salon of 1827, now Musée Wicar, Lille.

38. Translated into English in 1792, it may have influenced Wordsworth's *The Borderers* written in 1795. Later it provided the plot for Verdi's opera *I Masnadieri*, 1847.

39. C. Clément, *Léopold Robert*, Paris, 1875, p. 156.

40. ibid., 148. For Delacroix on Schnetz's *Femme de Brigand*, 1824, see his *Journal*, I, p. 50. Stendhal, *Salon de 1824*, praised this picture and Léopold Robert's *Mort du Brigand* (*Mélanges d'art et de littérature*, Paris, 1927, p. 171).

41. See the prose-poem by E.-B. de Bourdonnel in *L'Artiste*, II, 1831, p. 172. After describing the life of a Neapolitan fisherman, Bourdonnel continues: 'Et nous! quelle vie est la nôtre? Une activité dévorante au sein d'une société usée, des plaisirs factices, des désappointmens sans nombre, point de repos, une existence toujours inquiète et pourtant décolorée ...' The words curiously anticipate Matthew Arnold's 'Scholar Gipsy'.

42. Ascribed to Philothée O'Neddy (alias Théophile Dondey) by T. Gautier, *Histoire du Romantisme*, Paris, 1874, p. 101.

43. Hector Berlioz, *Mémoires* (1865), tr. David Cairns, London, 1970, p. 209.

44. ibid., p. 157.

7. ARTIST'S LIFE (*pages 245–75*)

1. For myths about artists from Antiquity onwards, see Ernst Kris and Otto Kurz, *Die Legende vom Künstler*, Vienna, 1934. For the idea of the artist before the Romantics, see Rudolf and Margaret Wittkower, *Born under Saturn*, London, 1963. For the late eighteenth-century development of the idea of the 'Bohemian', see George Levitine, 'The Eighteenth Century Rediscovery of Alexis Grimou and the Emergence of the Proto-Bohemian Image of the French Artist' in *Eighteenth Century Studies*, II, 1968–9, pp. 58–76.

2. Albrecht-Friedrich Heine, *Asmus Jakob Carstens*, Strasbourg, 1928, p. 112; see also Nikolaus Pevsner, *Academies of Art Past and Present* (1940), New York, 1973, p. 197.

3. Keynes, p. 600.

4. Samuel Johnson, *A Dictionary of the English Language*, 1755, *s.v.* Artist.

5. *Ideen* (1800); F. Schlegel, *Kritische Schriften*, p. 93.

6. Hector Berlioz, op. cit., p. 56. It has often been remarked that the early career of Berlioz as described in his memoirs has an uncanny similarity with that of the fictitious musician Joseph Berglinger in W. H. Wackenroder, *Herzensergiessungen eines Kunstliebender Klosterbruders*, Berlin, 1797.

7. This self-confidence was also in part a legacy of Neo-classical theory, which had elevated the artist above the craftsman.

8. A. W. Thayer, *Life of Beethoven*, rev. and ed. Elliot Forbes, Princeton, 1964, p. 1046. The remark was made to Hummel 1826–7, with reference to the popularity of Italian operas in Vienna.

9. A. W. Thayer, op. cit., p. 405. A few years earlier, in a letter to his brother Carl (ibid., p. 305), Beethoven expressed his sense of mission after referring to an accident caused by his deafness: 'Such incidents drove me almost to despair, a little more of that and I would have ended my life – it was only *my art* that held me back. Ah, it seemed impossible to

leave the world until I had brought forth all that I felt was within me. So I endured this wretched existence.'

10. William Dunlap, *Address to the Students of the National Academy of Design*, New York, 1831: 'Patronage! degrading word! Every artist who has the feelings of a man, or more especially of a republican man, will spurn from him the offer of patronage as debasing to himself, to his art and to his country ... If he truly loves his art, his pecuniary wants will be few, and the wise and virtuous will be happy to adminster to those wants, in fair exchange of their products for his, as equals, giving benefit for benefit.'

11. Musée Condé, Chantilly, see G. Wildenstein, *Ingres* (1954), London, 1956, no. 17.

12. National Portrait Gallery, London.

13. *Delacroix: Journal*, I, p. 391.

14. J. B. C. Grundy, *Tieck and Runge*, Strassburg, 1930, pp. 50–52.

15. Letter to Turpin de Crissé, *Nouvelles Archives de l'art français*, XVI, 1900, p. 196.

16. Alfred Einstein, *Music in the Romantic Era*, London, 1947, p. 144.

17. *Delacroix: Journal*, I, p. 366. He used the quotation from Michelangelo as the epigraph for his essay on him in 1830.

18. Heinrich Heine, *Religion and Philosophy in Germany* (1834), tr. J. Snodgrass, Boston, 1959, p. 99.

19. Werner Hofmann, *Art in the Nineteenth Century*, London, 1961, p. 237.

20. E. Delacroix, *Œuvres littéraires*, Paris, 1923, II, p. 52.

21. I am much indebted to Francis Haskell, 'The Old Masters in Nineteenth Century French Painting' in the *Art Quarterly*, XXXIV, 1971, pp. 55–85. For Italian paintings of similar subjects, see Sandra Pinto, *Romanticismo Storico*, exh. cat., Palazzo Pitti, Florence, 1973–4.

22. Angelica Kauffmann's painting is lost; Ménageot's is in Musée de l'Hôtel de Ville, Amboise, Bergeret's in Château de Malmaison: see F. Haskell, op. cit., p. 59.

23. Charles V picking up Titian's paintbrush was painted by Joseph-Nicolas Robert-Fleury in 1843 (lost) and by D. Pellegrini (Galleria Nazionale, Parma). Wilkie Collins (the son of a painter) refers to the story in *The Woman in White*. For Queen Christina and Guercino, see F. Haskell, op. cit., p. 70.

24. *Der Traum Rafaels* by Franz and Johannes Riepenhausen, 1821 (Muzeum Naradowe, Poznań), engraved 1833, was inspired by Wackenroder's *Herzensergiessungen*: see Claude Kleisch, *Der Ruhm ein Traumgesicht*, exh. cat., National-Galerie, Berlin (D.D.R.), 1972, p. 7.

25. Letter of 1818. E. Delacroix, *Selected Letters*, tr. Jean Stewart, London, 1971, p. 43. For the paintings by Ingres, see G. Wildenstein, op. cit., nos. 86, 88, 89, 231, 297. The earliest (lost) was dated 1813.

26. G. Wildenstein, op. cit., no. 104. The same subject was painted by Alexandre Menjaud (Salon of 1822). The story of Tintoretto scaring Aretino was told by Ridolfi, but Ingres and Menjaud probably took it from the account of Aretino in J.-C.-L. Sismondi, *De la littérature du midi de l'Europe*, 1813.

27. Gilbert and Chatterton both figured as martyr heroes in Alfred de Musset's *Stello*; Préault modelled a statue of the dying Gilbert, Salon of 1833.

28. Victor Hugo, *Les Contemplations*, Book V. For the image of Columbus, see Hugh Honour, 'L'image de Christophe Colomb' in *Revue du Louvre*, XXVI, 1976, pp. 255–67.

29. William Hazlitt, quoted in C. P. Brand, *Italy and the English Romantics*, Cambridge, 1957, p. 92. This book has a brief account of the cult of Tasso in England: for the cult in France, see Maurice Z. Shroder, *Icarus, The Image of the Artist in French Romanticism*, Cambridge, Mass., 1961.

30. *De l'Allemagne* (1813), Paris, 1968, I, p. 338.

31. Introductory note to *The Lament of Tasso*, 1817.

32. E. Delacroix, *Selected Letters*, edn cit., pp. 55–6.

33. A lithograph by Louis Boulanger of Paganini in prison was published in *L'Artiste*, I, 1831, p. 144 – illustrating the story that Paganini had learned the violin during an imprisonment of eight years (for *crime passionel* of course). A letter from Paganini, denying that he had ever been in prison and commenting on other fanciful stories about him, appeared in the next issue of *L'Artiste* (pp. 159–60) together with Boulanger's note of apology and 'justification'.

34. See P. E. Russell, '"Don Quixote" as a Funny Book' in *Modern Language Review*, LXIV, 1969, pp. 312–26. I am grateful to Nigel Glendinning for drawing my attention to this article.

35. Werner Brüggemann, *Cervantes und die Figur des Don Quijote in Kunstanschauung und Dichtung der deutschen Romantik*, Münster, 1958. See also Maurice Bardon, "*Don Quichotte*" *en France au XVIIe et au XVIIIe siècle*, Paris, 1931; for a selection of illustrations, *Don Quichotte*, exh. cat., Musée des Beaux Arts, Pau, 1955.

36. *Don Juan*, Canto XIII, lines 65–6.

37. *Mémoires d'outre-tombe* (1849), ed. M. Levaillant and G. Moulinier, Paris, 1951, I, p. 162.

38. Alfred de Vigny is quoted by Oliver W. Larking, *Daumier Man of his Time* (1966), Boston, 1968, p. 195; Balzac by M. Z. Shroder, op. cit., p. 111.

39. C. A. Sainte-Beuve, *Nouveaux Lundis* (1863–70), Paris, 1896, VIII, p. 37.

40. Painting of 1873, Musée des Beaux Arts, Dijon.

41. Painting begun 1824, present whereabouts unknown.

42. Illustrations to a translation by Louis Viardot, Paris, 1863.

43. For Thoré's comments, see P. Grate, op. cit., p. 172. Janin's remark is in *L'Artiste*, IX, 1835, pp. 50–51, but some of his words appear to have been lifted from Chateaubriand's description of Don Quixote as 'le plus noble, le plus brave, le plus aimable, et le moins fou de mortels' (*Itinéraire de Paris Jerusalem* (1811), ed. J. Mourot, Paris, 1968, p. 441).

44. Repr. *L'Artiste*, IX, 1835, p. 96.

45. Wilhelm von Kaulbach's drawing is in the print room of the Staatliche Museen, Berlin: see *La peinture allemande à l'époque du Romantisme*, exh. cat., Orangerie de Tuileries, Paris, 1976–7, no. 112. A print after it was widely diffused: repr. K. Koetschau, *Alfred Rethels Kunst*, Düsseldorf, 1929, p. 60. For Genelli's drawing (Museum für bildenden Künste, Leipzig), see Hans Ebert, *Buonaventura Genelli*, Weimar, 1971, p. 181.

46. Margaret Miller, 'Géricault's Paintings of the Insane' in *Journal of the Warburg and Courtauld Institutes*, IV, 1940–41, p. 160.

47. Hoffmann and also Tieck were indebted to such scientific writers as G. H. von Schubert and especially J. C. Reil, Professor of Pathology at Berlin and Halle and author of the curiously entitled *Rhapsodien über die Anwendung der psychischen Kurmethode auf Geisteszerrüttungen*, 1803.

48. F. Schlegel, *Kritische Schriften*, p. 111.

49. *Sketches of English Literature* (1837): see Oswald LeWinter, *Shakespeare in Europe* (1963), Harmondsworth, 1970, p. 76.

50. *William Shakespeare* (1864): see Oswald LeWinter, op. cit., p. 160.

8. THE MYSTERIOUS WAY (*pages 276–318*)

1. Nigel Glendinning, *Goya and his Critics*, New Haven and London, 1977, p. 86.

2. These works continued to be admired until well into the nineteenth century, but were sometimes interpreted in a distinctly Romantic way, by Blake among others. An extraordi-

 nary picture of 1804, by Pierre-Auguste Vafflard, of a scene from Young's *Night Thoughts* is in Musée National, Angoulême: see *French Painting 1774–1830*, no. 178.

3. Jean Paul (J. P. F. Richter), *Blumen- Frucht- und Dornstücke* (1796–7), tr. A. Ewing, London, 1877, p. 263.

4. ibid., p. 260.

5. R. Wellek, *Confrontations*, Princeton, 1965, p. 58.

6. ibid., p. 59; the translation is by Thomas Carlyle.

7. Ernst Cassirer, *The Philosophy of the Enlightenment* (1951), Boston, 1966, p. 163.

8. *Religion and Philosophy in Germany*, first published in *Revue des deux Mondes*, 1834, edn cit., p. 103.

9. E.-J. Delécluze, *Journal 1824–1828*, ed. R. Baschet, Paris, 1948, p. 213.

10. H. Girard, *Émile Deschamps: Un bourgeois dilettante à l'époque romantique*, Paris, 1921, II, p. 5.

11. Church of Saint-Paul-Saint-Louis, Paris; Delacroix Exhibition, no. 89. For a list of paintings executed for churches in Paris under the Restoration, see Léon Rosenthal, *La peinture romantique*, Paris, 1900, pp. 327–9. Most of them are unhappily disfigured by bitumen and grime.

12. *Contrasts*, London, 1836, pp. 3, 28.

13. *Blüthenstaub* (1797), p. 76: Novalis, II, p. 446.

14. F.-M. Granet began to paint church interiors in the 1790s, see pp. 161–2.

15. The most notable is in the Musée Royale des Beaux Arts, Brussels: see Elizabeth du Gué Trapier, *Eugenio Lucas y Padilla*, New York, 1940, p. 10.

16. The painting by Delaroche (Salon of 1824) is in a private collection in Paris; a sketch and reduced version are in the Wallace Collection, London. The painting by Granet (Salon of 1846) is in the Musées des Beaux Arts, Lyon. Scenes from the life of Savonarola were painted by several Italian artists. The twelfth-century heretic Arnold of Brescia was also popular with Italian painters but mainly, it seems, for his opposition to the temporal power of the Papacy (he was the hero of a tragedy by G. B. Niccolini, 1843): see Sandra Pinto, *Romanticismo Storico*, exh. cat. cit., pp. 38–40. Robert-Fleury combined the cults of the heretic and the misunderstood genius in *Bernard Palissy: ayant embrassé les opinions de Luther, il est arrêté par ordre du Conseil des seize*, Salon of 1839.

17. Keynes, pp. 383–96.

18. ibid., p. 476.

19. ibid., p. 605.

20. ibid., p. 617. The words bring to mind 'The Morning Star Sang' from *Illustrations to the Book of Job*. Blake also illustrated (with less artistic success) a Neo-Platonic text, Porphyry's *De Antro Nympherum*, in the watercolour now at Arlington Court: for interpretations of this puzzling work see Robert Simmons, Janet Warner and John E. Grant in *Studies in Romanticism*, X, 1970–71, pp. 3–26.

21. *William Blake 1757–1827*, exh. cat., Kunsthalle, Hamburg, 1975, with bibliography of earlier publications.

22. Keynes, p. 851.

23. Hoxie Neale Fairchild, *Religious Trends in English Poetry*, New York, 1949, III, p. 117, suggests that the 'spectrous fiend' was Blake's sexual urge.

24. See Martin Butlin, *A Catalogue of the Works of Blake in the Tate Gallery*, London, 1957, no. 25.

25. The difference of outlook seems to be marked in two images of the same subject, Ugolino in prison. Beneath the first, engraved 1793, he inscribed the angry legend: 'Does thy God, O Priest, take such vengeance as this.' In the second, one of the illustrations to

Dante on which he was at work in his last years (coll. Sir Geoffrey Keynes), angelic figures hover reassuringly above the group.

26. Alfred de Vigny had read a French translation of Jean Paul's vision, torn from its context and without the sentences which make the Christian point of the piece clear: see F. D. Klingender, *Goya in the Democratic Tradition*, London, 1948, p. 193.

27. R. Wellek, op. cit., p. 129.

28. F. Schlegel, *Gemäldebeschreibungen aus Paris und den Niederlanden in den Jahren 1802–1804* (1805), in *Kritische Schriften*, p. 584.

29. Rudolf Zeitler, *Klassizismus und Utopia*, Stockholm, 1954, p. 148.

30. S. Hinz, p. 92.

31. R. Wellek, op. cit., p. 59.

32. Kenneth Clark, *The Romantic Rebellion*, London, 1973, p. 218.

33. Eckart Klessmann, *Die Welt der Romantik*, Munich, 1969, p. 86.

34. Runge, II, p. 148.

35. Öffentliche Kunstsammlung, Basle; repr. *Das Dürer-Stammbuch von 1828*, exh. cat., Dürerhaus, Nuremberg, 1973, p. 37, and see also p. 127 for an apotheosis of Dürer by Joseph Wintergest. For the 'sanctification' of the artist in the nineteenth century see Renate Liebenwein-Krämer, *Säkularisierung und Sakralisierung*, Frankfurt-am-Main, 1977, pp. 222–94.

36. Quatremère de Quincy, *Raffaello*, tr. William Hazlitt, London, 1846, p. 274.

37. Hélène Toussaint, *Le Bain turc d'Ingres* (Musée du Louvre, les dossiers du département des peintures I), Paris, 1971. For an interpretation of the picture as an allegory of the five senses, see John L. Connolly, 'Ingres and the Erotic Intellect' in T. B. Hess and Linda Nochlin, eds., *Woman as Sex Object*, New York, 1972, pp. 17–31.

38. The earliest version (formerly Museum of Riga) was painted 1813; others are in the Fogg Museum, Cambridge, Mass., and Gallery of Fine Arts, Columbus, Ohio; see E. Camesasca, *L'Opera completa di Ingres*, Milan, 1968, no. 72.

39. E. H. Carr, *The Romantic Exiles* (1933), Harmondsworth, 1968, p. 17.

40. e.g. Friedrich Overbeck's self-portrait with his wife and child (Museen der Hansestadt, Lübeck). It is hard to decide whether William Mulready's *The Lesson* of 1858 (Victoria and Albert Musuem) represents the Madonna and Child or simply a mother and child.

41. The phrase seems first to have been used by Friedrich Schlegel in *Lucinde*, 1799.

42. Aargauer Kunsthaus, Aarau; see Gert Schiff, *Johann Heinrich Füssli*, Munich and Zürich, 1973, no. 720.

43. Österreichische Galerie, Vienna.

44. *Héro et Léandre*, *Roméo et Juliette* and *Apollo et Daphné* are all in the Louvre.

45. Novalis I, p. 104; see also M. H. Abrams, *Natural Supernaturalism*, New York, 1971, p. 247. Wordsworth used similar imagery to describe how the 'intellect of Man' might be 'wedded to this goodly universe' and described *The Excursion* as 'the spousal verse of this great consummation'. He exhorts hills to 'embrace' him and close him in; the vale extends to him 'a passionate welcoming'. Wordsworth's relationship with nature has all the elements of Romantic love – even if he was, as Shelley wrote, 'a kind of moral eunuch,/ He touched the hem of Nature's shift,/ Felt faint – and never dared uplift/ The closest all-concealing tunic'.

46. Géricault's painting is in a private collection in Paris; Delacroix's in the Atheneum, Helsinki; Chassériau's in the Musée des Beaux Arts, Strasbourg. Louis Boulanger exhibited at the Salon of 1827 a large picture of Mazeppa being tied to the horse (Musée des Beaux Arts, Rouen, sketch in Musée Fabre, Montpellier), and also published three lithographs of scenes from the story.

47. Aristide Marie, *Le peintre poète Louis Boulanger*, Paris, 1925, p. 25.

48. *Delacroix: Journal*, I, pp. 162–3.

49. In France, a number of artists, known as *Orientalistes*, specialized in North African and Near Eastern subjects, notably Adrien Dauzats, Gabriel-Alexandre Decamps, Eugène Fromentin and Prosper Marilhat.

50. Runge, I, p. 3.

51. It is perhaps significant that children figure prominently in all Constable's 'six-foot' pictures of the Vale of Dedham, where his own childhood was spent. For interpretations of the text from Matthew xviii, 1, see George Boas, *The Cult of Childhood*, London, 1966.

52. R. Trainer, 'The *Märchen*' in S. Prawer, ed., *The Romantic Period in Germany*, London, 1970, pp. 97–120.

53. *Biographia Literaria*, quoted by Peter Conrad in *Times Literary Supplement*, 10 December 1976, p. 1543.

54. Ronald Taylor, *Hoffmann*, London, 1963, p. 76.

55. *Caspar David Friedrich*, exh. cat., Tate Gallery, London, 1972, p. 105. The paintings described by Schubert are lost but seem to have been similar to a later cycle of watercolours in the Kunsthalle, Hamburg.

56. Fuseli's famous *Nightmare* (Detroit Institute of Fine Arts) is often cited in this context, but expresses distinctly eighteenth-century ideas about dreams: see Nicolas Powell, *Fuseli: The Nightmare*, London, 1973. There are several early nineteenth-century pictures of dreams which are literary illustrations, e.g. Moritz von Schwind, *Traum des Gefangenen* (Schack-Galerie, Munich). Such pictures as Joseph Guichard's *Le rêve d'amour* of 1837 (Musée des Beaux Arts, Lyon) can hardly be associated with Romantic attitudes to the dream world.

57. For an account of these strange works (mainly Tate Gallery), see Geoffrey Keynes, *Blake Studies* (1949), Oxford, 1971, pp. 130–35.

58. Fuseli's introduction to the 1808 edition of Robert Blair's *The Grave* with illustrations by Blake.

59. Lancelot Lew Whyte, *The Unconscious Before Freud* (1960), London, 1962, p. 124.

60. Novalis, II, p. 419.

61. Werner Hofmann, op. cit., p. 262.

9. EPILOGUE (*pages 319–23*)

1. The demand that the artist should 'be of his own time' does not, as is sometimes suggested, have any connection with the late seventeenth-century battle of the ancients and moderns. Nor does it owe anything to the practice of eighteenth-century artists who occasionally painted scenes from modern history in modern dress (Benjamin West's *Death of Wolfe*, J. S. Copley's *Death of Major Pierson* etc.). It seems to derive from the distinction between ancient and modern art (as expressions of paganism and Christianity) made by the Schlegels and Chateaubriand, to which Hegel's notion of the *Zeitgeist* is also related. The concept of modernity was narrowed down to the nineteenth century by Giovanni Berchet and his friends in Milan during the early years of the Restoration. Berchet demanded of writers: 'Rendetevi coevi al secolo vostro e non ai secoli seppelliti; spacciatevi dalla nebbia che oggidi invocate sulla vostra dizione; spacciatevi dagli arcani sibillini, dalle vetuste liturgie, da tutte le Veneri e da tutte le loro turpitudini; cavoli già putridi non rifriggeteli' (*Lettera semiseria di Grisostomo*, 1816, ed. N. Caccia, Milan, n.d., pp. 46–7). Gian Domenico Romagnosi coined a word for being of one's own time – 'Sono ilichiasto, se vuoi che te lo dica in greco, cioè adatto alle età' (*Il Conciliatore* I, 1818, p. 11). Stendhal introduced

the idea into France, identifying Romanticism with it. The demand for modernity in the arts was, however, most often expressed in criticism of architecture, with increasing frequency from 1830 onwards, e.g. a writer in *L'Artiste* II, 1831, p. 74, said that the Académie should inscribe on its façade 'Soyons français, soyons de notre époque'. For the development of this idea in Germany, see Klaus Döhmer, '*In welchem Style sollen wir bauen?*' Munich, 1976.

2. An article in *Ver Sacrum*, March 1898, is entitled 'Symbolists of a Hundred Years Ago', and calls on Tieck, Runge and Friedrich for justification of a new art. K. Scheffler, *Deutsche Maler und Zeichner im Neunzehnten Jahrhundert*, Leipzig, 1911, set the Romantics in the context of later German *Gedankenmaler*.

3. The notion of '*l'art pour l'art*' derives from the aesthetics of Kant: the first recorded use of the phrase is by Benjamin Constant in 1804. The best account of the history of the idea is still Albert Cassagne, *La théorie de l'art pour l'art en France*, Paris, 1906; see also John Wilcox, 'The Beginnings of l'Art pour l'Art' in *Journal of Aesthetics and Art Criticism*, XI, 1953, pp. 360–77. Plekhanov stated that the doctrine develops when artists feel 'a hopeless contradiction between their aims and the aims of the society to which they belong. Artists must be very hostile to their society and they must see no hope of changing it': see R. Wellek and A. Warren, *Theory of Literature* (1949), Harmondsworth, 1963, p. 101.

4. 1846, Kunstmuseum, Düsseldorf. Goethe had, of course, been the first to satirize the cult of *Werther* in *Der Triumph der Empfindsamkeit*, 1778.

5. *The Düsseldorf Academy and the Americans*, exhibition catalogue, High Museum of Art, Atlanta, Georgia, 1972.

6. See James Thomas Flexner, *That Wilder Image* (1962), New York, 1970, p. 250.

7. According to a contemporary he owned a house in Paris worth 200,000 francs and a country estate worth 70,000, which did not prevent him from 'crier toujours misere pour que chacun lui donne quelque chose': see Geneviève Lacambre, *Le Musee du Luxembourg en 1874*, exh. cat., Grand Palais, Paris, 1974, no. 99.

Books for Further Reading

GENERAL: The literature on Romanticism is vast but includes relatively few general accounts of the visual arts in Europe and America. Gustav Pauli, *Die Kunst des Klassizismus und der Romantik* (Propyläen Kunstgeschichte, XIV, Berlin, 1925) is still very useful, especially for its illustrations. In the new Propyläen Kunstgeschichte, Rudolf Zeitler, *Die Kunst des 19. Jahrhunderts* (Berlin, 1966) covers the whole nineteenth century. There are notable chapters on the Romantics in Fritz Novotny, *Painting and Sculpture in Europe 1780–1880* (Pelican History of Art, 1960; rev. edn, Harmondsworth, 1971). Werner Hofmann, *Das irdische Paradies: Motive und Ideen des 19. Jahrhunderts* (1960; rev. edn, Munich, 1974, tr. as *The Earthly Paradise*, New York, 1961, and *Art in the Nineteenth Century*, London, 1961) is largely concerned with Romantic themes. Ludwig Grote, ed., *Beiträge zur Motivkunde des 19. Jahrhunderts* (Munich, 1970) includes studies of such themes as hermits and monks, the open window and the shipwreck. Renate Liebenwein-Krämer, *Säkularisierung und Sakralisierung* (Frankfurt-am-Main, 1977) also discusses Romantic painting and sculpture thematically. The catalogue of the Council of Europe exhibition *The Romantic Movement* (Tate Gallery and Arts Council Gallery, London, 1959), with nearly a thousand items, provides an invaluable basis for a general survey, but has few illustrations. Numerous works are illustrated in Marcel Brion, *Romantic Art* (London, 1960) and *Art in the Romantic Era* (London, 1966). Klaus Lankheit, *Revolution und Restauration* (Baden-Baden, 1965) has a more perceptive text. William Vaughan, *Romantic Art* (London, 1977) provides a good general account of its subject. For an introduction to the ideas of the leading Romantic artists and theorists there is the excellent annotated anthology in the 'Sources and Documents in the History of Art' series, Lorenz Eitner, *Neoclassicism and Romanticism* (Englewood Cliffs, N.J., 1970).

The majority of publications on Romantic art are devoted either to single arts or to single countries. For painting, Henri Focillon, *La Peinture au XIXe siècle: Le retour à l'Antique, Le Romantisme* (Paris, 1927) is still very valuable, and Paul Colin, *La Peinture européenne au XIXe siècle, Le Romantisme* (Brussels, 1935) is also of interest. Kenneth Clark, *The Romantic Rebellion* (London, 1973) contains very perceptive studies of twelve painters and one sculptor (Rodin). Robert Rosenblum, *Modern Painting and the Northern Romantic Tradition* (New York and London, 1975) is both original and stimulating.

The best account of European and American architecture is in Henry-Russell Hitchcock, *Architecture: Nineteenth and Twentieth Centuries* (Pelican History of Art, 1958; rev. edn, Harmondsworth, 1971). Gothic Revival architecture is surveyed internationally by Georg Germann, *Gothic Revival* (London, 1972). For Romantic notions of Gothic there is Paul Frankl, *The Gothic: Literary Sources and Interpretations through Eight Centuries* (Princeton, 1960). For architectural theory in general there is Nikolaus Pevsner, *Some Architectural Writers of the Nineteenth Century* (Oxford, 1972).

The most interesting interpretations of Romanticism as an international phenomenon are in works which refer only marginally (sometimes not at all) to the visual arts. M. H.

Abrams, *The Mirror and the Lamp* (New York, 1953) is outstanding, and his *Natural Supernaturalism* (New York, 1971) is also very interesting. For literary theory, there is the indispensable René Wellek, *A History of Modern Criticism: The Romantic Age* (London, 1955). Paul van Tieghem, *Le Romantisme dans la littérature européenne* (1948; rev. edn, Paris, 1969) is a useful chronicle with extensive bibliography. Hans Eichner, ed., *'Romantic' and its Cognates: The European History of a Word* (Toronto, 1972) is as much concerned with theories as with etymology and has a final chapter on modern interpretations of Romanticism. René Wellek examines recent theories in Northrop Frye, ed., *Romanticism Reconsidered* (New York, 1963). Samples of twentieth-century interpretations of Romanticism with a commentary are in Anthony Thorlby, *The Romantic Movement* (London, 1966).

Mario Praz, *The Romantic Agony* (1933; rev. edn, London, 1960) is a brilliant study of eroticism in Romantic literature. Albert Béguin, *L'âme romantique et le rêve* (Paris, 1939) focusses on irrational elements in German and French literature. Erich Heller, *The Artist's Journey into the Interior* (London, 1965) is a series of essays on Romantic literature, art and philosophy. H. G. Schenk, *The Mind of the European Romantics* (London, 1966) is concerned mainly with writers and musicians. L. R. Furst, *Romanticism in Perspective* (London, 1969) is an excellent comparative study of English, French and German literature. There is an interesting and valuable Marxist assessment of Romanticism in Ernst Fischer, *Von der Notwendigkeit der Kunst* (1959, tr. as *The Necessity of Art*, Harmondsworth, 1963). Several books by Morse Peckham present interpretations of Romanticism which are both highly personal and stimulating: *Beyond the Tragic Vision* (New York, 1962), *The Triumph of Romanticism* (Columbia, South Carolina, 1970), *Romanticism and Behavior* (Columbia, South Carolina, 1976). Other books about Romanticism, mainly with reference to literature, include Jacques Barzun, *Classic, Romantic and Modern* (1943; rev. edn, New York, 1961); W. T. Jones, *The Romantic Syndrome* (The Hague, 1961); Donald Sutherland, *On Romanticism* (New York, 1971). Howard Mumford Jones, *Revolution and Romanticism* (Cambridge, Mass., 1974) is a study of cultural relations between Europe and America.

On music and Romanticism there are André Cœuroq, *Musique et littérature* (Paris, 1923); Fernand Baldensperger, *Sensibilité musicale et romantisme* (Paris, 1925); Alfred Einstein, *Music in the Romantic Era* (London, 1947); J. Chantavoine and J. Gaudefroy-Demombynes, *Le Romantisme dans la musique européenne* (Paris, 1955) and an excellent article by Friedrich Blume in the encyclopedia *Die Musik in Geschichte und Gegenwart* (Kassel, 1963, XI, pp. 785–845).

Historical surveys of the 'Romantic period' are numerous, and several refer to literature, music and the visual arts as well as to political and social history, notably Jacques Droz, L. Genet, and P. Vidalenc, *Restaurations et révolutions 1815–1871* (Paris, 1953) with extensive bibliographies; E. J. Hobsbawm, *The Age of Revolution: Europe 1815–1848* (London, 1962); Jacques Droz, *Europe Between Revolutions 1815–1848* (London, 1967); J. L. Talmon, *Romanticism and Revolt: Europe 1815–1848* (London, 1967).

INDIVIDUAL COUNTRIES

FRANCE: The key works for painting are still Léon Rosenthal, *La peinture romantique: Essai sur l'évolution de la peinture française de 1815 à 1830* (Paris, 1900) and *Du Romantisme au réalisme* (Paris, 1914). Walter Friedlaender, *David to Delacroix* (Cambridge, Mass., 1952) is also a work of fundamental importance. Essays reprinted in Frederick Antal, *Classicism and Romanticism* (London, 1966) are illuminating. The most important recent contribution to the study of French painting is the catalogue of the exhibition shown at the Grand Palais, Paris, as *De David à Delacroix* (1974) and at the Detroit Institute of Arts and Metropolitan

 Museum, New York (1975) as *French Painting 1774–1830: The Age of Revolution*, with notable essays by Pierre Rosenberg, Antoine Schnapper and Robert Rosenblum, as well as invaluable biographical accounts of the artists represented (the English language version corrects errors in the original edition). The frontiers between Romanticism and Realism in French painting are explored in two outstanding books by T. J. Clark, *Image of the People* and *The Absolute Bourgeois* (London, 1972, 1973).

On sculpture, the only work of importance is Luc Benoist, *La Sculpture romantique* (Paris, 1927); on architecture, L. Hautecœur, *Histoire de l'architecture classique en France*, VI (Paris, 1955). Art criticism is discussed in Pontus Grate, *Deux Critiques d'art de l'époque romantique* (Stockholm, 1959).

There are two accounts of Romantic attitudes to the eighteenth century and their reflection in the visual arts: S. O. Simches, *Le Romantisme et le goût esthétique du XVIIIe siècle* (Paris, 1964) and Carol Duncan, *The Pursuit of Pleasure: The Rococo Revival in French Romantic Art* (New York, 1976). Francis Haskell, *Rediscoveries in Art* (Ithaca, N.Y. and London, 1976) provides a more wide-ranging and deeper study of taste in old and contemporary art in both France and England.

The decorative arts and costume are discussed in V. Husarski, *Le Style romantique* (Paris, 1931), costume in Louis Maigron, *Le Romantisme et la mode* (Paris, 1911), the decorative arts in P. Schommer, *L'Art décoratif au temps du romantisme* (Paris, 1928) and J. Robiquet, *L'Art et le goût sous la Restauration* (Paris, 1937).

Literature and the visual arts are discussed in Maurice Z. Shroder, *Icarus: The Image of the Artist in French Romanticism* (Cambridge, Mass., 1961) and Malcolm Easton, *Artists and Writers in Paris* (London, 1964). For literature, R. Bray, *Chronologie du romantisme* (Paris, 1932) is very helpful; Philippe van Tieghem, *Le Romantisme français* (Paris, 1944) in the 'Que sais-je?' series provides a good brief introduction. There are brilliant studies of individual writers in Georges Poulet, *Études sur le temps humain* (Paris, 1952) and *Les Métamorphoses du cercle* (Paris, 1961).

GERMANY: For the visual arts, R. Benz and A. von Schneider, *Die Kunst der deutschen Romantik* (Munich, 1939) is still the fullest general survey. K. Scheffler, *Deutsche Maler und Zeichner im Neunzehnten Jahrhundert* (Leipzig, 1911) was a pioneer study and is still illuminating. The catalogue of an exhibition, *Deutsche Romantik* (Nationalgalerie, Staatliche Museen zu Berlin, 1965), has a valuable introduction by Gottfried Riemann. Eckart Klessmann, *Die Welt der Romantik* (Munich, 1969), which combines accounts of literature and painting, is well illustrated. Helmut Börsch-Supan, *Deutsche Romantiker* (Munich, 1972) presents interpretations of an interesting selection of paintings and drawings; Roger Cardinal, *German Romantics in Context* (London, 1975) a brief introduction to some leading writers and painters. An exhibition, *German Painting of the 19th Century* (Yale University Art Gallery, Cleveland Museum of Art and Art Institute of Chicago, 1970–71), had a useful catalogue and also provided the occasion for a symposium on German art (mainly Romantic), with papers by H. W. Janson, Robert Rosenblum and others published in the *Yale Art Gallery Bulletin* (1972). A more notable selection of paintings and drawings was included in the exhibition *La peinture allemande à l'époque du Romantisme* (Orangerie des Tuileries, Paris, 1976–7), with an excellent catalogue.

For the Nazarenes, there is Keith Andrews, *The Nazarenes* (Oxford, 1964) and the exhibition catalogue *Die Nazarener* (Städelsche Kunstinstitut, Frankfurt-am-Main, 1977). Connections between German and French painters are documented in Wolfgang Becker, *Paris und die deutsche Malerei 1750–1840* (Munich, 1971).

For architecture, there is Heinrich Beenken, *Schöpferische Bauideen der deutschen Romantik* (Mainz, 1952), for architectural theory Klaus Döhmer, '*In welchem Style sollen wir bauen?*' (Munich, 1976).

Among the numerous books on German Romantic literature Ricarda Huch, *Die Romantik* (1899–1902; repr. Tübingen, 1971) is still one of the best, though without notes or an index. Oskar Walzel, *Deutsche Romantik* (1926; tr. as *German Romanticism*, New York, 1966) is a standard work. Two books by Helmut Schanze provide a more modern interpretation of the movement, stressing liberal aspects and links with the Enlightenment: *Romantik und Aufklärung* (Nuremberg, 1966) and an annotated anthology *Die andere Romantik: Eine Dokumentation* (Frankfurt-am-Main, 1967). Some of the most important German texts are assembled with commentaries in English in Ronald Taylor, *The Romantic Tradition in Germany* (London, 1970). Siegbert Prawer, ed., *The Romantic Period in Germany* (London, 1970) contains illuminating studies on the major aspects of the subject.

An important aspect of aesthetic thought is examined in W. D. Robson-Scott, *The Literary Background of the Gothic Revival in Germany* (Oxford, 1965). Other notable studies of aesthetics include Israel Knox, *The Aesthetic Theories of Kant, Hegel and Schopenhauer* (London, 1958); B. A. Sørensen, *Symbol und Symbolismus in den ästhetischen Theorien des 18. Jahrhunderts und der deutschen Romantik* (Copenhagen, 1963); and Michael Podro, *The Manifold in Perception: Theories of Art from Kant to Hildebrand* (Oxford, 1972).

Political aspects of German Romanticism are investigated in Henri Brunschwig, *La crise de l'état prussien à la fin du XVIIIe siècle et la genèse de la mentalité romantique* (Paris, 1947) and Jacques Droz, *Le Romantisme allemande et l'état* (Paris, 1966). A. Gode von Aesch, *Natural Science in German Romanticism* (New York, 1941) explores an important but neglected topic.

GREAT BRITAIN: The exhibition catalogues *Romantic Art in Britain* (Detroit Institute of Arts and Philadelphia Museum of Art, 1968) with essays by Frederick Cummings, Robert Rosenblum and Allen Staley, and *La Peinture romantique anglaise* (Petit Palais, Paris, 1972) provide the best introduction to British Romantic painting. T. S. R. Boase, *English Art 1800–1870* (Oxford History of English Art, X, Oxford, 1959) contains brief accounts of the main painters, sculptors and architects. A thorough chronicle of artistic events is provided by William T. Whitley, *Art in England 1800–1820* and *Art in England 1821–1837* (Cambridge 1928 and 1930). Peter Quennell, *Romantic England: Writing and Painting 1717–1851* (London, 1970) is well illustrated but concerned mainly with literature. Leslie Parris, *Landscape in Britain c. 1750–1850* (exh. cat., Tate Gallery, London, 1973) and Karl Krober, *Romantic Landscape Vision: Constable and Wordsworth* (Madison, Wisconsin, 1975) are the most valuable recent studies of their subject. Peter Conrad, *The Victorian Treasure House* (London, 1973) is a fascinating discussion of art and literature. Artistic theory is discussed at length in the 1593 pages of Johannes Dobai, *Die Kunstliteratur des Klassizismus und der Romantik in England 1790–1840*, Bern, 1977, which appeared too late for me to be able to make use of it.

On architecture, there is the final section of John Summerson, *Architecture in Britain 1530–1830* (Pelican History of Art, 1953; rev. edn, Harmondsworth, 1977) and Henry-Russell Hitchcock, *Early Victorian Architecture in Britain* (London, 1954). Kenneth Clark, *The Gothic Revival* (1923; rev. edn, London, 1950) is still the best general account of its subject; J. Mordaunt Crook's introduction to the reprint of Charles L. Eastlake, *A History of the Gothic Revival* (1872; Leicester, 1970) is valuable; James Macaulay, *The Gothic Revival 1745–1845* (Glasgow and London, 1975) is mainly about buildings in Scotland. On sculpture, there is Nicholas Penny's very perceptive *Church Monuments in Romantic England* (New Haven and London, 1977).

For English Romantic literature, there are two volumes in the *Oxford History of English Literature*, W. L. Renwick, *English Literature 1789–1815* and Ian Jack, *English Literature 1815–1832* (both Oxford, 1963). Some of the most stimulating studies are in the 'comparative' works by M. H. Abrams and L. R. Furst cited above. René Wellek, *Confrontations* (Princeton, 1965) examines the relationship between specific English and German Romantics.

ITALY: For the visual arts, the first volume of Emilio Lavagnino, *L'Arte Moderna* (Turin, 1961) is indispensable. So also is the well annotated anthology of theoretical writings, Paola Barocchi, *Testimonianze e polemiche figurative in Italia. L'Ottocento dal Bello ideale al Preraffaelismo* (Messina and Florence, 1972). For Italian literary theory G. Borgese, *Storia della critica romantica in Italia* (Naples, 1905) is still valuable; E. Bellorini, ed., *Discussioni e polemiche sul romanticismo* (Bari, 1943) is a collection of sources. The main studies of literature include G. Citanna, *Il romanticismo e la poesia italiana* (Bari, 1935); and M. Fubini, *Romanticismo italiano* (Bari, 1953).

SPAIN: J. García Mercadel, *Historia del Romanticismo en España* (Barcelona, 1943) provides a general account. E. A. Peers, *A History of the Romantic Movement in Spain* (2 vols., Cambridge, 1940) and *A Short History of the Romantic Movement in Spain* (Liverpool, 1949) are concerned with literature. For the visual arts there are the opening chapters of A. de Beruete y Moret, *Historia de la Pintura Española en el Siglo XIX* (Madrid, 1926); J. F. Ráfols, *El Arte Romántico en España* (Barcelona, 1954); and J. A. Gaya Nuño, *Arte del Siglo XIX* (Ars Hispaniae, XIX, Madrid, 1966).

U.S.A.: Literature and the visual arts are discussed in G. Boas, ed., *Romanticism in America* (Baltimore, 1940). James Thomas Flexner, *The Light of Distant Skies: American Painting 1760–1835* and *That Wilder Image* (Boston, 1954 and 1962) provide a readable survey. A more sophisticated interpretation is presented by Barbara Novak, *American Painting of the Nineteenth Century* (New York, 1969). An interesting selection of pictures is assembled in D. C. Huntington, *Art and the Excited Spirit: America in the Romantic Period* (exh. cat., University of Michigan of Art, Ann Arbor, 1972). The relevant chapters of John Wilmerding, *American Art* (Pelican History of Art, Harmondsworth, 1976) are valuable. Landscape painting is discussed in a very stimulating way in *The Natural Paradise: Painting in America 1800–1950* (exh. cat., Museum of Modern Art, New York, 1976).

For sculpture, there is Albert TenEyck Gardner, *Yankee Stonecutters: The First American School of Sculpture 1800–1850* (New York, 1945); for architecture, James Early, *Romanticism and American Architecture* (New York, 1965); Phoebe Stanton, *The Gothic Revival and American Church Architecture: An Episode in Taste 1840–1856* (Baltimore, 1968); and for architectural theory a useful anthology, Don Gifford, ed., *The Literature of Architecture* (New York, 1966).

OTHER COUNTRIES: The best introduction to Danish painting is the exhibition catalogue *Das goldene Zeitalter der dänischen Malerei* (Kunsthalle, Kiel, 1968). For landscape painting there is H. Bramsen, *Landskabmaleriet i Danmark 1750–1875* (Copenhagen, 1935). On Denmark, Sweden and Norway there is Alfred Kamphausen, *Deutsche und skandinavische Kunst: Begegnung und Wandlung* (Schleswig, 1956). A general survey of Dutch painting is provided by Friedrich Markus Huevner, *Die Kunst der niederlandischen Romantik* (Düsseldorf, 1942);

more detailed accounts of individual artists are in J. Knoeff, *Tusschen Rococo en Romantiek* (The Hague, 1948). For Russia, there is *La Peinture russe à l'époque romantique* (exh. cat., Grand Palais, Paris, 1976–7).

Monographs on individual artists are cited in the Catalogue of Illustrations, pp. 372–409. Editions of the works of Romantic writers and theorists are cited in the Notes, which also include references to periodical articles on aspects of Romanticism.

Catalogue of Illustrations

1. THE CROSS IN THE MOUNTAINS. By Caspar David Friedrich, 1807–8. Oil on canvas, 115 × 110.5 cm., in a gilt-wood frame carved by Gottlieb Christian Kühn. *Dresden, Staatliche Kunstsammlungen, Gemäldegalerie.*

Recently published documents reveal that Friedrich began this painting without a commission and intended to send it to the Protestant King of Sweden, Gustav IV Adolf. He was, however, persuaded to sell it to the Catholic Graf Anton von Thun-Hohenstein, who said he wanted to place it in the private chapel of his castle, Schloss Tetschen, in Bohemia (though he did not in fact do so). The frame [Fig. v. Photo: Deutsche Fotothek

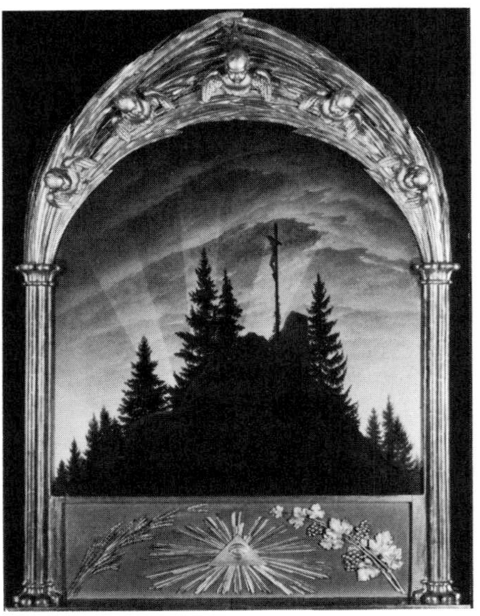

Figure v. *The Cross in the Mountains*, 1807–8. Caspar David Friedrich

Dresden] was carved to the design of Friedrich, who described its symbolism in his printed account of the picture: 'At each side the frame takes the form of Gothic columns. Palm branches rise up from these to make an arch over the picture. Amongst the branches are the heads of five angels, who all look down in adoration on to the cross. Above the central angel the evening star shines in the purest silvery lustre. Below, in a broad inset, the all-seeing eye of God is enclosed by the divine triangle surrounded by rays of light. Ears of corn and vines bow down on either side toward the all-seeing eye, indicating the body of Him who is nailed to the cross' (translation from the Tate Gallery exh. cat.).

Lit: S. Hinz, pp. 137–95; Börsch-Supan/Jähnig, pp. 300–302; *Caspar David Friedrich 1774–1840*, exh. cat., Tate Gallery, London, 1972, no. 33; Eva Reitharovà and Werner Sumowski, 'Beiträge zu Caspar David Friedrich' in *Pantheon*, XXXV, 1977, pp. 41–50.

2. THE LAUTERAARGLETSCHER. By Caspar Wolf, 1776. Oil on canvas, 55 × 82.5 cm. *Basel, Öffentliche Kunstsammlung.*

The second version of one of 170 oils and watercolours commissioned from Wolf by the Berne publisher A. Wagner (the earlier version, dated 1775, is in the Aargauer Kunsthaus, Aarau: cf. *Die Alpen in der Schweizer Malerei*, exh. cat., Odakyu Grand Gallery, Tokyo, 1977, no. 15). Engravings after the composition were published in 1777, 1782 and 1786. For the best account of Wolf, see '*Maegtiger Schweiz*', exh. cat., Thorvaldsens Museum, Copenhagen, 1973, nos. 43–9.

3. MORNING IN THE RIESENGEBIRGE. By Caspar David Friedrich, 1810–11. Oil on canvas, 108 × 170 cm. *Berlin, Verwaltung der Staatliche Schlösser, Schloss Charlottenburg.*

Lit: Börsch-Supan/Jähnig, pp. 78–80, 315–16.

4. THE FALL OF AN AVALANCHE IN THE GRISONS. By Joseph Mallord William Turner, 1810. Oil on canvas, 90 × 120 cm. *London, Tate Gallery.*

In the list of works issued when this picture was exhibited in Turner's own gallery in 1810, the following lines of verse were printed beneath the title of the picture:

'The downward sun a parting sadness gleams,
Portentous lurid thro' the gathering storm;
Thick drifting snow, on snow,
Till the vast weight bursts thro' the rocky barrier;
Down at once, its pine clad forests,
And towering glaciers fall, the work of ages
Crashing through all! extinction follows,
And the toil, the hope of man – o'erwhelms.'

Both the painting and the verses seem to have been inspired (as Jack Lindsay points out) by a passage in James Thomson's *Winter* (London, 1729), lines 413–22. The picture may also have had a political significance – a reference to the incorporation in the Napoleonic Empire of the Swiss Republic, so often associated with the notion of freedom, especially by James Thomson in *Liberty* (1734–36).

Lit: H. Finberg in *Burlington Magazine*, XCIII, 1951, pp. 383–6; J. Lindsay, p. 139; *La peinture romantique anglaise*, no. 261.

5. SNOW STORM: HANNIBAL AND HIS ARMY CROSSING THE ALPS. By Joseph Mallord William Turner, 1812. Oil on canvas, 145 × 236.5 cm. *London, Tate Gallery.*

Turner is said to have drawn inspiration from a (lost) painting of the same subject by John Robert Cozens and also from a thunderstorm he witnessed on the Yorkshire moors in 1810. John Gage suggests that the picture may also have been intended partly as an anti-heroic riposte to Jacques-Louis David's painting of Napoleon crossing the Alps, which Turner saw in Paris in 1802. Its pessimism is emphasized by Turner's verses (the first to be ascribed to his poem *Fallacies of Hope*) printed in the Royal Academy catalogue in 1812:

'Craft, treachery, and fraud – Salassian force,
Hung on the fainting rear! then Plunder seiz'd

The victor and the captive, – Saguntum's spoil,
Alike became their prey; still the chief advanc'd
Look'd on the sun with hope; – low, broad, and wan;
While the fierce archer of the downward year
Stains Italy's blanch'd barrier with storms.
In vain each pass, ensanguin'd deep with dead,
Or rocky fragments, wide destruction roll'd.
Still on Campania's fertile plains – he thought,
But the loud breeze sob'd, "Capua's joys beware!"'

Lit: A. J. Finberg, pp. 188–90; J. Lindsay, pp. 153–70; *La peinture romantique anglaise*, no. 262.

6. NAPOLEON ON THE BATTLEFIELD OF EYLAU. By Antoine-Jean Gros, 1808. Oil on canvas, 533 × 800 cm. *Paris, Musée du Louvre*. (Photo: Alinari.)

The battle of Eylau was fought on 8 February 1807. On 17 March 1807, artists were invited to submit sketches in competition for the commission of a picture to depict 'le moment où Bonaparte, visitant le champ de bataille, vient porter indistinctement des secours et des consolations aux innombrables victimes des combats'. A topographical view of the battlefield was made available. When the sketches were exhibited a police report protested: 'Les artistes ont accumulé tous les genres de mutilations, les variétés d'une vaste boucherie, comme s'ils eussent à peindre précisément une scène d'horreur et de carnage, et à rendre la guerre exécrable' (see *French Painting 1774–1830*, no. 128). Gros won the competition and finished his huge canvas in time for the Salon of 1808.

Lit: *Gros, ses amis, ses élèves*, exh. cat., Petit Palais, Paris, 1936, no. 40; P. Lelièvre, 'Napoléon sur le champ de bataille d'Eylau par A.-J. Gros' in *Bulletin de la Société de l'histoire de l'art français*, 1955, pp. 51–5; Robert Herbert, 'Baron Gros's Napoleon and Voltaire's Henri IV' in F. Haskell et al., ed., *The Artist and the Writer in France: Essays in Honour of Jean Seznec*, Oxford, 1974.

7. WOUNDED CUIRASSIER. By Théodore Géricault, 1814. Oil on canvas, 353 × 294 cm. *Paris, Musée du Louvre*. (Photo: Giraudon.)

The painting was clearly conceived as a pendant to *An Officer of the Imperial Guard* of 1812 (Louvre). Drawings (coll. Denise Aimé-Azam) and an oil sketch (Louvre) show that Géricault began with the more obviously melancholy image of a wounded soldier resting on a bank. There is an oil sketch for the definitive composition in the Brooklyn Museum, New York.

Lit: K. Berger, *Géricault et son œuvre* (1952), Paris, 1953, pp. 12–13; L. Eitner, *Géricault*, exh. cat., Los Angeles County Museum of Art and elsewhere, 1971–2, pp. 51–2; *French Painting 1774–1830*, no. 74.

8. THE RETURN FROM RUSSIA. By Théodore Géricault, 1818. Lithograph, 44.5 × 36.2 cm. *New Haven, Yale University Art Gallery, Gift of Charles Y. Lazarus, B.A. 1936*.

Lit: L. Eitner, *Géricault, an Album of his Drawings in the Art Institute of Chicago*, Chicago, 1960; Kate H. Spencer, *The Graphic Art of Géricault*, exh. cat., Yale University Art Gallery, New Haven, 1969, no. 6.

9. THE RAFT OF THE 'MEDUSA'. By Théodore Géricault, 1819. Oil on canvas, 491 × 716 cm. *Paris, Musée du Louvre*. (Photo: Archives Photographiques.)

On 2 July 1816, a French government frigate, *La Méduse*, carrying troops to Senegal, ran aground on the West African coast. The captain and the senior officers took the few sea-worthy life-boats, while the passengers and crew – 149 men and one woman – were cast adrift on a makeshift raft; fifteen men survived for thirteen days and five of them died shortly after they were rescued. As the captain was a returned *émigré* who owed his appointment to the ultra-royalist minister of the navy, the story became a political scandal. Two survivors wrote a brief book which told the whole horrifying story in full and gruesome detail, published in November 1817. Géricault, who had returned from Italy in September, interviewed the survivors and in the spring or early summer of 1818 probably made the first of his many sketches for the composition. He is said to have begun work on the canvas in November 1818. It was finished in July 1819, though he made one important last-minute alteration (the addition of the corpse in the lower right-hand corner) before it was hung in the Salon which opened on 25 August. It aroused widespread comment in the French press and reports of it were also published in Italy (*L'Antologia*, II, 1821, p. 313) and England (*Annals of the Fine Arts*, IV, 1819, p. 474), where the picture was re-exhibited in 1820. Many studies have been devoted to the artistic sources of *The Raft of the 'Medusa'* but G. Oprescu (*Géricault*, Paris, 1927, p. 114) seems to have been the only writer to have suggested the influence of Victor Schnetz. Géricault's friend and disciple A. A. Montfort recorded that when Géricault returned from Italy in 1817 and discussed with Horace Vernet the artists then working in Rome, 'L'un d'eux, Schnetz, fut celui dont le nom revint le plus fréquemment à la bouche de M. Géricault qui semblait faire un cas extrême de son talent' (P. Courthion, *Géricault raconté par lui-même et par ses amis*, Geneva, 1947, p. 183). The painting on which Schnetz was working while Géricault was in Rome is the heroic scale *Cain* [Fig. vi. Accademia di San Luca, Rome], which in handling of paint and manner

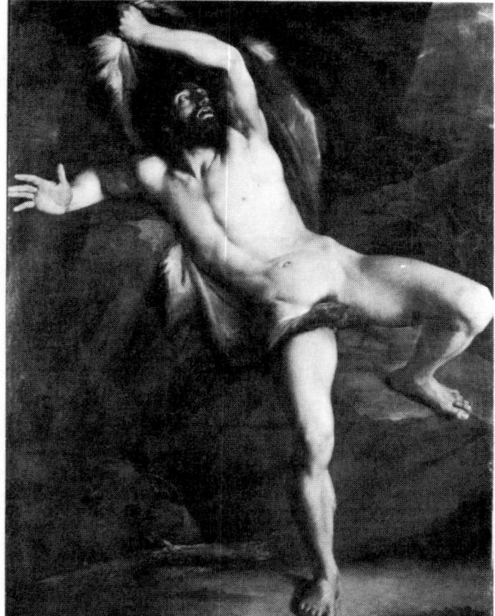

Figure vi. *Cain*, 1817. Victor Schnetz

of rendering the nude stands, perhaps significantly, between David's glabrously smooth figures and the more richly modelled men on *The Raft*.

Lit: L. Eitner, *Géricault's 'Raft of the Medusa'*, London and New York, 1972.

10. THE RETREAT FROM RUSSIA. By Boissard de Boisdenier, 1835. Oil on canvas, 160 × 225 cm. *Rouen, Musée des Beaux-Arts.* (Photo: Giraudon.)

Boissard was a poet and musician as well as a painter and also 'le maître du logis' of the *club des haschichins* frequented by Baudelaire. Théophile Gautier included a vivid description of him in his introduction to the 1868 edition of *Les fleurs du mal*, mentioning the success of *The Retreat from Russia.*

Lit: *Gros, ses amis, ses élèves*, exh. cat., Petit Palais, Paris, 1936, no. 138.

11. DRAGOON OF THE IMPERIAL GUARD. By Edouard-Alexandre Odier, 1832. Oil on canvas, 261 × 198 cm. *Amiens, Musée de Picardie.*

Entitled *Episode de Moscou* when shown at the Salon of 1833, and bought by the Crown for the Luxembourg. Described as 'Un dragon de la garde impériale, épuisé par ses blessures, s'achemine péniblement, s'appuyant sur son cheval' in the official catalogue *Explications des ouvrages de peinture et de sculpture de l'école moderne de France, exposée dans le Musée Royal du Luxembourg*, Paris, 1836, p. 45.

12. THE THIRD OF MAY 1808. By Francisco de Goya, 1814. Oil on canvas, 266 × 345 cm. *Madrid, Museo del Prado.* (Photo: MAS.)

On 24 February 1814, Goya petitioned the Spanish Regency Council to 'perpetuate with his brush the most notable and heroic actions or events of our glorious insurrections against the Tyrant of Europe'. He was commissioned to paint two pictures, *The Second* and *The Third of May 1808*, depicting incidents in the guerilla war against the Napoleonic army of occupation in Spain. They may have been conceived partly as a riposte to A.-J. Gros's *Capitulation of Madrid, The Fourth of December 1808* (now Musée de Versailles) which records the French re-occupation of the city: Goya could have seen a print of this in C. P. Landon, *Annales du Musée ... Salon de 1810*, Paris, 1810, p. 24. He may also have been influenced by English anti-Napoleonic prints (see E. H. Gombrich, *Meditations on a Hobby Horse*, London, 1963, p. 125).

Lit: Hugh Thomas, *Goya: The Third of May 1808*, London and New York, 1972.

13. STUDY OF SEVERED LEGS AND AN ARM. By Théodore Géricault, 1818. Oil on canvas, 52 × 64 cm. *Montpellier, Musée Fabre.* (Photo: Giraudon.)

Géricault is said to have made a number of similar studies while preparing to paint *The Raft of the 'Medusa'*. Six are recorded. That illustrated here seems to be identical with one mentioned by Delacroix (*Journal*, III, pp. 70–71). Comparing it with a portrait by J.-L. David he remarked: 'On y voit tout ce qui a toujours manqué à David, cette force pittoresque, ce nerf, cet osé qui est à la peinture ce que la *vis comica* est à l'art du théâtre ... Ce fragment de Géricault est vraiment sublime: il prouve plus que jamais qu'*il n'est pas de serpent ni de monstre odieux*, etc. C'est la meilleur argument en faveur du Beau, comme il faut l'entendre.' The words in italic are a quotation from Boileau's *Art poétique.*

Lit: L. Eitner, *Géricault's 'Raft of the Medusa'*, London and New York, 1972, p. 168.

14. THE BARQUE OF DANTE. By Eugène Delacroix, 1822. Oil on canvas, 189 × 246 cm. *Paris, Musée du Louvre.* (Photo: Alinari.)

Inspired by the eighth canto of the *Inferno* (lines 25–69), in which Dante and Virgil are ferried across the fifth circle of hell to the city of Dis by Flegias. The arrogant Florentine Argenti addresses Dante, who repulses him. It is not one of the more famous passages of Dante, and Delacroix appears to have been the first to illustrate it. Shown in the 1822 Salon, *The Barque of Dante* was bought by the Crown and hung in the Luxembourg. By 1860 its condition had deteriorated and Delacroix was authorized to have it relined and retouch it.

Lit: Lee Johnson, 'The Formal Sources of Delacroix's Barque de Dante' in *Burlington Magazine*, C, 1958, pp. 228–32; Delacroix Exhibition, no. 27.

15. THE MASSACRES OF CHIOS. By Eugène Delacroix, 1824. Oil on canvas, 417 × 154 cm. *Paris, Musée du Louvre.* (Photo: Giraudon.)

In April 1822, the island of Chios was taken by a Turkish force. Some 20,000 Christian inhabitants were massacred and others sold into slavery. In May 1823 Delacroix decided to commemorate the event in a picture he entitled *Scènes des massacres de Scio: famillies grecques attendant la mort ou l'esclavage.* Its progress can be followed almost day by day in his journal. After it was sent to the Louvre for exhibition in the 1824 Salon, he is said to have retouched it under the influence of paintings by Constable which he had recently seen in Paris, probably adding (as Lee Johnson suggests) highlights in brilliant colour, especially in the foreground.

Lit: Lee Johnson, *Delacroix*, New York, 1963, pp. 19–26; M. Florisoone, 'La genèse espagnole des Massacres de Scio' in *Revue du Louvre*, XIII, 1963, pp. 195–208; Delacroix Exhibition, no. 46.

16. STILL-LIFE WITH LOBSTERS. By Eugène Delacroix, 1827. Oil on canvas, 80 × 106 cm. *Paris, Musée du Louvre.* (Photo: Giraudon.)

Lit: Delacroix Exhibition, no. 98.

17a and b. TWO VERSIONS OF THE DEATH OF HECTOR (*La mort d'Hector* and *Encore la mort d'Hector*). Anonymous, *c.* 1824–30. Lithographs. *Paris, Bibliothèque Nationale.*

18. THE APOTHEOSIS OF HOMER. By Jean-Auguste-Dominique Ingres, 1827. Oil on canvas, 386 × 515 cm. *Paris, Musée du Louvre.* (Photo: Giraudon.)

Painted for the ceiling of the Salle Clarac of the newly named Musée Charles X in the Louvre, it was installed by December 1827. In 1855 it was taken down to be shown in the *Exposition universelle* and in 1860 a copy was provided for the ceiling so that the original could be hung vertically. According to Ingres's account of the iconographical programme (published by Raoul-Rochette in *Journal des Débats*, November, 1827), Homer is flanked by great writers and artists of Antiquity; also Raphael (with great prominence on the left) and Michelangelo (almost hidden behind Phidias on the right). On the left, Dante (with Virgil's arm round him) forms a link with the figures below, all but one of whom are moderns – Shakespeare, Tasso, La Fontaine, Poussin, Mozart and Corneille on the left, and Racine, Molière, Boileau, Longinus, Fénelon, Gluck and Camoens. In about 1840 Ingres began a revised version of the subject, for which he completed a drawing (Louvre) in 1865. Here he eliminated Shakespeare, Tasso and Camoens but added several others – Barthélémy (author of *Voyage du jeune Anacharsis*), Winckelmann, Giulio Romano, Jean Goujon, Lesueur, J.-L. David and John Flaxman.

Lit: N. Schlenoff, *Ingres, ses sources littéraires*, Paris, 1956, pp. 148–200; R. Rosenblum, *Jean-Auguste-Dominique Ingres*, London, 1967, pp. 130–133; *Ingres*, exh. cat., Petit Palais, Paris, 1967–8, no. 141; J. Whiteley, 'Homer Abandoned' in F. Haskell et al., *The Artist and the Writer in France: Essays in Honour of Jean Seznec*, Oxford, 1974, pp. 40–51.

19. THE DEATH OF SARDANAPALUS. By Eugène Delacroix, 1828. Oil on canvas, 395 × 495 cm. *Paris, Musée du Louvre.* (Photo: Réunion des musées nationaux.)

Byron's tragedy *Sardanapalus* (London, 1821, translated into French, 1825) probably drew Delacroix's attention to this subject, though it includes no description of the scene he painted.

 Lit: Jack J. Spector, *Delacroix: The Death of Sardanapalus*, London and New York, 1974.

20. INNOVATION ROMANTIQUE. Anonymous, *c.* 1830. Lithograph. *Paris, Bibliothèque Nationale.*

21. THE BARD. By John Martin, 1817. Oil on canvas, 213 × 155 cm. *Newcastle-on-Tyne, Laing Art Gallery and Museum.* (Photo: Philipson Studios.)

The picture illustrates the second stanza of Thomas Gray's 'The Bard, a Pindaric Ode' (1757). In a footnote Gray remarked that his image of the Bard ('Loose his beard, and hoary hair / Stream'd like a meteor, to the troubled air') was 'taken from a well known picture by Raphael representing the Supreme Being in the vision of Ezekiel' (i.e. that now in Palazzo Pitti, Florence). The lines were illustrated by several artists in the late eighteenth century: Paul Sandby (1760), Thomas Jones (1774), Philippe de Loutherbourg (early 1780s), Blake (*c.* 1797–9) and Fuseli (*c.* 1799). But Martin based his composition very closely on a painting of 1807 by Richard Corbould, merely adding the castle on the left and emphasizing the precipitousness of the mountains.

Lit: F. L. McCarthy, 'The Bard of Thomas Gray, its composition and use by painters' in *National Library of Wales Journal*, XIV, 1965, pp. 105–13; A. S. Marks, 'The Source of John Martin's "The Bard" ' in *Apollo*, LXXXIV, 1966, suppl. 'Notes on British Art' to August issue, pp. 1–2; W. Feaver, *The Art of John Martin*, London, 1975, p. 31.

22. A SCENE FROM BYRON'S *MANFRED*. By Thomas Cole, 1833. Oil on canvas, 127 × 96.5 cm. *New Haven, Yale University Art Gallery. John Hill Morgan, B.A. 1893, Fund.*

This illustrates scene 2 from Byron's dramatic poem *Manfred* (London, 1817), 'A lower Valley of the Alps – a Cataract'. The same poem inspired a painting by John Martin, 1837 (now Birmingham City Museum and Art Gallery).

Lit: H. S. Merritt, 'Studies on Thomas Cole' in *Baltimore Museum of Art Annual*, II, 1967, p. 88; T. E. Stubbins Jr, 'American Landscape: Some new acquisitions at Yale' in *Yale University Gallery Bulletin*, XXXIII, 1971, p. 12.

23. ROCKY MOUNTAIN WITH LANDSCAPE AND SHEEP. By Thomas Gainsborough, 1783. Oil on canvas, 116 × 143.5 cm. *Edinburgh, National Gallery of Scotland.*

This has been identified with a picture shown by Gainsborough at the Royal Academy, 1783, entitled *Landscape* and described in the *Morning Herald* as 'A romantic view, a precipice is the principal object in the foreground, with several figures, sheep, etc., descending to a rivulet that gushes through a cranny in the earth. The sky beautiful'.

Lit: L. T. Whitley, *Artists and their Friends, 1700–99*, London, 1928, II, p. 379; *The Romantic Movement*, exh. cat., Tate Gallery, London, 1959, p. 164.

24. DORDRECHT: THE DORT PACKET-BOAT FROM ROTTERDAM BECALMED. By Joseph Mallord William Turner, 1818. Oil on canvas, 157.5 × 233.5 cm. *Collection of Mr and Mrs Paul Mellon.*

Turner visited Dordrecht, Cuyp's native town, in 1817 and seems to have conceived this picture as both an act of homage to Cuyp and an attempt to rival his achievement – it is a much larger canvas than the latter's *View of Dordrecht*, already in an English collection (now Iveagh Bequest, Kenwood).

Lit: *The Shock of Recognition*, exh. cat., Tate Gallery, London, 1971, no. 44.

25. DEDHAM VALE. By John Constable, 1828. Oil on canvas, 145 × 122 cm. *Edinburgh, National Gallery of Scotland.*

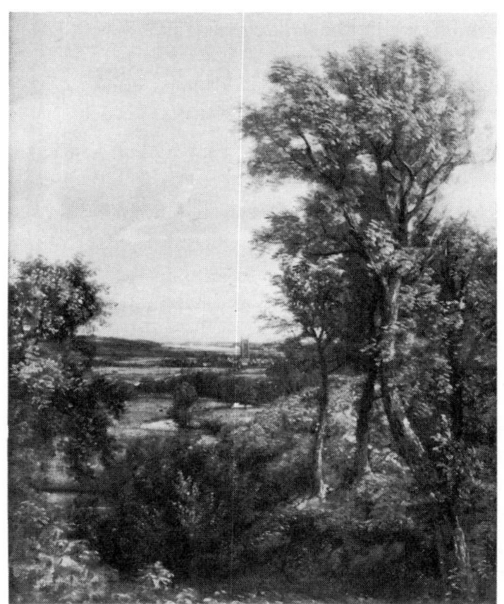

Figure vii. *Dedham Vale*, *c.* 1802. Constable

A small painting of the same view, *c.* 1802 [Fig. vii. Victoria and Albert Museum], is clearly influenced by Claude's *Hagar and Ishmael* which Constable had seen in Sir George Beaumont's collection. The bequest of the latter to the National Gallery in 1827 may have inspired him to return to the subject, though he now departed further from the Claudean composition.

Lit: Constable Exhibition, no. 253.

26. CLOUD STUDY. By Pierre-Henri de Valenciennes, *c.* 1780–86. Oil on paper, 23.8 × 38.8 cm. *Paris, Musée du Louvre.*

Lit: R. Mesuret, *Pierre-Henri de Valenciennes*, exh. cat., Toulouse, 1956.

27. CLOUD STUDY. By John Constable, 1821. Oil on paper, 21.2 × 29 cm. *Collection of Mr and Mrs Paul Mellon.*

In 1821–2 Constable painted some fifty studies of clouds, on several of which he noted date, time and weather conditions: see Kurt Badt, *John Constable's Clouds*, London, 1950. This study is inscribed, on the reverse: 'Augt 1. 1822/11 o'clock A.M./very hot with large climbing Clouds/under the Sun/wind westerly.' These studies were painted from nature, but cf. E. H. Gombrich, *Art and Illusion*, London and New York, 1960, pp. 175–78.

Lit: Ross Watson, *John Constable, A Selection of Paintings from the Collection of Mr and Mrs Paul Mellon*, exh. cat., National Gallery of Art, Washington, D.C., 1969, no. 51.

28. CASPAR DAVID FRIEDRICH IN HIS STUDIO. By Georg Friedrich Kersting, 1819. Oil on canvas, 51 × 40 cm. *Berlin, Staatliche Museen Preussischer Kulturbesitz, Nationalgalerie.* (Photo: Walter Steinkopf.)

Kersting exhibited an earlier version of this composition in 1811, together with a picture of another artist, Gerhard von Kügelgen, in his elegantly furnished apartment (now Staatliche Kunstsammlungen, Weimar): the striking contrast between the two was noted by contemporaries.

Lit: *Caspar David Friedrich*, exh. cat., Tate Gallery, London, 1972, no. 113.

29. ELM TREE TRUNK. By John Constable, *c.* 1821. Oil on paper, 30.6 × 24.8 cm. *London, Victoria and Albert Museum.*

Lit: G. Reynolds, *Victoria and Albert Museum, Catalogue of the Constable Collection*, London, 1973, p. 235.

30. THE WHITE HOUSE, CHELSEA. By Thomas Girtin, 1800. Watercolour, 30 × 51.5 cm. *London, Tate Gallery.*

Another version is in the collection of Sir Hickman Bacon. One of these views was known to, and greatly admired by, Turner.

Lit: F. W. Hawcroft, *Watercolours by Thomas Girtin*, exh. cat., Whitworth Art Gallery, Manchester, 1975, no. 60.

31. FOREGROUND STUDY. By Johann August Heinrich, *c.* 1818–20. Oil on paper, 21 × 26 cm. *Dresden, Staatliche, Kunstsammlungen, Gemäldegalerie.*

32. LANDSCAPE IN GUELDERLAND. By Wouter Joannes van Troostwijk, *c.* 1808–10. Oil on canvas, 52.5 × 63 cm. *Amsterdam, Rijksmuseum.*

Lit: J. Knoef, *Tusschen Rococo en Romantik*, The Hague, 1943, pp. 111–34.

33. ABINGDON: MORNING. By Joseph Mallord William Turner, *c.* 1810. Oil on canvas, 100 × 128 cm. *London, Tate Gallery.*

One of a group of Thames valley agricultural scenes painted between 1805 and 1811. Turner entitled another *Ploughing up Turnips, near Slough* (Tate Gallery), as if to draw attention to its workaday subject rather than to the skyline silhouette of Windsor Castle dimly glimpsed through the mist.

Lit: *The Shock of Recognition*, exh. cat., Tate Gallery, London, 1971, no. 43.

34. THE PLOUGHED FIELD. By John Sell Cotman, *c.* 1807. Pencil and watercolour, 24 × 36 cm. *Leeds, City Art Gallery.*

Cotman's watercolours and prints of this type initially met with little success: in 1811 a bookseller told him that subscribers did not like one of his etchings 'because it might have been *anywhere*. Two thirds of mankind, you know, mind more *what* is represented than *how* it is done.'

Lit: S. D. Kitson, *The Life of John Sell Cotman*, London, 1937, pl. 52.

35. MORNING (detail). By Philipp Otto Runge, 1808–9. Oil on canvas (whole work 152 × 113 cm). *Hamburg, Kunsthalle.*

On his death-bed in 1810, Runge asked his brother Daniel to cut up *Morning*, his largest and last work. Daniel refused to do this and the picture, though unfinished, seems to have remained intact until 1890 when it was cut into nine pieces which were reassembled in 1927.

Lit: J. Traeger, *Philipp Otto Runge*, Munich, 1975, pp. 156–68, 446–7.

36. LANDSCAPE WITH GRAVE, COFFIN AND OWL. By Caspar David Friedrich, *c.* 1836–7. Pencil and sepia wash, 48.5 × 38.5 cm. *Hamburg, Kunsthalle.*

Lit: Börsch-Supan/Jähnig, pp. 461–2.

37. THE LARGE ENCLOSURE NEAR DRESDEN. By Caspar David Friedrich, 1832. Oil on canvas, 73 × 102.5 cm. *Dresden, Staatliche Kunstsammlungen, Gemäldegalerie.*
Lit: Börsch-Supan/Jähnig, p. 431.

38. THE WANDERER ABOVE THE MISTS. By Caspar David Friedrich, *c.* 1817–18. Oil on canvas, 74.8 × 94.8 cm. *Hamburg, Kunsthalle.* (Photo: Arts Council of Great Britain.)
Lit: Börsch-Supan/Jähnig, p. 349.

39. THE CLIFFS OF RÜGEN. By Caspar David Friedrich, 1818–20. Oil on canvas, 90.5 × 71 cm. *Winterthur, Stiftung Oskar Reinhart.*
Börsch-Supan has identified the figures as the painter himself (looking over the cliff edge), his wife and his brother, Christian.
Lit: Börsch-Supan/Jähnig, pp. 353–4.

40. TWO MEN CONTEMPLATING THE MOON. By Caspar David Friedrich, 1819. Oil on canvas, 35 × 44 cm. *Dresden, Staatliche Kunstsammlungen, Gemäldegalerie.*
The two men are probably Friedrich himself and his pupil August Heinrich. When asked what they were talking about, Friedrich is said to have 'replied ironically' that they were 'hatching demagogic plots' (S. Hinz, p. 220). The 'old-German' costumes they wear were associated with Liberalism and the picture has thus been given a political interpretation (see p. 356, n. 10). It has also been read as a religious allegory (by Börsch-Supan). But as the two men have always been recognized as artists, a primarily artistic meaning seems more probable – with the dying oak tree perhaps signifying the art of the past (especially the German past) which cannot be revived.
Lit: Börsch-Supan/Jähnig, p. 356.

41. PILGRIM IN A ROCKY VALLEY. By Carl Gustav Carus, *c.* 1841. Oil on canvas, 28 × 22 cm. *Berlin, Nationalgalerie, Staatliche Museen Preussischer Kulturbesitz.* (Photo: Walter Steinkopf.)
Lit: M. Prause, *Carl Gustav Carus: Leben und Werk*, Berlin, 1968, p. 175.

42. THE ROMAN CAMPAGNA. By Martinus Rørbye, 1835. Oil on paper, 32 × 41 cm, *Gothenburg, Konstmuseum.*
Lit: M. Mackeprag, 'Kampagnen' in L. Bobé, ed., *Rom og Danmark*, vol. III, Copenhagen, 1942, p. 5.

43. THE GATEWAY BRIDGE. By Christian Købke, 1834. Oil on canvas. 79 × 93 cm. *Copenhagen, Ny Carlsberg Glyptotek.*

44. IN A SHOREHAM GARDEN. By Samuel Palmer, *c.* 1829. Watercolour and body-colour, 28.2 × 22.2 cm. *London, Victoria and Albert Museum.*
Lit: Geoffrey Grigson, *Samuel Palmer: The Visionary Years*, London, 1947.

45. VIEW OF DEDHAM. By John Constable, 1814–15. Oil on canvas, 55.3 × 78.1 cm. *Boston, Museum of Fine Arts.*
The mound by which the men are working in the foreground is a dunghill, of the type known in East Anglia as a 'runover dungle', which is given slightly less prominence in a preliminary sketch (Leeds City Art Gallery). Constable was not the only artist of his time to paint such a subject: in Denmark, Johan Thomas Lundbye depicted men muck-spreading (Statens Museum for Kunst, Copenhagen, no. 4774).

Lit: I. Fleming-Williams, 'A Runover Dungle and a Possible Date for "Spring"' in *Burlington Magazine*, CXIV, 1972, pp. 386–93.

46. SKETCH FOR 'THE LEAPING HORSE'. By John Constable, 1824–5. Oil on canvas, 129.4 × 188 cm. *London, Victoria and Albert Museum.*
Lit: Constable Exhibition, no. 236.

47. LANDSCAPE (THE LEAPING HORSE). By John Constable, 1825. Oil on canvas, 142.2 × 187.3 cm. *London, Royal Academy of Arts.*
Constable began work on this composition in November 1824 and showed it at the Royal Academy in 1825, but made some alterations after the exhibition was over. As the view is not topographically accurate the inclusion of Dedham church tower may have a symbolical significance.
Lit: Constable Exhibition, no. 238.

48. STONEHENGE. By John Constable, 1836. Watercolour, 38.7 × 59.1 cm. *London, Victoria and Albert Museum.*
Constable visited Stonehenge in 1820 and made a pencil sketch (British Museum). When exhibited at the Royal Academy, 1836, the watercolour was catalogued as: 'Stonehenge. "The mysterious monument of Stonehenge, standing remote on a bare and boundless heath, as much unconnected with the events of past ages as it is with the uses of the present, carries you back beyond all historical records into the obscurity of a totally unknown period."'
Lit: Constable Exhibition, no. 311.

49. SNOW STORM – STEAM BOAT OFF A HARBOUR'S MOUTH. By Joseph Mallord William Turner, 1842. Oil on canvas, 91.5 × 122 cm. *London, Tate Gallery.*
Exhibited at the Royal Academy in 1842, and described in the catalogue as: 'Snow-Storm – Steam Boat off a Harbour's Mouth making signals in Shallow Water, and going by the Land'. Ruskin, in *Modern Painters*, reported a conversation about the picture between Turner and the Rev. William Kingsley, who remarked that his mother had liked it:
'"I did not paint it to be understood, but I wished to show what such a scene was like: I got the sailors to lash me to the mast to observe it; I was lashed for four hours and I did not expect to escape, but I felt bound to record it if I did. But no one had any business to like the picture."

'"But my mother went through just such a scene, and it brought it all back to her."

'"Is your mother a painter?"

'"No."

'"Then she ought to have been thinking of something else."'

Joseph Vernet had been lashed to the mast of a ship on which he was sailing to Rome in order to study the effect of a storm at sea – an incident commemorated in a large picture by his grandson Horace in the Musée Calvet, Avignon: see G. Levitine, 'Vernet tied to the Mast in a Storm: The evolution of an episode of art historical folklore' in *Art Bulletin*, XLIX, 1967, pp. 92–100.
Lit: L. Gowing, *Turner: Imagination and Reality*, New York, 1966, pp. 45–8.

50. REGULUS. By Joseph Mallord William Turner, 1828–37. Oil on canvas, 91 × 124 cm. *London, Tate Gallery.*
Painted and exhibited in Rome in 1828 and again, with alterations, in London in 1837. As John Gage has pointed out, Regulus, who was exposed to the sun with his eye-lids cut

off, does not figure in the picture: the spectator is put in his place, staring into the light.
Lit: John Gage, *Colour in Turner*, London, 1969, p. 143.

51. THE BURNING OF THE HOUSES OF LORDS AND COMMONS, OCTOBER 16, 1834. By Joseph Mallord William Turner, 1835. Oil on canvas, 92.7 × 123.2 cm. *Cleveland, Museum of Art, Bequest of John L. Severance.*

Turner witnessed the burning of the Houses of Parliament, making several sketches on the spot and, probably later, a number of watercolours. In the following year he exhibited two paintings of the subject, one at the Royal Academy (illustrated here), the other at the British Institution (now in the Philadelphia Museum of Art).

Lit: A. J. Finberg, p. 354.

52. THE SLAVE SHIP (SLAVERS THROWING OVERBOARD THE DEAD AND DYING – TYPHON COMING ON). By Joseph Mallord William Turner, 1840. Oil on canvas, 90.8 × 122 cm. *Boston, Museum of Fine Arts.*

Lit: H. Honour, *The European Vision of America*, exh. cat., National Gallery, Washington D.C.; Cleveland Museum of Art; and Grand Palais, Paris, 1975–6, no. 315.

53. THE ANGEL STANDING IN THE SUN. By Joseph Mallord William Turner, 1846. Oil on canvas, 78.5 × 78.5 cm. *London, Tate Gallery.*

When he exhibited this picture (Royal Academy, 1846), Turner had two verses from *The Book of Revelations* printed in the catalogue (xix, 17–18) and also a quotation from Samuel Rogers, *The Voyage of Columbus* (Canto VI):

> 'The morning-march that flashes to the sun,
> The feast of vultures when the day is done.'

Lit: *Turner*, exh. cat., Royal Academy, London, 1975, no. 526.

54. CAMPO SANTO, VENICE. By Joseph Mallord William Turner, 1842. Oil on canvas, 62.2 × 92.7 cm. *Toledo, Ohio, The Toledo Museum of Art.*

Lit: A. J. Finberg, p. 390.

55. SEASCAPE. By Joseph Mallord William Turner, *c.* 1840–45. Oil on canvas, 91.5 × 121.5 cm. *London, Tate Gallery.*

One of several paintings found in Turner's studio after his death in 1851. When rediscovered in 1939, they were thought to be extraordinary precursors of non-representational art. As Kenneth Clark writes: 'They depend for their effect entirely on light and colour and have no identifiable subject – nothing to distract us from pure sensation. They are modern painting' (*The Romantic Rebellion*, London, 1973, p. 223). They are now thought to have been 'colour beginnings', canvases of the type which Turner took to the Royal Academy exhibitions and worked up into recognizable seascapes or landscapes on 'varnishing days'. However, this in no way detracts from their extraordinary power.

Lit: L. Gowing, *Turner: Imagination and Reality*, New York, 1966, p. 38; *La peinture romantique anglaise*, no. 271.

56. THE DEVOTION OF CAPTAIN DESSE. By Théodore Gudin, 1830. Oil on canvas, 210 × 295 cm. *Bordeaux, Musée des Beaux Arts.* (Photo: Réunion des musées nationaux.)

When exhibited at the 1831 Salon it was entitled *Trait de dévouement du capitaine Desse, de Bordeaux, envers le 'Columbus', navire hollandaise.* Despite great danger Desse had rescued the crew of a Dutch ship foundering in a heavy Atlantic storm.

Lit: *French Painting 1774–1830*, no. 92.

57. GUARDIAN'S HOUSE IN THE FOREST OF COMPIÈGNE. By Paul Huet, 1826. Oil on canvas, 116×148 cm. *Paris, Michel Legrand Collection.* (Photo: Réunion des musées nationaux.)

This may be one of the several pictures Huet unsuccessfully submitted to the 1826 Salon. It clearly reveals the impact of Constable's landscapes, about which Huet was later to write (see René-Paul Huet, *Paul Huet (1803–1869) d'après ses notes ...*, Paris, 1911, p. 95).

Lit: *French Painting 1774–1830*, no. 103.

58. IN THE SALZKAMMERGUT. By Johann Christian Erhard, 1818. Watercolour, 12.7×18.3 cm. *Bremen, Kunsthalle.*

The two figures are Johann Adam Klein and Ernst Welcker, who accompanied Erhard on a walking tour in the Salzkammergut.

Lit: *William Turner und die Landschaft seiner Zeit*, exh. cat., Kunsthalle, Hamburg, 1976, no. 345.

59. THE LANDSCAPE PAINTER ON HIS TRAVELS. By Johann Adam Klein, 1814. Etching. *Bremen, Kunsthalle.* (Photo: Stickelmann.)

60. CLOUD STUDY. By Adalbert Stifter, *c.* 1840. Oil on paper, 20.6×31.6 cm. *Vienna, Osterreichische Galerie.*

Stifter described a painter making cloud studies in his autobiographical short story *Feldblumen.*

Lit: F. Novotny, 'Zu einer "Wolkenstudie" von Adalbert Stifter' in *Mitteilungen der Österreichischen Galerie*, 1971, pp. 64–72.

61. VIEW OF HOUSES AND GARDENS. By Carl Blechen, *c.* 1830–37. Oil on paper, 20×26 cm. *Berlin, Staatliche Museen Preussischer Kulturbesitz, Nationalgalerie.* (Photo: Walter Steinkopf.)

Lit: F. Novotny, *Painting and Sculpture in Europe 1780–1880* (1960), Harmondsworth, 1971, pp. 223–4; Gertrud Heider, *Carl Blechen*, Leipzig, 1970, p. 32.

62. GRETA WOODS FROM BRIGNAL BANKS. By John Sell Cotman, *c.* 1805. Watercolour, 19.7×28.8 cm. *Leeds, City Art Galleries.*

Lit: *Romantic Art in Britain*, exh. cat., Detroit Institute of Arts, Philadelphia Museum of Art, 1968, no. 131.

63. THE ARTIST'S STUDIO IN PARMA. By Giovanni Battista De Gubernatis, 1812. Watercolour, 23.6×18.2 cm. *Turin, Galleria d'Arte Moderna.*

Lit: A. Passoni, *La Collezione G. B. De Gubernatis*, (Museo Civico) Turin, n.d.

64. A GARDEN IN VIENNA. By Erasmus Ritter von Engert, *c.* 1828–30. Oil on canvas, 31×26 cm. *Berlin, Staatliche Museen Preussischer Kulturbesitz, Nationalgalerie.* (Photo: Walter Steinkopf.)

Lit: *Park und Garten in der Malerei*, exh. cat., Wallraf-Richartz Museum, Cologne, 1957, no. 32.

65. CHAMONIX AND MONT BLANC. By Ludwig Ferdinand Schnorr von Carolsfeld, 1848. Oil on canvas, 24×42 cm. *Vienna, Österreichische Galerie.*

Symbols similar to that of the lonely traveller or 'wanderer' appear in other works by L. F. Schnorr von Carolsfeld. The moral improvement derived from the contemplation of nature is suggested by *Die 'Breite Fohre' bei Modling* (Österreichische Galerie, Vienna) in which a well-dressed couple seated on the grass give alms to a poor man.

66. PLATE. Königliche Porzellan-Manufaktur, Berlin, *c.* 1817–25. Painted porcelain, 24.5 cm diameter. *Berlin, Karl H. Bröhan Coll.* (Photo: J. Littkemann.)

The view is of a mountain landscape near Andermatt.

Lit: *Porzellan Kunst, Sammlung Karl H. Bröhan*, exh. cat., Schloss Charlottenburg, Berlin, 1969, no. 438.

67. GORDALE SCAR. By James Ward, 1811–13. Oil on canvas, 332×421 cm. *London, Tate Gallery.*

Gordale Scar in the West Riding of Yorkshire began to attract visitors in the eighteenth century. Thomas Gray in 1770 viewed it 'not without shuddering'; Wordsworth later wrote of 'Gordale chasm, terrific as the lair / Where the young lions crouch'. Several artists had depicted it before Sir George Beaumont declared it to be 'unpaintable'. Ward made numerous pencil studies (Tate Gallery) and at least two oil sketches (Leeds City Art Gallery and Bradford City Art Gallery) for the vast picture, shown at the Royal Academy in 1815.

Lit: P. Summerhayes, 'James Ward R.A. and *Gordale Scar*' in *Country Life*, CLXII, 1977, pp. 154–5.

68. LAKE WITH DEAD TREES. By Thomas Cole, 1825. Oil on canvas, 68.58×87.6 cm. *Oberlin College, Ohio, Allen Memorial Art Museum.*

Lit: *Allen Memorial Art Museum Bulletin*, XIII, 1956, pp. 165–7.

69. LANDSCAPE IN THE AUVERGNE. By Pierre-Etienne-Théodore Rousseau, 1837. Oil on canvas, 64.7×80.7 cm. *Toledo, Ohio, The Toledo Museum of Art.*

Lit: *Barbizon Revisited*, exh. cat., Palace of the Legion of Honor, San Francisco, 1962, no. 90; *The Past Rediscovered: French Painting 1800–1900*, exh. cat., Minneapolis Institute of Arts, Minneapolis, 1969, no. 75.

70. MORNING. By Philipp Otto Runge, 1803. Pen and ink, 71.7×48.2 cm. *Hamburg, Kunsthalle.*

Runge's final drawing for *Morning* in the series of four engravings *Die Zeiten*, published 1805.

Lit: J. Traeger, *Philipp Otto Runge*, Munich, 1975, pp. 46–52, 356–61.

71. THE SINGER'S DREAM. By Caspar David Friedrich, *c.* 1830. Pencil, 72×51.5 cm. *Hamburg, Kunsthalle.*

The drawing very closely corresponds to Friedrich's own description of one of four transparencies (now lost) which he was painting in 1830 for the Russian Imperial family (text in S. Hinz, p. 58).

Lit: Börsch-Supan/Jähnig, nos. 346, 437.

72. BEETHOVEN'S ROOM. By Johann Nepomuk Höchle, 1827. Pen and wash 25.8×21.1 cm. *Vienna, Historisches Museum der Stadt Wien.* (Photo: R. Stepanek.)

73. PAGANINI. By Eugene Delacroix, 1831. Oil on millboard, 41 × 28 cm. *Washington, D.C., Phillips Collection.* (Photo: Giraudon.)

Probably painted shortly after Delacroix attended Paganini's first concert in Paris, at the Opéra, 9 March 1831. For a vivid description of Paganini, corresponding closely with Delacroix's portrait, see Arturo Codignola, *Paganini intimo*, Genoa, 1935, pp. 321–2.

Lit: Delacroix Exhibition, no. 150.

74. WOTAN. By Bengt Erland Fogelberg, 1830. Marble, 312 cm high. *Stockholm, Nationalmuseum.*

The pose follows Antique statues of Zeus. A sketch model (also Nationalmuseum, Stockholm) shows Wotan wearing a more obviously Nordic plumed helm, which Fogelberg retained for a bust (Gothenburg Museum).

75. THE PRINCESSES LUISE AND FRIEDERIKE OF PRUSSIA. By Johann Gottfried Schadow, 1795–7. Marble, 172 cm high. *Berlin, Nationalgalerie.*

Schadow exhibited a full-size plaster model of the group at the Akademie in Berlin in 1795, but he made several revisions (notably the omission of a basket of flowers held by the elder princess) in the marble carved mainly by his assistant Claude Goussaut and exhibited at the Akademie in 1797. The work derives from two Antique groups, the 'Marbury Hall' *Bacchus and Ariadne* (now Museum of Fine Arts, Boston) and the San Ildefonso *Castor and Pollux* (now Prado, Madrid).

Lit: *Johann Gottfried Schadow*, exh. cat., Nationalgalerie, Berlin (East), 1964–5, no. 18.

76. PRINCESS LEOPOLDINA ESTERHAZY-LIECHTENSTEIN. By Antonio Canova, 1808–18. Marble, 150 cm high. *Eisenstadt, Schloss Esterhazy.* (Photo: Bundesdenkmalamt Vienna.)

Commissioned by the sitter's husband, Prince Moritz Liechtenstein, by 20 May 1808, the full-size model was completed in 1808, but the marble was not finished until 1818 (MSS. Canoviani, Biblioteca Civica, Bassano del Grappa).

77. THE SLEEPING CHILDREN. By Sir Francis Chantrey, 1817. Marble, life size. *Lichfield Cathedral.* (Photo: National Monuments Record.)

Commissioned as a monument to Ellen Jane and Marianne Robinson. The plaster model was exhibited at the Royal Academy in 1817.

Lit: M. Whinney, *Sculpture in Britain 1530–1830*, Harmondsworth, 1964, pp. 219–22; N. Penny, *Church Monuments in Romantic England*, New Haven and London, 1977, pp. 116–18.

78. THE LION OF LUCERNE. By Bertel Thorvaldsen, 1819–21. Stone. *Lucerne, Switzerland.*

In 1818 Thorvaldsen was commissioned to provide a model of a dying lion resting on a Bourbon coat of arms as a monument to the Swiss Guards killed at the Tuileries, Paris, in 1792. He made a drawing immediately and completed a large plaster model next year. It was originally intended that the monument should be carved in marble or cast in bronze and placed in front of a cliff-face. The proposal that it should be carved out of the living rock was made by a minor Swiss sculptor and writer in Rome, Heinrich Keller, and met with Thorvaldsen's enthusiastic approval. Lucas Ahorn carved it, enlarging the original model. Unfortunately it is not known who was responsible for the general design, which transformed the whole cliff-face and its setting into a work of art.

Lit: D. Helsted, 'Thorvaldsens Schweizerlöwe' in '*Maegtige Schweiz*', exh. cat., Thorvaldsens Museum, Copenhagen, 1973, pp. 144–7.

79a. STUDY OF A SEATED BOY. By Julius Schnorr von Carolsfeld, 1821. Pencil, 44.2 × 28.3 cm. *Munich, Dr Alfred Winterstein Coll.*

Lit: K. Andrews, *The Nazarenes*, Oxford, 1964, p. 113.

79b. SHEPHERD BOY. By Bertel Thorvaldsen, 1817–26. Marble, 149 cm high. *Manchester City Art Gallery.*

Thorvaldsen made the model for this July–October 1817. His first biographer, L. M. Thicle, stated that a boy who had been posing as Ganymede in Thorvaldsen's studio sat down to rest in this position, which caught the sculptor's eye. But this may be no more than an attempt to explain an unusual renunciation of literary subject-matter (a similar story was told about Canova's statue of Venus). Five marbles were carved from the model in Thorvaldsen's studio, the one illustrated having been commissioned by William Haldimand, probably in 1826.

Lit: *The Age of Neo-Classisism*, exh. cat., Royal Academy, London, 1972, no. 445.

79c. STUDY OF A SEATED BOY. By Julius Schnorr von Carolsfeld, 1822. Pen and ink, 43.9 × 29 cm. *Hamburg, Kunsthalle.*

Lit: *Die Nazarener*, exh. cat., Städelsches Kunstinstitut, Frankfurt am Main, 1977, E14.

80. ALFRED DE MUSSET. By Pierre Jean David called David d'Angers, 1831. Bronze medallion, 16.5 cm diameter. *Paris, Musée du Louvre.*

Lit: *David d'Angers 1788–1856*, exh. cat., Hôtel de la Monnaie, Paris, 1966, no. 122.

81. AUGUSTE-HILARION, COMTE DE KÉRATRY. By Honoré Daumier, *c.* 1832–3. Bronze, 12.4 cm high. *Milan, Private Collection.*

A bronze cast made shortly after 1925 from one of the 36 caricature busts modelled by Daumier. The features are similar to those of a lithograph by Daumier, *Caricature*, 19 September 1833. Kératry was a philosopher, art-theorist and politician who supported the July Revolution but later became an opponent of Liberalism.

Lit: D. Durbé, *Daumier Scultore*, exh. cat., Museo Poldi Pezzoli, Milan, 1961, no. 12.

82. LE GRAND CONDÉ. By Pierre-Jean David called David d'Angers, 1827. Bronze, 39 cm high. *Paris, Musée du Louvre.*

Reduction of an heroic-scale marble statue (destroyed 1944) which has a long prehistory. Before the Revolution, Philippe-Laurent Roland carved a statue of Louis II Prince de Condé for the Crown (plaster model exhibited in 1785 Salon, marble now at Versailles 1787). In 1815 he was given the commission to carve another for the pont Louis XVI (now pont de la Concorde), Paris, but as he was already ailing it passed to his pupil David, who exhibited a half-size plaster model at the 1817 Salon. David drew some inspiration from his master's statue but invested the figure with much greater vitality. According to Jouin, the pose exemplifies the principles of the Antique *Discobolos*. A more immediate source of inspiration was perhaps Bonaparte in A.-J. Gros's *Bataille des Pyramides*, even though this figure is on horseback.

Lit: H. Jouin, *David d'Angers, sa vie, son œuvre, ses écrits et ses contemporains*, Paris, 1878, I, pp. 118–24; F. H. Dowley in *Art Bulletin*, XXXIX, 1957, pp. 259–77.

83. TIGER DEVOURING A GAVIAL. By Antoine-Louis Barye, 1831–2. Bronze, 41 cm high. *Paris, Musée du Louvre.*

Barye exhibited the model for this work at the 1831 Salon, and a bronze cast of the following year was bought by the state in 1848. Although he had exhibited busts in the 1827 Salon, it was with this model that Barye first won critical acclaim.

Lit: *Barye*, exh. cat., Musée du Louvre, Paris, 1956–7, no. 3.

84. ORLANDO FURIOSO. By Jehan Du Seigneur, modelled 1830–31, founded 1867. Bronze, 130 cm high. *Paris, Musée du Louvre.*

Lit: H. Martin, T. Gautier et al., *Jean Du Seigneur Statuaire*, Paris, 1866, pp. 18, 26; L. Benoist, *La Sculpture romantique*, Paris, n.d., pp. 50–51.

85. TUERIE. By Auguste Préault, modelled 1834, founded 1850. Bronze, 109 × 140 cm. *Chartres, Musée Municipal.* (Photo: Bulloz.)

Préault submitted to the 1834 Salon two large medallions of Roman Emperors, a *Tête de Juif arménien*, the group of *Parias* [Fig. viii] and *Tuerie*. According to T. Silvestre: 'Tout cela fut mis à la porte, exceptée la *Tuerie* qui, sur l'avis de Cortot, devait rester exposé au Salon – comme un malfaiteur accroché au gibet – et effrayer le public sur l'avenir de l'école nouvelle, qui n'avait pas encore poussé le désordre si loin qu'elle le faisait cette fois'. Its subject has never been satisfactorily explained, and it was perhaps conceived simply as a scene of violence. In 1849 Delacroix recorded that he had been advised by Préault 'de faire pour l'année prochaine quelque sujet terrible. Cet élément est le plus fort pour frapper le monde' (*Journal*, I, p. 272).

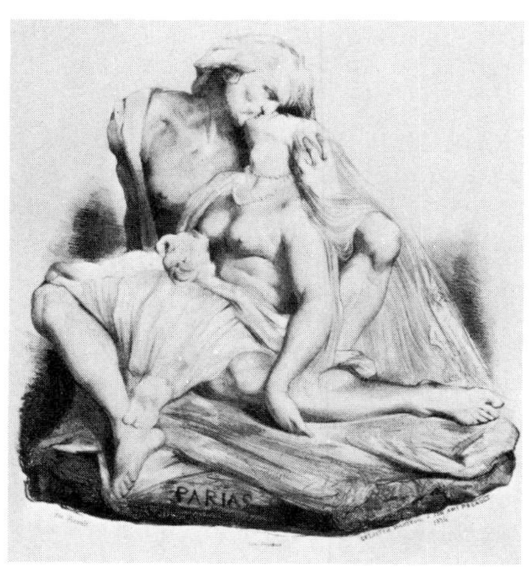

Figure viii. *Parias*, 1834.
Lithograph after A. Préault

Lit: T. Silvestre, *Les Artistes français, études d'après nature* (*1855–56*), Paris, 1878, pp. 291–2; E. Chesneau, *Peintres et Statuaires Romantiques*, Paris, 1880, p. 129.

86. SILENCE. By Auguste Préault, 1849. Plaster, 42 cm diameter. *Bayonne, Musée Bonnat.* (Photo: Archives Photographiques.)

Modelled and then carved in marble for the tomb of Jacob Robles in the Jewish section of the Père-Lachaise Cemetery, Paris. A bronze cast is in the Musée des Beaux Arts, Auxerre. For its influence on Odilon Redon's *Le Silence*, see T. Reff, 'Redon's *Le Silence*: an iconographic interpretation' in *Gazette des Beaux Arts*, LXX, 1967, pp. 365–6.

87. THE SALVATORKIRCHE AND WALHALLA. By Leo von Klenze, 1839. Oil on canvas, 84.3 × 126.5 cm. *Regensburg, Museum der Stadt Regensburg.*

The idea of building the Walhalla as a monument to the most famous Germans was originated in 1806 by Ludwig I of Bavaria (then Crown Prince), who began to commission busts for its interior from German and Italian sculptors in 1808, held a competition for the design of the structure in 1814, engaged Leo von Klenze to make designs *c.* 1821 and, shortly after he succeeded to the throne in 1825, selected the site above the Danube near Regensburg. The foundation stone was laid 18 October (anniversary of the Battle of Leipzig) 1830 and the building completed 1842. While work was in progress on the Walhalla, von Klenze was commissioned to 'restore' (in fact rebuild) the nearby Salvatorkirche (completed 1843) in the *Rundbogenstil* which he regarded as a development from Greek architecture. For the Walhalla, see L. Ettlinger, 'Denkmal und Romantik, Bemerkungen zu Leo von Klenzes Walhalla' in *Festschrift für Herbert von Einem*, Berlin, 1965, pp. 60–70.

88. THE CHURCH AMONG TREES. By Karl Friedrich Schinkel, 1810. Lithograph, 48.9 × 34.2 cm. *Bremen, Kunsthalle.*

The print is inscribed: *Versuch die liebliche sehnsuchtsvolle Wehmuth auszudrücken welche das Herz beim Klange des Gottesdienstes aus der Kirche herschallend erfüllt.* Eva Börsch-Supan very convincingly associates this lithograph with a passage in Ludwig Tieck's novel *Franz Sternbalds Wanderungen*, 1798. But, dating from the period of the French occupation of Germany, it may also have had the political significance attributed to it by Hans-Joachim Kunst, who suggests that the church is Gothic Revival (a style associated with liberal German nationalism) rather than Gothic.

Lit: Eva Börsch-Supan, 'Die Bedeutung der Musik in Werke Karl Friedrich Schinkels' in *Zeitschrift für Kunstgeschichte*, XXXIV, 1971, pp. 258–60; Hans-Joachim Kunst, 'Die politischen und gesellschaftlichen Bedingtheiten der Gotikrezeption bei Friedrich und Schinkel' in B. Hinz, H.-J. Kunst et al., *Bürgerliche Revolution und Romantik: Natur und Gesellschaft bei Caspar David Friedrich*, Giessen, 1976, pp. 26–7.

89. GOTHIC CATHEDRAL. By Karl Friedrich Schinkel, 1813. Oil on canvas, 94.4 × 126.6 cm. *Munich, Neue Pinakothek.*

Schinkel did two paintings of this imaginary cathedral, one for his friend C. W. Gropius (illustrated here), the other bought by the financier J. H. W. Wagner (destroyed 1931, copy of 1823 by Wilhelm Alhorn in Nationalgalerie, West Berlin).

Lit: R. Becksmann, 'Schinkel und die Gotik' in *Kunstgeschichtliche Studien für Kurt Bauch*, Munich, 1967, pp. 263–76.

90. FRIEDENSKIRCHE, POTSDAM. By Ludwig Persius, 1845–8. (Photo: Landesbildstelle, Berlin.)

Friedrich Wilhelm IV of Prussia seems to have played a part in determining the 'early Christian' style of the building (see L. Dehio, *Friedrich Wilhelm IV von Preussen*, Berlin, 1961, pp. 99–100).

91. CUMBERLAND TERRACE, REGENT'S PARK, LONDON. By John Nash and James Thomson, 1826–7. (Photo: Edwin Smith Estate.)

Lit: J. Summerson, *John Nash* (1935), London, 1949, pp. 194–6.

92. THE ROYAL HIGH SCHOOL, EDINBURGH. By Thomas Hamilton, *c.* 1826–9. Watercolour, 95.2 × 150 cm. *Edinburgh, Royal Scottish Academy.* (Crown copyright. Royal Commission on Ancient Monuments, Scotland.)

The Royal High School on Calton Hill, Edinburgh, was built to the design of Thomas Hamilton 1825–9. The version of the Choragic Monument to Lysicrates, shown in front of it in this watercolour, was also designed by Hamilton and erected to the memory of Robert Burns in 1830. Above the school, from left to right, the three buildings are the Observatory by Hamilton (1818), the tower monument to Nelson by Robert Burn (1807–16) and the National Monument designed by C. R. Cockerell, begun in 1822 but left unfinished in 1829.

Lit: A. Rowan, 'Georgian Edinburgh II' in *Country Life*, CXLII, 1967, pp. 1052–5.

93. THE PROPYLÄEN, MUNICH. By Leo von Klenze, 1848–60.

Inspired by the colonnaded entrance to the Athenian Acropolis (but with the addition of the two towers) the Munich Propyläen was conceived as a monument to the liberation of Greece from the Turks and its development under Otto of Bavaria. It stands in the Königsplatz formed by Klenze's earlier Ionic style (Palladian rather than Greek) Glyptothek of 1816–30 and Georg Friedrich Ziebland's more purist Corinthian exhibition building (now Antikenmuseum) of 1838–45.

Lit: O. Hederer, *Leo von Klenze*, Munich, 1964, p. 342 ff.

94. THE CATHEDRAL IN WINTER. By Ernst Ferdinand Oehme, 1821. Oil on canvas, 127 × 100 cm. *Dresden, Staatliche Kunstsammlungen, Gemäldegalerie.*

The architecture is similar to that of Meissen Cathedral. Artistically, Oehme was indebted to Caspar David Friedrich, but with an entirely different attitude to medieval Christianity.

Lit: R. Mattausch in W. Hofmann, ed., *Caspar David Friedrich und die deutsche Nachwelt*, Frankfurt am Main, 1974, pp. 28–9; *La peinture allemande à l'époque du Romantisme*, exh. cat., Orangerie, Paris, 1976–7, no. 151.

95. GOTHIC CHURCH IN RUINS. By Karl Blechen, 1826. Oil on canvas, 129 × 96 cm. *Dresden, Staatliche Kunstsammlungen, Gemäldegalerie.*

Lit: Gertrud Heider, *Carl Blechen*, Leipzig, 1970, p. 19; *La peinture allemande à l'époque du Romantisme*, exh. cat., Paris, 1976–7, no. 5.

96. CRYPT OF SAN MARTINO DEI MONTI, ROME. By François-Marius Granet, 1806. Oil on canvas, 125 × 158 cm. *Montpellier, Musée Fabre.* (Photo: Archives Photographiques.)

According to his own account, this was the first important picture Granet painted after going to Rome in 1802 (*Autobiography*, MSS. Musée Arbaud, printed serially in *Le Temps*, 28 September to 28 October 1872).

97. INTERIOR OF THE MUSÉE DES MONUMENTS FRANÇAIS. By J.-L. Vauzelle, *c.* 1815. Watercolour, 29.6 × 44.7 cm. *Paris, Musée du Louvre, Cabinet des dessins.* (Photo: Archives Photographiques.)

Lit: Marcel Aubert in L. Hautecœur, *Le Romantisme et l'art*, Paris, 1928, p. 30.

98. A CHURCH STEEPLE. By Joseph Mallord William Turner, *c.* 1826. Watercolour, 30.5 × 49 cm. *London, British Museum.* The church has been problematically identified as that of Grantham.

Lit: *Turner in the British Museum – Drawings and Watercolours*, exh. cat., British Museum, London, 1975, no. 108.

99. THE PRESENT REVIVAL OF CHRISTIAN ARCHITECTURE. By Augustus Welby Northmore Pugin, 1843. Engraving, 20.1 × 25.4 cm.

The frontispiece to Pugin's *An Apology for the Revival of Christian Architecture*, London, 1843, illustrating twenty-five churches which he had designed since 1836.

100. ST AUGUSTINE'S CHURCH, RAMSGATE. By Augustus Welby Northmore Pugin, 1845–50. (Photo: National Monuments Record.)

Pugin designed and built this church, at his own expense, near The Grange, the house he built for himself in 1844.

Lit: J. Newman, *North East and East Kent* (in N. Pevsner, ed., The Buildings of England, vol. 39), Harmondsworth, 1969, pp. 406–9.

101a. DEVICE OF THE *LUKAS-BUND*. Designed by Friedrich Overbeck, 1809.

The 'W' on the keystone of the arch stands for *Wahrheit*: the letters on either side, 'H W P O V S', are the initials of the members who formed the *Lukas-Bund* in Vienna in 1809: Hottinger, Wintergerst, Pforr, Overbeck, Vogel and Sutter.

Lit: K. Andrews, *The Nazarenes*, Oxford, 1964, p. 2.

101b. FRONTISPIECE TO *THE TRUE PRINCIPLES OF POINTED OR CHRISTIAN ARCHITECTURE*. By Augustus Welby Northmore Pugin, 1841. Engraving, 25.4 × 20 cm.

102. THE ENTRY OF RUDOLF OF HABSBURG INTO BASLE, 1273. By Franz Pforr, 1808–10. Oil on canvas, 90.5 × 118.9 cm. *Frankfurt-am-Main, Städelsches Kunstinstitut.*

Lit: *La peinture allemande à l'époque du Romantisme*, exh. cat., Orangerie des Tuileries, Paris, 1976–7, no. 169.

103. FRANZ PFORR. By Friedrich Overbeck, 1810. Oil on canvas, 62 × 47 cm. *Berlin, Staatliche Museen Preussischer Kulturbesitz, Nationalgalerie.* (Photo: Walter Steinkopf.)

Lit: K. Andrews, *The Nazarenes*, Oxford, 1964, p. 98; *Die Nazarener*, exh. cat., Städelsches Kunstinstitut, Frankfurt-am-Main, 1977, no. D15.

104. THE TRIUMPH OF RELIGION IN THE ARTS. By Friedrich Overbeck, 1831–40. Oil on canvas, 389 × 390 cm. *Frankfurt-am-Main, Städelsches Kunstinstitut.* (Photo: U. Edelmann.)

As Keith Andrews suggests, the painting was probably inspired by A. W. Schlegel's poem *Der Bund der Kirche mit den Künsten* (1811). Overbeck published a pamphlet in which he identified the figures in the painting and explained the significance of the other elements, including the unfinished Gothic church (reprinted in M. Howitt, *Friedrich Overbeck*, Freiburg, 1886, vol. II, pp. 61–72).

Lit: K. Andrews, *The Nazarenes*, Oxford, 1964, pp. 126–7; *Die Nazarener*, exh. cat., Städelsches Kunstinstitut, Frankfurt-am-Main, 1977, no. F19.

105. THE FAMILY OF ST JOHN THE BAPTIST VISITING THE HOLY FAMILY. By Julius Schnorr von Carolsfeld, 1817. Oil on canvas, 123 × 102 cm. *Dresden, Staatliche Kunstsammlungen, Gemäldegalerie.*

Lit: *La peinture allemande à l'époque du Romantisme*, exh. cat., Orangerie des Tuileries, Paris, 1976–7, no. 232.

106. GOOD AND EVIL. By Victor Orsel, 1823–32. Oil on canvas, 315 × 205 cm. *Lyon, Musée des Beaux-Arts.*

Lit: H. Dorra, '"Le Bien et le Mal" d'Orsel' in *Bulletin des Musées et Monuments Lyonnais*, V, 1975, pp. 291–302; idem in *Die Nazarener*, exh. cat., Städelsches Kunstinstitut, Frankfurt-am-Main, 1977, p. 340.

107. RIENZI VOWING TO OBTAIN JUSTICE FOR THE DEATH OF HIS YOUNG BROTHER, SLAIN IN A SKIRMISH BETWEEN THE COLONNA AND ORSINI FACTIONS.

By William Holman Hunt, 1849. Oil on canvas, 86.3 × 122 cm. *Collection of Mrs E. M. Clarke*. (Photo: Royal Academy of Arts.)

A quotation from Bulwer Lytton's novel *Rienzi, The Last of the Tribunes* was printed in the catalogue when first exhibited at the Royal Academy, 1849.

Lit: W. Holman Hunt, *Pre-Raphaelitism and the Pre-Raphaelite Brotherhood*, London, 1905, I, p. 114; *William Holman Hunt*, exh. cat., Walker Art Gallery, Liverpool, and Victoria and Albert Museum, London, 1969, no. 12.

108. FONTHILL ABBEY, VIEW OF THE WEST AND NORTH FRONTS. By T. Higham after John Martin, 1823. Engraving, 15.4 × 20.3 cm.

Published in John Rutter, *Delineations of Fonthill and its Abbey*, London, 1823, facing p. 66; on the building, see H. A. N. Brockman, *The Caliph of Fonthill*, London, 1956.

109. THE LÖWENBURG, SCHLOSSPARK WILHELMSHÖHE, KASSEL. By Heinrich Christoph Jussow, 1790–99. (Photo: E. Müller.)

A 'museum of Gothic antiquities from the time of Charlemagne to Albrecht Dürer' was assembled in Kassel by Professor Raspe before 1768. But the Landgrave Wilhelm IX von Hessen, for whom the Löwenburg was built, seems to have derived his taste for medievalism and landscape gardening from England (his mother was a daughter of George II), which he visited in 1775, and where he sent his court architect Jussow on a study tour in 1785. A mixture of styles was adopted for Löwenburg, giving it the appearance of a building gradually modified and enlarged over the years. Inside, genuine medieval objects stood among pieces designed by Jussow in a delicate neo-Gothic style.

Lit: Hans Vogel, *Heinrich Christoph Jussow*, exh. cat., Hessischen Landesmuseum, Kassel, 1958–9, pp. 18–23: Heinz Biehn, *Die Löwenburg im Schlosspark Wilhelmshöhe*, Berlin, 1965.

110. FRANZENSBURG, LAXENBURG, NEAR VIENNA. By Franz Jäger, 1798–1801. (Photo: Bildarchiv der Österreichisches Nationalbibliothek.)

Erected for Franz II, Emperor of Austria, partly out of fragments of medieval and later buildings, under the direction of Franz Jäger probably in consultation with the Emperor's private secretary Michael Riedel. The Gothic style had already been adopted for the redecoration of the church of the Deutsche Ritterordens (1720) and the Minoritenkirche (1784–9) in Vienna. But, designed as an element in a landscape park, the Franzensburg derives from the English Gothic Revival tradition.

Lit: J. Zykan, *Laxenburg*, Vienna, 1969.

111. THE HOLY ALLIANCE. By Heinrich Olivier, 1815. Gouache, 44 × 35 cm. *Dessau, Staatliche Galerie*. (Photo: Réunion des musées nationaux.)

Inspired by an article, 'Österreich und Deutschland', written by Metternich's official historian Hormayr in 1815, this represents the three signatories of the Holy Alliance: (left to right) Franz II of Austria, Alexander I of Russia and Wilhelm III of Prussia.

Lit: K. Lankheit, *Das Freundschaftsbild der Romantik*, Heidelberg, 1952, pp. 143–4; *La peinture allemande à l'époque du Romantisme*, exh. cat. Paris, 1976–7, no. 160.

112. WINDSOR CASTLE, BERKSHIRE. (Photo: British Tourist Authority.)

The exterior, as seen from a distance, is almost entirely due to Sir Jeffrey Wyatville, who heightened the Round Tower and Upper Ward and created the skyline of battlements and towers between 1824 and 1837.

113. SCHLOSS NEUSCHWANSTEIN, BAVARIA. By Christian Jank, Eduard Riedel and Georg Dollmann, 1869–86. (Photo: Studio Tanner.)

Ludwig II of Bavaria commissioned Christian Jank, painter of scenery for the court theatre in Munich, to design the castle in 1869, modified in course of construction under the direction of Eduard Riedel and, from 1874, Georg Dollmann.

Lit: H. Biehn, *Residenzen der Romantik*, Munich, 1970, pp. 288–99; *König Ludwig II und die Kunst*, exh. cat., Residenz, Munich, 1968.

114. THE HOUSE OF LORDS, THRONE ROOM, LONDON. By Augustus Welby Northmore Pugin, *c.* 1846. (Photo: A. F. Kersting.)

The competition to rebuild the Houses of Parliament after the fire of 1834 was won by Charles Barry with designs drawn by Pugin. In the creation of the building, Barry was responsible for the planning and structure, Pugin for the design of (mainly decorative) details.

Lit: P. Stanton: *Pugin*, London, 1971; J. Mordaunt Crook and M. H. Port, *The History of the King's Works*, VI, London, 1973, pp. 573–626; M. H. Port, ed., *The Houses of Parliament*, New Haven and London, 1976.

115. SIR FRANCIS SYKES AND HIS FAMILY. By Daniel Maclise, 1837. Watercolour, 112.3 × 64.7 cm. *Collection of Sir Francis Sykes Bart.* (Photo: National Portrait Gallery.)

Lit: Ann Crookshank and the Knight of Glin, *Irish Portraits 1660–1860*, exh. cat., Dublin and elsewhere, 1969–70, no. 110.

116. CRUET STAND. French, *c.* 1825. Gilt bronze and glass. *Paris, Musée des Arts Décoratifs.*

117. THE ROMANCE. By F.-S. Delpech after Alexandre-Evariste Fragonard, 1824. Lithograph. *Paris, Bibliothèque Nationale.*

118. PAOLO AND FRANCESCA. By Marie-Philippe Coupin de la Couperie, 1812. Oil on canvas, 101 × 82 cm. *Arenenberg, Musée Napoléon.*

Exhibited at the 1812 Salon and acquired in 1813 by the Empress Josephine. A print of it was published in C. P. Landon's *Salon de 1812*.

Lit: Wolfgang Hartmann, 'Dantes Paolo und Francesca als Liebespaar' in *Beitrage zur Kunst des 19. und 20. Jahrhunderts* (Schweizerisches Institut für Kunstwissenschaft, Jahrbuch, 1968–9), Zürich, 1970, pp. 13–15.

119. PAOLO AND FRANCESCA. By Jean-Auguste-Dominique Ingres, 1819. Oil on canvas, 48 × 39 cm. *Angers, Musée des Beaux Arts.* (Photo: Giraudon.)

Ingres painted the first version of this composition (now Musée Condé, Chantilly), *c.* 1814. The picture illustrated here is the second version, commissioned by the Société des Amis des Arts, whose members were, however, dissatisfied with it and exchanged it with Comte Turpin de Crissé for one of the latter's works. Four subsequent versions are recorded. The pose of the two principal figures (probably inspired by Flaxman's illustrations to Dante) is the same in all versions.

Lit: R. Rosenblum, *Ingres*, London and New York, 1967, p. 112; *Ingres*, exh. cat., Petit Palais, Paris, 1967–8, no. 110; Wolfgang Hartmann, 'Dantes Paolo und Francesca als Liebespaar' in *Beitrage zur Kunst des 19. und 20. Jahrhunderts* (Schweizerisches Institut für Kunstwissenschaft, Jahrbuch, 1968–9), Zürich, 1970, p. 15.

120. ROGER FREEING ANGELICA. By Jean-Auguste-Dominique Ingres, 1819. Oil on canvas, 147 × 190 cm. *Paris, Musée du Louvre.*

Although this painting was harshly criticized in the press when first exhibited at the Salon of 1819, it was bought for the collection of Louis XVIII on the advice of Comte de Blacas, French ambassador in Rome. Ingres painted two later versions of the subject (before 1839, National Gallery, London; 1841, Musée Ingres, Montauban).

Lit: *Ingres*, exh. cat., Petit Palais, Paris, 1967–8, no. 107.

121. ENTRY OF THE CRUSADERS INTO CONSTANTINOPLE, 1204. By Eugène Delacroix, 1840. Oil on canvas, 410 × 498 cm. *Paris, Musée du Louvre.* (Photo: Giraudon.)

One of the largest of the many paintings commissioned for the Salle des Croisades at Versailles, initiated in 1837 by Louis-Philippe as a tribute to legitimist nobility. (The coats-of-arms of French families which had included crusaders were incorporated in the decorations.) In 1885 Delacroix's painting was moved to the Louvre and a copy substituted for it at Versailles.

Lit: Delacroix Exhibition, no. 297; 'Le style néo-gothique sous Louis-Philippe, deux commandes officielles' in *L'Information d'histoire de l'art*, 1974, pp. 66–73.

122. JACQUES-LOUIS DAVID'S STUDIO. By Pierre-Nolasque Bergeret, *c.* 1805. Lithograph. *Berlin, Staatliche Museen Preussischer Kulturbesitz, Kupferstichkabinett.* (Photo: Walter Steinkopf.)

Lit: Thomas Arnauldet, 'Estampes satiriques' in *Gazette des Beaux Arts*, III, 1859, p. 113.

123. THE EXHUMATION OF THE BONES REMOVED FROM THE ROYAL TOMBS AT SAINT-DENIS. By Francois-Joseph Heim, 1822. Oil on canvas, 67 × 45 cm. *Sceaux, Musée de l'Ile de France.* (Photo: Bulloz.)

Sketch for or (more probably) reduced version of a picture by Heim in the sacristy of the Abbey church of Saint-Denis (now in a sadly darkened condition despite recent restoration). A royal ordinance of 24 April 1816 commanded that the bones, removed from the royal tombs at Saint-Denis in 1793 and thrown into a ditch outside the church, should be exhumed and replaced. They were ceremonially restored to the church 18 January 1817. Heim, on his own initiative, began a painting of the event on a canvas the same size as pictures already in the sacristy at Saint-Denis, subsequently receiving a commission to complete it from the Ministry of the Interior. This work was shown in the Salon of 1822 and the foreground figures identified in the *livret* as: the Chancelier de France, the Marquis de Dreux-Brézé, master of ceremonies, the Comte de Pradel, director general of the Maison du Roi, MM. Delaporte, Lalanne and Claire, *conseillers d'état*, MM. Sallier and A. de Pastoret, *maîtres des requêtes.*

Lit: 'M. de Saint-Santin' (Ph. de Chennevières), 'M. Heim' in *Gazette des Beaux Arts*, XXII, 1867, p. 44; J. Bottineau: 'Le décor de tableaux à la sacristie de l'ancienne abbatiale de Saint-Denis', in *Bulletin de la Société de l'histoire de l'art français*, 1973, pp. 276–7.

124. LE SOLDAT LABOUREUR. By Emile-Jean-Horace Vernet, 1820. Oil on canvas, 55 × 46 cm. *London, Wallace Collection.*

Painted as a pendant to *Le soldat de Waterloo* of 1818 (present whereabouts unknown) with which it was exhibited in the artist's studio in 1822.

Lit: Jouy and Jay, *Salon d'Horace Vernet*, Paris, 1822, pp. 96–100.

125. THE SWISS GUARD AT THE LOUVRE. By Théodore Géricault, 1819. Lithograph, 19.3×32.8 cm. *New Haven, Yale University Art Gallery.*

Said to have been inspired by an article published in the opposition newspaper *Le Constitutionnel* in 1817. According to Charles Clément, the background view of the Tuileries was drawn by Horace Vernet.

Lit: K. H. Spencer, *The Graphic Art of Géricault*, exh. cat., Yale University Art Gallery, New Haven, 1969, no. 11.

126. ALLONS, ENFANTS DE LA PATRIE! By Ary Scheffer, 1825. Oil on panel, 48×66.5 cm. *Dordrecht, Museum Ary Scheffer.* (Photo: Stijns Dordrecht.)

A sketch probably made in connection with the painting *La Chant de départ* (Museum Ary Scheffer, Dordrecht), of which a lithograph was published by Engelmann.

127. HENRI DE LA ROCHEJAQUELIN. By Pierre-Narcisse Guérin, 1817. Oil on canvas, 216×142 cm. *Cholet, Musée Municipal.* (Photo: Réunion des Musées Nationaux.)

Henri de la Rochejaquelin, at the age of twenty-one, became General in Chief of the counter-revolutionary Vendéan army, but was killed on 4 March 1794 by a Republican soldier whose life he had spared. The picture is one of a series of portraits of Vendéan generals, commissioned from a number of artists on behalf of Louis XVIII in 1816.

Lit: *French Painting 1774–1830*, no. 95.

128. HENRY IV AND THE SPANISH AMBASSADOR. By Richard Parkes Bonington, *c.* 1827. Watercolour, 16×17 cm. *London, Wallace Collection.*

A variant of, or preliminary study for, the oil painting which Bonington exhibited at the Paris Salon in 1827 (also Wallace Collection). In 1817 Ingres had exhibited the first of his several paintings of the same subject (now Petit Palais, Paris), derived from Hardouin de Beaumont de Péréfixe, *Histoire d'Henri le Grand* (1661), frequently reprinted under the Restoration – three editions were published in 1816.

Lit: A. Shirley, *Bonington*, London, 1940, p. 106.

129. CARDINAL DE RICHELIEU. By Paul Delaroche, 1829. Oil on canvas, 55×98 cm. *London, Wallace Collection.*

First exhibited at the 1831 Salon with *The Death of Cardinal Mazarin* (also in the Wallace Collection). Although the subjects had been described by earlier writers (notably Voltaire), Delaroche seems to have followed the highly coloured account given in Alfred de Vigny's novel *Cinq Mars ou une conspiration sous Louis XIII*, Paris, 1826, chap. xxv.

130. THE POMPEIIAN HOUSE, ASCHAFFENBURG. By Friedrich von Gärtner, 1841–6. (Photo: Verwaltung der Staatliche Schlösser, Gärten u. Seen, Munich.)

Gärtner was commissioned by Ludwig I of Bavaria to design the Pompeiian House in 1839. Work seems to have begun two years later and in 1844 Gärtner visited Pompeii.

Lit: K. Eggert, *Friedrich von Gärtner, der Baumeister König Ludwigs I*, Munich, 1963, pp. 171, 183; P. Werner, *Pompeii und die Wanddekoration der Goethezeit*, Munich, 1970, pp. 95–9.

131. REHEARSAL OF *LE JOUEUR DE FLÛTE* IN PRINCE NAPOLEON'S POMPEIIAN HOUSE. By Gustave Boulanger, 1861. Oil on canvas, 83×130 cm. *Versailles, Musée National.* (Photo: Bulloz.)

Le Joueur de flûte, a play by Emile Augier with a prologue by Théophile Gautier, was performed on 14 February 1860 in the recently completed house built for Prince Napoleon to the design of Alfred-Nicolas Normand.

Lit: Marie-Claude Dejean de la Batie, 'La maison pompéienne de Prince Napoleon, Avenue Montaigu' in *Gazette des Beaux Arts*, LXXXVII, 1976, pp. 127–34.

132. A DISCOVERY AT POMPEII. By Hippolyte-Alexandre-Julien Moulin, 1863. Bronze, 187 cm high. *Paris, Musée du Louvre*. (Photo: Alinari.)

133. THE ERUPTION OF VESUVIUS, 24TH AUGUST 79 A.D. By Pierre-Henri de Valenciennes, 1813. Oil on canvas, 147.3 × 195.6 cm. *London, Messrs. Marshall Spink.*

Lit: R. Mesuret, *Pierre-Henri de Valenciennes*, exh. cat., Musée Paul Dupuy, Toulouse, 1956–7, no. lvii: *Burlington Magazine*, December, 1972: supplement, 'Works of Art on the Market', pl. lviii.

134. THE LAST DAY OF POMPEII. By Karl Pavlovitch Bryullov, 1830–33. Oil on Canvas, 456 × 651 cm. *Leningrad, Russian Museum.*

Bryullov is said to have begun to sketch this composition immediately after attending a performance of Pacini's opera *Ultimo giorno di Pompeia* in Naples in 1827. He painted the vast canvas in Rome, completing it in 1833 when it was publicly exhibited in his studio and then in various Italian cities before being sent to Paris and St Petersburg. For a very enthusiastic Italian account, see G. Mosconi in *Ricoglitore italiano e straniero*, II, 1834, pp. 349–53.

Lit: *La peinture russe à l'époque romantique*, exh. cat., Grand Palais, Paris, 1977, no. 12 (sketch only exhibited).

135. ANTIOCHUS AND STRATONICE. By Jean-Auguste-Dominique Ingres, 1840. Oil on canvas, 57 × 98 cm. *Chantilly, Musée Condé.* (Photo: Giraudon.)

The subject, derived from Plutarch, had been painted by numerous artists since the Renaissance and, more recently, by J.-L. David (École des Beaux-Arts, Paris) and A.-L. Girodet-Trioson (lost). Ingres was attracted to it by 1807 (drawing in Louvre). In 1834 he was commissioned by the Duc d'Orléans to paint the picture illustrated here as a pendant to Delaroche's *Assassination of the Duc de Guise*. Numerous drawings for the composition survive (see *Ingres*, exh. cat., Petit Palais, Paris, 1967–8, nos. 184–9).

Lit: W. Stechow, 'The Love of Antiochus with faire Stratonica in Art' in *Art Bulletin*, XXVII, 1945, pp. 221–37; idem, 'Addenda to the love of Antiochus . . .' in *Bulletin du Musée National de Varsovie*, V, 1964, pp. 1–11; R. Rosenblum, *Jean-Auguste-Dominique Ingres*, London, 1967, p. 146; J. Conolly Jr, *Ingres Studies: Antiochus and Stratonice*, Ann Arbor, 1976.

136. THE JUSTICE OF TRAJAN. By Eugène Delacroix, 1840. Oil on canvas, 490 × 390 cm. *Rouen, Musée des Beaux Arts.* (Photo: Giraudon.)

Inspired by Dante's *Purgatorio*, Canto X, in the translation of Antony Deschamps (1829).

Lit: Delacroix Exhibition, no. 283.

137. CLEOPATRA AND THE CLOWN. By Eugène Delacroix, 1838. Oil on canvas, 98 × 127 cm. *Chapel Hill, North Carolina, The William Hayes Ackland Memorial Art Center.*

Inspired by the dialogue in the last act of *Antony and Cleopatra* between Cleopatra and the Clown. Lee Johnson suggests that Cleopatra is a likeness of the tragedienne Rachel.

Lit: J. C. Sloane, 'Delacroix's Cléopatre' in *Art Quarterly*, xxiv, 1961, pp. 124–8; Lee Johnson, *Delacroix*, exh. cat., The Art Gallery of Toronto, National Gallery of Canada, Ottawa, 1962–3, no. 6; Delacroix Exhibition, no. 280.

138. ATTILA FOLLOWED BY HIS BARBARIAN HORDES OVER-RUNNING ITALY. By Eugène Delacroix, 1843–7. Oil and wax on plaster. *Paris, Palais Bourbon, Library*. (Photo: Giraudon.)

Lit: Lee Johnson, *Delacroix*, New York, 1963, pp. 90–103; R. Huyghe, *Delacroix*, London, 1963, pp. 375–83.

139. MEDEA. By Eugène Delacroix, 1838. Oil on canvas, 260×165 cm. *Lille, Musée des Beaux Arts*. (Photo: Giraudon.)

'Médée m'occupe,' Delacroix wrote in his journal on 4 March 1824, but not until 1836 is he known to have begun work on a painting of the subject.

Lit: J. Seznec, *Essais sur Diderot et l'antiquité*, Oxford, 1957, p. 73; R. Huyghe, *Delacroix*, London, 1963, pp. 333–4, 348; Delacroix Exhibition, no. 245.

140. AT THE ADVANCE POST. By Georg Friedrich Kersting, 1815. Oil on canvas, 46×35 cm. *Berlin, Staatliche Museen Preussischer Kulturbesitz, Nationalgalerie*. (Photo: Walter Steinkopf.)

The three figures are Theodor Körner, Friedrich Friesen and Ferdinand Hartmann, who had been killed in the *Freiheitskrieg*.

Lit: K. Lankheit, *Das Freundschaftsbild der Romantik*, Heidelberg, 1952, p. 106.

141. THE 'CHASSEUR' IN THE FOREST. By Caspar David Friedrich, 1814. Oil on canvas, 65.7×46.7 cm. *Bielefeld, private collection*.

Painted during the French occupation of Dresden in 1813–14, it was shown in March 1814 at an exhibition of patriotic art in Dresden and later that year in Berlin.

Lit: Börsch-Supan/Jähnig, no. 207.

142. HERMANN'S TOMB. By Caspar David Friedrich, *c*. 1813–14. Oil on canvas, 49×70 cm. *Bremen, Kunsthalle*. (Photo: Stickelmann.)

The sarcophagus bore an inscription (no longer legible): 'Deine Treue und Unüberwindlichkeit als Krieger sey uns immer ein Vorbild'. In another painting of the same subject and date (Kunsthalle, Hamburg), a snake in the colours of the French tricolor slithers over the sarcophagus of Hermann, which is surrounded by the tombs of *Freiheitskrieger*.

Lit: Börsch-Supan/Jähnig, no. 206.

143. ULRICH VON HUTTEN'S TOMB. By Caspar David Friedrich, 1823–4. Oil on canvas, 93×73 cm. *Weimar, Staatliche Kunstsammlungen*.

Lit: Börsch-Supan/Jähnig, no. 316.

144. THE BEFREIUNGSHALLE, KELHEIM. Designed by Leo von Klenze and built 1842–63. (Photo: Verwaltung der Staatl. Schlösser, Gärten u. Seen, Munich.)

Ludwig I of Bavaria commissioned Friedrich von Gärtner in 1836 to design a memorial to the *Freiheitskrieg*. The foundation stone was laid in 1842, but little had been built before

 Gärtner's death in 1847. Leo von Klenze was then commissioned to take over the project, for which he made new and different designs. The statues representing the Germanic races (*Volksstämme*) on top of the piers outside were carved of local stone by Johann Halbig. The marble statues of goddesses of victory surrounding the interior are after models by L. M. Schwanthaler (see Frank Otten, *Ludwig Michael Schwanthaler*, Munich, 1970).

Lit: M. Fischer, *Befreiungshalle in Kelheim*, Munich, 1971.

145. MEMORIAL TO THE FREIHEITSKRIEG, BERLIN. By Karl Friedrich Schinkel. Engraving, *c.* 1820. (Photo: Landesbildstelle Berlin.)

The statues are of cast iron after models by Christian Daniel Rauch, Christian Friedrich Tieck and Ludwig Wilhelm Wichmann.

Lit: P. O. Rave, *Karl Friedrich Schinkel Lebenswerk*, vol. III, *Bauten für Wissenschaft, Verwaltung, Heer, Wohnbau und Denkmäler*, Berlin, 1962, pp. 270–96; P. Bloch, 'Sculptures néo-gothique en Allemagne' in *Revue de l'Art*, no. 21, 1973, pp. 71–9.

146. RECONSTRUCTION OF THE NAVE AND VESTIBULE OF COLOGNE CATHEDRAL. By Leissner, after Georg von Moller, 1813. Engraving.

Georg von Moller made a series of drawings of Cologne Cathedral and projects for its completion in consultation with Sulpiz Boisserée, who published engravings after them in *Ansichten, Risse und einzelne Theile des Doms von Köln*, Stuttgart, 1823.

Lit: W. D. Robson-Scott, *The Literary Background of the Gothic Revival in Germany*, Oxford, 1965, pp. 275–84.

147. MONUMENT TO HERMANN BY E. J. BANDEL. By J. Giere, 1875. Lithograph. (Photo: Landesdenkmalamt, Westfalen-Lippe, Münster.)

The idea of erecting a monument to the Germanic leader Hermann (called Arminius by Tacitus) was mooted in the 1780s and revived by Karl Friedrich Schinkel immediately after the *Freiheitskrieg*. In 1819 Ernst von Bandel (then aged nineteen) began to design a statue which he was finally commissioned to execute in 1835. The project was financed by the members of the Hermannsverein, a patriotic association with members throughout the German-speaking countries, and a site was selected in the Teutoburger Wald near Detmold in Westphalia. The large neo-medieval plinth was completed in 1846 and the statue finally set in place in 1875.

Lit: Hans Schmidt, *Das Hermannsdenkmal im Spiegel der Welt*, Detmold, 1975; M. Trachtenberg, *The Statue of Liberty*, London and New York, 1976, pp. 96–8.

148. THE HUSSITE SERMON. By Carl Friedrich Lessing, 1836. Oil on canvas, 230 × 290 cm. *Düsseldorf, Kunstmuseum.*

A scene from the war of 1419–36 between the Holy Roman Emperor and the Bohemian Hussites. Lessing subsequently painted several other scenes from religious history: *The Trial of Huss* (1842, Städelsches Kunstinstitut, Frankfurt), *Huss at the Stake* (1850), *Luther Burning the Papal Bull* (1853 and 1868), *Luther's Disputation with Eck* (1867, Staatliche Kunsthalle, Karlsruhe).

Lit: I. Markowitz, *Kataloge des Kunstmuseums Düsseldorf: Die Düsseldorfer Malerschule*, Düsseldorf, 1969, no. 228; H. Gagel in *Kunst der bürgerlichen Revolution von 1830 bis 1848/9*, exh. cat., Schloss Charlottenburg, Berlin, 1972–3, pp. 119–20.

149. COUNT FRANCESCO TEODORO ARESE IN PRISON. By Francesco Hayez, *c.* 1827. Oil on canvas, 151 × 116 cm. *Private Collection.*

Count Arese (1778–1835) was arrested in 1822, condemned to imprisonment in the Spielberg, pardoned and released in 1825.

150. GREECE ON THE RUINS OF MISSOLONGHI. By Eugène Delacroix, 1826. Oil on canvas, 213 × 142 cm. *Bordeaux, Musée des Beaux-Arts.* (Photo: Giraudon.)

Exhibited in Paris 'au profit des Grecs' in 1826, in London at Hobday's Gallery of Modern Art in 1829 and again in Paris at the Musée Colbert in 1830. The work was mistitled *La Grèce expirant* ... in the late nineteenth century.

Lit: *French Painting 1774–1830*, no. 39.

151. THE WOMEN OF SOULI. By Ary Scheffer, 1823. Oil on canvas, 23 × 30 cm. *Dordrecht, Museum Ary Scheffer.* (Photo: Stijns, Dordrecht.)

A preliminary sketch for the large painting (now Louvre) shown at the 1827–8 Salon together with two other Greek subjects, *Jeunes filles grecques implorant la protection de la Vierge pendant un combat* and *Les débris de la garrison de Missolonghi au moment de mettre le feu à la mine qui doit les faire périr* (sketch at Dordrecht). An undated painting by Scheffer of Greek refugees by the sea is in the Fodor Museum, Amsterdam. An account of the massacre of the Suliots at the command of Ali Pasha in 1804 appeared in F.-C.-H.-L. Pouqueville, *Histoire de la régéneration de la Grèce*, Paris, 1824, which inspired N.-L. Lemercier to write *Les Martyrs de Souli ou l'Epire moderne: Tragédie en cinq actes*, Paris, 1825. Lemercier complained that the play had not been performed because of opposition from the authorities.

152. RUSSIANS BURYING THEIR DEAD. By David Scott, 1832. Oil on canvas, 49 × 91 cm. *Glasgow, University of Glasgow Collections.*

Exhibited at the Royal Scottish Academy with the title *The Poles did Nobly, and the Russian General Craved an Armistice to Bury his Dead.* An inscription on the back (no longer visible) said that it was 'suggested by reading a paragraph in a Newspaper'.

Lit: *The Romantic Movement*, exh. cat., Tate Gallery, London, 1959, no. 329.

153. FINIS POLONIAE. By Dietrich Monten, 1832. Oil on canvas, 43 × 52 cm. *Berlin, Staatliche Museen zu Berlin, National-Galerie.*

154. THE POLISH OFFICER. By Léon Cogniet, *c.* 1831. Watercolour, 25 × 19 cm. *London, Wallace Collection.*

Perhaps the painting exhibited as *Poloniae* at the 1831 Salon. A lithograph of it was published in 1831 by Jazet. Other prints after it claim to represent a Pole, a Russian and a Hungarian. One, published in London in 1853, is inscribed with the name of Alexandre Rypinski, the poet who fought in the Polish insurrection of 1830–31. Henryk Rodakowski (a pupil of Cogniet) used the composition for a large painting of H. Dembinski, leader of the Hungarian uprising of 1848, exhibited in the Paris Salon 1852 and now in the National Museum, Cracow. Other French tributes to the Poles included a marble sculpture by Antoine Etex, *La Pologne enchainée implore ses libérateurs*, but this was re-titled *Olympia*, by order of the government, when exhibited at the Salon of 1842, and bought for the Crown (see Antoine Etex, *Souvenirs d'un artiste*, Paris, 1877, p. 317).

Lit: A. Ryskiewicz, 'Jean Gigoux i Romanty czny typ portreta wodza Zwyciężonej armii' in *Biuletyn Historii Sztuki*, XXIII, 1961, pp. 57–62.

155. THE 28TH JULY: LIBERTY LEADING THE PEOPLE. By Eugène Delacroix, 1830. Oil on canvas, 259 × 325 cm. *Paris, Musée du Louvre.* (Photo: Réunion des Musées Nationaux.)

On 18 October 1830 Delacroix remarked in a letter to his brother: 'I have undertaken a modern subject, a barricade ... and if I have not fought and won for my country at least I can paint for her.' In a letter of 6 December he stated that he had very nearly finished the work. It was shown in the 1831 Salon. It has often been suggested that the figure of Liberty was partly inspired by Auguste Barbier's poem *La curée*, published a few weeks before Delacroix began work.

Lit: *French Painting 1774–1830*, no. 41.

156. AUX ARMES CITOYENS! By Nicolas-Toussaint Charlet, 1830. Lithograph. *Paris, Bibliothèque Nationale.*

157. AMNESTY 1832. By Paul Huet, 1832. Lithograph, 25.8 × 36 cm. *Paris, Bibliothèque Nationale.*

First published in Philipon's journal *Caricature*, 8 November 1832, with the inscription 'Amnistie pleine et entière accordée par la mort en 1832, sous le règne de très-haut, très-puissant, très-excellent Louis-Philippe'. Probably in connection with it Daumier wrote from the Saint-Pélagie prison to Jeanron: 'Monsieur Philipon m'a demandé si je connaissais un paysagiste patriote, et je lui ai parlé de Cabat et de Huet' (see P. Miquel, *Paul Huet. De l'aube romantique à l'aube impressionniste*, Paris, 1962, p. 78). It alludes to the fate of the Republicans who had been imprisoned after the riot which broke out at the funeral (5 June 1832) of the Bonapartist General Lamarque. On 2 November *Le Temps* reported that the Ministry of Justice was proposing to commute the sentences by which many Republicans were to be sent to the galleys. But some of them had already died in prison. In Huet's print the largest monument is inscribed with the name of E. Richard-Farrat, author of political pamphlets published in 1830–31 (see J. Maitron, ed., *Dictionnaire biographique du mouvement ouvrier français*, pt I, Paris, 1966, vol. III, p. 311).

Lit: *William Turner und die Landschaft seiner Zeit*, exh. cat., Kunsthalle, Hamburg, 1976, no. 192.

158. THE DEPARTURE OF THE VOLUNTEERS 1792. By François Rude, 1833–6. Stone, approximately 1270 cm high. *Paris, Arc de Triomphe de l'Étoile.* (Photo: Archives Photographiques.)

The Arc de Triomphe was begun in 1806 to the designs of J.-F.-T. Chalgrin and others, and the final stage of construction in 1832–7 was supervised by G.-A. Blouet, who designed the attic. In 1833 Thiers (Minister for Commerce and Public Works) gave commissions for the sculptures to Rude, Antoine Etex and Jean-Pierre Cortot (see A. Etex, *Souvenir d'un artiste*, Paris, 1877, p. 200).

Lit: M. Legrand, *Rude, sa vie, ses œuvres, son enseignement*, Paris, 1856, pp. 134–7; L. de Fourcaud, *François Rude, ses œuvres, et son temps*, Paris, 1904, pp. 188–205.

159. NAPOLEON WAKING TO IMMORTALITY. By François Rude, 1847. Bronze, life-size. *Fixin (Côte d'Or), Parc Noisot.* (Photo: Prof. H. G. Evers.)

In 1844 Claude Noisot, formerly an officer of the Grenadiers and Commandant of the Imperial Guard on Elba in 1814, commissioned Rude (a personal friend) to model a statue of Napoleon to be placed, as he told the sculptor, at Fixin 'en face des Vosges at du Jura, en face de l'Italie, dominant les villes et les champs de la Bourgogne'. Rude's first model (Musée des Beaux Arts, Dijon) showed the Imperial eagle watching over the dead Napoleon, laid out on a rock. He was persuaded by Noisot to abandon this in favour of 'Napoleon waking to immortality'. The monument was cast at the foundry of Eck and Durand, and placed in Noisot's park near Dijon in 1847 with the inscription: 'À Napoléon, Noisot, grenadier de l'île d'Elbe, et Rude, statuaire.' Rude's first biographer M. Legrand, commenting on his having modelled statues to Napoleon and Godefroy Cavaignac at the same time, remarked, 'les deux termes qui nous semblent aujourd'hui inconciliables, étaient à peine séparés sous Louis-Philippe et se confondaient dans une identité absolue d'action sous la Restauration. On songera que l'Empereur était le *petit caporal* de la Révolution; en lui se personnifiait, par lui se réalisait l'égalité ...'

Lit: M. Legrand, op. cit., pp. 84–90, 146–9; L. de Fourcaud, op. cit., pp. 290–307.

160. BANDIT ON THE WATCH. By Léopold Robert, 1825. Oil on canvas, 47 × 38 cm. *London, Wallace Collection.*

Lit: C. Clément, *Léopold Robert*, Paris, 1875, pp. 155–6.

161. SELF-PORTRAIT. By Abel de Pujol, 1806. Oil on canvas, 71 × 55 cm. *Valenciennes, Musée des Beaux-Arts.* (Photo: Giraudon.)

Lit: *French Painting 1774–1830*, no. 146.

162. SELF-PORTRAIT. By Philipp Otto Runge, 1802. Oil on canvas, 37 × 31.5 cm. *Hamburg, Kunsthalle.*

Lit: J. Traeger, *Philipp Otto Runge und sein Werk*, Munich, 1975, pp. 323–4.

163. SELF-PORTRAIT. By Marcus Theodor Rehbenitz, 1817. Pencil, 19.6 × 16 cm. *Dresden, Staatliche Kunstammlungen, Kupferstichkabinett.*

Lit: *La Peinture allemande à l'époque du Romantisme*, exh. cat., Paris, 1976–7, no. 179.

164. SELF-PORTRAIT. By George Henry Harlow, 1818. Oil on canvas, 73.5 × 62 cm. *Florence, Galleria degli Uffizi.*

Lit: *Firenze e l'Inghilterra*, exh. cat., Florence, 1971, no. 72.

165. PORTRAIT OF CHATEAUBRIAND. By Anne-Louis Girodet de Roucy-Trioson, 1809. Oil on canvas, 130 × 96 cm. *Saint-Malo, Musée.* (Photo: Giraudon.)

Lit: *Girodet 1767–1824*, exh. cat., Montargis, 1967, no. 39.

166. JOHN KEATS. By Joseph Severn, 1821. Oil on canvas, 57 × 42 cm. *London, National Portrait Gallery.*

This portrait was painted in Rome, shortly after Keats's death. In a letter of 22 December (1858 or 1859), Severn told the secretary of the National Portrait Gallery: 'After the death of Keats the impression was so painfull on my mind that I made an effort to call up the last pleasant remembrance in this picture which is posthumous. This was at the time he first felt ill & had written the ode to the Nightingale (1819) on the morn of my visit to Hampstead. I found him sitting with the two chairs as I have painted him & I was so struck with the first real symptom of sadness so finely expressed in that Poem. The room, the open window, the carpet chairs are all exact portraits, even to the mezzotint portrait of Shakespeare, given him by his old landlady in the Isle of Wight ...' (National Portrait Gallery, Archive, by kind permission of the Director).

Lit: *La peinture romantique anglaise*, no. 249.

167. ALFRED DE MUSSET IN HIS MANSARDE. By Armand-Constant Mélicourt-Lefebvre, 1840. Oil on canvas, 22 × 27 cm. *Private Collection.*

Lit: *Le Parisien chez lui au XIXe siècle*, exh. cat., Paris, 1977, no. 630.

168. PORTRAIT OF R. P. DOMINIQUE LACORDAIRE O.P. By Théodore Chassériau, 1840. Oil on canvas, 146 × 107 cm. *Paris, Musée du Louvre.* (Photo: Giraudon.)

Painted in Rome where Lacordaire, already famous as a liberal theologian, was serving his novitiate as a Dominican, having decided that he could achieve independence by entering this order.

Lit: M. Sandoz, *Théodore Chassériau*, Paris, 1974, pp. 172–4.

169. PORTRAIT OF NESTOR VASILEVICH KUKOLNIK. By Alexandre Pavlovitch Bryullov, 1836. Oil on canvas, 117 × 81.7 cm. *Moscow, Tretyakov Gallery.*

Lit: *Apollo*, XCVIII, 1973, p. 417.

170. PORTRAIT OF BARON SCHWITER (detail). By Eugène Delacroix, 1826–30. Oil on canvas (whole work 218 × 143 cm). *London, National Gallery.*

Baron Schwiter, a painter of portraits and landscapes, was a personal friend of Delacroix. This portrait was submitted to the 1827 Salon but refused, and Delacroix subsequently made alterations to it.

Lit: Delacroix Exhibition, no. 75.

171. WIR DREI. By Philipp Otto Runge, 1804. Oil on canvas, 100 × 122 cm. *Formerly Hamburg, Kunsthalle.* The painting was destroyed in 1931.

Lit: J. Traeger, *Philipp Otto Runge und sein Werk*, Munich, 1975, pp. 83–4, 149–51, 374–5.

172. THE ARTIST'S STUDIO. By Horace Vernet, *c.* 1820. Oil on canvas, 52 × 64 cm. *Paris, Private Collection.* (Photo: Réunion des Musées Nationaux.)

Included in the exhibition held by Horace Vernet in his own studio in 1822.

Lit: Jouy and Jay, *Salon d'Horace Vernet*, Paris, 1822, pp. 166–70; P. Georgel and J. Baticle, *Technique de la peinture: l'atelier*, exh. cat. (Les dossiers du départment des peintures), Musée du Louvre, Paris, 1976, no. 100.

173. MYSTERIUM. By Buonaventura Genelli, 1868. Engraving. 18 × 22.5 cm.

Plate 24 (after a drawing of *c.* 1850–60 in the Museum der bildenden Kunst, Leipzig) in the series of prints published by Genelli in 1868 as *Aus dem Leben eines Künstlers.* In the accompanying text Max Jordan stated that the painting on the easel is inspired by Dante's description of Christ embraced by his bride Poverty: the woman who has posed for the model of Poverty stands behind the artist and both contemplate the cat playing with a crown of thorns.

Lit: H. Ebert, *Buonaventura Genelli*, Weimar, 1971, p. 30.

174. PORTRAIT OF A YOUNG MAN IN AN ARTIST'S STUDIO. By Théodore Géricault, *c.* 1818–19. Oil on canvas, 146.7 × 101.4 cm. *Paris, Musée du Louvre.* (Photo: Giraudon.)

Often erroneously described as a self-portrait, L. Eitner has persuasively suggested that it depicts Louis Alexis Jamar who assisted Géricault in painting *The Raft of the 'Medusa'*, for which he also posed.

Lit: L. Eitner, *Géricault*, exh. cat., Los Angeles and elsewhere, 1971–2, no. 56.

175. MICHELANGELO IN HIS STUDIO. By Eugène Delacroix, 1850. Oil on canvas, 41 × 33 cm. *Montpellier, Musée Fabre.* (Photo: Giraudon.)

Lit: C. de Tolnay, '"Michelange dans son atelier" par Delacroix' in *Gazette des Beaux Arts*, LIX, 1962, pp. 43–52.

176. GIOTTO AS A SHEPHERD BOY. By Ernst Förster, *c.* 1831–5. Oil on canvas, 32.5 × 25.5 cm *Düsseldorf, Kunstmuseum.*

177. TITIAN PREPARING FOR HIS FIRST ESSAY IN COLOUR. By William Dyce, 1856–7. Oil on canvas, 91.5 × 67 cm. *Aberdeen, Art Gallery.* (Photo: Studio Morgan.)

178. COLUMBUS IN CHAINS. After Gustaaf Wappers, 1846. Engraving. *Vienna, Österreichisches Nationalbibliothek.* (Photo: Bildarchiv, Vienna.)

179. MONTAIGNE VISITING TASSO IN PRISON. By François-Marius Granet, 1820. Oil on canvas, 98 × 73 cm. *Montpellier, Musée Fabre.* (Photo: Archives Photographiques.)

180. TASSO IN THE MADHOUSE. By Eugène Delacroix, 1839. Oil on canvas, 60 × 50 cm. *Winterthur, Sammlung Oskar Reinhart am Römerholz.*

Delacroix's first painting of this subject was exhibited at the Salon of 1824 (Bührle Collection, Zürich). In the following year he made a highly finished drawing of a more elaborate composition, with the addition of brutal warders and a Crucifix on the wall (collection of Dr Peter Nathan, Zürich; see A. Joubin, 'A propos du Tasse dans la maison des fous' in *Gazette des Beaux Arts*, 6/XI, 1934, pp. 247–9).

Lit: R. Huyghe, *Delacroix*, London, 1963, pp. 172–3.

181. DON QUIXOTE IN HIS STUDY. By Richard Parkes Bonington, *c.* 1825. Oil on canvas, 46 × 33 cm. *Nottingham, Castle Museum.*

Lit: *La peinture romantique anglaise*, no. 20.

182. DON QUIXOTE AND SANCHO PANZA. By Honoré Daumier, *c.* 1865. Oil on canvas, 100 × 77 cm. *London, Courtauld Institute Gallery.* (Photo: Courtauld Institute of Art.)

Lit: O. W. Larkin, *Daumier: Man of his Time* (1966), Boston, 1968, pp. 195–202.

183. THE YARD OF A MADHOUSE. By Francisco de Goya, 1793. Oil on tinplate, 43.8 × 31.7 cm. *Dallas, Meadows Museum, Southern Methodist University.* (Photo: MAS.)

One of twelve pictures of similar size submitted to the San Fernando Academy in Madrid by Goya in January 1794, and later augmented by two others. The series comprised eight bull-fighting scenes (formerly Torecilla collection, now dispersed), and pictures of strolling players (Prado), a marionette seller (coll. José Várez, San Sebastian), brigands attacking a coach (coll. Castro Serna, Madrid), a shipwreck (coll. Oquendo, Madrid), a crowd escaping from a fire (coll. José Várez, San Sebastian). Goya later painted another madhouse scene (Academia de San Fernando, Madrid): for an interesting interpretation of this work, see Michel Foucault, *Histoire de la Folie* (1961), tr. R. Howard, London, 1971, pp. 208–10, 279.

Lit: X. de Salas, 'Precisiones sobre pinturas de Goya' in *Archivo Español de Arte* XLI, 1968, pp. 1–16; Goya, exh. cat., Mauritshuis, The Hague, 1970, no. 15.

184. THE KLEPTOMANIAC. By Théodore Géricault, 1822–3. Oil on canvas, 60 × 50.1 cm. *Ghent, Museum voor Schone Kunsten.* (Photo: A.C.L.)

One of ten portraits of insane men and women painted by Géricault for Dr Georget. Only four others from the series are known to survive: *The Kidnapper* (Museum of Fine Arts, Springfield Mass.), *The Woman with a Mania for Gambling* (Louvre), *The Man with Delusions of Military Command* (Sammlung Oskar Reinhart am Römerholz, Winterthur) and *Woman Suffering from Compulsive Envy* (Musée de Lyon). Other physicians of the time also made use of portraits of the insane. In 1818 Esquirol employed a draughtsman to portray more than 200 *aliénés*. The Bibliothèque Nationale, Paris, has a slightly later volume of drawings of *aliénés* by G.-F.-M. Gabriel: see J. Adhémar, 'Un dessinateur passioné pour le visage humain, Georges-François-Marie Gabriel' in *Omagiu lui George Oprescu*, Bucarest, 1961, pp. 1–4.

Lit: M. Miller, 'Géricault's Paintings of the Insane' in *Journal of the Warburg and Courtauld Institutes*, IV, 1940–41, pp. 151–63; L. Eitner, *Géricault*, exh. cat., Los Angeles County Museum, etc., 1971–2, no. 123; A. Sheon, 'Caricature and the Physiognomy of the Insane' in *Gazette des Beaux Arts*, LXXXVIII, 1976, pp. 145–50.

185. OPHELIA. By Auguste Préault, 1843–76. Bronze relief, 75 × 200 cm. *Marseilles, Musées des Beaux-Arts.*

Préault made the plaster model for this in 1843 and exhibited it at the 1850 Salon. The bronze illustrated here was cast before 1876, when it was shown in the Salon.

186. NADA. ELLO DIRÁ. By Francisco de Goya, *c.* 1812–20. Etching, 15.5 × 20 cm. *Madrid, Biblioteca Nacional.*

Goya's inscription on the working proof, reproduced here, reads: 'Nada. Ello lo dice' – literally, 'Nothing. It says so' or 'Nothing. That is what is revealed'. But when it was published posthumously in 1863, as plate 69 of *Desastres de la Guerra*, the inscription was changed to: 'Nada. Ello dirá' – 'Nothing. It will be apparent'. Political as well as religious interpretations have been proposed for it: with the word *Nada* referring either to Napoleon who came from nothing and would return to nothing (a popular Spanish saying at the time of the Peninsular War), or alternatively to the constitution for which Spaniards fought but which was reduced to nothing by the Restoration. Nigel Glendinning has recently suggested that it was partly inspired by an illustration in a Spanish translation (1669 or 1672) of Otto van Veen's *Emblemata.*

Lit: N. Glendinning, *Goya and His Critics*, New Haven and London, 1977, pp. 86–8, 90; idem, 'Goya and van Veen' in *Burlington Magazine*, CXIX, 1977; Tomas Harris, *Goya: Engravings and Lithographs*, Oxford, 1964, II, p. 278.

187. THE PHANTOMS. By Louis Boulanger, 1829. Lithograph. *Paris, Bibliothèque Nationale.*

Lit: A. Marie, *Le peintre poète Louis Boulanger*, Paris, 1925, pp. 34, 123.

188. A VISITOR TO AN ANCIENT CHURCHYARD. By Philippe-Jacques de Loutherbourg, 1790. Oil on canvas, 81.5 × 71 cm. *New Haven, Yale Center for British Art.*

Inspired by a passage in Edward Young, *The Complaint or Night Thoughts* (1742–5), Night the Fourth.

Lit: R. Joppien, 'A Visitor to a Ruined Churchyard' in *Burlington Magazine* CXVIII, 1976, pp. 294–301.

189. PIETÀ. By Hippolyte Flandrin, 1842. Oil on canvas, 172.5 × 258.5 cm. *Lyon, Musée des Beaux-Arts.*

Painted at the time of the death of the artist's brother Auguste Flandrin, whose features are said to be recorded in the head of Christ. The composition was probably influenced by *The Entombment* by another Lyonnais painter, Louis Janmot (on loan to the parish church, Pugetville, Var). Antoine Etex may have been influenced by one or other of these

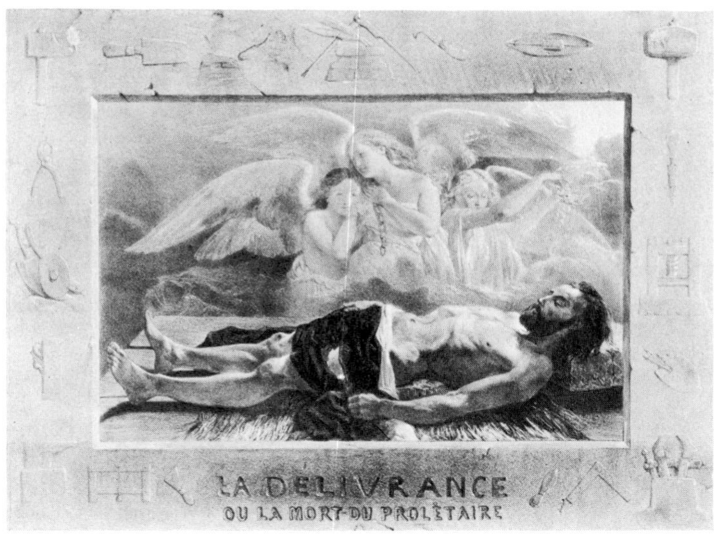

Figure ix. *Deliverance or The Death of the Proletarian*, 1844. Lithograph after Antoine Etex

works when he painted *Deliverance or The Death of the Proletarian* (Musée des Beaux Arts, Lyon) in which the traditional image of the dead Christ is given not merely a secular but a socialist interpretation [Fig. ix. Photo: Bibliothèque Nationale, Paris].

Lit: H. Dorra, 'Die französischen "Nazarener"' in *Die Nazarener*, exh. cat., Städelsches Kunstinstitut, Frankfurt-am-Main, 1977, p. 344.

190. CRUCIFIXION. By Pierre-Paul Prud'hon, 1822. Oil on canvas, 278 × 165.5 cm. *Paris, Musée du Louvre.*

Commissioned by the Ministère de la Maison du Roi for the Cathedral of Metz, but diverted to the Louvre. An early biographer states that Prud'hon was moved to paint it by the suicide of his pupil and friend Constance Meyer (Voiart, *Notice historique sur la vie et les ouvrages de P. P. Prud'hon*, Paris, 1824, p. 28).

Lit: J. Guiffrey, *L'œuvre de P.-P. Prud'hon*, Paris, 1924, no. 299.

191. SAINT THERESA. By Francois Gérard, 1828. Oil on canvas, 172 × 93 cm. *Paris, Infirmerie Marie-Thérèse.* (Photo: Réunion des Musées Nationaux.)

Commissioned for the chapel of the Infirmerie Marie-Thérèse, which was founded in 1819 by Mme de Chateaubriand as an asylum for distressed noble ladies and aged or infirm priests. Her friend Mme Récamier seems to have persuaded Gérard to paint it. A contemporary, A. Béraud, suggested that Gérard was influenced by Chateaubriand's chapter on 'la religion chrétienne considérée elle-même comme passion' in the *Génie du Christianisme.*

Lit: *French Painting 1774–1830*, no. 70.

192. THEN THE LORD ANSWERED JOB OUT OF THE WHIRLWIND. By William Blake, 1825. Engraving, 22 × 17 cm. *London, Tate Gallery.*

Blake drew illustrations to the Book of Job intermittently from 1793 onwards.

Lit: *William Blake*, exh. cat., Kunsthalle, Hamburg, 1975, no. 195.

193a. HECATE. By William Blake, 1795. Colour print finished in watercolour, 43 × 58 cm. *London, Tate Gallery.*

193b. NEBUCHADNEZZAR. By William Blake, 1795. Colour print finished in watercolour, 44 × 61.5 cm. *London, Tate Gallery.*

193c. NEWTON. By William Blake, 1795. Colour print finished in watercolour, 46 × 60 cm. *London, Tate Gallery.*

From a series of 12 monotypes, all of the same period.

Lit: M. Butlin, *A Catalogue of the Works by William Blake in the Tate Gallery*, London, 1957, nos. 12, 13, 18; *William Blake*, exh. cat., Kunsthalle, Hamburg, 1975, nos. 61, 63.

194. FRONTISPIECE TO *EUROPE: A PROPHECY*. By William Blake, 1794. Engraving finished in watercolour, 30.4 × 23.6 cm. *Manchester, Whitworth Institute.* (Photo: Manor, Kay & Foley.)

The subject is usually described as 'The Ancient of Days'.

Lit: A. Blunt, *The Art of William Blake*, New York, 1959, pp. 35, 56–7.

195. THE AGONY IN THE GARDEN. By Francisco de Goya, 1819. Oil on panel, 47 × 35 cm. *Madrid, Escuelas Pias de San Anton Abad.* (Photo: MAS.)

Lit: F. D. Klingender, *Goya in the Democratic Tradition* (1948), London, 1968, pp. 186–95; José Gudiol, *Goya*, Barcelona, 1971, no. 696.

196. CHRIST. By Bertel Thorvaldsen, 1821–39. Marble, 345 cm. high. *Copenhagen, Vor Frue Kirke.* (Photos: Ole Woldbye; Jonals Co.)

A statue of Christ was commissioned from Thorvaldsen for the chapel in the royal palace Christiansborg before 1819. But on his visit to Copenhagen in 1819, it was decided that this statue should stand above the altar of the Vor Frue Kirche, with statues of the Apostles, also by Thorvaldsen, in niches on either side of the nave. With the assistance of Pietro Tenerani he modelled all these statues in Rome in 1821.

Lit: Herbert von Einem, *Thorvaldsens 'Jason', Versuch einer historischen Würdigung*, Munich, 1974, pp. 39–41; *Bertel Thorvaldsen*, exh. cat., Wallraf-Richartz Museum, Cologne, 1977, no. 72.

197. THE CRUCIFIXION. By Eugène Delacroix, 1846. Oil on canvas, 81 × 65 cm. *Baltimore, Walters Art Gallery.*

Exhibited in the Salon, 1847. Delacroix wrote that on the opening day 'M. Van Isaker est venu me demander quels étaient ceux de mes tableaux à vendre. Le *Christ* et l'*Odalisque* lui convenaient ...' (*Journal*, I, p. 208)

Lit: Delacroix Exhibition, no. 360.

198. DÜRER AND RAPHAEL AT THE THRONE OF ART. By G. C. Hoff, 1832–5, after Franz Pforr, *c.* 1810. Engraving, 13.7 × 21.4 cm. *Berlin, Staatsbibliothek.*

One of the first of several images of Dürer and Raphael, probably inspired by Wackenroder's *Herzensergiessungen eines Kunstliebenden Klosterbruders*, 1797 (ed. C. Grützmacher, Munich, 1968, p. 53). Raphael and Dürer hold hands in front of the throne of art in a drawing by Friedrich Overbeck (Albertina, Vienna), and in a design for a transparency by Adam Eberle (Museen der Stadt, Nuremberg).

Lit: Jan Białostocki, *Stil und Ikonographic*, Dresden, 1966, p. 164; *Dürers Gloria*, exh. cat., Staatliche Museen Preussischer Kulturbesitz, Berlin, 1971, pp. 17–18.

199. THE VOW OF LOUIS XIII. By Jean-Auguste-Dominique Ingres, 1824. Oil on canvas, 421×262 cm. *Montauban, Cathedral of Notre Dame.* (Photo: Giraudon.)

Commissioned from Ingres 1820, and painted in Florence between 1821 and 1824, when it was taken to Paris and shown at the Salon prior to being sent to Montauban.

Lit: *Ingres*, exh. cat., Petit Palais, Paris, 1967–8, no. 131; Robert Rosenblum, *Jean-Auguste-Dominique Ingres*, London, 1967, p. 126; Pierre-Marie Auzas, 'Observations iconographiques sur le "Voeu de Louis XIII"' in *Colloque Ingres*, Montauban, 1969, pp. 1–13.

200. ON THE SAILING SHIP. By Caspar David Friedrich, *c.* 1818–19. Oil on canvas, 71×55 cm. *Leningrad, Hermitage Museum.* (Photo: Réunion des musées nationaux.)

Lit: Börsch-Supan/Jähnig, no. 263; *La peinture allemande à l'époque du Romantisme*, exh. cat., Orangerie des Tuileries, Paris, 1976–7, no. 66.

201. PAOLO AND FRANCESCA (detail). By Alexander Munro, 1852. Marble, 67 cm. high. *Birmingham, City Museum and Art Gallery.*

The plaster model for the group was shown at the Great Exhibition, 1851. Munro derived the composition for the group [Fig. x] from drawings by Dante Gabriel Rossetti, *c.* 1848–9. But Rossetti seems to have been influenced by one or more of the earlier renderings of the subject, by Flaxman, William Dyce, Ingres [119], etc.

Lit: J. A. Gere, 'Alexander Munro's "Paolo and Francesca"' in *Burlington Magazine*, CV, 1963, pp. 509–10.

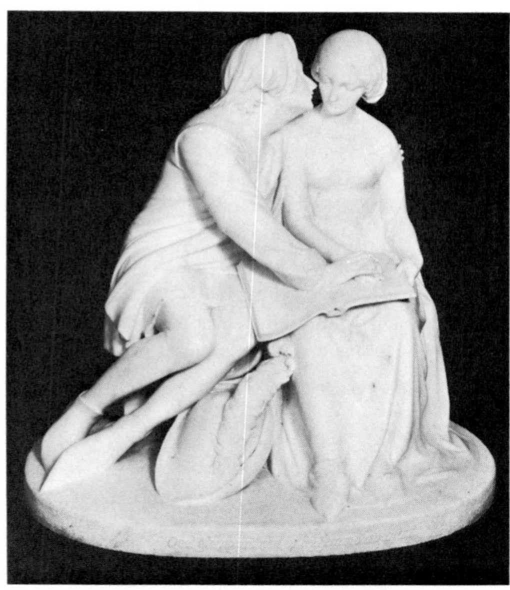

Figure x. *Paolo and Francesca*, 1852. Alexander Munro

202. THE WHIRLWIND OF LOVERS: PAOLO AND FRANCESCA. By William Blake, *c.* 1824–6. Watercolour, 37.4×52.9 cm. *Birmingham, City Museum and Art Gallery.*

One of the series of 100 illustrations to Dante, commissioned by John Linnell, 1824.

Lit: A. S. Roe, *Blake's Illustrations to the Divine Comedy*, London, 1953, pp. 63–5.

203. THE LEAP FROM THE ROCKS. By Ludwig Schnorr von Carolsfeld, 1833. Oil on panel, 74×44 cm. *Schweinfurt, Georg Schäfer Collection.*

The painting illustrates a poem by Friedrich Kind, *Der Kränzelbusche* (1825), describing how a young couple commit suicide rather than allow their feudal lord to exert the *droit du seigneur* (which though a dead letter was not, in fact, abolished in Austria until 1848).

Lit: *German Painting of the 19th Century*, exh. cat., Yale University Art Gallery, New Haven and elsewhere, 1970, no. 80.

204. MAZEPPA AND THE WOLVES. By Horace Vernet, 1826. Oil on canvas, 110×138 cm. *Avignon, Préfecture (on loan from Musée Calvet).*

In 1825 Vernet painted Mazeppa among a herd of wild horses. Next year he painted two almost identical versions of *Mazeppa and the Wolves* for a festival commemorating his grandfather Joseph Vernet in his native city of Avignon.

Lit: *French Painting 1774–1830*, no. 187.

205. LUISE PERTHES. By Philipp Otto Runge, 1805. Oil on canvas, 143.5×95 cm. *Weimar, Staatliche Kunstsammlungen.*

Luise was the four-year-old daughter of Runge's friend and publisher Friedrich Perthes.

Lit: Jörg Traeger, *Philipp Otto Runge*, Munich, 1975, pp. 91, 152–3, 376–8.

206. THE HÜLSENBECK CHILDREN. By Philipp Otto Runge, 1805. Oil on canvas, 131.5×143.5 cm. *Hamburg, Kunsthalle.*

Lit: Jörg Traeger, op. cit., pp. 84–6, 378–9.

207. COMÉDIE DE LA MORT. By Rodolphe Bresdin, 1854. Lithograph, 21.7×14.9 cm. *The Hague, Gemeentemuseum.*

Lit: *Die Schwarze Sonne des Traums*, exh. cat., Cologne, 1972, no. 7.

208. STUDIO SCENE. By Johann Peter Hasenclever, 1836. Oil on canvas, 72×88 cm. Düsseldorf, Kunstmuseum.

Lit: I. Markowitz, *Kataloge des Kunstmuseums Düsseldorf: Die Düsseldorf Malerschule*, Düsseldorf, 1969, pp. 116–17; H. Gagel, 'Die Widerspieglung bürgerlich-demokratischer Strömungen in den Bildmotiven der Düsseldorfer Malerschule 1830–1850' in *Kunst der bürgerlichen Revolution von 1830 bis 1848/49*, exh. cat., Schloss Charlottenburg, Berlin, 1972–3, pp. 119–134.

209. THE STUDIO OF THE PAINTER. By Gustave Courbet, 1854–5. Oil on canvas, 359×598 cm. *Paris, Musée du Louvre.* (Photo: Giraudon.)

Hélène Toussaint has recently proposed an elaborate and, to my mind, largely unconvincing interpretation of this work.

Lit: B. Nicolson, *Courbet: The Studio of the Painter*, London and New York, 1973; P. Georgel and J. Baticle, *Technique de la peinture, l'atelier* (Dossiers du département des peintures), Paris, Musée du Louvre, 1976, pp. 46–7; H. Toussaint, *Gustave Courbet*, exh. cat., Grand Palais, Paris, 1977, pp. 241–72.

210. THE STUDIO OF EUGÈNE GIRAUD. By Charles Giraud, *c.* 1860. Oil on canvas, 100×150 cm. *Compiègne, Musée National.*

Index

Numbers in *italic* refer to plates and Catalogue entries; Figs. i and ii are in the Introduction, iii and iv in the Notes, and v to x in the Catalogue.

'con Editions